KV-193-438

PRACTICAL NEEDLEWORK

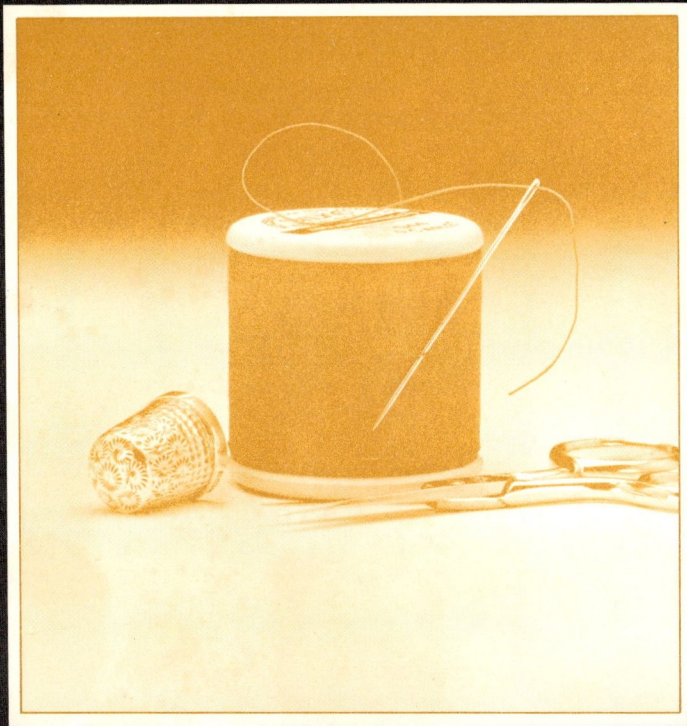

An illustrated guide

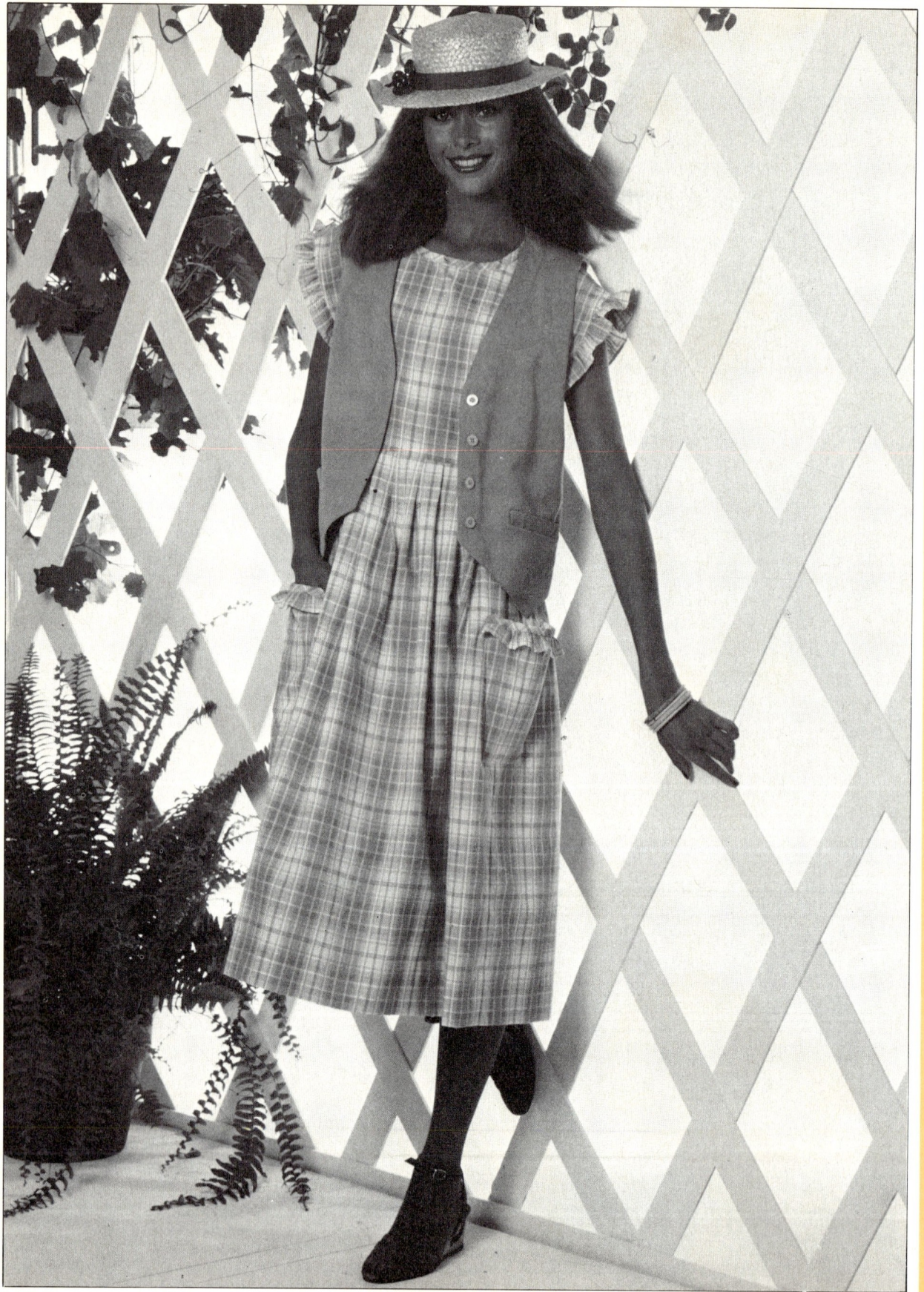

PRACTICAL NEEDLEWORK

An illustrated guide

HAMLYN

London · New York · Sydney · Toronto

The publishers would like to thank Simplicity Patterns Ltd., for their help and advice and for the illustrations used in the Dressmaking section

Line drawings by Janet Allen and Jill Shipley

Some of the material in this book has been revised and taken from The Big Book of Needlecraft and Odhams Encyclopaedia of Needlecraft Illustrated, both published by Odhams Press Ltd.
Additional copy and revision by Ethne Clarke, Patricia Jack and Eve Harlow

First published in 1980 by
The Hamlyn Publishing Group Limited
London · New York · Sydney · Toronto
Astronaut House, Feltham, Middlesex, England

Copyright © The Hamlyn Publishing Group Limited, 1980
All rights reserved. No part of this publication may be reproduced, stored in a retrieval system, or transmitted, in any form or by any means, electronic, mechanical, photocopying, recording or otherwise, without the permission of The Hamlyn Publishing Group Limited

Filmset in England by Photocomp Ltd., Birmingham in 11 on 12pt in Monophoto Baskerville

Printed in Italy

ISBN 0 600 33179 2

Contents

Getting organised

Sewing equipment · The sewing machine · Dress stands · Using commercial patterns · Choosing fabrics · Interfacing, lining and mounting fabrics

Construction methods   32–98

The important stages of dressmaking · Using the machine · Hand-sewing in dressmaking · Darts, tucks and gathers · Openings · Perfect finishes · Making fastenings · Handle with care

Introduction

For many people the needlecrafts conjure up visions of a secret society where the skills of dressmaking, home sewing and embroidery are available only to the initiated. How many times have you heard the exclamation, 'Aren't you clever, I wish I could do that!'? If this is an attitude you share with many others, *Practical Needlework* will go a long way towards changing it, as it is a comprehensive guide to all that is important in needlecraft—fabrics, stitches, and so on. And if you are an experienced needlewoman, you will find the book an invaluable work of reference, helping you to refresh your technique and increase your skill. Traditional approaches and time-honoured methods of the craft are clearly explained with text and illustration, and the professional tips and creative ideas add interest and flair to what is already a fascinating and very rewarding subject.

In *Practical Needlework* there is something for everyone. Some needlewomen prefer the practicalities of simple dressmaking, for in this way they can express their own personalities in the clothes they wear, and dress to suit their budget; others expend their energies on the adornment of the home with new and exciting soft furnishings. The more artistically inclined will take up embroidery and spend many happy hours arranging the wide variety of stitches in intricate patterns and vivid colour schemes, while others will be drawn to the rewarding amusement of toy making. Throughout the book you will find clear working diagrams, easy-to-follow instructions and beautiful photographs chosen to provide you with inspiration.

It is hoped that *Practical Needlework*, which has given such pleasure in its preparation, may bring equal pleasure to readers and help them to sew more easily and successfully.

Glossary

B

balance marks See notches.

baste See tack.

bias The diagonal direction of the fabric. True bias is created by folding the fabric back on itself, so that the lengthwise grain falls over the crosswise grain.

bias seam binding Bias cut strips of fabric with one or both long edges folded; used to enclose raw edges on seams and so on.

binding A strip of fabric, usually cut on the bias, used to enclose raw edges. Often used as a decorative finish on neckline openings and the armholes of sleeveless dresses.

bobbin thread The bottom thread on a sewing machine.

bodkin A large, blunt needle with an oversize eye, frequently used for threading elastic or rouleau through casings.

buckram Stiffened, coarse-weave fabric, used as a backing to give firmness to curtain headings and so on. (U.S., petersham.)

C

casing A hemmed edge which has been left with an opening through which elastic or ribbon can be threaded.

catch stitch Very small stitch used to secure a turned edge.

clean finish To turn under a raw edge 6 mm ($\frac{1}{4}$ in) and machine stitch close to the folded edge.

clip To cut into seam allowances on inner curves such as armholes, or where indicated on the pattern, so that corners and curves lie flat and smooth.

cording See piping.

crease A fold line pressed into the fabric.

crosswise grain The selvedge to selvedge direction of the fabric. The crosswise grain has more stretch than the lengthwise, but less than the bias.

D

dart A fold stitched into the fabric that tapers to a point at one or both ends. Darts shape the garment pieces to fit the body.

directional stitching To stitch fabric in the direction of the grain to avoid stretch and distortion of the fabric piece.

drape The way in which many fine, soft fabrics fall naturally into folds; it may be controlled by carefully placed gathers or pleats.

dress stand, form or dummy A plastic, padded fabric or wire model of the human torso used to aid fitting and cutting in dressmaking.

dressmaker's shears A pair of very sharp scissors, with handles curving up and away from the cutting surface so that the bottom blade can be guided smoothly through the fabric. These shears should be used only for cutting fabric.

dressmaker's squared paper Large sheets of paper divided by measurement into a uniform number of squares; available in metric – one square equaling 5 cm and subdivided into 1 cm squares, and imperial (standard) measure. Used for cutting paper patterns and designing embroidery.

dressmaker's tracing paper Sheets of coloured carbon paper used to transfer markings to fabric.

E

ease To distribute fullness evenly along a seam without creating gathers, or otherwise pleating the fabric.

ease allowance Additional amount added to a pattern to allow for a comfortable fit.

edge finish To neaten a raw edge. Hemming, overcasting and pinking are methods of edge finishing.

edge stitch To neatly stitch close to a folded edge.

elastic thread Very thin elastic, wound on a spool or reel, frequently used for shirring.

extension Additional width to fabric piece that extends beyond the seam line.

eyelet A small hole punched into fabric. The edges may be neatened with either a metal ring or decorative stitches. A pattern formed by eyelets is called broderie anglaise (U.S., eyelet embroidery).

F

facing A straight or bias-cut piece of fabric used to finish openings. It is applied to the right side of the main fabric piece and then turned to the wrong side, thus concealing the raw edge.

fastening Any system of closure for an opening in garments, soft furnishing, or other sewing project.

finger press To open out a stitched seam or crease a fold by the pressure of fingers and thumb only.

G

gather To distribute fullness by drawing up the fabric on parallel rows of long stitches.

gimp A heavy-duty thread, frequently used for hand-worked buttonholes.

grain The lengthwise and crosswise direction of the fabric threads. To be on the true grain, these threads must be at right angles.

gusset A piece of fabric set into seams to help shaping or add ease; in home sewing, a band of fabric forming the sides of a cushion cover.

H

haberdashery Sewing accoutrements such as pins, needles, threads, ribbons, fastenings and so on. (U.S., notions.)

heading The section of fabric above a row of gathers or pleats, used most in connection with curtains.

hem To finish a raw edge by turning the fabric to the wrong side and stitching in place by hand or machine.

I

insertion A piece of lace or other straight edge trimming set into the main fabric for decoration.

inset Any piece of fabric let into a garment.

interfacing A piece of fabric, usually applied to the wrong side of the facing, which gives added body and shape to openings. Interfacings must be chosen according to the weight and type of the main fabric.

interlining A fabric cut to fit the main fabric, and placed between it and the lining for added body and shape.

L

lap To lay or fold one piece of fabric over another.

layering To trim seam allowances to different widths, thereby reducing bulk along seams.

layout Plan for placing pattern pieces on prepared fabric for cutting out.

lengthwise grain The direction of the fabric running parallel to the selvedge.

lining Fabric applied to the wrong side of the main fabric. Dressmaking: the lining is cut as the main fabric, but constructed separately. Soft furnishing: used to protect the wrong side of curtains and add body to bed covers.

M

marking The transfer of pattern symbols to the main fabric.

mercerised The finish given to cotton thread which makes it stronger and more lustrous.

mitre The diagonal line or fold formed when a corner is hemmed or bound.

mounting A lining cut to the same size as the main fabric piece and stitched with the main fabric seams. Also called underlining.

N

nap A raised, soft surface on fabric made by fibres pulled away from the weave and brushed in one direction.

neaten To finish a raw edge or otherwise complete a sewing procedure, e.g. tying in loose thread ends.

notches Diamond shaped symbols on the cutting line of paper patterns, used for matching seams and fabric pieces.

notions See haberdashery.

O

overcast To finish raw edges with small slanting stitches.

overwrap (overlap) An area of garment that extends over another area, usually at an opening.

P

pile Loops or tufts of yarn raised from the fabric weave.

pin baste To pin together, rather than stitch, two pieces of a garment prior to final sewing.

pinking shears Toothed scissors that leave a serrated edge on the fabric. Used only for trimming seam allowances on fabrics that do not readily fray.

pivot To turn the work on the machine needle to achieve a sharp corner. The presser foot must first be raised.

Q

quilting To sew several layers of fabric together, making a decorative pattern with the lines of stitching; often padded to accentuate the pattern.

R

raw edges The unfinished edge of fabric after the pattern has been cut out.

reinforce To strengthen seams at areas of stress, and at corners with additional rows of stitching or a small piece of fabric.

rip To undo a stitched seam by carefully cutting and removing the sewing thread.

S

seam The join formed by stitching two fabric pieces together. Also, to join two fabric pieces.

seam allowance The amount of fabric between cutting line and seam line, usually 15 mm ($\frac{5}{8}$ in) on commercial patterns.

self fabric The main fabric.

selvedge (selvage) The manufactured finished edges along the length of the fabric.

shirring Two or more rows of decorative gathers, often elasticated.

slash To cut the fabric evenly along a straight line for purposes of making an opening or an insertion.

stay stitch To stitch just within the seam allowance of a fabric piece prior to final sewing to prevent bias-cut and curved edges stretching out of shape.

straight of grain The exact lengthwise or crosswise grain of fabric.

T

tack To hold two pieces of fabric together with long hand or machine stitches, prior to final sewing.

tailor's tack To transfer pattern symbols to fabric by thread marks made through paper and fabric.

taping To stitch fabric tape to seams to strengthen areas of stress.

tension The looseness or tightness of both the bobbin thread and needle thread. If the tension is correctly adjusted, the stitches will lock evenly within the fabric.

toile The pattern made up in muslin or calico before the actual garment is sewn; done to check for correct fit and style.

top-stitching Line of decorative stitching on the right side of the garment, usually following a seam or opening edge.

tuck A series of small folds stitched into the garment to gather up fullness.

turnings See seam allowance.

U

underlap An area of a garment that lies under another area.

underlay A piece of fabric stitched under the main fabric to strengthen areas of stress.

understitch To stitch through a facing and seam allowance, close to the seam allowance to prevent the facing rolling out to the right side.

W

warp The lengthwise yarn in a woven fabric.

weft The crosswise yarn in a woven fabric.

with nap Indicates that all pattern pieces must be placed on the fabric in one direction only for cutting; includes pile and one-way direction designs on printed fabrics.

Getting organised

Sewing is such a popular craft nowadays that the range of tools and gadgets available in the sewing departments of stores is wider than ever. Good tools are an investment and will save you both time and money. But think twice about some of the gadgets in the shops, not all of them are necessary to your basic sewing equipment. Here is a list of the essential equipment you will need from the start, and some items that can be added later that will help save time and help you to achieve a professional finish.

Threads

Buy several spools of sewing thread in colours to match the fabrics at the start of every sewing job. The list below gives you some guidance about the suitability of the different types of thread on the market. You will also need a large spool of tacking thread.

Types of thread

Button thread (buttonhole twist) A heavy silk thread used for sewing on buttons and making hand-worked buttonholes. Used also for topstitching.

Heavy-duty machine thread Used for stitching fabrics such as canvas or similar sturdy fabrics.

Mercerized sewing thread Used for sewing fine and medium weight natural fibre fabrics. For home dressmaking you will use gauge 50, but you will need a heavier gauge for home sewing projects.

Silk thread Used for sewing silk fabrics, wool and man-made fibre fabrics that feel like silk, and also for tacking sheer fabrics, velvets and for tacking pleats (silk thread is far less likely to leave marks after pressing).

Synthetic threads Made of polyester and used for hand or machine sewing all man-made fibre fabrics of any weight. Use twisted polyester thread for heavy work.

Transparent nylon thread is available for invisible sewing, but should be used with caution as it tends to stretch and can melt under the heat of an iron.

Needles

Hand sewing needles

It is advisable to have a selection of different kinds of needles in your workbox, so that you always have the right type on hand for a particular sewing job. Needles come in a range of sizes; the higher the number, the finer the needle and are available in packs of assorted sizes.

Betweens These are sometimes called quilting needles. Shorter than sharps, use these needles whenever you want to make small fine stitches.

Crewel needles Although these are embroidery needles, some needlewomen like to use them for dressmaking because their long eye makes them easy to thread.

Milliner's needles These long needles with a small round eye are ideal for tacking, gathering etc.

Sharps These medium length needles with a small round eye are the most common and can be used for any sewing job.

Sewing machine needles

Keep a selection of these in your sewing basket. British needle sizes go from 9 to 14, and then 16. 16 is the coarsest, used for heavy fabrics. Continental sizes range from 70 to 100, which is used for sewing heavy fabrics.

There are specialized sewing machine needles for special fabrics: ballpointed needles are used for sewing knitted fabrics, spear pointed needles are used for sewing leather and suede.

Indispensible Tools

Bodkin Used for pulling elastic or tape through a casing, and also for turning rouleau to the right side.

Brown paper strips Cut a dozen brown paper strips about 5 cm (2 in) wide and keep them rolled with a rubber band around them ready for pressing seams etc.

Dressmaker's carbon paper Used for transfering pattern markings. Sold in packs, containing blue, yellow, white and red. Not advised for use on fine fabrics.

Dressmaker's graph paper Used for drawing up patterns, the paper is most readily available in metric size and divided into 5 cm (2 in) squares which are subdivided into 1 cm ($\frac{3}{8}$ in) squares.

Dressmaker's shears Use exclusively for cutting out fabric. Choose the very best quality you can afford and then look after them carefully. Have shears sharpened about twice a year.

Hem gauge Used for turning hems, it is a card of plastic marked with different depths so that turning is kept even as you pin.

Metrestick (or yardstick) Choose one made of wood or clear plastic and use for drawing up patterns, measuring fabric, checking grain lines and when marking darts and pleats.

Needle threader Even if you have perfect eyesight, a needle threader makes life easier. Buy two or three and keep them in your work basket. Bend the tip of one threader for threading the sewing machine needle.

Paper scissors Buy a pair of large scissors and keep them just for cutting paper. Tie a piece of brightly coloured yarn to the handles so that you do not confuse them with fabric cutting scissors.

Pins Choose fine, stainless steel dressmaker's pins. The kind with coloured glass heads are made from broken needles and are therefore very sharp and should always be used on fine fabrics. The heads also make it easy to see them if they are dropped.

Pincushion The pincushion should be filled with sawdust to prevent the pins becoming blunt. A pincushion on an elastic wrist band will be useful when you are doing a fitting.

Seam ripper Essential for unpicking machine-stitched seams.

Sewing gauge This is a useful piece of equipment and helps you to measure and mark short distances, such such as buttonholes or a seam allowance, accurately.

Tailor's chalk Available in small, flat squares or pencil form and used for making markings on fabric during fitting. The chalk will launder or dry clean out of fabrics and marks will brush out of napped fabrics.

Tape measure Choose one that will not stretch – fibreglass is best. Double-sided tape measures are convenient to use, having inches on one side and centimetres on the other.

Thimble Try to get used to using a thimble for hand sewing, especially on heavy fabrics. Choose a good one which fits your middle finger exactly and feels comfortable.

Tissue paper White tissue paper is used to assist the cutting out of sheer fabrics and to prevent some fabrics catching on the feed teeth of the machine.

Tracing wheel Used with dressmaker's carbon paper, the serrated wheel leaves a dotted line on the fabric, marking seam lines, darts etc.

Useful extras

The following items are not absolutely essential, though they can, in some cases save time, or make a perfect finish easier to achieve.

Buttonhole scissors These have notched blades so that the cut is made into the fabric leaving the edge uncut.

Clear adhesive tape Use it for mending torn patterns and for altering them, and for holding paper patterns on fabrics such as leather and suede.

A dressmaker's squared cutting out board Made of firm, thick cardboard it is used for extending a table top for cutting out. It is also useful for drafting graph patterns. You simply pin tracing paper on top and then draw out your pattern, without having to mark in the squares first. Squared boards are also useful when altering commercial paper patterns.

Embroidery scissors These are quite small scissors, with sharp pointed tips, about 10 cm (4 in) long, used for small work.

Hem marker You will need one of these if you take hems up without help. The most popular type has a hand operated bulb which puffs chalk onto the garment at the hem line as you turn around.

Pinking shears These have serrated blades and are used for trimming seam allowances on non-fray fabrics. Never use them for cutting out other types of fabric.

Thread clipper These have a simple spring-type action; simply pick them up in one hand and close the blades together.

Trimming scissors Smaller than shears, with about 15 cm (6 in) long blades and round handles, they are used for all trimming jobs.

The sewing machine

If you enjoy sewing for yourself, your family and home, your sewing machine is the single most important piece of your equipment. Perhaps you are still using an old hand or a treadle operated machine and wish to buy a new electric powered machine; then you must think carefully about the type of machine that would best suit your needs.

There are three main types on the market; there may seem to be more as machines vary greatly in appearance, and the manufacturers will claim that their machines have certain qualities which others in the price range do not have – but basically, there are still only three types.

Straight stitch

These machines will do straight stitching only, but they cannot do zigzag stitch for sewing jersey fabrics, nor make buttonholes. If you simply want a machine to sew straight seams and little else, this is the type to choose. These are the least expensive kind.

A straight stitch machine is quite basic. Reliable machines can be purchased secondhand.

A lightweight semi-automatic machine will meet the needs of most families.

A fully automatic machine with electronic 'brain' will perform almost any sewing job at the touch of a button.

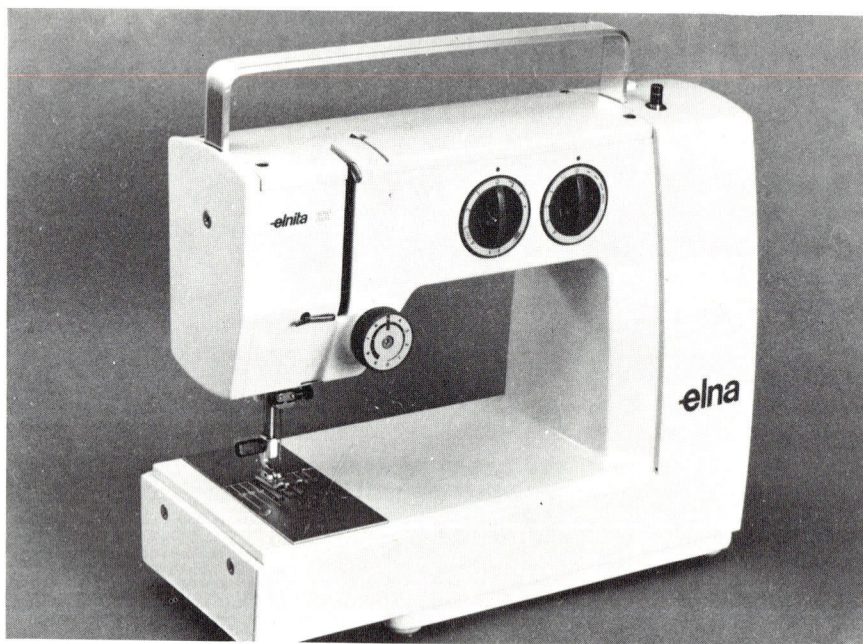

Semi-automatic and swing needle

Both of these have a stitch width regulator which enables the needle to work from side to side. By operating the stitch length adjustment with the stitch width, you can work close satin stitch for appliqué and a zigzag stitch.

The range of facilities of swing needle machines is considerable: they will do most things from simple straight stitching to some decorative stitches for embroidery. By winding special threads on the bobbin, swing needles can be used to work a range of machine embroidery effects. Many manufacturers have a range of attachments available to increase the scope of their machines.

These machines will do all that the home dressmaker requires, and they are well worth considering. If you are sewing for young children, look at the models which have removal extension tables. When the table is removed, the machine can be used for sewing small armholes etc.

Automatic machines

These are the most expensive machines on the market, but they are undoubtedly the quickest and easiest to use and they do so much more than the semi-automatics. A home dressmaker would not be likely to use all the facilities these machines have, but a keen needlewoman would find them exciting to use.

Most dealers will demonstrate the machines for you and allow you to try them yourself. Bring along several fabric scraps of different weights and fibres to try the machine on. Consider the variety of stitches, the lengths of stitch available and the speed the machine is capable of.

No matter which type of machine you choose it will come with an instruction booklet. Read this through carefully before you begin to sew. It will tell you not only how to get the best performance from the machine, but how to care for it properly. This is extremely important if you want the machine to last and give consistently good performance.

Machine problems

Here are a few of the more common problems experienced by dressmakers, although it is best to check with the instruction booklet for your particular machine:

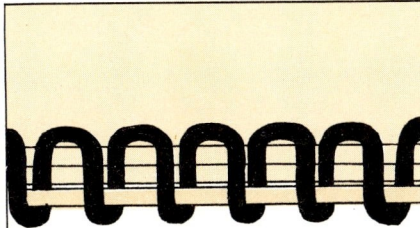

Upper thread tension too loose or bobbin thread tension too tight.

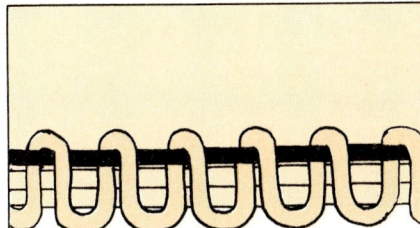

Upper thread tension too tight or bobbin thread tension too loose.

A perfectly locked stitch

Needle breaking

The needle may not be inserted correctly or a pin in the fabric has been hit while stitching. (With some machines you can stitch easily over pins, but they must be in the fabric horizontally.)

The needle may be bent–always raise the needle to highest point when pulling work out of the machine, do not force the needle over too thick a seam. Never pull the work towards you when pulling work out. This bends the needle and will eventually break it.

Thread breaking

The thread will jam, knot on the wrong side or break if the thread take up lever is not raised to its highest point when beginning a line of stitching.

If the needle thread is breaking it may be that the top tension is too tight. Balanced tension is when the needle thread and the bobbin thread lie evenly within the fabric. If the thread seems to lie on top of the fabric, the needle thread is too tight. If it is too loose, the bobbin thread seems to lie along the under surface. Check also that the needle is inserted correctly and that it is not rusty.

If the *bobbin* thread breaks, it may be unevenly wound or else overwound.

Looped stitches on the underside

This is either incorrect threading or the upper tension is too tight.

Puckered fabric

Either the lower tension or upper tension is too tight, or the presser foot pressure is too great for the fabric.

Jumped stitches

The needle may not be inserted properly; may be blunt, or it is the wrong size for the fabric.

Always unplug the machine when it is not in use. If it is the type where the light can be switched off independently you may not notice that the power is still switched on and, if it is left plugged in all night, you may ruin the motor.

Have your machine serviced at least once a year.

Dress stands

A dress stand, sometimes called a dressmaker's dummy, is an essential piece of equipment for all serious seamstresses. It is a model of the human torso, and can be adjusted or padded to conform to the figure details of the dressmaker or person for whom she is sewing.

With a stand it is possible to fit a garment perfectly without assistance, and to see and make alterations to style or cut where necessary. There are three types of stand on the market, and varieties of each type.

Adjustable Although this is the most expensive type of stand, it is the most popular. The body is firm and fabric covered and is made in sections which are adjusted by wheels or dials. You simply take your measurements and then adjust the stand until it is your size. Some stands can also be adjusted to length of waist and neck measurements.

Front-buttoning mesh To adjust this type of stand to your measurements, the torso form is put on like a jacket and fastened. Then the wire frame is pushed with the hands until it moulds to the figure. Some dressmakers find that the uneven wire surface is difficult to work with, but you might make a fitted cover of stretch fabric once you have shaped it to your figure.

Firm body This is the most familiar type, often found in the corner of grandmother's attic. If you are an average size and your figure does not alter, this may be the type for you. The body is padded and covered with fabric so that pins can be pushed in very easily. This type can also be altered by adding pads.

Padding a dress stand
Although no dress stand when purchased will exactly resemble your figure and must be adjusted, greater differences will be found if you have a distinct figure detail such as a large bust and small hips or perhaps a dowager's hump. If this is the case, you should buy the standard, firm-bodied type of stand slightly smaller than your measurements, rather than larger, and then pad it accordingly. To do this, make a calico bodice and ask a friend to fit it to your body carefully. Stitch the bodice at the side seams and shoulders but leave the back open.

Put the bodice on the stand and

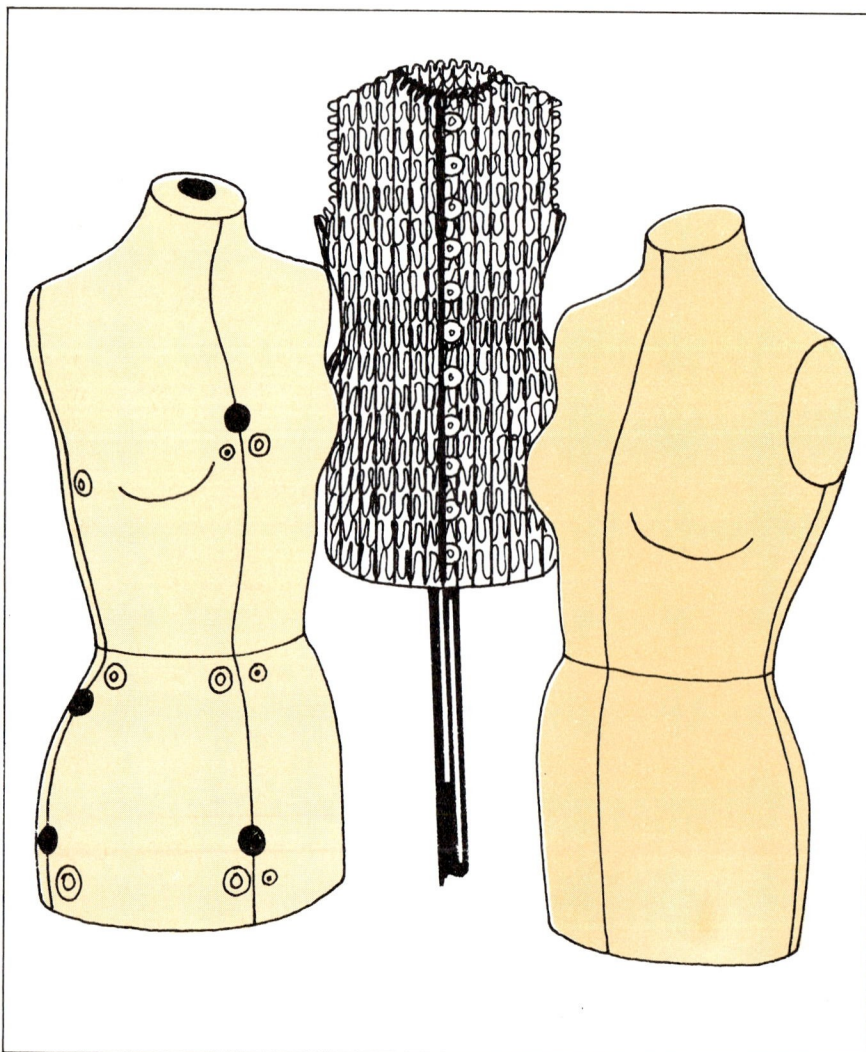

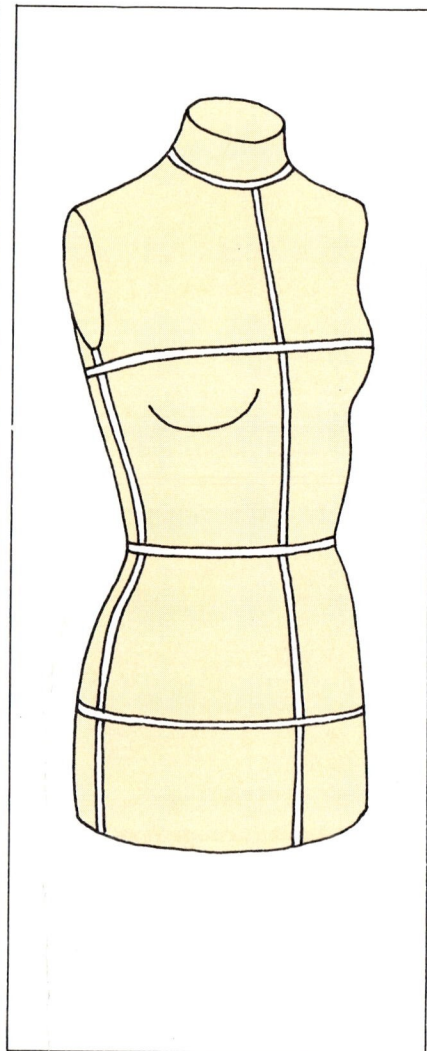

close the back with pins, you will immediately be able to see the places where the bodice is too large for the stand. Mark the shape of the places on the stand with dressmaker's chalk. Cut a big shape from a roll of cotton wool and then smaller shapes. Take the bodice off the stand and pin the cotton wool to the stand at the marked areas, the largest shape first and then the smaller shapes so that you are building up the contours. Put the bodice on the stand and check the fit. Add more padding if necessary.

When the bodice fits correctly, cut pieces of lawn or cotton on the bias and stretch these over the padding. Sew the fabric to the stand with herringbone stitch using a small, curved upholstery needle. Take out the pins.

The hipline of a dress stand is altered in exactly the same way, using a basic straight skirt in calico to position the padding.

Taping a stand If the stand you buy is without grain tapes, you should add these because they are helpful in fitting and making sure that garments are hanging straight. Use 6 mm ($\frac{1}{4}$ in) wide cotton tape. Mark the body as shown. With horizontal tapes around the bust, waist, hips and neck and then vertical tapes down the centre front and back and down the sides from where the underarm would start. Sew the tapes to the body with herringbone stitches using a small curved upholstery needle.

A dress stand is as invaluable a piece of equipment today as it evidently was in 1910. Notice the attachment for fitting long, full skirts, and compare the figure shape with the contemporary outlines opposite

Far left Fully adjustable dress stand.
Centre Front buttoning mesh type.
Left Traditional firm body stand.

CLARK'S
DRESS STANDS

have been supplied to 15 Royal Families, hundreds of Titled Ladies and Nobility, over 60 Technical Colleges, Town and County Councils, H.M Government, and the London County Council.

This *clientèle* is a guarantee to ladies of the stability of **CLARK'S** (established 60 years).

All the Costume Stands shewn are made to measurements, padded and covered for pinning, supplied with Skirt Markers, and packed in boxes without extra charge.

For fuller particulars of

CLARK'S GOOD FIT DRESS STANDS

send for our 40 page Catalogue, with photographic design, post free. Mention *Delineator.*

Complete Costume Stand in Box. With Padded Arms, **16/6**

Complete Costume Stand in Box. With Armlets, **14/6**

Expanding Dress Stand in Box. Expands from 19 ins. to 30 ins. waist; 32 ins. to 40 ins. bust. Complete with Armlets, **27/6** Without Armlets, **25/-**

Complete Costume Stand in Box. With Jointed Arms, **25/6**

Complete Costume Stand in Box **12/6**

Long Hips — with Armlets, *as sketch,* **8/6** Without Armlets, **6/6** With Padded Arms, *as sketch,* **10/6**

Folding & Expanding Skirt Stand. Expands from 17 ins. to 36 ins. waist. Packs in small space of 3 ins. by 36 ins. long, **10/6**

CLARK'S make Shapes to suit all Figures.

3 TOTTENHAM STREET TOTTENHAM COURT Rd LONDON W

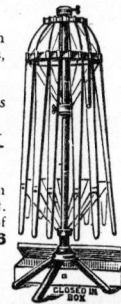

Using commercial patterns

Buying a pattern

Choosing a paper pattern is the first important decision a dressmaker makes and a successful choice depends upon knowing the correct size to buy. Make quite sure that you have an up-to-date note of your measurements. This is best done by having someone else take the measurements for you.

Pattern sizings

Sizes in the pattern industry do not correspond to those of the ready-to-wear garment industry. Paper patterns are sold according to standardized sizings for a range of figure types. Your measurements will closely match one of the pattern sizes, unless you have a special figure difference. Take the following measurements as described and use them in comparison to the pattern sizing established by the manufacturer of the pattern you have chosen.

For a *high bust*, measure straight across the back, directly below the armpit and above the bust.

Take the *bust* measurement straight across the back over the fullest part of the bust.

Find the natural *waistline* and take the measure comfortably round at this point. Do not pull it tight.

The *hip* measurement should be taken 23 cm (9 in) down from the waist.

The *back* length is taken from the nape of the neck, to either the waist or the knee.

Your measurements are highly unlikely to be exactly the same as those given on the pattern, so for fitted bodices (blouses, jackets etc.) choose according to bust size; skirts and trousers by waist and hip. Measure for men's patterns as follows: For the *chest*, take the tape measure straight across the back and around the fullest part of the breast.

Measure the natural *waistline* (even for hip-slung trousers) over a shirt.

Measure the hips of mature men 20 cm (8 in) below the waistline, and younger men 18 cm (7 in) below.

Add at least 12 mm ($\frac{1}{2}$ in) to *neck* measurement for neckbands. Obviously, do not pull the tape too tight or the resulting collar will be uncomfortable.

Sleeve length is determined by measuring the *arm* length from the collar bone, over the shoulder and bent elbow to the wrist.

For trousers you must have the *inside leg* – from crotch to desired hem and *trouser length* – from natural waist to desired hem.

Ease If you have noticed that patterns sometimes seem large in spite of careful measuring, you may be overfitting the ease which has been designed into the garment. Ease is extra centimetres added to make the garment comfortable and allow freedom of movement. Generally, 7.5 cm to 10 cm (3 in to 4 in) has been allowed at the bustline, 12 mm ($\frac{1}{2}$ in) at the waistline and 5 cm (2 in) at the hipline. Coats and jackets have more ease because they are intended to be worn over other garments. However, do not attempt to use this ease to get a better fit, you will probably find the finished garment is a little uncomfortable.

When choosing a maternity pattern, stick to the size you would normally choose if you were not pregnant, the extra ease is designed in.

The pattern

Everything a dressmaker can want to know about a paper pattern is printed either on the envelope or

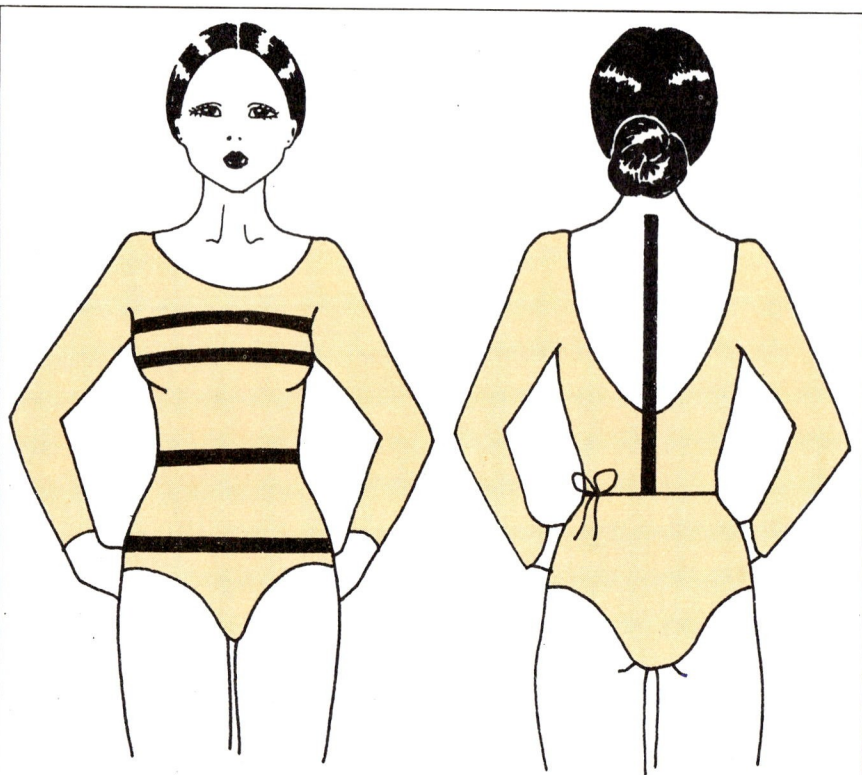

Left The correct position for high bust, bust, waist and hip measurements.
Right Neck to waist measurement taken down centre back.

The essential measurements for men's patterns: chest, waist, hip, inside leg and trouser length. Inset shows neck and shirt sleeve length.

2548
12 PIECES

CHILD'S DRESS AND PINAFORE: High-waisted dress, with flared and gathered skirt, has back zipper fastener, rounded collar and ribbon neck tie. Long sleeves, View 1 and 2, and short sleeves, View 3, are gathered at head and elasticated at lower edge. View 1 features contrast collar, and bias-cut bodice and patch pockets. View 2 and 3 have deep frill around lower edge. High-waisted pinafore View 4, with button and loop back fastening, has "scooped" neckline, flared and gathered skirt cut without side seams and patch pockets. View 3 and 4 are completed with trimming.

Suggested fabrics — View 1, 2 and 3 in cotton types, rayon, crepe, wool/cotton blends, silk types, fine wool, fine jersey and synthetics. View 1 also in gingham, seersucker and tartan. View 4 in lawn. voile, broderie anglaise and dotted swiss. View 1 unsuitable for obvious diagonal fabrics.

To complete garment — Thread. View 1, 2 and 3 25 cm zipper for size 2, 30 cm zipper for sizes 3-5. 35 cm zipper for size 6. 6 mm wide elastic. 1.00 m of 1.3 cm wide ribbon. View 4. Bias binding, three 1.3 cm buttons.

Back of a pattern envelope.

The back of the envelope has a great deal of useful information on it. First there is a garment description. This tells you the design features of the garment and something about the variations which can be adapted from the basic pattern.

There is a note about the number of pattern pieces in the envelope and sketches showing the back views.

Body measurements

These are the basic body measurements used by the pattern house to establish the size. Check your measurements against them before choosing the correct pattern size.

Yardage chart

This chart is divided into columns by size reading across, and by fabric width reading down, thus telling you how much fabric is required for each view. Also indicated is whether allowance has been made for nap, shading and one- or two-way design.

Below the main fabric requirements there is the amount of interfacing needed, and the types of fabric print that are not suitable.

on the instruction sheets inside. They are specially written and designed to be easy to understand. Take time to look over everything before starting on a garment. It pays dividends in increased confidence at a later stage.

Reading the envelope

This has a sketch or a photograph of the garment and variations, called views, which can be made with the same pattern. The size, price and pattern number are also given here.

Dressmaking – Getting organised

Finished measurements
This information is particularly useful to know. If the garment is long enough, too full or not full enough, you know and can then allow more or less fabric.

Fabric advice
Here the pattern house tells you which fabrics are best suited to the cut of the garment so that you will not make the mistake of, say, buying stiff polished cotton for a dress with a bias-cut skirt.

Sewing notions
This shopping list details all the bits and pieces you need – buttons, zippers, trimmings – to finish the garment.

Inside the envelope
Inside the envelope besides the pattern tissues, there are several sheets of printed paper. These sheets are the sewing instructions and they tell you exactly how to put the garment together in the right order. This is very important. To make a success of your garment, you should work the various stages in the order recommended.

To ensure that you cut the fabric economically and correctly, follow the layout for the pattern pieces precisely. Look at these carefully to see which one corresponds first with your pattern size and then with the width of your fabric. You will be given a key showing right and wrong side of fabric and this is to help you see which pieces are cut double and which single. Unless you are very experienced, you should follow these fabric layouts without changing them. You may feel sometimes that patterns are extravagent with fabric and you can see ways of economising, but remember that paper patterns are standardized and, as far as possible, have been designed to be foolproof. Layouts are there to make life simple for the home dressmaker. You won't go wrong if you follow them.

From the sewing direction sheets, you can also check the number of pattern pieces you will be using to make up your particular style. You

are also given some hints on altering patterns and a key to understanding the various symbols and lines on the pattern. Some patterns even tell you how to prepare your fabric for cutting out.

Reading the pattern pieces
Take out one of the pattern tissues and carefully unfold it. If it has more than one pattern piece printed on it, they will have to be separated. Do this by cutting around the pieces, leaving a margin of tissue around the outline. *Do not cut on the solid black outline.* This is the cutting line and must be followed only when cutting out the fabric.

Spread out the pattern pieces and look for the following symbols:

Short solid line from cutting line to stitching line. This is a *clip*, the seam allowance is snipped along this line to relax the seam.

The position of the centre front and centre back. This helps to position the pattern piece on printed fabric. Often the centre front is placed on the fold of fabric, but do check carefully for 'place on fold' elsewhere on pattern pieces. Pattern pieces cut on a fold do not have a seam on that edge.

A triangle formed by the cutting line and two dotted lines. These are *darts*; the dotted lines are brought evenly together and stitched along the dotted line. Often there is a

solid line down the centre of the dart – this is the fold line.

Squares, small and large circles. These are marks to assist matching seams etc.

Small triangles along the cutting line. These are *notches* and should be cut into the fabric, not into the seam allowance. They are used to match pieces for seaming and are sometimes numbered so that you place the correct pieces together. Pay particular attention to notches at sleeve heads to avoid putting the sleeve in backwards.

Heavy, solid line within the pattern piece with arrowhead at each end; known as the *grain line*, this must be aligned with the straight grain of the fabric and be absolutely parallel to it. A grain line lying across the pattern piece usually indicates that the piece will be cut on the bias.

Dotted line running parallel to the solid cutting line. This is the *seam line* and normally falls 15 mm ($\frac{5}{8}$ in) from the cutting line. If there is an arrowhead on the line, the seam must be stitched in the direction indicated. *Ease* and *gathering* along seam lines are also indicated by lines broken into varying lengths – ease or gather will be printed on the line.

Heavy solid line running across

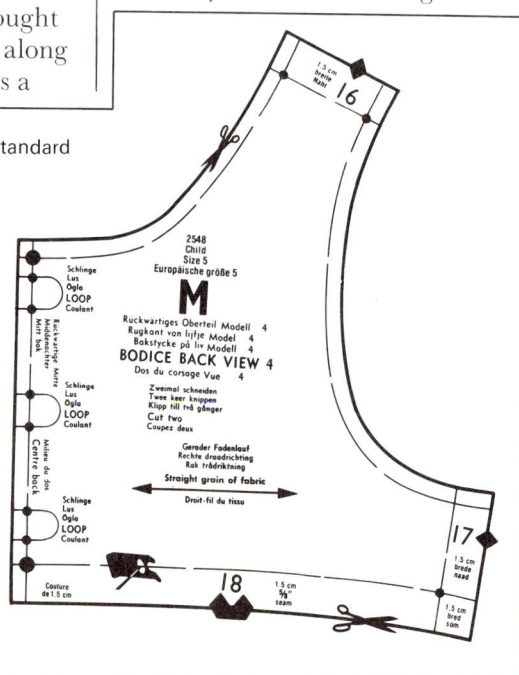

A typical pattern piece showing standard construction markings.

the pattern from cutting line to opposite cutting line. This is the *lengthening* or *shortening* line and is what the name implies.

Adjusting paper patterns

Before making any adjustments to the paper pattern it is essential to measure the various pieces and compare them with your own measurements. Remember the designed-in ease on the pattern pieces and allow for it in your comparison.

You will need the following measurements in addition to those you took originally:

Shoulder From the base of the neck to the point of the shoulder.

Upper arm Sleeves usually have about 10 cm (4 in) ease built in. Measure around the heaviest part of the arm.

Wrist Measure around the wrist above the actual joint and below the bottom thumb joint.

Armhole On a garment you consider fits well, measure from the shoulder seam to the underarm seam.

Rise Important for making trousers. The measurement should be taken while sitting upright on a straight hard seat. Measure from the back natural waistline to the chair seat.

Front waist line From the base of the neck at the shoulder to the natural waistline, over the fullest part of the bust.

Shoulder to bust From the base of the neck to a line at the bust point. You need this measurement to check the placing of the dart.

Back width From armhole to armhole about 12 cm (5 in) below the neck base.

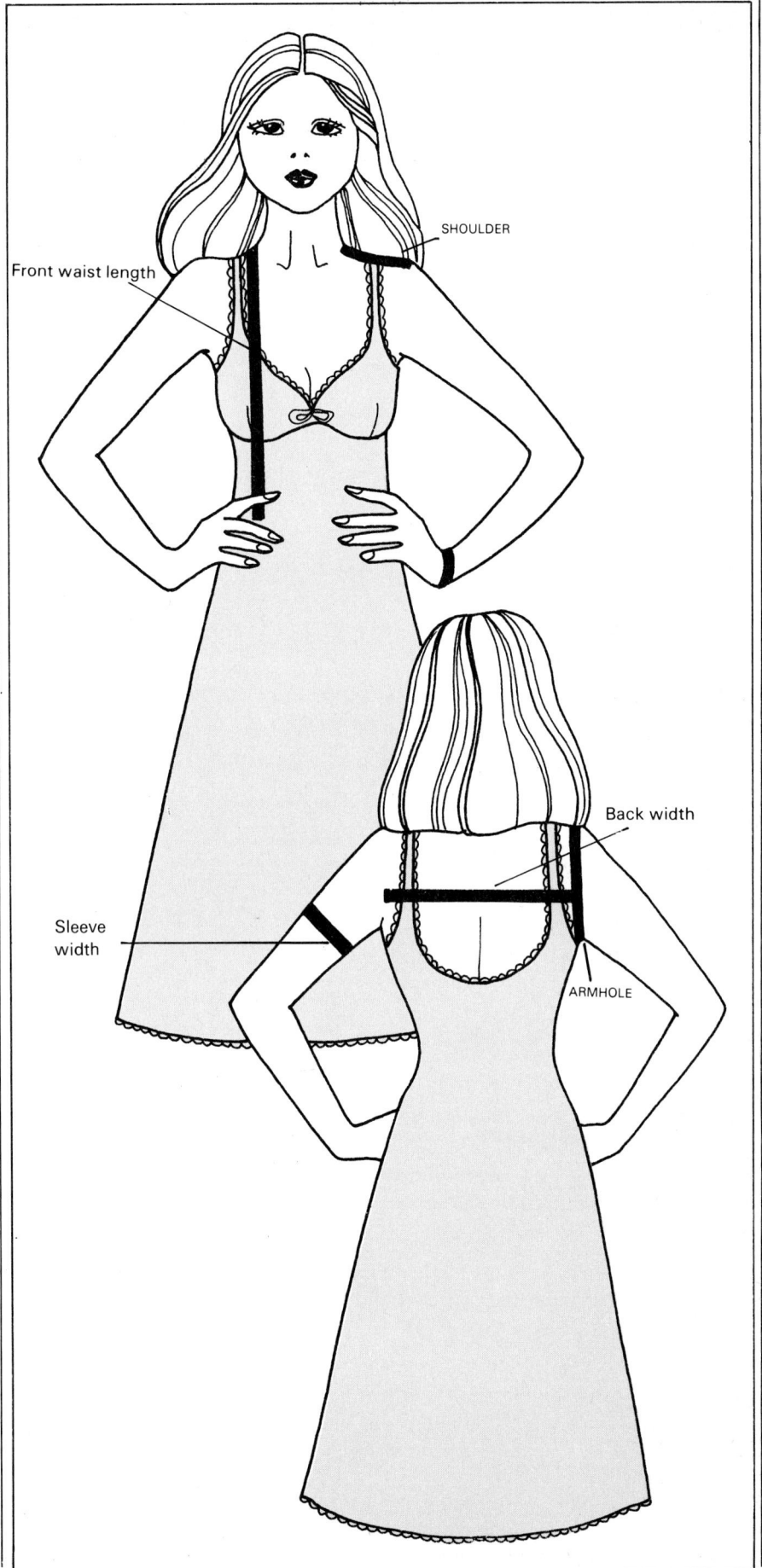

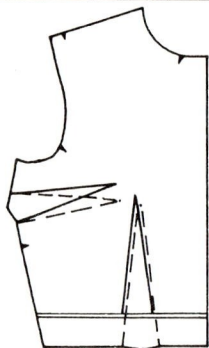

Raising bust and waist darts

Raising the darts on a dress

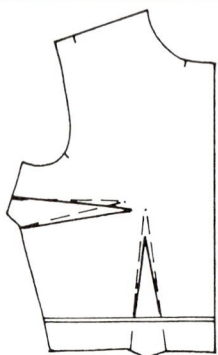

Lowering the bust and waist darts

Lowering the darts on a dress

Having checked the measurements of the pattern, you have a rough idea where adjustments are going to be needed. Very few can be made to a garment at fitting stage, so that important alterations must be made to the paper pattern.

Reinforce the armholes and neckline with adhesive tape. Fold the darts and pin them. Pin the pattern together and slip the half pattern on over undergarments and foundation garments. You get a general idea of the fit of the pattern

and this, combined with the measurements you have checked, gives you an idea about the adjustments you are going to be making to the pattern before cutting out.

Bust darts

The point of a dart must rest on the fullest part of the bust. If it does not, the point must be raised or lowered.

To raise a dart, measure from the widest point of the dart to the new point and re-draw the lines. If there are waistline darts, extend them by the same amount.

To lower a dart, measure the new point down from the dart point and then measure the length, re-draw the lines. Move waist darts to correspond.

Shoulders

If your shoulders are broad and will cause strain across the shoulders of the garment, you need to widen the shoulder seam. Cut the back pattern pieces as follows: From the centre of the shoulder seam line, keeping it parallel to the sleeve seam, draw a line down the pattern piece, to the top of the underarm seam curve. From this point draw another line to the sleeve seam line. Cut the pattern along these lines, from the edge of the shoulder to the sleeve seam line. Lay the pattern on a piece of tissue

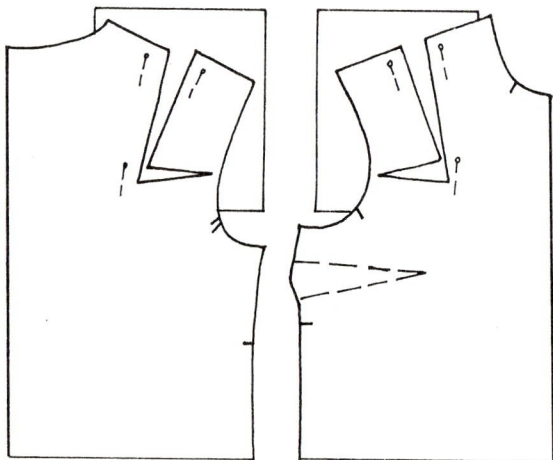

Altering front and back pattern pieces to fit broad shoulders.

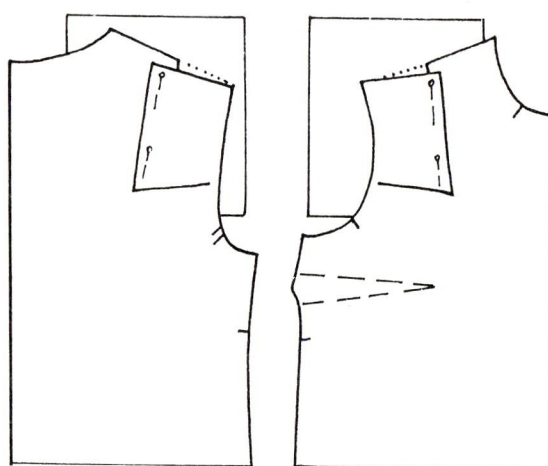

Altering front and back pattern pieces to fit narrow shoulders.

paper and spread the cut to *half* the desired increase. Repeat with the front pattern piece.

To decrease the shoulder measurement if you have narrow shoulders, cut the pattern in the same way, and then overlap the cut edges by half the desired decrease.

Altering length

Generally, the alteration most needed on a pattern is increasing or decreasing the length. Patterns are ·clearly marked lengthening/ shortening lines, and this is where the adjustment should be made. Remember, if you shorten or lengthen a main pattern piece, alterations must be made in corresponding pieces – facings for example. To shorten a paper pattern, take a pleat to the desired decrease (the depth should be *half* the measurement being deducted) and pin it. Straighten the seam line

if required.

To lengthen a pattern piece, cut the pattern through on the marked line. Lay the pattern on tissue paper, and spread to the new depth. Sleeves are altered in the same way.

Increasing width

Minor adjustments, up to 5 cm (2 in), can sometimes be made simply by adjusting the cutting line, by drawing a new line either outside or inside the old. The measurement should be divided equally on all seams so that half of the measurement is distributed on the front of the garment and half on the back, in other words, add $\frac{1}{4}$ the desired increase to the cutting line. 12 mm ($\frac{1}{2}$ in) is the maximum amount that can be added to a

A pattern envelope from the 1920s is similar, but somewhat more fanciful than those to which we are accustomed.

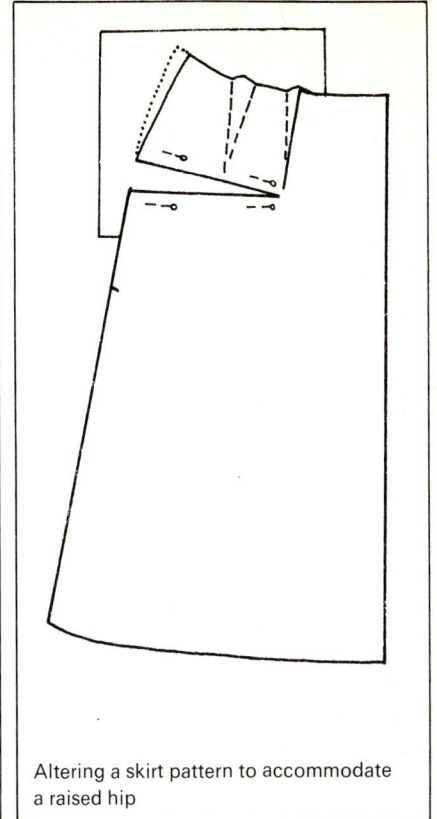

Altering a skirt pattern to accommodate a raised hip

seam. This type of alteration should only be made on skirts at hip or on trousers.

Skirt alterations

Sometimes a skirt appears to hang crookedly and this is caused by one hip being higher than the other. To correct it, first cut another pattern of both back and front and transfer all the markings. The adjustments are made only to the front and back patterns for the high-hip side. If the pattern is cut on a fold, you will have to cut a complete front or back.

Draw a line from the side seam to the point of the waistline dart nearest to the centre front. Cut the pattern along this line and along the dart stitching line nearest to the centre front. Lay the pattern on tissue, spread the horizontal slash by the required amount. The dart slash will overlap, making the dart smaller. Pin the pattern to the tissue and draw in the new seam line and increase the waistline by the amount that the dart was decreased by. Alter the back piece of the skirt pattern in the same way.

Pattern No. 1,843 For you, my lucky Spring bride, I would choose all white for your wedding gown. Soft satin and georgette trimmed with tiny pearls, a veil of lace and tulle, and a bunch of fragrant lilies-of-the-valley.

Pattern No. 1,844 To give a touch of colour to this Spring wedding, let the bridesmaid wear primrose-yellow georgette, with subtle touches of pale-green velvet ribbon, and carry primroses.

Choosing fabrics

A guide to care and use

Fabrics can be grouped under four headings: cotton, wool, silk, and synthetic. In each group there are many types, each named according to the weave, process or chemical treatment used in the manufacture. Linen is another group but it is becoming difficult to find.

Keeping pace with ever-changing fashion, many advances in the colour, weave and texture of fabrics have been made.

Each season produces something new and attractive in synthetic fibres. The use of new processes improves and adds variety to all kinds of textiles. Today, there are crease-resistant synthetics imitating natural fibre textiles. There are also plastic-based fabrics which make attractive accessories. They are especially suitable for raincoats, being waterproof and can easily be sponged clean.

Because of the variety of weaves, patterns and fibres it is easy to become bewildered when choosing a fabric to suit a particular purpose. There is one golden rule to remember: it is always better to buy a good, well-made fabric. A dress made in poor quality fabric will soon look shabby, lose its shape and obviously not be worth the time and care spent in sewing.

The choice of fabric is influenced by the purpose and style of garment to be made. The fabric used for children's clothes and sportswear should launder easily without shrinking, so that it always looks fresh; it must be durable and able to withstand hard wear. Lingerie obviously needs to be made of something light and sheer that will also launder easily.

Clothes that are worn only on rare occasions, such as evening dresses, need not necessarily have good washing qualities; they will probably not become very soiled and can usually be dry cleaned.

For daytime dresses, softly draping materials are a good choice, while fine woollens make smart suits and tailored dresses.

Tweeds are especially suited to outdoor wear. There are many kinds of wool fabric, from the very finest to the coarsest weaves.

Firm, closely woven fabrics are more suitable for skirts than loosely woven ones, and patterned fabrics are more practical than plain, as they show spots and dirt less easily.

Fabric	Description and qualities	Uses	Fibre	Description and qualities	Uses
COTTONS					
Gingham	Woven in plaids, stripes, and checks. Washes and wears well and looks crisp. Needs ironing.	Dresses, blouses, shirts, summer skirts, children's clothes, also some simple home furnishings.		beautifully; hard-wearing.	
Seersucker	Similar patterns and qualities to gingham, but woven with a knobbly or crinkled surface. Needs no ironing.	Dresses, blouses, shirts, summer skirts, children's clothes. Useful also for easy-care household linens such as tablecloths.	Organdie	A very stiff transparent cotton, plain or with embroidered patterns. Sticks out when gathered, but pleats beautifully.	Blouses, children's dresses, collars, cuffs.
Piqué	Corded surface, in various plain colours, rather bulky and not suitable for gathers, but tailors well.	Suits, skirts, sportswear, collars, cuffs.	Sateen	Imitation satin, has a shiny surface, is strong and wears well but it is rather bulky.	Coat linings and loose skirt linings.
			Winceyette	Cotton flannel woven in large striped patterns or plain. Warm and durable.	Nightwear, children's underclothes.
Voile	Semi-transparent in plain, spotted or striped weaves, very soft and drapes	Blouses, dresses, evening wear, children's clothes, nightdresses.	Velveteen	Thick cotton pile like velvet; strong and washable.	Dresses, suits, children's coats, skirts; corduroy good for sportswear.
			Corduroy (Needlecord)	A fine or coarse ribbed velveteen.	

Fibre	Description and qualities	Uses	Fibre	Description and qualities	Uses
	SILKS			threads and silk, in various patterns or plain. Tarnishes and will not wash.	
Crêpe de chine	Very fine silk, slightly crinkled, suitable for gathers; wears and washes well.	Blouses, lingerie, evening wear, linings.	Brocade	Stiff heavy-woven fabric, with rich patterns, often satin or taffeta backed. Does not drape or wash.	Evening coats, dresses and blouses.
Shantung	Fine or coarse corded surface, slightly rough; very strong and washable.	Dresses, blouses, suits, coats, and children's wear.	Velvet	Very soft with fine silky pile, drapes beautifully.	Evening wear, skirts, coats and accessories.
Taffeta	Very stiff, shiny surface. May be plain or patterned with embroidery, sometimes woven in stripes or plaids; does not wash.	Evening wear, blouses, children's party clothes, petticoats.	Panné velvet	Has similar qualities with a flat pile.	
			Cloqué	A double woven fabric with crinkled patterned surface and muslin backing, but is not reversible. Drapes nicely.	Evening wear, blouses.
Georgette	Very fine, semi-transparent crêpe, with a crinkly surface; does not crush; drapes and gathers well.	Blouses, lingerie, evening wear.			
Chiffon	Similar to georgette, but more transparent; plain or printed.	Evening wear, scarves, nightdresses, blouses.		**WOOLLENS**	
			Tweeds	May be hand or machine woven, rough or smooth surfaced. Available in plain colours, it is also woven in multi-coloured stripes, checks and plaids; strong and hard-wearing.	Suits, coats, skirts, children's outdoor clothes.
Marocain	Fine, corded or crinkled surface; satin or crêpe de chine backing; drapes and hangs well.	Dresses, summer coats.			
Satin	Strong weave, very shiny surface, crêpe backing. Various qualities – lingerie satin, very soft and thin; double-sided satin, shiny on both sides and hangs heavily; duchesse or slipper satin with very stiff taffeta back and thick, shiny surface, used for very full evening skirts.	Underclothes, blouses, evening wear, accessories.	Mohair	Silky wool, woven with a mixture of fine yarn hair from the Angora goat. Drapes well and is very warm and soft.	Dresses and blouses.
			Jersey cloths	Tubular woven stockinette; drapes well if it is finely knitted.	Evening wear, dresses, blouses, accessories.
Lamé	Soft draping fabric, woven with metal	Evening coats, blouses and dresses.	Flannel	Fine felt-like cloth, plain weave, strong and washes well, often woven with stripes.	Children's clothes, suits, dresses.

Fabric	Description and qualities	Uses	Fabric	Description and qualities	Uses
Velour cloth Face cloth	Pile fabrics; velour is heavier in texture, face cloth is very fine with a slightly shiny surface.	Coats and suits.		knobbly surfaced fabric; hard-wearing.	
Bouclé	A fancy weave,	Coats and suits.	Delaine	A fine printed woollen, washes well and will drape and gather.	Dresses, blouses, children's clothes, nightdresses.

Synthetics

Fabrics made from synthetic fibres are especially useful for their easy-care properties and are suitable for making all kinds of garments. The following list gives brief descriptions of the main types together with advice on how to care for them.

Fibre	Description and qualities	Washing details	Fibre	Description and qualities	Washing details
Acetates	Fibres are silk like in texture and woven into satins, surahs and taffetas. Brand names include Dicel and Lansil.	Not easy to care for: wash by hand in warm water and iron with a warm iron on the wrong side while damp.		fibre which is often blended with a natural fibre to give it easy-care properties. There are different finishes and brand names include Terylene, Crimplene, Trevira, Tergal and Dacron.	carefully and drip-dried. If necessary iron with a cool iron.
Acrylics	Sometimes used for tweeds. They look like jersey when used for knits. Brand names include Acrilan and Courtelle.	Easily washed but need a final cold-rinse to help prevent creasing. Iron when dry if necessary.			
Modacrylics	Strong, closely woven fabrics which are sometimes flameproofed. Brand names include Teklan and Dynel.	Wash and dry easily. If necessary, iron with a cool iron when dry.	Triacetates	Used to make crisp fabrics with a silky feel which are generally crease-resistant. Brand names include Tricel and Arnel.	Washes easily and dries quickly. No ironing needed. Must not be dry cleaned.
Nylon	Strong, crease resistant fibre which can be woven, or knitted into a jersey. Brand names include Perlon, Celon and Enkalon.	Washes easily. Needs no ironing.	Viscose Rayon	These come in two finishes; either with a brushed surface or a crisp shiny look for linings. Also blended with natural fibre. Brand names include Sarille and Erlan.	Care depends on the way the fabric has been processed.
Polyester	Good wearing	Should be washed			

Fabric terminology

Special finishes

Crease resistant The yarn or the finished fabric has been treated so that it has the ability to shed creases. The fabric may crease, as other fabrics do, but the crease should drop out without ironing.

Drip dry, minimum iron, minimum care The garment will dry without creases if it is not wrung out after washing. Most washing machines have a special programme for these finishes. Sometimes a light smoothing with an iron is required.

Durable press or permanent press The garment can be washed in a washing machine, will shed wrinkles and creases while drying, and keep its shape.

Fire resistant, flame-proof The fabric has been chemically treated so that if it catches fire, will either simply smoulder or extinguish itself once it is taken away from the naked flame. Ideal for children's clothes. Laundering instructions should always be followed carefully to retain the flame-proof finish.

Moth-proof This is a permanent proofing which makes the fabric unattractive to moth larvae. The proofing is not affected by dry cleaning or laundering.

Non-iron finish A term used for a special finish on cotton or blended fabrics. They should not have to be ironed after washing, but laundering instructions provided with these fabrics should be closely followed.

Permanently pleated Many fabrics can be given this process and, if the manufacturer's instructions are followed for cleaning and laundering, pleats should stay in a garment almost indefinitely.

Shrink-resistant, pre-shrunk This means that the fabric has been pre-shrunk during finishing. Several types of shrink-resistant finishes are available, and some of these will be guaranteed by the manufacturer. Fabrics which are treated in this way include wool, cotton, linen and blends of these with man-made fibres.

Choosing dressmaking fabrics

Clothes can be stylish even if their lines do not follow the latest fashion trends.

Well-cut clothes have beauty of line and require little superficial decoration to add to their charm. A cleverly cut garment can make a plump woman look slim, a short woman look tall and so on.

Diagonal lines in the design and narrow striped fabrics, cut on the cross, have a slimming effect, while wide frills, gathers, wide sleeves and yokes, horizontal stripes and added decoration tend to shorten a tall figure or make a slim figure look heavier.

Shiny fabric and large patterns should be avoided by the plump woman, but she should be able to wear softly drapes styles in small-patterned and dull-surfaced fabrics.

So, for successful dressmaking, remember that what suits one woman will look ludicrous on another. When planning your wardrobe, study your good points and choose styles which will enhance your figure and hide the defects.

Choosing the right fabric for each project is the key to successful sewing.

Interfacing, lining and mounting fabrics

Interfacings

Most garments have an interfacing in them somewhere, to give strength or crispness to certain areas. Lapels, collars, jacket and coat edges, cuffs, pockets and necklines are usually interfaced.

Choosing fabrics

It is important that the top fabric is not dominated by the interfacing. To test suitability, hold a piece of the top fabric over the edge of the interfacing. If it is too stiff, the fabric will just fall over the edge. If it is too soft, both will collapse together. If the interfacing weight is correct, the top fabric will gently roll over it.

As a general rule, interfacings fall into two categories: woven fabrics and non-woven (Vilene [Pellon]).

Non-wovens have a number of advantages. They wash and dry easily, they are non-fray and do not lose their shape, and they are economical to use because, as they have no grain, they can be cut in any direction. There are three types: straight non-woven, available in several weights; fusible, which is ironed onto the fabric (also available in widths for stiffening waistbands and for finishing hems); stretch, especially designed for interfacing knitted fabrics. When using the iron-on type you should bear in mind that it tends to stiffen the fabric and should, therefore, never be used on the outside of the garment.

Many dressmakers prefer to use woven fabrics for interfacing, and a guide to suitable interfacings of both kinds is given below:

Light to medium weight natural fabrics (lightweight wool, cotton, linen and linen type fabrics) Use pre-shrunk lawn, lightweight cotton, iron-on and standard non-woven interfacing of suitable weight.

Fabrics made from man-made fibres Use non-woven standard interfacing.

Stretch fabrics Use fabrics of suitable washing qualities and weights, cut on the bias, special non-woven interfacing.

Sheer fabrics Use silk organza, soft organdie, transparent iron-on, non-woven interfacing.

Silk Use lawn, pure silk organza, thin pure silk, suiting weight fabrics.

Coat weight fabrics Use non-woven interfacing of suitable weight, special tailoring canvas.

Linings

Linings are used to finish off the inside of a garment, to help to prevent the fabric stretching out of shape and sometimes, to replace facings. Any fabric which is inclined to fray or is very loosely woven should be lined. Dresses made of wool fabrics which have a rough finish are more comfortable if they are lined.

Lining fabrics are usually smooth and rather slippery so that they are comfortable to wear, and help the garment to slip on and off more easily.

Generally, the lining should be a little lighter in weight than the outer fabric and have the same care requirements – a washable garment should have a washable lining and a garment which is going to be dry cleaned should have a lining which will stand dry cleaning.

When choosing lining fabrics, match the colour to that of the top fabric as closely as possible, or choose one which makes an interesting, attractive colour contrast. Before buying a lining, hold the outer fabric against it to make sure that the lining does not show through. If you are fully lining a garment, you will need the same amount as of the top fabric.

Mounting

Mounting, sometimes called underlining, is a layer of fabric attached to the wrong side of the top fabric before making up. Both layers of fabric are then treated as one. Mounting, or underlining, is used for the following reasons or effects:

To give extra support or opacity to lightweight or sheer fabrics.
To support loosely woven fabrics.
To conceal construction details on sheer fabrics.
To give support to some areas of an otherwise soft garment – a blouse or dress of a sheer fabric where the sleeves are left sheer, and the body is underlined to become opaque and firm.

Choosing fabrics for mounting

Here are some of the uses of underlining and a guide to suitable fabrics:

Backing sheer fabrics Use jap silk, lawn, of soft net.

Giving body Use cotton, calico, holland or lawn, depending on the fabric weight.

Shaping Use holland, tailor's canvas or Vilene (Pellon) for areas to be shaped such as a standing hem.

Spring folds Use net, fine Vilene (Pellon) or domette to pad out a fold.

Controlling grain Use jap silk, lawn or soft net to control fabric cut on the cross.

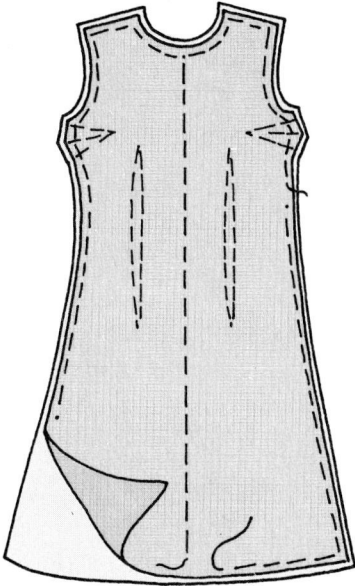

When mounting, the full lining is tacked to the garment pieces, and they are then treated as one fabric.

Technique of mounting

After cutting out the garment piece, use the same pattern piece for cutting the underlining or mounting piece. Lay it on the wrong side of the fabric, pinning at corners and down the middle. Single-thread tack all around the edges and down the centre of the two fabrics. Single-thread tack all the fitting lines as well. Make up both layers of fabric together.

Hints on cutting underlinings

Some fine fabrics, such as silk jersey, silk, crêpe de chine and georgette are inclinded to slip about when being cut, and the shape is therefore likely to be different from that of the pattern. Here is a way of cutting both top fabric and underlining more accurately.

Allow a little more fabric than recommended in the yardage requirements. Cut out the top fabric and the underlining a little larger than the pattern – about 6 mm ($\frac{1}{4}$ in) outside the cutting line. Lay the two fabrics together on a flat surface, matching grain lines and notches and symbols. Pin down the centre and across the width and

then baste two fabrics together diagonally, starting at the middle and working out towards the edges.

Keep the work absolutely flat and keep the diagonal basting inside the seam lines. When you have finished, re-pin the paper pattern to the fabric and match the grain lines again. Cut accurately along the pattern lines. Neaten the edges of the sections and apply any staystitching the pattern requires before proceeding with making up the garment.

A lining always helps a tailored skirt to hang well and prevents ugly 'seating'.

Preparation of the fabric

To make a success of dressmaking every effort should be made to get the most out of the fabric.

It always pays to buy best quality fabric, as it will make up more satisfactorily, be worth the work involved and wear better.

Shrinking

Many woollen fabrics, some cottons, and linen fabrics require shrinking before cutting.

This is done to prevent ugly cockled seams which appear after pressing and detract from the good finish of the garment.

The best method of shrinking is as follows. Damp a clean sheet thoroughly and evenly, open it out flat on a table. Place the fabric (still folded double as when purchased) very smoothly on top of the sheet. Roll up loosely with fabric inside and leave for about twelve hours. Then hang the fabric up to dry thoroughly. Always let it dry naturally, do not dry it in a tumble-drier or with an iron. Handle the fabric as little as possible while it is damp.

Straightening

The cut edge of the fabric should be straightened before cutting out the pattern. Draw out a weft thread of the fabric near to the cut edge, then cut straight along this thread. Press out any deeply marked creases or folds.

Press out the creases in the pattern, with a cool iron, especially if adaptations have been made.

Pattern layout

The way that the pattern is laid out is different for each type of fabric. If this is done with care and thought a great saving in fabric can be made.

Lay the fabric smoothly on a table. Make sure that the weft threads lie absolutely straight and exactly one over the other, when the fabric is doubled. If this is not exact it will cause the garment to hang badly, a mistake that cannot

be rectified.

If a commercial pattern is being used, follow the manufacturer's instructions for laying out. If, however, the pattern is being altered or it is a home-cut pattern, then it is necessary to plan the layout entirely.

Place the main pieces of the

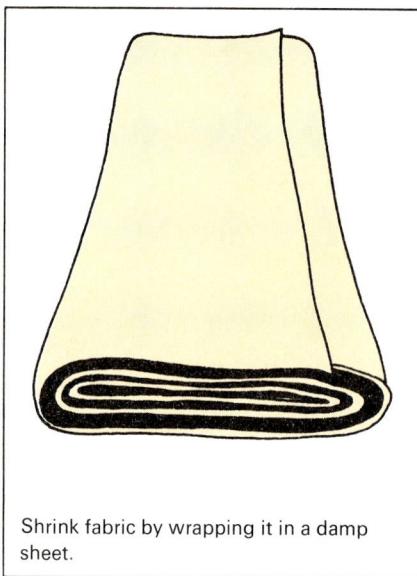

Shrink fabric by wrapping it in a damp sheet.

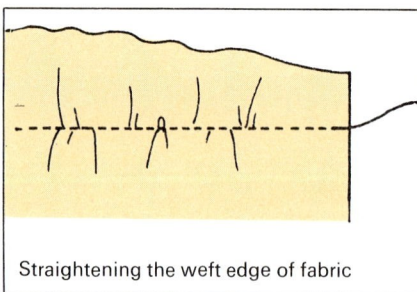

Straightening the weft edge of fabric

pattern on the fabric first, making due allowance for any extra length and turnings required.

It may be necessary to allow extra turnings of about 12 mm ($\frac{1}{2}$ in) when using fabrics that fray badly, particularly on all lengthwise seams.

When arranging the layout of the pattern, take great care to ensure that the fold edges are placed exactly on the fold of the fabric. The lengthwise grain marking should lie on the straight grain of the fabric, exactly parallel to the selvedge. Special care should be taken with fabrics with nap or one-way designs as shown. Pieces to be cut on the bias should lie

diagonally to the grain of the fabric.

When the layout of the pattern has been planned satisfactorily, pin all the pattern pieces to the fabric. Insert the pins at right angles to pattern edges (10 cm to 13 cm) (4 in to 5 in) apart. Pin at straight grain indicators (usually an arrow on

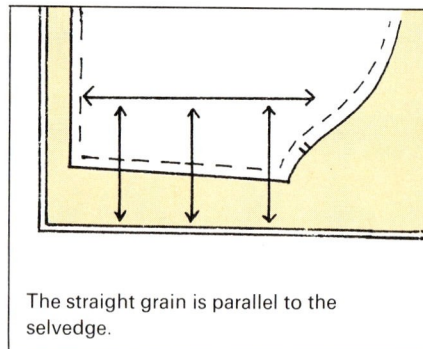

The straight grain is parallel to the selvedge.

commercial patterns) before fixing along edges.

If it is necessary to unfold or re-fold parts of the material to cut out the pattern, plan the layout carefully, then cut out pieces on the first fold. Re-fold, making sure that all the threads are even and that the selvedge is parallel to the new fold, then cut out the remainder.

If left and right sides are cut separately on a single thickness of fabric make sure that the pattern piece is turned over to prevent cutting two left-hand or two right-hand pieces.

Patterns on fabrics without nap or one-way design can often be dovetailed to save material.

Cutting out

Do not cut out a pattern in a hurry. If your time is limited, then leave it to another day.

Cut with good, even strokes, using large dressmaker's shears, leaving turnings as directed in the instructions if you are using a homemade pattern. Hold material firmly with the other hand. Keep all corners sharp.

Certain fabrics require very careful cutting, especially those with a nap surface which should be cut with the pile running downwards, except in the case of velvet, where the pile should run upwards in order to give a richer appearance.

When cutting on the cross make sure that the exact bias is obtained, otherwise the garment will hang incorrectly. Often it is easier to cut each piece on the cross separately, especially if a striped fabric is being used.

When each piece of pattern has been cut out, the markings for fitting lines, darts, pockets and so on should be transferred from the paper pattern to the fabric.

Patterned fabrics

If the fabric has a one-way design every piece of garment pattern must be carefully placed on the material so that the design lies in one direction only, thus avoiding a jumbled appearance when made up.

Large Prints

The motifs of a fairly large design should be so planned that they lie in the centre of each main part. They should also be placed so that motifs match up across seam lines wherever possible. Remember to choose a pattern with as few seam lines as possible in the bodice and the skirt, when using boldly patterned fabrics.

Raised pile

Treat fabrics with nap or pile in the same way as patterned fabrics with a one-way design, letting the nap stroke the same way on every section of the garment.

To determine the direction of the nap stroke the fabric with the finger: it should feel smooth when running with the pile and rough when running against it.

The pile of velvet, corduroy or needlecord should brush upwards for maximum wear and richest colour tone. Napped fabrics such as cashmere and certain other types of wool should have the pile running downwards.

Slippery fabrics

There are a number of these, principally woven from nylon and other synthetic yarns. It is a

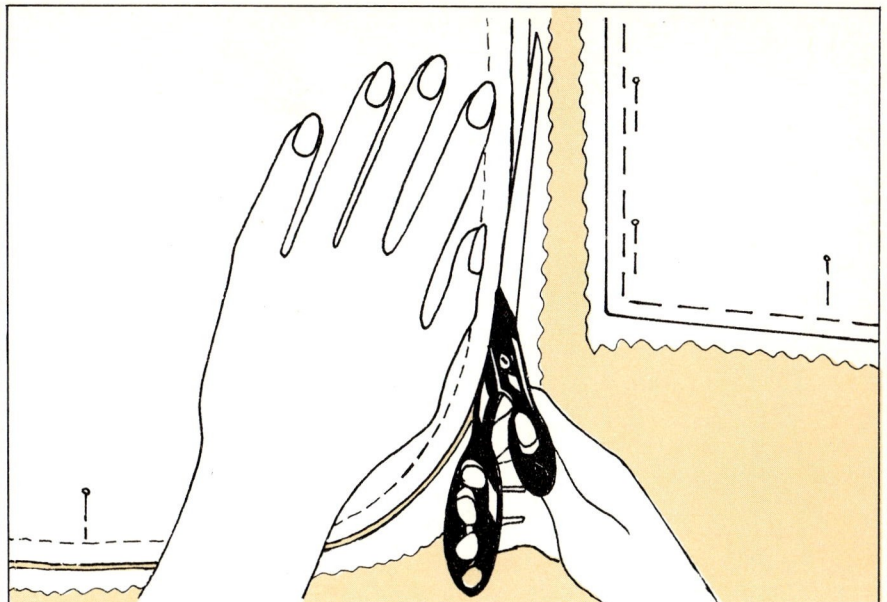

Cut out with smooth even strokes.

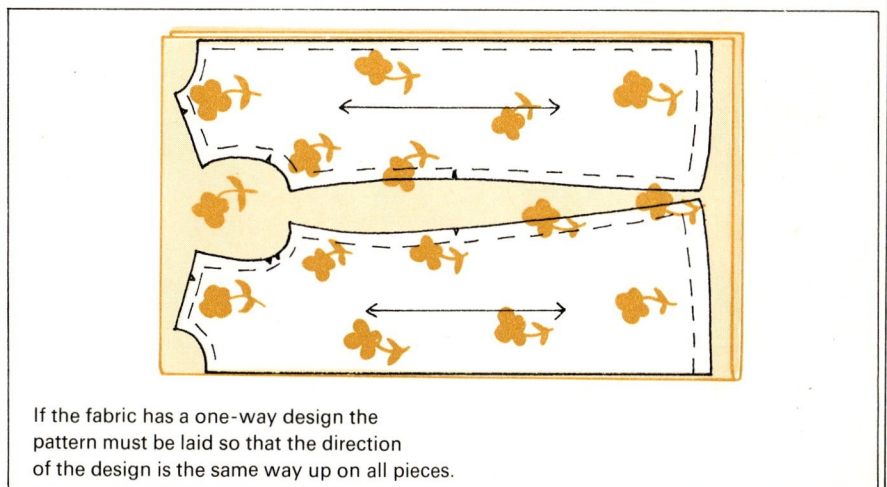

If the fabric has a one-way design the pattern must be laid so that the direction of the design is the same way up on all pieces.

good idea to pin or tack the folded material together before laying on the pattern. Cut out on a cloth or rough surface to prevent slipping.

Stretch fabrics

Treat as slippery fabrics; great care must be taken to prevent stretching when cutting out.

Striped or check fabrics

Checks and stripes should match at the centre front and back, and underarm seams of bodices and jackets, at skirt seams and at shoulder and sleeve seams. It is wiser, therefore, to cut out every main part of the pattern in single fabric. The fabric is then reversed, and the pattern, still pinned to the first pieces cut, is placed over it so

that the stripes or checks match. Re-pin to the double fabric and cut out.

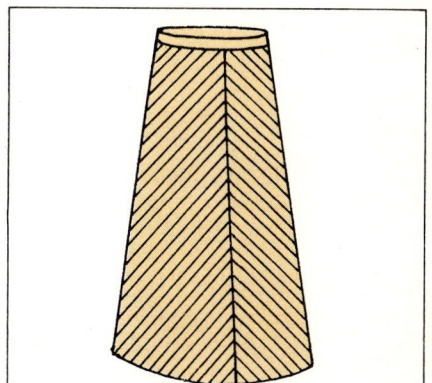

Stripes should match up at the centre front seam of a skirt.

schnittlinie
kniplijn
klipplinje
linea del corte
ligne de coupe
cutting line

5 cm saumzugabe
5 cm zoomtoeslag
5 cm fålltillägg
dobladillo de 5 cm.
ourlet de 2"
2" hem allowed

schnittlinie
kniplijn
klipplinje

5 cm saumzugabe
5 cm zoomtoeslag
5 cm fålltillägg

de la poche
del bolsillo
richtlinie

place on straight grain of
placez sur le droit-fil du ti
colóquese en el hilo de la
Im geraden Fadenlauf auf
Op de rechte draadrichtin
Lägg i den raka trådrikt

30

cutting line
ligne de coupe
linea del corte

schnittlinie
kniplijn
klipplinie

Simplicity
7688
Child
size 3

front
devant
frente
vorderteil
voorkant
framstycke
grösse

cutting line for lining
ligne de coupe pour la doublure
linea del corte para el forro
kniplijn voor voering
schnittlinie für futter
klipplinje för foder

nahtlinie
naadlijn
sömlinje

line
couture
costura

cut two
coupez deux
córtese 2 piezas
zweimal schneiden
twee keer knippen
klipp till två gånger

stitch seams in direction of arrows
piquez les coutures dans la direction des flèches.
coserse las costuras en la direccion de las flechas.
die nähte in der durch pfeile
richtung steppen
de naden in de met pijlen aangegeven
richting stikken
sy sömarna i pilarnas riktning.

fabric

The important stages of dressmaking

Marking

Having cut out your pattern, the next most important stage in making a garment is marking. Leave the pattern pinned to the fabric until you have transferred all the symbols and construction lines. A good method of doing this is to mark all the symbols – dots, spots, squares – with tailor's tacks, and to then mark fold-lines, pocket placings, centre front and back, interfacing lines and so on with chalk lines or thread tracing. Beginners might also thread-trace curved seam lines to make machine stitching easier.

Chalk lines should not be made on sheer or semi-transparent fabrics, and thick, tweeds or fabrics with a pile will not take chalk marks. These should be marked with thread tracing.

Dressmaker's carbon paper

This is a quick but very accurate method of marking both construction lines and symbols, marking symbols with a small cross. The technique works best on smooth fabrics and is ideal for marking lining fabrics.

The marks should be made on the wrong side of the fabric, so if you are working with doubled fabric, you will have to work with the paper folded.

Remove the pins around the area to be traced so that you can slip the carbon paper between the layers of fabric. Working on a firm, hard surface, roll the tracing wheel firmly over the lines. Move the carbon paper as you need to. Make crosses or intersecting lines on the construction symbols if you are not using tailor's tacks for these.

Tailor's chalk

This method is useful for marking seam lines and darts on single layers of fabric. Pin the pattern piece along the seam line, fold the edge over the pins, and lightly sketch in the lines with the chalk edge. If you prefer, use a tailor's chalk pencil.

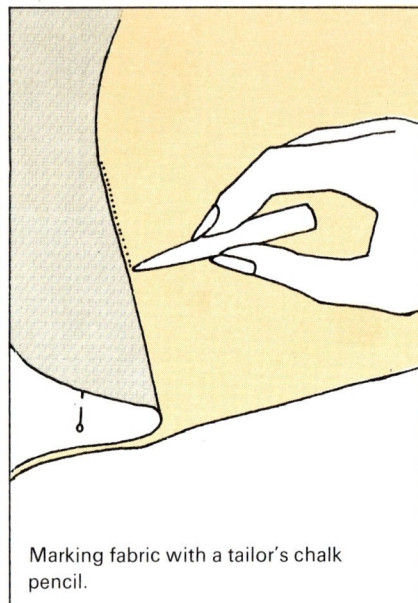

Marking fabric with a tailor's chalk pencil.

Tailor's tacks

Double thread a needle with tacking thread but do not tie a knot. When working tailor's tacks on fine fabrics, such as sheers, satins, and silks, use a good sewing thread instead of tacking cotton. To mark a single construction symbol, take a small stitch on the symbol through paper and fabric, leaving about 3.5 cm ($1\frac{1}{2}$ in) of thread ends. Make another small stitch immediately and leave a large loop on the surface. Cut the thread leaving about 3.5 cm ($1\frac{1}{2}$ in) of thread. Finally, clip the loop. To mark seam lines, darts and other construction lines take the needle to

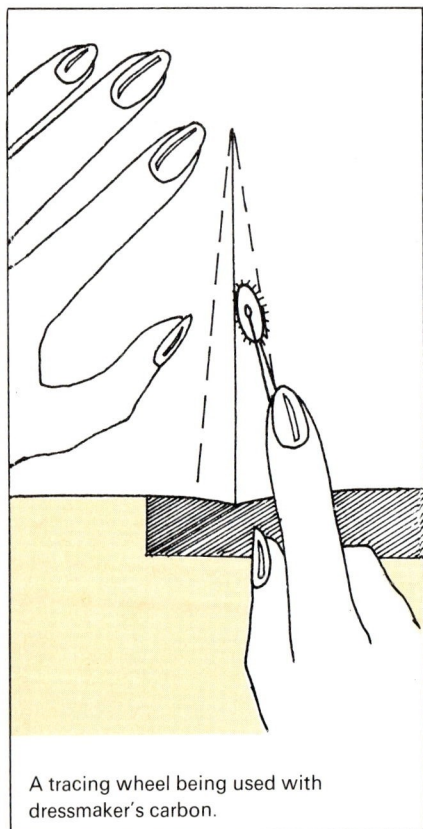

A tracing wheel being used with dressmaker's carbon.

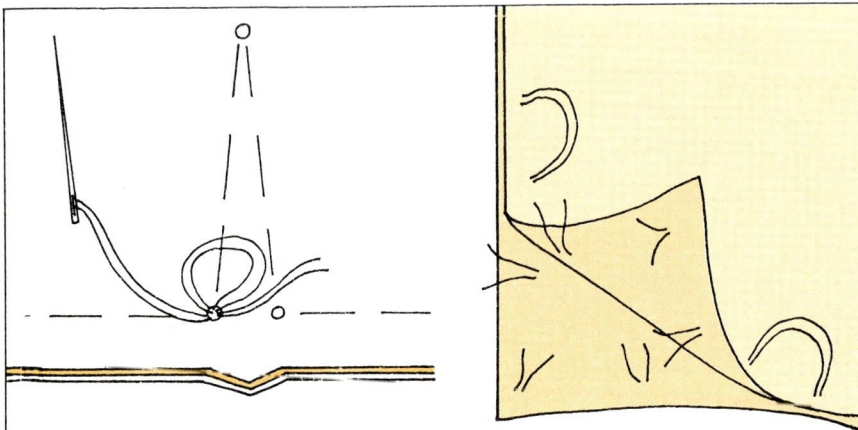

Left Tailor's tack
Right Cut the loops and gently pull the layers apart.

the next symbol, leaving the thread slack. Do not cut the thread. When all the symbols are marked, unpin the pattern and carefully break the tissue paper over the loops to release it. Gently ease the two layers of fabric apart and snip the threads leaving small tufts of thread along the marked lines.

If you want to be sure of the marks, make a small chalked cross on the wrong side of the fabric, just in case the tailor's tacks drop out while putting the garment together.

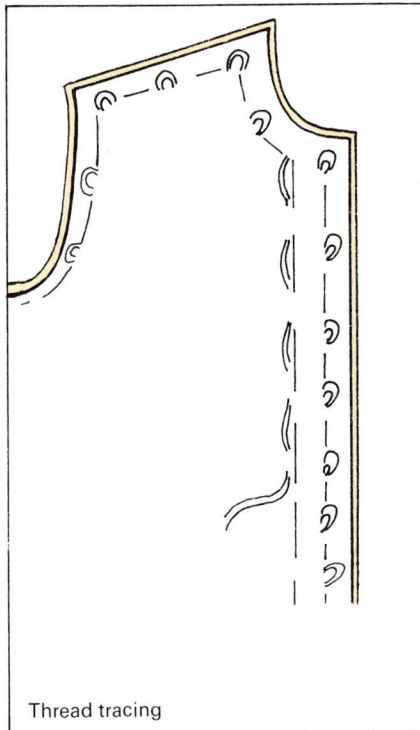

The arrows show the correct directions for stay stitching.

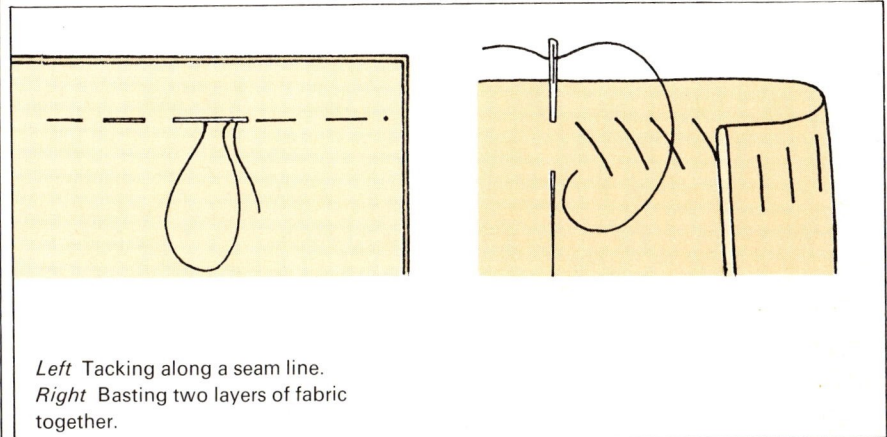

Left Tacking along a seam line.
Right Basting two layers of fabric together.

Thread tracing

Thread tracing
This technique is used by many professional dressmakers primarily for marking seam lines and grain lines on single layers of fabric. Work tailor's tacks for all the symbols. Double thread a long, fine needle with tacking thread. Work uneven tacking stitches along the lines, making small stitches on the pattern side so that when the pattern is pulled off, it is not damaged too much.

To mark seam lines on double fabric with thread tracing, fold the edges of the pattern back along the lines and work even tacking stitches, leaving large loops on the surface through both thicknesses of

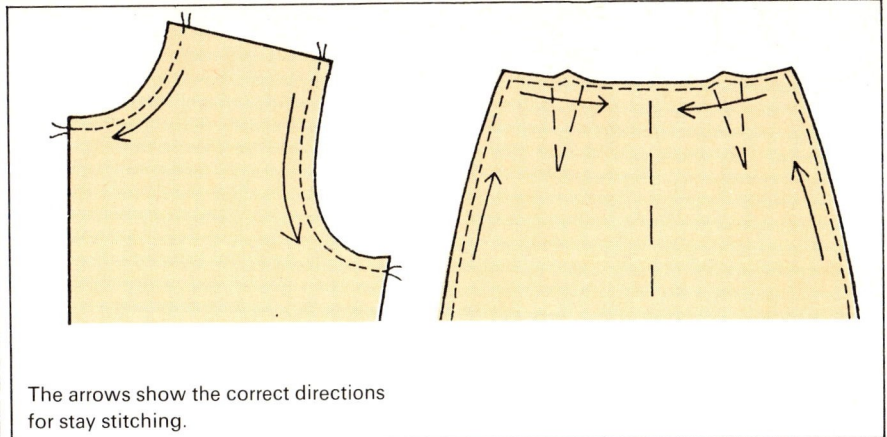

fabric. Pull the layers apart and snip the threads.

The second stage
Staystitching
Staystitching is a line of straight machine stitching worked 3 mm ($\frac{1}{8}$ in) from the seam line and within the seam allowance.

Staystitching is the next step in putting the garment together after the construction symbols and marks have been transferred. It is important because curved and diagonally cut edges can easily be pulled out of shape during fitting.

Use the sewing thread you have chosen for the garment because staystitching stays in the garment permanently.

Method
Obviously, you must work on a single layer of fabric, otherwise you will be seaming the garment pieces together. To staystitch properly so that the fabric does not pucker, stitch curves as follows:
Armhole From shoulder to underarm.

Hipline seams From hip to waist. Jersey and other knit fabrics must be stitched from the edges of the curve to the centre. This way the fabric will not be stitched as you sew.
Neckline From the outer edges to the centre.

Tacking and basting
Some needlewomen get confused over these two techniques. Tacking is the stitching technique used to hold two seam edges together. Basting is the stitching technique used for holding two large pieces of fabric together. The stitches used are different.
Tacking
After pinning the garment pieces together on the seam line, thread a needle with tacking thread and work even stitches about 6 mm ($\frac{1}{4}$ in) long and the same distance apart just 2 mm ($\frac{1}{8}$ in) inside the seam allowance. When stitching the seam, take care not to machine over the tacking, it would make the tacking difficult to remove

33

afterwards. When tacking a very long seam, make a backstitch occasionally to take the strain during fitting. Tacking stitches around curved seams should be a little shorter and closer together so that the fabric is easier to manipulate during fitting and stitching.

Basting

This technique is used mainly for holding pieces of fabric together, as when applying an interfacing. Single thread a needle and knot one end. Lay the work flat and, bringing the needle up from the wrong side, make a line of 2.5 cm (1 in) long stitches, putting the needle through the fabric at right angles to the edges. The stitches will lie diagonally on the fabric. When basting plaids, stripes, complicated curves or alterations made from the right side of the garment, use *slip-basting*.

Crease the seam allowance of one garment piece to the wrong side. With right sides facing lay this piece over the corresponding piece, with the folded edge against the seam line. Match the print, pin in place and then begin stitching from the upper fold through to the lower fabric piece. Make the stitches very small and even.

The fitting stages

It is most important that, when you are in the process of making a dress or other garment, you continually try it on to see how the work is progressing: are the seams even, are darts positioned correctly, does it hang properly and fit neatly? These are just a few of the questions you should ask as you fit a garment during construction.

As mentioned earlier, only minor adjustments can be made now, so if you were careful when making pattern adjustments, you should not have too much work to do now.

Fitting is divided into two stages, and at each stage you should take the time to change into good foundation garments and put on

the shoes you are likely to wear with the garment.

Dressmaker's toile

This is a trial garment made up in muslin or calico to check the fit of pattern before making it in the actual fabric. Although this may sound like a tedious task, it is not the time-waster you might think. If you have chosen an elaborate pattern and very expensive fabric for a special dress, you could save yourself making uncorrectable errors and the expense of possible ruining the fabric. If you find that the adjustments you must make to the pattern are quite complicated you can simply unpick the toile and use it for your cutting out.

First stage Mark all main pattern pieces with thread tracing along the grain lines. Tack the main garment pieces together along major seam lines. Leave openings untacked. Press the seams open lightly because it helps you to get a better impression of fit.

Try on the garment, right side out and fasten the openings. Stand

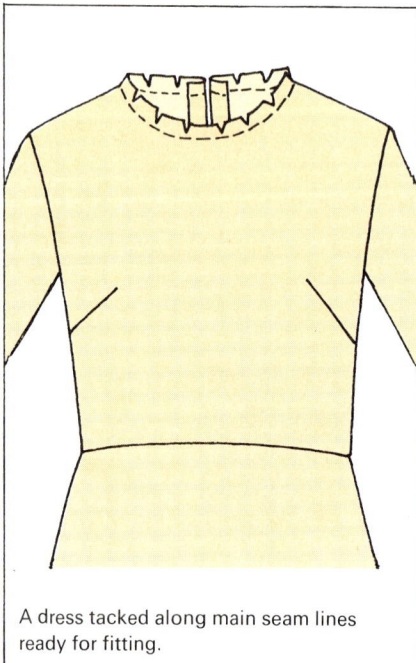

A dress tacked along main seam lines ready for fitting.

in front of a full length mirror and check the following: thread-traced grain lines are vertical to the floor; that the centre front is in the right place, and then that the centre

back lies down the spine. Next, look for folds and wrinkles down the length which indicate too much width, any across the figure means either tightness, or that there is too much length in that particular

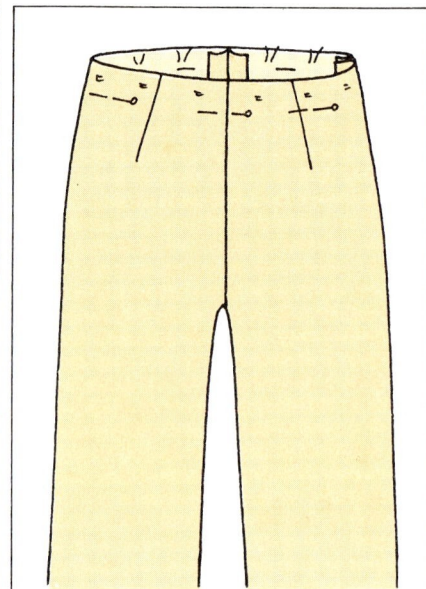

Trousers tacked together for fitting with waistline clearly marked.

piece. For instance, when a jacket or bodice is too long in the waist, a series of crosswise creases will occur between the shoulder and the armpit or between armpit and waist – or even at both places. An armhole which is too tight will make creases across the chest and across the back. Diagonal creases indicate that shaping is faulty, the most common place being from the bust to the side waist. This could mean remaking a dart.

Incorrect cutting out may make a garment hang incorrectly. The weft threads of the fabric should run straight around the body. If these threads are out of true, the garment will never fall properly.

First stage alterations
Shoulders

The back shoulder should always be eased a little to the front. This gives a little moulding and helps the garment to sit well. The seam should lie exactly on the top of the shoulder. If you stand particularly erect, it may be necessary to lift the back shoulder at the seam.

Necklines

To correct a baggy neckline, increase the shoulder seams at the neck edge and taper off towards the armhole edge. To ease a tight neckline, clip into the seam allowance until the neckline lies flat, but take care not to clip beyond the staystitching. Mark the new seam line with pins and then thread-trace or use tailor's chalk. Remember to make a similar alteration to the neckline facing or the collar.

Skirts

Skirt seams should fall away slightly from the waist and not fall in below the knees. Try sitting down to make sure that the skirt does not ride up.

Trousers

Generally, alterations for fitting should be made to the pattern. However, if the crotch of trousers seems too low, lift the trousers at the waist and mark the new waistline with pins and tacking.

Darts should not extend beyond the centre of the bust. If the point seems in the wrong place, remove the tacking stitches and refold and pin the dart until the point falls in the right place. Mark the new stitching lines on the wrong side, then tack the dart into the new position and try on again to double check.

Seams should fall absolutely straight. If a seam has to be altered, remove the tacking, correct the seam by overlapping the edges from the right side and re-pin. When you take the garment off, mark the new seam line with thread tracing or tailor's chalk on the wrong side and then re-pin, tack and try-on again before stitching.

Having made any alterations necessary, baste facings in position, stitch the main seams, and finish the darts.

Second stage Tack the sleeve seams ready for fitting into the armholes. Similarly, have a waistband ready for fitting to a skirt. Check the grain lines again to make sure that they are still hanging straight.

Lay the work flat and smooth the fabric towards the seams. If wrinkles appear this means that the fabric has slipped while sewing. To correct this, unpick the seam and restitch it. Turn up the hem to roughly the correct length.

Pin the sleeves into the armholes. Alterations should be made on the armhole allowance not the sleeve itself. If the underarm seems tight, take off the garment and re-cut it a little lower. Once you are happy with the sleeves, tack them into

place. If you have made alterations to the neckline, make sure that you do not have to alter the placing of buttons. Check all fastening placements at this fitting.

Finish sewing the garment, but before you actually finish off – stitching the hem, sewing on buttons and other fastenings – try the garment on one last time to be sure that everything is to your satisfaction. See that the hem hangs evenly and that there are no seams to be eased.

Fashion, like history, repeats itself – particularly if the style relies on a good fit and uncluttered lines. Bear this in mind when choosing patterns and fabrics.

Using the machine

Practising stitching

Many beginners will be impatient and eager at once to be making something, and will be tempted to miss the straight stitching practice, necessary on all types of machine, before starting serious work. This should be done on paper, without threading the machine, until the operator can follow a straight line with ease. Crooked sewing ruins the appearance and fit of a garment.

Rule straight parallel lines 12 mm ($\frac{1}{2}$ in) apart, and then practise following these lines with stitching (without thread) until perfect results are obtained.

The next step is to practise turning corners. Begin by stitching along one edge, keeping the right-hand edge of the presser foot even with the edge of the paper. When near the corner, stop the machine with the needle in the paper, raise the presser foot and turn the paper ready to stitch along the next side. Follow the four sides of the paper and then use the first line of stitching as a guide, making a nest of squares.

This gives excellent practice in turning corners, as well as in straight stitching by using the edge of the presser foot as a guide.

By following these suggestions, the beginner will acquire a knowledge of speed and control of the machine.

The instruction book supplied with every new sewing machine has been carefully compiled by the manufacturer as the result of years of experience, and if it is read and followed closely you should not go far wrong.

Finishing sewing

Finishing off a seam correctly is as important as beginning it in the right way.

When finishing a seam, never sew beyond the end of the material. Stop the machine just before the end is reached; this will prevent the thread becoming caught in the bobbin case.

Before releasing material, see that the take-up lever is at the highest point; then raise the presser foot lever (which also releases the upper tension) and remove the material by drawing it back and to the left. Hold threads in both hands and cut them by a quick downward movement over the thread cutter fixed to the presser bar, or with scissors.

Three or four inches of thread should always be left to prevent the needle becoming unthreaded when a fresh seam is started.

Reinforcing a seam

The beginning and end of the seam can be reinforced if you have an electric sewing machine that sews in reverse. Lower the needle into the fabric about 12 mm ($\frac{1}{2}$ in) from the point where the seam is to begin and backstitch to that point. Sew the seam as above and at the end reverse 12 mm ($\frac{1}{2}$ in) back along the seam line.

Sewing seams

Always keep the bulk of the fabric to the left of the needle. This allows greater freedom of feeding than when it is all allowed to pass under the arm of the machine.

If a sewing machine is correctly adjusted it should sew straight without effort, but if the needle is bent or the foot is out of level, the line of stitching will have a tendency to curve. Any machine that will not stitch approximately straight should be adjusted professionally; it is difficult to turn out perfect work if the material has to be continually guided to preserve a straight line.

Neatening and finishing seams

Some seams such as the French seam or flat fell seam require no further finishing as they leave no raw edges. Other seams, including the ordinary plain seam, require extra neatening to prevent fraying and to strengthen the seam.

Binding

This is suitable for fabrics which fray very easily such as woollens and linen. Use commercial binding or thin strips cut on the bias of the fabric.

If using your own binding, fold one-third of the binding over along its length and press the crease. This may be ironed to keep it flat. Slip the raw edge of seam between the edges of binding, keeping the narrow edge uppermost. Tack and machine stitch on right side exactly on the edge. One row of machine stitching holds both edges of the binding, the under edge being wider than the top.

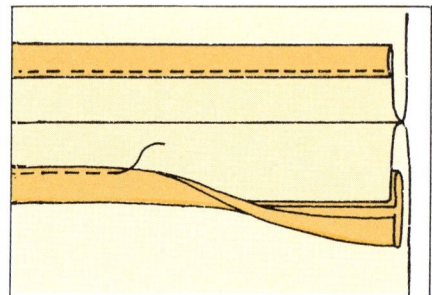

Bound seam edge

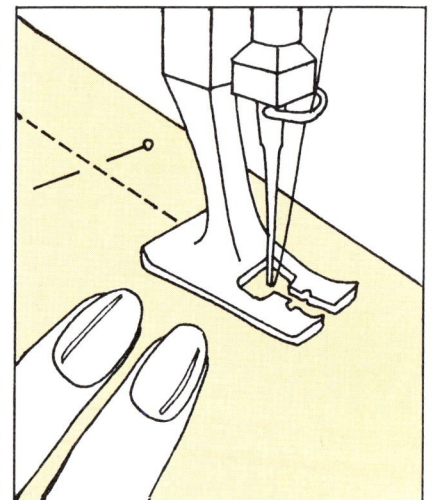

Sewing a seam with the bulk of the fabric to the left of the needle.

Blanket stitch
Used on seams in all kinds of woollen fabrics. It is worked as buttonhole stitch over the raw edge.

Overcasting
The overcast stitch is worked over the edge of the fabric. This is used on closely woven woollen materials.

Notched or pinked
Trim the seam allowances with pinking shears and, if desired, strengthen by running a straight line of stitching close to the notched edge. This method is used on very thick or closely-woven materials; never on fabrics which fray easily.

Edges turned in
Only suitable for fine woollens, silk, cotton or linen fabrics. Fold back the single edge of each turning to wrong side of material. Finish with running stitch, by hand, if the material is inclined to fray. Machine sewing can be used if the material is closely-woven and not too fine.

Zigzag
If you have a swing-needle machine, seams can be neatened by simply using a zigzag stitch on the two raw edges. After neatening in this way press the seam open and trim close to stitchings. This method is especially suitable for jersey and other stretch fabrics.

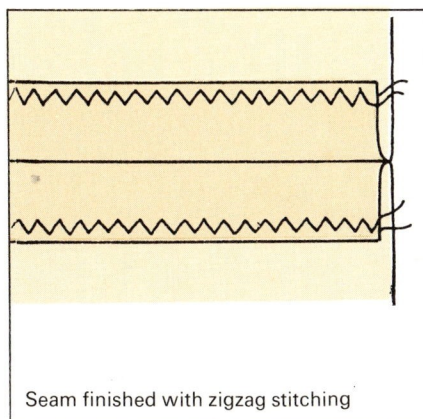
Seam finished with zigzag stitching

Seams

Seams are used to join two or more pieces of fabric together, the type of seam used is governed by the garment and the texture of the fabric.

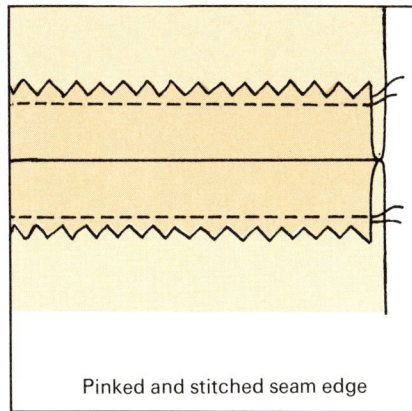
Pinked and stitched seam edge

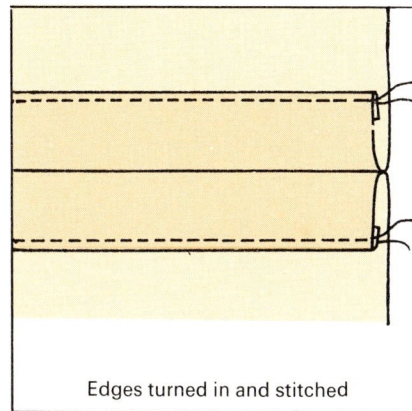
Edges turned in and stitched

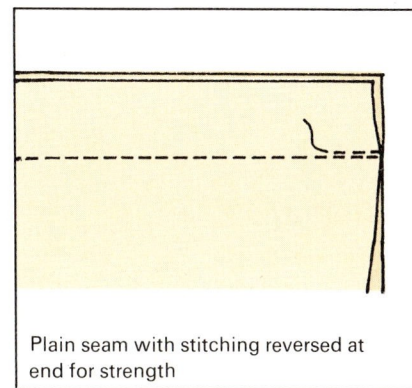
Plain seam with stitching reversed at end for strength

Plain seam
Tack and machine stitch the seam along the fitting line, trim and neaten as desired.

Raised seam
This is used on woollen material, it is a more decorative method than the plain seam.

Place right sides together, with edges meeting, and tack on the wrong side along the fitting line. Lay both turnings to one side and tack down on the right side. Machine stitch on the right side 6 mm ($\frac{1}{4}$ in) from fold. Both turnings are finished together with binding.

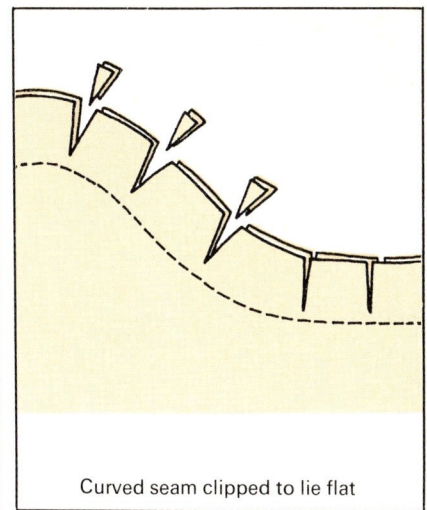
Curved seam clipped to lie flat

Curved seam
To sew a curved seam a shorter stitch should be used than that for a straight seam to give greater elasticity. Curved seams must be clipped if they are to lie flat.

Open seam
This is the simplest of all seams to make, and is used mainly on woollen fabrics.

Place right sides together with edges meeting. Tack and machine stitch along fitting line. Press open flat and finish the raw edges by overcasting or binding with bias binding.

Channel seam
This is a popular method of making seams when the style lines are to be emphasized. Two overlaid seams are arranged over a straight strip, or a shaped section, so that the folds lie towards each other, forming a channel. The stitching which holds the seam in place should be worked at an even distance from the fold.

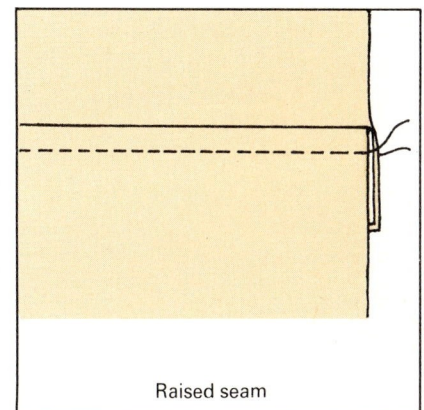
Raised seam

Construction methods

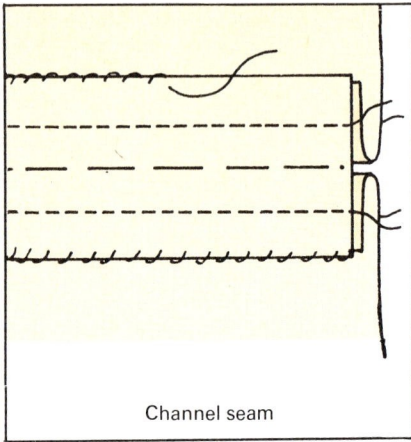
Channel seam

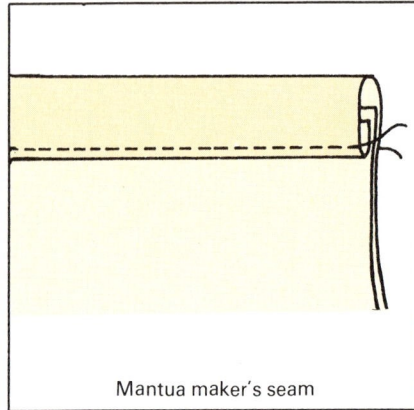
Mantua maker's seam

Whipped seam

A light finish for short seams in fine materials. The seam line is machine stitched with wrong sides together. One edge is cut to within 3 mm ($\frac{1}{8}$ in) of the stitching. The other edge is trimmed to the same amount above the first and whipped over the inner edge to make a neat seam. For fabrics that fray easily, the outer edge should be rolled over the inner edge before whipping.

Mark the centre of the strip with a line of tacking. Tack along the seam line and press open as for the plain seam. Place the strip under the seam and pin and tack along lines an equal distance 6 mm to 12 mm ($\frac{1}{4}$ in to $\frac{1}{2}$ in) from the seam. Machine stitch along these lines, remove tacking threads and press. Trim the turnings level and overcast to neaten.

French seam

This is used for any fine fabric when a neat appearance on both sides is required; it is not suitable for thick fabrics or curved seams. Stitch the seam on the right side of the material, trim the edges as narrow as possible and press. Turn the seam onto the wrong side and tack just outside the trimmed edges, then stitch.

Flat fell seam

This may be used on overalls, skirts, shirts and cotton suits; it is firm and decorative.

Stitch along the fitting line with wrong sides together. Trim one edge so that it is about half as narrow as the other, press both turnings to one side with the wider one covering the other and turn in the wider edge and machine stitch or hem by hand.

This seam can be made with right sides of the fabric together, in which case an ordinary seam appears on the outside of the fabric with one parallel row of stitching.

Mantua maker's seam

A quickly made seam which is suitable for overalls, petticoats, and strong cotton garments.

Tack the seam on the fitting line with right sides together. Trim the turning of one edge, leaving the other wide enough to turn over the edge just cut. Make a single turning on the wider edge, which is then folded over, to make the hem lie along the original tacking line; machine stitch through all thicknesses. The neatening and the seam are finished with one row of stitching.

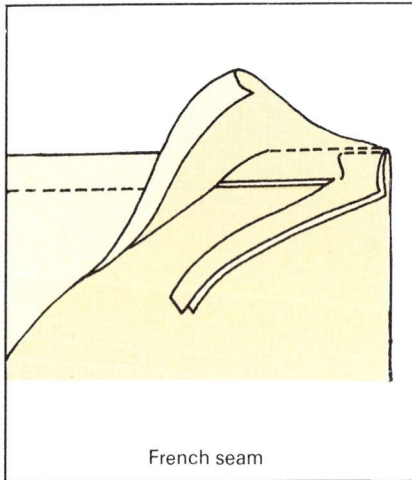
French seam

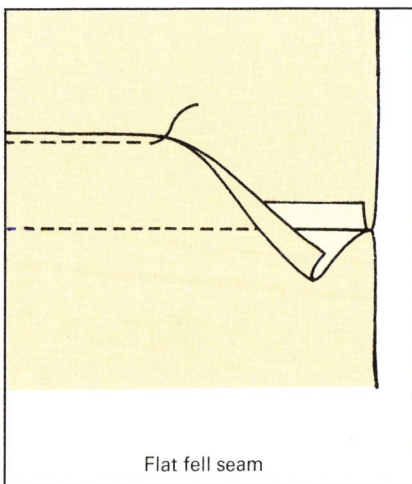
Flat fell seam

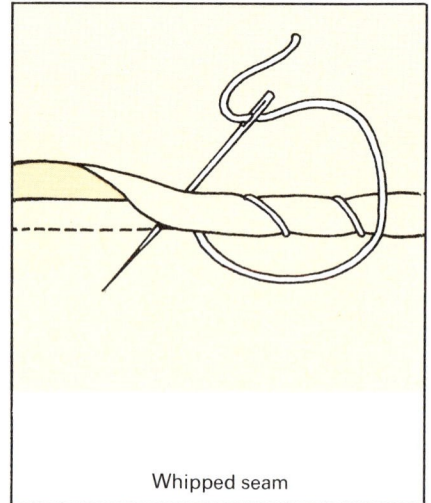
Whipped seam

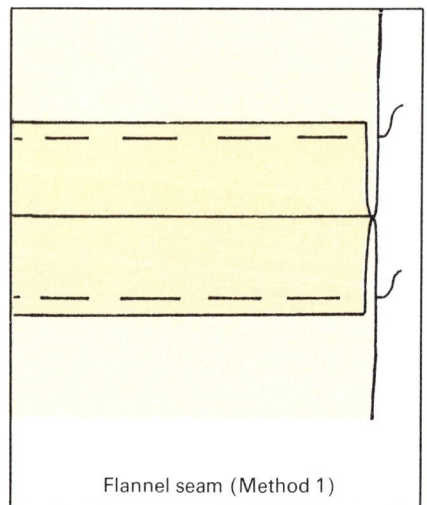
Flannel seam (Method 1)

Flannel seam

Used to make very flat seams on rough or bulky fabrics. There are two methods of working:

Method 1 To make a flannel seam place the two edges of the garment exactly together, warp threads running the same way and the right sides inside. Tack about 9 mm

($\frac{3}{8}$ in) from the edge, and run and
back stitch immediately above.
Open and flatten the seam, and
tack and herringbone the two
edges.

Method 2 Place one edge of the
seam about 6 mm ($\frac{1}{4}$ in) lower than
the other. Tack, and run and back
stitch 6 mm ($\frac{1}{4}$ in) from the lower
edge. Flatten down the upper part
so as to cover the lower one. Tack
and herringbone stitch. If the
garment is worn next to the skin it
is advisable to put the seams on the
outside.
The herringbone stitch serves two
purposes, for it covers the raw edge
and holds down the turnings. Work
from left to right as shown, see also
page ooo for full details of working.
Hand-sewn flat seam
The flat seam is very useful for
general work. It is strong and flat if
neatly done. Turn down a narrow
fold of 6 mm ($\frac{1}{4}$ in) onto the right
side and press it well. Raise the fold
and place the outer edge of
garment along the crease, right
sides together. Turn the fold down
again and pin and tack through the
three thicknesses. Run and back
stitch just under the raw edge,
which serves as a guide to even
sewing. When this is done, flatten
out the seam well, turn down the
fold, and tack and hem on the
wrong side of the material as for a
flat fell seam.

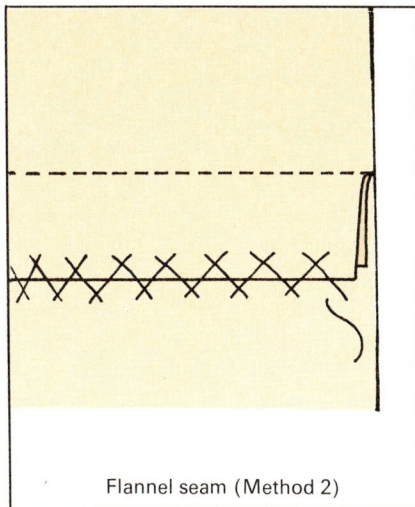

Flannel seam (Method 2)

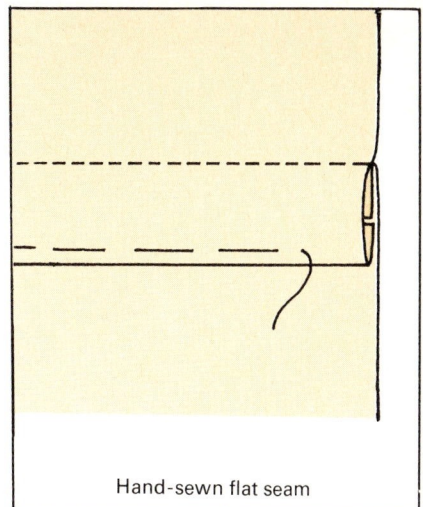

Hand-sewn flat seam

As seams in stretch fabric usually benefit
from being taped, why not turn them into a
fashion feature by using a contrasting colour
to tape the seams on the outside? Here taped
seams add racing stripes to a velour track
suit.

Handsewing in dressmaking

The thread used for sewing should be chosen with care, to suit the fibre, weight and colour of the fabric. Natural fibre threads, such as mercerized cotton, should always be used with natural fibre fabrics – cotton, linen, wool and mixtures of natural fibres. Mercerized cotton can be obtained in Nos. 40 or 50; No. 40 is used for medium weight fabrics and No. 50 for fine, lightweight fabrics. Always use synthetic thread for synthetic fabrics, or fabrics that contain some synthetic fibres.

Needles are important, too, a 7–8 is used for ordinary fabrics, while a 9–10 is best for the finer fabrics. Ball-point needles should be used on stretch fabrics.

Back stitch
Used for seams and other joins where strength is required. It has the appearance of machine stitching on the right side and stem stitch on the wrong side of the work.

Work from right to left. Make a small stitch in the line of sewing, then insert the needle back into the first hole on the right side and bring it out beyond where the thread emerges, making a space equal to the stitch.

Finish off by darning the thread through the stitches on the wrong side.

Decorative stitches
Many decorative stitches are ordinary sewing stitches used in a decorative way, these are not to be confused with the traditional embroidery stitches.

One of the most usual plain sewing stitches to be used in a decorative way is tacking stitch. This is known as saddle stitch. It should be worked in a straight line with a fairly thick thread, the same amount of fabric being picked up as is passed over.

Feather stitch is frequently used on garments for the sewing of hems or tucks decoratively.

When working decorative-stitch borders, always begin and end by darning the thread into the hem or seam or by leaving an end of thread to be darned into the wrong side of the stitches, after the work is completed. Joins in the thread are worked in the same way.

Blanket or loop stitch
This stitch is useful for finishing raw edges of thick material and making buttonholes. It is also used when making up lock-knit fabrics as well as for neatening scalloped edges.

Work from left to right. Keep the edge to be loop stitched towards you. Begin by making a back stitch a little way up from the edge. Insert the needle into the material, bring it out again under the edge and through the loop of thread which starts from the previous stitch. Do not pull tightly. Continue making stitches in this way, close together on a firm edge as for scallops, or spaced apart on thick fabric.

Hemming
There are several variations of this stitch. Real hemming has slanting stitches, goes right through all thicknesses of the fabric so that small slanting stitches are seen on both sides of the work.

Work from right to left on the wrong side. Prepare the hem with traditional double fold and tack it; press lightly. Begin by passing the needle up under the hem edge and through the sewing fold. Stroke the end of thread out of sight between hem and garment. Insert the needle just under the fold and through the work, taking a forward slanting stitch through all thicknesses. Fasten off with a small slanting back stitch and darn the end into hem edge.

Herringbone
A stitch which can be used to hold down a single-fold hem and in the making up of garments from stretch fabrics. Work from left to right.

Begin with a back stitch on the hem about 3 mm ($\frac{1}{8}$ in) above the raw edge. Cross the thread diagonally over the edge and take a small stitch into the garment from right to left. Cross the thread diagonally again and insert the needle from right to left into the hem, level with the last top stitch. Continue in this way.

Overcasting
A stitch used for neatening raw edges, principally on seams and other inside parts of garments.

Work from left to right. Take the stitch through from wrong to right side of seam edge with the needle sloping downwards slightly from

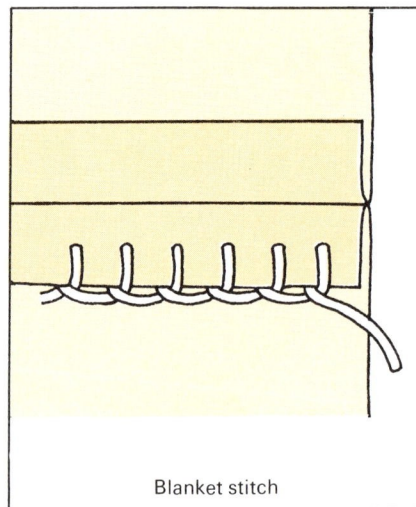

Blanket stitch

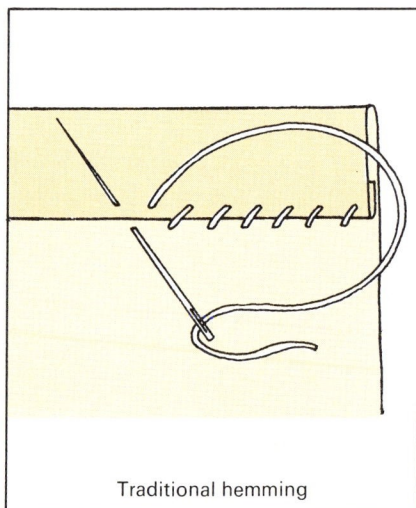

Traditional hemming

right to left. Continue in the same way. Do not make the stitches too deep or too far apart; they should lie over the edge and should not look drawn up in any way.

Oversewing

This is similar to overcasting, but the stitches are made closer together. Place the two edges to be joined together and tack. Working from the right, join the thread to the edges and make small, even stitches over and over at regular intervals. The stitches should be kept close together.

This stitch can be used to sew a fine seam. Turnings are made on both the edges to be joined and tacked. The two sides are placed together, with the folds level, and the oversewing stitches are worked over the folds. After the sewing is completed the turnings are trimmed close to the stitches on the wrong side.

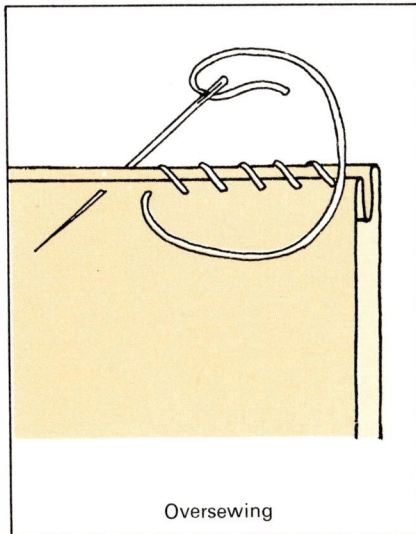

Oversewing

Running

This is the most simple of all stitches and it is suitable for many purposes. Its main uses are for joining seams, sewing hems and inserting gathering threads. A small piece of the fabric is picked up on the needle and passed over alternately. The spaces and stitches should be equal in size and very small. Insert the needle right through the work evenly and firmly. Always begin and end with a back stitch.

Slip hemming

This is a variation of ordinary hemming in which the stitches are invisible on the right side of the work. It is therefore very useful for hemming skirts and trousers.

Work from right to left. Begin as for hemming, then pick up a tiny piece of the surface of the fabric just below the fold, working forward insert the needle through the fold of the hem. Continue in this way, working loosely.

Slip stitch

Slip stitch is worked in a similar way to slip hemming, but the long stitch is made into the turning of the hem, so that no stitches are visible. It is suitable for sewing hems that are turned on to the right side.

Whipping

A stitch used either for neatening an edge on fine fabric such as silk or chiffon, or for drawing up fullness. It is used, too, for neatening edges after applying lace. Work from right to left, turning the edge towards you. Use a fine needle.

Trim the turning or edge to be whipped to within 6 mm ($\frac{1}{4}$ in) from the fitting lines. Begin with a back stitch, then roll the edge over towards you, with the thumb and first finger, making a small slanting stitch over the roll at the same time. Bring the needle through just below the roll and pull the thread fairly tightly. If gathers are required, draw up the thread as the work proceeds.

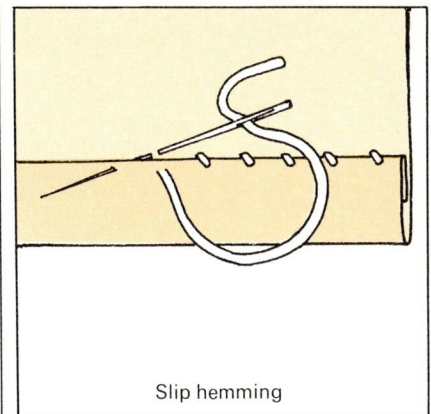

Slip hemming

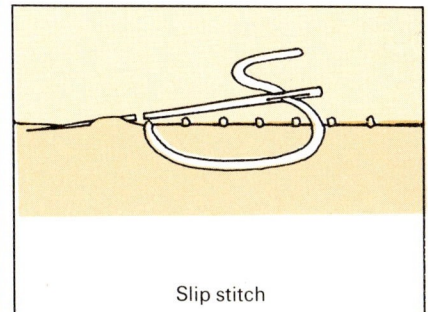

Slip stitch

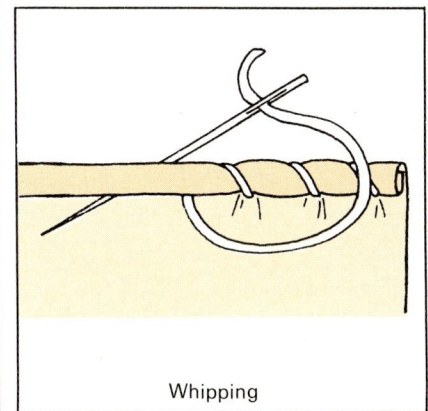

Whipping

A hand sewn flat fell seam is a suitable seam finish for delicate fabrics.

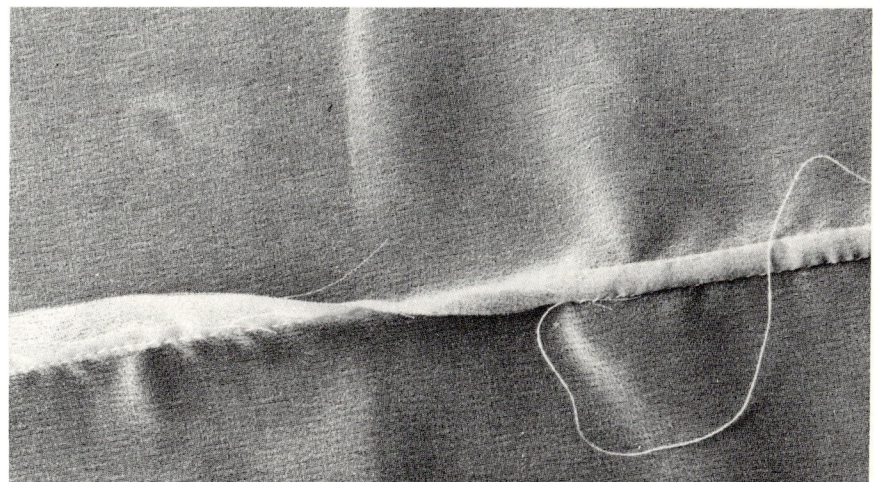

Darts, tucks and gathers

Darts

Darts are used to dispose of fullness and to give a good fit to a shaped garment. These may be arranged as follows:
From the shoulder tapering to the bust-line.
From the waist upwards, tapering towards the bust-line.
From the waist downwards, tapering towards the hip-line.
From the wrist, tapering towards the elbow.

Sometimes small darts are made at the front underarm seam in order to give sufficient ease across the bust and yet gives a neat, plain appearance. Darts are sometimes made at the neck and these must always radiate from the neck curve.

If a dart is made at the wrist of a dress, tapering upwards and downwards, it is cut across the middle up to the machine stitching, then a slit is made along the fold ready for pressing. This is necessary to prevent a puckered appearance.

Darts must not extend beyond the hip, bust, or elbow, and they must always taper gradually to a thread. If this rule is not observed an ugly pleat will appear on the right side, which no amount of pressing will shrink away.

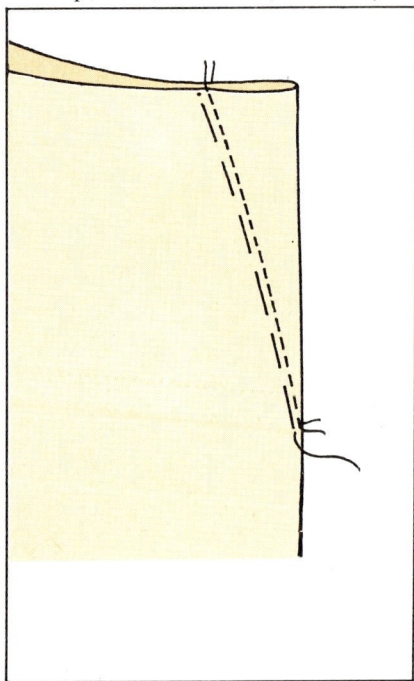

How to make a dart

Darts are thread-marked, or chalk marked on to the material before the pattern is removed. Find the centre of the dart, and mark with a pin, then fold from this point down to the end of the dart. Pin along the dart markings towards the end of the dart. Replace the pins with tacking stitches, there should now be a piece of material tacked in a wedge shape. Fit, and alter if necessary. Machine stitch close to the tacking thread, beginning at the wide end and tapering off to nothing at the point.

Gathers

Gathers are used to introduce fullness into a garment in a decorative way. Even distribution of fullness is essential if the smart appearance of a garment is to be retained.

Careful consideration should be given to the choice of fabric, when gathers are a feature of the design. They should be light and soft in character so the fullness will fall into attractive folds. More than one row of gathering stitches is necessary in order to provide a fairly flat surface for setting in. It is an advantage, on most fabrics, to have three rows, one on the fitting line and two on the turnings above, about 6 mm ($\frac{1}{4}$ in) apart. For a more decorative finish, additional rows can be made below the seam line. These must be absolutely parallel and equal distances apart.

Setting in gathers

The most usual method of setting in gathers is with an overlaid seam.

Insert the lines of stitching as required, making the first one on the fitting line and the others at equal distances above and below, 3 mm to 6 mm ($\frac{1}{8}$ to $\frac{1}{4}$ in) apart to suit the design and the material being used. Use small even running stitches or set the machine to a long stitch and sew without reversing or neatening the ends of the threads. Draw up the gathers, by pushing the fabric along the thread, into tiny pleats, to the correct length and fasten off the ends of the thread. The gathered portion should be approximately 6 mm to 12 mm ($\frac{1}{4}$ in to $\frac{1}{2}$ in) longer than the section of the garment into which it is to fit. Stroke the gathers into tiny pleats.

If the overlaid seam method is being used, turn under the garment edge to the seam line and lay this over the gathered edge, with fold to seam line, and tack, taking care to keep the fullness evenly distributed. If the seam is long, mark halves and quarters of both sections and match them together. If machine stitching is being used for the sewing it should be made close to the folded edge.

For invisible sewing hem the fold

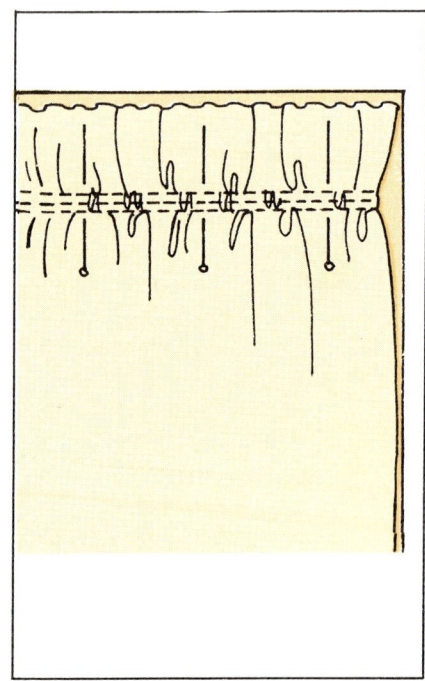

Left A dart tacked and stitched.

Right Gathers pinned into place for joining with a plain seam.

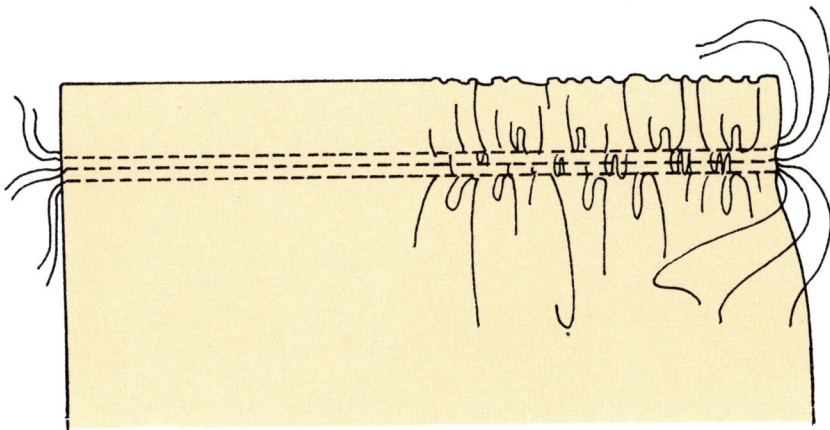

Three rows of gathering stitches give small, even gathers.

by hand, making one tiny stitch into each pleat.

When joining gathers with a plain seam work from the wrong side of the garment, keeping the fullness towards you in order that distribution may be seen and manipulated easily. Distribute the gathers evenly, place balance marks together, right sides facing, and stitch. When stitching by machine, keep the gathered part uppermost so the fullness can be regulated.

To neaten, trim the turnings to within 9 mm ($\frac{3}{8}$ in) and finish with fine overcasting.

Band or yoke

Gathers are frequently set into bands or double yokes, especially on children's clothing, when a slightly different method is used.

Use a plain seam method, sewing the right side of band to right side of garment first. On the wrong side of the band, turn in the raw edges slightly inside the fitting lines, and tack firmly. Trim all turnings evenly, to within 9 mm ($\frac{3}{8}$ in). Fix the wrong side of band over the gathers with the fold to seam line and hem lightly, picking up one gather at a time and taking care not to allow stitches to be caught through to the outside of the work. Press carefully, using just the tip of the iron in order that the gathers are not flattened.

Making tucks

A tuck is a fold of fabric held firmly in position by means of running stitches or machine stitching. Tucks may be used as a decoration only, as are cross tucks, to dispose of fullness, or to reduce the length of a garment. The amount of material required for tucking is three times the tuck width; the under part of the fold, the upper part, and the fabric on which it lies have to be taken into account. If a space is to be left plain between each tuck, then this amount will have to be added to the calculation, remembering it is only one layer thick.

Tuck Guide

A very good and easy method of preparing tucks is with the aid of a tuck marker made out of cardboard or stiff paper. Cut notches to indicate the width of a tuck as shown. If there is a space between the tucks, then the tuck marker should be notched to give the depth of tuck, the under part of tuck, and the width of the space between. Indicate these widths with pins, then tacking stitches.

Pin Tucks

When tucks are used as a decoration they are very tiny, about 3 mm ($\frac{1}{4}$ in) wide, and are called pin tucks. They are easily worked following the straight warp threads. Regularity of stitches and even spacing are essential to the beauty of these tucks.

They should be measured in the same way as ordinary tucks.

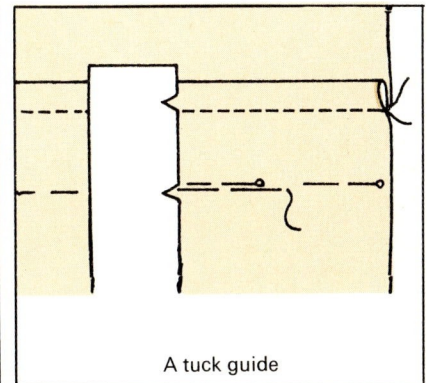

A tuck guide

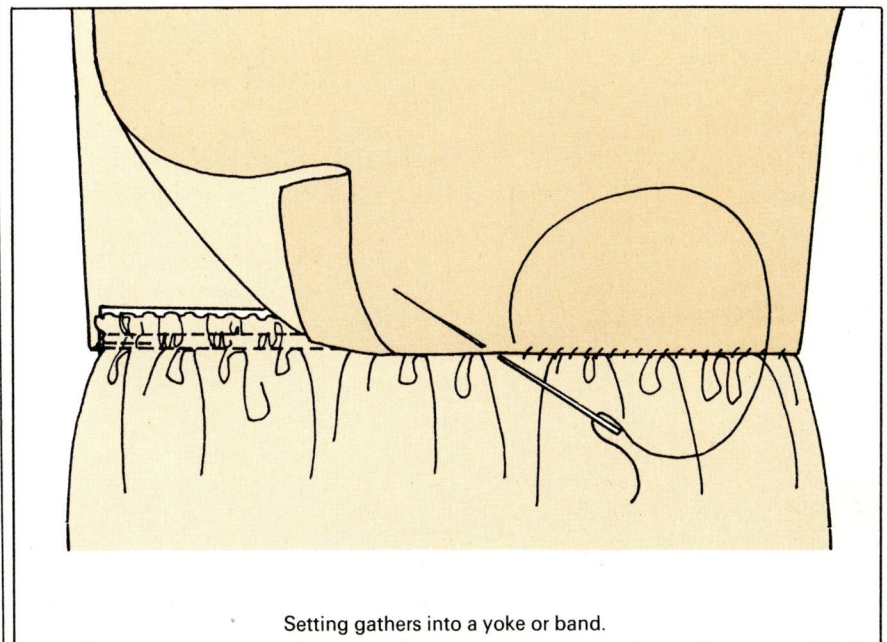

Setting gathers into a yoke or band.

Construction methods

Pressing and Pressing aids

For the best results in dressmaking and home sewing, it is essential to press every stage of your work as you finish it. Press a section before you join it to another; press seams open before crossing them with another, and press darts before you join seams. You will never get the same result by pressing after the sewing is complete.

Apart from the ironing board and iron you will need other pieces of equipment for handling different parts of a garment. Some of them you buy – others you can make yourself.

Iron

Although dry irons are less expensive than steam/dry combination irons, and can be satisfactorily used for pressing with a moist cloth, the steam iron is really the best choice: it is far more efficient, has a wide variety of settings and the steam is more easily controlled.

Ironing board

Adjustable boards are recommended, and should be covered with a padded, closely fitted sleeve.

Padded mitt

This is fitted over the hand for pressing curved areas of a garment, such as darts or shoulder seams. You can also use it on the end of your sleeveboard. Mitts can be bought in haberdashery shops and department stores but it is a simple matter to make your own.

Cut two pieces of unbleached calico 19 cm × 15 cm ($7\frac{1}{2}$ × 6 in) and another piece 22 cm × 15 cm ($8\frac{1}{2}$ in × 6 in). Round off the corners on one end of all three pieces so that they are the same shape. Join the two smaller pieces on the two sides and round the curved end; stuff with kapok or cotton wool and oversew the straight end to close. Press a narrow hem on the straight end of the long

piece and then stitch a 15 mm ($\frac{5}{8}$ in) hem. Lay this piece wrong side out on the padded section. Stitch all round taking a 6 mm ($\frac{1}{4}$ in) seam allowance. Turn right side out.

Point presser

This is not an essential piece of equipment, but it is quite useful if you do a lot of sewing. It is a narrow piece of wood shaped to a point and is used for pressing points in collars and waistbands.

Pressing cloths

These should be about 45 cm (18 in) square, and you need three types. Make two or three muslin cloths, one cloth of white, medium-weight flannel and a third in heavy cotton. It is a good idea to stitch a piece of unbleached calico to the flannel cloth and then use it flannel side down. The calico comes into contact with the hot iron and the flannel acts as a diffuser of the steam so that there is no shine on the fabric.

Seam roll

This is a bolster-shaped cushion used for pressing seams and places which are hard to get to. It is an important piece of pressing equipment because if a seam is pressed over the roll, you will not get ridges showing through. To make a seam roll, pad a length of broomstick or 2.5 cm (1 in) dowelling with an old blanket.

Tailor's clapper

Once you have got used to using a clapper you will find it invaluable when pressing seams and faced edges on woollen and other heavy fabrics. The technique used is as follows: create as much steam as you can with a hot iron and a damp cloth over the fabric. Lift the cloth and then quickly pound the area with the clapper, forcing the steam back into the fabric, making a good, firm crease.

Tailor's ham

This large, ham-shaped cushion is essential for pressing curved seams

and shaped areas. It is easy to make your own: cut two egg-shaped pieces of calico, stitch side seams leaving an opening, stuff with kapok and stitch closed.

Pressing for a professional finish

Pressing is a distinctly different technique from ironing in that, rather than moving the iron back and forth on the surface of the fabric, it is lifted up and put down repeatedly on the area being pressed, always moving in the direction of the fabric grain. When you press on the right side of fabric, always use a pressing cloth. Always remove pins and tacking stitches before pressing, except when pressing pleats.

When pressing with a steam iron, cover the fabric with the pressing cloth and press the steam into the fabric. Remove the pressing cloth, switch the iron from steam to dry and press the work until the fabric is dry. Never handle sewing until it is completely dry. To press with a dry iron, lay the pressing cloth over the work and then lay a damp muslin cloth on top. Press to force steam into the fabric. Remove the muslin and press again until no steam rises from the material.

Pressing different fabrics

Always test fabrics before doing any pressing at all, using scraps left over from cutting out, to ascertain whether the fabric shrinks, whether it marks with water, how much pressure and heat are required and whether dry pressing or damp pressing are needed to get a crease or remove a crease. A too-hot iron or a cloth that is too damp will cause iron-shine marks.

Natural fibre fabrics

These fabrics require more heat than synthetic fibre fabrics and should be pressed with a damp cloth. Care should be taken when pressing silk: to avoid water-spotting cover the area being pressed with a dry cloth. Use a low- to medium heat setting. Wool should be pressed with steam or a damp pressing cloth (when pressing napped wools, use a piece of the same fabric, it helps to keep the nap raised).

Press linen on the wrong side with a hot iron, using a pressing cloth and a dampened muslin. Take care with linen because it is easily spoiled with iron-shine. Cotton fabrics should be pressed under a dampened cloth first, then pressed until quite dry. Dark-coloured cottons are best pressed on the wrong side to avoid iron-shine.

Press as you sew
Pressing as you sew is called construction pressing. The secrets of doing this successfully lie in the way the garment is positioned on the ironing board, and the special techniques used for each area.

Seams
To press armhole seams, turn the sleeve inside out, lay the crown of the sleeve on the edge of the sleeveboard and with the tip of the iron, press the seam allowance only, avoiding the stitching line.

Gathers in seams should be pressed by first pressing the gathered fabric piece in the seam allowance only. Machine stitch the seam, then press on the wrong side, moving just the tip of the iron up between the gathers.

Shoulder seams are pressed in

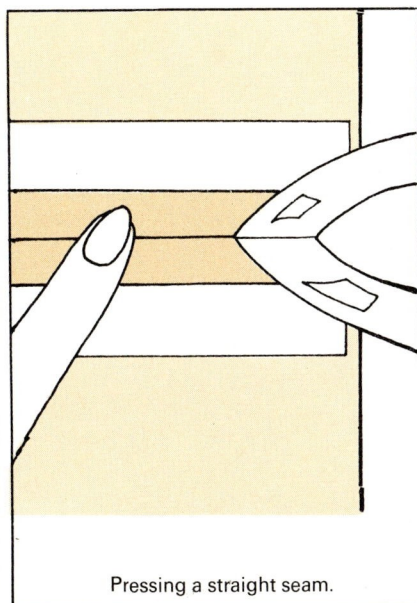
Pressing a curved seam over a tailor's ham.

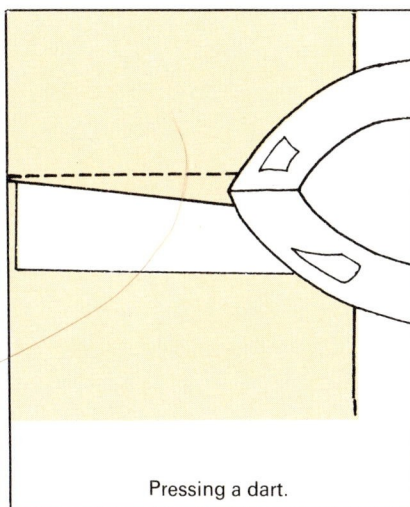
Pressing a dart.

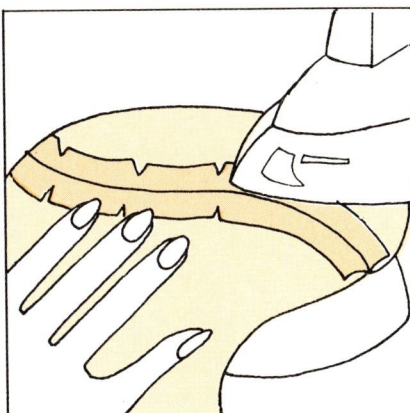
Pressing a straight seam.

the same way as straight seams, working from the neck edge towards the shoulder edge. On the final, right side pressing, use the tailor's ham and press on the lengthwise grain of the fabric so that you shape the work to follow the body's contours.

To press a straight seam, remove all tacking threads after stitching the seam. Then, with wrong side facing, lay the seam along a seam roll. Open the seam by creasing along the stitching line with your fingers. Lay strips of brown paper under the seam edges and dry-press, using just the tip of the iron, along the stitching line. Turn the work to the right side. With the paper strips in position and on a seam roll as before, press using a little steam and a pressing cloth.

Shaping
Curved seams are pressed over a

tailor's ham or a mitt using the technique for straight seams.

Press darts that have been slashed in the direction they were stitched. Unslashed darts must be pressed in the direction recommended in pattern instructions. Use a tailor's ham or a mitt and press away from the stitching, and with a piece of brown paper under the fold. Make sure that you do not press beyond the dart's point.

After the pleats have been tacked, dry press on both sides to set the fabric. After fitting the

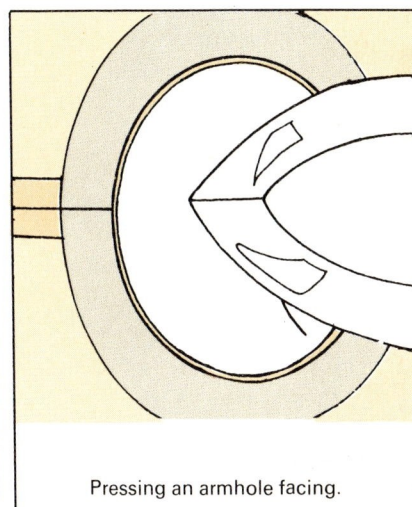
Pressing an armhole facing.

garment, press the pleats with strips of brown paper under the folds, to within about 15 cm (6 in) of the hem. Finish the hem and then press the pleats again.

Edge finishes
Beginning on the wrong side, turn the facing so that the edge rolls neatly and favours the wrong side. Press very lightly. Turn work to the right side, press lightly, keeping the edge perfectly rolled. To prevent a ridge showing on the right side of the garment, avoid pressing the hem edge of the facing.

Hems also require extra care in pressing to avoid an unsightly ridge showing on the right side of the garment. Tack the hem in place 12 mm ($\frac{1}{2}$ in) from the raw edge and then slip strips of brown paper under the edge. Press, using steam to shrink in any fullness.

45

Interfacings and facings

An interfacing is a fabric applied to a garment between top fabric and facing to give it extra strength or crispness. The interfacing is cut from the same pattern piece as the section, or from the facing. Sometimes it is applied to the main garment, as in front facings. In other designs it is applied to the facing section, as a neck or armhole facing.

To apply interfacings, tack or baste diagonally to the wrong side of the fabric just outside the seam lines. Treat top fabric and interfacing as one from then on. After seams have been stitched, trim the seam allowance of the interfacing close to the stitching line.

Facings

Facings are used to neaten raw edges of fabric on a garment. They can be either straight cut or bias cut strips of fabric.

Applying facing strips

Facing strips can be made from ready-made bias binding of a matching colour, or bias strips can be cut from the same fabric. Cut the strips at least 2.5 cm (1 in) wide and join them to the required length. To prepare the garment for facing turn a single narrow hem to the wrong side, snipping into the edge of curves so that the turning lies flat. Press the fold. Turn both edges of the strip to the wrong side and press. Lay the edge of the strip just below the folded edge of the garment. Tack and then hem neatly. Slip stitch the other edge of the strip to the garment.

Alternative method

Strips can also be applied with machine stitching. Snip into the garment edge on curves. Lay the strip along the garment edge, right sides facing, the raw edge of the strip just below the snips. Pin and then tack together. Machine stitch 6 mm ($\frac{1}{4}$ in) from the edge. Turn the strip to the wrong side so that it does not show from the right side. Press and then tack along the fold.

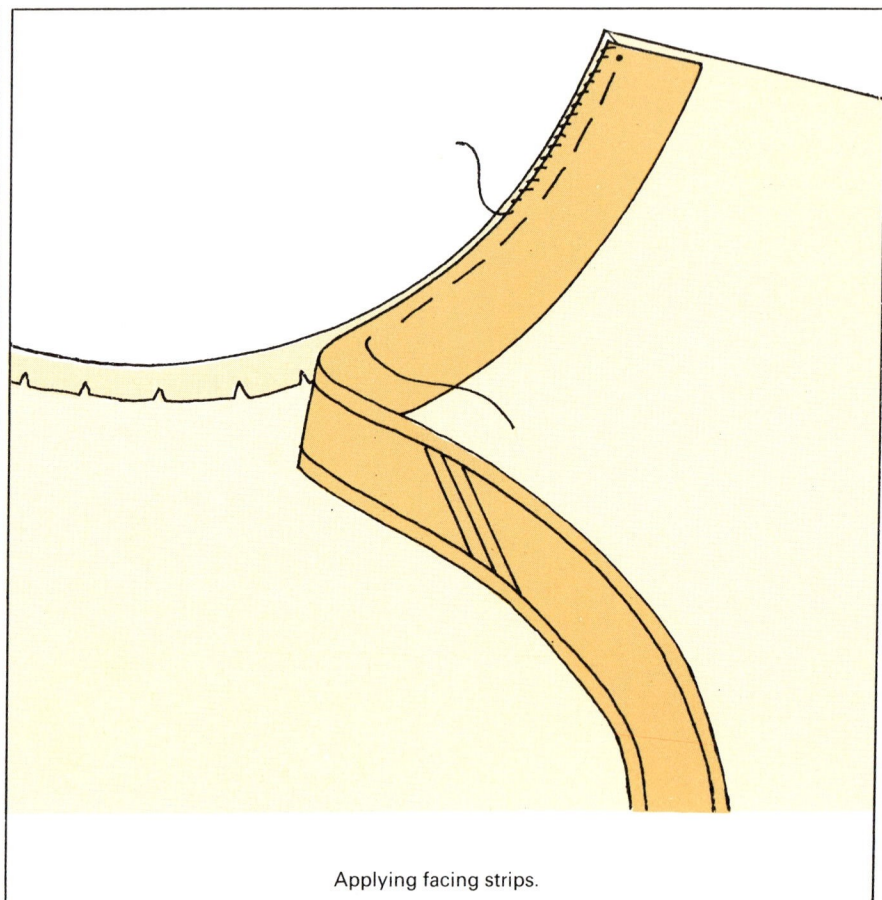

Applying facing strips.

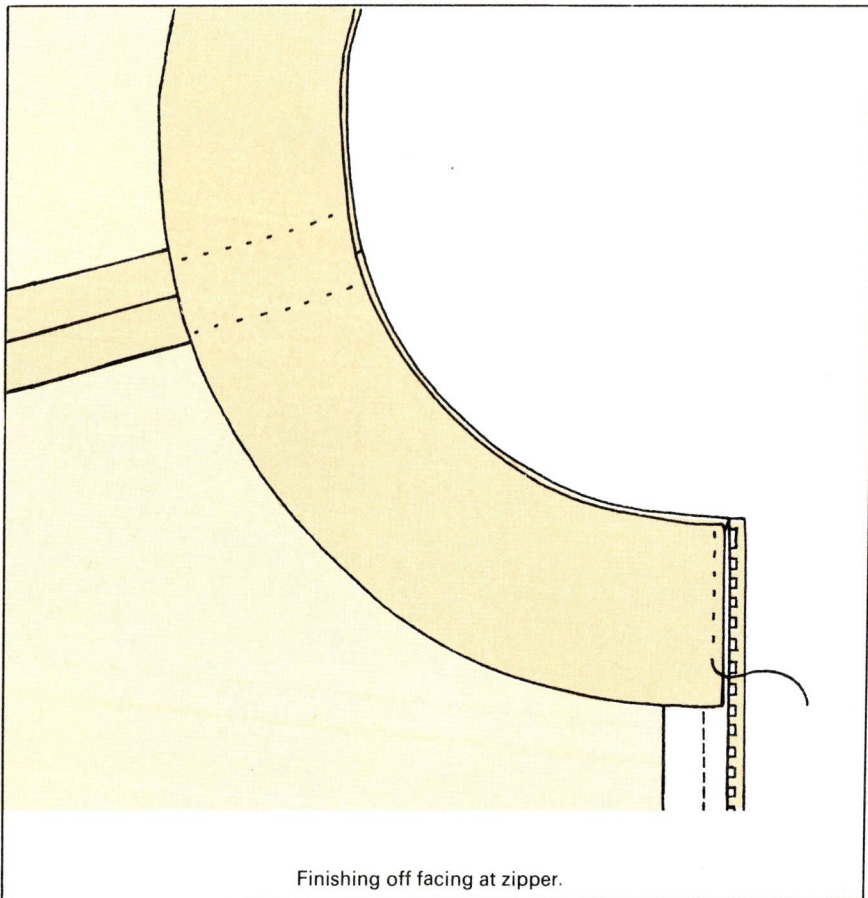

Finishing off facing at zipper.

Turn a narrow hem on the other edge of the strip and slip stitch to the garment.

Neck openings

A slit neck opening is faced with a simple facing. Mark the slit on the garment with thread tracing. Cut a piece of fabric for the facing at least 3.5 cm (1½ in) deeper than the slit and so that there is a turning of 3.5 cm (1½ in) on each side of it. Make a neat hem on the sides and bottom edges of the facing.

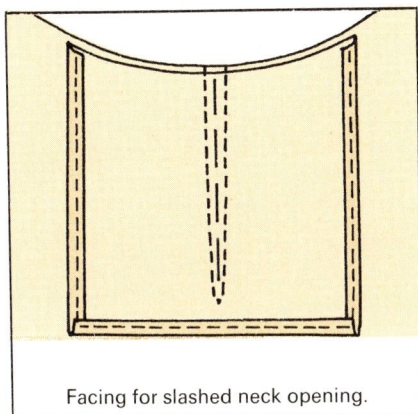

Facing for slashed neck opening.

Mark the centre of the facing and pin it to the marked slit, right sides of the fabric together. Tack and then stitch on each side of the slit, beginning 6 mm (¼ in) from the marked line at the top of the slit and tapering to 1 mm (1/16 in) at the end of it. Unpick the tacking.

Cut the slit through both thicknesses of fabric. Turn the facing to the wrong side of the garment and tack along the fold. Press. Unpick tacking.

This facing technique can also be used on long sleeves to make a cuff opening.

Shaped facings

A scalloped edge is finished with bias cut strips. If the edge of the garment is cut to an intricate shape, such as points or squares, the facing is cut to the same shape as the garment edge and about 2.5 cm (1 in) wider.

Finish the straight edge with a single machine stitched hem or just press and tack it. Lay the facing on the garment edge, right sides together and matching the edge. Tack and then machine stitch, working about 6 mm (¼ in) from the edge. You will have to snip into corners and curves.

Trim corners off diagonally so that the facing turns to the wrong side neatly. The fold should be exactly on the edge. Tack about 12 mm (½ in) from the fold. Press carefully and catch stitch the hem to the wrong side.

A simple faced neckline is very effective on a light broderie anglaise type fabric.

Construction methods

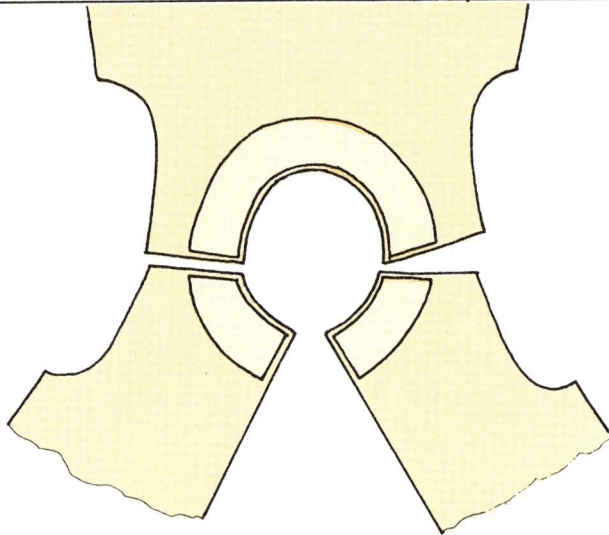

Facing for round neckline cut in three pieces.

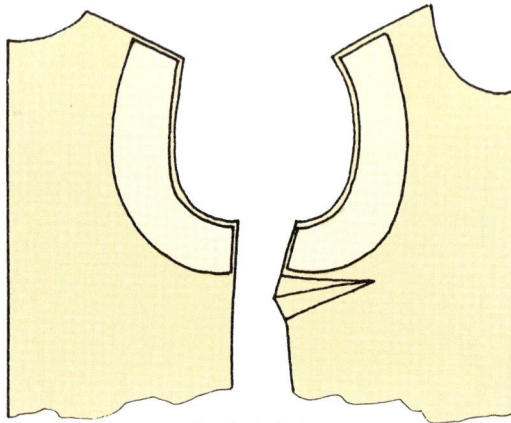

Armhole facing

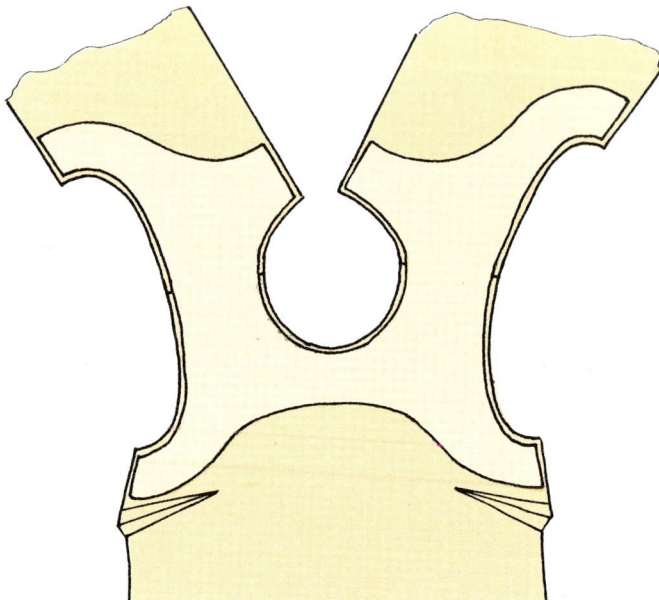

One piece facing for neck and armholes.

Alternative method

Mark the pattern line on the garment edge on the wrong side but do not cut it out. Cut a facing strip and tack it to the right side of the garment. Work diagonal basting to hold the two layers together. Machine stitch on the pattern line. Cut out the edge about 3 mm ($\frac{1}{8}$ in) away from the stitching line. Unpick the basting. Snip into curves and corners for a smooth turn to the wrong side. Finish the facing as before, making a neat hem on the loose edge.

Garment facings

Commercial paper patterns supply either pattern pieces for cutting neck, armhole and front facings, or instruct you to use the garment pattern to cut the facing.

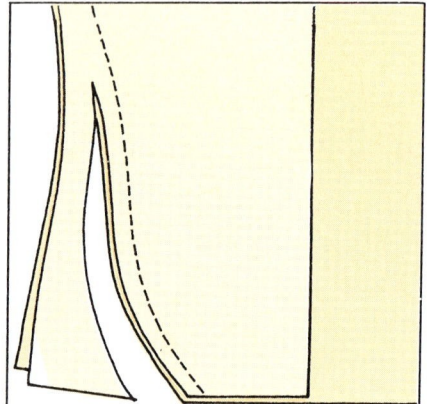

The seam is trimmed before the facing is turned to the wrong side.

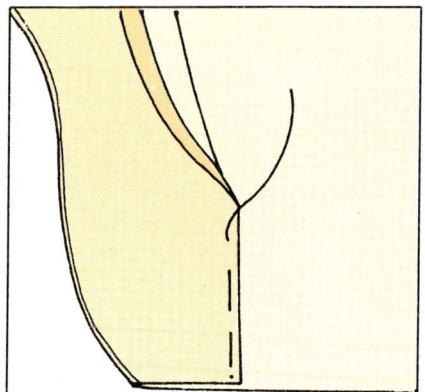

Tacking the facing to the garment edge before pressing.

If you have altered a garment style so that it requires facings, perhaps taking off a collar or making a dress sleeveless, you can make your own facing patterns from the garment pattern.

Fold any darts on the paper pattern and press them flat. Lay a piece of tracing paper over the pattern and hold it down with weights. Trace the outline of the pattern, using a ruler for the straight edges. Mark a line 7.5 cm (3 in) down from the edge to be faced. Mark in any symbols or construction lines and grain line.

For a neck facing on a back-zipped dress you will need to make the front neck facing in one piece and the back neck facing in two pieces.

For armhole facings, cut the front bodice facing from the front bodice pattern and the back facing from the back pattern.

Combined facings, where the neck and armhole facing are one piece are cut from the front pattern and the back pattern.

Making neat facings

It is not difficult to apply a facing as long as you are careful when transferring pattern markings to the garment pieces, and have transferred any adjustments made to the main pattern pieces to the facings.

When you position the facing on the main garment, match all notches and be sure that the seams are matching. This is extremely important and can be checked by pinning through the facing seam line to the garment seam line. Always tack a facing very carefully into position before machine sewing.

Turning a facing to the wrong side is tricky, but providing that the seams are graded properly and curves clipped it can be done neatly. Understitching the facing to the seam allowance will prevent it from rolling to the right side; do this by hand with small prick stitches or by machine.

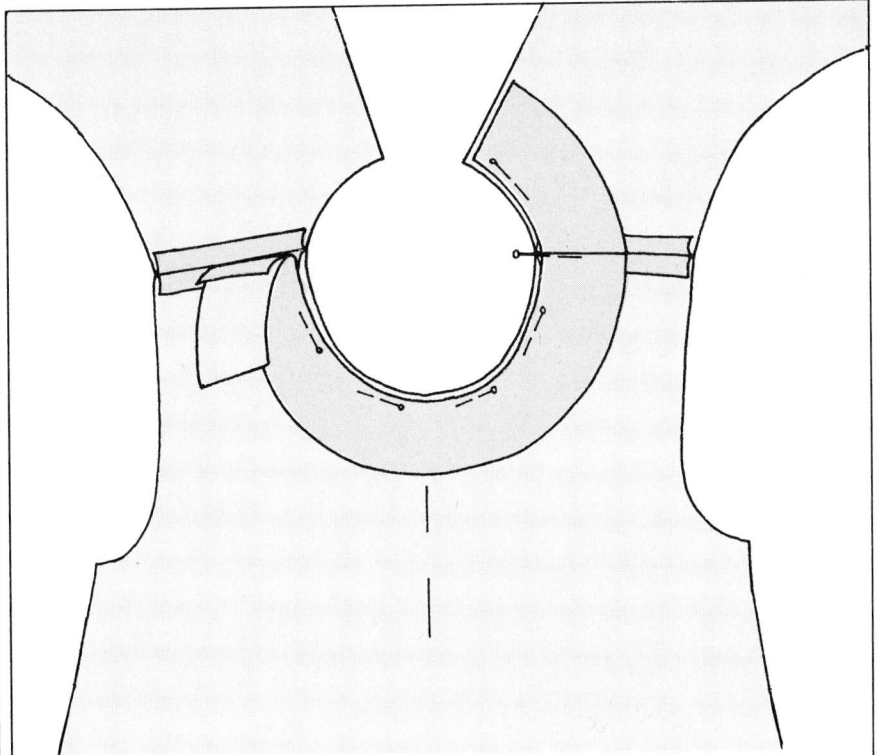

Check that seams will match by pinning the facing to the wrong side of the garment, through the seamline.

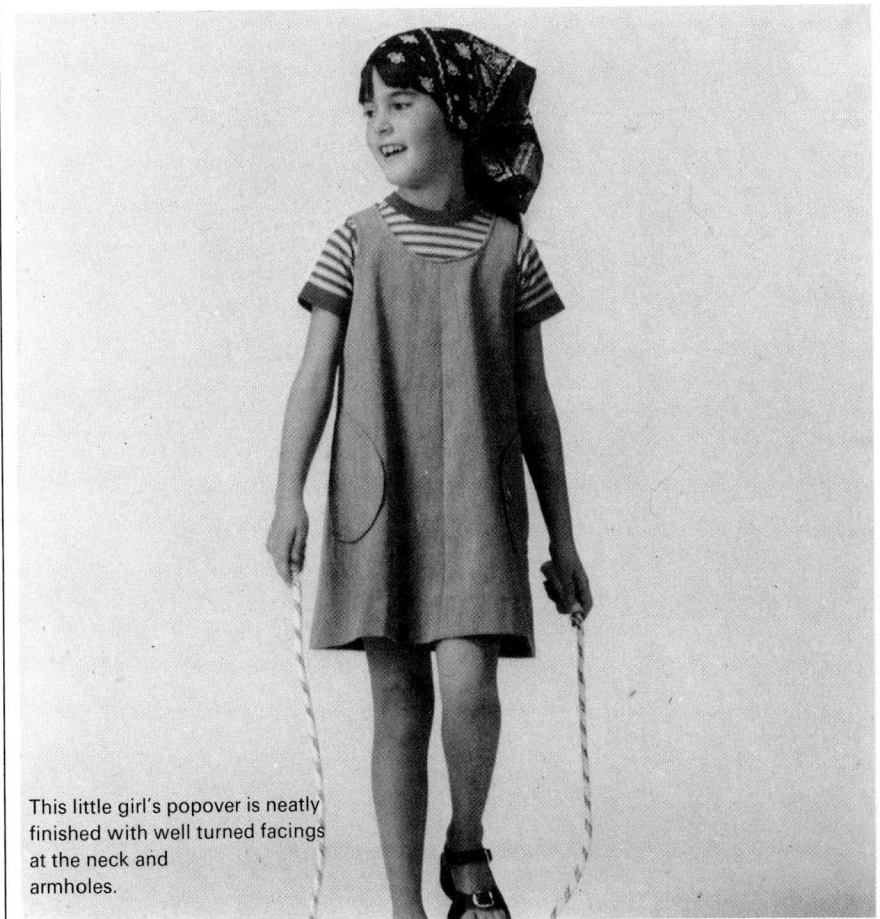

This little girl's popover is neatly finished with well turned facings at the neck and armholes.

Construction methods

Linings

Commercial paper patterns usually give instructions for making up linings if they are intended as part of the garment. You may sometimes want to line a garment

A full, well-fitted lining in a homemade jacket gives the garment a professional finish.

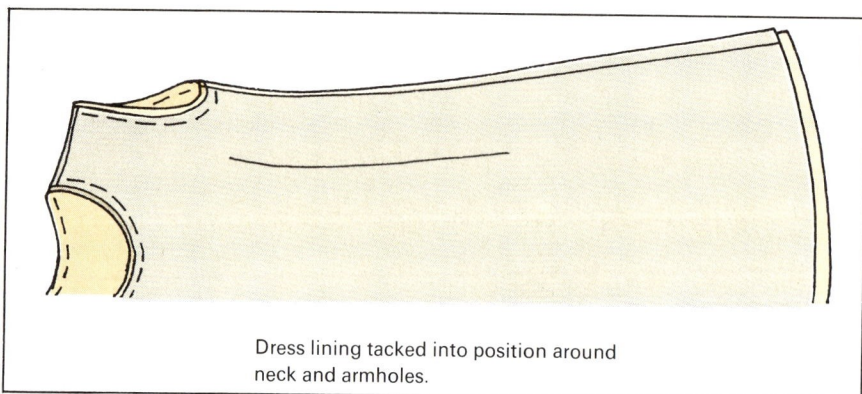

Dress lining tacked into position around neck and armholes.

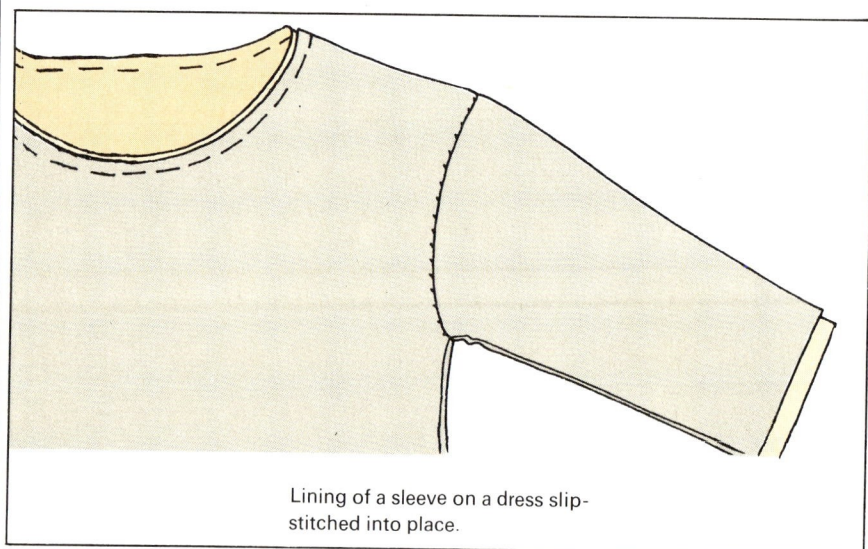

Lining of a sleeve on a dress slip-stitched into place.

where lining has not been included in the pattern, or you may want to line a garment you have bought. Garments are sometimes fully lined or, if you wish, they can be only partly lined. A dress for instance, may have unlined sleeves or just the skirt lined; trousers might be lined from the waist down to the knees; a skirt may have just the back lined to prevent seating. If you are dressmaking, use the same pattern for cutting the lining pieces. If you are lining a purchased garment, either try to find a commercial paper pattern with similarly shaped pieces or make a paper pattern from the garment itself. To do this, turn the garment inside out. Spread it as flat as possible. Pin tissue paper to the garment along the seam lines. Pencil along the pinned line marking darts with a pencil. Unpin the paper. Spread the pattern and cut into the marked dart lines. Lay the tissue pattern on brown paper

or tracing paper and draw around the shape, adding a seam allowance. Complete the darts with a 'V' on the seam line. Cut out and use the pattern to cut your lining. Make up as you would a garment.

Making and inserting linings
Sleeveless dress

Stitch any darts. Join the front and back bodice at the shoulders on both dress and lining. (Join bodice piece to skirt if there is a waistline seam on both dress and lining.) Place lining on the dress, right sides facing and matching seams. Pin on the seams. Pin and tack together around the armholes and around the neckline. Machine stitch the armholes and neckline. Turn garment pieces to the right side and press the edges of the neck and armhole carefully, rolling the lining to the wrong side slightly. Tack along the edge.

Tack the two layers of fabric together along the garment's side seams. Stitch the side seams, working both layers together as one. Neaten the seam edges. Stitch the dress back seam separately from the lining and then stitch the lining's back seam. Insert the zipper into the dress. Turn under the edges of the lining and hem the zipper tape.

Sleeved dress

Make the lining in the same way as the garment. Put the garment on a dress stand, wrong side out and slip the lining over the garment, right side out. Tack together around the armholes and neck. If the sleeves are unlined, simply apply them to the double layer of fabric at the armhole. If they are lined, do not tack the lining to the garment around the armhole, but put in the sleeves and then turn the edges of the lining under and slip stitch the sleeve lining to the dress lining. On a lined dress with a faced neckline, tack the lining to the garment around the neck and then apply the facing in the normal way.

Hemlines Take up the dress hem. Take up the lining hem so that it is

2.5 cm (1 in) shorter and machine stitch it. Work buttonhole stitched ties at the seams to hold the lining to the dress hem.

Jackets

Use the garment pattern to cut out two fronts and one back. Add an extra 2.5 cm (1 in) at centre back for a pleat. If the back is in two pieces, cut the back lining on folded fabric, placing the pattern piece 12 mm ($\frac{1}{2}$ in) from the fold.

Make up all darts and slit them

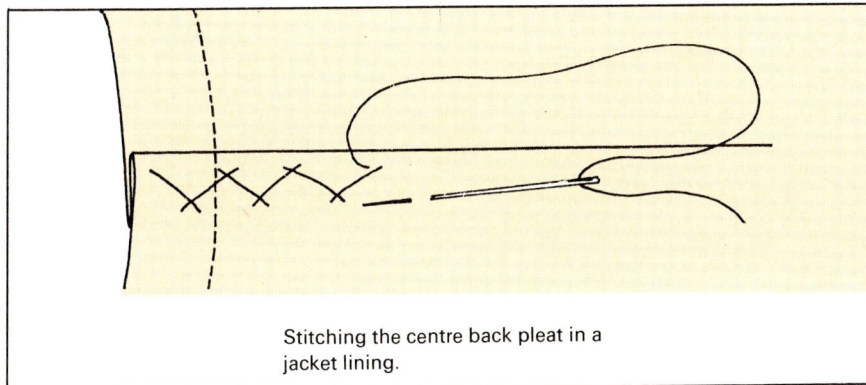

Stitching the centre back pleat in a jacket lining.

on the fold. Press open and oversew the raw edges. Stitch the side seams and shoulder seams. Press open. Make the centre back pleat and tack at both ends to hold the pleat.

Turn the jacket to the wrong side and put it on the dress stand with the collar and lapels turned up. Chalk the lining line on the facing, starting 3.5 cm (1$\frac{1}{2}$ in) from the neck and curve to 7.5 cm (3 in) at the bust level. Continue straight down the front and then draw a line 3 cm (1$\frac{1}{4}$ in) up from the hem fold. Mark the back neck on the seam line.

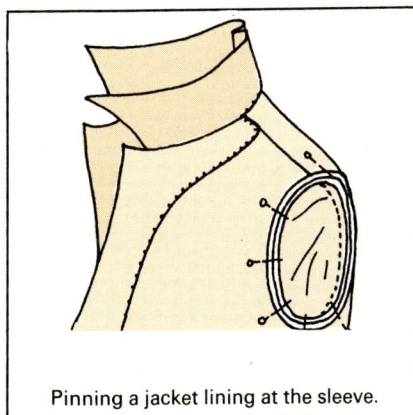

Pinning a jacket lining at the sleeve.

Slip the lining onto the jacket. Make sure that the grain lines of the lining are true and straight.

Pin the lining from armhole to armhole across the back, working about 20 cm (8 in) down from the neck. Pin around the armholes and pin to match seams on the shoulder line. Fold under the back neck, shoulder and front edges and pin on the chalk line. Tack the lining around the armholes, down the fronts and around the hem. Remove all the pins. Slip-stitch the lining to the jacket leaving the armholes free.

Sleeve lining Make up the sleeve lining as for the sleeve. Turn the sleeve to the wrong side and chalk a line 3.5 cm ($\frac{1}{2}$ in) from the cuff. Lay the sleeve flat on the table and

lay the lining on it, inside it. Pin the turnings of the sleeve and lining together, working from the sleeve head down to the cuff. Starting and finishing 7.5 cm (3 in) from each end, hand-sew the turnings together with small running stitches. Turn the sleeve right side out. Turn the lining up at the cuff and hem to the chalk line. Insert the sleeve into the jacket, leaving the lining free. Turn the jacket to the wrong side leaving the sleeves on the right side. Pull the sleeve linings through and turn in the edges of the lining so that they cover the lines of machine stitching. Allow a little fullness to prevent a drag. Pin and then slipstitch.

Hints on linings

Before making up a lining, test the fabric with an iron to check the heat you need to press open the seams.

Always make sure that lining pieces are cut on exactly the same grain of fabric as the garment pieces.

Lining fabrics are likely to fray. To extend the life of your lining it is worth oversewing the seams to finish them off. Alternatively, work a line of machine stitching or zigzag stitching along the raw edges.

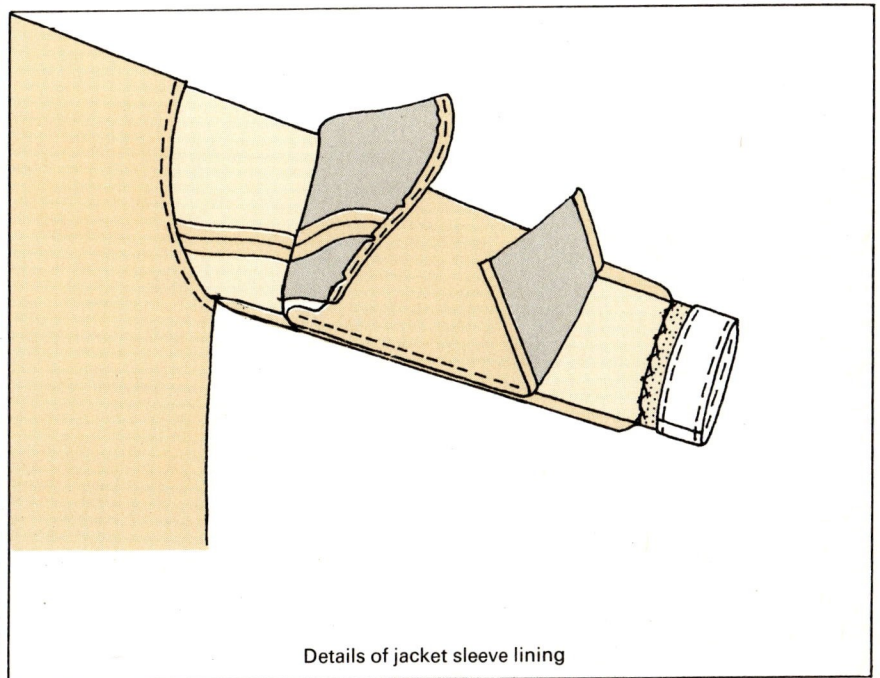

Details of jacket sleeve lining

Openings

Openings are made so that the garment may slip on and off easily, and yet have a good fit and neat appearance. The opening should either be decorative or if hidden, should be as inconspicuous as possible. All openings on women's garments fasten right over left, and men's clothes the opposite way. Some are made in a seam, others are cut into the fabric of the garment.

Continuous Opening

There are different methods of making an opening, according to the purpose for which it is used and its position on the garment. A continuous opening is the most adaptable as it is flat and can be made invisible.

The length of the opening depends upon the position, but it must be sufficiently long to allow the garment to slip on and off easily. When made in a seam, the lay or turning on the wrong side must be snipped where the opening is to end; this allows the false piece to lie flat. If the opening is cut into the fabric the end of the cut should be strengthened with a few buttonhole stitches.

Underlay

A 'false piece' to be used as backing is cut along the selvedge, twice the length of the opening plus 12 mm ($\frac{1}{2}$ in) to avoid any discrepancy in length at the top of the opening. The width is twice the finished width of the binding plus turnings. A usual finished width is 15 mm ($\frac{5}{8}$ in) as it allows space for fastenings.

Place the continuous strip to the edge of the opening, right sides together. When fixing hold the garment towards you. On no account must the strip be eased, otherwise the opening will be untidy. On a specially cut opening the smallest possible turning should be taken from the garment at the corner. Elsewhere the machined seam should be 3 mm ($\frac{1}{8}$ in).

Fold the continuous strip to the wrong side. Turn in the raw edge, and tack just above the machining. This will create a portion which projects from the opening and will form the underlay.

Upper edge Cut away half the width of the false piece on the remaining portion which is to form the overlap, then fold this flat onto the garment and hem or machine stitch it down. Make the end neat and strong with a row of hand or machine stitching.

For a short opening where absolute flatness is not the first consideration, the continuous strip may be retained intact and merely folded under against the upper edge of the opening. The under portion projects as before. The finished width of the false piece is narrower, about 9 mm ($\frac{3}{8}$ in), for this arrangement of the continuous opening.

There should not be any machining showing on the right side.

Neck openings
Bound

This method is suitable for use on cottons, fine woollen fabrics, silks, and some pile fabrics.

Cut the opening down the centre front in line with the straight grain, using a thread as a guide. Cut a bias strip 18 mm ($\frac{3}{4}$ in) or 2.5 cm (1 in) if the fabric is loosely woven.

Place the right side of the binding to the right side of the opening with edges meeting, taking care to have the end of opening unpuckered. Machine stitch, or run and back stitch 6 mm ($\frac{1}{4}$ in) from the edge, tapering towards the bottom end of opening. An extra stitch or two should be made here to give extra strength. Snick into the corners of the binding and press.

Make a fold along the edge of

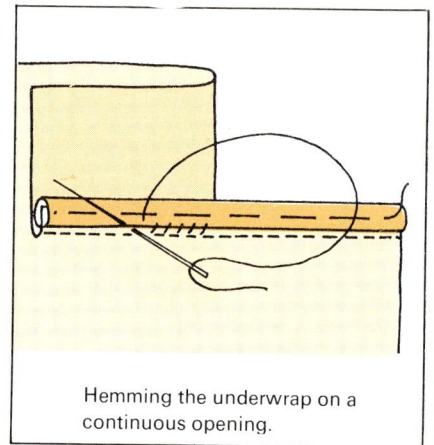

Hemming the underwrap on a continuous opening.

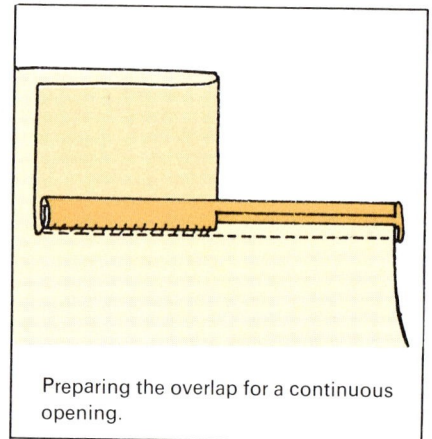

Preparing the overlap for a continuous opening.

the strip, then fold it over to touch the stitching. Hem the fold just above the stitching; these stitches should not go through to the right side of the garment. The bias strip should be stretched tightly at the bottom of the opening to ensure that it lies flat.

Faced opening

This is effective both as an opening and a trimming and has the added advantage of being easy to handle.

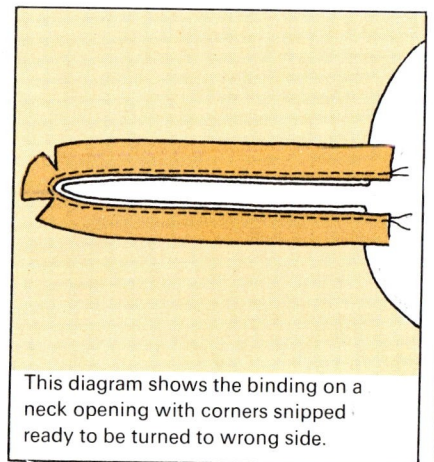

This diagram shows the binding on a neck opening with corners snipped ready to be turned to wrong side.

Cut a strip of fabric on the straight grain 2.5 cm (1 in) longer than the opening and about 5 cm (2 in) wide. Make a crease to mark the centre. Place right sides together over the line of the opening. Machine stitch each side of the crease, about 3 mm ($\frac{1}{8}$ in) away from it, making a neat square at the end.

Cut between the machining, clipping the corners, and turn the facing onto the wrong side, creasing along turning edge. The raw edges are trimmed, turned in and secured with hemming.

Decorative faced opening

When contrasting material is used the process is reversed, the facing being sewn onto the wrong side and turned onto the right with wrong side facing to right side of garment. Many decorative necklines can be made in this way and it is also a useful finish for cuffs.

Shoulder opening

When there is to be an opening on one shoulder only it is made on the left shoulder before the neckline is finished.

Leave the shoulder seam unstitched for 8 cm to 10 cm (3 in to 4 in), insert a straight cut strip of lining, about 2.5 cm (1 in) longer than the opening and 2.5 cm (1 in) wide, under the back shoulder edge. Tack it along the raw edge and then machine stitch it to keep the edge firm. The lining is inserted in order to strengthen the edge of opening as the shoulder seam is, as a rule, on the bias. Bind the raw edge and slip stitch to the garment.

Press the seam of the shoulder open. Cut a straight piece of lining the length of the seam 5 cm (2 in) wide, and place it along the front edge with right sides together. Machine stitch, continuing the line of the seam, and turn the lining over the edge onto the wrong side. Slip stitch the edge to the garment invisibly. This forms the overlap of the opening.

Fasteners are then sewn on, or buttons and buttonholes can be

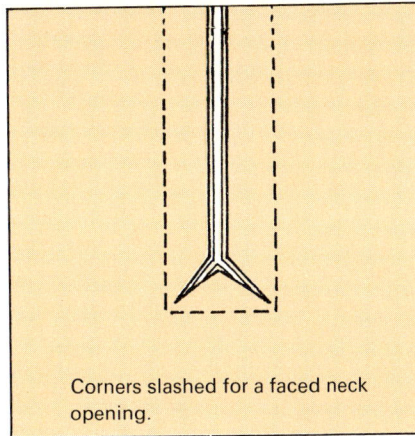

used if a more decorative finish is desired.

Waist opening for a dress

When a dress fits closely at the waist it is necessary to make an opening to enable the dress to be slipped on and off easily. This should be as neat and inconspicuous as possible.

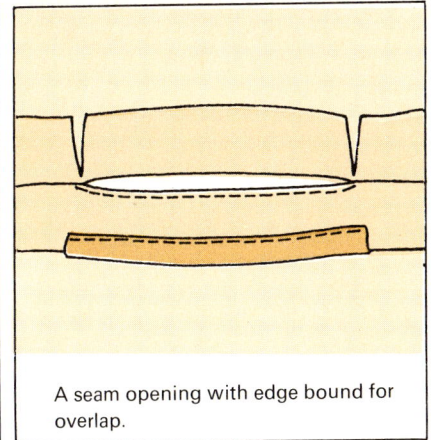

Corners slashed for a faced neck opening.

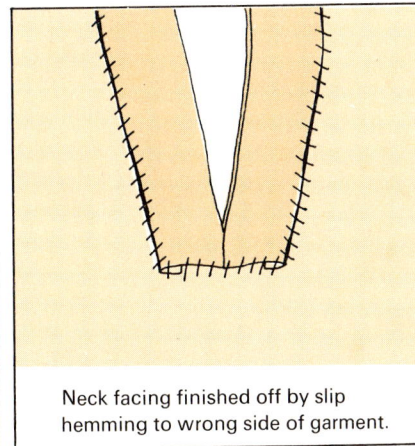

Neck facing finished off by slip hemming to wrong side of garment.

Shoulder opening with snap fasteners.

A seam opening with edge bound for overlap.

Seam opening

The simplest, best and neatest method is to make an opening in the seam at the left-hand side, fastening the right over the left, that is front over back.

The length of the opening varies according to the requirements, but 10 cm (4 in) below and 10 cm (4 in) above the waistline is a good average. For the overlap cut a strip of lining 2.5 cm (1 in) longer than the opening and 4 cm (1$\frac{1}{2}$ in) wide. Insert the edge of strip in the crease of the top seam and sew with running stitch.

Turn the seam over along the seam line and sew with machine stitching down the edge on the right side to keep it firm. Bind the lining strip and edge of turning together.

To make the under lap, snip the seam allowance up to the machine stitching 12 mm ($\frac{1}{2}$ in) above and below the opening. Cut a strip of lining the length between the slits and 5 cm (2 in) wide. Place right

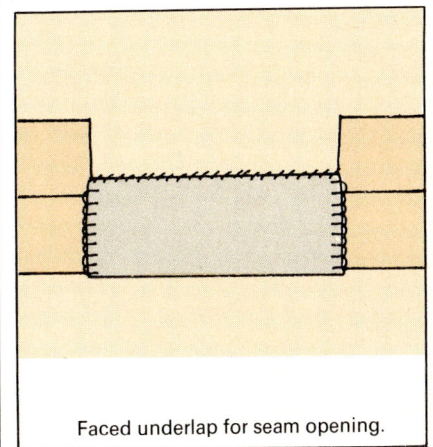

Faced underlap for seam opening.

53

side of lining to right side of turning and machine stitch 6 mm ($\frac{1}{4}$ in) from the edge. Turn lining over the edge of seam onto the wrong side and slip stitch or neatly hem the turning down onto the garment.

Lay the under lap against the overlap and buttonhole stitch the turnings at top and bottom.

Sew snap fasteners at regular intervals along the opening with one at each end of the opening to keep it perfectly flat.

Skirt opening or placket

The placket in a skirt should be made before the turnings of seams are neatened. The seam at the left side is left unstitched from the waist for about 20 cm (8 in).

For the overlap, cut a strip of lining 23 cm (9 in) long and 4 cm ($1\frac{1}{2}$ in) wide. Insert the strip under the turning and sew with running stitch alongside the turning of the seam.

Fold along the line and machine stitch by the edge on the right side, keeping a continuous line with the side seam. If the seam is top stitched the machining on the placket edge should be a continuation of this line. Bind the raw edges of lining and fabric together.

For the underlap, cut a piece of the skirt fabric 23 cm (9 in) long and 5 cm (2 in) wide. Bind one side and one end with seam binding.

Place the wrong side of strip to the wrong side of underlap, raw edges meeting. The bound end of the strip should be 2.5 cm (1 in)

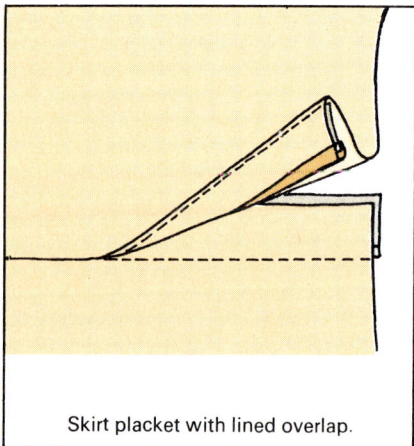

Skirt placket with lined overlap.

below end of opening. Bind the two edges together and carry the binding right down the skirt seam to the hem.

Stitch across the closed end of opening to keep the upper and under parts together, making stitches that do not show on the right side.

This opening is suitable for fastenings such as snap fasteners and hooks and eyes.

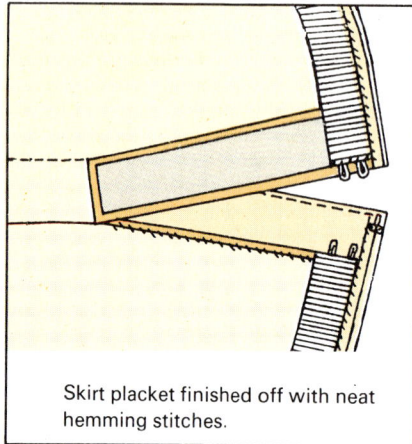

Skirt placket finished off with neat hemming stitches.

Sleeve openings

With a tight-fitting cuff it is necessary to have an opening at the wrist to enable the sleeve to be pulled over the hand. These openings may be made in one of several ways.

Opening for two-piece sleeve

Open the back seam, or dart, for 9 cm ($3\frac{1}{2}$ in) above the wrist. Tack back the seam allowance of the sleeve and bind with lining or seam binding. Snip the allowance of the under sleeve seam level with the

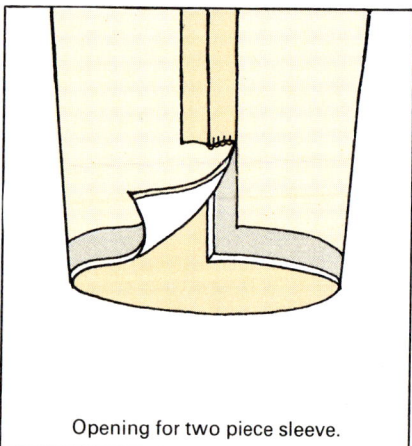

Opening for two piece sleeve.

top of opening and bind the edge. Turn up the wrist edge and face as for other openings. Lay the upper part of opening over the underpart and buttonhole stitch across the cut and the seam turnings. A tailored sleeve may be finished with buttons and buttonholes if desired.

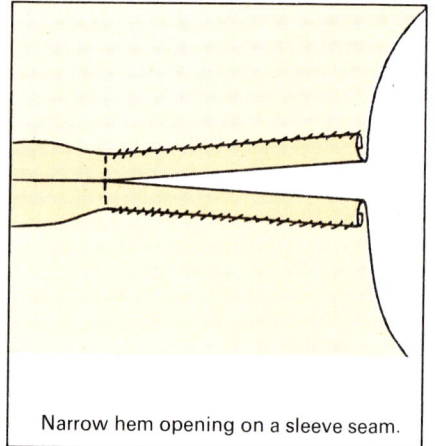

Narrow hem opening on a sleeve seam.

A Narrow Hem

Suitable for fine woollens or cotton materials. The opening is made 8 cm (3 in) from the sleeve seam on the under side. Cut a slit 4 cm ($1\frac{1}{2}$ in) long at right angles to the sleeve edge and make a 3 mm ($\frac{1}{8}$ in) hem all around the slit. Gather the wrist edge ready for cuff.

Continuous Opening

Make the opening 8 cm (3 in) long following a lengthways thread. Cut a strip of fabric 18 cm (7 in) long and 5 cm (2 in) wide, and continue in the way described above.

Tack the top part of binding back on the wrong side of sleeve. The under part projects and forms the under wrap. For a link cuff, tack both pieces back onto the edge of sleeve at the wrist.

Zippers

A zipper is a neat and secure method of fastening which can be used invisibly or decoratively for many purposes. Zippers are made in various lengths and weights to suit many requirements and types of fabric. They either have metal teeth or nylon teeth. The latter are preferable as they are not too obvious when properly inserted.

The tape on which the fastener is mounted is strong and firm in texture; therefore, it is not always advisable to use a zip on very thin fabric. If the fastener is too heavy for the fabric the garment will fall away from the figure causing it to drag. However this can generally be avoided by careful choice from the variety available.

Setting in a zipper

There are a few general instructions which apply to all methods of setting in zips. When selecting a zipper for an opening allow clearance at each end of the fastener, 3 mm to 6 mm ($\frac{1}{8}$ in to $\frac{1}{4}$ in), and a small amount for easing onto the fastener. This ease is particularly necessary when dealing with thin fabrics. The zipper itself tends to stretch in wear, so try to set it in taut. If using a commercial pattern, directions for type and length of zip to be used and method of setting in should be followed carefully.

When pinning a zip into a placket, place pins at right angles with the points to the fastening. Then tack right across the pins. Always measure and mark with a line of tacking the position of the stitching on the placket. The zip can then be tacked firmly in

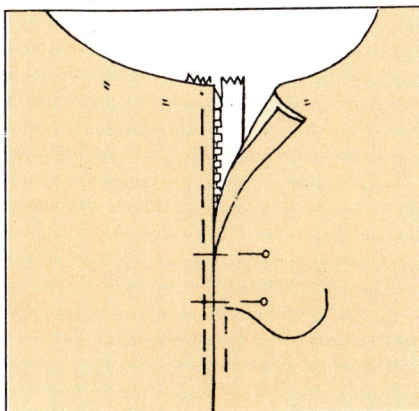

Using a zipper foot to stitch zipper into final position.

position and the stitching line will remain clear and easy to follow.

The most effective way of sewing in a zip is by machine using a medium length stitch and special zipper foot. This will give a strong, neat finish. Zips can also be sewn in by hand using small neat stitches.

Concealed Method
Stitch the seam up to the ends of the opening. Turn under the seam allowance down each side of the opening. Tack the turnings and press the folds. Mark the stitching lines 6 mm ($\frac{1}{4}$ in) each side of the opening. Place the closed zip under the folds so that they meet exactly in the centre of the teeth. Pin and tack the folds in this position to the zipper taking care to keep the folds meeting in the middle, and stitch along the marking tacks and across the closed end of fastener, making a neat square.

If the zip is very long it is a good idea to roughly tack the two edges together until the stitching has been made. This keeps them even.

Lapped Method
With this method only one line of stitching is made on the right side, the second edge being sewn from the inside of the work.

Fold under the turnings of the overlap, tack them and press the fold. Mark the stitching line

parallel to the edge and straight or slanting across each end. The stitching should be at least 9 mm ($\frac{3}{8}$ in) from the edge to allow the fold to cover the teeth. Place the closed zip under the fold, tack it firmly and stitch along the marking line.

Turn under the second edge level with the seam line, tack and press. Place the fold over the zipper tape close to the teeth, tack in position, and stitch on the edge of the fold.

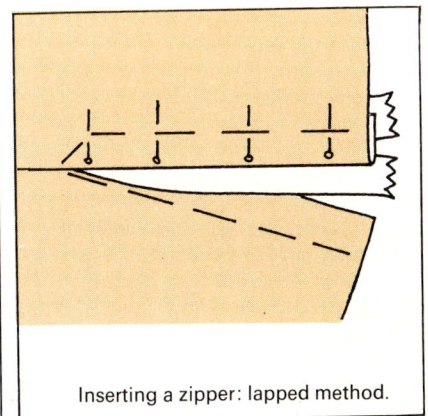

Inserting a zipper: lapped method.

Visible
This method is used when a zipper is to be set into an opening which is specially cut, and not into a seam.

Mark the position of the opening on the garment, cut it to within 6 mm ($\frac{1}{4}$ in) of the end. At the end of the slit, make two diagonal snips, to form a V shape, each 3 mm ($\frac{1}{8}$ in)

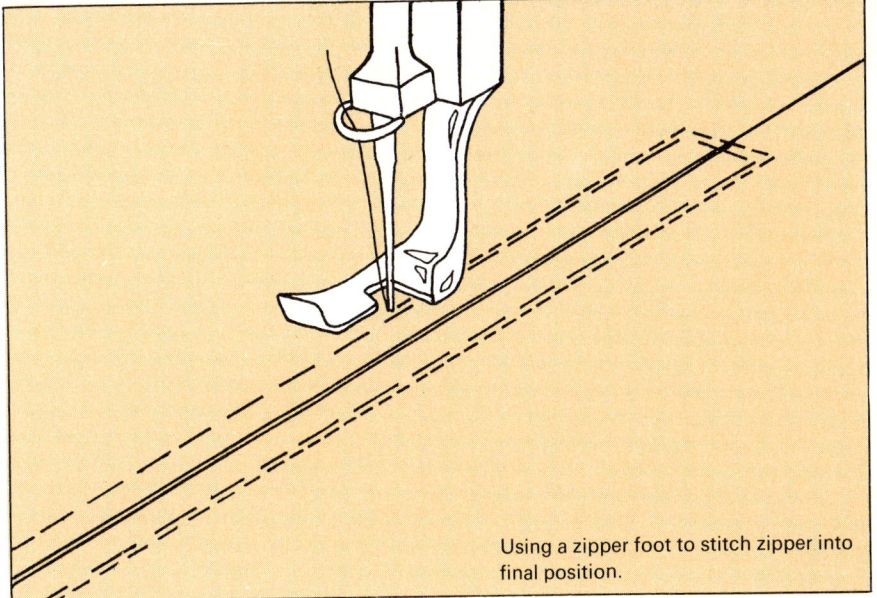

Tacking a zipper into position for concealed method.

long. Turn under onto the wrong side, 3 mm ($\frac{1}{8}$ in) turnings at each side of the opening. Tack firmly with small stitches. Turn under the small V-shaped tab at the end of the slit. Strengthen this end by hemming a small piece of seam binding right across the tab, thus hiding the raw edges of the diagonal snips. Press.

Working from the right side, lay the slit over the closed zip, with the folds equal distances from the teeth each side. Pin and tack in place. Stitch close to the edge of the garment all round. Remove tacking and press.

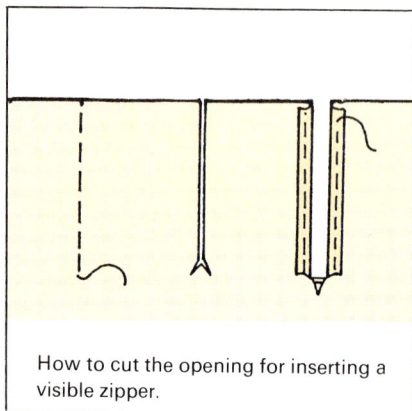

How to cut the opening for inserting a visible zipper.

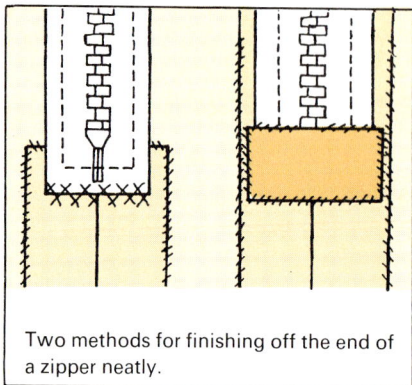

Two methods for finishing off the end of a zipper neatly.

Finishing

Whichever method is used, it is necessary to neaten the end of the tape on the wrong side. On thick fabrics straighten the tape and herringbone it down to the seam turnings. On other fabrics neaten by hemming a piece of seam binding over the ends.

Where the fastening is visible a shaped facing can be applied so that all but the teeth is covered on both sides of the work. The facing

should be cut and snipped in exactly the same way as the garment and the turned-in edges are hemmed to the tape close to the teeth.

Waistbands

Straight waistband

This is the most common sort of waistband usually made in the same fabric as the skirt. It generally requires some form of interfacing.

To make a waistband without a pattern cut a strip of fabric on the straight grain 10 cm (4 in) longer than the waist measurement to allow for the wrap. Mark centre front, centre back and side seams.

Sew ends of the band to seam allowance. Interface as required, tacking interfacing to notched or bottom edge of band. Fold in the seam allowance on the unnotched or top edge and press into place.

With right sides facing pin and tack the band to the garment, easing in fullness and matching markings. Trim seam allowance and clip curves. Fold band over and slip stitch the raw edge into place along the seam line, continuing along edge of wrap. Sew fastenings into place.

Faced waistband

This gives a neat appearance as it is not visible from the right side of the garment. The most common fabric to use is petersham ribbon (or grosgrain) which is obtainable in 2.5 cm to 10 cm (1 in to 4 in) widths. A faced band can also be made from lining or other light fabrics.

Both ends of the band are finished with a small hem, and hooks and eyes are sewn on the right side. The right side of the band is next to the wearer, and should fasten right over left.

Mounting skirt onto band

Mark the centre front centre back and sides of both skirt and band.

Place the wrong side of the band to the wrong side of the skirt, with

the corresponding points on band and skirt matching. Keep the skirt 12 mm ($\frac{1}{2}$ in) above the top edge of the band, and pin all round. Insert the pins downwards, as in this way they are easier to remove when fitting. Fit the skirt and arrange the fullness to lie neatly and regularly all round. Remove the top hook before sewing. Tack with diagonal stitches, then back stitch the skirt onto the band. Use a strong needle and thread for this process.

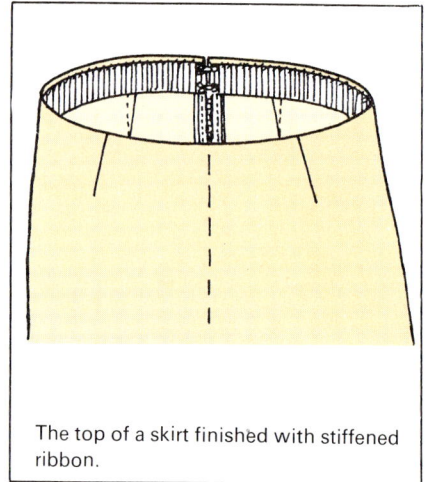

The top of a skirt finished with stiffened ribbon.

The 12 mm ($\frac{1}{2}$ in) turning at the top of the skirt is turned over the edge of the band and rough hemmed down. At the end of the band the top edge of the placket is turned down inside, to be in a line with the top of the band. Finish the raw edges by binding with straight seam binding or a strip of matching lining.

Sew on the top hook.

Casing

When elastic or tape is to be inserted into the waist line of a garment the casing is made first, a little wider than the elastic or tape. The hem is turned onto the wrong side and machine stitched along the inner edge. A second line of stitching is made 3 mm ($\frac{1}{8}$ in) inside the fold of the hem to form the casing into which the elastic is inserted.

Inserting elastic

In a garment that does not require much laundering it is not necessary

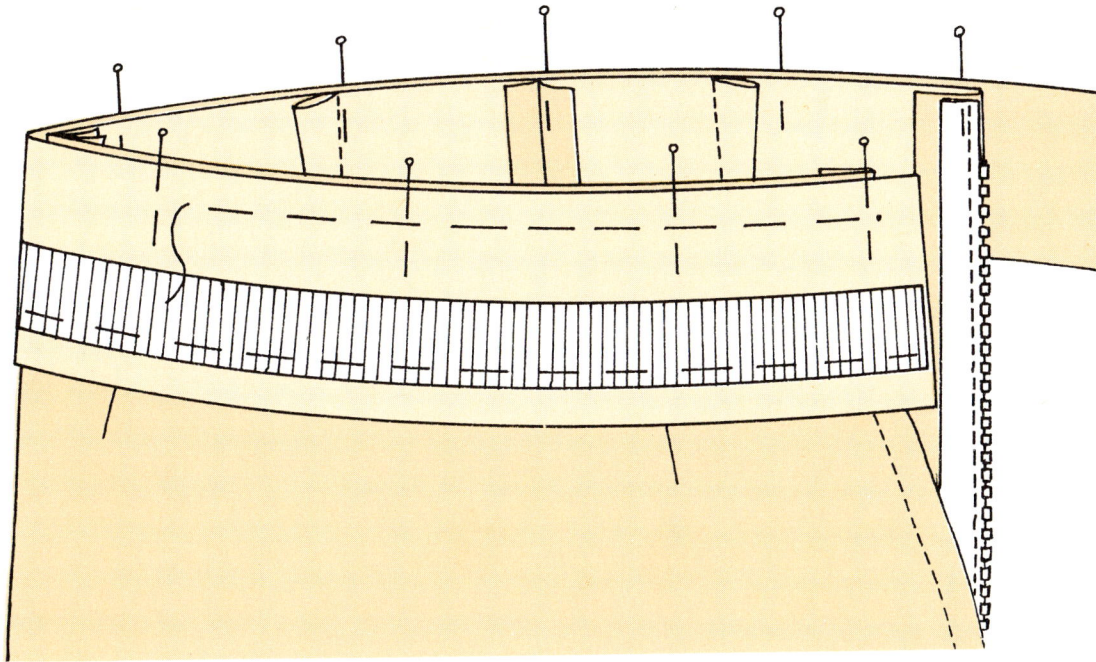

Applying an interfaced waistband.

to make the elastic removable; in this case a small portion of the hem is left unsewn until the elastic has been inserted; the ends are sewn together and the hem is completed.

Method 1 It is much easier when washing, drying and ironing a garment if the elastic can be removed first, also this saves the elastic from wearing out. In this instance two buttonhole slots are made in the heading, about 4 cm (1½ in) apart, and each side of a seam. These should be made through one thickness of material only and on the wrong side of the garment. A small button is sewn half-way between the slots, and a buttonhole loop, as described on page 86, is made each end of the elastic, which is cut 2.5 cm (1 in) less than the waist measurement. The elastic is then threaded into the hem and the loops are slipped over the button.

Method 2 Hem both ends of the elastic and sew a button or eye onto one end of it and make a loop or sew a hook onto the other. One end then fastens onto the other.

Method 3 For a blouse or garment that opens down the front the method is slightly different. The buttonhole slots are made each side of the opening and a button is sewn on the outer side of the slot. The loops at the end of the elastic fasten onto the two buttons.

Drawstring

All sorts of cord or decorative ribbon can be used in a casing as a drawstring. The length should be equal to the waist measurement plus an allowance for tying a knot or a bow. When a drawstring is being used the buttonhole slot method is used and the ends of the tape tie over the space between.

A few small back stitches may be made through the hem and the elastic, or tape, to prevent it from pulling out.

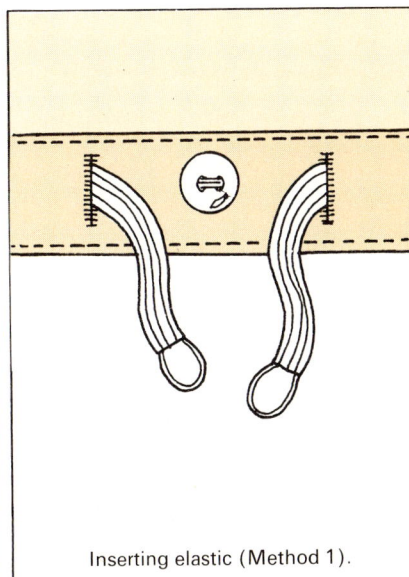

Inserting elastic (Method 1).

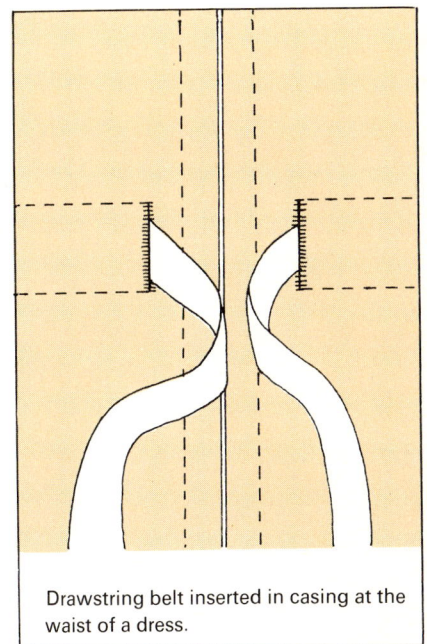

Drawstring belt inserted in casing at the waist of a dress.

Construction methods

Cuff finishes

Cuffs may be made any width and shape desired, but they must be designed to suit the sleeve on which they are being used.

Straight cuff

This is the most simple type of cuff. There is no slit made into the sleeve of the garment. If using a commercial pattern a pattern piece will be provided for the cuff. To make a cuff without a pattern, cut a piece of fabric the length around your wrist plus turnings, and wrap over if necessary. It should be cut twice the width of the cuff plus turnings both sides. Fold the fabric in half lengthwise and press the crease.

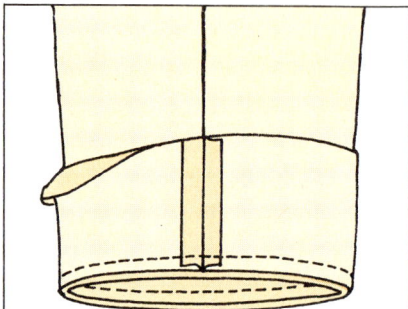

Straight cuff applied to right side of sleeve.

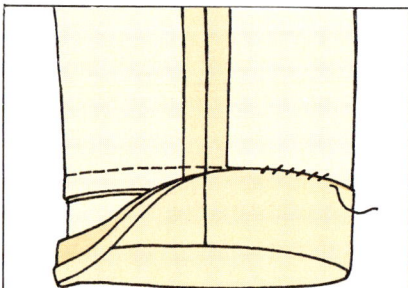

Straight cuff turned and hemmed inside sleeve.

Place one edge of the cuff to the edge of the sleeve, right sides facing. If the sleeve is gathered the fullness should be evenly arranged. Tack the cuff piece in place, then machine stitch. If preferred the cuff

Left A classic shirt cuff with monogram.
Right The cuff on this blouse is enhanced by a lace insertion.

seam can be opened out and the machining can be made on the right side, close to the edge. Fold the cuff along the centre crease, turn under the raw edge and neatly hem the fold to the turnings just above the machine stitching. Sew on buttons and make buttonholes or loops, or sew on fasteners.

Shaped cuff

This is an easy method of fixing a shaped cuff to a very full sleeve. Gather the bottom edge of the sleeve before the sleeve seam has been sewn up. Draw up the gathers to fit the cuff. Make a turning along the top edge of the cuff. Lay the top edge of the cuff over the gathered edge of the sleeve right

sides uppermost, taking care to keep the ends of the cuff and sleeve in a continuous line. Machine stitch close to the top edge of cuff. Oversew the turnings of sleeve and cuff together.

Fold sleeve over so that the right sides are together and side seams meet, taking care to have the seam of cuff meeting exactly. Machine stitch and press the seam perfectly flat. Finish the edges of the turnings with top stitching, buttonhole stitch, or a narrow hem. If the cuff is too wide, fasten as described for a fold over opening.

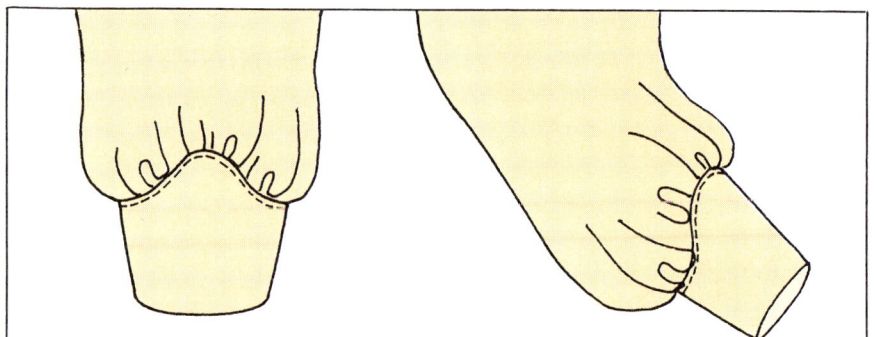

An attractive shaped cuff emphasises the gathers in this sleeve.

Frilled cuff

Turn up a hem sufficiently deep to allow about 2.5 cm (1 in) for the frill, more may be left if wished 12 mm ($\frac{1}{2}$ in) is needed for the double hem and 6 mm ($\frac{1}{4}$ in) for turnings. That will mean an extra 4.5 cm ($\frac{3}{4}$ in) must be added to the length of the sleeve when cutting.

.Machine or slip stitch the edge of the hem and run or machine 12 mm ($\frac{1}{2}$ in) from the edge. If elastic is to be used, work a buttonhole in the hemline on the inside of the sleeve at the under arm seam; with a drawstring make it on the outside.

Thread the elastic or drawstring through the hem and pull up.

Plain buttoned cuff

Make a slit in the sleeve 8 cm to 10 cm (3 in to 4 in) long, unless the seam is being used as an opening. This slit is faced with a piece of fabric cut on the straight of grain. The right side of the facing is placed to the right side of the sleeve with the slit closed. Machine around the edge of the slit, as for faced openings (page 53), cut through facing, clip the corners, turn the facing to the wrong side of the sleeve and press. Neaten the edges and attach the cuff.

Cut a straight band twice the finished width, plus turnings and the length around wrist, plus wrap over and turnings. Fold band in half and cut one end to a point. Slit the buttonhole at the point and prepare for working. Fold the cuff in half with the points matching and right sides together, stitch both the pointed and the straight ends, turn right side out and press. Finish the buttonhole in the chosen manner to match the rest of the shirt.

Gather the sleeve edge. Placing the right side of the outside of the cuff to the right side of the sleeve, pin and tack edge to edge arranging the gathers evenly. Stitch the two together. Turn the sleeve inside out, pin the turned-in edge of the cuff over the gathers and slip stitch along the stitched line. Sew

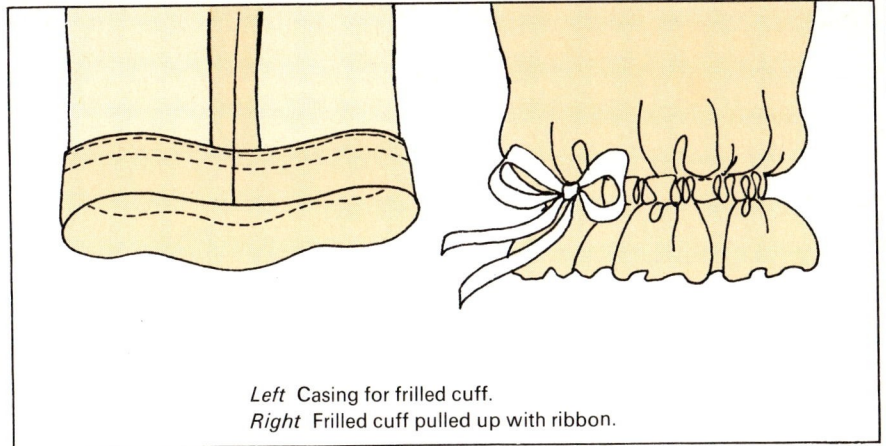

Left Casing for frilled cuff.
Right Frilled cuff pulled up with ribbon.

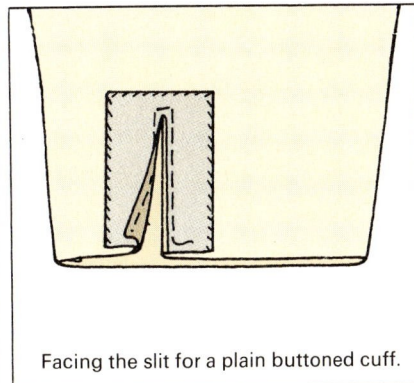

Facing the slit for a plain buttoned cuff.

on button to match buttonhole. A line of top stitching may be made all round cuff 3 mm ($\frac{1}{8}$ in) from the edge.

Shirt cuff

This opening and cuff are traditionally used for a shirt. The slit is bound with two separate strips of fabric. The under one with a narrow crossway strip, the upper one with a wrap-over piece which should be 2.5 cm (1 in) longer and 12 mm ($\frac{1}{2}$ in) wider than the facing when finished. Stitch the wide

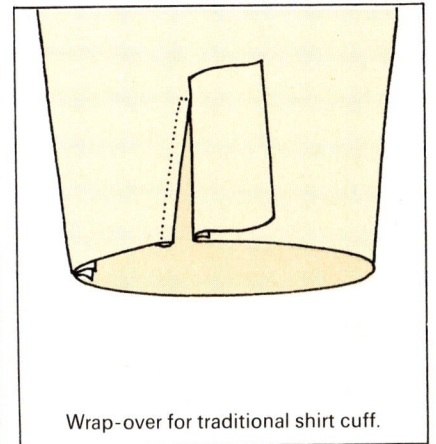

Wrap-over for traditional shirt cuff.

piece with right side to the wrong side of garment, sewing about 3 mm ($\frac{1}{8}$ in) from the edge. Turn this piece to the right side of the sleeve and press with the seam at the edge. Turn in the facing all round, tack and stitch making a cross at the head of the opening. The head of the facing illustrated is square but it may be pointed or rounded.

The cuff is sewn over the gathered sleeve as for straight cuff.

Plain buttoned cuff completed.

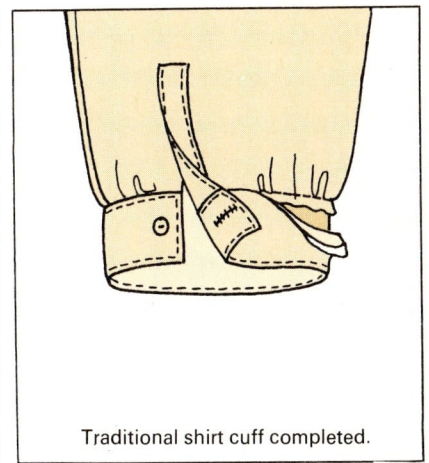

Traditional shirt cuff completed.

Construction methods

Pockets

Pockets can be decorative as well as functional. There are several methods of fitting pockets to garments, but for ease of handling they should be attached before main seams are joined.

Bound Pocket

Method 1 Have the position and side of the pocket clearly marked on the fabric. Tack a strip of linen or lining to wrong side of garment against mark so as to strengthen the work. Cut two pieces of fabric 5 cm (2 in) longer than the pocket and 8 cm (3 in) wide.

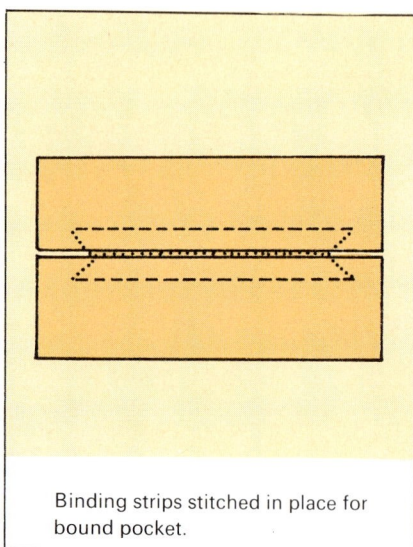

Binding strips stitched in place for bound pocket.

On the right side of garment place one binding piece to top of mark, with the edge along the line to be cut, the other pocket piece to the under side of line. With right sides together. Machine stitch along both pieces 6 mm ($\frac{1}{4}$ in) from the edges, beginning and ending in exactly the same place on both strips and leaving 2.5 cm (1 in) free at the ends of each strip. Cut through the pocket mark to within 12 mm ($\frac{1}{2}$ in) from each end, then cut a V-shape to the machine stitching.

Press seam open and pull the pieces through to the wrong side. Form a lip on each side of opening, taking care to tuck the ends well in. Tack and machine stitch along the sides and across the ends.

Cut two pieces of fabric the size of the pocket. Place one piece to top part of pocket binding and the other to the under part and machine stitch. These two pieces lie on top of each other, and are stitched around the edges to form a pocket. If the garment fabric is too bulky for this, a piece of lining can be used for the under part of pocket.

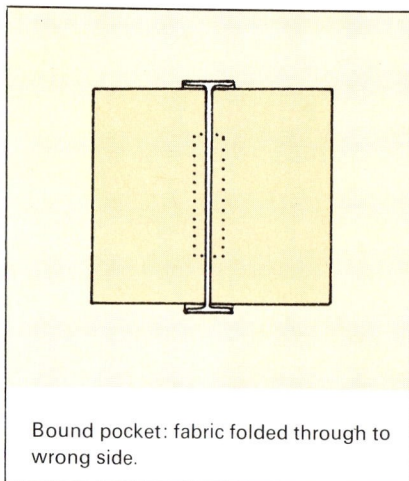

Bound pocket: fabric folded through to wrong side.

Method 2 Mark size and position of pocket carefully on garment.

Cut a piece of material 19 cm ($7\frac{1}{2}$ in) long and 4 cm ($1\frac{1}{2}$ in) wider than the length of pocket opening. Place right side of this piece to right side of garment, with 10 cm (4 in) above pocket mark, 9 cm ($3\frac{1}{2}$ in) below and 2 cm ($\frac{3}{4}$ in) over at each end. Machine stitch 6 mm ($\frac{1}{4}$ in) along each side of pocket mark, and across the ends. Cut along the pocket mark and clip the corners as shown, taking care to cut right to the machine stitching.

Trim the edges very slightly. Pull the material through to the wrong side and open it out over the cut edges. The folds of the binding should meet exactly in the centre. Press the turnings at the ends of pocket well back and arrange the fullness into little inverted pleats. Tack around the seam of the binding neatly and from the right side machine stitch along the joins at the sides and ends. Fold the top part of material over to lie on the under part and machine stitch 12 mm ($\frac{1}{2}$ in) from the edge all

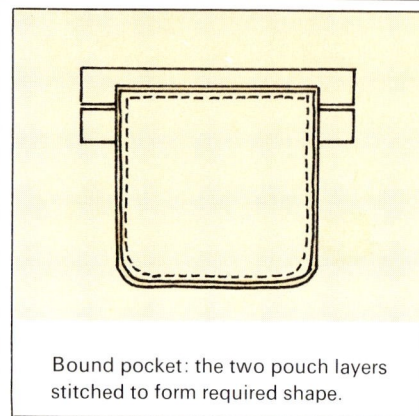

Bound pocket: the two pouch layers stitched to form required shape.

around to form a pocket of the required shape. Turn the raw edges in against each other and oversew. This method cannot be used on thick woollen fabric, but is excellent for cotton, linen, silk or artificial silk.

Flap pocket

To make the flap, cut a piece of material 10 cm (4 in) long and 14 cm ($5\frac{1}{2}$ in) wide, taking care to match the pattern stripes, or checks of fabric at the pocket marks. Fold this piece in two lengthwise and stitch up the ends, rounding the corners if desired. Turn right side out and tack. Press perfectly flat and machine stitch around the edge.

This pocket is now made in exactly the same way as a bound pocket. Use the flap as the top binding piece keeping it on the right side.

Patch pockets

Patch pockets can be varied in shape and size. There are a number of ways of finishing the edges: binding, facing and simple hems.

Generally a pattern of a pocket is included with the garment pattern, but it is simple to adapt the basic patch pocket and add it to a plain pattern if desired.

Cut out the pocket on either weft or selvedge way of the fabric. If the fabric is plaid or striped, the pocket can be cut crossways to give a decorative effect. If the top is hemmed a wide turning is allowed. Allow narrow turnings on the other edges.

Mark position of pocket on garment. Make the first turning of the top hem on the wrong side of the pocket piece and tack. Fold the second hem over to the right side and stitch it at the sides of pocket for the exact width of the hem. Turn right side out after trimming turnings to 6 mm ($\frac{1}{4}$ in). Do not trim all around the pocket.

Turn raw edges on remaining sides of pocket onto wrong side, tack and catch-stitch, or machine around edge. Hem the top edge, or finish with one or more rows of machining. Press. Pin and tack the pocket in position on the garment. Sew close to the edge with machine stitching or running stitch. Strengthen the top corners of the pocket by sewing a small triangle in each one or with a few tack stitches into the seam.

Lined patch pockets

A decorated pocket, or one which stands out from the garment a little, requires a lining. Turn all four turnings of the pocket onto the wrong side. Cut a lining the same size and following the same direction of the grain. Baste the lining to the wrong side of the pocket, turn in the edges together and hem the folds. Press and attach to garment.

If the pocket is to be finished with decorative stitches on the outside, these should be completed before attaching.

Patch pocket with flap

First cut a strip of material or binding and sew it to the wrong side of the garment between the marks indicating the top of the pocket, to reinforce the fabric. Cut out and prepare the pocket as for patch pocket, binding the top edge or making a narrow hem. If preferred, the pocket many be lined. Sew it to the garment.

Cut out the pocket flap, making it about 3 mm ($\frac{1}{8}$ in) wider than the pocket at each side and about one-third the depth of the pocket. Two pieces will be needed for the flap, one in the same fabric as the garment, and one in lining. Place the two together, right sides facing,

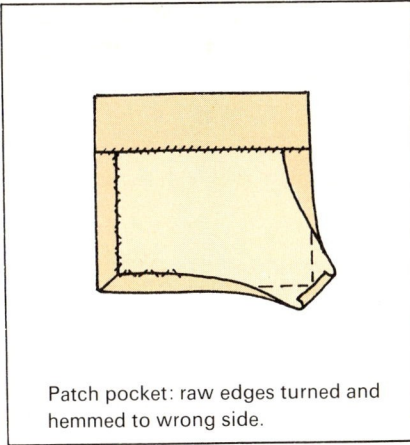

Patch pocket: raw edges turned and hemmed to wrong side.

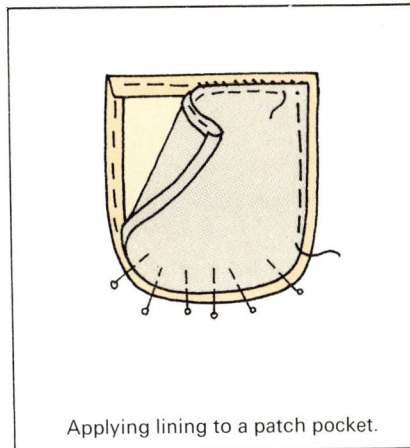

Applying lining to a patch pocket.

and sew along the two sides and bottom edge. Trim turnings narrow, turn right side out and press.

Place the flap, face down, on the right side of the garment with the raw edge level with the top of the pocket. Stitch through surface material only, press. Then turn under the edge of lining, enclose the turnings and hem the fold to garment. Press.

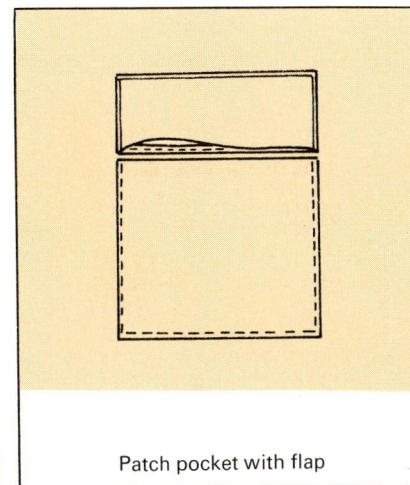

Patch pocket with flap

Welt pocket

This pocket has the edge bound with a fairly wide strip. It is a method which gives interest to pocket openings which run lengthwise from the waist in skirts. Mark the position of the pocket on the garment. Cut the welt strip parallel to the selvedge. The strip should be the length of pocket line, plus turnings and the width of the welt plus 2.5 cm (1 in). A west is usually 18 mm ($\frac{3}{4}$ in) deep when finished. The two pocket pieces are cut the same length as the pocket, plus 2.5 cm (1 in), by the depth of pocket; they are shaped as required.

The two pocket pieces are sewn together around the edges and the loose turnings are neatened on the wrong side with overcasting. Fold under the ends of the welt strip to make it fit the pocket slit, tack the turnings down and trim them to about 6 mm ($\frac{1}{4}$ in).

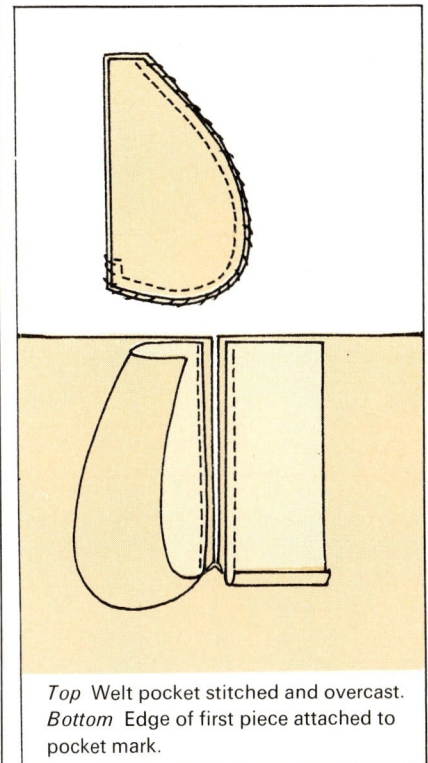

Top Welt pocket stitched and overcast.
Bottom Edge of first piece attached to pocket mark.

Place one edge of the strip, right side facing outside of garment 6 mm ($\frac{1}{4}$ in) below the pocket mark, tack and stitch. Put the edge of one pocket piece to the other side of pocket mark, level with welt, tack and stitch. Fasten off the ends carefully and secure the edges of welt and pocket with a few back stitches. Cut the pocket slit and snip diagonally into the corners. Press the seam open.

Fold the pocket piece through to the wrong side. Fold the welt strip in two along the length, slip stitch the folds at the two ends neatly.

Fold the loose edge over the turnings, encasing them and stitch into place. Then stitch the second pocket piece to the welt. Press.

Welt is turned to the wrong side and second pocket piece is attached to it.

Collars

Collars may be tailored and discrete or frilly and extravagant. There is a wide choice of fabrics that are suitable for collars; they may be similar to the garment, or of a contrasting fabric. Collars can be permanently attached to the garment or they can be made detachable.

Suitable fabrics for plain and tailored collars are piqué, linen, shantung, taffeta, fine wool, while fine crêpe, silk, voile, muslin, lace and taffeta make more dressy neckwear. Various weights of interfacing are available for collars that need stiffening.

Whatever the shape of the collar, the pattern should be carefully cut, so that it fits snugly around the neck and lies flat on the garment.

To make a collar for a finished dress

Fold the dress in half down the centre back and front, pulling one

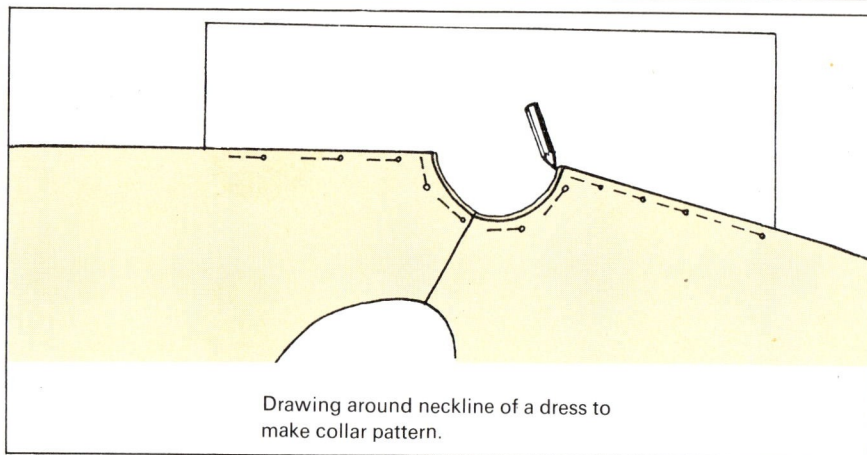

Drawing around neckline of a dress to make collar pattern.

sleeve inside the other and fitting the shoulders exactly. Pin the two sides together carefully and lay the neck on a sheet of strong paper. Pin the centre back fold firmly to the edge of the paper for at least 8 cm (3 in). Smooth out the dress so that the neck lies quite flat, and pin the centre front to the paper. With a firm line, draw around the neck and along the centre back and front folds for about 10 cm (4 in) using a coloured pencil.

Remove the dress and the neckline should be clearly and accurately marked on the paper. Draw the shape of the collar onto this outline.

Any style of flat collar can be designed on this basic outline, and some variations are shown here, all taken from the same pattern.

Peter Pan or flat collar

This style fits snugly to the neck and it is one of the easiest collars to make. Measure all around from the neck curve the width of collar wanted, usually about 8 cm to 10 cm (3 in to 4 in). Join the centre back line to the centre front with a curve parallel to the neckline. To avoid a point at centre neck on the outer edge, rather than follow the curve exactly, draw the outside curve at right angles to the back line, for 6 mm ($\frac{1}{4}$ in) from the edge of the paper.

At the front edge of the collar extend the neckline 6 mm ($\frac{1}{4}$ in) for a turning, and mark a point 12 mm ($\frac{1}{2}$ in) from the centre front on the outside line. Join this point to the point where the 6 mm ($\frac{1}{4}$ in) turning

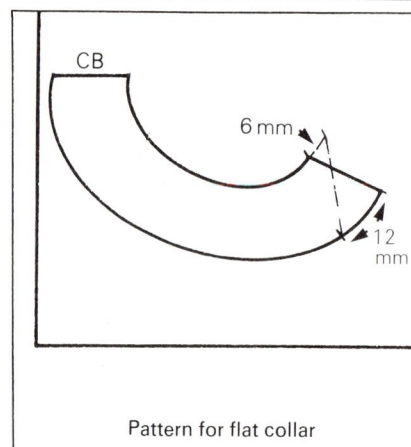

Pattern for flat collar

was marked on the neck edge with a straight line to form the front edge of the collar. This is half the Peter Pan pattern and the centre back should be marked to avoid confusion in cutting.

If the collar is being made for a dress which opens at the back instead of the front, place the centre front fold along the edge of the paper when drawing the collar pattern and then proceed as before.

To make variations of this pattern, re-draw the outer edge as indicated or make up your own designs.

To calculate material required

The amounts of material required for collars vary with the styles chosen. A straight collar takes less than a rounded or shaped collar.

Measure the neckline of the garment and add 8 cm to 10 cm (3 in to 4 in) according to the shape of the points; call this measurement (a). Then measure from the neckline to the bottom of the points and multiply this by two for measurement (b). The amount of material required is a rectangle (a) × (b), cut with the selvedge right across the width of the pattern as shown.

Flat or shaped collar

Place the centre back of the pattern to the edge of the table, draw a square enclosing the collar pattern, then measure at right angles from the table edge to the end of the pattern, to obtain depth and width required. The amount required is 45 cm to 70 cm ($\frac{1}{2}$ yd to $\frac{3}{4}$ yd) according to the style.

Making collars

To cut out a collar

Place the centre back of the pattern to the fold of material absolutely straight on the weft way of the weave. Allow turnings of 6 mm to 12 mm ($\frac{1}{4}$ in to $\frac{1}{2}$ in). Pin down firmly and cut out. With a double collar of similar material, two pieces must be cut exactly alike. If the lining material is short, it may be cut in two pieces with a central seam. If the collar is of thick material, the lining should be thin.

Interlining

This is not often required on dress collars, although it adds crispness to a tailored design. Cut without turnings.

To fix an interlining This must be fixed to the lining of the collar before making up. Lay the collar lining on the table, wrong side uppermost, place the interlining on top with an equal amount of turning showing all around, pin and tack in position.

Tailor's pad stitching Hold the collar with the neck edge towards the right and work from centre front to centre front, from left to right, then back from right to left, without altering the position of the collar. Work with a thread that matches the lining. Pad stitching is a form of tacking with long stitches on the working side and tiny

stitches picking up the two fabrics so that they scarcely show on the under side of the collar lining. Continue in this way until the whole collar has been covered with rows of stitches.

To make up a collar

These instructions apply to any shape of double collar, whether an interlining is used or not.

Place the two right sides of the collar together, and tack and stitch 6 mm ($\frac{1}{4}$ in) in from the edge all around the outer edges. Remove the tacking and press, cutting the turnings very narrow, and snipping off the points of corners. Clip in between scallops or points, just down to the stitching. Turn right side out, tack carefully around the edge so that no lining shows from underneath, and press again on the wrong side.

On a short collar a row of stitching, about 6 mm ($\frac{1}{4}$ in) from the edge, is often made at this stage to give greater firmness.

Single collar

The edges of this collar are bound, picot edged or roll hemmed, according to the fabric used. It is attached in the way described below.

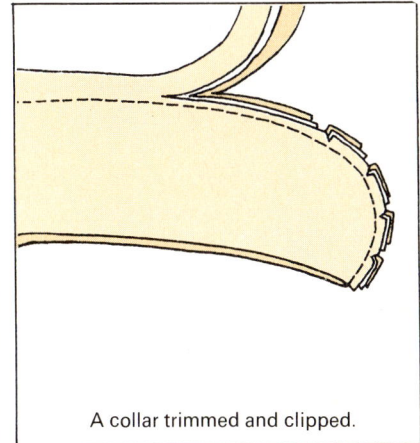

A collar trimmed and clipped.

A white Peter Pan collar brightens a plain dress. It is decorated with a bow made from velvet ribbon.

Construction methods

Detachable collar

A collar that may be removed for laundering can be made to suit any style of neck. The neck edge must be bound neatly. A shaped collar is bound with a bias cut strip of material about 2.5 cm (1 in) wide, a straight collar is finished with a strip on the straight or it can be inserted onto a specially cut neckband. A thin material should be used for the crossway strip, this should be cut 5 cm (2 in) wide.

Method When the collar has been made, tack around neck edge. Place the right side of collar neck edge and strip together, leaving 12 mm ($\frac{1}{2}$ in) of binding projecting at each end. Tack and stitch 3 mm ($\frac{1}{4}$ in) in from edge. Remove tacking and press the material over the stitching, then fold it over. Turn in the two ends and the raw edge and hem or machine stitch just above the first line of stitching. This binding now forms the stand of the collar which is tacked inside the neckline.

Always finish the neck edge of a dress with a cross-cut binding or facing, before attaching this type of collar to it.

Attaching a collar

There are some points which should be observed when fitting and attaching any collar. Do not stretch the neck of the garment or it will be pulled out of shape; the neck edge of the collar should be slightly stretched to make it lie flat when finished; the binding should be eased on, as it forms a facing over the raw edges and is turned down over the neckline of the dress.

Shaped collar

For this a bias strip about 2.5 cm (1 in) wide is needed. Find the centre back of the dress and of the collar and mark with thread or pins. Place the under side of the collar to the right side of the dress. Pin the centre back and the two

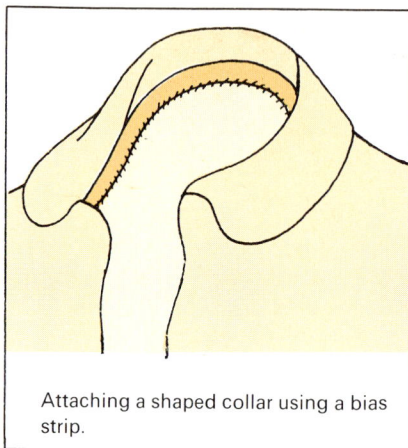

Attaching a shaped collar using a bias strip.

centre fronts in position, and tack around. Take the bias strip and tack it to the right side of the collar with the wrong side uppermost. Leave 12 mm ($\frac{1}{2}$ in) of binding at each end, and stitch 6 mm ($\frac{1}{4}$ in) in from the edge all around.

Remove the tacking, and press the turnings open carefully. Holding the collar in the left hand and away from the dress, turn the facing over the seam, flattening it very carefully. Tack the facing just below the join to give greater firmness when fixing the loose edge, then press again.

Turn in the raw edge of the facing and tack to the dress, taking care to hold it flat; slip stitch or hem the fold. Machine stitching should never be used on this edge as it is clumsy and does not have sufficient give.

This shirt-style overblouse is neatly finished with a stand up collar and simple band cuffs. These styles of collar and cuff are especially well-suited to casual wear and lightweight fabrics.

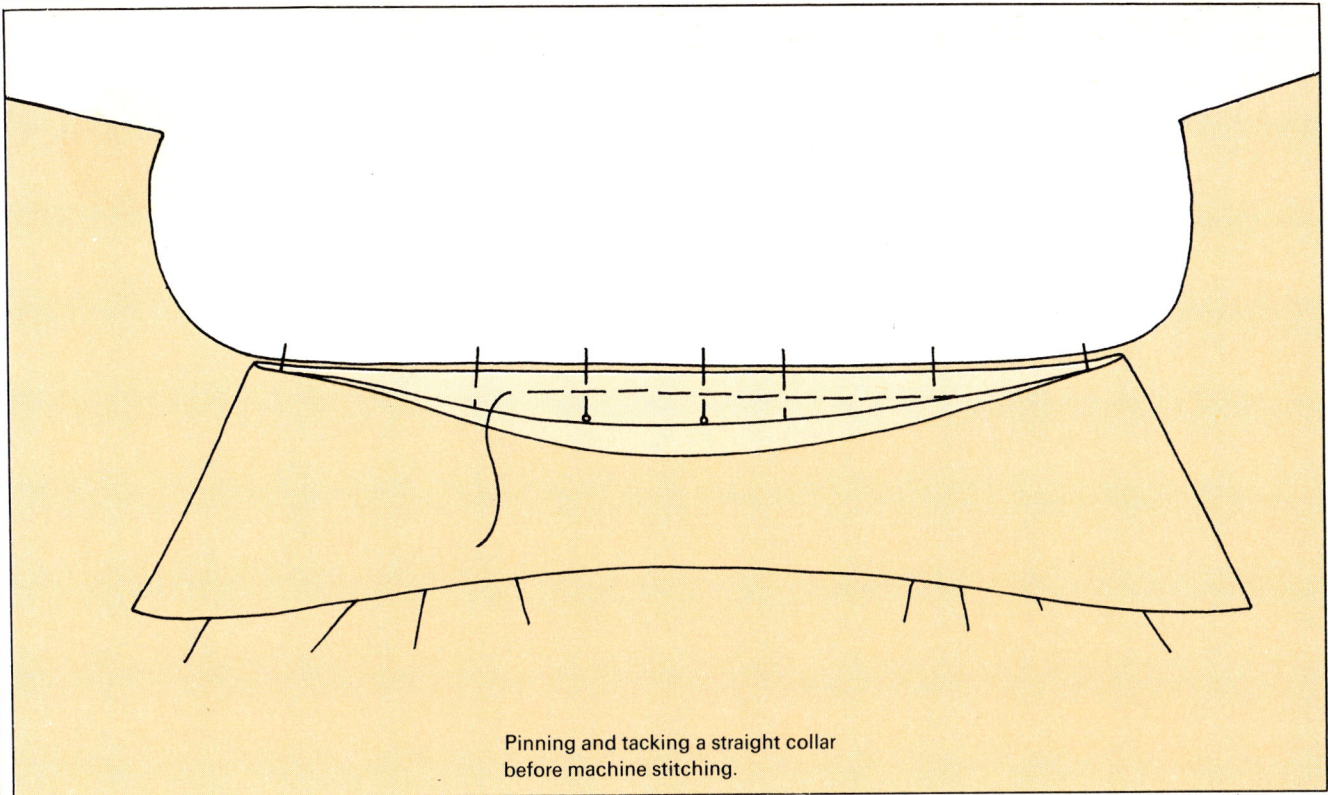

Pinning and tacking a straight collar
before machine stitching.

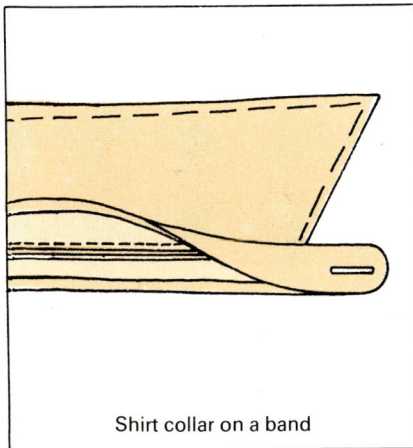

Shirt collar on a band

Shirt collar on a band

Make the collar as described above.
The band should be the length of
the neck measurement plus 2.5 cm
(1 in) for fastening overlap and
18 mm to 3 cm ($\frac{3}{4}$ in to $1\frac{1}{8}$ in) wide.
Cut two bands following the grain
of the collar, use one as the band
and one as band facing. Turn in
the edge of the band all around and
tack it down.

Insert the neck edge of the collar
over the top edge of the band, and
place the neck edge of the garment
over the bottom edge of the band
and tack them in place. Tack
around the edges of the band

facing, place it over the neck band
exactly, covering up to raw edges of
the collar and the neck of the
garment, and tack through the
three thicknesses. The band may
then be slip stitched all around by
hand, or machine stitched;
according to the type of garment
being made.

Straight collar

Make up as a double collar.
Working with the right side of dress
outside, pin the right side of upper
part of collar only to the inside of
dress, centre back points together
and edges exactly even. Then pin
the ends of collar in position and
pin all around the neck edge. Tack
and machine stitch 6 mm ($\frac{1}{4}$ in)
from edge.

Remove tacking, and press the
turnings into the collar. Lift the
collar in left hand, lining on tip,
and turn in the loose edge until the
fold lies just above the machine
stitching. Pin carefully and tack,
then hem the fold onto the
turnings. The hemming stitches
should not be visible on the right
side of the dress. Remove tacking
and press once again.

When the ends of this collar are
to be continuous with the edge of
opening, pin the collar onto the
neck edge before machine stitching
the ends.

Perfect finishes

Sleeves

There are three basic types of sleeves: the kimono, the raglan and the set-in sleeve.

The easiest to sew is the kimono. This is cut in one with the garment or as part of a yoke. Sometimes kimono sleeves have gussets let into the underarm seam for a better fit.

Raglan sleeves are also quite simple to handle. On these, the sleeve joins the bodice of the garment with a diagonal seam.

The set-in sleeve, which can have a variety of styles from a straight slim-fitting sleeve to a full bishop sleeve gathered into a cuff, is the type which needs the most care in handling. Setting in a sleeve is not difficult, but it does require a knowledge of how to handle the garment during this stage of construction.

The plain set-in sleeve has a smooth roll on the sleeve head and no gathers. Although it is a popular style for tailored dresses and soft jackets, it is the style which gives home dressmakers the most problems.

Plain, set-in sleeves

Before making up the sleeve, work thread tracing lines down the straight grain of the sleeve and on the crosswise grain. The straight grain line should be in line with the third finger of the hand when the sleeve is on the arm. These lines of tacking will help you to check whether the sleeve is properly set at fitting stage and at the final trying on stage.

Finish all the work on the sleeves before putting them into the garment. Turn the garment inside out. Put the sleeve inside the armhole so that right sides of sleeve and garment are facing. You will notice immediately that the sleeve is too big for the armhole. The extra fabric is so that the sleeve will fit over the roundness of your shoulder and you are going to ease in this extra fabric by pinning.

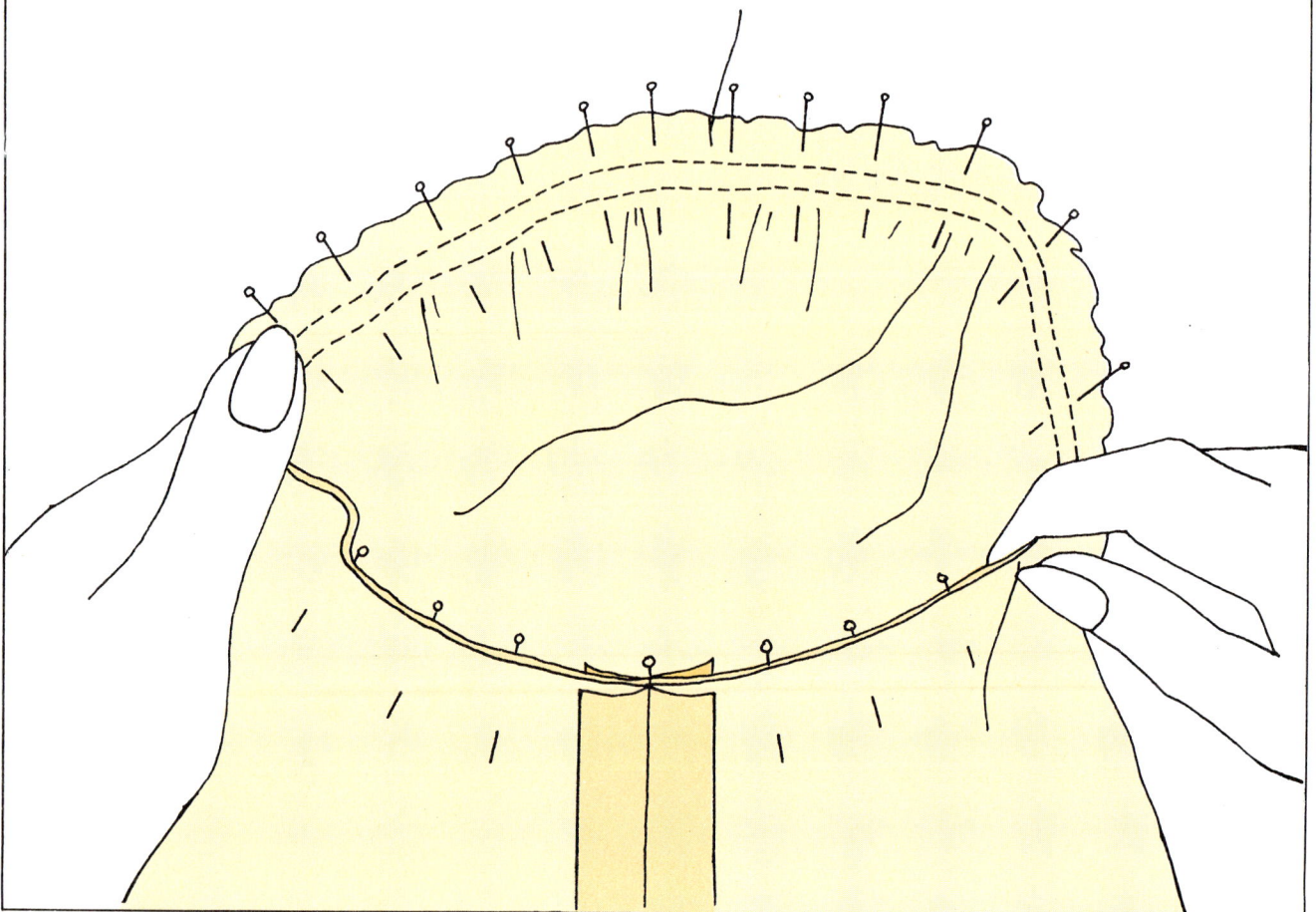

Pinning a set-in sleeve into armhole opening to ease in fullness.

Start pinning

Have a lot of pins ready; long, glass headed dressmaker's pins are best for this job. First pin the underarm seams together. Then insert pins vertically on each side of the first pin until you are within 75 mm to 100 mm (3 in to 4 in) of the shoulder seam on back and front. Make sure that you match notches and markings as you pin. Tack the seam where pinned with small, firm stitches and take out the pins. Put in one pin at the shoulder seam to hold the garment and sleeve together temporarily. The next stage is important and success depends on your holding the garment and sleeve properly.

Making a 'shoulder'

Pick up the garment, holding it at the shoulder seam and sleeve head, so that the sleeve is on top. Turn your hand so that the sleeve lies over your closed hand. Your hand makes a 'form' for the sleeve and you will see that the sleeve now appears to fit the armhole. Your hand has made a curve similar to a shoulder. Keeping your hand in position, start pinning the sleeve into the armhole. Pins must lie across the seam, not along it. Place them about 12 mm ($\frac{1}{2}$ in) apart at first and then add others between. As you pin, adjust the fabric so that the back and front of the armhole is smooth and that there is a smooth, flat area on the shoulder seam. Most of the ease will be either side of this spot.

Tacking in

Now tack the sleeve into the armhole, using small stitches and working them over the pins, removing each pin in turn. If you use small stitches, there will not be pleats in the fabric where you have eased. If the fabric is one that can be steam-shrunk, such as wool, you can steam out any puckers that show on the right side, using a hot iron and a damp cloth, working over a pressing mitt.

Try the garment on and make sure that the thread traced lines on

Plain set-in sleeves are generally used for traditional shirt patterns as in this photograph.

the sleeve are perfectly horizontal and vertical. If they are not, you know that the sleeve is not positioned properly and will have to be unpicked and re-positioned.

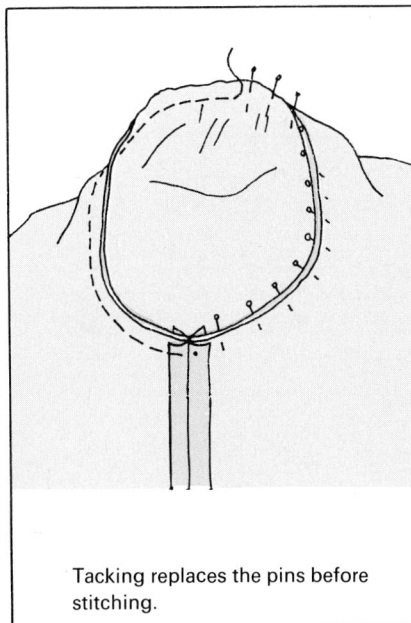

Tacking replaces the pins before stitching.

Sewing in the sleeve

You can sew sleeves in by hand or by machine. Hand sewing enables you to keep some control over the easing as you stitch. Small, half back stitch is used. (Garments made of woollen or jersey fabrics are often best stitched by hand.)

If you prefer to machine stitch, begin at the undrarm seam and work from the sleeve side. You can control the ease better if you can see it. Stitch as slowly as possible. Keep a pair of small scissors near you, and use the points to move the fabric if you see that the presser foot is making a pleat out of an eased area. Stitch right round the sleeve and then carefully unpick the tacking. Press the seam allowances towards the sleeve but do not press the sleeve head itself.

When setting sleeves into children's and baby clothes, use a narrow French seam.

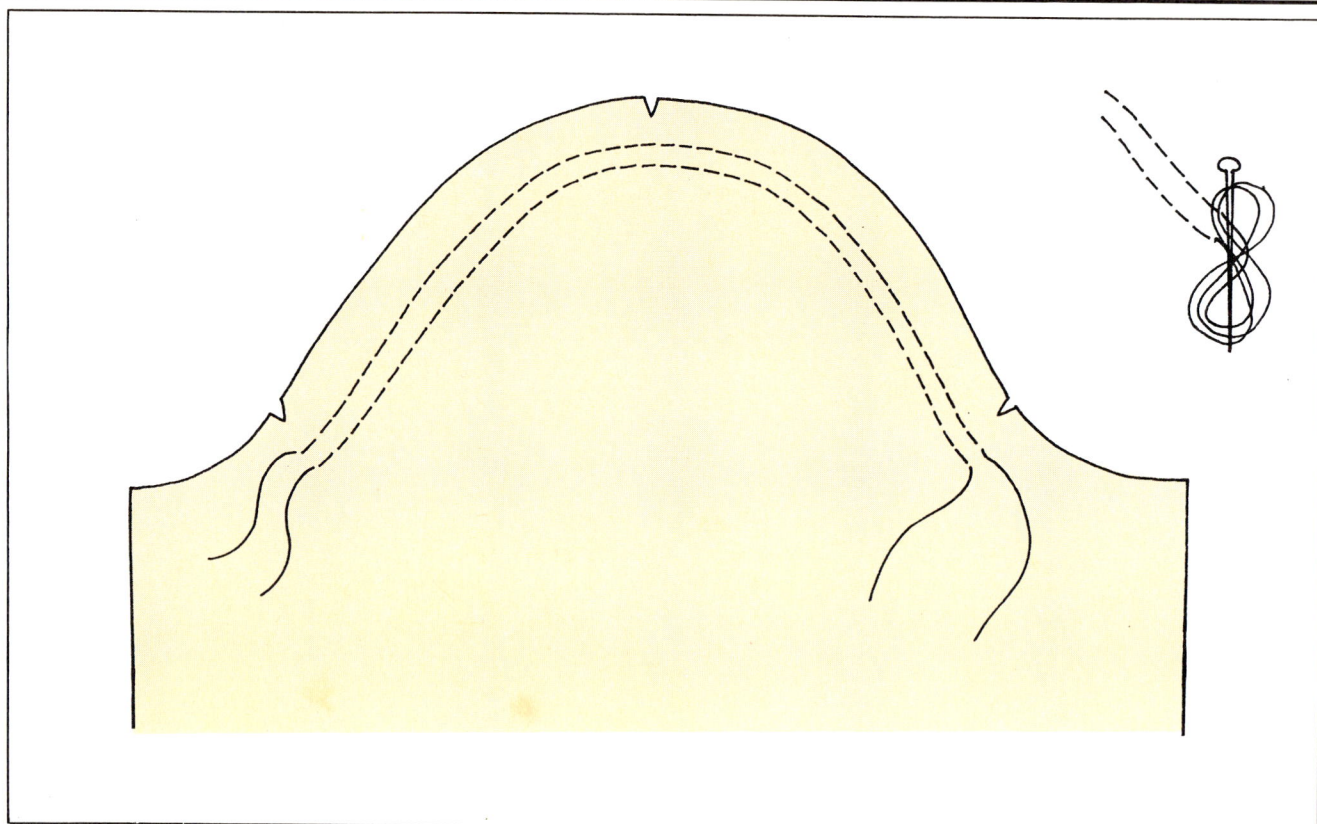

Finishing

There are several ways of finding armhole seams. If the fabric is thick or has sharp edges, such as lace or nylon net, trim the seam allowance back to 9 mm ($\frac{3}{8}$ in) and bind the edge with bias cut strips of a soft fabric. Non-fray materials can be overcast by hand or finished with machine zigzag stitch. Very soft fabrics or those which are lightweight and inclined to fray need two rows of stitching. Work the second row inside the seam allowance about 6 mm ($\frac{1}{4}$ in) away from the first. Trim the fabric close to the second stitched line and then overcast by hand or finish with zigzag stitching.

Gathered sleeve head

Sometimes a commercial paper pattern will instruct you to gather between dots on the sleeve head before inserting the sleeve. Your aim is still to achieve a smooth, rounded sleeve cap (unless the sleeve is of the type where the gathers are part of the style and are to be seen). Here is the best method of working a gathered sleeve head.

Two rows of stitches

Before making up the sleeve, work two rows of gathering stitches between the dots marked on the sleeve head, one just inside the seam line and the second 6 mm ($\frac{1}{4}$ in) away in the seam allowance. Two lines of gathering give better control for even gathering. Wind each pair of thread ends around a pin in a figure-of-eight. Now you can make up the sleeve.

Pinning the gathers

Put the sleeve into the armhole as before, right sides of the garment facing. Pin the underarm seams. Match the notches and pin both back and front of the armhole just short of the gathering.

Pull up the gathering stitches until the sleeve fits neatly into the armhole. Wind the thread ends around the pins again. Pin the remainder of the sleeve, inserting pins vertically between the gathers. Adjust the fullness evenly but try to ensure that there is a flat area on the shoulder seam. Tack firmly along the seam with small stitches removing pins as you stitch.

Two rows of stitching give even distribution of fullness on a gathered sleeve head.

Try the garment on to see if any adjustments have to be made. If not, tie the gathering threads off tightly.

If the fabric is of a type which can be steam-shrunk, press lightly on the right side to remove any puckers, using a damp cloth and a pressing mitt. Let the fabric cool off. Now hand sew or machine stitch the sleeve into the armhole and then finish off the seam edges.

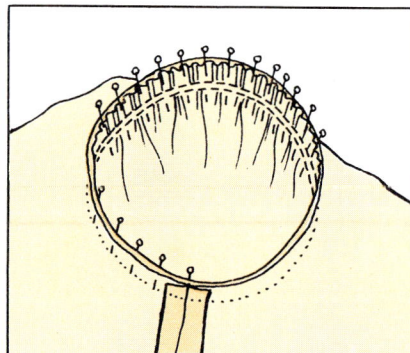

Setting in a gathered sleeve.

Hems

Hems are used in varying forms to neaten raw edges. The name is also used to describe the lower edge of a garment, whether or not it is finished with a hem.

Sewing hems

While nearly all dress and skirt hems are held in place by some form of hemming, those used on lingerie may be secured with hemming, slip-hemming or running stitch. The disadvantage of hemming is that the stitches show on the right side as disconnected dots, while slip-hemming is not a strong method to use upon garments which have to be washed frequently.

Running stitch is an effective method as the stitches form a continuous line, are strong and suitable for use on fine rayon, nylon and other fabrics of this type.

Plain hems

Plain hems should have the traditional two folds or turnings, the second of which is sewn to the garment by some form of hemming.

Make a line of tacking or chalk where the second fold is to come; this is known as the hemline. Turn over to the wrong side and tack about 6 mm ($\frac{1}{4}$ in) below the edge.

Mark the width of the hem, measuring from the fold at the edge, insert pins or make a chalk line. Turn under below the line and tack again. Pin the hem to the garment, inserting pins at right angles, then tack and sew with hemming or slip-hemming along the edge of the fold or, if the hem is turned onto the right side, machine stitch on the very edge.

Slip-hem method

Mark the fold and turn under the hem, cutting the turnings very even. Make a line of tacking about 12 mm ($\frac{1}{2}$ in) from the raw edge. When working the slip-hemming take one stitch into the garment, one into the hem turnings; pull up the thread to turn the edge under.

The second turning should always be quite even, about 6 mm ($\frac{1}{4}$ in) in width. This is especially important when making hems on sheer fabrics.

For narrow hems less than 2.5 cm (1 in) wide, when the width of the turnings will be even, it is simpler to turn and tack the first turnings, then to pin and hem or to tack and machine stitch the second.

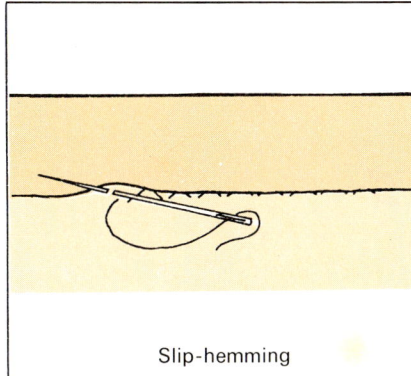

Slip-hemming

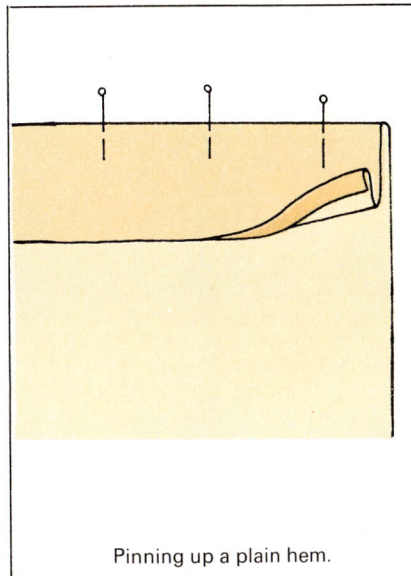

Pinning up a plain hem.

Rolled hems

Extremely narrow hems which are only used on thin, fine fabrics are rolled between the fingers. They are not easy to make, especially if the fabric is at all springy.

Cut the edges to be hemmed very evenly, allowing about 6 mm ($\frac{1}{4}$ in) for the roll. Work from right to left. With the thumb and first finger of the left hand, roll the raw edges towards you. Slip-hem the roll closely, but do not make it at all tight. The stitches should be as invisible as possible so very little of

the garment fabric should be picked up. For greater security take the needle right through the roll diagonally, insert it again, making a tiny stitch, and bring it out diagonally through the roll, then pick up a very tiny stitch in the garment. Do not pull the stitches tight.

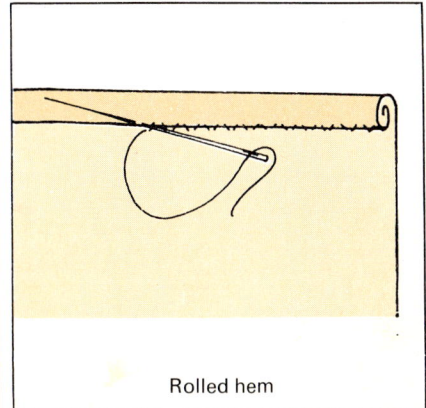

Rolled hem

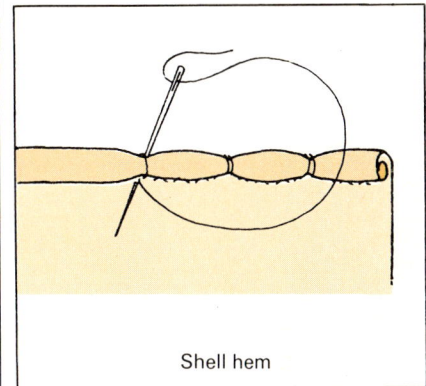

Shell hem

Shell hem

This is a decorative way of finishing a narrow rolled hem. Roll the hem edge between the thumb and first finger of the left hand, slip stitch the roll to the garment and take two over-stitches over the roll, at regular intervals.

Single hems

This type of hem is suitable for use on heavy fabrics, and when a hem is to be faced with lining. There are several stitches which may be used for the sewing; each has a special quality which lends itself to different types of material.

Catch stitch This method is suitable when the hem is to be covered by a lining or a facing.

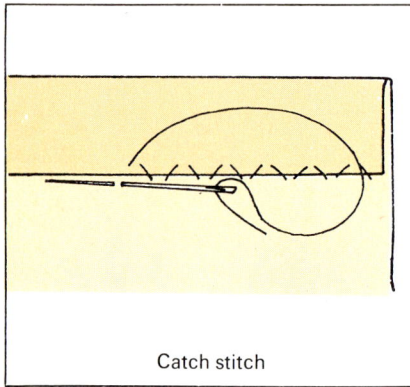

Construction methods

Catch stitch

Mark the fold line of the garment hem as already described, make the turning and tack it down. Sew it in place by loosely catching threads from hem and garment in turn.

Herringbone Used on heavy fabric hems which are not to be neatened.

Mark hemline, tack turnings and cut hem edge absolutely even. Pin in place and tack.

Sew the hem in position with loosely worked herringbone stitches.

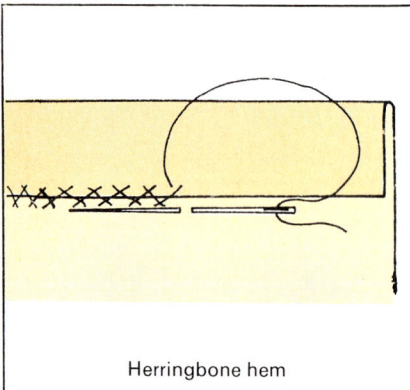

Herringbone hem

Hemming a skirt or dress

The appearance and hang of a skirt can be ruined if the hem is incorrectly turned up or sewn. Very careful measuring is needed to get it absolutely level with the ground all round.

There are several gadgets on the market for measuring hems but it is perfectly possible to do without one of these if you have a long ruler and someone to help you. The person being fitted stands still and erect while the fitter measures the distance from the ground with the ruler and makes a chalk mark at

the correct spot. The ruler must be kept firmly on the floor and moved round the skirt for each mark. Care must be taken not to pull the skirt to one side when measuring or the hem will be uneven.

After the hemline has been measured and marked in this way turn up the hem and tack it, then try it on again to make quite sure it is the correct length and even all round. Fix and stitch it, using one of the methods described.

When there is no one to measure the skirt length for you, yet another method may be used. Measure from a fixed point on the garment such as waistband of a skirt or neckline of a loose dress to the desired hemline making sure it is the same distance all round. When using this method, it is important to keep checking the hem by trying on the garment in front of a full length mirror.

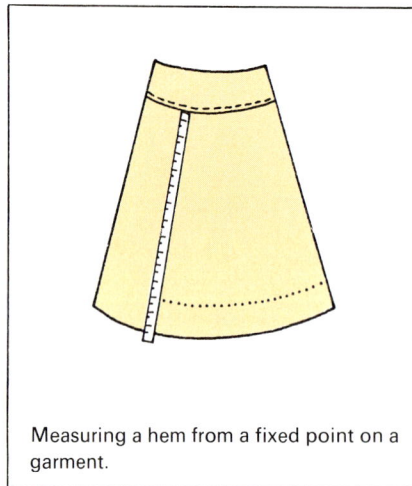

Measuring a hem from a fixed point on a garment.

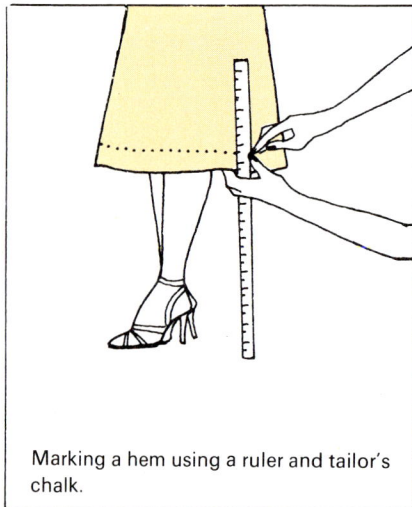

Marking a hem using a ruler and tailor's chalk.

If you have used a commercial pattern and cut the bottom of the garment carefully it is possible to use the markings indicated to turn up the hem. Always check the length of the garment in front of a mirror when doing this.

Flared skirts

Skirts that are cut on the bias, particularly circular skirts, must have the hemline measured very carefully, but before any measuring is done at all they must be allowed to hang for several days. This is necessary as the part of the fabric that is on the bias will drop more than the part that is on the straight grain, thus making the lower edge of the skirt uneven. When the skirt has been left to drop in this way the hem is measured by one of the methods described above.

Pleated skirts

Hand-pleated skirts are measured for the hem length after the pleats have been fixed. The tacking in the pleats at the hem edge will have to be removed when the hem is being made, the pleats are pressed out around the hem, then re-fixed, tacked and pressed again, after the hem has been sewn and completed.

Machine-made pleats, such as accordion and sun-ray pleats, are treated in the same way as a flared skirt, being left to hang for a few days. The pleats will have to be pressed out and re-fixed around the hem edge while it is being turned.

Trousers

When marking the hem on trousers it is not possible to measure from the floor. Trouser hems should rest on the shoe at the front and slope down slightly towards the back. Pin both legs, checking the length by trying on in front of a mirror.

Take the trousers off and mark the hemline with pins or tailors chalk. Proceed as for an ordinary hem.

Faced hems

These are used on an edge where it is impossible to make an ordinary hem, they can be made on the right

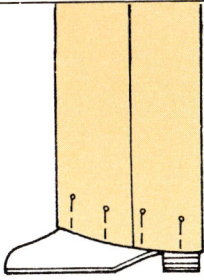

The correct shape for a trouser hem.

or the wrong side. They have the advantage of not further reducing the cut length of the garment. When turned onto the right side, they are usually of contrasting fabric to add a decorative interest.

Cross-cut facing

Turn up the bottom edge of the garment about 6 mm ($\frac{1}{4}$ in). Cut the crossway strip about 5 cm to 8 cm (2 in to 3 in) wide and join to make sufficient length for the hem. Turn in both edges about 6 mm ($\frac{1}{4}$ in) and tack one edge over the skirt turning. Slip stitch, or hem this edge.

If the skirt is quite straight, the top edge of the crossway facing is tacked in place as it will fit without easing.

If the skirt is slightly shaped, the top edge will have to be eased slightly or darted to give a smooth finish. Pin the easing in place all around the skirt, before tacking, to get an even distribution of fullness. Join the two ends of the crossway strip together. Then tack and slip stitch the upper edge in place. Press well, removing tackings.

Shaped facing

A shaped or circular skirt must have a shaped hem. The pieces of material must be cut so that they fit the skirt edge exactly when joined together to make the whole band. Mark the outline of the skirt edge on paper and measure from this line to the width of facing desired. Place the pattern on the fabric matching the straight grain on the garment.

Place right side of the facing to right side of garment matching the

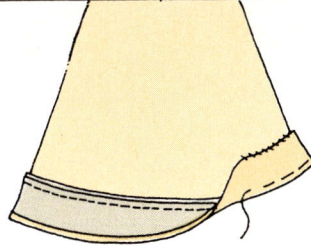

Faced hem

grain of fabric, stitch around the edge carefully and turn to wrong side. Neaten the facing with a tiny hem and machine stitch round, joining seam, or slip stitch edge to garment.

This facing may also be used on necks and sleeve edges, but it must be cut to the shape of the edge on which it is being applied.

When using a faced hem as decoration the right side of the facing is placed to wrong side of garment. The corners are clipped and the facing is finished on the right side with machine stitching, or slip stitching.

Pleats

A pleat is a fold of fabric used to dispose of fullness in a decorative manner. These may be used on all kinds of fabric. The preparation of pleats is similar to that of tucks, the only difference being that pleats are never stitched all the way down. They usually hang free from the top fixture but can be machine stitched along the pressed edge for part of the way, falling free at the bottom edge.

Knife pleats

This method has the pleats arranged so that the top edge of one pleat falls along the under edge of the next pleat. The amount of fabric required is three times the finished width.

Box pleats

These pleats have the appearance of a double pleat with one edge

facing towards the right and one towards the left. The amount of fabric required is three times the finished width.

The quickest method of making these pleats is to make and tack a large tuck twice the width required. Crease-mark, chalk-mark, or thread-mark the edge of this tuck, then flatten it down so that the marking is in the centre and lies along the tacking.

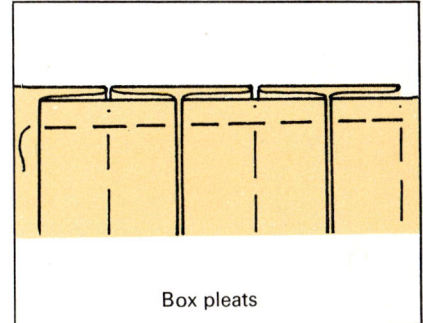

Box pleats

Inverted pleats

This method of pleating is the reverse of box-pleating. Proceed as directed for a box pleat, but tack and flatten pleat on the wrong side instead of the right side.

Frills and flounces

These are decorative and are mainly used to trim a garment. Frills and flounces may be used to add length to a garment at the hem or to sleeves, but they are most attractive if added to the surface as neck, sleeve or skirt trimmings.

Making frills

These are used on skirts and sleeves to give a full, fluffy effect. They may be cut straight, on the bias, or

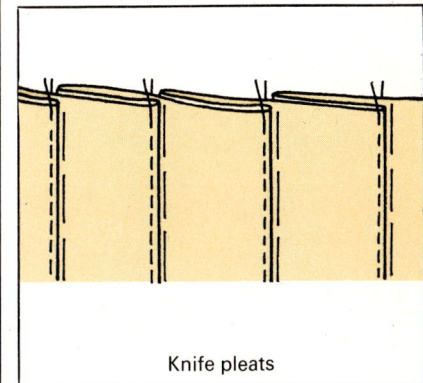

Knife pleats

Construction methods

shaped. Narrow frills are better cut on the straight or bias. If straight they should be cut with the straight grain of the material. Frills must hang gracefully, if cut the wrong way they will poke out and have a stiff appearance. Light soft fabrics are more suitable for frills than stiff heavy ones. For a straight frill allow one and half to twice the finished size.

The bottom edge of a frill may be finished with a very narrow stitched or rolled hem, binding or picot edging. The joins in frills should be made with a single seam.

Application of frills

Method 1 Mark the half and quarter points along the top of the frill and the line on the skirt to which the frill is to be attached. Gather each quarter of the frill separately. Place the quarter points of frill and skirt together with the frill upside down and right sides facing. Machine stitch along the gathering thread.

Turn the frill down into position and the raw edges are hidden.

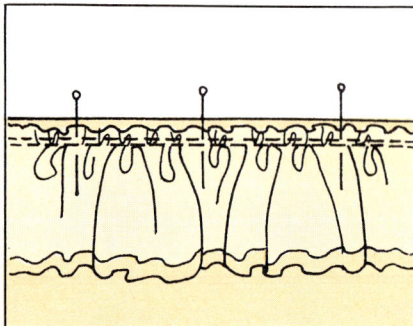

Application of frills (Method 1).

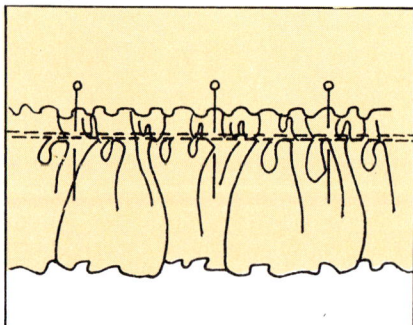

Application of frills (Method 2).

Method 2 Prepare as for first method. Make a narrow turning along top edge of frill and gather each quarter separately, through the turning. Place corresponding points of frill and skirt together. In this way the fullness of the frill is evenly arranged. Tack and back stitch to skirt along the gathering line.

Pleated frills

These make a delightful trimming and look best when 2.5 cm to 3.5 cm (1 in to $1\frac{1}{2}$ in) wide.

First cut strips of material perfectly straight to the depth required and about three times the finished length. Machine stitch a very narrow hem along the bottom edge. The pleats are then made in the way described on page 71.

Flounces

These are similar to frills only much deeper. They may be cut straight, on the bias, or shaped. Prepare and finish the bottom edge as for narrow frills.

A straight flounce is treated and applied in the same way as a gathered frill.

Shaped flounces are very graceful without any fullness at the top edge; they are full and very frilly at the bottom edge. They are cut on the bias in the same way as a flared skirt.

Flounces are mounted onto a foundation skirt and there may be two to six or even more, one above the other as fashion or personal preference decrees. To apply a shaped flounce to a skirt make a narrow turning along the top edge of the flounce, as second method of applying gathered frill, then tack it to the skirt and machine stitch along the edge.

Above right A frilled hem gives flair to a plain dress.
Below right A frill added to the sleeve head is an unusual feature.
Far right Frilled pocket tops echo the pretty sleeves on this dress.

Construction methods

Decorative seams

When making fine lingerie or blouses of good fabric it is worthwhile hand-sewing the seams. Decorative seams are fun to make and add interest to the work, besides being suitable for the purpose and more hard wearing. Such seams are almost entirely hand-worked, therefore there is more elasticity than with machining, which has no give and cuts the fabric, sometimes causing it to tear away. Some of these seams give the effect of openwork, while others provide a delicate tracery of stitches along the seam line.

There are several stitches which can be used, many of which are described in detail in these pages.

Faggot-stitched seam

There are two methods of working this seam, both are decorative and suitable for fine light garments such as lingerie and blouses.

First mark the seam lines, then trim the turnings to within 3 mm ($\frac{1}{8}$ in) of the lines. Turn under the 3 mm ($\frac{1}{8}$ in) turnings once, onto the wrong side and press. Turn under 3 mm ($\frac{1}{8}$ in) again and tack firmly. This edge should come 3 mm ($\frac{1}{8}$ in) inside the fitting line. Press lightly.

Cut a strip of strong paper about 5 cm (2 in) wide. Using a tracing wheel or tailor's chalk, mark parallel lines slightly less than 6 mm ($\frac{1}{4}$ in) apart down the centre.

When the seams or parts to be joined are shaped (however slightly) the paper strips should be cut to the same shape or the line of

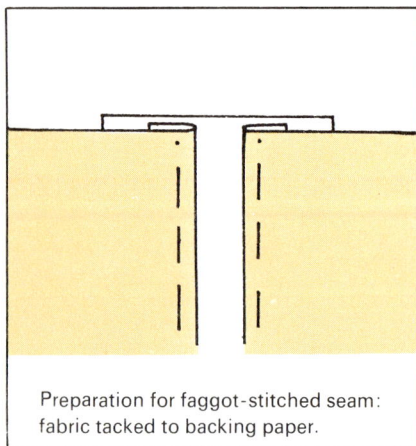

Preparation for faggot-stitched seam: fabric tacked to backing paper.

faggoting will not lie flat.

Tack the garment to the traced lines, with the wrong side facing the paper. Join the edges with either of the following faggot stitches.

Crossed faggoting

Work from the left, making stitches alternately into the top and lower hem, always keeping the point of the needle away from the gap and making a loop of thread around the point.

To join the thread, darn in the ends into the hems and bring out the new thread in exactly the same place as the previous stitch. Continue the stitch.

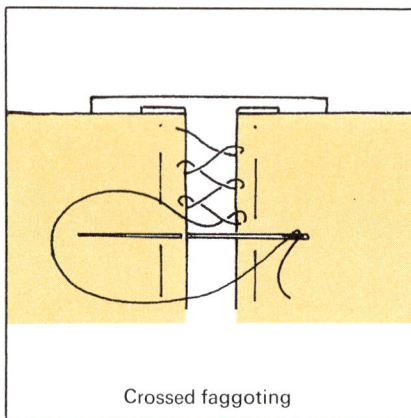

Crossed faggoting

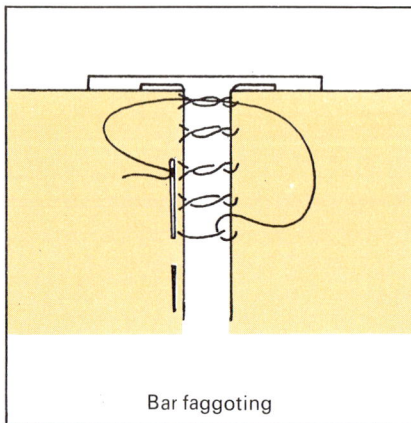

Bar faggoting

Ladder faggoting

Use a heavier thread than for ordinary seams and a No. 8 crewel needle. Begin at the right; darning the thread into the top hem, work a tiny stitch over the hem edge. Hold the thread down with the left hand to form a loop, pick up a tiny stitch in the lower hem and bring the needle through the loop. Insert the needle from the gap outwards on

the lower edge.

Bring the needle through and insert it again into the hole of first stitch, passing it along the hem fold for the length of one stitch. Make a second bar and continue in this way.

To finish off, press carefully, keeping the paper next to the iron. This helps to preserve the shape of the seam. Remove tacking threads, but the ends of joining threads close. Press again.
Press again.

The tiny hems should be held by the faggot stitches; no other stitching is necessary.

Hemstitch seam

This is a decorative seam which can only be worked on fabric that has both weft and warp threads fairly even in texture and a seam which is absolutely straight to a thread.

Threads of the fabric are drawn away for the width required, along the seam line, on one of the pieces to be joined. Fold the turnings of the second piece under and tack. Place the fold of this piece to the drawn threads of the first and tack together.

Use a fine needle with silk or very fine cotton thread for the hemstitching. Working from right to left, pick up about three loose threads from right to left, then insert the needle to the right of threads again, as if to make a back stitch, taking a diagonal stitch up onto the fold. Pick up another five threads, back and up diagonally.

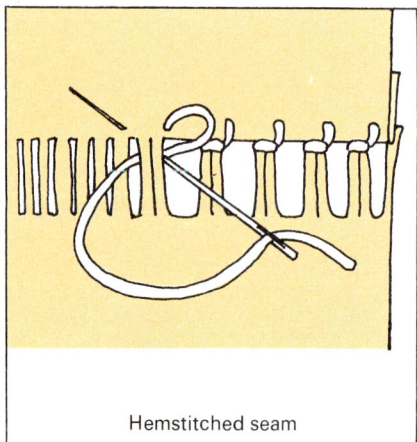

Hemstitched seam

Continue in this way. Hemstitch the lower edge to match. Trim the turnings on the inside close to edge and whip finely.

Point turc or pin stitch

This is one of the most delicate decorative stitches and a useful one as it can be used on any shaped seam. It is easily and quickly manipulated and the finished result is very effective, rather like hemstitch in appearance.

Prepare the garment as for an overlaid seam, sewing along the folded edge on the outside, with fine running stitches; use a fine needle and fine silk or cotton for this. For the point turc stitch a fine carpet needle is ideal.

It should be emphasized that this stitch is strong, and when well and evenly worked no neatening is necessary.

Join the thread to the right hand end of the seam and work from right to left, keeping the single thickness fabric as the lower part. Pick up a small stitch, close to the edge of the hem, in the single material and make a back stitch from 1 to 2, taking the needle up diagonally through the triple thickness of the fold to 3. Insert the needle again down into the first hole of the backstitch 4, and pick up another small stitch along the edge of the fold. Continue in this way for the length required, making a series of closely worked stitches along the seam.

The thread should be drawn fairly firmly but not tight.

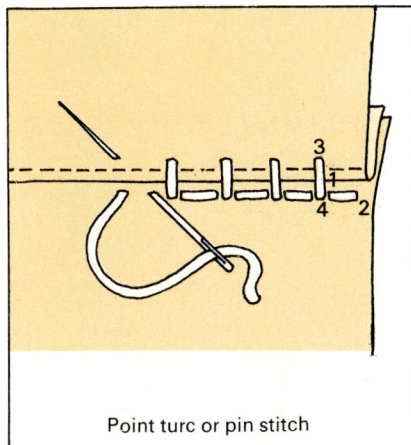

Point turc or pin stitch

To finish the seam, remove any tacking threads. Press, then cut away the turnings on the inside of the work very close to the stitchery. These turnings may be whipped if the fabric is one which frays easily.

Punch stitch or Bermuda faggoting

This is another decorative seam which resembles hemstitching in appearance, holes being made by a large needle and the pulling of the stitches.

Prepare the work and begin with an overlaid seam in the same way as point turc. Bring the thread out at 1 and make a back stitch between 1 and 2. Insert the needle at 2 again and bring it out at 3; make a backstitch between 2 and 3. Pass the needle diagonally from 2 to 4 and make two backstitches between 1 and 4; then repeat the procedure, working over 3, 4, 5 and 6, and then over the next four holes and so on to complete a continuous line of stitching.

Follow the diagram carefully, keeping the distance between the rows of holes and the stitches about 1 mm ($\frac{1}{16}$ in). Draw up the stitches firmly and keep the tension even.

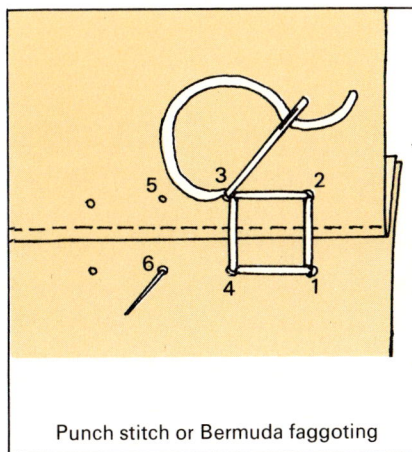

Punch stitch or Bermuda faggoting

Piping

This is a method of finishing a seamed edge and it is also a means of adding decoration and colour. There are two ways of making a piped edge, one with a cord inserted which gives a strong, rounded effect, and one with a plain bias strip folded into two.

Corded edge

Special piping cord can be obtained for this and it is made in several thicknesses. Choose one that is suitable for the purpose and fabric being used. Shrink it by steeping it in water, then hang it out to dry. When quite dry, pull it over a wooden edge (such as a chair back) to straighten and remove knots and twists.

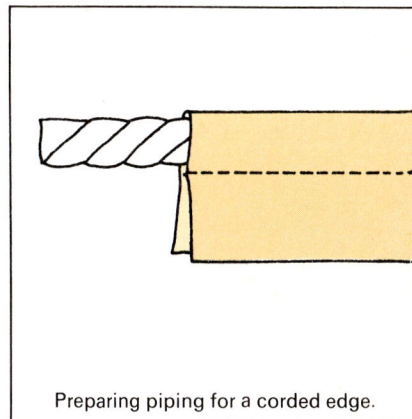

Preparing piping for a corded edge.

Method 1 Make a length of bias-cut strip wide enough to fold around the cord and allow double turnings. The strip should be long enough to pipe the whole seam. Fold the strip right side outside, round the cord and sew with running stitch, close to the cord.

The seam can be worked as a lapped seam. The top section of the garment has the turnings folded under to the wrong side. If the seam is shaped the turnings must be clipped to allow them to lie flat. The hem fold is placed close to the piping, pinned and tacked.

Place this section over the under piece, with the inner edge of the piping to the seam line. Pin and tack, then sew with machine stitching or slip-hemming.

The piping should be eased slightly to prevent stretching.

It is sometimes easier to stitch the piping to the under section of the garment; if this method is used the top part is applied as a facing with slip-hemming, the turnings being folded under and tacked as for the lapped seam method.

Construction methods

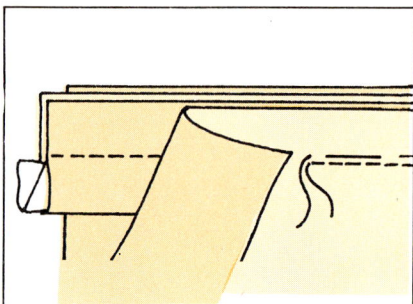

Applying piping to a straight seam.

Method 2 In a seam that has no shaping, and when a plain piping is being used, it is possible to work a plain seam. The piping is tacked to the right side of one edge of the garment, raw edges together. The second section of the garment is placed so that the piping is enclosed along the seam line. Sew with machine stitching.

Whichever method of inserting the piping is used the turnings are always neatened in the same way, on the wrong side. Cut down the turnings to about 6 mm ($\frac{1}{4}$ in) and overcast them.

The piping is folded around the corner; if it is an inside corner the turning must be slit to avoid bulk, if an outside corner it is snipped to prevent puckering. The facing is cased or mitred as necessary.

Plain piping

This is made with a bias-cut strip of fabric twice the width of the piping plus double turnings. It is folded into two along the length and tacked. The method of inserting this piping is the same as for corded piping.

Right Piped edges are used on this blouse to emphasise the unusual shapes of pockets, collar and epaulettes.
Far right The lace trim contrasts well with the clean lines and plain gingham fabric in this fresh summer dress.

Lace and net

French stemming
A method of attaching lace, net borders, and insertions. Embroidery silk or stranded cotton, matching either the fabric or lace, should be used. The stitch is worked on the right side of the fabric, from left to right, with the work held flat over the first finger of the left hand. First tack the insertion or edging onto the fabric then oversew the edges with small stitches. If the fabric is folded as for oversewing, the edge is more liable to stretch in working. The surplus material is afterwards cut away on the wrong side.

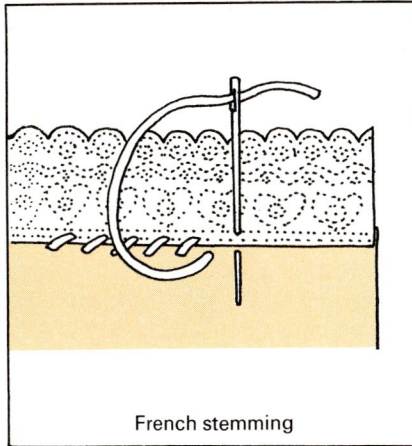

Lace appliqué
If you can obtain it, handmade lace is the best sort to use for appliqué. If machine-made lace is used choose a clearly defined pattern so that it can be followed for an edging or border, and, in the case of motifs, small complete

French stemming

Lace edging applied with point turc

designs which can be cut out.

A very lightweight lace should be used on lingerie. The lace should have surplus net and unwanted patterns cut away before application to the garment, but care must be taken not to cut the fine outlining cord.

Place the lace in position, right side uppermost, over the fabric. In the case of a neckline, the lace should be cut to the correct shape first, to ensure a good line on the garment. To match the pattern at a

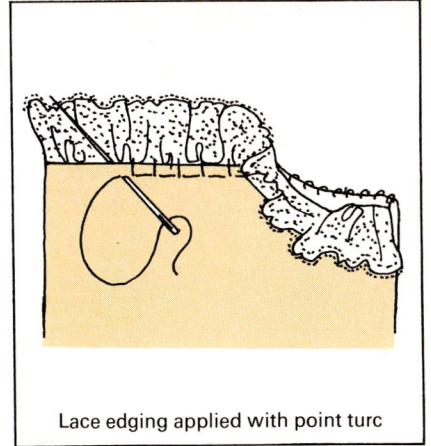

join overlap one edge and whip stitch around neatly with one thread of stranded cotton, or sewing silk, matching the lace.

The inner edge of the lace is stitched from right to left, following the outline of the pattern. Afterwards the surplus material is cut away on the wrong side close to the whipping. To prevent fraying, the raw edge may be neatly oversewn on the wrong side.

Punch stitch or point turc can be used instead of whipping.

Lace and net edging
Tiny frills of lace and picot-edged net provide a delicate finish and are simple to attach. Lingerie lace with a net ground has a thread woven into the edge for easy gathering. Ready-frilled lace and net can also be bought by length. The edging should be gathered and joined into a circle, if necessary, before application.

The seam in the net is made by placing one end over the other, turning under both edges and

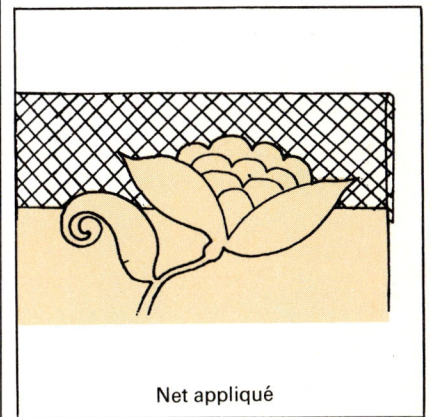

Net appliqué

neatly hemming them. This is called a counter seam and is the best means of joining picot-edged net, since there is no design to match and overlap. Punch stitch, point turc or french stemming may be used for sewing the join.

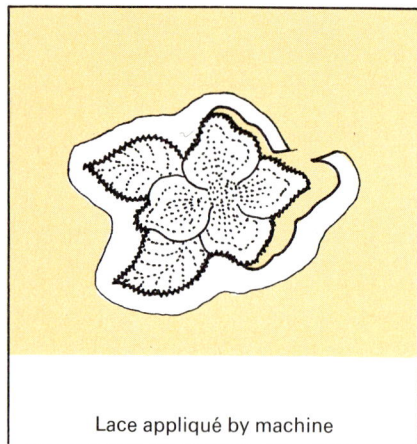

Lace appliqué by machine

Net appliqué

The term appliqué is used in embroidery when one kind of material is applied upon another to form a pattern. In net appliqué it is the garment edge which is imposed on the net. A fine net is most suitable for this purpose. Georgette may be used in place of the net.

The design, which should be clear and simple in outline is lightly traced onto the garment. Double net is then tacked behind the design with the fold to the garment edge. Where the outline is irregular, the net edge is neatly bound.

Lace appliqué by machine

Lace motifs may be applied by machine using a small, closely spaced zigzag stitch. Trim around the motif to be applied but do not trim right to the edge of the design. Tack into position. Straight stitch around the outside of the design and then zigzag over this line. Trim away surplus fabric carefully.

It is also possible to cut out the design first, tack it into place and then zigzag around the edges. It is advisable when using this method to place an extra piece of a fine fabric behind the appliqué design to provide a strengthened backing.

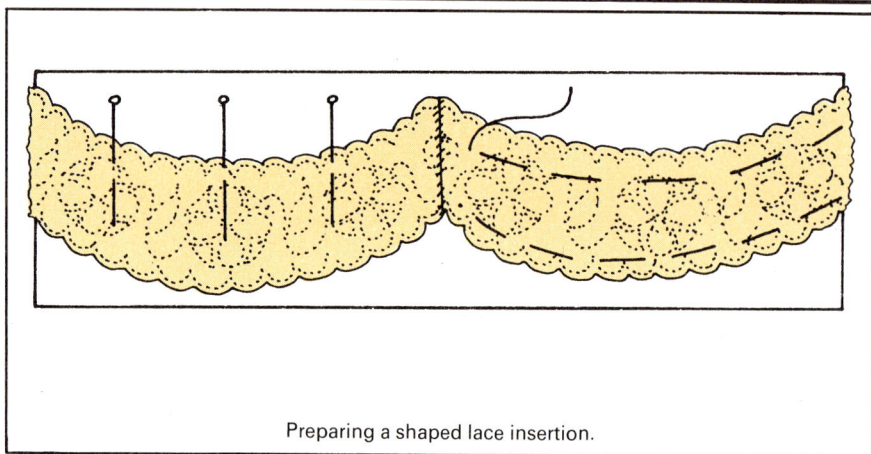

Preparing a shaped lace insertion.

Insertions

The method of applying a lace insertion is slightly different from applying lace. If it is to be inserted into a shaped section work as follows: trace the shape of the insertion onto brown paper, leaving generous turnings around all the edges. The edge of the lace insertion should be clearly marked with chalk, tracing wheel or tacking. Pin the lace onto this shape, easing and stretching where necessary to get a perfect fit. Tack firmly onto the paper and shape the lace further with darts and seams, using the appliqué method of joining. Make all these adjustments over the paper shape, but take care that the stitches do not penetrate through it. Press, placing the lace over a pad and a damp cloth keeping the paper next to the iron. Remove paper by cutting the tacking and press again, on the wrong side.

Cut away the turnings on the wrong side close to the stitches; if the net is of a fraying kind overcast the turnings neatly.

Place the insertion over the edge of the garment and apply by the satin stitch or hemming method.

Threading ribbons

Ribbon can be used decoratively when it is threaded through slots or holes and tied in a neat bow. It can also be used for drawing up fullness. The slots used for this purpose can be added to the surface of the fabric or as holes, cut into the material.

Latches or loops

These are formed by making a loop of half a dozen loose strands over the fabric. The strands are caught into the fabric at each end by a small backstitch. The loop is strengthened by a closely worked buttonhole or loop stitch, as for a buttonhole loop. The ribbon is threaded under the loops.

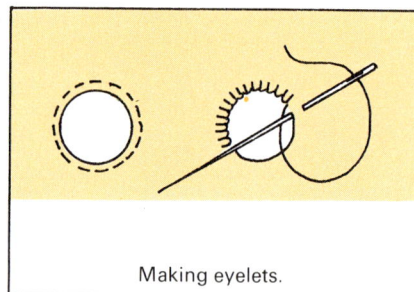

Making eyelets.

Eyelets

These are little round holes which are pierced with a stiletto, and sewn with a deep, tightly drawn, overcast stitch, worked from right to left. They can be used as holes for cords or ribbons around the neck of a garment or around the top of a bag.

Blanket stitch may be used with the loop either at the raw edge or outside the edge of the eyelet. A better finish is obtained if the eyelet is first encircled with small running stitches.

Bows

These are frequently used as trimming for dresses as well as for fastenings of belts. There are several ways of making them.

French bow

Cut two pieces of ribbon, both the same length and slanting at one end. Fold each one to make a loop and tail, making the loop slightly shorter and at an angle to the tail. Sew the end to the fold with oversewing. The second loop is sewn as the first but the tail should slope in the opposite direction to give a crossed effect. Place the two loops together and oversew the folds.

For the tie cut a short piece of ribbon, a little longer than the ribbon width, and make a fold in it. Wrap this around the centre of the bow and sew the two ends neatly on the wrong side.

French bow

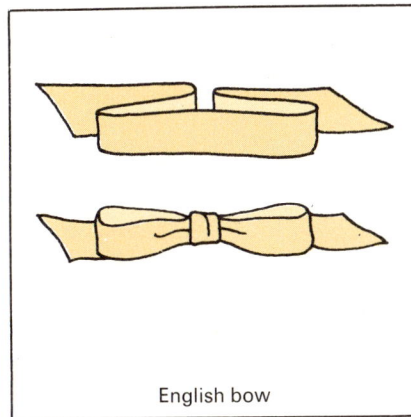

English bow

English bow

This is made from one length of ribbon folded so that the loops fall in the centre. The loops should be a little shorter than the tails. Stitch the centre and gather it slightly. A small length of ribbon is pleated and wrapped round the centre, and the two ends are sewn together on the wrong side.

Scalloping

Scallops make attractive finishes to hems, sleeve edges and necks of undergarments. They may be any shape and size to suit the purpose and they can be worked in loop stitch or finished with binding or facing.

Transfers in various sizes and designs are available, but a pattern drawn to fit a given outline is more accurate and satisfactory.

The design

Method 1 Two parallel lines are drawn for fine work, these should be not more than 3 mm ($\frac{1}{8}$ in) apart. A small button or coin is used to define the scallop. Place the edge of

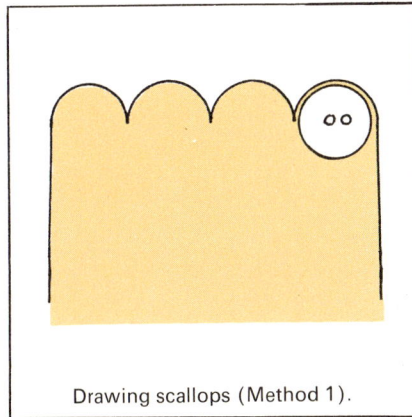

Drawing scallops (Method 1).

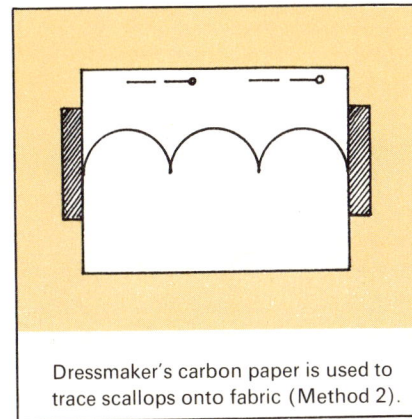

Dressmaker's carbon paper is used to trace scallops onto fabric (Method 2).

the circle to the top line and draw the shape as far as the bottom line. Only the tip of the disc should be outlined, otherwise the scallops will lose much of their beauty and be more difficult to embroider. The entire area must be planned so that the junction of two scallops or a complete pattern falls at the centre of the garment. The corners should

be two-thirds of a circle, extending from one side to the other. When the edge is planned a template of two or three scallops can be made and repeated for the full length.

The design may be lightly traced directly onto the garment, using tailor's chalk to follow the scalloped edge of the template.

Method 2 Another method is to place a small piece of dressmaker's carbon paper between the template (the scalloped edge of which is not cut out) and the garment. A knitting needle is then used to follow the outline. Pins should never be passed through carbon paper to the fabric or an unwanted mark will result. Only the paper pattern should be pinned to the garment, the small piece of coloured carbon is then slipped underneath.

Faced scallops

These provide an excellent finish for a hem or where a heavier treatment is desired.

A facing of the same fabric is cut to correspond in shape with the edge of the garment. Allowance must be made for the depth of the scallops, also a hem if required, and turnings. Place the false piece in position, right sides together, centres and seams matching.

Plan the number of scallops necessary for the given length. These may be drawn with a compass to the required size with two parallel lines to act as guide or outlined around a section of a large coin, cup or saucer. The former is the better and more accurate method. Trace the pattern onto the facing.

Machine stitch around the scalloped outline, through facing and garment. The surplus fabric beyond the scallops is cut away to 3 mm ($\frac{1}{8}$ in) from the machining. Each corner must be clipped to allow the facing to be turned onto the wrong side. Pull each scallop into shape, tack and press. Fold in the free edge and machine or lightly hem.

Making fastenings

Well-made fastenings on a garment are important to successful dressmaking. Badly made buttonholes or hooks stitched on clumsily will detract from the fine finish that hand-made clothes should have.

There are several styles of fastenings and each of them fulfils a different function: some are intended to be decorative as well as functional, others are concealed.

Buttons

Buttons are manufactured from many materials and come in a wide variety of shapes and sizes; the colour range is vast and you should have little difficulty in finding a colour to match your fabric. If the buttons are made of synthetic material, such as nylon, you must be careful when ironing as they will melt if the hot iron touches them.

Buttons can be bought loose in odd quantities or on a card. If you are using a commercial paper pattern, the notions box on the envelope (see pages 16-19) will tell you the diameter and quantity of buttons you will need. Always buy three or four more than you need and keep them on a large safety pin for replacements. Beautiful buttons, made of silver, ivory or carved wood, can still be found in specialist shops. These are worth buying if you want a very individual look.

Choosing button sizes

Always buy buttons before working buttonholes or loops. Buttons should slip through a buttonhole easily without straining the fabric. It is therefore important that you buy exactly the size designated in the pattern. Remember that thick or domed buttons need a larger buttonhole and allowance should be made for this. Domed and ball buttons are best if used with loops.

Threads for sewing on buttons

Generally, choose a thread suitable for the fabric, but not too fine. For heavy weight fabrics, use strong button thread.

Marking the position of buttons

The approximate position for buttonholes and buttons will be marked on the pattern, and you should transfer these to the fabric, either with tailor's tacks or with crossed chalk marks.

Make the buttonholes and then try the garment on, pinning as if to close it, taking care that the centre front lines or centre backs, as the case may be, lie over one another.

Mark the position for the button with pins. For a horizontal button, put two crossed pins, half the diameter of the button from the rounded end of the buttonhole. For a vertical buttonhole, pin across the centre.

Unpin the opening, easing the marker pins through the buttonhole. Sew on the button where the pins cross, or on the spot where the vertical pin picked up the fabric.

Sewing on buttons

Fasten the thread to the wrong side of the fabric with two or three back stitches. Do not tie a knot. Do not use the thread doubled to try to save time; the thread will snarl up. Bring the thread through to the right side of the fabric.

The holes of a two-hole button should lie in the same direction as the buttonhole. Work stitches between the two holes, and right through to the back of the fabric.

Four-hole buttons can be worked with the stitches making two bars or as a cross.

Work about five stitches to fasten on the button then finish off with two or three back stitches on the wrong side.

Shanked buttons have either a short stem pierced with a hole, or a metal loop shank, and are stitched on by passing the needle through the hole or loop and then through the fabric.

Work four or five stitches through the shank and then fasten off on the wrong side with back stitches.

Buttons on thick fabric

Coat buttons or any button being stitched to a thick fabric must be stitched on with a shank of thread to allow for the fabric thickness in the buttonhole.

To make the shank put a matchstick or a pin between the button and the garment while the stitches are being made. Then remove the stick or pin and wind the thread around the strands between button and garment. Take the thread through to the wrong side and finish off with back stitch.

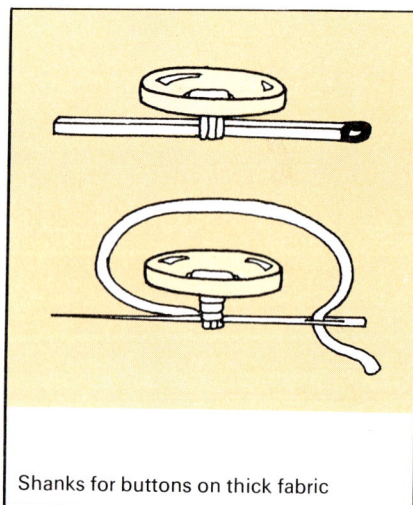

Shanks for buttons on thick fabric

Types of button fastenings

Self-cover buttons

These buttons are made on button moulds which are covered with fabric. You can buy the moulds and cover them yourself or have them professionally made.

Mould buttons sometimes have a metal loop for sewing to the garment, but some types are almost flat and simply have the area of gathered fabric at the back instead of a shank. With this type you can work stitches through the fabric cover of the button itself, pulling the button onto the garment with the stitches, but a better way is to make a thread loop. It takes longer to work but the strain on the button is lessened. Work three or four strands of thread across the button back and then make a bar by working buttonhole stitch along the strands (see page 190). The sewing-on stitches are worked through the bar.

Detachable buttons
Detachable buttons are used on garments which will be laundered frequently, such as overalls and work coats.

Make a hole at the button position with a stiletto. Work tiny running stitches around the hole and then overcast or buttonhole stitch the edges neatly, working the stitches very close together.

Left Rouleau loops for a pretty fastening.
Top Snap fasteners work well on denim.
Bottom A chunky zipper for a sporty look.

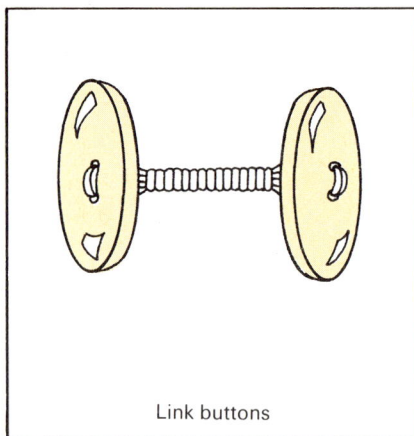
Link buttons

Link buttons

Link buttons look very pretty on the cuffs of shirt blouses.

Work three or four strands of thread between two buttons, leaving the thread end long. Work buttonhole stitch over the strands and over the thread end.

Finish by darning back into the buttonhole stitches before snipping the end of the thread.

Link closures

Large buttons are sometimes used as link closures on heavy capes or cloaks. They are linked with a piece of rouleau or braid passed through the holes of the button or shank loops, and then stitched securely at each end of the rouleau.

Double buttons

On fabrics which are loosely woven or on leather and suede, a second smaller button is stitched behind the button, stitches being worked through both buttons at the same time. This prevents the outer button from pulling a hole in the fabric.

Making soft buttons

Linen buttons without holes used to be available for household linens, but are not generally available now. A similar type of soft button can be made with a plastic or metal ring and fabric.

Cut two circles of fabric to the diameter of the ring plus 3 mm ($\frac{1}{8}$ in) all around. Work gathering stitches around the edge of one circle. Put the ring in the middle and pull up the gathering stitches.

Fasten off securely. Hem stitch the second circle to the ring, turning a 3 mm ($\frac{1}{8}$ in) hem to the wrong side as you stitch. The resulting soft button is stitched to the garment with small stitches crossing in the middle.

Chinese ball buttons

These are generally used with frog fastenings. Use Russian braid or hand-made rouleau. Follow the diagram for making the loops. Pull the ends gently to form the ball. Turn the ends under and secure with small stitches. Sew to the garment.

Buttonholes

First mark the position and size of the buttonhole on the garment. To do this place the button flat on the fabric and insert a pin each side. Make a line of tacking between the pins. If following a commercial pattern transfer the pattern markings using tailor's tacks or chalk.

Bound buttonholes

Cut a strip of fabric on the straight grain 4 cm ($1\frac{1}{2}$ in) longer than the buttonhole and 5 cm (2 in) wide. Place the centre of the strip to buttonhole mark with right sides facing. Machine stitch 3 mm ($\frac{1}{8}$ in) along both sides of the buttonhole mark and across the ends. Cut through the two thicknesses of fabric along the centre of the buttonhole, and then snip diagonally into the ends of the stitchings. Pull the strip through to the wrong side, press it out

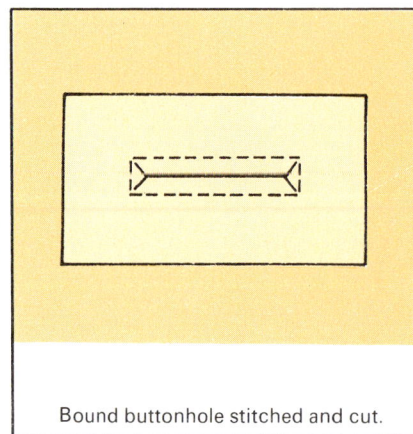
Bound buttonhole stitched and cut.

perfectly flat, and tack around the slit. The strip should be quite flat and form a neat binding on the right side. Two tiny inverted pleats will be formed at each end of the buttonhole on the wrong side.

If the garment is unlined turn the raw edges of facing strip and slip stitch the strip to garment.

If there is a facing, merely tack the strip into position at the back. Place the facing over the top, and cut a slit exactly opposite the buttonhole. Turn in the edge and hem to wrong side of buttonhole. This method is also used when making slots for pulling through a decorative ribbon.

Worked buttonholes

Buttonholes may be worked by hand or by machine. They should lie in the direction of the greatest strain, and remember that women's garments button right over left, men's left over right.

Worked buttonholes should always be made in double cloth. There are two different kinds: those on bands and underclothing have usually one rounded end and one square end; those on the fronts of shirts, shirt-blouses, and on some night-dresses have two barred ends.

Hand-worked buttonholes

Place the button on the band, half its diameter from the end, and make a tiny mark at right and left of the broadest part. With sharp-pointed scissors, preferably buttonhole scissors, cut a slit between these two marks, plus 3 mm ($\frac{1}{8}$ in) for ease. If the button is very thick a little more than 3 mm ($\frac{1}{8}$ in) will be necessary.

The buttonhole will be very much stronger if overcast stitches are worked over the cut edge before the buttonhole stitch. This is especially recommended for fabric that frays easily.

Using a fine needle and ordinary thread work in small stitches around the buttonhole starting at the left on the right side of the fabric. For a rounded end work in a semicircle taking slightly shorter stitches. For a barred end work in

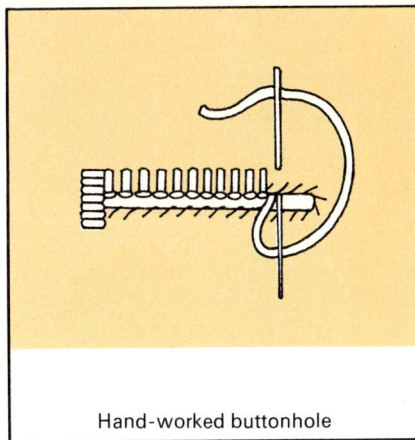

Hand-worked buttonhole

satin stitch taking stitches the depth of both rows of working.

Buttonholes worked by machine

Buttonholes may easily be worked by machine if you have a swing-needle model. They can also be worked with a straight stitching machine with the appropriate buttonhole attachment. As machines vary in detail it is best to follow the instructions given in the manufacturer's booklet.

Snap fasteners

These fasteners are made in sizes ranging from large to very small and should be chosen to suit the fabric of the garment. It is better to use too small a fastener rather than have a large, heavy one which looks and feels clumsy. They are made in two pieces, an upper section which has a projecting bump in the centre, and an under section which has the corresponding depression. The upper section is always sewn to the overlap of the garment first.

Marking the position

Mark the position of the fastener on the overlap with chalk and two pins crossed. Sew the fastener with stab stitch. When it is possible take the stitches right through to the wrong side, with the stitches passing from hole to hole or over the edge of the fastener at each hole.

If this method would cause the stitches to show on the right side, pick up one thickness of material

only slipping the needle between the two fabrics. A small circle of fabric as backing is usually necessary in this instance. Finish off with a back stitch under the fastener, darning in the end of the thread.

The under section

Sew on all the upper-section pieces first. Fix the overlap over the underlap correctly in the closed position and pin. Mark the exact spot where the bump of the upper section touches the underlap, with pins. A little french chalk rubbed on to the bump of the fastener will make a spot on the fabric of the underpart and give the exact position for the pins. Sew on the under section of the fastener with stab stitch so that the depression is exactly over the pin-mark. Care must be taken to sew on fasteners strongly and neatly, but not so tightly as to pucker the garment.

Hooks, eyes, loops and bars

Hooks, eyes and bars

These are made of either silver or black coloured metal, and are used for openings on garments, household linens and furnishings. Hooks and eyes are used on edge-to-edge fastenings and hooks and bars on overlapped fastenings.

Thread loops or bars can take the place of metal bars on delicate fabrics.

There is a range of sizes in hooks and eyes and they should be chosen in relation to the style of garment and fabric, and suitable thread should also be used. For instance, size 2 is used on stiffened waistbands, and sewn on with buttonhole twist. Size 1 is used on heavy and medium weight woollens. Use No. 40 mercerized cotton thread. No. 0 is suitable for fine wool, cotton fabrics, linen etc.

Sheer or fine fabrics require sizes 00 or 000, sewn on with fine polyester or pure silk thread.

Positioning hooks

Hooks and eyes are used for extra strength on waistband fastenings, the hook positioned on the overlap (see diagram). On neck openings the hook is again on the overlap. The flat side of the hook lies on the fabric, the hook towards the opening. The eye also faces towards the opening.

Sew the hooks on first. Position them 3 mm ($\frac{1}{8}$ in) from the edge, spacing them accurately by measuring and marking with pins. There are two methods for sewing on hooks and eyes. Method 1 is used for only one or two hooks. Method 2 is used when there are several in an opening.

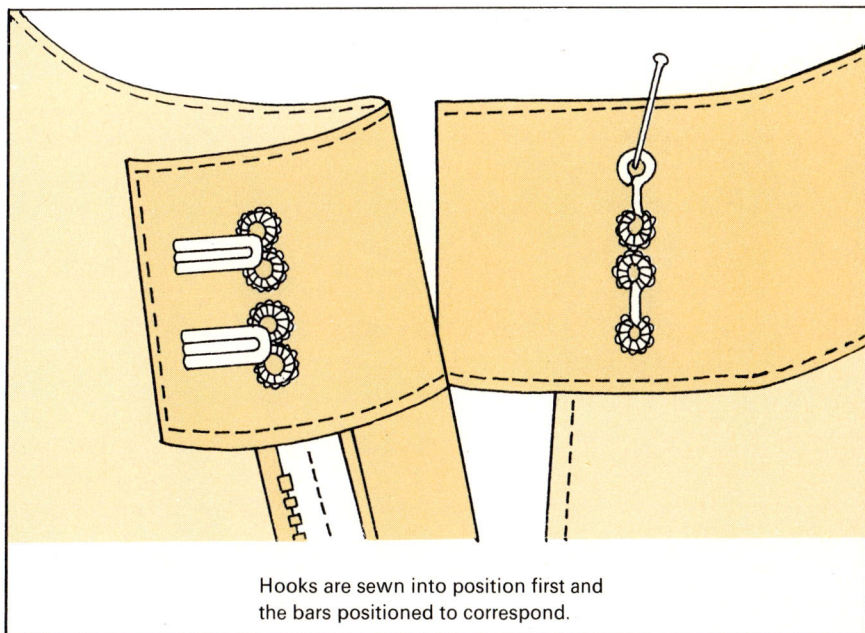

Hooks are sewn into position first and the bars positioned to correspond.

Above The cool, soft lines on this dress are created by gentle frills and gathers.

Left A tailored skirt with pleats looks smart and professional, but is not difficult to make.

Right A variety of pretty touches, including tucks and ribbon bows, have been used in the making of this traditional christening robe.

Far right The main feature of this dress is the tucked bodice which controls the fullness of the skirt.

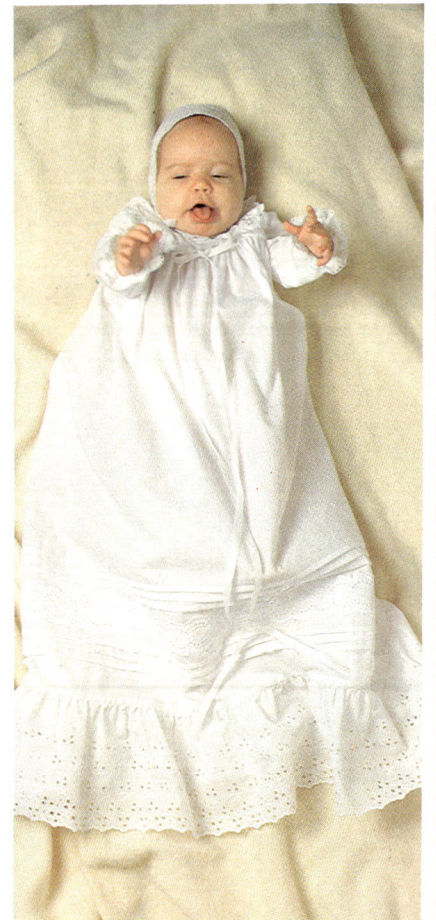

Construction methods

Method 1 Open the hook slightly with the scissor blades. Stitch to the garment, working blanket stitch over the rings, covering the metal completely.

After completing the blanket stitch, slip the needle under the fabric to the hook and work three stitches horizontally across the bend of the hook. Finish with small back stitches.

When sewing hooks to elastic or stiffening, stitches should be stabbed right through, front to back and back to front. This takes time, but the effect is neater and the result stronger.

When the hooks are sewn on, close the opening with a pin. Then slip a pin through each hook into the fabric, thus making bars of the pins. Unhook and unpin the opening.

Round eyes are sewn onto the wrong side of the opening with the loop of the eye projecting slightly beyond the edge of the garment. Stitch around the rings using blanket stitch.

Method 2 In this method the sewn-on hooks and eyes are covered with a strip of seam binding or the garment lining.

Sew on the hooks and eyes using radiating oversewing stitches in the rings. Work three or four horizontal stitches at the bend of the hook.

Slip the seam binding under the hooks and hem stitch along both edges. The seam binding is stitched on the wrong side of the opening, covering the eye rings, in the same way.

Metal bars
The bars are positioned so that the curve is towards the hook. Sew round the loops with blanket stitch.

Worked bars
Mark the length of the bar. Tie a knot in the thread end. Bring the needle out on the fold of the opening edge (the knot inside the fold). Work three or four strands about 3 mm to 6 mm long ($\frac{1}{8}$ in to $\frac{1}{4}$ in) depending on the size of the

hook. Work buttonhole stitch over the strands, the knots towards the hook. Finish with a back stitch.

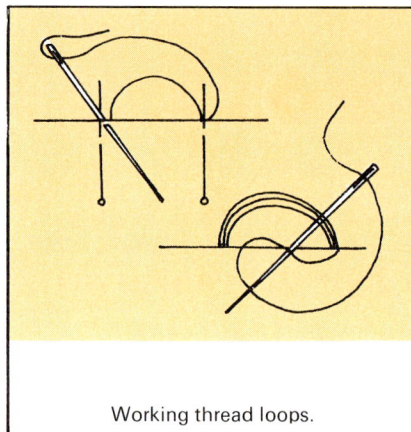
Working thread loops.

Thread loops
Thread loops for buttons are made in a similar way to worked bars. They are not a very strong fastening but they are very suitable for small buttons, or very fine fabrics where bound or machine-made buttonholes would be impractical. The edge of the garment is first finished with a tiny hem or with the lining, then carefully pressed.

Measure for the width of the loop, it should be a little less than half the width of the button. Mark this distance on the correct opening edge with two pins placed at right angles to the edge; mark all the loops. Attach the thread end with back stitches at the first pin. Pick up a small piece of fabric at the second pin, leaving a small loop. Make a back stitch. Go back to the first pin. Make a back stitch. Work three loops for a fine fabric, four for a heavier fabric.

Now work buttonhole stitch over the threads, keeping the stitches close together. Make sure that the knots are always on the same side of the loop and not allowed to twist.

If you are working a row of loops, work all the loop threads first, then go back and work the buttonhole stitches on each loop. Finish off securely with back stitches.

This technique is also one of the methods used for belt carriers.

Button loops
Fabric or braid loops are used on edge to edge fastenings, and are particularly suitable for ball or domed buttons.

Fabric loops
The loops are made with lengths of bias cut fabric stitched to form a tube known as *rouleau*.

Making rouleau There are two methods of making rouleau. The first and better-known method is for fine fabrics.

Cut bias strips 2.5 cm (1 in) wide. Place raw edges together, right sides facing. Machine stitch or work running stitches 3 mm ($\frac{1}{8}$ in) from the edge. Taper one end and then thread the tapered end into a bodkin and tie a knot. Push the fabric back over the bodkin so that the tube is turned right side out.

For heavy fabrics, another method is used. Cut strips 3 cm to 4 cm ($1\frac{1}{4}$ in to $1\frac{1}{2}$ in) wide. Fold under the raw long edges and tack close to fold. Press flat. Now fold the tacked edges to the centre of the strip and slip stitch together.

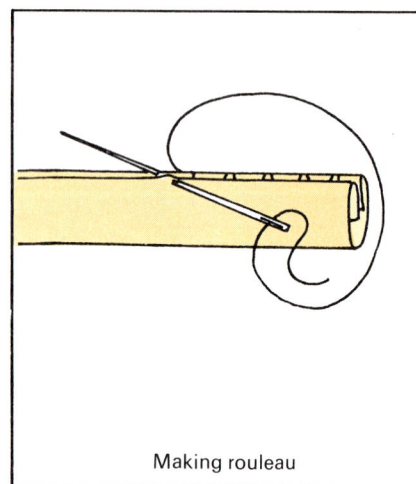
Making rouleau

These charming children's dresses utilise various fastenings. The dress on the left has pretty buttons and a velvet bow, while the school dress on the right is more functional with a front zipper which is easy for the younger child to manage.

Stitching single rouleau loops Single rouleau loops are sewn to seam binding. Mark the width of the loop on the binding with pins. Cut the rouleau to length so that the ends are just inside the edge of the binding, machine stitch.

Fold under the edge of the garment and tack. Place the prepared binding strip on top, the cut ends of the loops to the garment. The loops should project over the folded edge. Hem stitch the binding along long edges.

Continuous loops You need one long strip of rouleau or decorative braid.

Turn the garment opening edge under. Arrange the loops along the opening, the edge of each loop touching the previous. Pin, tack and then hand stitch in place. Finish with a bias cut strip of the same fabric stitched over the rouleau at the opening. Note: if the button loops are on a faced edge, such as on a dress front, the loops are positioned on the garment facing away from the edge and then the facing is applied. When the facing is turned to the inside of the garment, the loops are turned towards the edge in the correct position.

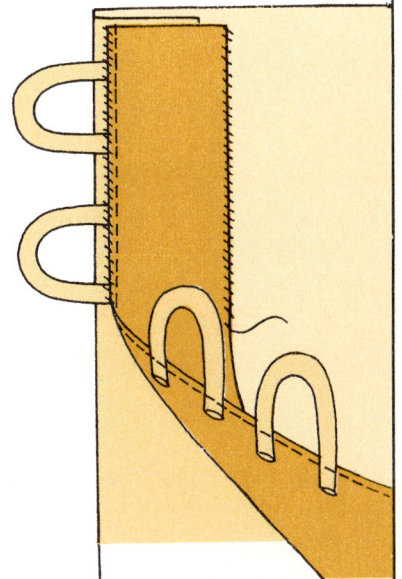

Single rouleau loops are attached with seam binding

Construction methods

Belts

A greater variety of changes can be made to dresses with the use of belts than with any other accessory. They can be neat and narrow matching the frock or in a contrasting fabric. A gay splash of colour can be introduced with the wide, shaped and stiffened variety. Belts that are plain and made of luxurious fabrics or dull fabrics or felt that are enhanced with embroidery, studs, beads, sequins or braid, all help to brighten up a plain dress.

They are simple to make and odd lengths of fabric can be used.

Straight belts

Method 1 This type is suitable for woollen, cotton and linen garments. It is made in double material. Cut a strip of fabric lengthways on the straight grain 13 cm (5 in) longer than the waist measurement, and twice the width required, plus turnings for seams. Fold the strip in two lengthwise with right sides together, and machine stitch 6 mm ($\frac{1}{4}$ in) from the edge. Press the seam open, and pull through to right side. To do this fasten a safety pin to one end of the belt, slip the head of safety pin inside the belt and pull through.

Flatten the belt with the seam down the centre and tack. Finish the end with a point.

For the point sew across the end when right sides are together. Trim the turnings, turn right side out and flatten. Fold both points to the centre seam and hem. This method should only be used on fine fabric.

Method 2 Cut the material as directed above. Fold the strip in two lengthwise, with right sides meeting and machine stitch 6 mm ($\frac{1}{4}$ in) from the edge, also stitch one end to form a point.

Cut the turnings from the point and turn right side out. A ruler is very good for this purpose. Begin at the point and pull the belt over the ruler until it appears at the open end. Tack with one seam along edge, taking care to poke out the point well to make a good line.

Turn in the edges of the straight end and stitch. Sew a buckle onto this end. Sometimes a fastener is sewn onto the point to keep it perfectly flat when the belt is being worn.

Covered buckle

It is possible to buy metal buckles ready to cover. To make a buckle to match a belt, cut the shape in cardboard first. Then cut several lengths of material on the cross, about 2.5 cm (1 in) wide. Join into one long strip and press the seams. Fold one edge of the strip under for

Straight belt (1st method)

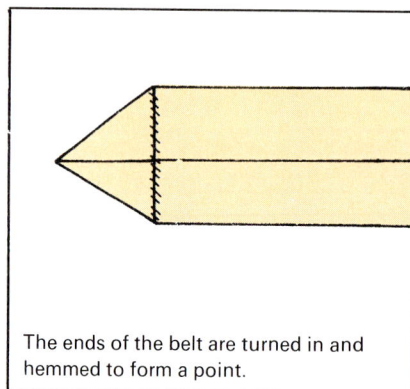
The ends of the belt are turned in and hemmed to form a point.

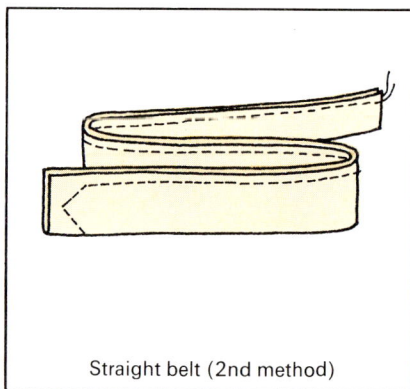
Straight belt (2nd method)

half the width lengthwise, and with right side out cover the cardboard foundation by winding the material over it, covering the raw edges with the fold.

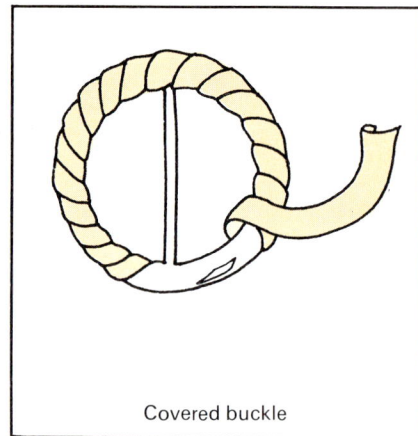
Covered buckle

Belt carriers

These are made at the side seams in order to hold a belt in position, and are made of the same fabric as the dress about 6 mm ($\frac{1}{4}$ in) wide. Cut a strip of material 2.5 cm (1 in) longer than width of belt and 18 mm ($\frac{3}{4}$ in) wide. Fold over and hem down on the wrong side. Make a turning at the top and bottom of tab and sew it firmly to the side seams in the position of the belt.

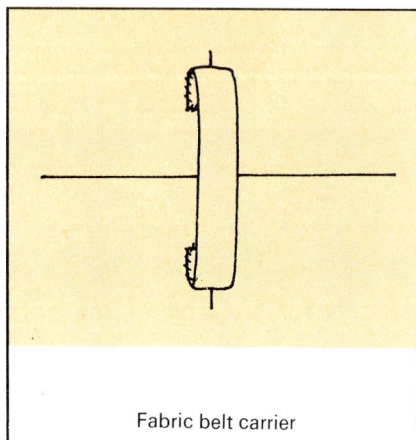
Fabric belt carrier

Thread loop carrier

With a strong thread make three strands along the seam, wide enough to take the belt, work loop stitches close together across these strands. This is less bulky than the cloth supports and suitable for very light fabrics such as silk.

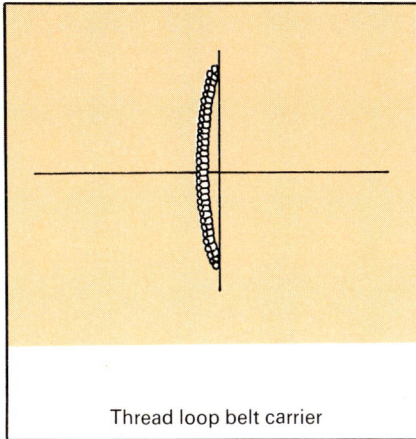

Thread loop belt carrier

Ribbon and material belt

This may be made of one colour, to match a dress, or of two contrasting colours. If the belt is to be reversible, a laced fastening will be the most suitable.

One colour belt

Cut a piece of petersham ribbon the required length, plus wrap-over and an extra inch for turnings. Also, cut a piece of matching material 12 mm ($\frac{1}{2}$ in) wider than the petersham all round, turn in the edges so that the strip is the same width as the ribbon, tack and press the turnings. Now tack the petersham over the material to cover the turnings, and stitch by hand with small running stitches. Shape one end as required, thread the other end through a buckle and fix in position. Work one or two eyelet holes at the shaped end of the belt for fastening.

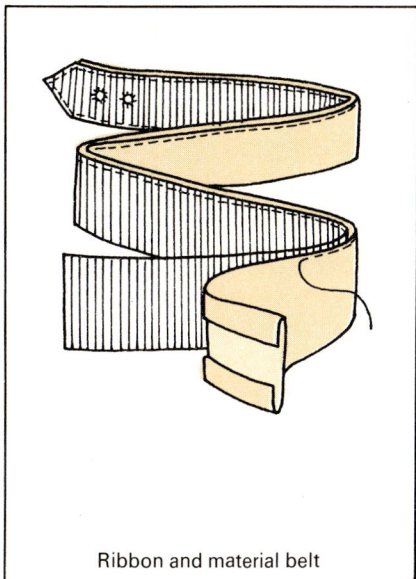

Ribbon and material belt

Reversible belt

Use a fabric to match the dress with a contrasting petersham ribbon. Make up as for a one-colour belt, but without a wrap-over and making both ends similar. Neaten the ends and work eyelet holes into each through which cord or narrow ribbon can be threaded.

Shaped and stiffened belt

An infinite variety of shaped belts may be made, and they are suitable for day or evening wear; there are many methods of fastening them.

A wide straight belt may need some kind of stiffening to hold its shape. A very wide shaped belt could be cut from the bodice pattern, otherwise cut as for the unlined belt.

Cut out the fabric for the belt itself, also the lining of the same or different fabric, both with 12 mm ($\frac{1}{2}$ in) turnings. Join the seams and press. Cut out interlining to the exact size of the pattern, allowing turnings only where there are seams. All the pieces are cut on the straight grain for this type of belt. It is possible to buy a special stiffening for belts called 'belting'. If using this follow manufacturer's instructions.

Place the interlining on the wrong side of the belt lining, lapping the seams and matching them with the lining. Tack the two together.

Pad stitch the interlining and lining together as for collars. If the belt is not reversible, rows of machine stitching may be used

instead of pad stitch; this will give a stiffer foundation for a very wide belt. Turn the lining over the interlining, tack and sew with catch stitch.

On the belt fabric, turn in all the edges so that the finished piece is exactly the same as the lining, tack it in position over the canvas and slip stitch the edges by hand, or machine stitch around the edge. If the belt is not very stiff and only shaped a little, the right side of the belt may be placed to the right side of the fabric and the edges machined. The turnings of the curved parts are clipped, then pressed and turned right side out, a short end having been left unsewn for this purpose. This end is then turned in and slip stitched.

Fastenings

For a laced fastening, eyelet holes are worked through the belt and cord is threaded through.

Large hooks and eyes may be sewn to the ends or loops of cord with buttons sewn to match. Ribbon ties make a good fastening for a fancy belt.

Decoration

Embroidery decoration should be applied to the fabric before the belt is made up. Braiding or stud trimmings can be added after the belt is completed as they need the firmness of the interlining as a foundation.

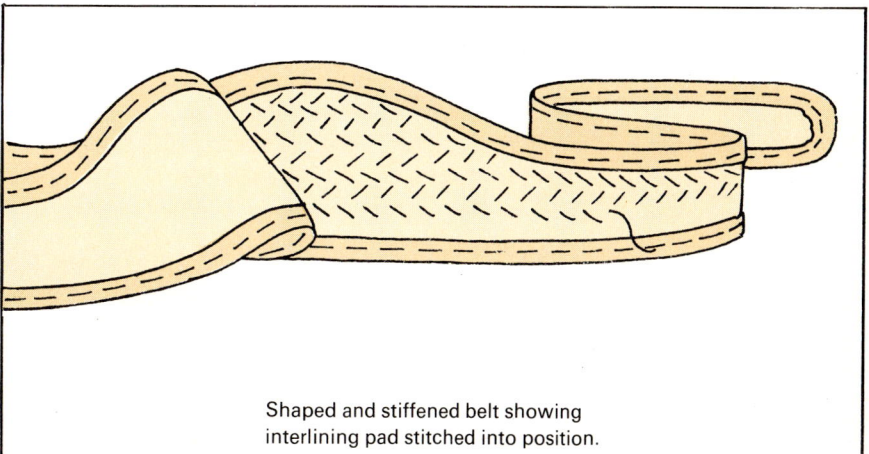

Shaped and stiffened belt showing interlining pad stitched into position.

Handle with care

Certain fabrics have a special weave, knit or finish and using them helps to make simple patterns look distinctive and smart. These fabrics need a different kind of handling at every stage of dressmaking to achieve satisfactory results.

Stretch fabrics

Some stretch fabrics are woven, while others are knitted – jerseys, double knits, rashels and so on, and their most important feature in home dressmaking is that they can be fitted over body curves. Knits are comfortable to wear and are used for casual clothes and for children's wear. The range of effects and finishes is wide but most have to be handled in a similar way.

Knits have different degrees of stretch, and you need to know what kind of stretch you are working with. Most patterns for use with knit fabrics will indicate which type to choose:
stable knit = suitable for knits;
moderate stretch knit = for patterns with cling;
stable unbonded knit = for patterns that have very little ease designed into them.

Some patterns give a gauge on the pattern envelope so that you can judge the degree of stretch before buying a length of fabric.

Some knit fabrics are sold in a tube so you will have to cut carefully along one folded edge in order to lay the fabric flat. Check if the knit is washable; if so, pre-shrink it before cutting out.

Pinning and cutting out
Lay the fabric flat on the table and study the loops of the knit. Chalk in a line following the loops as a guide or work a line of thread-tracing. There is no grain in knitted fabric so follow the rib for the straight of fabric. You will find it better to cut jersey and stretch fabrics out single, one layer at a time. Look to see if the knit has a nap – many have.

Lay your pattern pieces out on the right side of the fabric and use either ballpoint pins or very sharp dressmaker's pins. Support the weight of the fabric so that it does not hang off the table onto the floor. Drape the ends over a couple of chairs. Try not to stretch the fabric as you pin, and take up only a thread or two of the fabric. As knit fabrics are inclined to curl on cut edges, cut all the vertical seams a bit wider – as much as 2.5 cm (1 in). Use only very sharp dressmaking shears for cutting out and never use pinking shears.

Interfacings
You can use woven or non-woven fabrics for knits and jerseys. Non-woven includes a special all-bias stretchable interfacing.

Linings
If the garment is to retain its stretch qualities, the linings must be stretchable as well. If the garment is to hold a shape, choose a lining which will support the fabric: heavy taffeta, crêpe-backed satin, crêpe, or silk shantung, selecting a weight to suit the top fabric.

Fitting knits
You will find fitting easier to do, especially with very stretchy fabrics, if you tack loosely so that you can adjust the stitches. Tack with double thread, using a ball-point or very sharp needle. Start at the top of a seam and tack down towards the hem of the garment. Make the stitches fairly loose and then, at the end of the seam, make a single back stitch and leave a length of thread hanging. When you have the garment on, ease the fit by redistributing the fabric along the thread.

Sewing knits
It is important that seams have some give to them so that the stitches do not break. If you have a sewing machine that only works straight stitch, set the machine to a fairly large stitch and stretch the

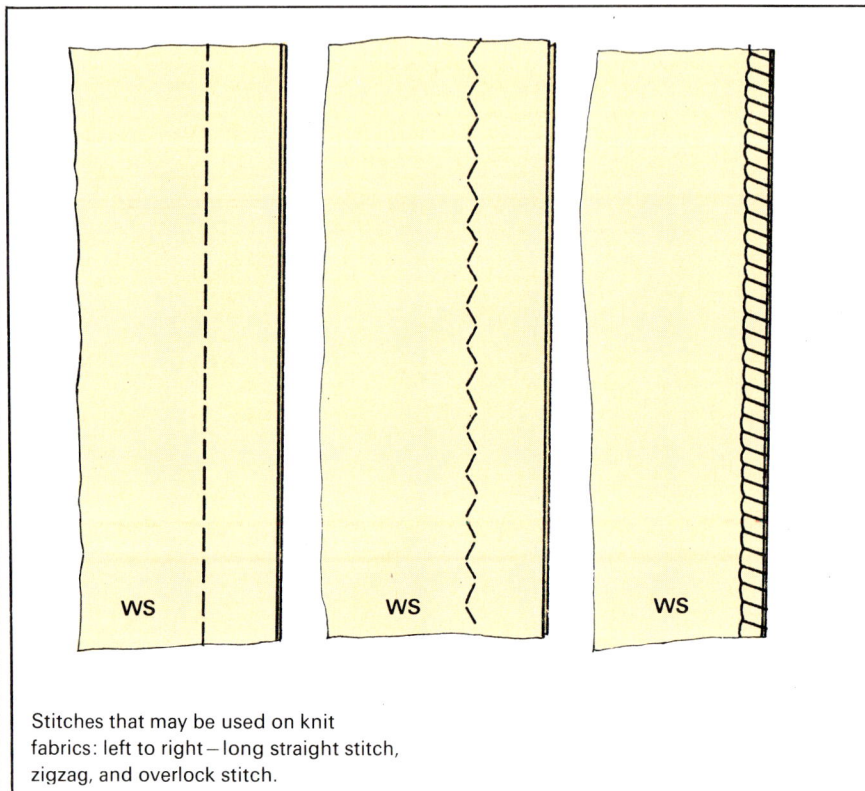

Stitches that may be used on knit fabrics: left to right – long straight stitch, zigzag, and overlock stitch.

fabric slightly as you sew.

A semi-automatic machine set to a narrow zigzag stitch can be used satisfactorily. If it has a setting for overlock stitch, use this for seams that will receive some strain. Experiment with various settings on scraps of the fabric to find the best possible stitch setting; pull the test seam lengthwise and then try to pull the two pieces of fabric apart.

Thread the machine with a pure polyester or a polyester sheathed cotton, and use ballpoint needles.

Check the machine tension and adjust it so that it is perfectly balanced – otherwise the seam will rip the first time you wear the garment. A good way to test this is to stitch a sample seam and then, with top thread facing, pull the seam apart. On a balanced seam both threads break together; if the bottom breaks first the tension is too loose, if the top thread, the tension is too tight.

Make sure that you do not stretch the fabric while you are working. After working on the seam line, work another row in the seam allowance 3 mm ($\frac{1}{8}$ in) away from the first. Trim away the seam allowance almost up to the second line of stitching.

Staystitching
Knitted fabrics should be staystitched as soon as possible after cutting out. Work staystitching from the widest part of the section to the narrowest. Then, to check that the fabric has not been distorted by the stitching lay the pattern on the fabric piece. If it is smaller, release the staystitching by clipping a thread or two. If it has stretched, pull up the staystitches with a pin.

Seam taping In places where there should not be any stretch, such as shoulder seams and waist seams, ribbon seam binding should be tacked along the seam line and stitched with the seam. Use bias binding for curved seams, shaping it before applying to the edge.

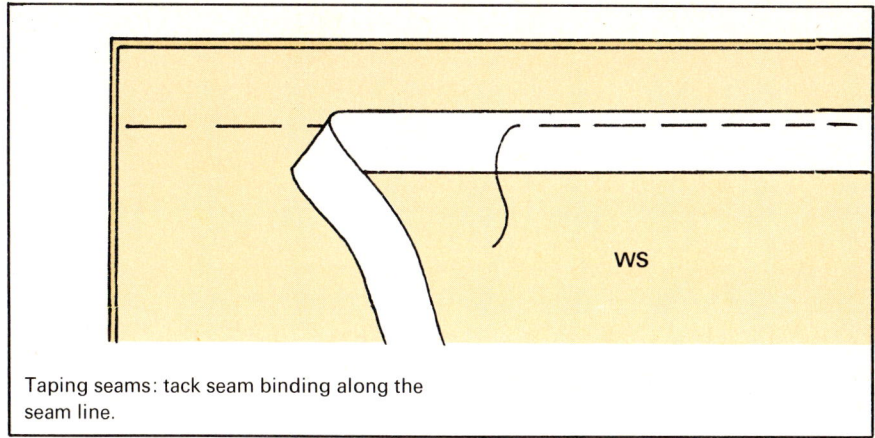

Taping seams: tack seam binding along the seam line.

Finishing details
It is advisable to hang a knit fabric garment for at least a day before taking up the hem.

Use interfacing on button placements and always for making machine buttonholes.

When inserting zippers, stretch the fabric a little as you sew in the zip. Knits with a large loop should have coil zips rather than the kind with teeth.

Delicate fabrics
These lovely fabrics – chiffon, pure silk, organdie, soft muslin, georgette illusion nets – are wonderful to wear, but they do need special handling in dressmaking.

Pinning, cutting out and marking
Use only the finest, sharpest pins and very sharp shears. If you are mounting (underlining) parts of the garment, follow the technique described on page 27 and cut both layers of fabric to exactly the same shape.

Pinning patterns to sheer fabric is difficult because the layers are inclined to slip against each other and are hard to keep straight, so spread tissue paper on the work table and then have another sheet of tissue between the fabric layers.

Pin the two layers of fabric together first. Pin along the selvedges together and then pin across the width before pinning down the paper pattern. Alternatively, work diagonal basting stitches across the fabric.

Tailor's tacks are the best marking method for symbols, with thread tracing for construction lines. Use silk sewing thread for making tailor's tacks. Be careful with chalk because it may permanently mark the fabric. Never use a tracing wheel on sheer or fine fabrics. If you are working with mounted fabric, you can make chalk marks on the wrong side of the mounting.

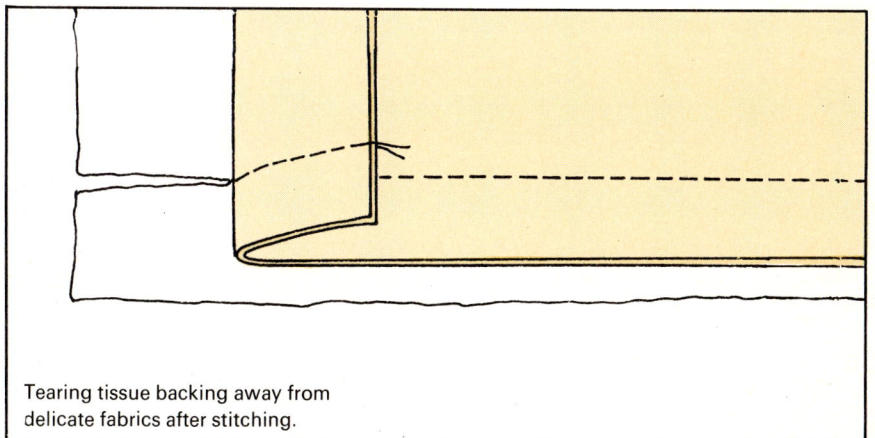

Tearing tissue backing away from delicate fabrics after stitching.

Construction methods

Sewing

Choose a fine needle and the correct thread for the fabric. Work test pieces first so that you choose the best stitch length for the fabric.

Machine stitching can be difficult to do because the layers of fabric tend to slip about under the presser foot. Slip a layer of tissue paper between the layers, and then tack the layers of fabric together carefully just outside the stitching line and again in the seam allowance. Machine stitch with tissue paper on top if the fabric still shows signs of slipping.

If the fabric seems to catch in the teeth of the feed dog, lay tissue paper over the teeth. Tear tissue paper away from the stitches after stitching.

Finish the ends of seams by weaving the thread ends back in and out of the stitches, rather than running the machine backwards and forwards.

Seams to use

Enclosed seams such as French seams are best as many fine fabrics are inclined to fray, double-stitched seams can be used for putting in sleeves.

Finishing details

If the fabric is underlined, an ordinary hem finish can be used. If the fabric is unmounted, the hem should be either deep and exactly doubled or very narrow so that it is unnoticeable. Hems can be finished with hand rolling. If the garment has two or more layers of sheer fabric, the outer skirt should be the longest with subsequent layers about 9 mm ($\frac{3}{8}$ in) shorter, so that the innermost layer is the shortest.

Bound buttonholes are recommended if the garment is underlined. Machine-made buttonholes should be used on unmounted sheers. Button loops are very suitable for all fine fabrics.

Zippers can be put into garments made of firm sheer fabrics but not for floaty sheers. Use a lapped closing and snap fasteners or hooks and eyes. A lightweight zipper can be used on underlined garments.

Above This dramatic watered silk dress has a deeply flounced skirt.

Right A delicate, lacy fabric is ideal for a traditional, white wedding dress with floating sleeves and skirt.

Construction methods

Shiny fabrics

Satin

Satin should always be treated as a napped fabric because the light catches the surface threads, producing a one-way effect.

Pin holes made in satin cannot be removed so always pin in the seam allowance only. Use a fine needle and sewing thread to mark symbols with tailor's tacks but, again, make tacks within a dart and within the seam allowance to prevent holes showing. Satin can be marked with chalk lines on the wrong side, using tailor's chalk and a ruler. Do not use a tracing wheel as this may damage the surface fibres.

Sewing

Use pure silk thread or pure polyester thread. Satins should be stitched with a medium length stitch. Hold it firmly between your hands to prevent it puckering while stitching.

Seam finishes

Satin garments should always have beautifully finished seams. Binding the raw edges with a matching underlining fabric is the couture finish.

Finishing details

Ordinary hem finishes are used on satin garments but the finished effect is better if no stitches show on the right side. A soft edge rather than a sharp looks better. Use a soft interfacing in the hem so that you get a rolled edge.

You can work bound or machine-stitched buttonholes on a satin garment, and covered buttons usually look best. Zippers can also be used, and a better finish is achieved by inserting a zipper by hand using prick stitch.

Taffeta

Taffeta is easy to handle at the cutting out stage, although light-coloured taffetas should have pins inserted in the seam allowance as for satin.

Use tissue paper between layers if the fabric shows signs of slipping while being machine stitched.

Be extremely careful when pressing. Many taffetas are spoiled with heat and with water marks. Make several tests on scraps of fabric before attempting to press seams. Always use a seam roll and strips of brown paper to prevent iron-shine.

Brocade

Generally, handle brocade as for satin. Press right side down over a thick soft surface so that the raised design is not flattened.

Metallic finishes

The first thing to remember when working with fabrics woven with metal threads is that the metal will blunt shears, needles and pins. Rather than spoil your best shears, use an old pair and replace machine needles several times during a sewing project.

Pinning

Most metallic fabrics have a one-way effect so follow the pattern layouts for napped fabrics.

Facings

If you are making a dress with neck and armhole facings or a combination facing, you will find that the garment is more comfortable if the facing is made from a matching lining fabric rather than self fabric. If you are careful to roll the edges of the facing gently to the wrong side, the lining should not show.

A jersey knit fabric is a good choice for a plain winter dress.

Sewing

Polyester threads and fine needles are best with these fabrics.

Pressing metallic fabrics may damage the metal threads and must be done very carefully. To be sure of not damaging the seams, open them with your fingers and run a thimble down the stitching lines on the wrong side to press them open.

Metallic threads can be uncomfortable against the skin so seams should be finished off with seam binding, unless the garment is being lined.

Finishing details

Metallic threads are not only uncomfortable against the skin, they can also snag tights and stockings. Make a plain fabric bias-faced hem so that the finish on the inside of the garment is smooth.

Bound buttonholes should be avoided because metallic fabrics are inclined to fray. Put zippers in by hand using prick stitch. Machine insertion may crease the fabric too sharply and cause the metal threads to break.

Napped fabrics

Napped fabrics usually include any fabric with a surface which lies smoothly one way, but this section deals with those fabrics where there is a definite pile or surface. Velvet, corduroy, needlecord and fleece, plush and velour are just a few of the fabrics in this category.

To get the best effect from a napped fabric – velvet particularly – the nap should run up the body so that you get a richer colour effect. Panné velvet, where the pile has been flattened in processing should be used with the nap running down the garment so that the surface shimmers.

To find the direction of the pile, lay the fabric on a table and smooth it with your hand, following the straight of grain up and down. In one direction it will feel rough – this is the 'up' of the nap; in the other direction, smooth – this is the 'down' of the nap.

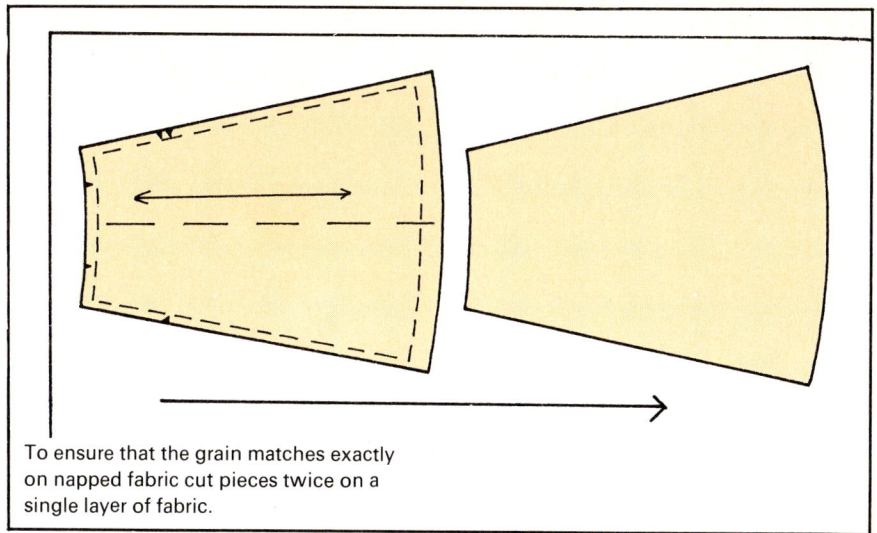

To ensure that the grain matches exactly on napped fabric cut pieces twice on a single layer of fabric.

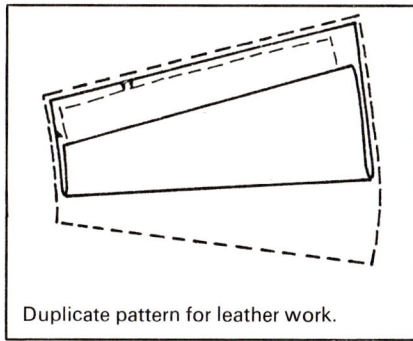

Duplicate pattern for leather work.

When working with napped fabrics, always follow the layout supplied in the pattern. Beginners should choose simple styles with few details and not too many darts.

Pinning, cutting out and marking

Velvets, like sheers, are inclined to slip about while cutting out, so lay sheets of tissue paper between the layers to minimise this. Cut thick velvets singly. Thinner velvets can be cut out double.

Professional tip If you have to cut pieces single it is worth making a duplicate pattern piece and marking the reverse. This prevents you making a mistake and cutting two pieces the same way around.

Tailor's tacks and thread tracing are the best methods of marking velvet fabrics; use silk thread.

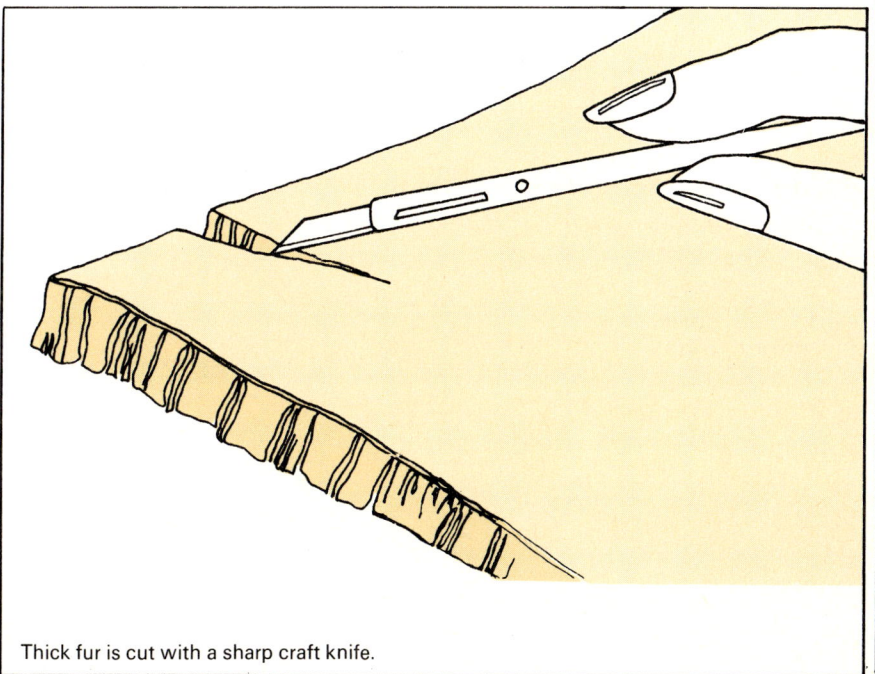

Thick fur is cut with a sharp craft knife.

Construction methods

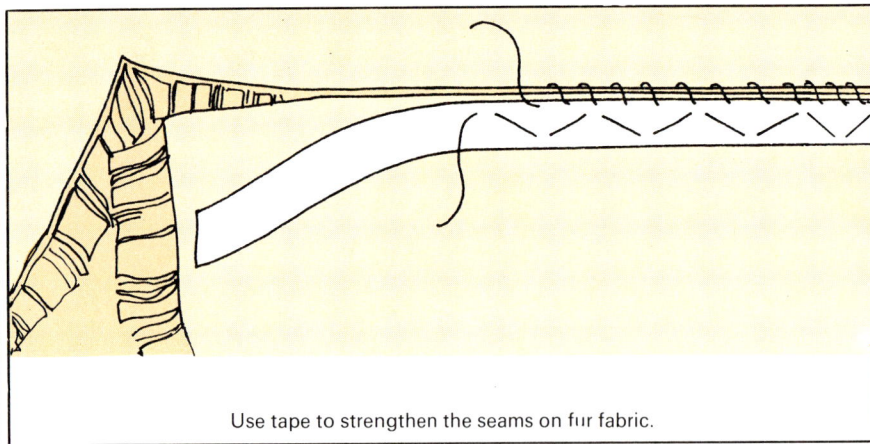
Use tape to strengthen the seams on fur fabric.

Chalk marking can be done on the wrong side of the fabric but do not use a tracing wheel on velvet.

Sewing

Use silk thread for tacking and work two rows, one just inside the stitching line and the other 6 mm ($\frac{1}{4}$ in) away. Make small even stitches.

Always try out the stitch length and machine tension on fabric scraps and stitch in the direction of the nap. Hold the fabric taut as you stitch. If the fabric starts to pucker, adjust the presser foot.

Raw edges should be either overcast or bound.

Fur and fur fabrics

Real fur skins are cut out and stitched using the same techniques as for leather and suede. The only other difference is the handling of the pile. The techniques of working with fake fur fabrics should be read through before working with real fur.

Fake furs have either woven or knitted backings; sometimes the back has a thin sheet of polyether foam laminated to it to give the fabric more body; it also increases warmth. Knit-backed furs are more flexible than the woven kind and easier to work with.

The choice of pattern is important when you are using fake fur fabric. Choose styles with as few seams and details as possible because these will make bulk. If the back has a centre back seam, trim off the seam allowance and cut the back on the fold of fabric so that it is in one piece. Try to arrange that facings are cut in one with the fronts also so that there is no seam on the edge. Avoid facings at the hem of a jacket. Plan to take the lining down to the edge.

Pinning, cutting out and marking

The nap of the fabric should run down the body. Before cutting out, look at the fabric to see if there is a fabric design which should be centred on the back and front pieces. Duplicate pattern pieces where you have to cut two (fronts and sleeves) and reverse one pattern. Lay the fabric pile side down.

Thin furs with a short pile can

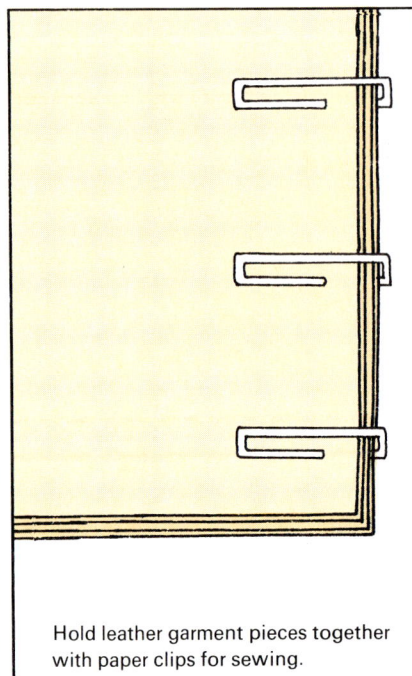
Hold leather garment pieces together with paper clips for sewing.

have the pattern pinned to them. If you are using a thick fur, tape the pattern to the backing.

Use very sharp shears for cutting out, and cut through the backing only. Thick furs may need to be cut out with a razor blade in a holder or a sharp craft-knife.

Use chalk or soft pencil for marking all symbols and construction lines on the wrong side.

Sewing

Try various stitch lengths on scrap pieces; generally, the thicker the fur, the stronger the needle and the longer the stitch. Use a pure silk thread or a pure polyester thread.

Fur fabrics with a knitted back should be treated as knits, using a narrow zigzag stitch. Thinner furs can be tacked together for seaming; thick furs are held together with clothes pegs or large paper clips.

Always stitch in the direction of the pile. If seams are going to be under strain, such as shoulder seams, tack seam tape along the seam and stitch through in one.

After stitching, shave the pile from the seam allowances, using either a safety razor or scissors. Then use a needle to tease out the pile from the seam on the right side. To open seams on the wrong

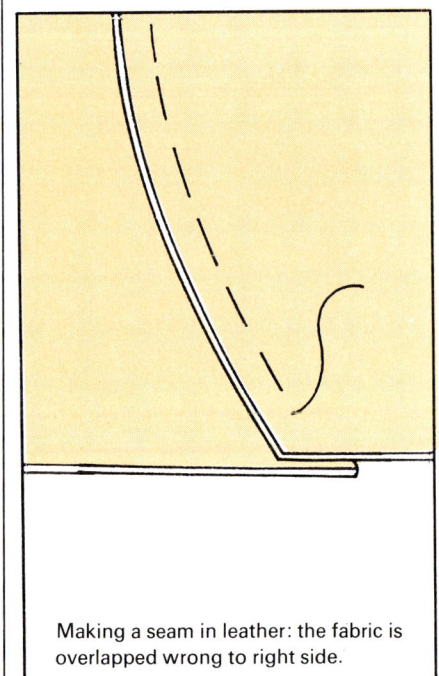
Making a seam in leather: the fabric is overlapped wrong to right side.

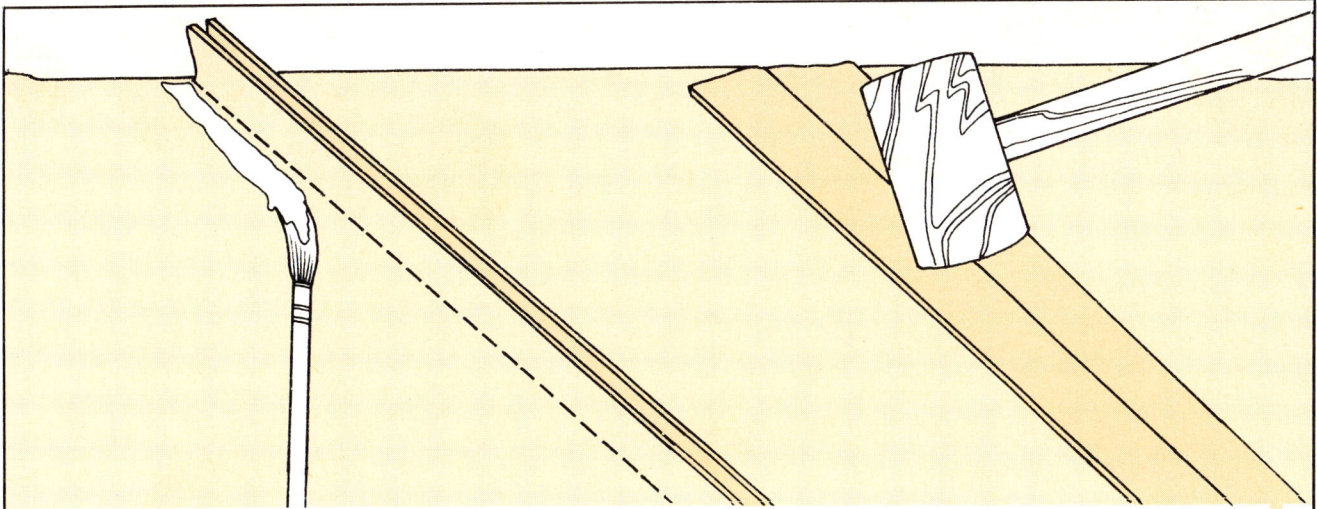

Spread rubber-based adhesive under seam allowances on leather.

Then pound seams flat with a wooden mallet.

side, run a thimble along the stitching line.

Cut darts open and then shave seam allowances.

Finishing details

Bound buttonholes are best on fur fabrics, using leather or soft vinyl. You can also use large snap fasteners for an opening with a large button stitched on the right side. Zippers on fur fabric garments should be stitched in by hand.

Leather and similar fabrics

Leather and suede are sold by the skin and paper patterns which are intended for these materials will tell you how many skins to buy. However, skins almost always have some thin or imperfect places in them. Consequently you may have to adjust the pattern slightly to make the best use of the skin, for example cutting a skirt panel with an extra piece in a seam.

Suede has a nap and should be treated as a napped fabric. Leather may have a distinctive grain in it and should be looked over carefully before placing pattern pieces.

Cut leather and suede singly and make duplicate pattern pieces where you need to cut two pieces.

Cutting out and marking

Leather and suede cannot be pinned because holes would be made which cannot be removed. Lay pattern pieces on the wrong side of the skin and secure them with strips of adhesive tape. Cut leather and suede with sharp dressmaker's shears. Mark all the cutting lines and darts with a ballpoint pen.

Sewing

Hold pieces together with paper clips or bulldog clips. Alternatively, staple pieces together for seaming, placing the staples in the seam allowance.

Fitting is very important and should be done before stitching as the needle leaves holes which cannot be removed. Use a special spear-pointed machine needle and silk, synthetic or mercerised thread, these can be used on both leather and suede. Have another needle on hand ready to change over when the needle in the machine becomes blunt. If you handsew any part of the garment, use a special glovers' needle. Set the machine to a stitch length of between 8 and 10 stitches to 2.5 cm (1 in). Reduce the pressure of the presser foot so that the leather moves easily under the foot. If you have to force the leather to stitch it you will either break the needle or spoil the surface of the skin. Spread a piece of tissue paper over the feed teeth to prevent them from damaging the skin. Tie thread ends off when starting and finishing. Do not run the machine backwards and forwards because the needle will make too many holes and weaken the seam.

At corners, do not pivot the needle but work a rounded corner for ease when turning a shaped seam right side out.

Seams

Ordinary seams are used for dressmaking with leather and suede but if a seam is going to take a lot of strain, tape a length of seam binding over the seam and stitch through it. Use lapped seams for shaped sections.

Cut darts open and run a thimble over the back of the stitching. Glue down the turnings with a rubber-based adhesive.

Finish seams in the same way, but if the leather is thick, pound the seams open with a wooden mallet.

Linings

Leather garments have a long life and you should choose a strong, good quality lining fabric such as silk or acetate. Linings cannot be slipstitched into garments in the normal way. The best way to insert linings is to stitch with seam tape to a facing edge or hem and then slipstitch the lining to the tape.

Construction methods

Needle and thread chart

Fabric type	Type of thread	Needles for hand sewing	Needles for machine sewing
Fine to medium weight Chambray, chiffon, cotton knits, batiste, crêpe, georgette, lawn, nets, ninon, organdie, silk, surah, silk jersey knits, tulle, voile.	Silk thread on silk and silk-like fabrics. Synthetic threads for all fabrics.	Sharps, betweens, sizes 8, 9, 10.	British sizes 9-12. Continental sizes 70-80 (some machines require size 60). Ballpoint for knits.
Medium to heavy weight Brocade, challis, cotton, fleecy fabrics, gingham, jerseys, needlecord, piqué, pongee, poplin, shantung, single knits, satin, seersucker, taffeta, tweed (lightweight), fine wool.	Mercerized cotton nos. 40, 50 for natural fabrics. Synthetic thread for all fabrics, especially knits.	Sharps or betweens 7, 8.	British sizes 12, 14, 16. Continental sizes 80, 90, 100. Ballpoint for knits.
Heavy fabrics Denim, corduroy, furnishing repp, tweeds and coat weight wools.	Sewing cotton 36, 40. Synthetic threads for all fabrics.	Sharps 5, 6, 7.	British sizes 14, 16, 18. Continental sizes 90, 100.
Very heavy fabrics Canvas, duck, leather, sailcloth, suede, ticking, vinyl.	Sewing cotton 36, 40. Heavy duty thread. Button thread.	Sharps 1, 2, 3, 4.	British sizes 16, 18. Continental size 100. Spear-pointed needles for leather and vinyls.

Fabrics and fitting

Even if you have not sewn since you were at school, you will love sewing for a baby. The garments are tiny, so they do not take long to finish, and the fabrics you use are light and a pleasure to work with.

As babies grow older there are more things which can be sewn for them – little girls particularly. And when girls grow older still, it is good training for them to help to choose their own pattern styles and fabrics. They may be able to help with simple sewing jobs and thus develop their own interest in sewing.

Choosing suitable styles

If you are going to enjoy sewing for your children, choose simple patterns with construction techniques which are within your capabilities. Avoid styles that will quickly date, except for older children, and concentrate on well-cut designs with simple seams and not too much detail. Remember the reasons you are undertaking sewing for your children: probably first for economy – it is still cheaper to make clothes than buy them; secondly, to achieve a better fit. Finally, you will be sewing for pleasure and for your children's appreciation; make a success of everything you undertake and there will be no distress or embarrassment.

Children vary a great deal in their build, so ignore the age groupings on commercial patterns and choose by measurements. Very small girls look charming in full skirted styles with a fitted bodice for best wear, while popover tunics and smocks are more comfortable playwear. Tall, thin girls can wear puffed sleeves, gathered skirts and frills; smocking adds an attractive finish. Plump girls with a high tummy should wear straighter lines, preferably styles which hang from the shoulder. Pleats are better than gathers in skirts.

Choose clothes which are easy to wear. Even party dresses should be able to be forgotten once they are on.

Children's heads are larger than you think. Check the size of the neck opening before you apply the facing and finish it off. Generally, avoid cuff fastenings.

Choose styles with front openings wherever possible and avoid collars or neckline finishes which can irritate the skin. Some children are allergic to fabrics such as angora, wool and velvet and will naturally refuse to wear a garment which makes them uncomfortable.

Anticipate the child's growth, which is usually upwards rather than outwards. Make doubled hems on skirts, cuffs and trouser hems. Include extra fabric in linings too.

When joining a skirt to a bodice, make the bodice 5 cm (2 in) longer, but attach the skirt at the natural waistline. Later alterations can then be made from the waist.

Coats

Children often dislike wearing coats. The fabric is thicker and so they feel constricted. If you can, choose a pliable fabric for outdoor garments, such as a jersey knit. Always fit the garment over the child's clothing, so that armholes and sleeves are not too tight. Listen to the child's opinion about the collar fabric and how it affects him in wear.

Fabrics for children's clothes

There is a wide range of fabrics that wash easily, tumble dry with very little creasing and so need little or no ironing. Obviously, if comfort in wearing is also a feature, this is the type of fabric to choose for children's clothes. Here are some of the fabric types to look for and the kinds of clothes each type will be used for.

Pretty, small print fabrics are suitable for a girl's party dress. This picture shows three classic designs which could all be adapted from basic patterns.

Broderie anglaise An eyelet embroidered cotton fabric which will make pretty pinafores or smock tops. Thin fabric can be used for babies' angel tops.

Cambric Lightweight cotton for dresses, blouses or shirts.

Cheesecloth Cotton fabric for casual summerwear. Needs little or no ironing.

Clydella Lightweight fabric, 80% cotton, 20% wool. Can be used for nightwear, shirts, babies' dresses.

Corduroy Made of cotton or cotton mixture – napped fabric. Will make girls' skirts, trousers for both sexes and coats and jackets.

Cotton and cotton mixes Even weave or surface finished fabric, usually with easy-care properties. Lightweight to medium weight and suitable for most kinds of children's clothes except warm outdoor garments. Brushed cotton is soft and is suitable for warm nightwear.

Denim Touch cotton fabric, usually in blue but sometimes in colours. Used for trousers, skirts, jackets and so on.

Flannel Wool fabric with a napped surface. Suitable for suits and coats.

Flannelette Cotton fabric with a brushed surface. Used for warm shirts and nightwear.

Gabardine Wool or cotton with a twill weave. Used for coats.

Gingham Cotton with distinctive weave of checks or stripes. For dresses, skirts, shirts, blouses, summer nightwear.

Jersey Knitted stretch fabric, often crease resistant. Can be of a man-made fibre, cotton or silk. Choose from various weights for coats, suits, trousers, casual wear and playwear for young children.

Lawn Sheer fabric in cotton or cotton mixes. Pretty for party dresses, blouses, underwear.

Madras Indian cotton in woven stripes or plaids for dresses, shirts, blouses.

Mohair Usually blended with other fibres. Used for coats or cloaks.

Muslin Fine, loosely woven cotton. Ideal for infant summer clothes.

Needlecord A fine corduroy. Suitable for dresses, skirts, suits, trousers, jackets.

Nun's veiling Fine wool fabric. Can be used to make classic winter dresses.

Piqué Firm cotton fabric with a raised surface. Good for sports clothes, tennis skirts, shorts; also for collars and cuffs.

Poplin Hardwearing cotton fabric with a sheen. Used for dresses, shirts, blouses.

P.V.C. Synthetic finish on woven or knitted fabric. Use for rainwear.

Seersucker Cotton or cotton mixture with a textured surface. Needs no ironing. Use for dresses, playwear, summer suits, shirts.

Serge Hardwearing fabric of wool or wool mixtures. Use for classic coats.

Terry cloth Towelling finish in woven or knitted fibres. Use for beach clothes, sportsclothes, bathrobes. Stretch variety good for young children's playsuits.

Tweed Woven or knitted wool or wool mixtures. Choose light, soft variety for children's coats.

Velour Woven fabric with a short pile. Use for coats.

Velvet Pile fabric made from silk, cotton or man-made fibres. Use silk or cotton velvet for party clothes. Velveteen is less dense and often better for children's clothes.

Viyella Woven fabric, 55% wool – 45% cotton. Used for dresses, shirts, blouses.

Wincyette Brushed woven cotton, suitable for nightwear.

Wool A wide variety of weaves and finishes. Choose New Wool fabrics if available – they are softer and easier to care for.

Fabric designs
When choosing patterned fabrics for children, avoid large splashy prints, big floral designs, strong geometric patterns, wide stripes and bold checks. Choose small motifs and simple patterns. Take the child's colour preferences into consideration – but do not be guided entirely by them.

Measuring for pattern sizes

A child's measurements will change quite quickly. Keep a small notebook with all of his measurements in it and check them before every sewing project. Once you have the measurements, choose patterns according to these, not to the age of the child. If you have to alter patterns, alter them in length rather than in width.

Measure a child in his underwear. If you are sewing for a baby who still wears a nappy, measure him over this.

Commercial paper patterns usually give the following measurements:
Breast (chest) Measure around the chest just under the shoulder blade.

Waist Measure where the waist goes in or where it should be. Get the child to bend sideways so that you can see where it is – then measure him upright.

Hip Measure around the buttocks over the fullest part.

Back waist Measure from the nape of the neck, down the back to the natural waist.

Length Dress length is measured from the nape down the back; skirt length from the natural waist and over the bottom. Trouser measurements on patterns are usually outside leg from waist to ankle with shoes on.

Other measurements to take

When you get the pattern home, measure it against the following body measurements, remembering that all paper patterns have ease built into them, so that the finished garment is comfortable to wear.

Neck Measure around the base of the neck. Add 12 mm ($\frac{1}{2}$ in) for ease.

Shoulder Measure from side of neck to end of shoulder.

Inside leg Measure from the crotch to the ankle.

Crotch Measure from back waist between legs to front waist and add 2.5 cm (1 in) for ease.

Stomach Measure just below the waist over the top or fullest part of the stomach.

Thighs On plump children you may need to measure around the upper thigh for fitting trousers.

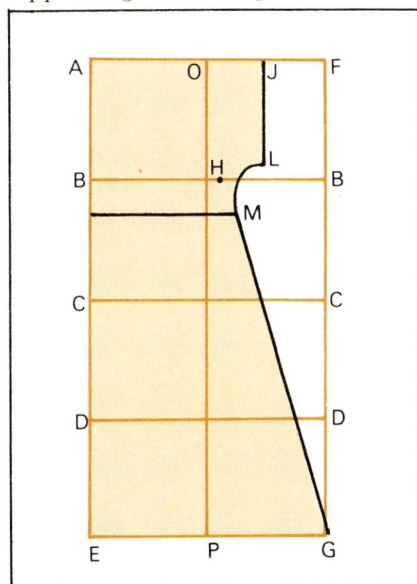

Fitting children

As far as possible, make alterations to the paper pattern rather than aiming to do a great deal at the fitting stage.

Having cut out the pattern, tack the pieces together. Do not use pins anywhere. Inevitably there will be a scratch and fitting sessions will become distressing for everybody.

To tack for fitting, fold one seam allowance under and lay the fold along the seam allowance of the matching piece. You will find it easy to snip tacking stitches and re-tack for fitting, working on the right side.

Hints on sewing

Generally, seams should be neatened and finished off, particularly if the garment is going to be laundered frequently. Use French seams on baby clothes so that there are no rough edges to chafe the skin. Bind the seams if fabric frays easily. Finish all hems off neatly and securely.

It is easy for shoe buckles to catch in hems so be sure they are closely stitched. Use sturdy zippers and plain washable buttons. Sew buttons on tightly and firmly. Make strong button loops if they are needed.

Always sew hanging loops into skirts and trousers so that they are easy to hang up. Iron-on tapes for easy hems and cuffs should be avoided on childrens' clothes; they will not last. Never use clear, nylon thread for hems or cuffs. The ends can become loose and scratch legs and wrists.

Drawing your own patterns

Although you can buy well-cut paper patterns almost everywhere, it is useful to be able to make your own simple paper patterns, especially for children's clothes. If you know the basic principles of pattern drafting, you will find it easier to alter patterns to fit, besides being able to take advantage of inexpensive fabric remnants or of

outgrown clothes, cutting them up to make new clothes for smaller children.

Tools and equipment

You do not have to invest in expensive equipment, but some things are essential. You need a fairly large flat surface to work on and some squared dressmaker's paper for drawing out patterns. You can use white shelf paper if you like, but you will have to use a set square to mark out an absolutely square graph. You will also need a long ruler, at least 60 cm (24 in) long, several HB pencils and a soft eraser. Invest in a drawing aid called 'French curve'. This is a piece of plastic with varying degrees of curve along its edges. It is a help when drawing armholes and similar curves. Have a pair of pencil compasses as well.

Magyar garment

This garment has sleeves cut in one with the bodice and no waist. It will make a simple dress, top or nightdress.

For this block pattern you need two measurements: the length of the intended garment from the nape of the neck to hem and the chest, taken under the child's arms.

Left Magyar pattern – steps 1-5.
Right Magyar pattern – step 6.

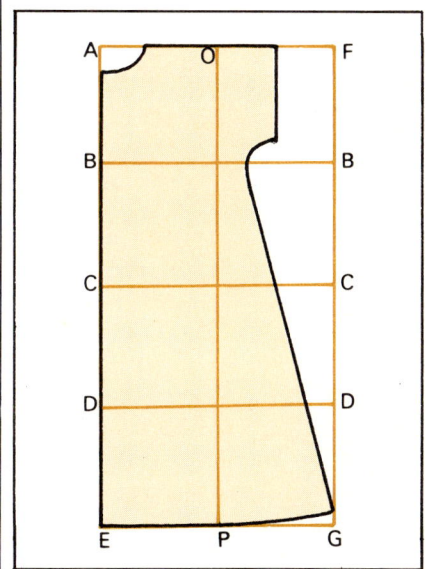

To determine the area of the pattern, draw a rectangle to the length of the garment by half the width. Divide the rectangle in half with a line vertically and in thirds with three lines horizontally to make eight squares.

1. Mark the points of the rectangle as shown.
2. Divide the chest measurement by 4 and add 2.5 cm (1 in) to the result. Draw a line to this length from point B. Mark the end H.
3. *Sleeve* From point F, mark a point halfway across line F–O, mark it J.
   Draw a line down from J, stopping about 12 mm ($\frac{1}{2}$ in) above the chest line B–H. Mark it L.
4. From the chestline B–H, measure and mark a line one-third of a square down. Draw the line to end 2.5 cm (1 in) beyond point H. Mark the end M.
5. Now draw a line lightly joining L and M. Draw it into a curve. Then join M to corner G. This is the side seam.
6. To curve the hem, mark a point a quarter-square up from corner G (g) and draw a curve from the side seam to the middle line (A–E) of the pattern.
7. *Neckline* Mark a point one-third of a square along on the line A–O. Mark the same distance down from A on the line A–B. Join the points lightly, then curve them for the front neck. Mark the back neck a little higher as shown in the diagram. If you prefer, you could draw the neckline as a 'V' neck or as a square neck.

Now you have drawn out the block pattern. To make the paper pattern which you will use, trace off the front of the garment with the lower neckline, marking line A–E as the centre front to be placed on the lengthwise fold of the fabric. Trace the block again for the back of the garment, marking the higher neckline, again marking line A–E as centre back, to be placed on the fold of the fabric. At this stage it is a good idea to add notches or balance marks on the paper pattern at shoulder seams and side seams, so that matching up pieces will be easier.

Cutting out

The paper pattern pieces for the maygar garment are pinned to doubled fabric in the usual way, laying centre front and centre back on the lengthwise fold of fabric. As you cut out, you add seam allowances and hem allowance. Children's clothes do not usually need much more than 9 mm ($\frac{3}{8}$ in) for seams unless the fabric is thick. Cut out 9 mm ($\frac{3}{8}$ in) from the pattern edge, and allow an extra 4 cm ($1\frac{1}{2}$ in) for the hem.

Extra pieces
When you are planning a garment made from your own block patterns, you must always think about the extra pieces of pattern which may be needed to make up the garment. You might, for instance, decide to face or to bind the neckline and sleeve ends with self fabric bias strips. You may want to add pockets or perhaps cuffs to a long sleeved nightgown. The pieces must be included on the block.

Adapting the block pattern
To make a roomier garment, a nightdress for example, a new line is added – the waistline. Measure the child from shoulder to waist – you might have to get a young child to bend sideways to find his waist. Draw the sleeve longer and the underarm seam deeper as shown. Extend the length of the pattern to the desired length of the nightdress. If you want to make the nightdress very full skirted, extend the length of the line E–G before joining the side seam to the sleeve and hem.

Pattern for Magyar garment: Step 7 with back and front neckline drawn in.

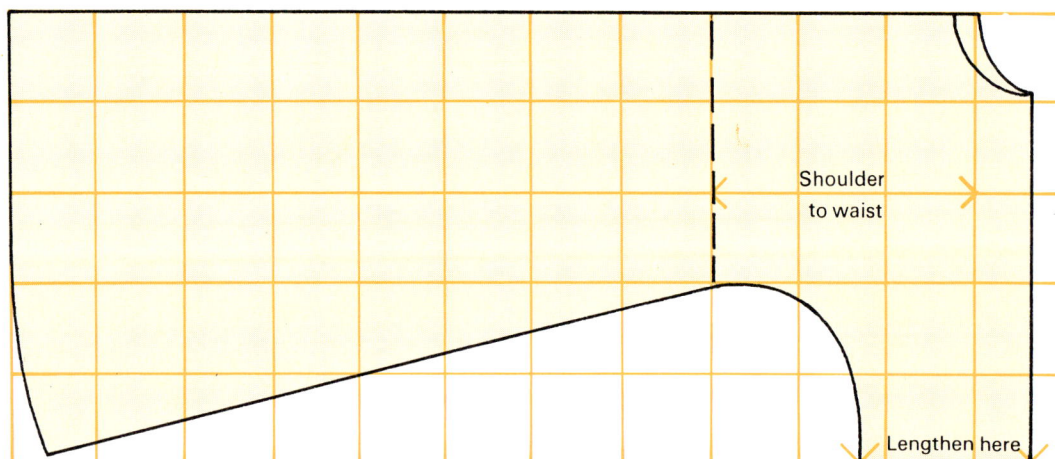

Shoulder to waist

Lengthen here

Children's patterns

In this section there are some basic patterns for young children, with chest sizes from 53 cm to 64 cm (21 in to 25 in). They are all easy clothes to make and require no detailed finish. There are also some ideas for adapting the patterns to make other clothes.

The patterns are given as graph patterns but you draw the grid to the size you want. To do this involves you in a little mathematics.

Each pattern has been reproduced smaller than life size and with a grid of squares over it. To enlarge the pattern, you have to produce a grid of squares and copy the lines of the pattern onto it.

To get a grid of the right size, you measure the child, either around the chest for tops and dresses, or around the waist for trousers and skirts. Using the popover on page 104 as an example, suppose your child has a chest of 53 cm (21 in). To this you would add the ease, in the popover this is 7.5 cm (3 in).

The pattern gives you half of the front and half of the back. Your chest measurement then has to be divided by 4 to get a quarter measurement – 15 cm (6 in).

You next divide the quarter measurement by the number of squares in the grid – 14 in the popover. The measurement you get is about 11 mm ($\frac{7}{16}$ in). Draw a grid of squares to this size and then copy the pattern onto your grid.

If the pattern needs any adjustment, you can make the pattern a little bigger on the seams, or smaller.

It is suggested that you draw your pattern out on thick paper to make a master pattern, and then trace off the patterns on tracing paper. Thus you can make any adaptations you like to the master pattern to suit the child's figure or make alterations to the style.

Popover

This is a sleeveless, scoop necked garment which can be made up as a cool summer pinafore dress or as a popover to wear over a blouse or jumper. It has a back zipper. On the pattern you will also see a dotted line for a higher neckline to make a more classic dress.

Suitable for children with a chest measurement of 51 cm to 53 cm (20 in to 23 in). The ease is 7.5 cm (3 in) across the chest measurement.

Fabrics requirements

You will need between 1.20 cm (for the smallest size) and 1.30 cm (for the largest size) of 90 cm wide fabric ($1\frac{1}{4}$ yd to $1\frac{1}{2}$ yd of 36 in wide fabric).

Notions 30 cm (12 in) zipper.
Binding for the neckline and sleeves. This could be ribbon, braid, bias binding or bias cut strips of the same or contrast fabric.

Making the Popover

1 Draw up the pattern and cut two backs and one front, allowing 12 mm ($\frac{1}{2}$ in) seam allowance on all edges except armholes and neckline. Transfer all markings.
2 Staystitch the front neck and back necks.
3 Join the shoulder seams.
4 Join the back seam up to the dot for the zipper.
5 Put in the zipper.
6 Join the side seams.
7 Bind the neckline, neaten the edges and sew on a hook and eye.
8 Bind the armholes making the join under the arm.
9 Take up the hem.

References   Zipper insertion
Hooks and eyes
Staystitching
Hems

Alternative styles from the pattern

The alternative neckline enables you to make a high-necked style, in which case you will need a slightly longer zipper.

A bought collar could be slipstitched to the bound neckline,

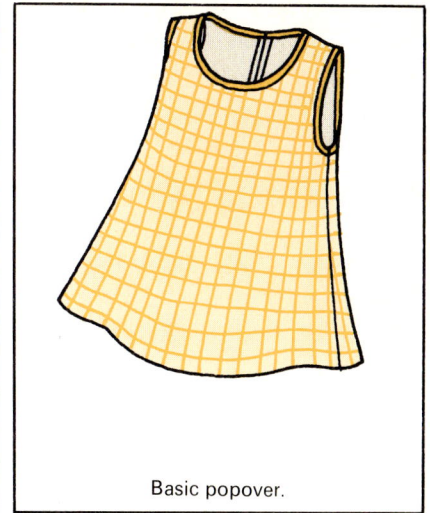
Basic popover.

Popover with pockets and trim.

High-necked popover with skirt.

and small patch pockets could be applied to the skirt front. A small girl could have a trim of broderie anglaise on the hem.

For playwear, leave the side seams open for about 10 cm (4 in), round off the seam edges and bind with matching braid.

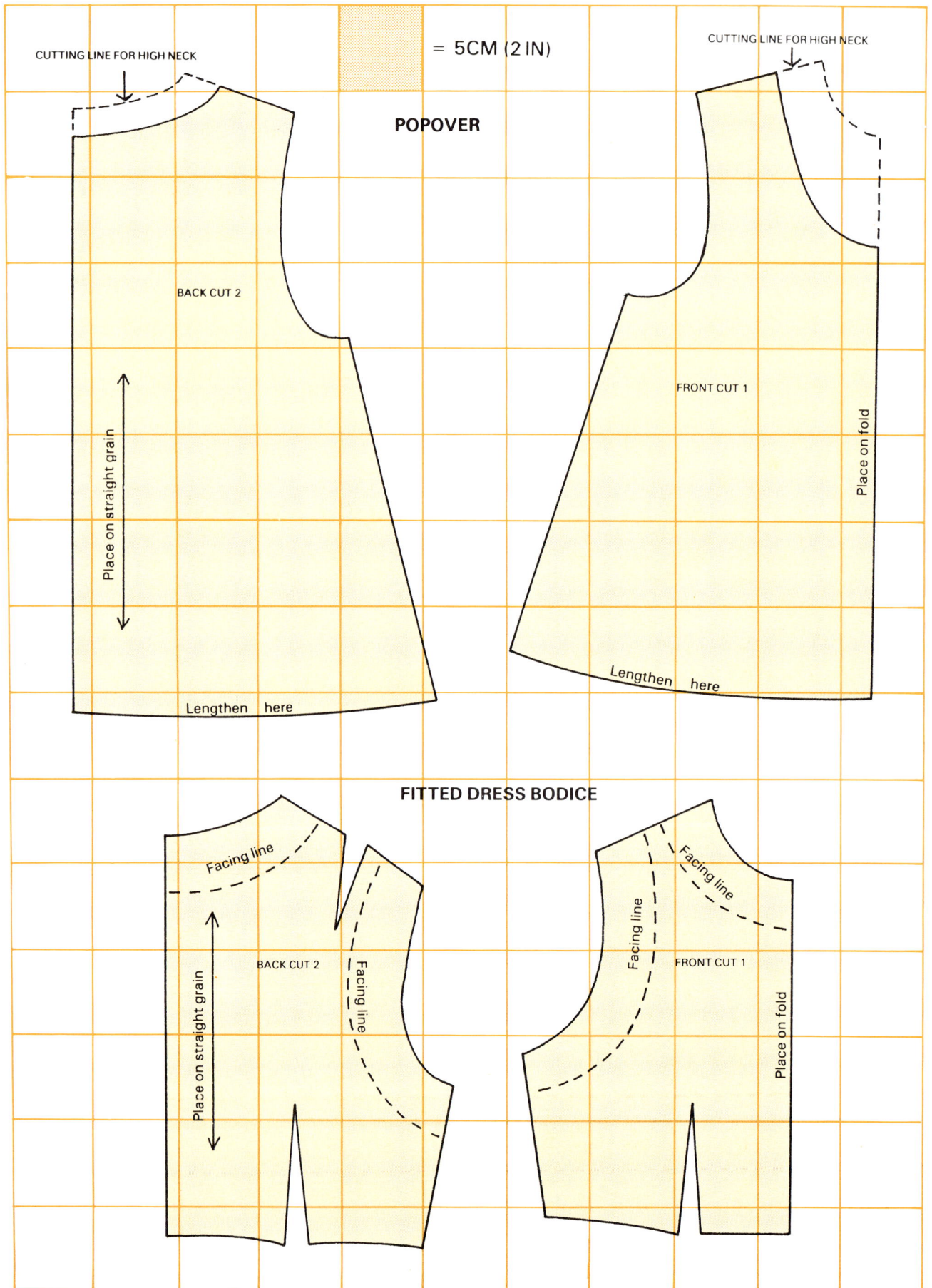

Dressmaking for children

CUTTING LINE FOR HIGH NECK

= 5CM (2 IN)

POPOVER

CUTTING LINE FOR HIGH NECK

BACK CUT 2

Place on straight grain

Lengthen here

FRONT CUT 1

Place on fold

Lengthen here

FITTED DRESS BODICE

Facing line

BACK CUT 2

Facing line

Place on straight grain

Facing line

Facing line

FRONT CUT 1

Facing line

Place on fold

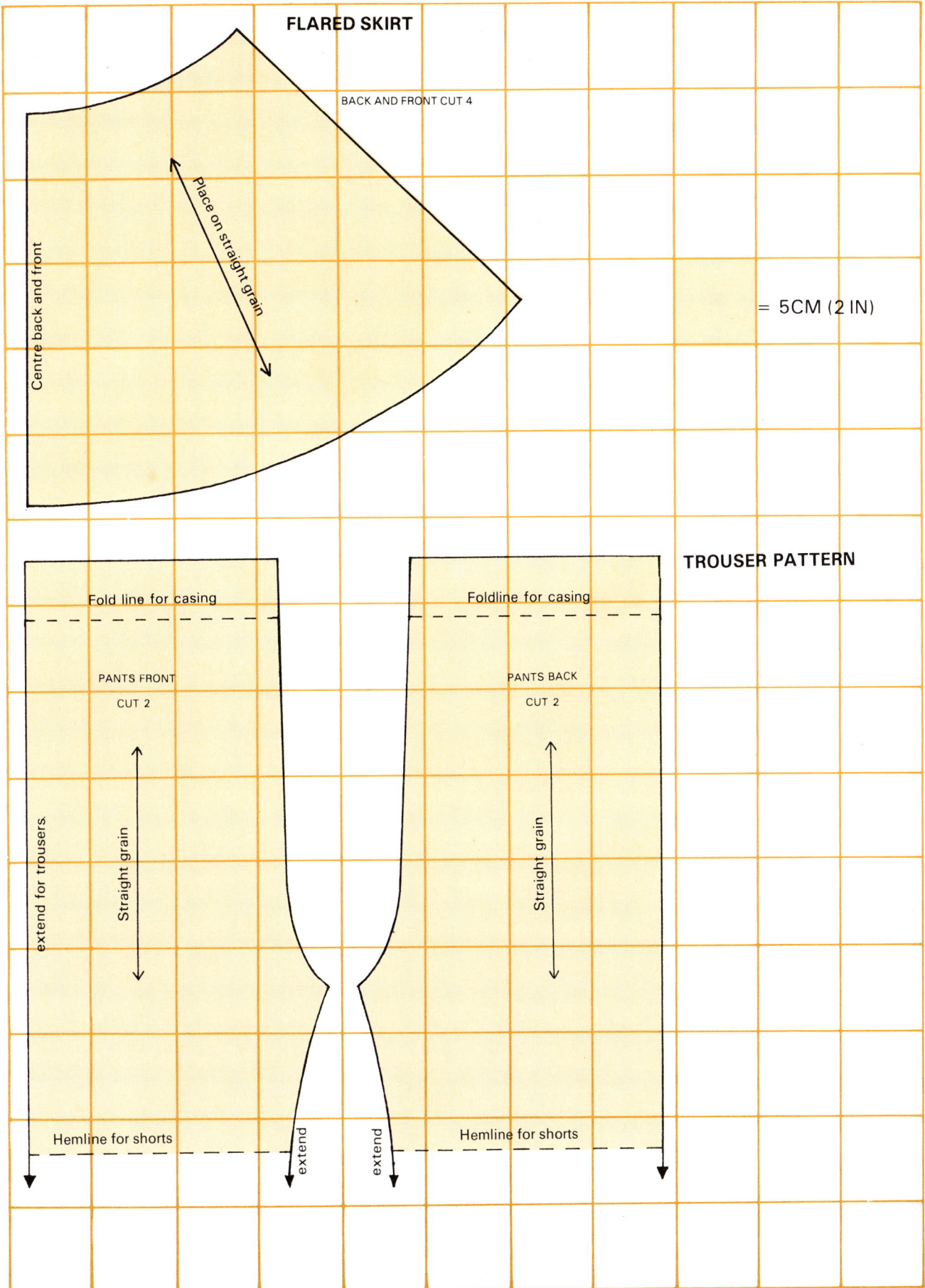

FLARED SKIRT

BACK AND FRONT CUT 4

Place on straight grain

Centre back and front

= 5CM (2 IN)

TROUSER PATTERN

Fold line for casing

PANTS FRONT

CUT 2

extend for trousers.

Straight grain

Hemline for shorts

extend

Foldline for casing

PANTS BACK

CUT 2

Straight grain

extend

Hemline for shorts

Cut the top a little shorter for a playtime top to wear with trousers.

The top of the popover can be cut off under the armholes to make a sleeveless yoke for a gathered skirt.

Fitted dress bodice.

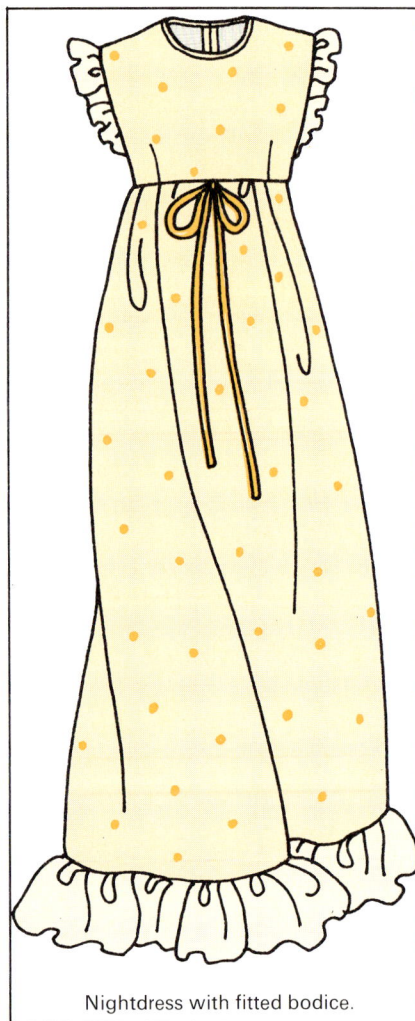

Nightdress with fitted bodice.

Fitted dress bodice

This is a useful pattern for any needlewoman who likes to make pretty little summer dresses. It is designed for girls with a chest measurement of 53 cm to 64 cm (21 in to 25 in). The bodice only is given here. On the next page there is a skirt pattern which can be used with the bodice to make a waisted dress. Alternatively, a simple gathered skirt can be attached to the bodice. The bodice has 7.5 cm (3 in) ease at the chest.

Fabric requirements

The bodice takes just under 45 cm of 90 cm wide fabric ($\frac{1}{2}$ yd of 36 in wide fabric). If you were adding a gathered skirt, you would need another 45 cm ($\frac{1}{2}$ yd).

Notions The bodice has a back zipper which should be measured from the nape of the neck to about 7.5 cm (3 in) below the natural waist.

You will also need a hook and eye.

Making the dress

1 Draw up the pattern to size and cut out two backs and one front, with 12 mm ($\frac{1}{2}$ in) seam allowance all round. Transfer all markings.
2 Staystitch the neck edges on back and front pieces.
3 Make the darts on the front and on the back.
4 Stitch bodice front to back at side seams.
5 Make up the skirt with a back seam and side seams. Leave the back seam open 7.5 cm (3 in) at the waist edge for the back zipper.
6 Tack the skirt to the bodice waist. Matching side seams.
7. Machine stitch the waist seam in one action. Insert the zipper.
8 Either bind the neckline and armholes or cut facings from the dotted line on the pattern. For a party dress, trim armholes with a gathered frill. Remember to add seam allowances to the facings so that you can join them. Cut facings on the bias of the fabric.

Apply the facings and finish the edges.
9 Put on hooks and eyes for the back neck.
10 Take up the hem.

References   Staystitching
Darts
Gathering
Zipper
Facings
Hems

Alternative styles from the pattern

This dress will make a short school dress or a long party dress.

The front bodice can be trimmed with ribbon, braids or lace appliqué.

The bound neckline can have a bought collar attached, which could be matched with a wide binding on the armholes.

To make a summer nightdress, cut the bodice shorter – about 5 cm (2 in) under the armholes. Make a long or short gathered skirt to the gown. Finish the back opening with a narrow bound edge and a tie at the back of the neck.

Flared skirt

This pattern can be matched up with the bodice on the previous page or made up as a simple flared skirt. The pattern is in four pieces so the zipper can be at centre back (as for the dress) or on the side for a skirt.

Cut the skirt to any length desired, short for a play skirt or a sports skirt, longer for party wear. Notice that the pattern is cut on the cross of the fabric. The ease on this garment is 2.5 cm (1 in) at the waist.

Fabric requirements

You will need about 45 cm of 90 cm ($\frac{1}{2}$ yd of 36 in) wide fabric for the skirt.

Notions Iron-on waistband interfacing, 10 cm (4 in) zipper. Hooks and eyes.

Two types of flared skirt.

Making the skirt

1 Make two patterns from the grid pattern to size, one for the front, one for the back.
2 Cut out on doubled fabric to make two fronts, two backs, adding 12 mm ($\frac{1}{2}$ in) seam allowance all round.
3 Stitch centre front seam and then the centre back seam.
4 Stitch side seams leaving 10 cm (4 in) open for the zipper on the skirt's left side.
5 Insert the zipper.
6 Cut a strip of fabric 6 cm ($2\frac{1}{2}$ in) wide by the child's waist measurement plus 3.5 cm ($1\frac{1}{2}$ in). Make up a waistband, ironing the interfacing to the wrong side of the waistband.
7 Stitch the waistband to the skirt, overlapping the end and sew on a hook and eye fastening.
8 Take up the hem.

References Zipper
Applying a waistband
Hooks and eyes
Hems

Alternative styles from the pattern

The skirt could have patch pockets applied to the front.

For a peasant-style skirt, make the skirt in a patterned cotton and add a doubled frill at the hem.

Add shoulder straps to the skirt

and make the zipper opening at centre back.

Trousers

This trouser pattern is for children with waist measurements from 51 cm to 56 cm (20 in to 22 in). The trousers have an elastic casing waistline and could be made in all kinds of soft, stretchy fabrics as well as hard-wearing cotton or denim.

The trousers could be worn with the popover top for an outfit.

The pattern is suitable for both boys and girls.

The waist of the trouser pattern is 61 cm (24 in), so 2.5 cm (1 in) ease allowance would be sufficient at the waist.

Fabric requirements

You will need about 1.10 cm ($1\frac{1}{4}$ yd) for the smallest size in 90 cm (36 in) wide fabric and 1.40 cm ($1\frac{1}{2}$ yd) for the largest size, depending on the trouser length. Cut the pattern and then measure for more accurate fabric quantities.

Notions 2 cm ($\frac{3}{4}$ in) wide elastic to fit the waist.

Making the trousers

1 Draw up the patterns and cut two fronts and two backs adding 12 mm ($\frac{1}{2}$ in) seam allowance on all edges except the waist edge.
2 Stitch the front pieces together.
3 Stitch the back pieces together.
4 Seam the back to the front at the side seams.
5 Press and tack a 6 mm ($\frac{1}{4}$ in) turning on the waist edge.
6 Turn on the fold line (marked with a dotted line on the pattern). Tack and then machine stitch on the fold and again on the edge of the casing, leaving a gap in the seam for inserting elastic.
7 Insert elastic, using a safety pin to pull it through the casing. Overlap the ends and machine stitch.
8 Take up hems.

References Casings
Elastic insertions
Hems

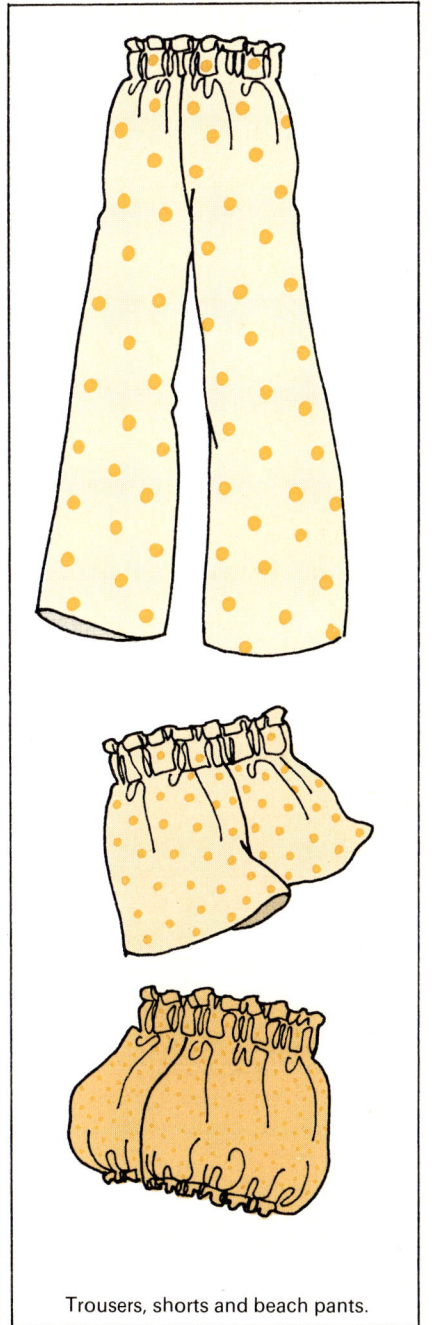

Trousers, shorts and beach pants.

Alternative styles from the pattern

Cut the pattern with an extra seam allowance – up to 2.5 cm (1 in) – and use the pattern for making pyjama trousers. Cut the popover top larger for a pyjama top.

Cut the trouser pattern short for a pair of summer shorts for either a boy or a girl.

For beach pants for a girl, cut the legs really short and make casings for narrow elastic at the leg hems.

Poncho

Warm poncho or party shawl

Both little girls and little boys will wear warm ponchos if the fabric is carefully chosen; soft wool or mohair are recommended. This pattern can also be used to make a towelling beach wrap, so that a child can dress and undress on the beach.

To make the pattern, have the child stand straight, with his arms at his sides. Measure from the wrist, up the arm, across the back, down the other arm to the wrist.

Cut a square of pattern paper to this size. Draw a line diagonally from corner to corner. Fold the paper in half along this line. Bring the two furthest corners together and fold in half again. The 90° angle is the exact centre of the square, and where the neckhole will be positioned.

Measure across the childs' neck and divide this measurement in half, then add 2.5 cm (1 in). Measure and mark this distance on both sides, from the neckhole corner. Put the edge of a plate over the corner and against these marks, then trace a curve around the plate edge. Cut away the corner for the neckhole. Slash the pattern from one corner to the hole.

Measure the pattern to ascertain how much fabric you need. If necessary, you could make the poncho in two pieces with a diagonal seam.

Notions The poncho could be made of double fabric or lined with a smooth contrast fabric. Trim the edges with braid or bias binding.

The edge could also be trimmed with bought fringing.

Making the poncho

1 Machine stitch the seam to within 10 cm (4 in) of the neckline.
2 Bind the neck edge and the neck opening with one continuous binding.
3 Sew a ribbon loop on one side of the neckline and a button on the other. Alternatively, bind the neckline and then the neckline opening separately, leaving long ends on the neckline for a tie.
4 Stitch fringing around the hem or bind the edges to match the neck binding.

Shawl for a party

Little girls often need a lightweight and pretty shawl to go over a party dress so that they do not have to wear a school coat. Cut a square of lightweight fabric from the same pattern. Do not cut the neck hole or the front seam.

Cut strips of fabric 12.5 cm (5 in) wide and join ends to make a strip

You could use the same method of measurement taking to make an adult-size poncho.

Shawl

long enough to go around two sides of the square, gathered. Fold the strip, wrong sides together and gather the raw edges and the short ends. Pin the gathered strip along two adjacent sides of the square on the right side, matching raw edges.

Fold the square diagonally so that the frill is sandwiched. Pin and tack along both sides. Machine stitch, leaving about 10 cm (4 in) in the middle of one side for an opening to turn to the right side. Turn right side out and finish off the open seam with small slip stitches. The shawl can be worn simply wrapped across or tied in front.

Christening robe

The bodice pattern and sleeve pattern only are given because the skirt of the robe is just two straight pieces, shaped under the arms and gathered onto the bodice.

Choose a very soft, lightweight fabric for the robe, one that is comfortable to a baby's skin and gathers easily.

Fabric requirements
You will need about 1.40 m (1½ yd) of material for the underskirt, and the same quantity of soft silk net for the over dress.

Notions Lace edging, lace appliqué trim, narrow white ribbon and 3 small buttons.

Making the robe
1 Cut two yoke pattern pieces, one for the front yoke and one for the back.
2 Cut the front yoke on the fold of fabric, adding 9 mm (⅜ in) seam allowance all round.
3 Cut out two back pieces with the same seam allowance plus an extra 9 mm (⅜ in) at centre back for a opening facing.
4 Cut the two under skirt panels to 60 cm × 75 cm (26 in × 30 in) wide. Cut two panels of net 10 cm (4 in) longer. Cut 2 sleeves with 9 mm (⅜ in) seam allowance all round.

6 Using the same patterns, cut the yoke and sleeves from net. Mount the net on the under fabric with diagonal basting, then work as one layer of fabric.
7 Join the shoulder seams with a French seam. Turn the opening allowance on centre backs with a narrow hem and then turn again to neaten hemstitch. The back opening edges overlap about 3 mm (⅛ in).
8 Bind the neck edge with bias cut self fabric. Make a thread loop at neck for a button.
9 Gather up the sleeve heads, leaving about 3.5 cm (1½ in) ungathered at each end.
10 Sew the gathered part into the armhole of the bodice with a French seam.
11 Sew the two side seams of the skirt panels. Sew the side seams of the two net skirt panels. Make a slit 15 cm (6 in) long down the centre back of the skirt and turn a tiny doubled hem. Hemstitch. Do the same with the net overskirt.

Cut the corners from the skirt panels diagonally about 3.7 cm (1½ in).
12 Put the net overskirt on the underskirt and gather up along the waist edge leaving the diagonally cut corners.
13 Attach the skirt to the bodice from the diagonal corners which

now become the underarm seam of the sleeves. Top stitch the waist seam.
14 Finish off the underarm seams. Gather the sleeve edges, bind, and trim with lace.
15 Trim the neckline with lace. Shell-edge the underskirt hem and trim with lace.
16 Turn a doubled hem on the net overskirt and hem. Trim with appliqué lace. Make two more thread loops at back opening. Sew on buttons.

Finish the robe with a rosette of ribbons at front waist, leaving long ribbon ends.

References Binding edges
French seams
Mounting fabric
Shell edging
Gathering
Thread loops
Tucks
Appliqué lace

Alternative styles from the pattern
The yoke of the dress can be tucked by hand. Make the yoke pattern and then cut it into strips 18 mm (¾ in) wide. Pin and then tape tissue paper behind the strips spacing them 12 mm (½ in) apart. Cut the pattern from this widened pattern. Cut the fabric. Make tiny 6 mm

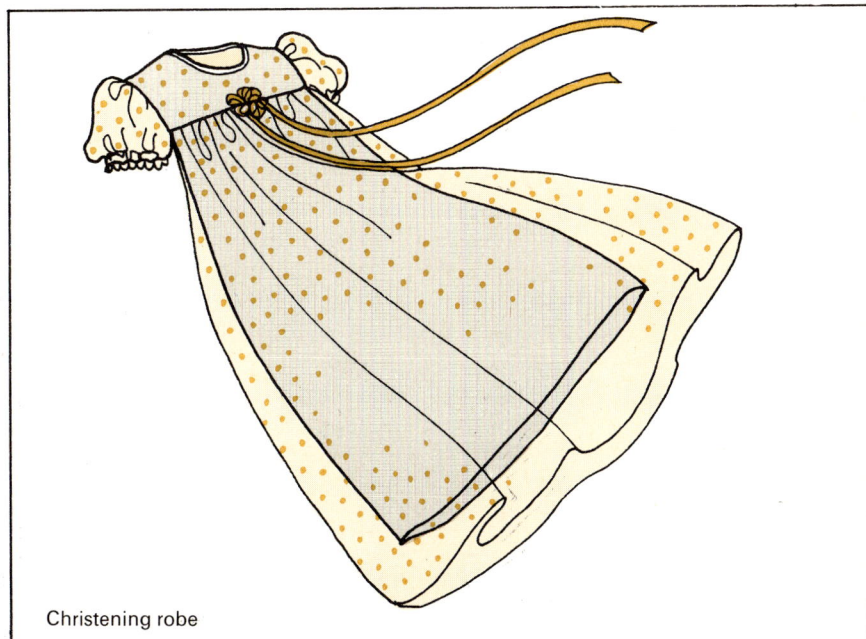
Christening robe

Dressmaking for children

($\frac{1}{4}$ in) tucks in the fabric across the yoke, turning towards the sleeves from the centre front. Insert narrow lace under each tuck for prettiness. Stitch tucks with prick stitch or running stitch.

Baby gown

This raglan sleeved gown is for a new baby and can be used to make a sleeping gown, a sleeping bag or an angel top.

Use soft, fleecy fabric for the sleeping bag, soft cotton and wool mixture for the nightgown. Angel tops can be made of pretty lightweight cottons.

Cut the nightgown pieces 64 cm (25 in) long. Cut the gown back piece 87 cm (34 in) long for the sleeping bag. The dotted line on the pattern is for the dress or angel top. Cut the dress a little shorter for a boy and make a pair of matching elastic-legged pants. Cut the dress sleeves shorter on the dotted line.

Fabric requirements

You will need approximately 60 cm (24 in) of 90 cm (36 in) wide fabric for the dress, 1.10 m ($1\frac{1}{4}$ yd) for the nightdress, 1.40 m ($1\frac{1}{2}$ yd) for the sleeping bag.

Notions You will also need some narrow elastic for the wrist finish, three buttons for the sleeping bag. Tape for the nightgown.

1 Cut two backs and one front on the fold.
2 Cut two sleeves. Seam allowances 9 mm ($\frac{3}{8}$ in) to be added to all seams.
3 Stitch the front to the backs on the side seams.
4 Stitch the underarm sleeve seam.
5 Turn a narrow hem on the sleeve edge and then turn again to make a casing. Insert elastic.
6 Insert the sleeves into the gown.
7 Sew the centre back seam up to the beginning of the facing fold.
8 Turn in the facing fold and hem stitch.
9 Gather up the neck edge and bind with self bias-cut fabric.
10 Make thread loops and sew on buttons for the angel top back opening.
11 Alternatively, trim the neck with self fabric binding to make a casing for tape insertion for a drawstring neck. After gathering the neck, apply one edge of bias strip cut to 31 mm ($1\frac{1}{4}$ in) wide. Trim the seam allowance of the gathered edge and handsew the bias trim in place on the inside of

Top left: The basic baby gown.
Bottom left: Shortened gown with pants.

By lengthening the back pattern piece you can make a sleeping gown from the baby gown pattern.

the garment. Fold in the open ends of the casing and hem. Insert tape on a safety pin. Hem the tape ends.

12 Turn up and finish the hem of the dress and gown.

13 For the sleeping bag, fold up the end of the bag back onto the front. Mark where the hemmed edge falls on the bag with pins. Turn in the sides and bottom and hand sew a hem. Make machine stitched buttonholes and sew on three buttons to match.

References Binding
Inserting elastic and tape
Machine-made buttonholes

Alternative styles from the pattern

The nightgown pattern could be used to make a very pretty and

simple christening robe, using a dotted swiss cotton or lawn. Gather the cuffs into a bias-cut binding instead of elastic and perhaps embroider the front of the gown with tiny flowers in white satin stitch. The front of the gown might also have a small panel of smocking to take up the fullness. Stitch three rows of lace around the hem, 7.5 cm (3 in) apart.

Bib or feeder pattern

If you are making a gown for a new baby, add a feeder bib for good measure. The pattern is a simple shape. Make it from doubled towelling or towelling mounted on thin plastic sheeting.

1 Cut a pattern for the bib shape.
2 Cut it out twice in towelling or once in towelling and again in plastic sheeting.
3 Tack the two layers together around the edges, wrong sides facing.

4 Bind the outer edge of the feeder with washable binding.
5 Cut a length of binding for the neckline and ties. Pin the middle of the binding to the middle of the neck edge. Stitch the binding to the neck and then hem the tie ends.

Babydress pattern

This pattern is for babies of about 12 months old but it could be made larger for babies 6 months older, or a month or two younger by adding to or decreasing at the seam edges. Make the garment in cotton or thin fabrics for a summer dress, in a washable fabric for a popover pinafore or in a soft Viyella fabric for a warm, winter overdress.

The pattern could also be used to make a pretty petticoat to wear under a semi-sheer dress.

Fabric requirements

You will need 90 cm (36 in) square piece of fabric for the overdress or pinafore, slightly less for a petticoat. Add extra fabric for a self frill on a summer dress hem.

Notions Button for back neck fastening, bias trim; lace trim for neck and sleeves.

1 Cut a pattern for back and front.
2 Cut one front on the fold. Cut two backs.
3 Cut bias strips for binding edges if required.
4 Staystitch the front and back neck edges.
5 Stitch the centre back seam to within 10 cm (4 in) of the neck.
6 Turn a narrow hem on the back neck opening and machine stitch.
7 Join front to back at shoulders and side seams.
8 Bind the neck edge and the armholes.
9 Make a button loop at the back neck edge and sew on a button to correspond.
10 Turn up the hem.

References Staystitching
Thread loop
Binding raw edges

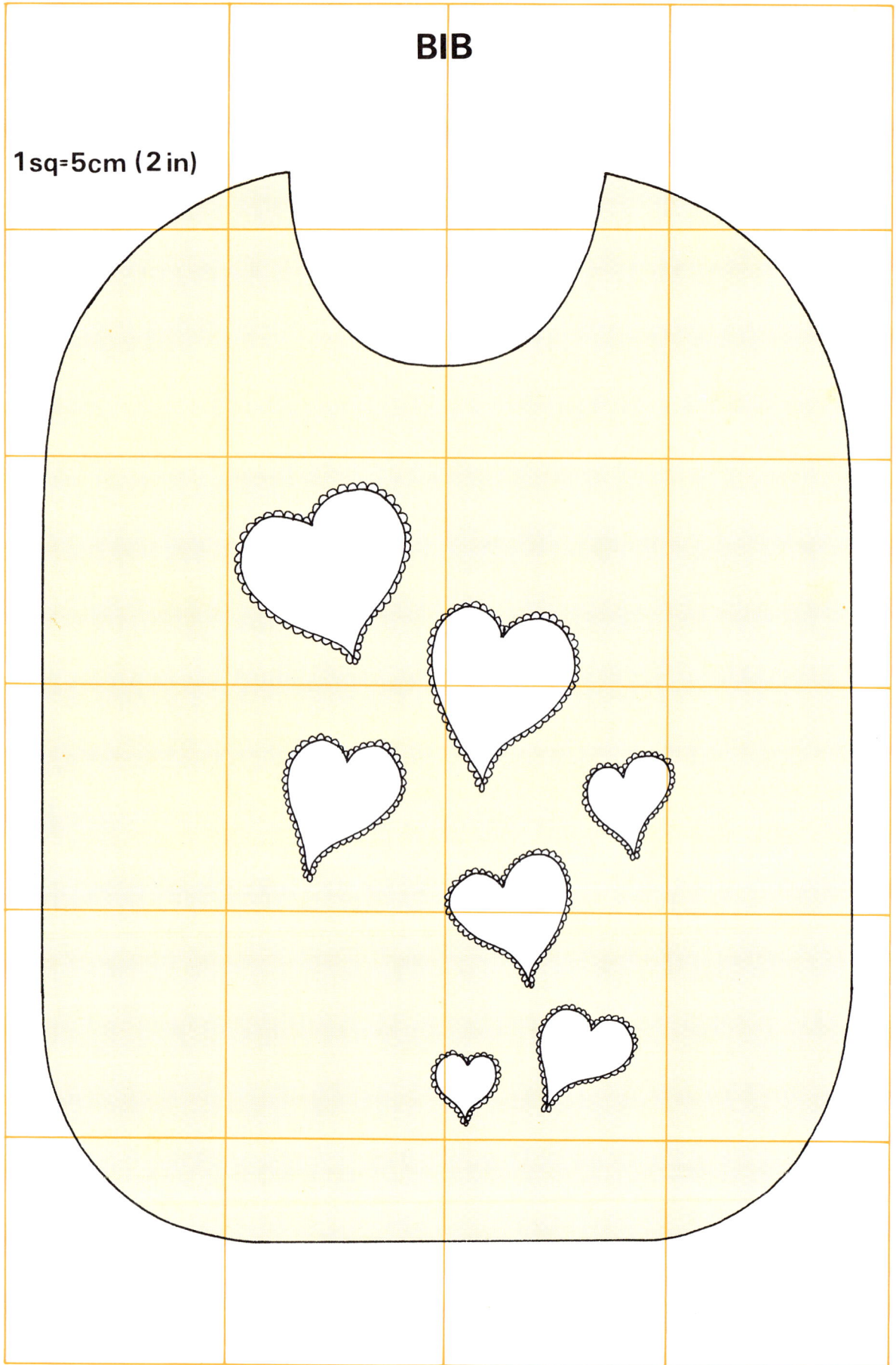

BIB

1sq=5cm (2 in)

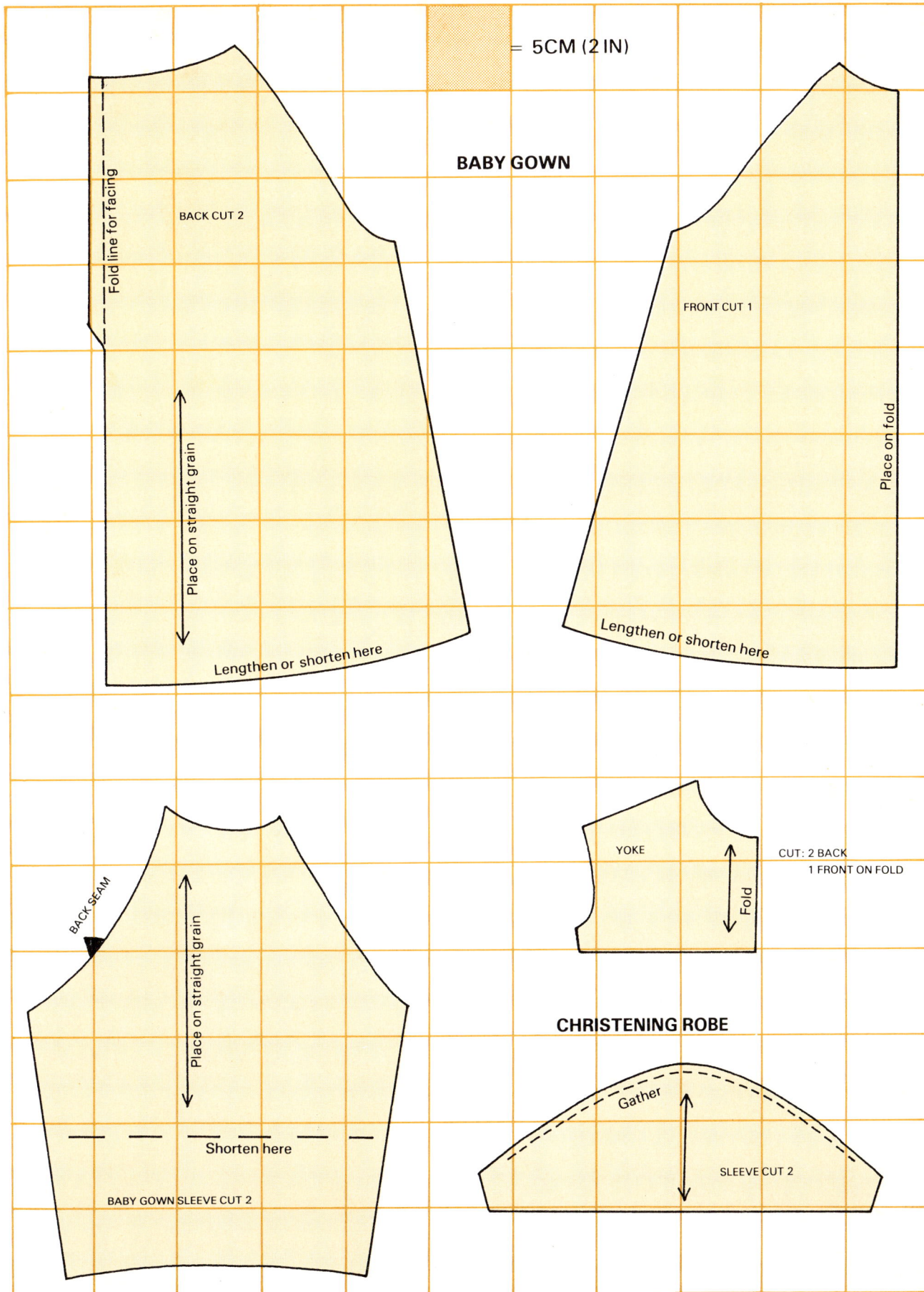

= 5CM (2 IN)

BABY GOWN

BACK CUT 2

Fold line for facing

Place on straight grain

Lengthen or shorten here

FRONT CUT 1

Place on fold

Lengthen or shorten here

BACK SEAM

Place on straight grain

Shorten here

BABY GOWN SLEEVE CUT 2

YOKE

CUT: 2 BACK
1 FRONT ON FOLD

Fold

CHRISTENING ROBE

Gather

SLEEVE CUT 2

113

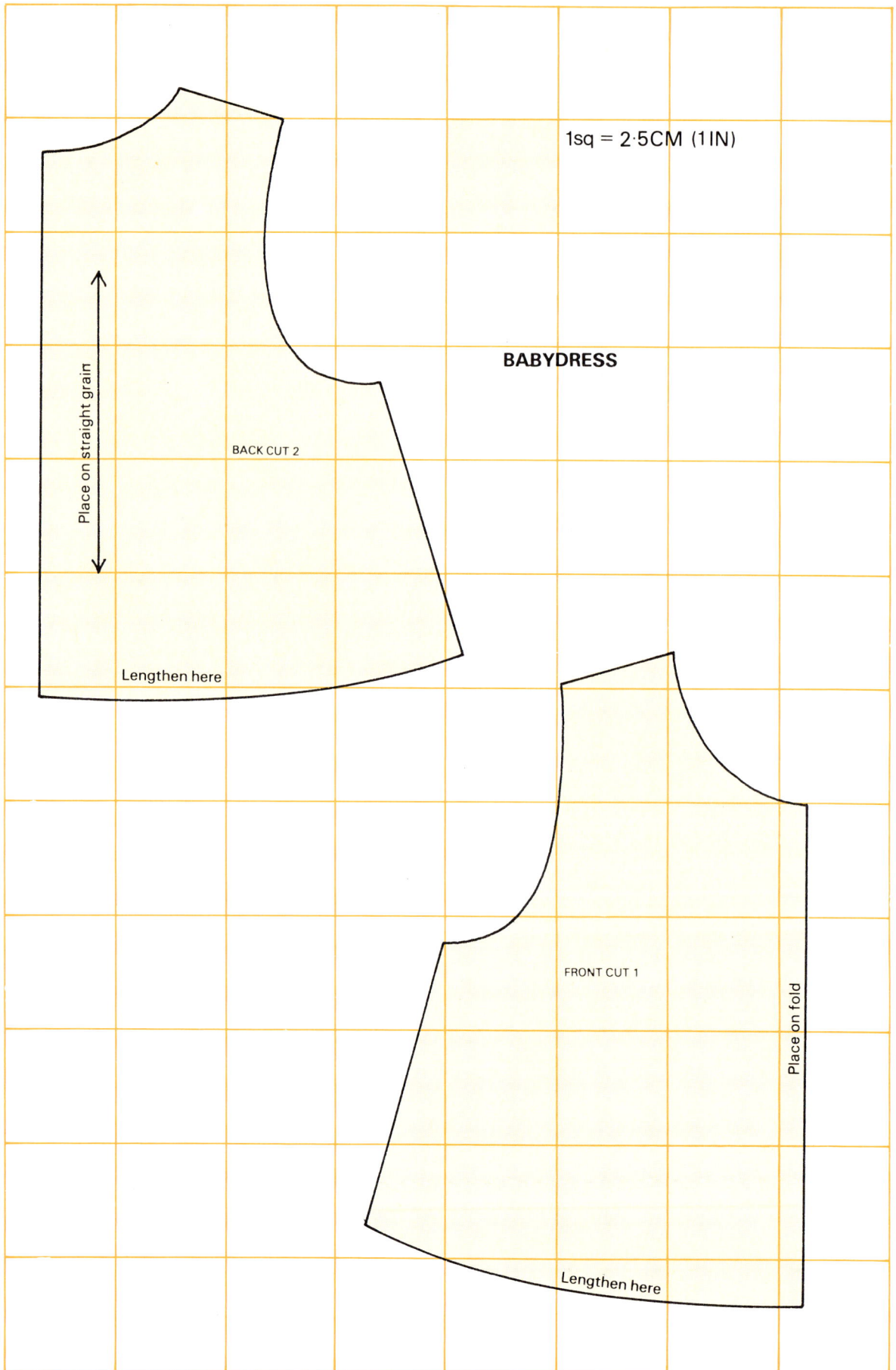

1sq = 2·5CM (1IN)

BABYDRESS

Place on straight grain

BACK CUT 2

Lengthen here

FRONT CUT 1

Place on fold

Lengthen here

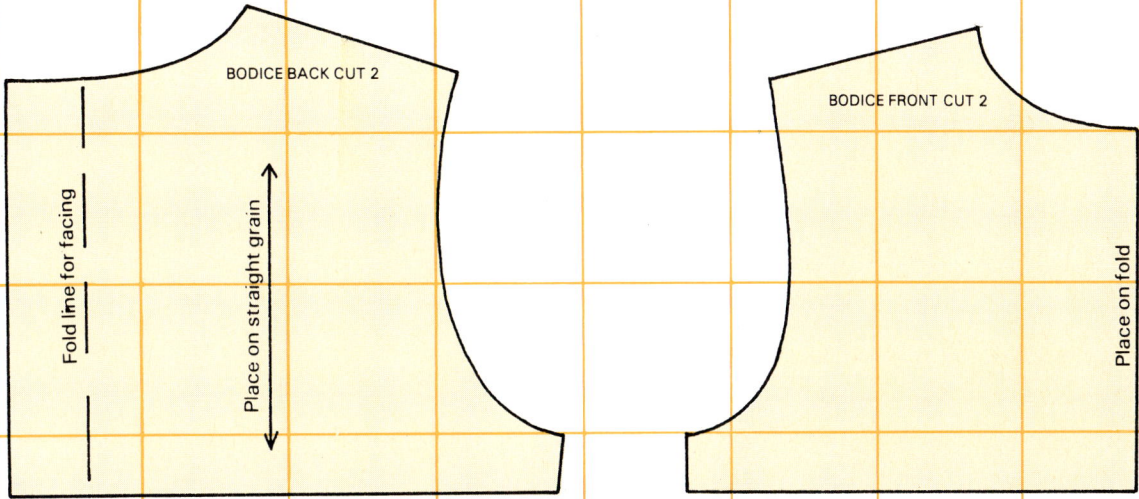

SUMMER DRESS

BODICE BACK CUT 2

Fold line for facing

Place on straight grain

BODICE FRONT CUT 2

Place on fold

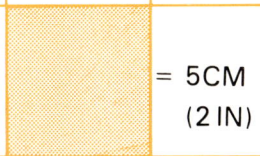

= 5CM
(2 IN)

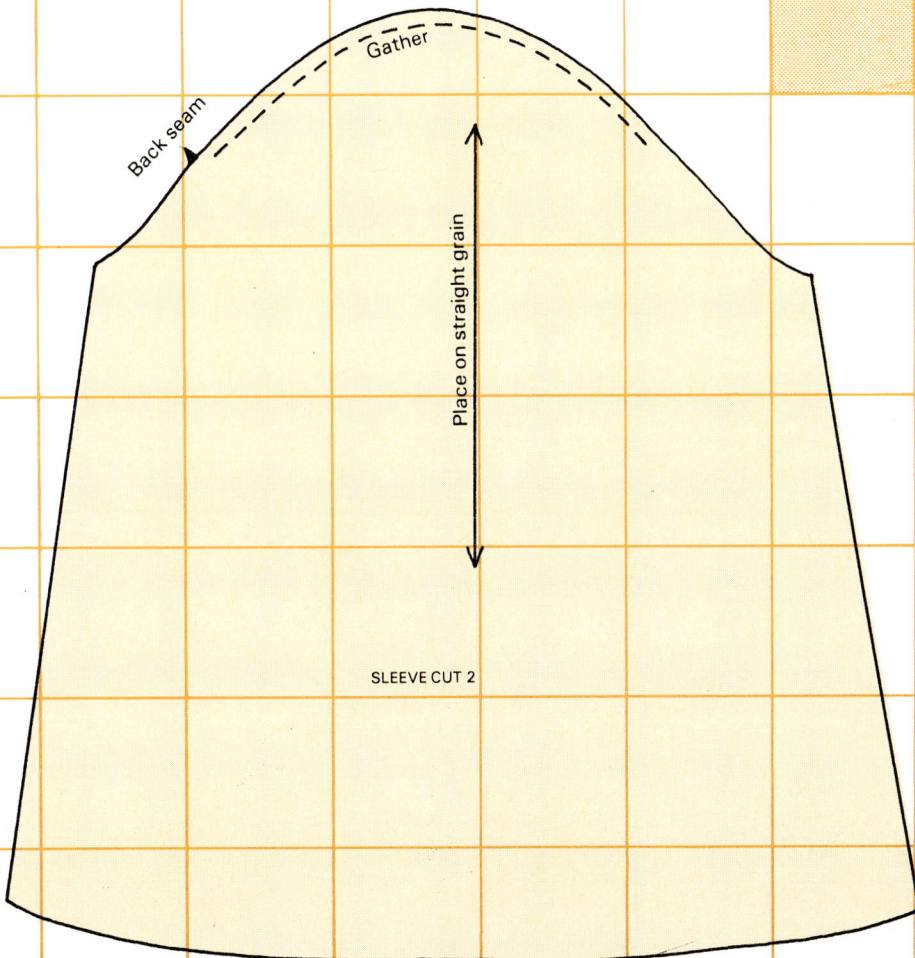

Gather

Back seam

Place on straight grain

SLEEVE CUT 2

Babydress

Alternative styles from the pattern

Make the petticoat of fine lawn or fine Tricel jersey; trim the armholes, neckline and hem with narrow lace. The petticoat hem could also be embroidered with rosebuds and finished with shell-edging.

Make a self fabric frill for a summer dress or trim with bought broderie anglaise. Cut a frill with tapered ends for the armholes to make a party popover. Finish the neckline with bias binding and then make a small bias bow for the front neck.

Cut the pattern into six or eight strips and insert 18 mm ($\frac{3}{4}$ in) wide strips of paper to make the pattern suitable for tucking. Tuck from the shoulder down the front for about 15 cm (6 in).

Summer dress for a baby

This is a pretty pattern to make for a little girl about 18 months old. A sleeve pattern is also given so that you can make a warmer dress for cool weather.

Fabric requirements

You will need about 1.30 m ($1\frac{1}{4}$ yds) for the summer dress and about 1.40 m ($1\frac{1}{2}$ yds) for the winter dress.
1 Cut out two bodice backs and one bodice front on the fold of fabric. Add a seam allowance of 12 mm ($\frac{1}{2}$ in) all round.
2 Staystitch the front and back necks.
3 Join the shoulder seams.
4 Turn a narrow hem on the centre back edges and machine stitch a hem. Turn again on the fold line (marked in a dotted line on the pattern) and press. Make three machine stitched buttonholes on the back, the top about 12 mm ($\frac{1}{2}$ in) from the neck edge and the bottom 2.5 cm (1 in) from the bottom of the bodice edge. Position them about 9 mm ($\frac{3}{8}$ in) in from the opening edge.
5 Bind the neckline of the dress.

6 Cut two pieces for the skirt front and two for the back, 62.5 cm × 33 cm (25 in × 13 in). Join the front seam. Join the centre back edges with a seam 2.5 cm (1 in) wide and leave the top end open for about 7.5 cm (3 in).
7 Gather the top edge of the skirt front and the skirt back.
8 Pull up the gathers so that the skirt front and back fits the bodice. Stitch in place. Join the underarm seam and the skirt side seam in one stitching.
9 Bind the armholes.
10 Sew on buttons so that the back opening overlaps and the buttons match the buttonholes.
11 For the frill, cut two strips of fabric 45 cm (18 in) long. Finish three raw edges with a machined hem, gather remaining on long raw edge. Top stitch the frill from the front waist to back waist, placing the gathered edge exactly halfway across the shoulder. Apply the frill by laying it wrong side to right side of fabric. Cover the stitching with a strip of ribbon or braid, hemming it to the dress on both edges.

Dress with sleeves

12 Cut two sleeves. Join the underarm seams. Gather the sleeve heads and insert into the armhole at stage 8 above.
13 Turn a hem on the cuff edge for a casing and insert elastic. Alternatively, gather the cuff into a self-fabric bias binding cuff edge.
14 Take up the hem.

References   Buttonholes
Bias binding
Gathering
Elastic casing
Gathered cuffs into binding
Hems

Top Babydress with tucks.
Middle and bottom Variations on the summer dress.

Renovating children's clothes

If you sew for children you can plan ahead to give their clothes a longer life. Make extra wide seams, particularly at the waistline of dresses and in side seams. Give dresses and trousers deep hems and make deeper cuff hems so that you can let down to lengthen them later. Always reserve at least $\frac{1}{2}$ m ($\frac{1}{2}$ yd) of the fabric after sewing a garment and occasionally launder it with the garment so that colours fade a little.

Letting down hems

If a worn line shows when a hem has been let down, stitch a length of braid or ribbon trim along the line.

Unpick the hem and press it carefully to remove the old crease entirely. On sleeves and trouser cuffs, make sure you do not press over the seam and thus mark the fabric. Unless the hem allowance is very deep, you should make a false hem so that the hem hangs properly when it has been let down.

False hems and cuffs

Ideally, the false hem facing should be the same fabric as the garment. If this is not possible, choose a plain fabric of about the same weight or lighter and as close in colour as possible. Cut the facing on the same grain as the garment hem and make seams to correspond with those of the garment.

With right sides together, tack and stitch the facing to the garment. Turn a narrow hem on the opposite edge of the facing and tack. Press, and then turn the new false hem up so that the joining seam is inside the garment and about 9 mm ($\frac{3}{8}$ in) above the new hemline fold. Finish with slip-hem as described on page 69.

Inserted hems

A short skirt can be lengthened by inserting a contrast band of fabric just above the hem, or with a band of the same fabric. Cover the seams with ribbon or braid.

Added hems

Add a gathered frill of a similar fabric to the unpicked hem of a full skirt.

Pleated skirts

False hems on pleated skirts are difficult to do well. If you have some spare matching fabric, consider making a new top to the skirt.

Cut off the old waistband and as much of the skirt as you need to. Make a new top with a commercial pattern. Join the skirt to the new top. Alternatively, make a long waist bodice in contrasting fabric and cut the skirt so that the pleats hang from the hip.

Cuffs and trouser legs

Lengthen jacket cuffs with a false hem. If the sleeve is too short for this, or the style is not suitable for this kind of alteration, cut the sleeve shorter. Finish the new length sleeve with a straight cuff (see page 58) or a frill of contrasting fabric or lace.

Alternatively, gather the edge of an elbow-length sleeve into a bias-cut binding or apply a casing for elastic.

Trouser legs usually wear on the hem, so letting down the hem does not solve the problem. Apply a deep binding of new fabric to jeans or sports trousers.

Jeans can take an added section of denim without looking odd. The colour does not have to match exactly.

Open the leg seams sufficiently and press the fabric flat. Trim off any worn part. Lay the garment on the new fabric matching grain and chalk in the new leg sections. Tack and stitch the new sections to the legs with a straight seam. Then remake the flat fell seams. Finish the new hems.

Cutting trousers short

If trousers or jeans fit everywhere but the length is wrong, cut them back to make a pair of shorts. Make neat hems or, on cotton and denim fabrics, work a line of straight machine stitching all around and then fringe back to the stitching line. Alternatively, cut trousers back to just below knee length and gather onto a band to make pedal pushers. Use remaining cotton or denim fabric to make a totebag to match, or a brimmed summer hat.

Sleeves Lengthen or shorten sleeves as described. Sleeves which are tight across the chest and back should be removed entirely and the armhole cut to a comfortable size. Bind the edges with strips cut from the sleeve or with a contrasting fabric. Make a tunic dress by removing the collar and cutting the neckline lower.

Small or high waists

On dresses, let out bodice and skirt side seams to their maximum. Sew new tape over the new seams to strengthen them. On princess line garments insert a band of new fabric at the waistline.

If a small girl's dress has a good skirt but the waist is too high because she has grown, unpick the skirt and make a new, simple top from a plain fabric, or knit a sweater top and stitch the skirt to it.

Use fabric from an unpicked full skirt to make a new, simpler dress. Use a panel from a full skirt to make a strapped, shirred-top sundress.

Keep all scraps of good cotton fabrics cut from children's clothes for patchwork and appliqué.

Dresses which fit except at the waist can be remodelled to make a skirt and a bolero top. Use fabric from sleeves to make the skirt waistband and facings.

Straight dresses will make new pinafores.

Long skirts

Long, floor length skirts with a too-small waist can be remodelled into a sundress. Measure around the chest. Cut off the waistband and top of the skirt. Unpick the zipper and keep it for future dressmaking.

Re-stitch seams and make a casing on the top edge for wide elastic. Add straps and a broderie anglaise frill. Use odd scraps to make a triangular head scarf.

Make a long skirt into a shorter, mid-calf length skirt by remaking the waistband. Unpick the old waistband and discard. Unpick the zipper. Cut fabric from the hem for a new waistband, joining pieces if necessary. Measure the waist. You will probably find that very little has to be cut off to make it big enough. Do not cut too much – it is easily done. Replace the zipper. Make a new waistband and stitch it to the skirt. Take up the hem to the desired length.

Remodelling jackets

Generally coats and jackets are too worn to do much remodelling. Try cutting out the sleeves and removing collars. Bind the edges with bright braid and replace buttons to match braid. Sometimes, new knitted sleeves can give an outdoor garment a new life. Use a heavy yarn and a toning colour. Knitted ribbed cuffs sometimes work on casual coats and jackets.

Shirts and blouses

Too-short shirts and blouses can be remodelled to make sun-tops or blouson tops. Make a casing for elastic or apply a new waistband, gathering the shirt onto it. If the garment is also too tight around the chest, but it is worth the work of remaking, consider putting in a zipper to replace the buttons.

Renovating knitted clothes

Purchased knitwear is usually machine knit, consequently it may not be easy to unpick and renovate. You might find it better to cut the fabric up and sew it to make play garments for young children. The sleeves of a raglan sweater in a soft knit could make a pair of long crawlers for a baby. Alternatively, cut the good pieces of knitted fabric up and machine stitch them together to make warm interlinings for bed covers.

Planning ahead

When you are knitting for a growing family, think about possible changes to the garment and buy extra yarn for future alterations to waist and sleeve length.

Experienced knitters find the best way of knitting sleeves is to start at the shoulder crown and knit down to the cuffs. In this way, worn or outgrown sleeves can be easily unravelled from the cuff edge and re-knitted introducing new yarn to make them longer. Use the same yarn for new cuffs and welt or change the look of the garment entirely with a different colour.

Re-knitting for extra length

This technique works best with stocking stitch, garter stitch and patterns worked on plain and purl ribs. It is difficult to do on fancy knit patterns.

Note where you will be adding new knitting and work tacking stitches across the garment. Unpick the seams carefully, enough for you to be able to work easily.

Make a note now of any shaping so that you can reproduce the stitches. A good way to do this uses squared graph paper. Count the number of stitches in a row. One square will represent each stitch. Count off the rows you will be re-knitting and shaping. Every line of squares will be a row of knitting. Mark crosses in the squares where you will be decreasing and diagonal lines where you will be casting off to shape. Number the rows on the graph and use the graph as a re-knitting pattern.

Unpicking

Insert a knitting needle into the loop of the third stitch from the edge. Pull on the stitch until it becomes a loop. Cut the loop and very gently pull the knitting apart along the row. Unravel until you have a row of complete loops on the main section.

Pick up the stitches, checking with your graph pattern to make sure you have picked them all up.

The crinkles in yarn are steamed out before re-using.

Recycling yarn

Unravel the lower section and wind it into a loose ball. It will have kinks in it and must be steamed or washed to remove them.

Wind the yarn between your thumb and index finger and round your elbow to make a skein. Tie the skein twice. Hang the skein in the steam from a boiling kettle or swish it in warm, fresh water. Fold the skein in a dry towel to remove excess water. Hang to dry naturally away from heat. Wind into balls for re-knitting.

Re-knitting

If you are not certain of the needle size originally used to knit the garment, knit a test piece first using a similar yarn. You will need to knit a square of at least 10 cm (4 in). Count the number of rows in 5 cm

(2 in) and then the number of stitches across 5 cm (2 in). If there are more than you need, use smaller needles. If less, use a larger size.

Start re-knitting on the picked-up stitches, using the recycled yarn. In fact, the new knitting will be upside down but it will not be easily detectable. Introduce the new yarn for the cuff or welt.

For a different look to the garment, you could introduce stripes of colour using new yarn immediately, keeping the recycled yarn for the cuff or welt.

Something new from something old

In families where there are several children, partly worn clothes are handed down to the youngest. Where there are young adults in the family, there may be an opportunity for using clothes which have been cast aside for style reasons. The fabric may have plenty of wear left in it and can be cut up to make new clothes for younger children.

Suitable fabrics

Generally, children do not like thick, scratchy fabrics and some dislike big patterns. Patterns should be in scale with the child's size and colours acceptable to them. Lightweight, soft tweed, woven and knitted wool fabrics, velours, corduroy and needlecord and face cloths will make coats, jackets, trousers and so on. Lightweight woollens, jersey, woven fabrics of cotton and cotton mixtures will make dresses, skirts, trousers, shirts, blouses, shorts and playwear.

Preparing fabrics

Wash or dry clean the garment and then unpick every part carefully. Throw out any parts which are worn. Press or iron the rest. Keep buttons, zippers, hooks and eyes if they are re-usable. Do not be tempted to keep a collar whole for re-use. Unpick the pieces and cut a new collar. Wool fabrics may still

look grubby even after dry cleaning. A gentle wash in warm suds will probably do no harm. There may be a little colour run, but if the water is just warm, the fabric will not suffer from washing and careful drying.

Man-made fibres which are designed to hold creases and pleats may be difficult to re-use because it is impossible to get the crease marks out altogether. Use only the uncreased parts.

Choosing patterns

The most satisfactory re-make depends on a simple rule: choose a pattern in a related style with the same or fewer number of pieces. For instance, an adult shirt or blouse with long sleeves will make a new child's shirt with sleeves. A straight adult dress without a waist seam will make a princess styled or shift-style dress for a little girl. An adult smock has enough fabric to make a smock for a little girl. The sleeves of an adult's raglan coat have sufficient fabric of the right shape to make a similarly styled coat for a boy.

It is not wise to try to re-use linings. They wear first in a garment and may not stand up to a child's treatment.

Measure the unpicked, pressed pieces, then measure the child. Study pattern books and look carefully at the shapes of the pattern pieces before deciding on a pattern. Take particular note of pieces cut on the bias of the fabric or facings cut in one piece as these may be difficult to fit onto the fabric pieces. Make sure that bodice or jacket fronts can be cut from the unpicked fronts when the old buttonholes have been discarded. Never try to utilize buttonholes or pockets. They will almost certainly be in the wrong place and too far apart for a child. Keep remakes simple in style and suitable for the fabric.

Try to think of the project as an original make and give it as much sewing time as you would normally.

Cutting up to cut down

Household furnishings

Worn furnishings and linens can be used to make new things. Use your needlework skills to make the most of good fabric.

House linens

Cut up table linens to make table napkins, traycloths and so on. Make double hems, each 6 mm to 9 mm ($\frac{1}{4}$ in to $\frac{3}{8}$ in). Finish corners evenly.

Bed linens

Cut worn sheets down the middle. Cut the worn parts away. Join up the good parts on the outside seams, making a flat fell seam. Turn a double hem on the outside edges.

T-sheets

Cut the top end from the sheets. Cut the worn part down the middle. Trim the worn parts away and re-seam with a flat fell seam. Make the top part to a width to fit the re-made sheet.

Using sheet cuttings

Use good parts of sheets for patches and other repairs; tie-dye and dip-dye remnants and use them for patchwork.

To get a graded effect on dip-dyed sheets, put one side of the sheet into the dye and leave for several minutes, then gradually introduce the remainder of the sheet for paler effects.

Use dyed sheeting to make short-length curtains, appliqué motifs from printed fabrics along the hem.

Pillow and cushion covers

Use the good parts of sheets for housewife pillowcases or cushion pad covers.

Use good pairs of old sheets for the base for crazy patchwork or as backing for quilting.

Keep small pieces for pressing clothes. Stitch pieces of sheeting together to make a floor runner to protect carpets on rainy days.

Blankets

Cut and re-make blankets for baby blankets, edging them with buttonhole stitch or binding with ribbon binding.

Use good parts of blankets for ironing pads and for interlining small household projects such as tea cosies. Dip-dye a blanket in a cold water dye. Embroider it with chain stitch patterns for a throw-over cover.

Warm interlinings

Machine stitch together scraps of blanket and wool clothing to make large pieces of fabric to use for interlining warm capes or for making bedcovers.

Curtains

Use the good parts of curtains to make cushion covers and bedcovers. Use plain weave fabric curtains to make cushions for the garden.

Towels

Cut good parts away to make bath mitts and face cloths. Cut towelling into strips to make hooked rag rugs for the bathroom.

Machine stitch squares of towelling to make bathtub cleaners. Crochet over the edges with crochet cotton to make them neat.

Nylon tights and stockings

It is a long tedious job, but snipped up tights and stockings make a good filling for soft toys. Boil them first to remove the colour.

Altering readymade clothes

Even if you are an accomplished needlewoman and make most of your clothes, you will occasionally buy garments. You can use your needlecraft skills to alter readymade clothes for a better fit.

When you are trying on clothes in a store, do not buy a garment which fits badly at the neck or across the shoulders. These are difficult and time consuming alterations to make and often not worth the effort.

Hems can be shortened or lengthened, cuffs can be taken down or turned up, skirts can be eased for a more comfortable fit and trousers altered for a neater fit.

An unlined garment might be a budget buy and you can give it a luxurious lining once you get it home.

Hems

The technique for lengthening with a false hem is on page 118.

Shortening a hem

Unpick the stitches holding the hem and unpick any seam binding. Press the crease out. Put the garment on and get someone else to mark the new hem line with pins and then tacking stitches. Measure the hem depth – between 6.5 cm and 7.5 cm ($2\frac{1}{2}$ in and 3 in) from the tacked line. Cut off the surplus fabric. Finish the raw edge as it was originally finished. (See hem finishes, pages 69-71).

Lengthening or shortening a coat

Check first that the fabric has not been trimmed away under the facing at the front corner. If it has, you cannot lengthen the coat satisfactorily.

Unpick all the stitching in the coat hem, the lining, and the lining where it is attached to the facing. Press out all creases. Put the coat on and have someone else pin the coat and lining together about 30 cm (12 in) above the hem. This makes sure that you don't end up with the lining longer than the coat.

If you are lengthening the coat with a false hem, add this to the hem and facing now, matching seams.

With the coat on, pin and tack mark the new hem line. Turn the hem and tack along the fold. Tack up the hem. Put the coat on again and check that the corners are level. Check that the turned up hem lies smoothly. If it does not, you may need to pin the seams of coat and hem together then run a gathering stitch along the raw edge. Press the fullness out with steam pressing.

Finish the raw edge as it was originally finished and hand finish the hem.

Turn the front facing back and slip stitch lower edges together. Finish the raw edge of the facing onto the hem with herringbone stitch.

If the lining is insufficient for a lengthened seam on additional lining, match the seams, turn and stitch the lining hem so that it is about 18 mm ($\frac{3}{4}$ in) shorter than the coat. Make a series of French tacks to hold the lining to the hem.

French tacks are bars of threads worked between the lining and the hem, about 2.5 cm (1 in) long and then covered with buttonhole stitch.

Shortening coat sleeves

Pin the coat and lining together at the elbow. Turn the sleeve inside out and unpick the lining at the lower edge. Unpick the cuff hem and press out the crease, removing any interfacing.

Put the coat on and have someone else mark the new sleeve length with pins. Tack and turn on the fold line. Tack along the fold line. Mark the depth of the new hem and cut off the excess fabric.

Press the new edge.

Replace interfacing. Turn up the lining so that it is 18 mm ($\frac{3}{4}$ in) shorter than the cuff. Cut off excess fabric and then slip stitch in place.

Altering waists

If a garment is too loose at the waist, unpick the waist seam, the darts and the side seams in the bodice and skirt and re-fit them. Make the new waist seam.

For a garment which is too tight, make sure that there is sufficient fabric in the seams to let them out to give the additional ease.

Unpick the waist seam and remove the zipper. Unpick the darts and side seams. Re-fit the side seams on the bodice and skirt first, then re-fit the darts for a perfect fit.

Make the waistline seam.

Skirts

Skirts are shortened in a similar way to other garments, although if there is hem interest, you may have to shorten the skirt from the waist.

Put the skirt on and pin a tuck so that the skirt is the desired length. Remove the waistband and zipper. Cut off the amount marked for the new depth but leaving 12 mm ($\frac{1}{2}$ in) for a seam. Open up the darts and seams. Put the skirt on and re-fit on seams and darts. Re-stitch. Replace the waistband and re-insert the zipper.

Fitting the hipline

If the skirt has become baggy around the seat, the excess fabric must be taken up into all the seams. Take the zipper out and unpick the seams around the fullest part of the hipline. Put the skirt on and pin the seams, distributing the fullness equally on all the seams. Re-stitch and put back the zipper.

Adjusting a thrown hip

On straight skirts particularly, differing hip levels can throw the hem of a skirt out of true.

Unpick the waistband and remove the zip. Lift the skirt waist until the hem hangs evenly. Mark the new waistline with pins and tacking. Replace the waistband and insert the zipper.

Swaybacked waist

A hollow waist at the back makes wrinkles across the top of a skirt. To remove them, the skirt must be raised into the waistband, sometimes as much as 18 cm ($\frac{3}{4}$ in). Unpick the waistband and lift the skirt. Pin, tack and restitch.

Trousers

A badly-fitting crotch is one of the major fitting problems with trousers. To correct, remove the waistband and let down the hems. Lift the trousers until they fit the crotch comfortably. Mark the new waist with tacking stitches. Unpick and re-make darts and seams. Cut away any surplus fabric from the waistline and re-apply the waistband. Take up the hems or make false hems.

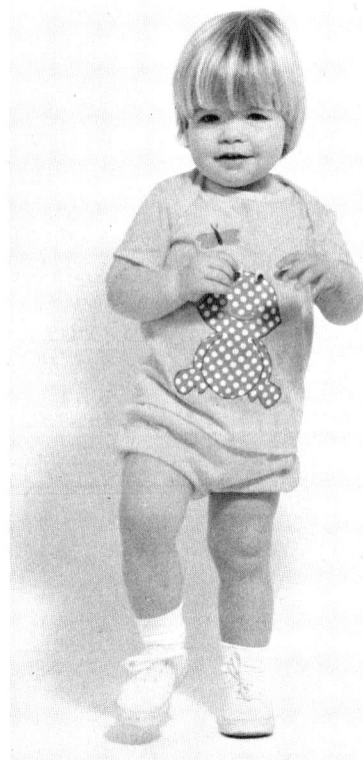

An appliqué picture such as this can be used to rejuvenate old clothes or perhaps to cover a stained area.

Mending

Every homemaker has to mend something at some time or another. This section tells you how to give extra life to household linens, soft furnishings and clothes that are worn, frayed, ripped or torn.

Reinforcing

If a button has been pulled off and the fabric is weakened, tack a piece of hem tape on the wrong side and then work the stitches through the tape.

Buttonholes

If machine-made buttonholes become worn, unpick the threads, and rework the stitches over a laid thread of buttonhole twist. If they are badly worn and seem past repair, you might try making them into bound buttonholes.

Button loops

Unpick the old stitches and remake loops. (See technique on page oo.)

Collars and cuffs

The wear on shirts occurs most frequently on the collar and cuffs. Tailored shirts have stiffenings in the collar, or an arrangement for inserting bones and so cannot be turned. A sports shirt collar can sometimes be turned.

Turning a collar

Unpick the collar from the shirt. Press it flat and then darn over the worn place with tiny stitches using a matching thread. If the wear has become a hole, make a neat patch using fabric from the hem or tail of the shirt. Reverse the collar and stitch it onto the shirt. (See page 64 for applying a collar.)

Turning cuffs

Double cuffs Unpick the cuff from the sleeve. Tack the pleats or gather the sleeve end. Press the cuff flat and darn or patch the worn place. Replace the cuff so that the repaired place is outside and hidden when the cuff is folded up.

Repairing single cuffs Remove the cuff from the sleeve. Gather the sleeve end. Unpick the entire cuff including the buttonhole which will be stitched through the interfacing. Cut off the worn edge and remake the cuff. Restitch the buttonhole and replace the cuff.

Alternative renovation Remaking a single cuff makes it shorter by at least 18 mm ($\frac{3}{4}$ in) and the other sleeve must be shortened to match. You might feel that the effort involved is not worth the result. An alternative renovation is to make the shirt short-sleeved. Try the shirt on and measure the new length plus 15 cm (6 in). Turn a single 3 mm ($\frac{1}{4}$ in) hem to the wrong side and machine stitch. Turn again for 7 cm ($2\frac{3}{4}$ in) hem and slip stitch to the wrong side. Press the folded edge and turn the cuff up on the right side.

Darning

Darning is a technique using small stitches to strengthen a thin place in fabric or fill a hole. Generally, darning threads should be the same colour, texture and thickness as the fabric threads.

For the re-weaving technique, draw threads from turnings in a hidden place in the garment.

Reinforcing darning
This is used to strengthen threads which are wearing thin, but where a hole has not yet occurred. Generally, reinforcing darns are worked on the wrong side of the fabric, but if the area is going to be next to the skin, you might decide to work the darn on the right side of the fabric to prevent possible chafing. Work on the weft (horizontal) threads only unless the area is so thin it needs darning both ways. Work tiny running stitches in close rows using a matching, fine thread. For an almost invisible

darn in garments, draw threads from the weft in a hidden place, such as the hem.

In heavy fabrics, such as on curtains, you can strengthen a darn by tacking a piece of net or muslin on the wrong side and then working stitches through it.

When reinforcing a woollen fabric with wool yarn, leave small loops at the end of each row of stitches to allow for shrinkage.

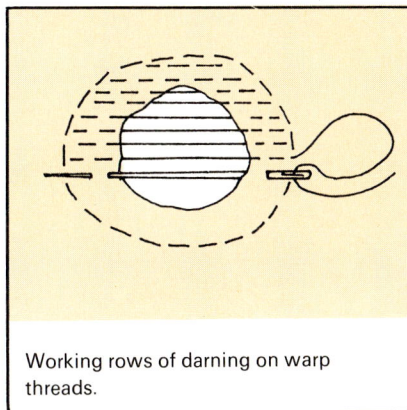

Working rows of darning on warp threads.

Web darning
Web darns are worked on knitted and woven fabrics to fill small to medium sized holes; you will need a darning egg or mushroom. Use an extra-long needle for web darning. Outline the hole with small running stitches, working on the good fabric. (A worn-through hole has a thin area around it.) If the edges of the hole are very ragged, trim them neatly but try not to make the hole larger. Holes in knitted fabrics, such as on socks, are better left untrimmed.

Start by working reinforcing darning on the warp (vertical) threads first. Work on the right side. As you get to the edges of the hole, take the darning threads across the hole and then continue working reinforcing running stitches to the outlining stitches.

Each row of darning warp stitches should go over, then under the edge of the hole alternately for a neat finish. Continue until the hole is filled with closely worked vertical threads and go on to fill the remaining thin area with reinforcing stitches.

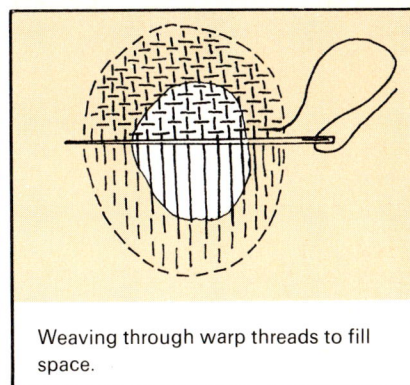

Weaving through warp threads to fill space.

For the second stage, work weft stitches, first in the reinforced area as running stitches and then weaving over and under the warp stitches. Complete the remaining reinforced area.

Darning knitted fabrics
When darning holes in knits, pick up the whole loops on the edges of the hole as you work the warp threads. This prevents the stitches unravelling later.

Darning net
Holes in net can be darned in three stages. Use a thread to match the net as closely as possible in colour and thickness.

For the first stage work the horizontal stitches first, working about three holes beyond the hole.

Stage 2 is worked upwards, diagonally from left to right. Fasten the thread end by tying it around a net thread. Darn across the horizontal darning, looping the thread once around each stage 1 row.

Stage 3 is worked downwards from left to right, taking the thread once around each intersection of stages 1 and 2.

Cross cut darn
This is used to repair a slit or straight tear in fabrics. First draw the edges of the slit together with fishbone stitch. (This used to be done with a human hair but nowadays, fine gauge, colourless nylon thread is used.) This drawing-together technique is called *stoteing*, and you can use it for mending a very small slit or tear

with a matching or drawn thread.

To work fishbone stitch, start on the wrong side of the fabric. Fasten the thread end with back stitches. Pass the needle through the slit to come out about 3 mm ($\frac{1}{8}$ in) from the edge. Take it back through the slit again in the opposite direction. Once the edges of the slit have been drawn together, tack an area round the slit as shown. With tiny running stitches, darn the warp way first to fill the tack-marked area. Then darn the weft-way to complete the darn.

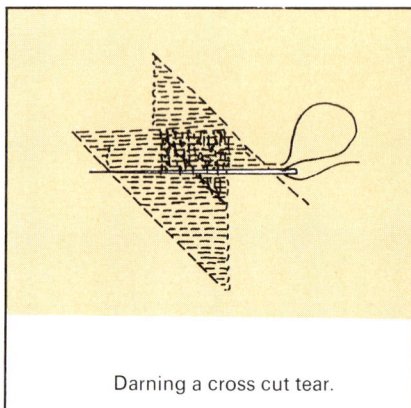

Darning a cross cut tear.

Hedge tear darning

Hedge tear is the term given to three-cornered rips. Draw the edges of the rip together with nylon thread. Tack an L-shaped area around the rip. Withdraw some weft and warp threads from a hidden part on the garment if you can, or use closely matching thread. Start darning at A-B, using small running stitches. Work almost to the corner of the rip then stop, leaving the thread hanging. Start darning on the other leg of the L and darn towards the corner. Stop just before the corner. Now complete the first leg to finish the first stage of the darn, then finally work the second leg to finish the darn. By working in this way you keep the grain of the fabric true across the corner of the rip, which is its weakest place, and so strengthen it while darning.

Darning ladders or runs

Ladders or runs in jersey fabrics can be machine stitched. Lay the two edges of the ladder together, right sides facing and stitch just beyond both ends of the ladder, using a small stitch.

Alternatively, you can repair the ladder with a small crochet hook. Pick up the loop at the bottom of the ladder and hook it over the next thread above. Pick up the thread loop and hook it over the thread above and so on until the ladder is repaired. Fasten the final loop off with backstitches on the wrong side.

Linen darns

Use linen thread of a size which will match the texture of the fabric. Size 16 is a good general thickness. Work with a long, thin darning needle on the wrong side of the material.

Mark the limit of the darn all around the thin place with small tacking stitches, including enough of the stronger fabric to allow the darning thread to sink into the weave.

Work parallel to the selvedge and make the darn an uneven shape: zigzag, lozenge, or diamond. Leave loops at the ends of each row of stitches in case the thread shrinks in washing. Begin at the right-hand end, take a few evenly spaced stitches on the needle, draw the needle up and out. Work the second row by beginning either higher or lower according to the shape required. Work down, alternating stitches and spaces with those previously worked.

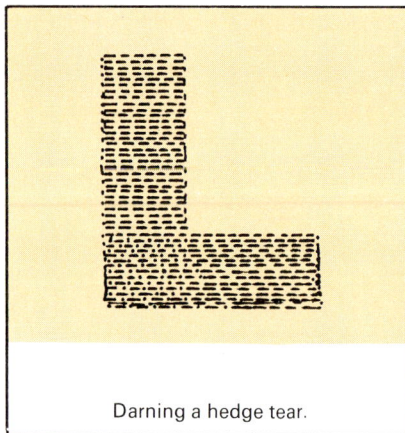

Darning a hedge tear.

Continue in this way, working well into the less thin border.

Re-weaving darns

These are usually worked on clothes made of woven fabrics. It is a useful technique for mending small holes such as cigarette burns, and properly done, the mend can be almost invisible.

Study the weave of the fabric through a magnifying glass so that you know how the colours and weave work. Draw threads for both warp and weft from seams allowances and hem. You will be able to use quite short lengths.

Put the work in an embroidery frame, wrong side up. Darn the new threads in using a fresh thread for each row and leaving the ends free on the work, matching colours and weave. Trim the ends off to 3 mm ($\frac{1}{8}$ in) and press the darn.

For a really professional invisible darn, you would have to unpick threads back from the hole on the warp, and darn in the new threads. Then unpick back from the hole on the weft and darn in new threads.

Swiss darning

This is used to mend thin places in knitted garments. Run tacking stitches around the place first so that you can see where you are working. Thread a needle with matching yarn. Start at the top of the area and pick up loops in the knitting, working from right to left. When you get to the edge of the area, turn the work upside down and pick up a second row of loops linking them to the first row. Continue until the weak area has been reinforced with stitches.

Machine darning

Fit a darning foot on the machine. Check with the manufacturer's handbook for lowering the feed teeth. Thread the machine with matching embroidery thread and set the stitch length to 0. Tack around the area to be darned and put the fabric in an embroidery frame, right side up, so that the fabric is flat on the machine bed.

Work parallel stitches in the surrounding worn area first and then across the hole, keeping rows of stitches close together. (Page 215 tells how to place your fingers on the hoop to move the work under the needle.) When the vertical stitches have been worked, turn the work to be ready to stitch the other way. This time make the rows a little wider apart. Finally work a third darning, turning the work to the first position again.

When darning a woollen fabric, thread machine with woollen yarn by hand. Work ordinary straight stitching for the first darn, then zigzag stitching for the second. Do not stitch a third time.

Darning furnishings
Worn places on upholstered furniture can be darned if you use a small-sized, curved, mattress needle.

Repairs to elastic

Elastic waistbands
The elastic in the waists of underpants and some children's garments perishes with frequent laundering, and can be replaced.

Unpick the worn elastic. Cut new, openweave elastic to fit the waist comfortably, plus about 3 cm ($1\frac{1}{4}$ in). Measure and mark the waistline of the garment into eighths, using pins. Seam the ends of the elastic. Mark it into eighths with pins. Pin the elastic to the garment, the join at the back and the elastic just over the seam line, matching pins. Set the sewing machine to a narrow zigzag. Stitch along the edge of the elastic, working from the elastic side and stretching it as you work so that it lies flat on the fabric.

Finish the cut ends of the elastic by catching them down with herringbone stitch.

Elastic in casing
If you are making a casing for elastic, leave a gap in the machine-stitched seam at the back of the garment, insert the elastic and then close the gap with hem stitch. When elastic has to be replaced, the hem stitches can be unpicked easily. On ready-made garments you will probably have to unpick the machine stitching to open the casing.

Pull out the worn elastic. If it has been stitched into the seams, unpick the casing at the seams, release the elastic and restitch the casing at these points.

Cut new elastic to the waist measurement. Put a safety pin on one end and push the closed pin through the casing, gathering the casing over the pin and onto the elastic. Pin the ends of the elastic together and make sure the elastic lies flat in the casing all round. Overlap the ends of the elastic and stitch, by machine or hand back stitching, first in a square over the ends and then in a cross over the square. Close the casing seams.

Frayed hems and cuffs

Trouser hems
Trousers with worn cuffs can be renovated by doing away with the cuff. Unpick the hem and press all the creases out. Try on the trousers and mark the new hem line with tacking stitches. (See page 71 for turning hems.) Turn up the new hem and cut off the surplus, worn fabric.

Trousers without cuffs
Unpick the hems and press flat. Machine darn the worn place. Turn up a slightly deeper hem so that the darned place is above the fold on the inside of the trouser leg. Cover the darn with trouser-kick tape, stitching it by hand just above the fold of the hem.

Jeans and casual trousers
The worn edges should be trimmed neatly first. If the hems have worn because the trousers are too long, turn a new hem to the correct length. Alternatively, bind the hem with wide commercial binding, or with a new piece of fabric to contrast decoratively. This gives a very pretty effect to clothes.

Frayed pleats
When a pleat wears away from its stitches at the top, repair it with an arrowhead. Mark the arrowhead in pencil. Fasten thread on the wrong side. Bring the needle out on the left-hand corner and take the thread to the apex of the triangle. Make a stitch and then take the needle to the right-hand corner, passing it from the right to left-hand corner. It is now in position to make the next stitch to the apex, to the right of the first stitch. Continue until the triangle is filled.

Frayed cuffs and edges
Worn cuffs, coat opening edges, pocket welts and so on, can be repaired with binding. Repair fur garments and clothes made of heavy tweed fabrics with leather or suede. Use commercial binding, ribbon or braid to repair other fabrics.

Binding with leather or suede
Measure and mark strips of skived (thin) leather to fit edge being repaired, and about 2.5 cm (1 in) wide. Mark both leather and suede on the wrong side of the material and cut out with a sharp craft knife and a metal-edged ruler. Do not use scissors. If you are repairing cuffs, add 2.5 cm (1 in) for a seam.

Apply the leather strip to the garment by taping it over the worn edge to hold it in position. Machine stitch, using a special spear-pointed needle in the machine and strong thread, working through the leather, the garment and the leather inside in one working. Alternatively, leather and suede can be glued over a worn edge using a suitable fabric adhesive.

When binding sleeves, stitch the strip into a circle first and then apply to the cuff.

Iron-on mending tapes
These are useful for quick mends on clothes and are particularly suitable for raincoats and similar heavy fabrics. Iron-on interfacing can be used to repair tears in

lightweight fabrics.

Pull the edges of the tear together with fishbone stitch or oversewing. Cut a piece of mending tape or interfacing to size and iron onto the wrong side of the garment.

Fur and fur fabric

If the fabric is thin and worn, do not attempt to sew areas of real skin together. The stitches will simply pull the remaining fabric apart. A rent in fur can be repaired on the wrong side by oversewing the edges together with silk thread, using a leather needle. Afterwards, apply adhesive-backed fabric tape over the stitching. Pick strands of fur out of the mend with a needle.

Seams

If the seams on a fur garment weaken, the skin pulls away from the overcast seam. Glue seam tape along both sides of the seam using a rubber-based adhesive. When it is quite dry, oversew the seam edges together, taking the stitches through the tape.

To patch a hole

Mark a neat triangle or diamond shape around the hole on the wrong side. Cut the shape out with a sharp blade, cutting through the skin only and not the fur pile. Lay the cut-out piece on a new piece of fur so that you can match colour and pile direction, then place it on the wrong side of the new fur. Mark and cut the new shape. Spread a rubber-based adhesive on the edges of the patch and insert it into the hole in the garment from the back. Lay the garment flat while the glue dries, but make sure that no strands of fur are caught in the join; if this should happen, they can be freed with a needlepoint. When the glue has dried, oversew the edges of the patch with silk thread and a leather needle, working on the wrong side.

Patching

Patching is the best method for mending large holes, whether they are worn or torn. Patches should be as invisible as you can make them so they are not noticeable when completed.

Use fine needles and matching thread for working patches. When repairing woollen fabrics it is sometimes worth unravelling the material, but this must be carefully done.

General method

With small tacking stitches, carefully mark the exact size and shape of the patch on the item, making it large enough to include the hole and worn part.

Cut the patch with or without turnings so that it fits into the marked area. Turnings on patches should be quite generous. Be sure to match the thread, weave and design of the fabric. If new material has to be used it may be necessary to fade, wash and shrink it before beginning the work.

Position of patches

The position of a patch is important. Sometimes a patch put onto the right side of a garment is less noticeable than if it is on the wrong side; this applies particularly to printed fabric when the design must be matched.

Shape of patches

The shape and size of a patch depends almost entirely upon the position and size of the part to be mended. Sometimes the applied piece is sufficiently large to be an actual part of the garment – a patch does not necessarily have to be square, rectangular, or even to have four sides; it can have two or three sides or be let into a seam. All patches must be flat and unpuckered.

Types of patches

Blanket patch

Mark out the size of the patch on the blanket. Cut the patch plus about 5 cm to 7.5 cm (2 in to 3 in) all the way around. Fix the patch in position on the wrong side.

Using a darning needle and fine wool, darn over the edges of the patch, making the stitches cover a border of about 2.5 cm (1 in) all around. Cross the darning at the corners. Cut away the hole and worn part, leaving about 5 cm (2 in) of double fabric all around.

Darn down the inner edge on the right side, again making the stitches in a 2.5 cm (1 in) wide border. Press.

Darned patch

Use a ruler and chalk to mark the area of the patch on the wrong side of garment. Mark an area of the same size on the patch, adding a very generous allowance for turnings when cutting. Fray these turnings carefully.

On the garment, cut along the lengthwise threads on one side of the area to be patched. Tack the patch in position on the wrong side. Insert a long, fine darning needle into the garment immediately below the cut, and weave it into the fabric surface. Then thread the needle with a frayed thread from the patch and pull it through, being careful not to draw it too tightly. Use every thread in turn, keeping the darn even. Work opposite sides until the patch is darned and fits neatly. Use this method on plain closely woven woollen fabrics such as worsteds and suitings. Press the finished patch.

Dress patch

Mark the area of the patch allowing 12 mm ($\frac{1}{2}$ in) turnings beyond the mark. Then cut away the hole and surrounding worn part. Cut the patch the same size plus turnings. Turn in the edges of both garment and patch, snipping diagonally into the corners of the garment. Join with a plain seam, or an oversewn seam worked on the right side.

Whether the patch is inserted on the wrong or the right side depends upon the fabric, its texture and weave. On a soft, dress cloth, straight seaming together on the right side is not satisfactory. Trim away the surplus material from the corners of the patch on the wrong side. Catch the folds together with tiny herringbone stitches then overcast raw edges around both garment and patch. Press.

Flannel patch

Apply on wrong side. Use mercerized cotton for sewing. Cut away the hole and worn part to the exact shape and size required. Cut the patch the same size plus 9 mm ($\frac{3}{8}$ in). Tack onto wrong side of garment. Herringbone stitch the sides of the patch and the edges of the hole.

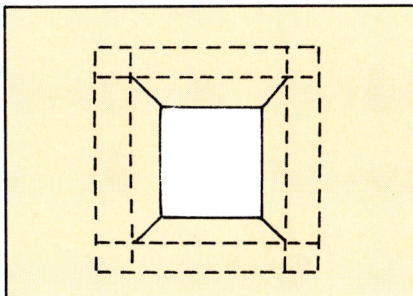

Preparing the hole in fabric for patching.

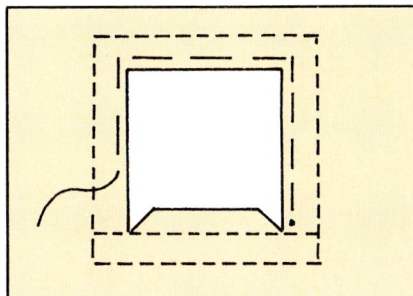

The patch is tacked into position behind the fabric.

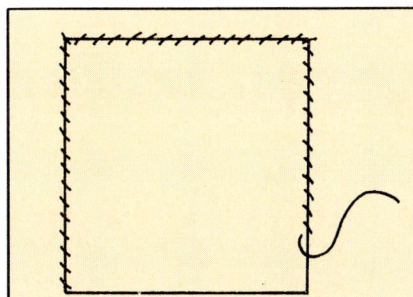

On the wrong side of fabric the patch is hemmed neatly.

Knitted fabric patch

The stitch used must have a certain amount of give. Follow the procedure as for the flannel patch, using either herringbone stitch or loop stitch to hold the edges in place.

Machined patch

A machine stitched version of a fabric patch which is very useful, particularly for household linen and strictly utilitarian garments such as overalls, dungarees, winceyette and cotton nightgowns.

Prepare and proceed in the same way as for a hand stitched patch and tack in place. Machine stitch very near the edges of the patch on both wrong and right sides.

Patterned patch

Match the pattern carefully when cutting the patch, then proceed in the same way as for the plain fabric patch; work on the right side as it is easier to match the patterns of the print. On some fabrics (such as haircord) it will be found more satisfactory to use a form of hemming which produces a straight vertical stitch over the edge of the patch; this will merge into the cord or weave and is consequently less visible than a series of slanting stitches. Stitches should be very small and the thread fine.

Wrong side Cut the turnings of both patch and garment to 9 mm ($\frac{3}{8}$ in), using the method of cutting away beyond the hole described for a plain fabric patch. Loop stitch the edges of turnings together. This is a good patching method to use for furnishing materials.

Plain fabric patch

Used for cotton, linen and rayon fabrics; apply on the wrong side, sewing with matching thread. Cut the patch to the size required with 12 mm ($\frac{1}{2}$ in) turnings all around. Turn in the raw edges and tack the patch in position, making sure that the lengthwise threads of patch and garment are matching. Hem or seam the edges of patch on the

wrong side, using whichever stitch seems to accommodate itself to the weave. Turn to the right side. Crease twice diagonally across the patch. Trim down the hole of the garment to 9 mm ($\frac{3}{8}$ in) from the hemming stitches. Turn under the turnings of each side after cutting towards each corner along the creased lines, to within 4 mm ($\frac{1}{6}$ in) of corner. Pin or tack and hem.

Table-linen patch (inserted)

Method 1 This patch is also sewn with darning, but the edges of the darn are usually made uneven to avoid strain.

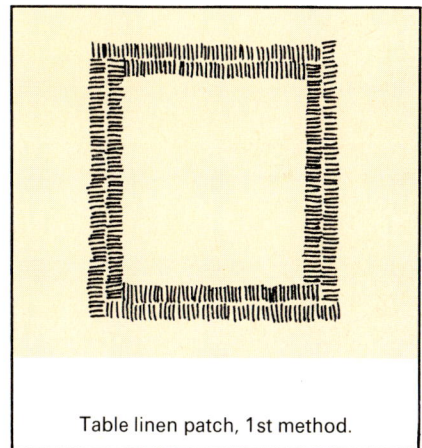

Table linen patch, 1st method.

Cut the patch; cut away hole and worn part to allow 12 mm to 9 mm ($\frac{1}{2}$ in to $\frac{3}{8}$ in) double fabric all around. Tack the patch firmly in position.

Darn all round, working one side at a time and crossing the corners. Darn right across the double border.

Method 2 Crease around hole and worn part. Cut patch to fit exactly, pin and tack patch in position, edges of patch to creased lines, matching the threads. Cut away a little of the hole at a time, allowing sufficient to be darned. Continue in this way, making double stitches at the corners. This method requires great care in handling and is recommended only for use upon table-linen of the best quality. It is unsuitable for rayon types of damask.

Table-linen patch, cont'd.

Method 3 This method is suitable for thick, firm damask. Prepare as for method 2. Insert and make closely worked fishbone stitches, drawing them firmly but not tightly to keep the patch in place.

Machine-stitched patch

Use this patch on bed sheets, tea towels and so on. Cut the patch fabric from a similar article. Cut the patch 3 cm (1¼ in) larger than the hole. Tack over the hole, turning in the edges. Machine stitch around the patch. On the wrong side cut away the worn fabric surrounding the hole. Turn in the raw edges and tack. Machine stitch on the folded edge.

Patching worn knees

Go over the worn place with machine stitching. Machine stitch a shaped patch of contrast fabric over this area.

Patching torn pockets

Unpick the pocket. Mend the tear with fishbone stitch. Sew seam tape behind the tear and replace the pocket.

Decorative patches

Holes worn in casual clothes can be repaired so that the mend becomes a decorative feature. Buy decorative patches or cut motifs from printed fabrics for appliqué. Reinforce the fabric with iron-on interfacing. Sew patches on with zigzag stitch or decorative hand stitches.

Straps and tapes

For replacing a shoulder strap on lingerie or a tie tape, turn a narrow hem on the end of the tape or ribbon and place it so that the fold is below the garment edge. Pin and back stitch just inside the hem edge, then turn the tape back so that the edge is level with the garment and hem to the band. Slip the needle through to the wrong side and hem the remaining three sides. When working tie tapes, finish the other end with a narrow hem.

Loops for hangers

Loops for hanging towels and tea towels. Place them at the corners. Turn both ends of 15 cm (6 in) of tape to the wrong side. Pin the ends side by side and hem as shown.

Pockets

Holes in pockets can be darned if the hole is small, otherwise buy a replacement for the entire pocket.

Trim away the worn part. Turn a narrow hem on the top edge and machine stitch to the cut pocket edges.

If the entire pocket needs replacing you will need a new pocket bag. Unpick the stitching where the pocket bag joins the seam. Tack the new bag, right sides together, to the seam. Machine stitch. Complete the seam of the pocket edging to the new bag.

Seams

Wherever seams break, the repair should reproduce the original stitching. If a simple machine-stitched seam breaks, start machine stitching (or hand-back stitching) before and beyond the good stitching.

Fell seams Jeans have run and fell seams. Either repair them with machine stitching working over the old stitched lines or hand hem the folded edges to the garment.

Zippers

Zip replacement Unpick the stitches holding the broken zip. Press the opening edges. Re-insert the new zip following techniques described on page 000.

Zip repair If the teeth of the zip break apart, take the slider to the bottom. Snip into the tape below the last zipper tooth on the side that has broken away from the slider. Lift the tooth and push it into the top of the slider. Gently move the slider up so that it closes the teeth. Work a bar of stitches across the zipper teeth above the gap.

Thrifty makes

Rag rugs

Making a rag rug is a good way of using up dressmaking remnants and the good parts of worn furnishings. Wash fabrics to remove dirt – even woollens – and press them before cutting the strips.

Nylon tights and stockings make good quick-dry bathroom rugs. Boil the colours out and then re-dye.

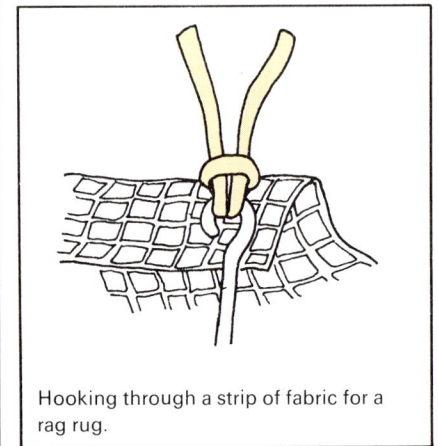

Hooking through a strip of fabric for a rag rug.

Methods

Hooked rugs

Work on a hessian background with a hooking tool. Cut strips of fabric 10 cm to 15 cm (4 in to 6 in) long and 12 mm to 15 mm (½ in to ⅝ in) wide. Thin fabrics should be cut to twice the width and worked folded lengthwise.

Tack a 5 cm (2 in) hem all round and work through double fabric to within 2.5 cm (1 in) of the edge. Turn the unworked edge to the wrong side and slip stitch. Back the rug with hessian, oversewing the edges.

Looped rugs

Cut fabric in long strips and 12 mm (½ in) wide. Insert the hook through the hessian and pull the first loop through, which can be anything from 2.5 cm to 5 cm (1 in to 2 in) long. Make the loops about 6 mm to 12 mm (¼ in to ½ in) apart.

Plaited rugs

Cut or tear strips of fabric 7.5 cm (3 in) wide and as long as possible. Fold in the raw edges and then fold the sides in as you wind the strips around strips of cardboard. Prepare strips of different colours.

Join two strips on the bias as shown then join the third strip. Secure the end of the three strips in a drawer and plait the strips, keeping the folded edges to the middle. As each colour strip finishes, join in a new one with a bias seam.

When you have plaited about 2 m (2 yd) you can start stitching. Use fine twine and a heavy needle. Lace through the loops, pulling coils tightly together to make a circular or oval rug. To finish, cut the strips of the last plait down in width to taper them. Slip stitch the ends to the last round.

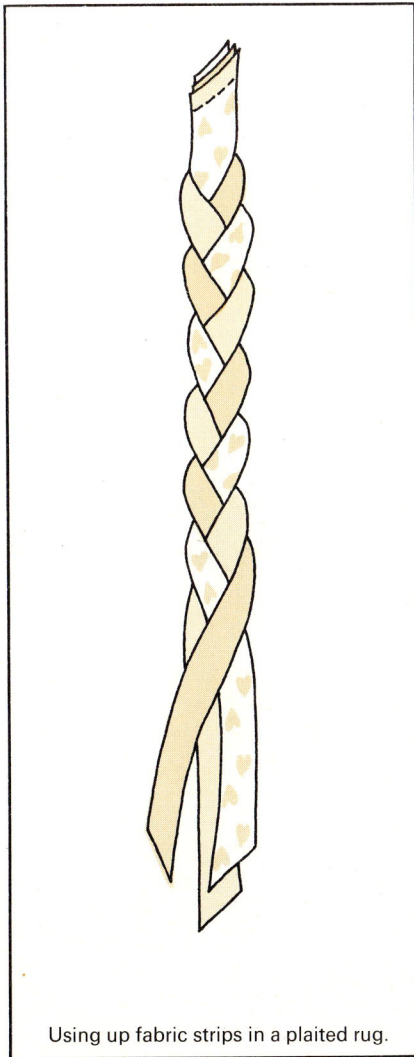

Using up fabric strips in a plaited rug.

Stain removal

If stains on carpets, household furnishings and clothes are treated quickly, they are more likely to be removed. If you do not know the origin of a stain, take the item to a reputable dry cleaner.

There are two basic methods of cleaning.

Water-soluble stains

Some stains will come out if they are soaked first in cold water then washed in the normal way.

Other stains

The chart shows the chemical solvents and stain removers that are used on various stains. They are used as follows. Place a piece of folded clean rag under the stain. Dip a clean pad of cloth in the solvent and dab around the outside edge of the stain, gradually working towards the centre. Rinse fabric afterwards to remove solvent.

Remember that many solvents are highly inflammable, so always work in a well-ventilated area and away from any kind of flame.

If you are in doubt about the effect of a chemical on a fabric, perhaps one made of acetate rayon, try out the solvent first on a concealed corner.

Most solvents are poisonous so keep them in clearly labelled bottles and well out of the reach of children. *Never* store a dangerous chemical in a bottle which is recognisable to a child as a container for something pleasant to drink, such as a soft drink bottle.

Key to the chart
dilute 1 tbs to 600 ml ($\frac{1}{2}$ pint) of water**
dilute 1 to 1 *

Dangerous chemicals

I stands for inflammable liquid
V stands for a vapour which could be inflammable or dangerous to inhale
C stands for a corrosive liquid

Beer Clean with peroxide solution** then soak in cold water.
Blood Soak in cold water first, then in hot enzyme detergent solution.
Carbon paper Methylated spirits (I).
Chewing gum Rub with ice cube to remove most, then commercial dry-cleaning fluid (V).
Chocolate Cold water first to remove surface stain, then wash in enzyme detergent solution.
Cocoa As above.
Coffee Soak in cold water first, then peroxide**. If the background fabric would be damaged by peroxide, sponge with tepid borax solution**.
Creosote Dry-cleaning fluid, then try white spirit (I) or try glycerine, rinsing afterwards in lukewarm water.
Egg Soak first in cold water, then in tepid salty water – 1 tsp to 600 ml (1 pint). Finally wash in enzyme detergent solution.
Fruit juice Cold water first, then try glycerine and a lukewarm wash. If this fails, peroxide**.
Grass Clean with surgical methylated spirit (I).
Grease Press area first between clean blotting paper with warm iron. Then sprinkle on French chalk and leave overnight before brushing out. Finally, dry cleaning fluid (V).
Ice cream Soak in cold water, then wash in enzyme detergent solution.
Indelible pencil Clean with surgical methylated spirit (I).
Ink Wash in cold water immediately then apply:
Ballpoint: surgical methylated spirit (I).
Duplicating ink: Dry-cleaning fluid (V).
Felt tip: surgical methylated spirit (I).
Indian Ink: white spirit (I).
Marking ink: cloudy ammonia (V, C)*.

Red ink: methylated surgical spirit (I).

Mildew Wash first, then peroxide**.

Lipstick Cold water first, then warm soapy water. If stain persists, eucalyptus oil, or methylated surgical spirit (I).

Nail varnish Clean off with amyl acetate (I) first. Leave for a while then try surgical methylated spirit (I).

Oil, clear Dry-cleaning fluid (V).

Paint emulsion: water as soon as possible.
oil based: thinner, turpentine (I).

Perspiration cold water first, weak cloudy ammonia (V, C)* solution or vinegar. Wash afterwards in warm soapy water.

Milk Cold water first, then enzyme detergent solution.

Plasticine Rub with an ice cube first to remove surplus. Then dry-cleaning fluid (V).

Wax polish Try dry-cleaning fluid, then surgical methylated spirit (I).

Rust Soak in lemon juice and water for 30 minutes. Sprinkle oxalic acid on stain and pour hot water through treated area. (Do not use this method on coloured fabrics).

Scorch Dab with peroxide**.

Spirits Cold water first then wash in enzyme detergent solution.

Tar Remove as much as possible then try glycerine. White spirit (I) may remove the stain.

Tea Rinse in cold water immediately. Sprinkle with powdered borax. Pour hot water through and wash.

Urine, vomit, faeces Cold rinse, then enzyme detergent wash.

Wine On the carpet or table cloth, sprinkle with salt immediately. Brush up next day. Try glycerine if stain persists and then peroxide** on suitable fabrics.

Accessories

Bags

A bag plays an important part in completing the general appearance of an outfit. The design must be suitable for the occasion, with emphasis on two main points. Firstly, size and shape with a view to the purpose for which the bag is to be used; whether it is to be a finish to the outfit for formal occasions, and to contain the minimum of contents, as in the case of an evening bag, or whether it is to be a completely practical bag made to hold everything that might be considered necessary for use during the day. Secondly, a good design that is in keeping with the style of dress. Formal bags can incorporate intricate details of finish, such as tucks and fullness, ornate catches and handles. Practical, tailored bags, which rely on simplicity of line and quality of material, need a minimum of decorative detail and tone well with tweeds and heavy fabrics for casual wear. Generally speaking, for whatever purpose the bag may be used, a good design relies for effect on beauty of shape, simplicity of line and fine workmanship.

Any firm, closely woven material may be used as long as it is suitable for the design. Strong, practical bags can be made of felt, linen, sail-cloth, plastics, leather, corduroy, face-cloth, or any evenly woven material. Stiff taffetas, moiré or wide gros-grain ribbon, velveteen, velvet, brocade and lamé, may be used for the more elaborate type of bag. Attractive shopping bags can be made of gay furnishing fabrics if lined with tailor's canvas, for strength, or with plastic to make a waterproof, lined beach bag.

Beadwork bag

The Victorian fashion of a bead bag, made entirely of beads sewn onto a net foundation, is coming into its own again. This is fascinating work, but it is a long, slow process.

Another type of beadwork, which is not so tedious, is that of sewing a group of different-shaped beads on to a smooth surface. Some very beautiful and rich effects can be obtained with the use of these sparkling 'jewels': spangles, sequins, jet, bugles, and all the other glittering fragments of glass and tinfoil that are made for the purpose.

Although the work looks complicated, you will find that the sewing on of the various beads and gold thread is very easy, needing no more experience than simple embroidery. A certain amount of patience is needed, but you will be well rewarded for your trouble.

The work can be done held in the hand, but it is easier if the material is mounted in a square needlework frame. Do not cut the shape out before working, but mark the outline on the material with tacking, and cut out after the beading is finished.

This black velvet bag with beadwork decoration, makes a smart accessory all the more striking for its originality.

Materials required: 2 pieces black velvet 25 cm × 30 cm (10 in × 12 in).
1.80 m (2 yd), 5 cm (2 in) wide, black velvet ribbon.
One 20 cm (8 in) zip-fastener (black and very fine).
2 squares of buckram for interlining.
20 cm × 25 cm (8 in × 12 in).
Black thread.
35 cm (⅜ yd) taffeta.
6 small brass rings.

Materials required for embroidery:
Gold thread: Japanese thread (a fine thread of gold twisted over yellow silk); gold twist or fine gold lurex embroidery thread.
Embroidery thread: 1 skein each gold, green and red stranded cotton.

Beads: small, round red; small, round, light and dark green; small, gold metal; 3 light green, thick and flat, with holes through centre; 1 long drop-shaped jet with holes each side.

Bugles: 3 long red; 20 long dark green; 20 short gold.

Sequins: 18 flat light; 66 medium and 20 dark green; 4 flat gold (a little larger); 2 thick button-shaped white pearl (or white pearl buttons); 1 heart-shaped, ribbed black.

Stones: 3 green, round with 9 mm ($\frac{3}{8}$ in) holes each side.
Fine bead needles.

Cutting the pattern

Draw the pattern on tracing paper, following the diagram, then cut it out. Lay the pattern on the velvet and tack all round the edges, repeat this for the second side – do not cut out.

Using the same pattern cut two pieces of taffeta for the lining, allowing 12 mm ($\frac{1}{2}$ in) turnings all round, and cut a strip 8 cm × 80 cm (3 in × 30 in). Cut two pieces of buckram for the interlining, allowing 12 mm ($\frac{1}{2}$ in) turnings round the two sides and at lower edge, but not at the top.

Complete the beadwork before cutting out the velvet.

To trace the design

It is difficult to trace a design on to velvet owing to the long pile.

Trace the diagram on to tracing paper, copying the outline and main points of the design to size required (the fewer details drawn,

— 28 cm —

Pattern for beadwork bag.

the better in this case). Prick along all the lines on the wrong side, with a needle.

Pin the velvet to the smooth surface such as a drawing board or the back of a wooden tray, pile side up. Place the design in position on the velvet and pin in place, handling the velvet very carefully.

Shake powdered chalk on to the paper and pad it gently with a wad of cotton-wool, so that the chalk sifts through the pricked holes. A very little is enough to make a fine, pin-point line of chalk. Remove the tracing paper carefully.

Trace along the lines lightly with a tailor's chalk pencil to give the outline of the dragon. It is important not to mark the velvet too heavily as it may be difficult to remove marks later.

To work the design

The chart is numbered to show the

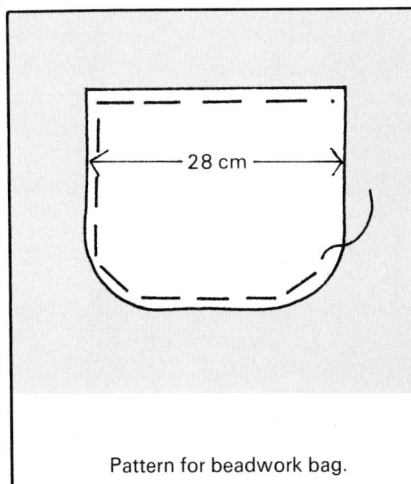

A dragon embroidered with beads and sequins on black velvet forms the main feature of a luxurious evening bag.

placing of the various beads, sequins and gold thread. Handle the velvet very carefully and use two strands of a matching colour of stranded cotton for the stitching.

The normal way to sew beads and bugles is to thread each one on the cotton, which has been attached to the material in the right spot, and then take a back stitch into the fabric. Any deviation from this method is described where it applies.

A long, fine bead needle is the best to use for this work, and in all cases care should be taken not to force the bead on to the needle, as it is liable to split.

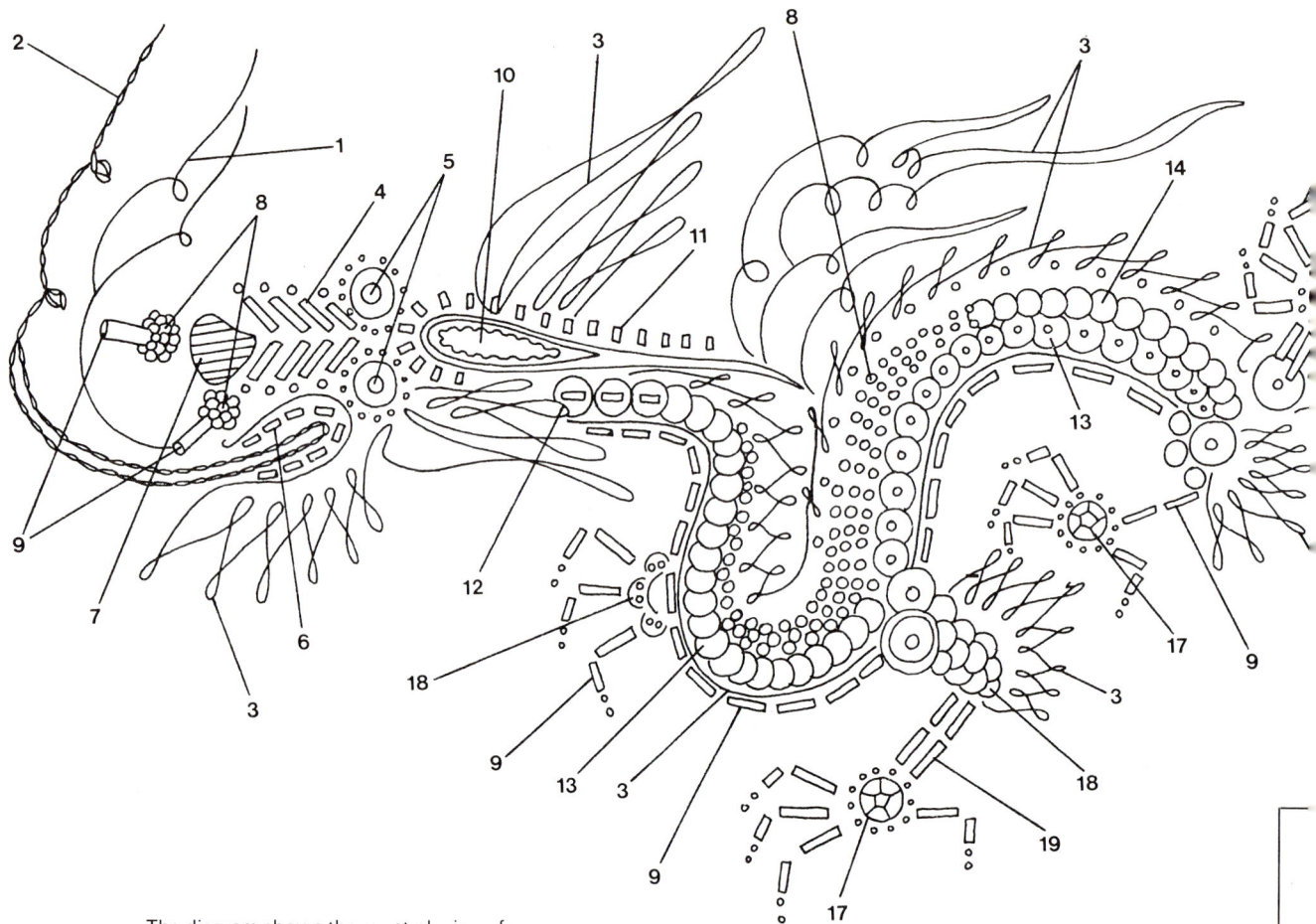

The diagram shows the exact placing of the coloured beads and sequins. Work through from low to high numbers.

Begin by sewing on the gold thread. This is couched, as described on page 195.

1 The tongue – gold thread couched with red.

2 The lower tongue and jaw – gold thread couched with yellow.

3 The wings, tail and legs – gold twist couched with yellow.

4 The dragon's head – long, dark-green bugles with a red bead at outer end. The thread is brought through at end of one stroke in the centre of the head, a bugle and a bead are threaded on to it, insert the needle again so that the bugle and bead lie flat on the material.

5 The eyes – white pearl sequins with red bead in centre and light green beads round. The thread is attached through centre of eye; the sequin, then the red bead, are threaded on to it and the needle is passed back through sequin and material.

The little green beads are sewn on separately, quite close together, round the sequin.

6 Three long, red bugles surrounded by smaller, green ones.

7 Black, heart-shaped sequin – sewn on with green cotton, the stitches being taken along the ridges of the sequin.

8 Nostrils and top of back – small dark-green beads sewn on with raised-bead method. Several beads are threaded on to the cotton, which is brought out at one end of the stroke and taken to the back again at the other end. The number of beads on each thread is regulated by the length of the stroke; they should lie in a gentle curve on the surface of the fabric.

9 Centre of nostrils, legs and under part of body – long, green bugles. Two tiny gold beads are sewn at the ends of the claws.

10 Centre of neck – drop-shaped, black, jet bead.

11 Neck – short, gold bugles, radiating round jet bead.

12 Back – three light green, thick, flat beads.

13 Scales, back and tail – medium green sequins. These

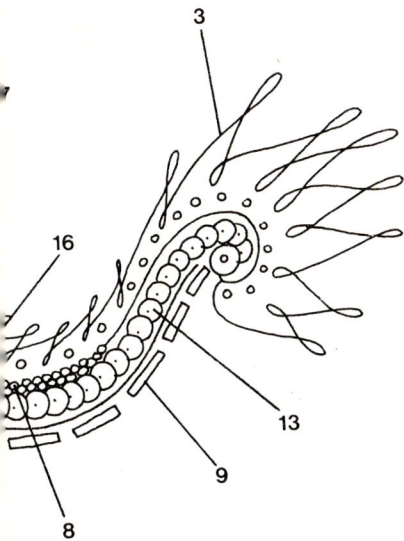

3

16

13

9

8

sequins are sewn on over-lapping each other. The thread is brought through at the tail end of the section and taken over one side of the sequin, through the centre and back into the material, emerging again at the edge of the sequin, ready for the next one.

14 Back scales – light green sequins, applied as 13.

15 Scales on under-body – medium green sequins with red bead in centre. The thread is fastened to tail end of section and a sequin is threaded on to it, the needle is then passed through a red bead and through centre of sequin to back of fabric, emerging again at edge of sequin.

16 Small, red beads.

17 The heels – flat, green stones surrounded by tiny gold beads.

18 Legs – dark green sequins sewn on as scales as 13.

19 Gold sequin under a dark green sequin, with red bead in centre, applied as 15.

When the beadwork is

completed, cut out the velvet for the bag, allowing 12 mm ($\frac{1}{2}$ in) turnings all round.

To make up

Lay the interlining on the wrong side of the velvet pieces, letting the velvet overlap 12 mm ($\frac{1}{2}$ in) at the top edges. Tack them together firmly all over. Turn the 12 mm ($\frac{1}{2}$ in) turnings on to the wrong side and sew with catch stitch. Attach the zip-fastener in the normal way. Tack the velvet ribbon all round the sides and lower edge of back and front of bag, matching the centre of ribbon strip to centre of bag. Take 6 mm ($\frac{1}{4}$ in) turnings only on the ribbon and trim the 12 mm ($\frac{1}{2}$ in) bag edges down to this width after stitching. Stitch lining strips to lining in same manner. Turn the lining right side out and slip the finished outer part of bag into it, with the raw edges and buckram side against the inside of the lining. Make a small hem at the top of lining and slip-stitch firmly to binding of zip-fastener, leaving the two small seams at the ends open. Push the ends of the zip down these openings. Turn right side out.

Fold the long ends of the velvet ribbon double, into loops, pushing the cut ends between bag and lining each side of the zip-fastener. Catch down firmly and sew the hem of the lining gusset. Slip two small brass rings down to the bottom of each loop and catch. Slip the top of the two loops through two more rings and sew to form a short bow effect.

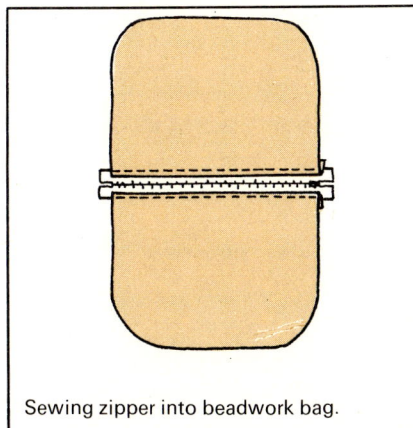

Sewing zipper into beadwork bag.

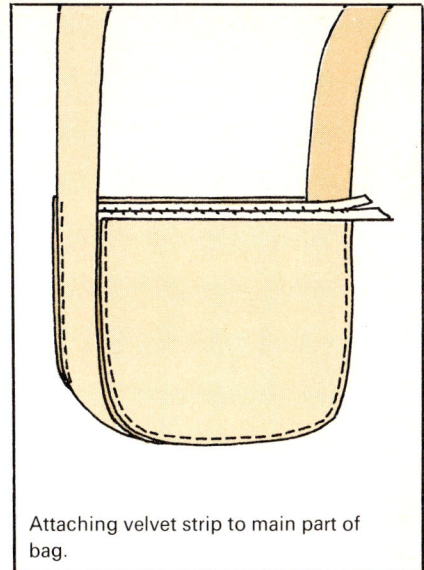

Attaching velvet strip to main part of bag.

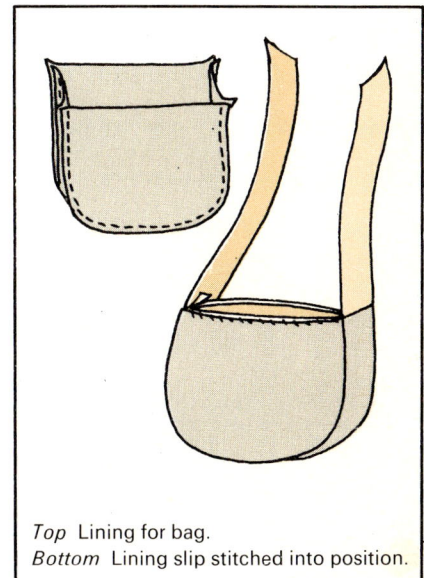

Top Lining for bag.
Bottom Lining slip stitched into position.

The velvet strip is threaded through the gold ring to form a handle.

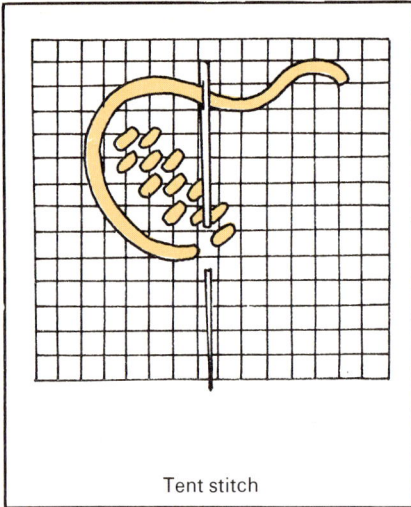

Tent stitch

Petit-point bag

Petit-point is a fine canvas embroidery suitable for bags: tent stitch worked on a single-thread canvas produces work of great delicacy and beauty. Complete bags may be made in this manner but with endless hours of work, and an equally attractive bag, taking far less labour, is made by incorporating a panel of petit-point into a plain cloth shape of simple design, as in the pochette.

The pochette is a convenient shape for a handbag and it is the simplest to make. It is a shape which can be adapted for all occasions from a very large, flat one without gussets to the small compact one with gussets, which gives a roomy inside.

Materials required: 1 piece black felt 50 cm × 62 cm (20 in × 24 in). 1 piece tailor's canvas 50 cm × 62 cm (20 in × 24 in). 1 piece taffeta 50 cm × 62 cm (20 in × 24 in). Stranded embroidery threads. Small piece single-thread canvas (about 18 squares to 2.5 cm (1 in)). 1 large press-fastener.

Cutting the pattern

Draw a paper pattern from the diagram; then cut the following:
A main body of bag: one piece black felt; one piece in taffeta for lining; one in tailor's canvas 3 mm ($\frac{1}{8}$ in) less all round, for interlining; the side flaps are cut on both lining pieces.

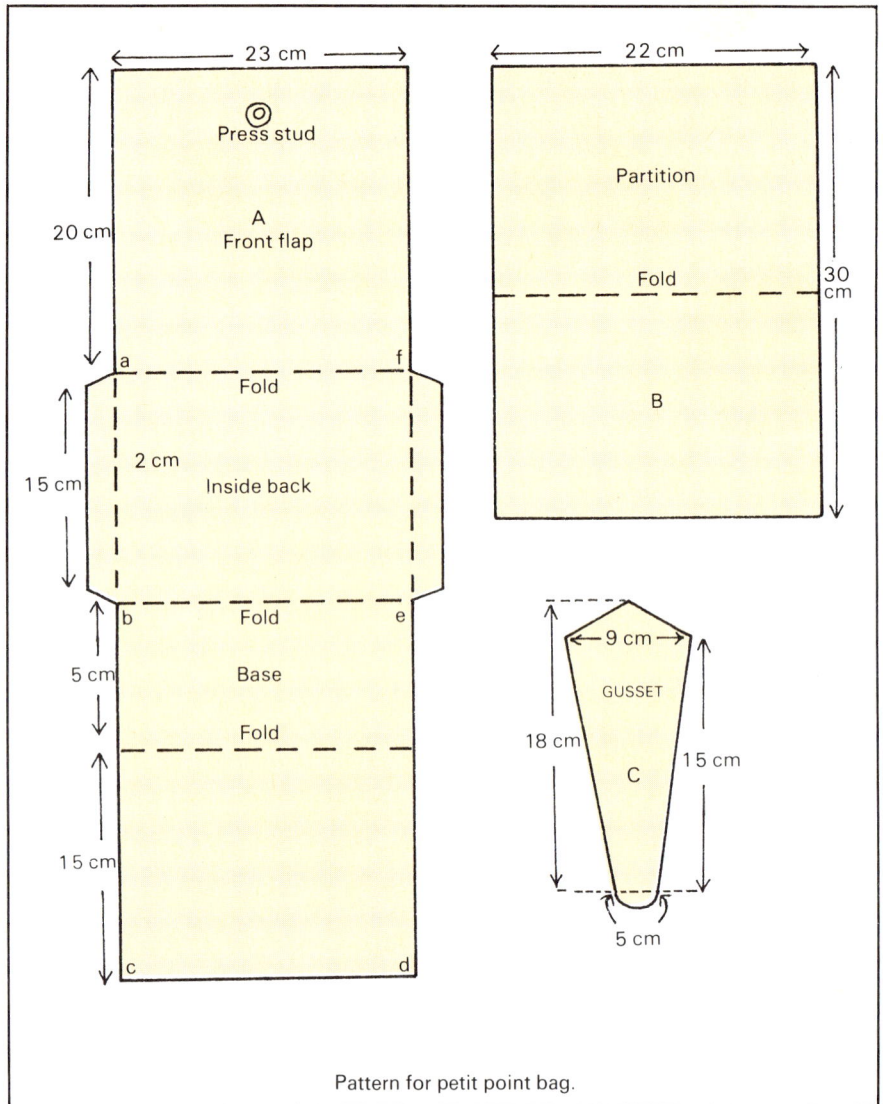

Pattern for petit point bag.

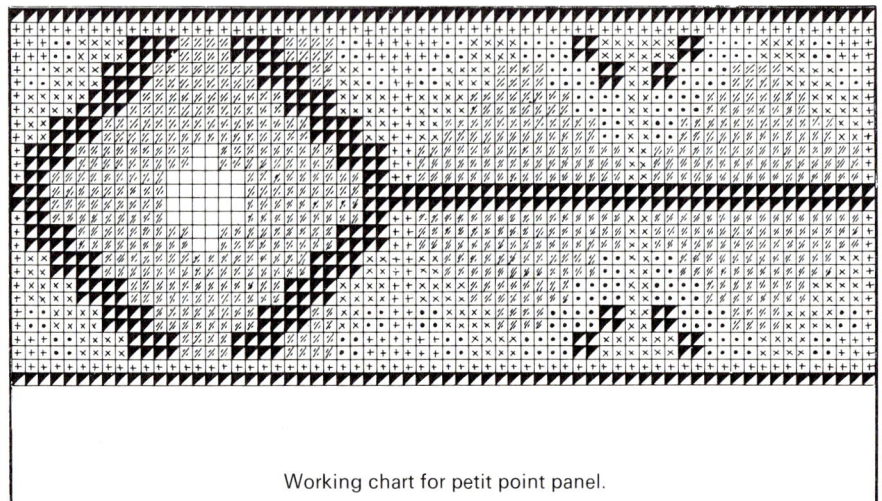

Working chart for petit point panel.

B partition for compact and purse: one piece in felt; one in taffeta.
C gusset: two pieces in felt; two in taffeta. No allowance for seams is made on the diagram.

Panel

Work the petit-point panel, following the chart. Cut right across the felt flap about 4 cm ($1\frac{1}{2}$ in) from front edge. Trim off the

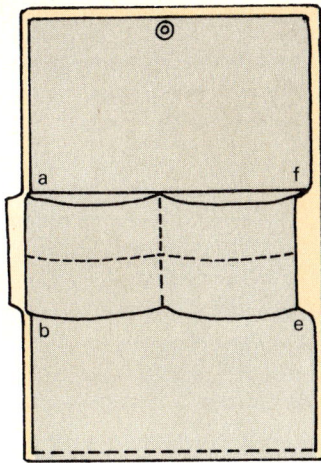

Details of inside of petit point bag.

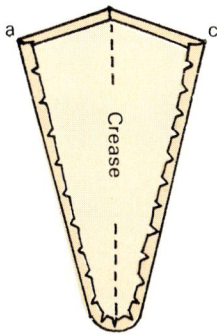

Gusset with edges snipped.

width of panel, less 6 mm ($\frac{1}{4}$ in) turnings, from the large piece of flap. The canvas ground of the petit-point should extend an inch or so all round under the edge of the felt. The panel is tacked in position on the interlining piece, A. The edges of the outer fabric are turned under and tacked, and placed close to the embroidery each side of the panel. A line of neat machine stitching or back stitch is then worked close to the fold, and the bag is ready for making up.

If press-fasteners are used, they must be fixed before the main part of the bag is stitched. Special press-studs, suitable for the purpose, may be bought together with simple

tools for fixing.

Place lining and interlining of flap together with lining extending 3 mm ($\frac{1}{8}$ in) all round the edge and tack well. Fix top part of press-stud on lining side; a small square of canvas placed under the stud acts as strengthening. Fix the lower part of fastening to the front of bag on the outside. Careful measuring will be necessary to find the exact position of fasteners.

If preferred, the fasteners can be fixed just before the front edge of the flap is finished.

Partition

Place the lining and felt together and sew the top and bottom edges. Turn right side out and press the seams flat, then machine-stitch down the two sides. Fold in half and stitch, as diagram, to form two compartments for purse and compact.

If lining is used for both sides of the partition, then it will be necessary to have a canvas interlining. This is cut as B with 3 mm ($\frac{1}{8}$ in) less all round.

When making up, place both pieces of lining together on the interlining and, when the ends have been sewn, turn so that the canvas is sandwiched between. Then continue as for felt.

The main body of bag

Take the felt piece, A, and place lining and interlining on it, the latter uppermost; tack.

Stitch round flap from a to f, sewing very close to edge of interlining and fastening ends of stitches securely. Turn right side out and press with a warm iron. At points a and f shape lining slightly by taking a bigger turning; if necessary, trim the edges of interlining to prevent extra bulk at sides of bag.

Between points a-b and f-e stick edges of lining down with rubber solution, leaving flaps of outside fabric protruding.

Between points b-c and e-d turn outside fabric over interlining and stick lining over it, on the same

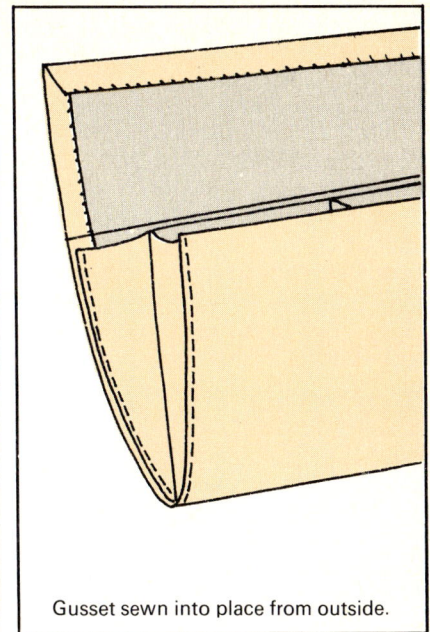

Gusset sewn into place from outside.

level as at a-b and f-e, leaving slight margin of outside fabric showing.

Turn in edges at c-d and machine-stitch neatly together, strengthening ends by reverse stitching for 9 mm ($\frac{3}{8}$ in), cut threads close to fabric.

Place partition on bag between points a-b and e-f. Turn flaps of outer fabric over raw edges of partition. Stick with rubber solution and press between boards under a heavy weight for twelve hours. Where two surfaces are to be stuck together, without added bulk, an excellent alternative to rubber solution is plastic tape, this melts under a hot iron and fuses the two together.

The gusset

Snick side edges of felt round point from a to c, turn them over and stick with rubber solution.

Snick and turn under edges a-c of lining and stick to wrong side of felt.

Make a snick at point b, turn under and stitch top edge a-b-c of the two fabrics together. Crease down centre of gusset to help it lie flat when fixed in bag.

Working on the right side of bag, fix point a of gusset to a of bag and c of gusset to c of bag, tack into place using stab stitch, easing base of bag round end of gusset. Machine- or hand-stitch carefully,

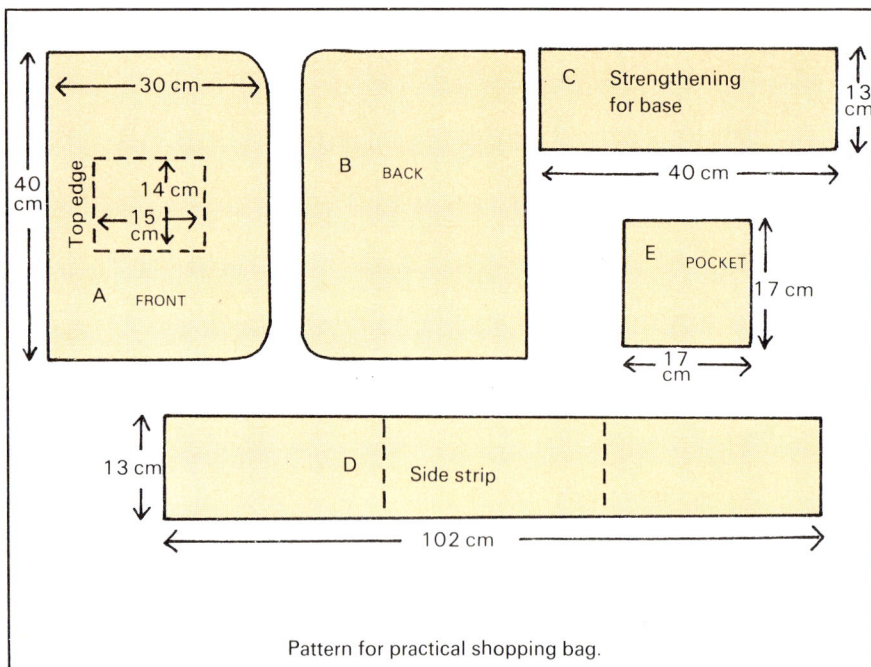

Pattern for practical shopping bag.

A main front piece.
B main back piece.
C strengthening layer to cover plywood or base of bag.
D long side strip to join back and front pieces together.
E pocket.

Making up
Bind top edges of front and back pieces, with webbing or leather strips, tacking through all thicknesses. Leave a raw edge at each end, as this will be covered by binding on sides. Then machine-stitch.

Make a narrow turning 12 mm ($\frac{3}{8}$ in) on top edge of small pocket and machine-stitch it to lower edge of zip-fastener. Place pocket, with zip-fastener attached, above pocket position, as in diagram, and stitch top tape of fastener to front of bag on line A-B, finishing off end firmly. Fold pocket back again on to dotted line, make a small turning on lower edge only and stitch.

The gusset
Stitch short strengthening piece, C, to wrong side of the base of gusset, with the plywood stiffening between the two layers.

reverse stitching at each end to strengthen, finish off.

Repeat for opposite side.

The bag is now completed. Crease gusset down centre, fasten the bag and place it under weights for twelve hours to press into a flat, smooth shape, or, if preferred, it may be ironed under a damp cloth with a moderately hot iron.

Practical shopping bag
This bag with a separate compartment to hold pocket-books and purse will give good service for many years.

Materials required: 112 cm (1$\frac{1}{4}$ yd) strong coloured canvas or duck, 72 cm (28 in) wide.
Strong sewing thread (no lighter than No. 40).
9 m (10 yd) 2.5 cm (1 in) wide webbing, or soft leather strips for binding.
Thin plywood for stiffening base 9 cm × 37 cm (3$\frac{1}{2}$ in × 14$\frac{1}{2}$ in).
13 cm (5 in) zip-fastener.
74 cm (29 in) lengths of 12 mm ($\frac{1}{2}$ in) rope, for handles.

Cutting the pattern
Draw out the patterns, following the diagram, on paper and cut out, then arrange the pieces on the canvas and cut:

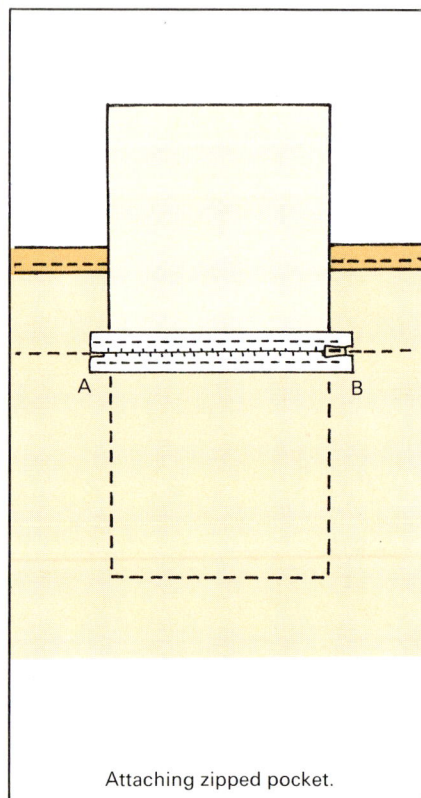

Make a useful, neck-slung pouch bag, and decorate it to co-ordinate with a casual outfit.

Attaching zipped pocket.

Stitch the same 41 cm (16 in) of the gusset, which forms the base, to bottom edges of front and back pieces, on the right side, leaving the two side strips loose. Bind the part just stitched with webbing.

The handles

The handles and supporting webbing are joined into one piece for strength. Cut four lengths of webbing, each 74 cm (29 in) long, for the supporting straps, and four short lengths, each 30 cm (12 in) long, for handles. Cut the ends of each piece to a point. Lay a 23 cm (9 in) length of rope between two 30 cm (12 in) pieces of webbing, leaving 4 cm (1½ in) at each end of double webbing. Stitch all round rope and close to it.

Stitch two 74 cm (29 in) lengths of webbing together, sewing down each side.

Fix the points neatly inside the pointed ends of the handle-piece, and machine round points and across centre.

Make the second handle in the

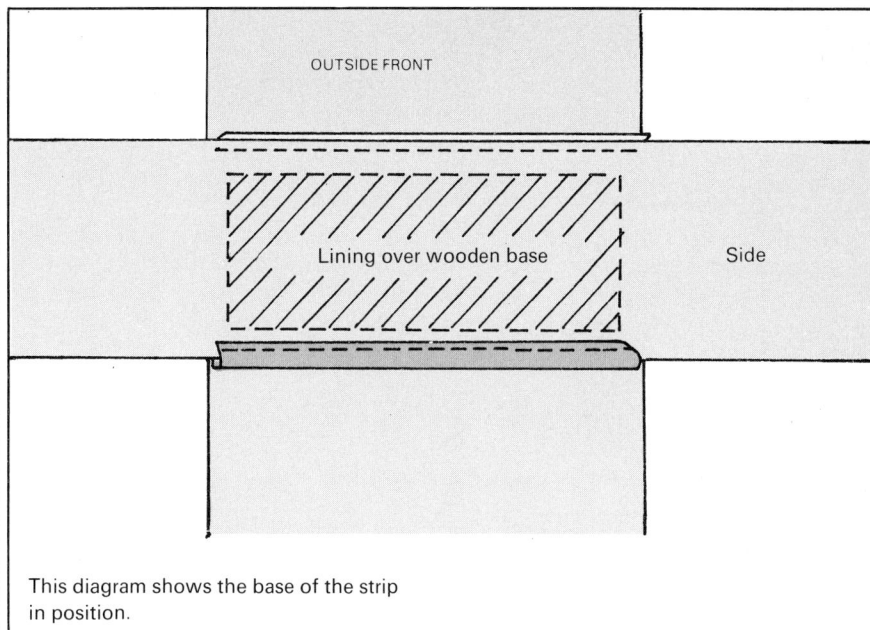

OUTSIDE FRONT

Lining over wooden base   Side

This diagram shows the base of the strip in position.

same way.

To join supports to bag

Lay the two supports round the bag, covering the edges of the pockets and placing the points of the handle about 2.5 cm (1 in) below the top edge of the bag. Pin in place and tack. Stitch the supports firmly along each edge as far as the binding on lower edge, fasten off securely. Carry strap across base of bag and stitch again above the binding on back.

To complete the bag, stitch side

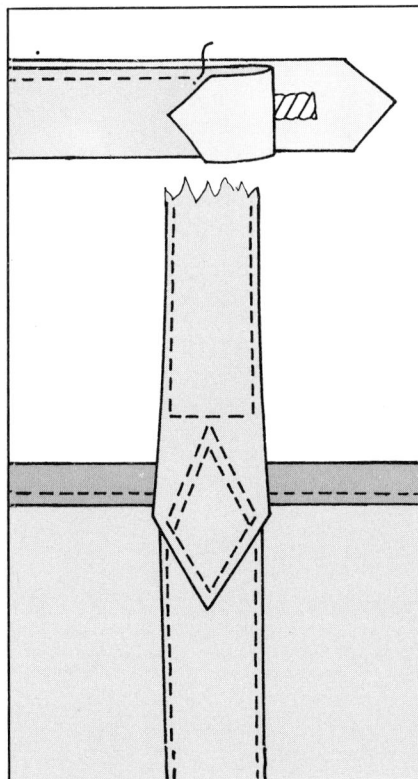

Above Handle stitched around rope.
Below Attaching a handle to rest of strap.

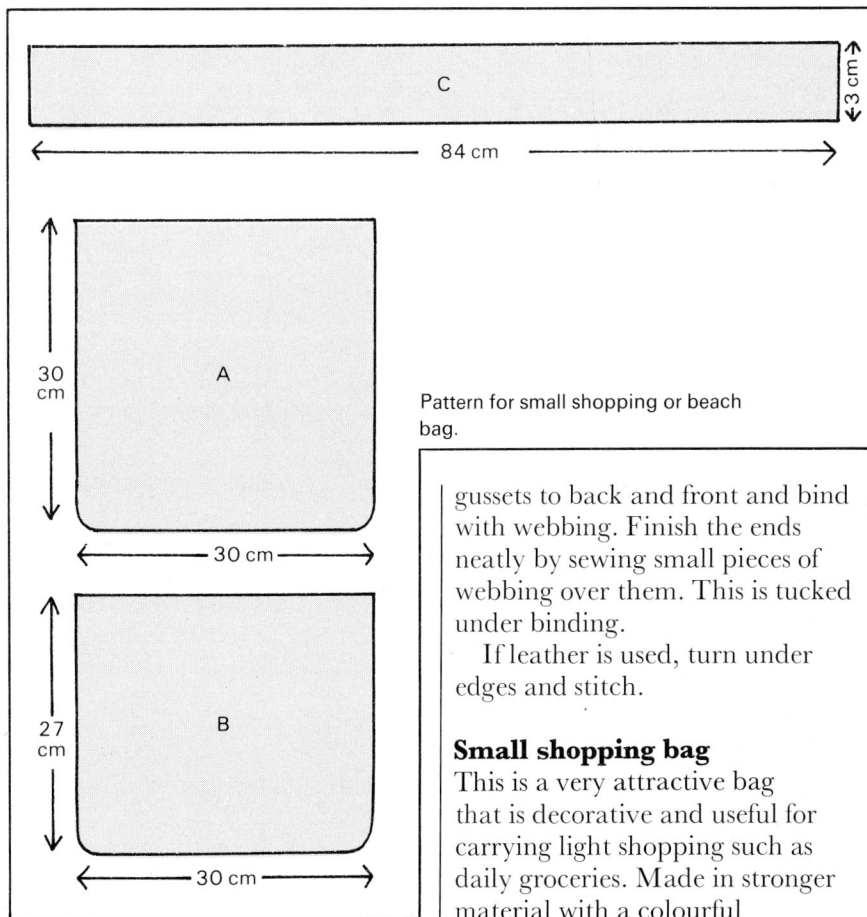

C

84 cm

3 cm

A

30 cm

30 cm

B

27 cm

30 cm

Pattern for small shopping or beach bag.

gussets to back and front and bind with webbing. Finish the ends neatly by sewing small pieces of webbing over them. This is tucked under binding.

If leather is used, turn under edges and stitch.

Small shopping bag

This is a very attractive bag that is decorative and useful for carrying light shopping such as daily groceries. Made in stronger material with a colourful waterproof lining, it is an excellent beach bag.

For a shopping bag choose something to tone with your outfit, plain or printed silks and rayons are most attractive, but almost any light-weight fabric may be used. Soft tailor's canvas is used for the lining and all inside turnings are neatened with bias binding. Ribbon lines the mouth of the bag to strengthen the eyelet holes.

Materials required: 2 pieces of material 30 cm × 30 cm (12 in × 12 in).
45 cm (½ yd) tailor's canvas for lining.
90 cm (1 yd), 8 cm (3 in) wide, grosgrain ribbon.
90 cm (1 yd), 5 cm (2 in) wide, ribbon.
180 cm (2 yd) bias binding.
180 cm (2 yd) of silk cord.
16 large, brass eyelets.
Draw the pattern, following diagram, and cut it out.

Directions for cutting
Cut two pieces of main shape, A, in outside fabric.

Cut two pieces, B, in tailor's canvas.

Cut one strip of canvas, C, 8 cm × 86 cm (3 × 34 in), joining where necessary.

Making up
Place outside fabric on top of canvas lining and lightly tack together to prevent them slipping out of position. Keep the two rounded edges of the base level, leaving the extra 4 cm (1½ in) of the outside fabric loose at the top edge.

Place the 8 cm (3 in) wide ribbon over the canvas strip and leave 4 cm (1½ in) free each end. Placing ribbon to fabric, tack the strip for gusset all round one side of bag, taking the narrowest possible seam allowance, machine-stitch round edge from a to b. Neaten turnings with bias binding.

Make sure the ends of the canvas strip are level with the top of the canvas lining B.

Join the other side of bag to second side of gusset strip.

Finish open edge of bag by

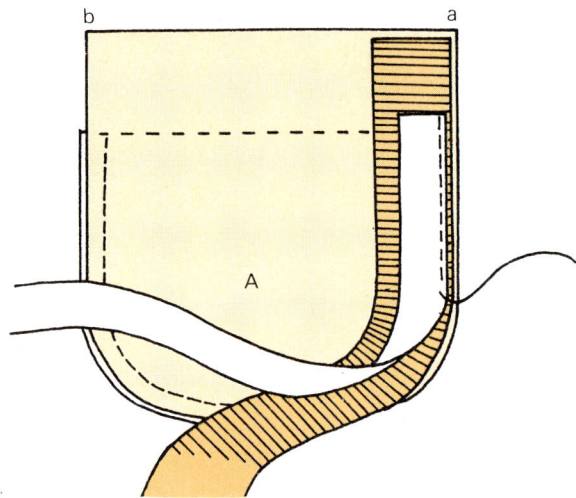
Placing the canvas, fabric and ribbon for stitching.

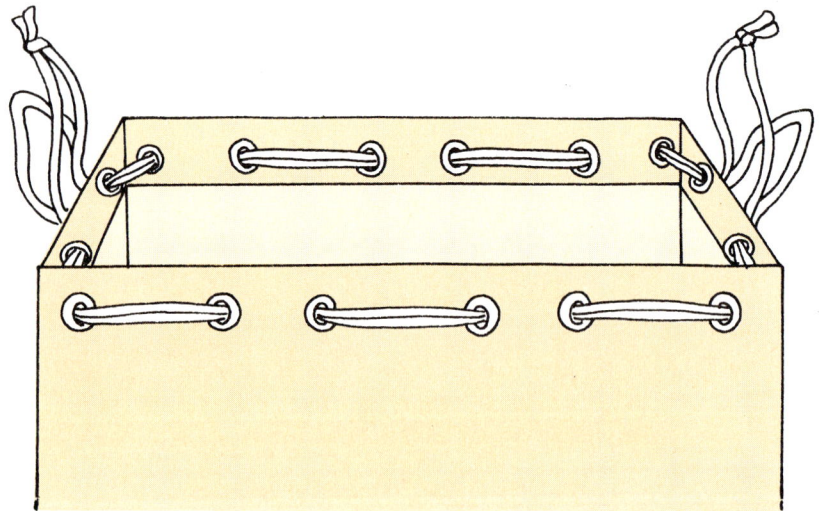
Cord is threaded through the eyelets in a double circle.

making a 12 mm (½ in) single turning on the outer fabric. Tack this down, neaten with the 5 cm (2 in) wide ribbon, hemming the top edge to the turnings and the lower edge to the canvas.

Have 16 large, brass, sailmaker's eyelets fixed for strength and easy movement of the cord. (These eyelets can usually be obtained and fitted at a blind-maker's or upholsterer's shop).

Thread the cord through eyelets, in a double circle and knot, as in diagram.

Fringes
There are two ways of making attractive fringes.

First method Wind yarn round a book or piece of cardboard and cut through the strands with scissors. The length of the fringe is determined by the breadth of the article round which the yarn is wound. Take these strands in groups and insert them into the edge at even distances.

The number of threads in the groups can be varied to suit the size of fringe being made. Fold each group in half, insert a crochet hook into the edge of the fabric, place the loop over the hook, draw it through, and pull the ends through the loop. Trim the lengths even.

This type of fringe is suitable for the edge of scarves, shawls or table cloths.

Second method Draw out the weft threads of a piece of coarse material, leaving a fringe of warp threads. With a long fringe these threads can be knotted in bundles; the knots should be close to the material in an even line. The number of threads in each bundle depends on the type of material and thickness of the threads. A second and third row of knots may be made by taking half or two consecutive groups together and knotting them again.

Either of these two fringes may be made in more than one colour or texture. The first type can have extra strands inserted at intervals among the warp threads, and the second type may consist of so many strands of one colour or texture, and so many of another. Used with care, a fringe can make a plain edge much more attractive.

Gloves

Leather is the most suitable and durable material for gloves, but various fabrics, chosen to match or tone with a certain outfit, may be used. It takes a little practice to become proficient in glove-making, so it is a good idea to start with a simple slip-on pair in skin. When all the snags have been realized and overcome, then more exciting styles may be attempted, incorporating punched or embroidered decorations.

Materials: A skin, a pattern, a large pair of sharp scissors, a pair of nail scissors, a sharp pencil, No. 6 or 7 needle and thread.

Glove needles are not recommended, unless for very thick leather, as they tend to cut the skins. A good silk thread should be used, or an ordinary buttonhole twist; if this becomes untwisted in use, draw it over a piece of beeswax to keep in good condition when working.

Choice of skins
The type of skin used will depend on the purpose and design of the glove, but always choose good leather. There is a great variety of gloving leathers; the most suitable are made from sheep or lambskin.

Chamois leather This is the most popular and it is made from the split lamb or sheep skins. These are put through a process of fish-oil dressing which makes the leather soft, hardwearing, and pliable.

Originally this leather was made from the chamois, now almost extinct.

Suede Sheep skins dyed and finished on the flesh side by means of a dry emery wheel, which gives a suede effect.

Tan cape Sheep skins tanned by dipping and specially treated to give a glossy finish.

Originally this leather was made from the skins of South African sheep.

Care must be taken when selecting a skin. Hold it up to the light and choose one of even thickness, and one that stretches one way only. Test the stretch of the skin in the centre between neck and tail, as it is only down the spine that the skin is firm. In chamois, do not choose a spongy skin as there is usually too much stretch in it. Select one with a smooth finish which will not soil so readily. For hand-made gloves only the best quality skins should be used.

Pattern
A good pattern is essential and the simplest and most popular glove is the slip-on type. It is a good plan to unpick a favourite, well-fitting, worn, glove and use it as a pattern.

The pattern consists of three pieces: (1) the hand; (2) thumb; (3) fourchette. The fourchette joins front and back of finger. These are cut to average sizes, but sometimes a little alteration in length is required. This must be very carefully done. Test the pattern, width round knuckles, length from fork of thumb, i.e. midway between B and D to base of first finger. If the pattern is too long, make a small tuck round the hand, midway between the fork of thumb and base of fingers; if it is too short, slash and insert a piece of paper the required width.

The base of the fingers on the back of the hand should be 9 mm to 12 mm ($\frac{3}{8}$ to $\frac{1}{2}$ in) lower than the front.

Arranging pattern on skin
Hold the skin up to the light and mark lightly with tailor's chalk or pencil, on the right side, any defects so that they may be avoided when placing the pattern. Stretch the skin both ways before laying it out on a smooth wood surface. The stretch must go across the hand.

Place the skin right side uppermost so that any discoloured parts are easily detected, and pin it in place with a few drawing pins. If the pattern is crushed, press it with a warm iron until it is smooth.

It is a good plan to cut rough duplicates of the pattern in paper and use these for arranging the layout on the skin. Each part of the pattern must be placed in the same way as the hand, with the stretch across; this is most important, and care must be taken to avoid thin and stained parts of the skin. The stretch at the base or tail end of the skin is sometimes 5 or 8 cm (2 or 3 in), up and down.

Place the hand, the largest part of pattern, towards the centre where the skin is thickest. Place a weight over the thumb hole to keep it in position. Outline the pattern, using a finely pointed pencil, taking care not to stretch the skin. For chamois the outline should be dotted lightly with a pencil or stiletto. Mark round the top of

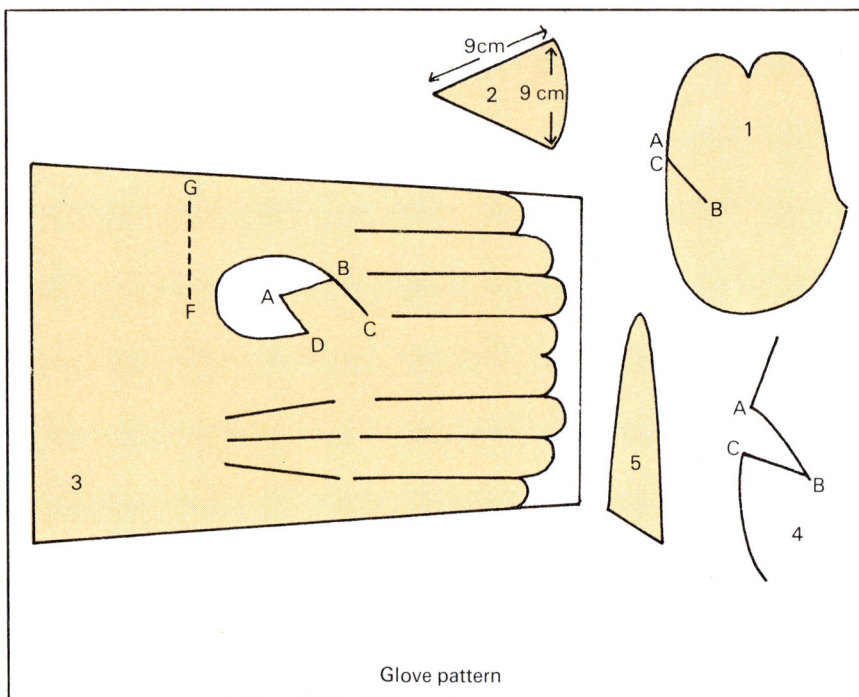

Glove pattern

fingers and firmly at the base of each. Remove the weight and draw round the thumbhole, marking point c. Mark nips on back of hand, with dots each end, before removing the pattern. Reverse the pattern for the second hand. Place thumb also with the stretch going across. Outline the pattern, 1, marking point B. Reverse the pattern for the second thumb. Six pairs of fourchettes, 5, are required for the fingers. The waste pieces of skin can be used for cutting the fourchettes. They are all cut the same length at first. The stretch must go across as in other parts.

Cutting out

Use large sharp scissors for cutting out. To avoid a jagged edge, do not close the points of the scissors. Cut the fourchettes first to get accustomed to the cutting, then cut up the sides of the hand part of pattern, taking care to cut exactly on the marking line or dots. Cut straight across the top, as shown, do not curve, or slit down the fingers. Insert the point of scissors in the centre of the thumb-hole. Cut along line BA to D, do not slit to C until thumb is cut out. Draw lines on the wrong side from the top of the fingers to the base.

Cut out the thumb patterns,

marking points AC and B, but do not slit. Check measurements on thumb and thumb-hole. AB and BC on thumb-hole should equal AB and BC on thumb. Slit B to C on thumb-hole and AC to B on thumb. Successful glove making depends greatly on the pattern being cut accurately.

The gusset pattern, 2, may be omitted.

Making up

The stitch most often used is stab stitch. The two wrong sides of the skin are placed together, and the stitching is kept equidistant from the edge throughout. The stitches must be even, not too small and of equal length on both sides. Do not curve the skin over the fingers to sew, as it is inclined to stretch.

Alternatively the edges may be overcast giving a rolled effect. Two stitches are made through one hole and diagonally across to the next stitch. It gives a more decorative result and could be worked in a contrasting colour, such as black on white or vice versa.

Nips or points Fold the glove in a straight line, to the base of the second finger at the centre dot, wrong sides together. Stab stitch close to the edge to form a little

tuck; this should extend to within 6 mm ($\frac{1}{4}$ in) below the finger base. Commence with a knot about 5 cm (2 in) from end of thread. This end is darned in on the wrong side after sewing for added strength. Always begin sewing in this way when making a glove.

All the stitches should be very even and the needle is inserted at right angles to the edge. Care must be taken that the stitches at the knuckles are not drawn too tightly, as the full width of the glove must be left here. The sewing should be made tighter at the lower end to give shaping. Finish off the thread on the wrong side with a loop, and back stitch, then darn through the last few stitches. If a continuous line of stitching is desired, a second row can be worked on the reverse side, filling up the spaces of the first row. The other two tucks are worked in the same way from the dots to 6 mm ($\frac{1}{4}$ in) below the base of the first and third fingers.

Thumb Point A on the thumb is placed to point A on the thumb-hole, wrong sides together.

Begin with a knot as before, bringing the thread out between the folds at A. Stab stitch to B, then to C, pulling the stitches taut at the points. Continue stitching to about 25 cm (1 in) down the side of the thumb-hole, then make a stitch on one side only, bringing the thread out on the wrong side between the

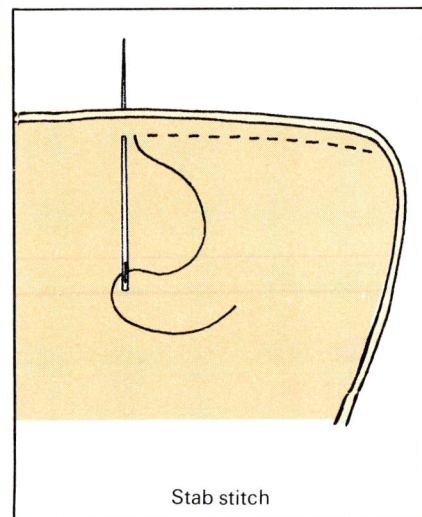

Stab stitch

folds. Cut off the thread, leaving about 5 cm (2 in).

Fold the thumb, wrong sides together taking care that the top is well shaped.

Commence at the top, and stab stitch down through A and round the thumb-hole until the end of the last thread is reached. Make a stitch on one side opposite the stitch on the other. Take the thread between the folds to the wrong side and tie the two ends together with a reef knot. Darn in the ends.

Elastic Insert the elastic at the wrist while the glove is flat. If the position is not marked on the pattern, measure 12 mm ($\frac{1}{2}$ in) down from the base of thumb-hole and 6 mm ($\frac{1}{4}$ in) in towards palm, then straight across to within 12 mm ($\frac{1}{2}$ in) of the side seam.

Turn in the raw edge of elastic and hem the end firmly to the glove at F. Herringbone over the elastic to G, taking the stitches through to the right side for strength. Draw up the elastic a little and secure with a pin, but do not fasten off until the glove is completely finished.

Fourchettes Oversew the base of a pair with right sides together from H to I. Take a double stitch, but do not finish off thread. This when opened out forms the fork.

The fourchettes are sewn to the back of the hand first. Cut down between the first and second fingers and curve the top with nail scissors.

Point I is placed to the base of the first finger, with the same needle and thread, stab stitch the fourchette and the finger together halfway up. Measure the fourchette and cut it exactly the same length as the finger, tapering it, using the paper pattern as a guide. Continue sewing to the end of the fourchette. Finish off on the wrong side, darning in the end of the thread. Curve the point of the second finger. Re-start at the base and sew the fourchette to the left side of second finger, measuring and tapering as before. Care must be taken that the fourchettes are not

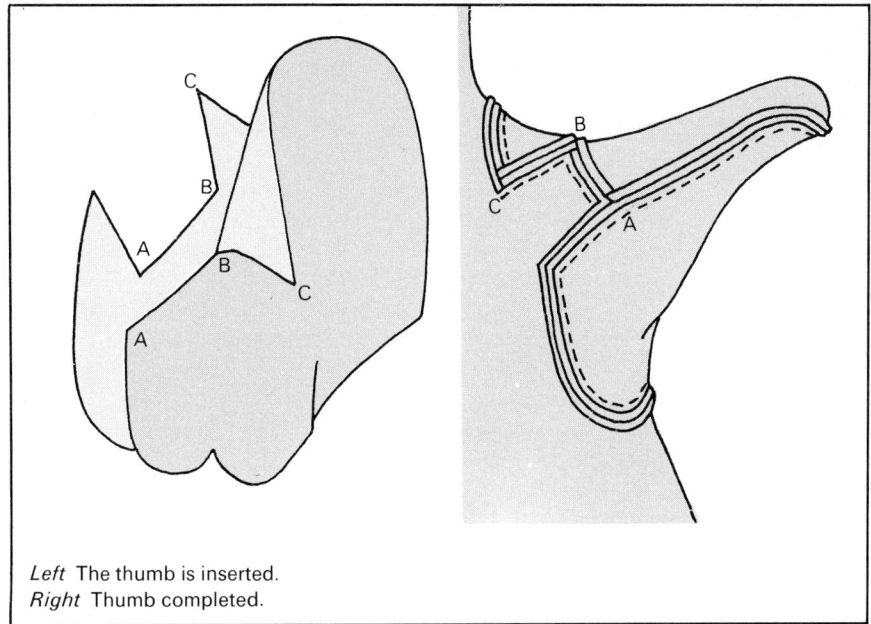

Left The thumb is inserted.
Right Thumb completed.

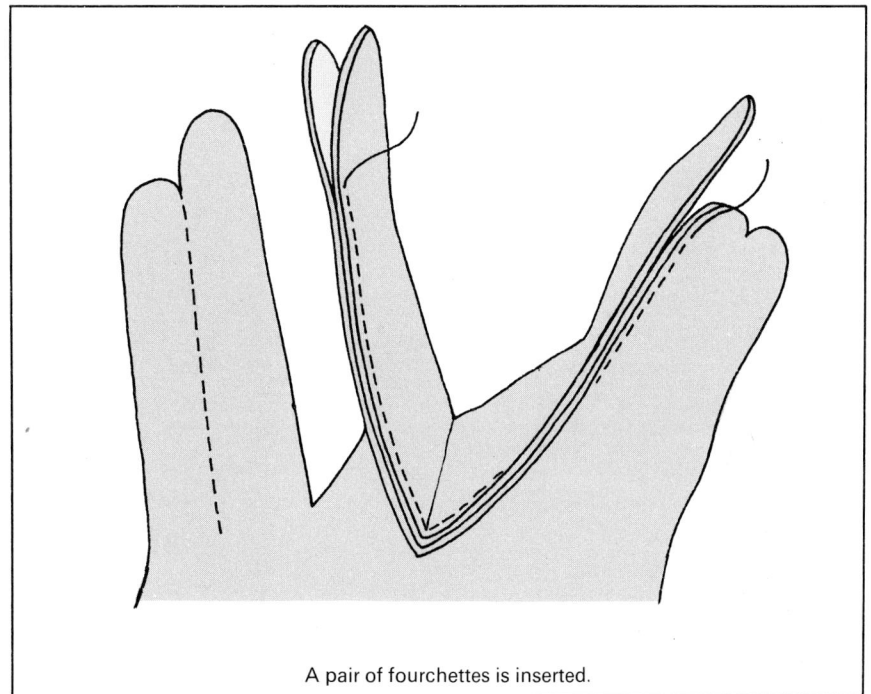

A pair of fourchettes is inserted.

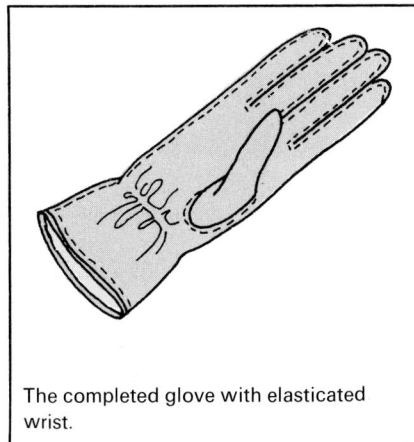

The completed glove with elasticated wrist.

cut too short. They should be just long enough to allow the width of two stitches at the tips. Insert all the fourchettes in this way and then sew the points.

Finishing off Fit the glove and test the width of the elastic, turn in the end at G and fasten off securely. This may be omitted in a non-fitting type of glove, in which case a gusset may be needed in the side seam. Insert this before the stitching is completed.

Cushions

Cushions are one of the most versatile furnishing accessories in the home and for the needlewoman who likes decorative sewing, they present almost endless opportunities.

Practically any kind of fabric can be used to make cushions; they can be made of patchwork, be quilted or appliquéd. A wide variety of embroidery techniques can also be used on cushions and yet the basic techniques for making these useful accessories are very simple and straightforward. The only expertise required is careful machine stitching.

Fillings and cushion pads
Cushions generally fall into three types: soft pillows or cushions which are used for decorating or simply for comfort, firm pillows and cushions made on a latex or polyether foam base and used for chair seats and casual floor seating, and block cushions which usually come in cube or other geometric shapes, and are made of dense, latex foam.

Soft cushion pads can be purchased in a limited range of sizes, in square, rectangular, round and oval shapes. Latex cushion pads and blocks can be purchased from large department stores and specialist shops and come in a variety of sizes, usually square or round in shape but some geometric shapes, for bolsters, are available. Polyether foam is available in a range of thicknesses, from 12 mm ($\frac{1}{2}$ in) up to about 15 cm (6 in). It can be bought by the sheet or, more often, as offcuts, which are more economical.

Use an array of easily made cushions to add colour and pattern to a room.

It is generally cheaper to make your own soft cushion pads, particularly if the cushion is an in-between size. Animal-shaped cushions or other fancy shapes must obviously have their own specially-made cushion pads.

Fillings
Down Down is a fine, feathery, substance from a bird's breast. It is beautifully soft and light when used in cushions but is becoming more difficult to obtain and is thus very expensive. It is sometimes mixed with feathers.

Feathers Curled chicken or duck feathers are sold by weight for filling cushion pads but occasionally it is possible to purchase an old eiderdown and decant the feathers from this to make your own cushions. For a cushion 46 cm (18 in) square you will need 1 kilo (2 lb) of feathers.

Kapok This is a vegetable fibre, fairly inexpensive and easily obtained. Its drawback for use in cushions is that it tends to become lumpy. It is ideal for cushions which are used out of doors as it does not absorb moisture.

Polyester fibre filling This is soft and resilient and is completely machine-washable. It is an ideal filling for cushions and pillows which are going to be laundered. When used in a large cushion, wrap it round a foam pad for firmness combined with softness.

Foam chips and shreds Foam chips are a good filling for large cushions and for box cushions for use in the garden but they are inclined to produce a lumpy surface. Choose a really firm fabric for the inner cushion cover if you are using foam chips. Foam shreds are finer and make a better filling.

Wood shavings Wood shavings, sometimes mixed with sawdust, make a good filling for pouffes and big floor cushions. The inner cover must be made of a strong, closely-woven fabric.

Polystyrene granules Polystyrene granules are purchased as minute, glass-like beads which are prepared for use with boiling water and steam. (Instructions are given on the can.) Polystyrene granules are used mostly for large, squashy floor cushions, such as sag-bags, but with continuous use they are inclined to disintegrate and have to be replaced. If you decide to use polystyrene, the cushion inner cover should have a zip fastener so that you can refill or replace the granules easily. Use with care – they are highly inflammable.

Covers for cushion pads
Whatever type of filling you choose, the cushion pad should be in a separate cover, especially if a loose filling is being used.

In the case of feather or down fillings, the inner cover prevents the material from seeping out of the cushion. If foam chip filling is being used, the inner cover will help to produce a smoother surface on the finished cushion. Latex and foam pads or blocks are easier to handle if they are fitted with a close-fitting cotton cover first.

Choose a down-proof calico for the pad cover. Alternatively, closely woven curtain lining can be used. The method for making a cushion pad is the same as for making a basic square or rectangular cushion.

Cushion pad cover or basic square cushion
For either a cushion pad or a square cushion, first decide on the size and shape required. (For a complex shape you will have to cut a paper pattern first.) Add 12 mm ($\frac{1}{2}$ in) all round for the seam allowance. For a plump-looking cushion, make the pad 12 mm ($\frac{1}{2}$ in) larger all round than the cushion cover.

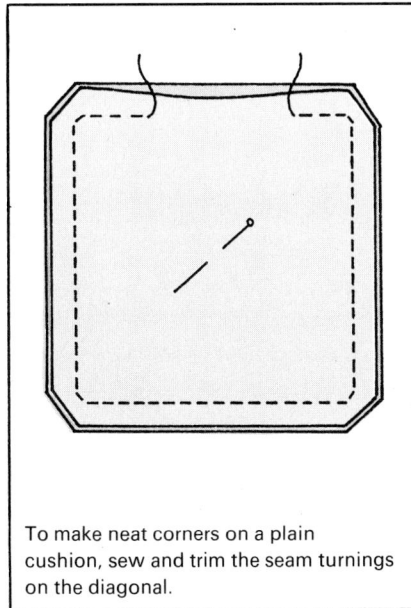

To make neat corners on a plain cushion, sew and trim the seam turnings on the diagonal.

Cut two pieces of fabric to size on the straight grain, taking the selvedges off the fabric first. Place the two pieces together with the right sides facing. Put one pin in the middle to hold the pieces together then pin round the edges, inserting the pins at right angles and without puckering the fabric.

Work tacking stitches along the seam line, remove the pins, and then machine stitch the seams or stitch them by hand using small back stitches. When doing this, secure the thread end firmly and begin stitching about 8 cm (3 in) from one corner. Stitch to the corner, pivoting the work on the machine needle to make a small diagonal stitch across the corner, then stitch the remaining three sides, but after pivoting on the fourth corner stitch for only 8 cm (3 in) along the fourth side. (The diagonal stitch on the corner helps to give a clean point to the corner when the cover is turned.) This leaves part of the fourth side of the cushion open for inserting the cushion pad.

Trim the seam allowances back to 6 mm ($\frac{1}{4}$ in) and trim the corners off diagonally, almost to the stitching. Leave the fourth, partly stitched side untrimmed. Press the seam allowances open and press the seam allowances on the unfinished seam flat. Turn the cushion or pad cover to the right side, poking the corners through with a blunt pencil.

For a cushion pad, fill the pad at this point. Pin the edges of the opening together and oversew neatly.

If you do not mind unpicking and re-stitching the seam every time you take the cushion cover off for laundering, the opening can be simply closed with handsewing. Insert the cushion pad, adjusting it to fit fully into the corners. Pin the open seam edges together and then sew them together with slip-stitches. Alternatively, use tiny oversewing stitches and a closely matching thread.

Square or rectangular cushion covers can be closed with a zip fastener, snap fasteners or touch-and-close fastening (Velcro), but closures of these kinds must be added before all the seams are completed.

Filling with feathers

Here's a way to transfer feathers from an existing cushion or bag into a cushion pad without the inconvenience of having them fly about. Tack the opening of the pad over the opening of the bag that holds the feathers. Then work the feathers into the cushion pad. Put some pins along the seam line of the pad's opening before unpicking the tacking stitches. Turn in the edges of the opening and oversew or slip-stitch them together tightly. This trick can also be used when recovering pillows.

Making piped cushions

In soft furnishing, piped cording is used to give a neat, defined edge to seams. It also strengthens those areas where there is likely to be more wear, such as corners. Piping helps to give cushion covers a good, professional finish and it is worth learning how to make it properly. Practise on oddments of fabric until you feel absolutely sure of the techniques. You will then be ready to make your first piped cushion. Try a round cushion first, without angles or corners.

Piping

Piping cord is made of cotton in six thicknesses and is purchased by length. Thicknesses gauged 2 and 3 are mostly used in cushions. The cord is covered with cross-cut strips of fabric and then stitched between two layers of fabric in a seam. Piping cord has a tendency to shrink when it is first washed. To prevent this happening, and spoiling the effect of a neatly made cushion, boil the piping cord in hot water for about five minutes and then allow it to drip dry.

Cross-cut strips for piping casing

The strips of fabric (the casings) used for covering the piping cord are cut on the bias of the fabric so that the fabric stretches smoothly on corners and curves. It is important, therefore, that the strips

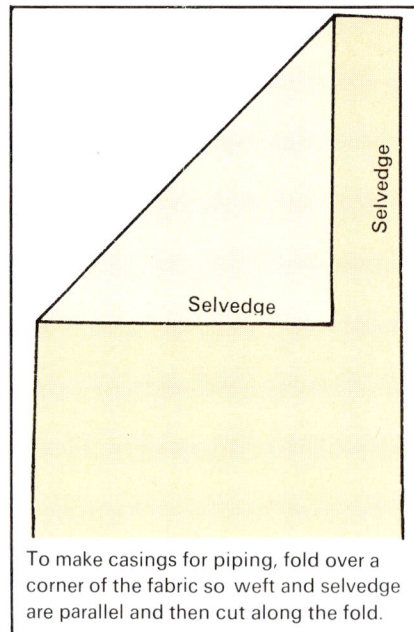

To make casings for piping, fold over a corner of the fabric so weft and selvedge are parallel and then cut along the fold.

are cut on the true bias of the fabric.

The cross-cut strips can be cut from the same fabric as the cushion cover or can be in a contrasting colour. Loosely woven fabrics are not suitable for piping so if the cushion cover is made of tweed or something similar, choose cotton or silk for the piping.

Cutting bias strips Find the bias of the fabric first. To do this fold the fabric diagonally so that the selvedge edge lies parallel with the weft, press the fold and then cut along it. Cut the selvedges off. All the strips used must be of exactly the same width – 4 cm ($1\frac{1}{2}$ in) is the usual width for piping casing. Cut a length of stiff card 4 cm ($1\frac{1}{2}$ in) wide. Lay one edge of the card along the diagonally cut edge of the fabric and mark along the other edge. Continue in this way, moving the card and making a series of parallel chalked lines across the fabric. Alternatively, you can measure and mark chalked lines from the cut edge 4 cm ($1\frac{1}{2}$ in) apart. Leave the ends cut on the diagonal, do not cut them off straight.

Joining strips for piping casing Cross-cut strips are joined on the straight grain of the fabric. Lay two strips, right sides facing, at right angles to

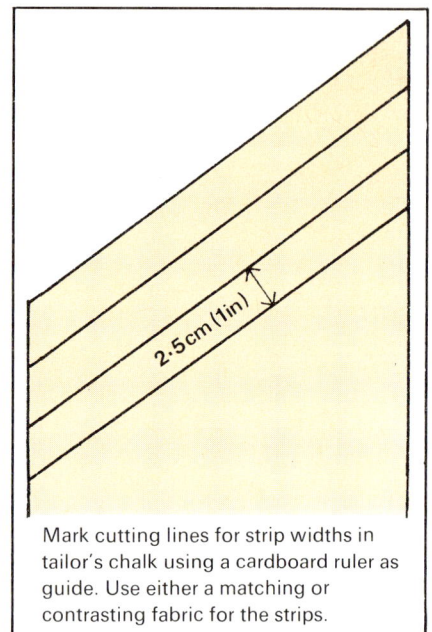

Mark cutting lines for strip widths in tailor's chalk using a cardboard ruler as guide. Use either a matching or contrasting fabric for the strips.

each other. Pin, tack and then machine stitch. Trim the small protruding corners. Join as many strips as you need to make a piece long enough to go round your cushion cover.

Inserting cord into casing

Lay the pre-shrunk piping cord along the centre of the cross-cut strip, on the wrong side. Fold the casing over the cord and tack along close to the cord, so that it is firmly held in position. Then, following the line of tacking, work small running stitches along the length of the cord using a closely matching thread. Remove the tacking. These running stitches can be left in position after the piping is finished and, if the colour of the thread is well-matched, they will not show.

If preferred, you can machine stitch the casing instead of working running stitches, using the piping or zipper foot on your sewing machine.

Positioning the piping

Pin the prepared piping to one piece of the cushion fabric on the right side, positioning it so that the cord is lying exactly along the seam line 12 mm ($\frac{1}{2}$ in) from the raw edge. The raw edges of the casing and the raw edge of the fabric should be parallel. The second piece of cushion fabric is laid on top, right side down, and tacked

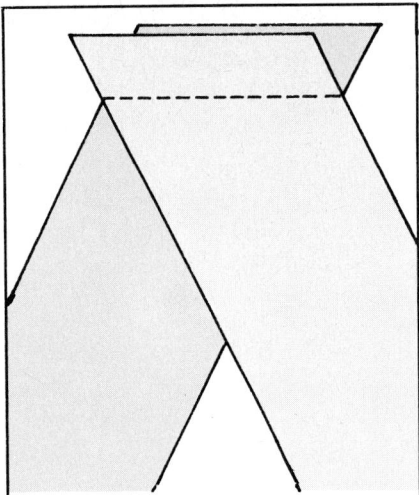

To make a continuous strip, place the strips with right sides facing and ends together as shown here and stitch. Press the seam open.

exactly along the inside edge of the cord over the casing stitches.

It is very important that these tacking stitches be carefully worked and placed because they are your only guide to accurate machine stitching of the seam. You may find that it helps to mark the seam line in chalk before pinning and tacking.

Stitching the piped seam

Using the piping or zip foot on the machine, machine stitch exactly on the seam line, as close to the cord as possible. On the right side, the piping will lie smoothly and neatly in the centre of the seam. If piping is being inserted into a seam which is going to be left partially open for turning, such as on a cushion cover,

machine stitch the piping to the base fabric *before* putting the second piece of fabric on top. This will ensure that the piping is held securely in position while you are closing that section of the seam by hand.

Piping curves and corners

When fitting piping around a corner, such as on a square cushion, clip into the seam allowance of the piping casing, so that the piping turns the corner.

Joining ends of piping When you have pinned and tacked the piping round the cushion corner, the ends must be joined so that they do not show when the cushion is finished.

To do this, cut off the excess

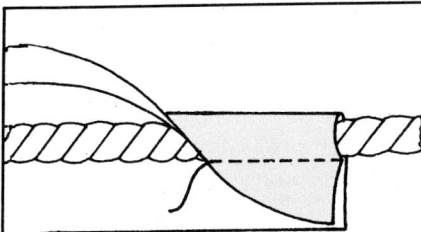

Place piping cord in centre of strip and machine stitch the fabric casing close to cord.

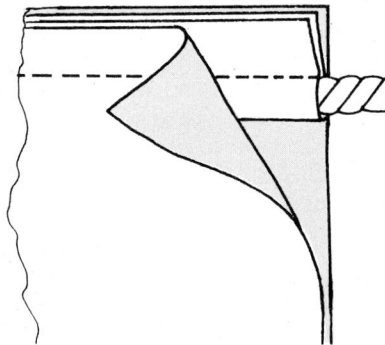

To insert piping into a seam, sandwich the cased piping between the main fabric pieces, then pin and tack the layers together.

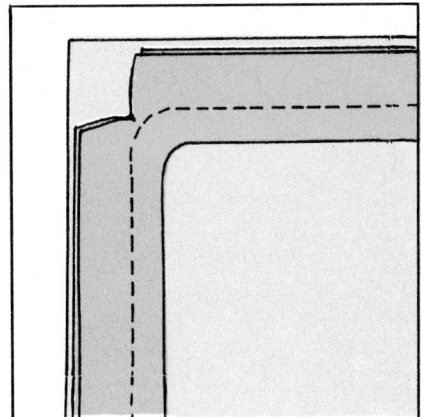

Clip into casing overlap at corners so that the piping sits comfortably around the curve.

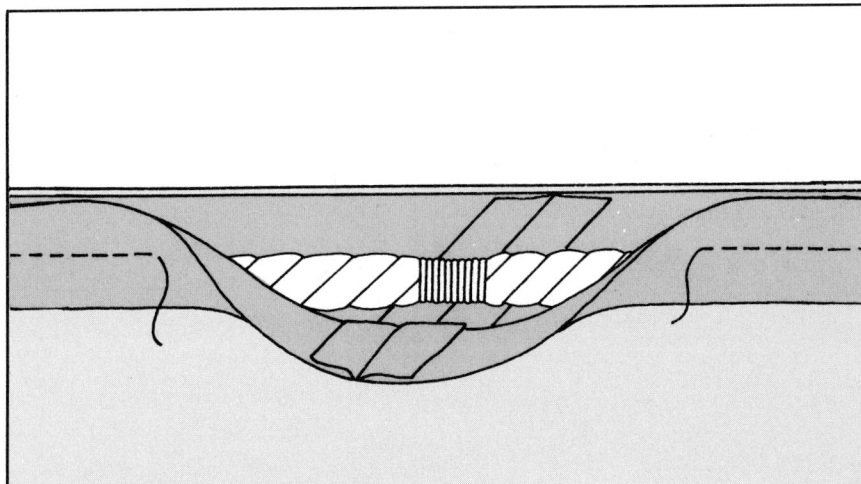

casing but leave about 5 cm (2 in) extra at each end. Unpick the running stitches in the casing for these 5 cm (2 in) and open up the casing so that it lies flat. Overlap the cut ends and mark diagonal pencil lines for the joining seam. Machine stitch the seam and trim off the excess material. Unravel the ends of the cord and cut two threads from one end and two threads from the other. Lay the remaining threads together and bind them tightly with thread. Re-stitch the casing and complete the tacking.

To join piping, seam casing ends and then butt cord ends together. Wrap the join with thread to secure it. Restitch the casing around the cord and complete tacking.

Cushion closures

Although you can simply sew up the seam of a cushion cover, it is not the ideal way to finish the opening. No matter how carefully you do it, the stitches show and, if the cushion is going to need frequent laundering or dry cleaning, it is time-wasting to be forever unpicking and sewing up the seam. Zippers are the most popular closure but there are other methods which you might prefer.

Zippers

Choose the lightest weight of zipper available and in a colour closely matched to the material – a lighter tone rather than a darker if an exact match is not possible. The zip should be 2.5 cm (1 in) shorter than the length of one side of the cushion.

Inserting zippers

Un-piped, knife-edge cushions Pin the two cushion pieces together, right sides facing, and tack along one edge only on the seam line, using fairly small running stitches. Press the seam open and lay the fabric flat, wrong side up. Lay the closed zip fastener, right side down, positioned on the seam and so that the centre of the zip teeth lies exactly along the stitching line. Tack the zip in position and then machine stitch, working close to the zip teeth and using a zipper foot on the machine. (Alternatively you can sew by hand using small running stitches or prick stitch.) Remove the running stitches from the seam and unzip about 5 cm (2 in). Finish making up the cushion as described on previous page, machine stitching the remaining three sides.

Note Prick stitch Prick stitch is worked in the same way as back stitch, except that only two or three threads are picked up by the needle.

Piped cushions To insert a zip fastener into a piped seam, first pin the piping casing all round the front of the cushion fabric (as

described). Open the zip fastener and place one side of the zip, wrong side up, along the piping casing or one edge of the cushion fabric. The edges of the zipper teeth should lie along the folded edge of the piping casing. Pin and tack the zip in position. Using the zipper or piping foot, machine stitch all round the cushion cover as close to the piping as possible. Remove the tacking stitches and trim the excess fabric at the corners. Now pin and tack the other half of the zip to one edge of the cushion back. Machine stitch again, working close to the zipper teeth.

Complete tacking the cushion back to the cushion front and, with the zip open, machine stitch on the remaining three sides. Neaten the raw edges inside the cushion and finish the ends of the zip tape ends by sewing them together.

Lapped zip fastening If a zip fastening is being inserted into a central back seam of a cushion, the seam edges can be lapped so that the zip is more or less hidden, or the zip can be simply centred on the seam. For both methods, cut the back piece of the cushion in two pieces with an extra seam allowance on the centre edges. Insert the zip as you would for a skirt side seam (see page 55), completing the seam above and below the zip.

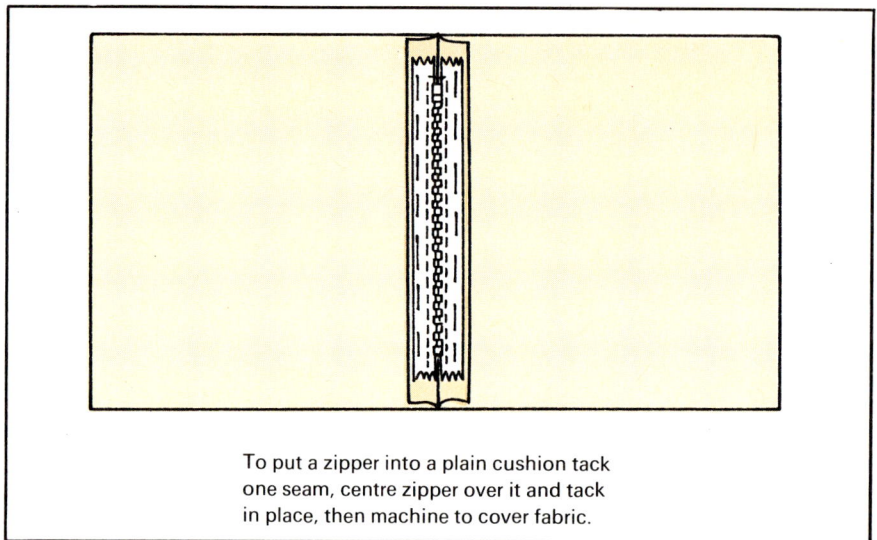

To put a zipper into a plain cushion tack one seam, centre zipper over it and tack in place, then machine to cover fabric.

Touch-and-close fastening

Cushions can also be closed with the type of nylon hook and loop closure which clings to itself (Velcro). It is a useful closure for covers which require a quick opening, such as those used for divan day pillows or bolsters.

Cut the cushion back in two pieces, adding an overlap on each piece. On one side add 12 mm ($\frac{1}{2}$ in) and on the other add the width of the tape plus 12 mm ($\frac{1}{2}$ in). Press 6 mm ($\frac{1}{4}$ in) under on each overlap. Machine stitch the hooked surface of the tape to the underside of the top overlap and the loop surface to the lower lap before making up the cover.

Tack zipper over piping as shown, and then tack the remaining cover piece in place. Machine stitch together through all layers.

Cushions can be made to express a theme.

Snap fastener strip

Snap fasteners can be purchased already fitted into a strip of tape. This makes a quick and useful closure for cushion covers and for loose covers. Sew on strips of snap fastener tape in exactly the same way as for the touch-and-close nylon tape.

Simple overlap opening

An overlap without fastenings can be used on pillow or cushion covers which are likely to be removed frequently, such as on day bed pillows or bolster covers.

The overlap opening is made at the back of the cover. Cut the back in two pieces with an extra allowance on both of between 4 cm to 8 cm ($1\frac{1}{2}$ in to 3 in) depending on the size of the cushion. Turn and stitch a double narrow hem to the wrong side on the left side of one piece and the right hand side of the other. Pin and baste the two pieces together, hemmed edges overlapping so that the cushion back is exactly the same size as the cushion front. Now make the cushion up in the usual way. For a pretty effect, the top edge of the overlap could be trimmed with lace or ribbon.

Strap facing for hook and eye closure

For the strap, cut a piece of the cushion fabric on the straight grain to the width of the cushion plus 2.5 cm × 8 cm (1 in × 3 in) deep. Then cut the strap *facing* to the same width but only 5 cm (2 in) deep.

When the piping has been machine stitched to the cushion front piece, pin the strap facing, (the 5 cm (2 in) deep piece), along one edge of the cushion, right sides of fabric together, and raw edges matching. Machine stitch close to the piping, using a zipper or piping foot on the machine. You should be stitching about 12 mm ($\frac{1}{2}$ in) from the edge. Turn the facing to the inside of the cushion piece and turn the remaining raw edge under 12 mm ($\frac{1}{2}$ in) and press. Slip-stitch to the wrong side of the cushion cover.

Next work on the cushion back piece. Lay the strap (the 8 cm (3 in) deep piece), along one edge, right sides together. Stitch as before 12 mm ($\frac{1}{2}$ in) from the edge. Fold the raw edge under 12 mm ($\frac{1}{2}$ in) and then bring the fold over to the wrong side of the cushion piece so that the fold lies along the first row of stitches. Slip-stitch in place.

Place the cushion back to the cushion front, matching corners. The strap on the back piece will extend above the strap facing on the front piece. Pin, baste and stitch the remaining three sides of the cushion. With the cushion cover still wrong side out, turn the strap onto the facing and stab stitch (page 140) the two together at each side of the cushion. Turn the cushion to the right side and sew hooks and eyes to correspond.

Box tassels

It is rather fun to make your own tassels for cushions and bolsters. Here is how it is done: cut strands of wool or embroidery thread to twice the depth the finished tassel is to be. Fold across the middle. Judge the size of the bunch and add more threads if required. Tie the bunch tightly just below the fold and leave a long end of thread. Thread a needle with the same yarn or thread and work buttonhole stitch all round the tie. Then work buttonhole stitch into the row of loops made by the previous stitches, and continue in this way, working round and round until the knob of the tassel is covered. Take the long end of thread up through the knob to the top of the tassel and use this for stitching the tassel to the cushion.

Gusseted cushions

There are two ways of making cushions with sides or gussets. Round or oval cushions, such as those made for stools and tied on with strings, have a one-piece gusset. Box cushions, usually made for armchairs or for casual floor seating, look better with a four-piece gusset.

Round or oval cushion

Make a cushion pad first from 5 cm (2 in) thick foam. Cut a paper pattern to the desired shape from the stool or chair seat and use it for cutting out both the pad and the cushion cover pieces.

Cut out the two cushion pieces from the fabric with a 12 mm ($\frac{1}{2}$ in) seam allowance all round. Prepare piping if you are using it; gusseted cushions look better if they are piped. Cut a piece of fabric for the gusset 8 cm (3 in) to the circumference of the paper pattern plus a 2.5 cm (1 in) allowance for the seams.

Tack the piping to one piece of cushion on the right side of the fabric, snipping into the piping casing at intervals so that it curves and lies neatly. Join the ends of the piping (see page 145). Now pin one edge of the gusset over the piping, so that the right side of the fabric is facing the right side of the cushion piece and all the edges are parallel. Again, you'll have to snip into the seam allowance to get a neat fit. Pin the short sides of the gusset together so that the gusset will stand perpendicularly. Mark the seam line with soft pencil or chalk. Unpin the gusset and machine stitch the seam. Re-pin to the cushion cover, tack and then finally stitch.

Making the ties

Lay the second cushion piece on the stool top and pin to mark the positions of the stool legs. Cut four strips of fabric 60 cm long × 5 cm wide (24 in × 2 in). Fold in the ends and press. Fold along the length and turn in the edges to make a strip about 12 mm ($\frac{1}{2}$ in)

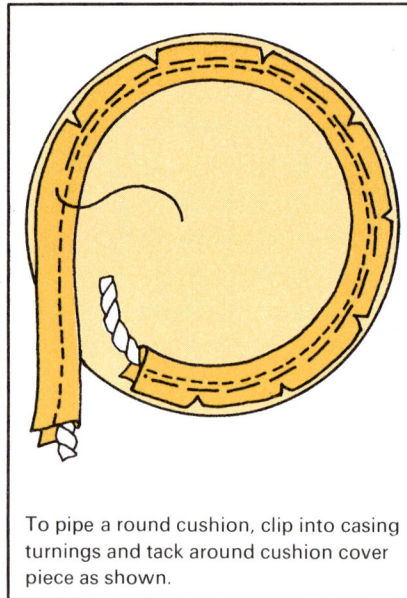

To pipe a round cushion, clip into casing turnings and tack around cushion cover piece as shown.

wide; press and machine stitch close to the turned-in edges. Fold across the middle and tack the fold to the right side of the cushion piece on the seam line, in the places marked with pins. These strips will be the ties which hold the cushion to the stool.

Prepare the piping and tack and then machine stitch it to the cushion piece, catching in the ties as you stitch.

Now pin and tack the cushion piece to the remaining edge of the gusset. Machine stitch but leave enough of the seam open to allow for inserting the cushion pad. You will find it squashes up quite small and 10 cm (4 in) is usually a sufficient gap. You will have to pull and push at the pad to get it positioned inside the cover properly. Finally, close the open seam with neat slip-stitches.

Piped box cushions

Box cushions are usually made on solid foam pads and they look better if they are piped. They can be left unpiped for casual seating especially if the fabric used is patterned and the seams do not show clearly.

Four-sided box cushions

Measure the dimensions of the foam pad exactly. Cut the top and base in fabric, adding a 12 mm ($\frac{1}{2}$ in) seam allowance all round.

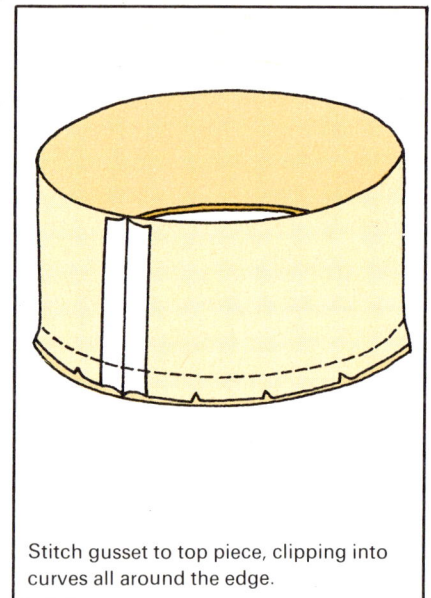

Stitch gusset to top piece, clipping into curves all around the edge.

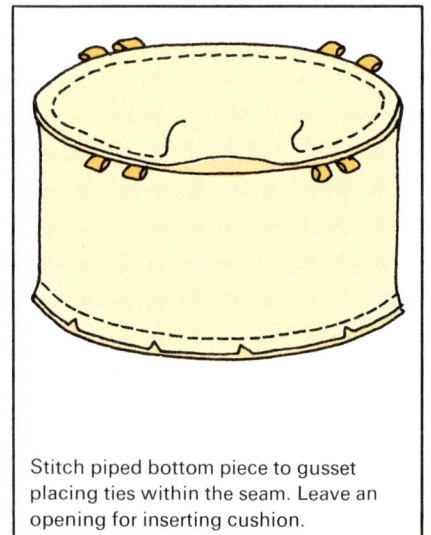

Stitch piped bottom piece to gusset placing ties within the seam. Leave an opening for inserting cushion.

Measure the dimensions of the cushion sides. (Remember that if the foam pad is rectangular there will be two different sets of measurements.) Add 12 mm ($\frac{1}{2}$ in) on all four edges of each side panel for seam allowances.

Cut out four side panels. Pin the pieces together, working on the foam pad with the material wrong side up, so that you can check the fit. Pin and then chalk along the marked line. Unpin, and then tack the four pieces together along the chalked lines. Machine stitch to make a circle of fabric for the gusset. Press the seams open. Tack the gusset to the cushion base, matching the corners and snipping into seam allowances for a neat fit.

Machine stitch and then try the piece on the foam pad to see if any adjustments have to be made.

Tack and stitch the top cushion piece to the gusset but stitch on two sides only. This is necessary because it is almost impossible to push a dense foam pad into a cushion cover. You can slip-stitch the remaining seams together or insert a long zip that will run on the two adjacent sides of the cover.

If you are piping a box cushion the piping must, of course, be inserted into the seam before the gusset is attached.

Zipped box cushion
This is a little more difficult to do but it does produce a professional-looking finish.

Cut the top and base of the cushion and apply piping to the right side of both pieces. The joins in the piping should be positioned at the back of the cushion. Measure the depth of the cushion pad and the circumference. Cut a strip of material to the depth measurement plus 2.5 cm (1 in) by half the circumference plus 2.5 cm (1 in). This is for the front gusset. Cut a second piece for the back gusset which is going to have a zip fastener inserted into it. Cut this to the same depth as the front piece but with 5 cm (2 in) added instead of 2.5 cm (1 in), and to the same length as the front piece.

Choose a zip fastener long enough to extend from the middle of one side of the cushion across the back and round the corner to the middle of the other side. This will ensure the widest possible opening for the pad. Cut the back strip in two lengthwise. Tack the two pieces together with small stitches, press the seam open and apply the zip fastener (see page 146 for technique).

The back and front gusset pieces should now be the same depth. Pin the back and front gusset pieces to the cushion back to match the side seams. Match them, pin and mark. Stitch the seams along the marked lines. Press open. Attach the top and bottom cushion pieces to the gusset, stitching on the machined line which secures the piping. Turn the cover to the right side through the zippered opening.

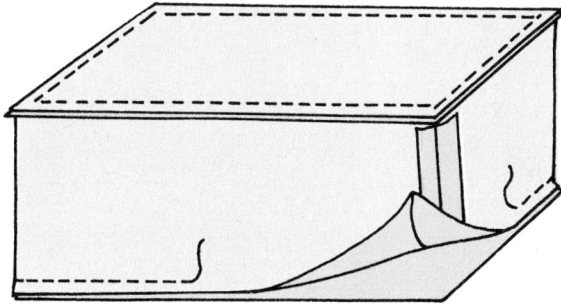

Leave one corner of a box cushion open for inserting the cushion pad.

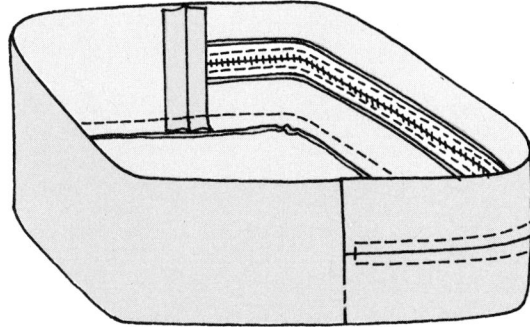

A zipper fastening for a box cushion is put into the gusset.

To make inexpensive but eye-catching seating use a selection of cushion shapes and sizes. Foam rubber pads and expanded polystyrene granules are just a few of the fillings which may be used. But do check safety warnings and also durability before making a choice.

Curtains

Any woman who can sew a straight seam can learn to make curtains which look almost as professional as those made by an interior decorator or by a furnishing store. The most important factor for successful curtain making is working space. It is important that your work surface is large enough to allow you to spread the fabric out. An ordinary large-size dining-room table will do if a chair is stood at each end to support the length of the fabric. If you do not have a table large enough, work on an uncarpeted floor.

The only materials and equipment you will need, other than the fabric itself, is a large supply of sharp dressmaker pins, No 7 betweens needles, tacking thread, dressmaker shears, tailor's chalk, a tape measure, long ruler and a sewing machine.

Choosing curtain fabrics

If you are making curtains yourself, you are saving quite a lot of money on the making up and this is a good reason for not economising on fabric. Curtains get a great deal of wear and are exposed to strong light. Choose quality fabrics both for their wearing qualities and colourfastness and your curtains will last as long as those which are professionally made.

The type of fabric you choose – patterned cotton, velvet, figured satin or textured weave – depends on the style of the room.

Most people have an idea of the look of the fabric they want but are not always sure that they are putting the right name to it – which can be very confusing to the salesman who is trying to help! Here are a few of the fabrics and fibres you are likely to meet in a furnishing store.

Fabrics and fibres

Fabrics used for soft furnishings fall into two distinct categories. First there are the heavyweights, which

are usually used for upholstery and, secondly, there is a large range of fabrics which are used for loose covers, bedspreads, cushions and curtains. If you are planning to make loose covers to match the curtains, make sure that the fabric you choose is a suitable weight for both.

Printed cotton

This is used for curtains, bedspreads and cushions. It is washable if it does not have a glazed finish, and if it bears the name of a reputable company, it is usually shrink-proof and colour fast. If the fabric does not have a brand name woven into the selvedge or if it is an imported fabric, obtain a sample about 10 cm (4 in) square, wash and iron it for colourfastness and then measure the square to check the amount of shrinkage.

Linen-union

This is a thick cotton, mixed with linen (or sometimes a man-made fibre), heavy enough for loose covers and for upholstering furniture which does not get a great deal of wear.

Curtains do not have to be restricted to use on windows and can be used to hide shelves or divide rooms, and they may be pleated and hung in many ways to achieve the desired effect.

Cotton satin (sateen)

This is cotton which has been woven so that the surface has a lustrous finish, looking rather like satin. It is a high quality fabric and can be used for bedspreads, loose covers and for curtains.

Chintz

Chintz is cotton with a special surface treatment which makes it shiny and thus dirt-resistant. Chintz is used for curtains – it is a little stiff for other kinds of furnishings.

Cotton repp

Repp is 100 per cent cotton and is very hardwearing. It is sometimes finished with acrylic to improve the crease-resistant properties. Repp is closely woven with a horizontal ribbed effect and comes only in plain colours. Repp can be used for loose covers and curtains.

Twill

Twill is 100 per cent cotton and has a diagonal ribbed effect.

Brocade

Brocade is a richly figured Jacquard weave fabric with a pronounced design on a satin-like ground. It can incorporate several colours and is usually a mixture of cotton and rayon. Brocades are suitable for both curtains and light upholstery.

Cotton damask

This is a glossy, Jacquard weave fabric similar in appearance to brocade but the raised pattern is flatter. It can also be woven from cotton and rayon mixtures. Usually, damask is regarded as a curtain fabric but it can be used for light upholstery.

Velour

Curtain velour is made of cotton and looks rather like velveteen with a short, close pile. Sometimes it has a silicone finish. Velour is suitable for curtains and drapes.

Upholstery velvet

Usually of rayon and cotton mixture, upholstery velvets wear extremely well. Most are plain colours but some types have figuring in the surface of the pile which produces an attractive, patterned effect. Velvets are rather heavyweight and can be used for both curtains and upholstery.

Moiré

When sold as a furnishing fabric, moiré is a mixture of rayon and cotton which has been processed with heat to produce the watered effect on the surface. It can only be dry-cleaned and is suitable for curtains, bedspreads and cushions.

Dupion

This can be a mixture of different fibres but the best for furnishings is a mixture of silk and Terylene, thus combining the beauty of silk with the easy-care qualities of a man-made fibre. Dupion is mostly used for curtains and cushions.

Sheers

This term covers a wide range of curtain fabrics which are either semi-transparent or are loosely woven so that there is a see-through effect. Most sheers nowadays are easy-care and some are flame-resistant.

Other fabrics to look for

The man-made fibres which are mostly used in soft furnishings include *nylon*, usually appearing as a velvet fabric or mixed with other fibres. *Viscose rayon* is a versatile and moth-proof fabric with several different weaves and finishes. *Acetate* when finished looks rather like silk. *Acrilan* produces strong, mothproof and mildew-proof fabrics in a variety of finishes. *Dralon* is well-known as a superb furnishing velvet. *Merkalon* appears as a chunky, stain-resistant fabric which is very hardwearing for upholstery and loose covers. *Tapestry*, once a woven wool fabric, means nowadays a machine-made fabric with an all-over pattern. *Furnishing tweed* is heavy to handle but invaluable in room schemes where texture is required. *Genoa velvet* is a velvet with a multicoloured pile combined with a satin ground. *Moquette* also has a pile, either cut ot uncut, on a wool or cotton ground.

Calculating fabric quantities

First, decide how long the curtains are to be. Curtains should begin and end at a structural part of the window or wall, so they begin at either the ceiling level just beneath the cornice or from a rail above the top of the window frame. They end at window-sill level, at the apron, the top of the skirting board or on the floor. The width of the curtains is decided by the width of the rail or curtain pole and the fullness of fabric you require.

The two measurements which you will take, therefore, are the width of the curtain rail and the depth from the curtain rail to wherever the curtains end.

There are several factors to be considered in working out fabric quantities. It is a good idea to draw a plan of the window and write in the measurements. Take the plan with you when you are buying fabric and the salesman will help you to estimate the quantity needed.

These are the factors which must be taken into consideration:
I The total fabric width in each curtain is decided by the amount of fullness you want. Very sheer curtains require three times the measured width. For medium or heavyweight fabrics 2 to 2½ times the width is required. Thus, for windows wider than 1.20 m (4 ft), it will be necessary to join widths to make one panel.

Make sure that you know the exact width of the fabric you are

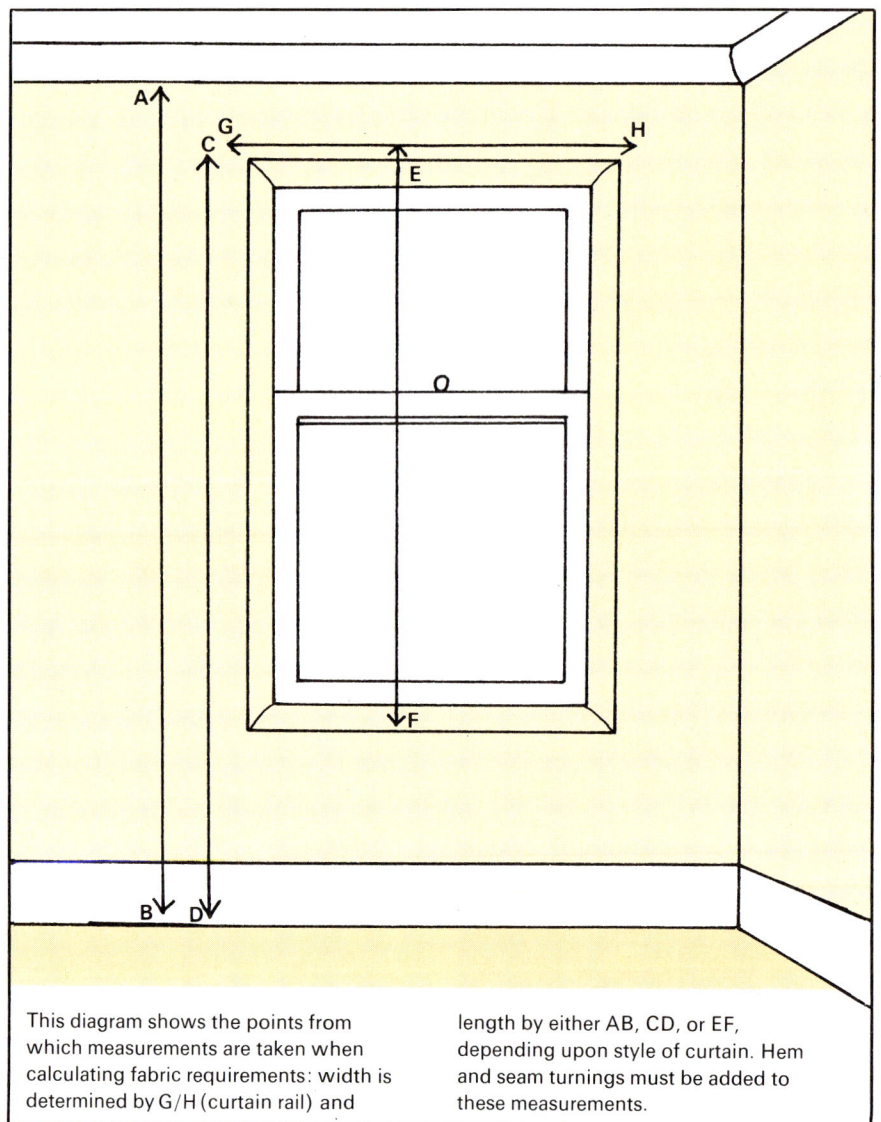

This diagram shows the points from which measurements are taken when calculating fabric requirements: width is determined by G/H (curtain rail) and length by either AB, CD, or EF, depending upon style of curtain. Hem and seam turnings must be added to these measurements.

buying because some imported fabrics come in odd measurements. Generally, furnishing fabrics are made in 120 cm, 130 cm and 150 cm (48 in, 52 in and 60 in) widths. Sheers are available in a wide range of widths up to 150 cm (60 in).

To the width required by the fullness, add an allowance for seams and for side seams.

2 If the fabric is patterned with a large repeat, allow at least one repeat extra for matching up widths. It is also important that the motif be placed so that the effect when hung is pleasing. On long curtains, an unbroken repeat should be at the top of the curtain because it does not matter if a broken repeat is near the floor. On short curtains, the bottom repeat is

more important and this should be the complete one.

3 To the length of the curtains, an allowance must be added for top and bottom hems. Top hem allowances vary with the type of heading being used. A double bottom hem is a distinct advantage; it not only makes curtains hang better but also provides extra fabric for letting down if shrinkage occurs or if the curtains have to be used on a deeper window later.

The following table provides a guide to hem allowances:

Top hems
Straight hems used with rings: 10 cm (4 in)
Casing for wires or rods: 8 cm (3 in)
Ready-made gathering tapes of all kinds: 2.5 cm (1 in)

Bottom hems (double)
Sheer curtains: 15 cm (6 in)
Medium weight fabrics: 18 to 23 cm (7 to 9 in)
Heavyweight fabrics for long curtains: 23 to 30 cm (9 to 12 in)

Linings
When considering the style and fabric for your curtains, you will also think about whether you need light and privacy. If the room is overlooked, you will probably decide to have sheer curtains with heavier curtains to pull at night. If, on the other hand, the window is a feature of the room and not overlooked, you may decide to have beautiful semi-sheers which are intended to allow in as much daylight as possible.

Curtains made of fabrics with a pattern on both sides, such as cotton gingham, which are usually used for informal settings, do not require lining.

Curtains made of medium and heavyweight fabrics, used for formal settings, look better if they are lined. The lining gives the fabric more substance and weight so that the folds hang better. Also, linings help to protect fabrics from fading by the sun and present a more attractive look from outside. Thin fabrics, such as silk, can be interlined with 'Bump' – a special curtain interlining which looks like fleecy flannelette.

Buy lining fabric at the same time as the top fabric. Linings for curtains are usually made of cotton with a slightly shiny surface and are available in a limited range of colours as well as white and cream.

Estimating lining quantities
To the finished curtain length measurement add 2.5 cm (1 in) for the top hem plus the same allowance as the top fabric for the bottom hem. For width, add 4 cm (1½ in) for each side hem (this allows for a 2.5 cm (1 in) hem and a 12 cm (½ in) turning). Add 2.5 cm (1 in) to each width in the panel for joining with 12 mm (½ in) seams.

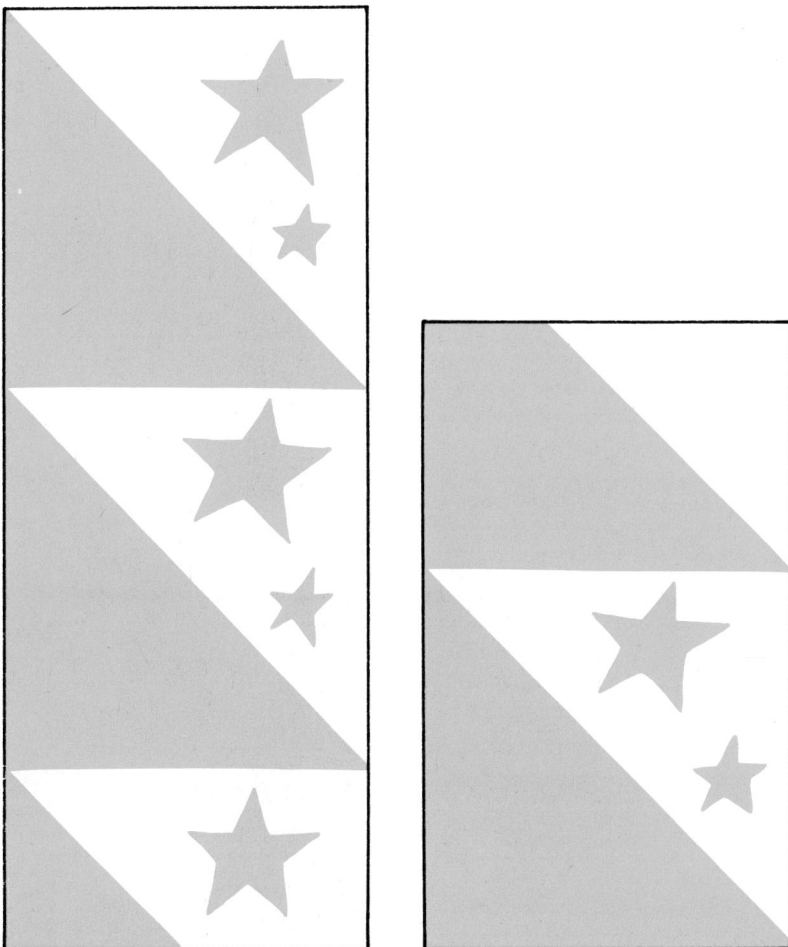

Unbroken repeats should be at the top of long curtains and at the bottom of short curtains. Make allowance for this when buying the fabric.

Curtain headings

Professional curtain makers sew pleats into curtain headings by hand. The advantage is that the stitches do not show on the right side of the fabric, but this method does take a great deal of time and you need a mathematical mind to work out the pleats exactly.

Home sewers can achieve almost the same effects by using one of the special gatherings or pleating tapes available. The standard gathering tape is simply stitched to the

curtain heading and the gathers drawn up on cords. The pleating tapes used for deep curtain headings are stiffened and some of them require special hooks. These tapes have a pre-set formula for calculating how much fabric is required for a window width and you should purchase the heading tape and hooks at the same time as the fabric.

Cutting the fabric

Accuracy is of the utmost importance when cutting curtains. Press or iron the fabric first to remove all creases. Lay the fabric on a large flat surface right side up. Decide which way up the pattern or pile runs and make sure that you mark all pieces as you cut them. The fabric must run the same way on all panels. Draw a thread along the top edge and cut along this line. Measure and mark the top hem allowance with chalk. From the line, measure the finished length of the panel. Measure and mark the bottom hem allowance. Draw a thread and cut straight across.

If the fabric is of a type where threads cannot be drawn, line up the selvedge edge with the long side of the table so that the cut edge of the fabric lies just over the short side of the table. By drawing the chalk across the fabric on the edge of the short side of the table you will get a straight line across the width.

Cutting panels for joining

Spread the remainder of the fabric right side up. Lay the cut panel on

The success of a room's décor depends largely on the window treatment, but you will never go wrong if the curtains are well-made. Accurate measuring and preparation will ensure that curtains hang gracefully and are full enough for the window they cover.

it right side down. Match the design carefully on the edges. Using the cut panel as a pattern, cut the other lengths required.

Joining curtain widths

Clip into the selvedges every 10 cm to 12.5 cm (4 in to 5 in). This is to make the seams lie more smoothly. Pin the lengths together carefully matching the pattern. You will probably find that slip-stitching is best for keeping the pattern matched while joining the seams but machine stitching can be used, provided that tacking is done firmly. Stitch all the joining seams in the same direction, from top to bottom. Press seams open.

Join lining lengths in exactly the same way making sure that the seams of curtains and linings will match.

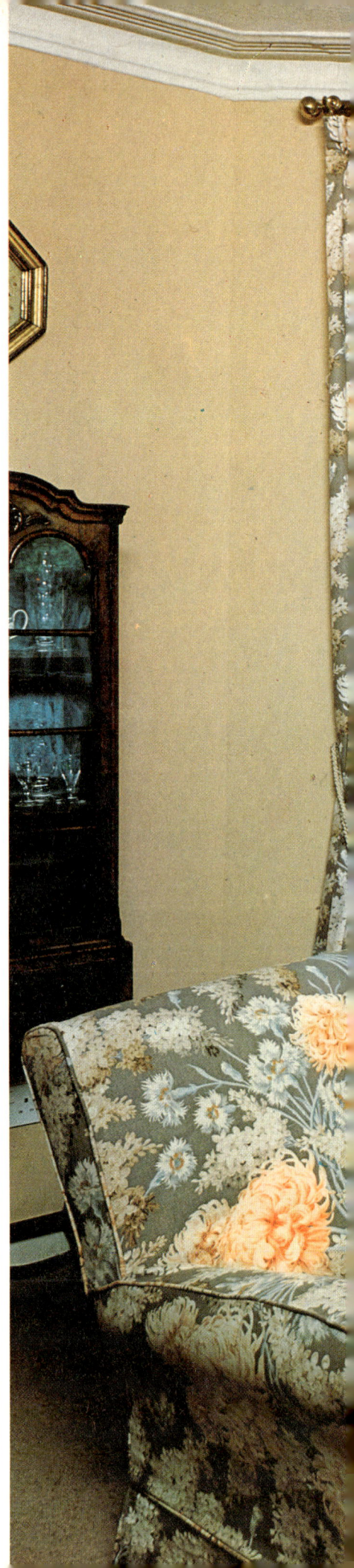

Making lined curtains

There are two methods of making lined curtains. The 'bag' method is used for making short curtains of a single width of fabric. Long, heavy curtains are 'locked' to the lining (i.e. stitched to the lining at intervals, so that the two fabrics hang as one).

Bag method

Cut the lining fabric so that it is 10 cm (4 in) narrower and 8 cm (3 in) shorter than the curtain fabric. Mark the centre of both lining and curtains with tacking stitches. Turn in 12 mm ($\frac{1}{2}$ in) and then a 2.5 cm (1 in) hem on the bottom edge of the lining and machine stitch.

Lay the curtain fabric right side up and arrange a fold down the centre so that the curtain is the same width as the lining. There is no need to pin or tack the fold. Place the lining on the curtain, right side down, and with the top of the lining about 4 cm ($1\frac{1}{2}$ in) below the top edge of the curtain. Pin lining and curtain together down the sides. Tack and machine stitch both sides to within 5 cm (2 in) of the lining hem. Press seam allowance towards the lining.

Turn the curtain to the right side. Arrange the curtain on a flat surface with the lining uppermost so that the lining is centred on the curtain. Press. Turn the top edge of the curtain down onto the lining and tack.

Attaching the heading tape

Gathering tapes Cut a piece of gathering tape to the width of the finished curtain plus 2.5 cm (1 in). Withdraw the cords at both ends and turn under 12 mm ($\frac{1}{2}$ in). Knot the cords together on the end of the tape which will lie to the inner edge of the curtain. Tack the tape to the curtain so that the upper edge of the tape just covers the raw edge of the curtain. Machine stitch along both edges of the tape, making sure that you do not catch in the cords. Finish off the open ends of the tape with slip-stitches.

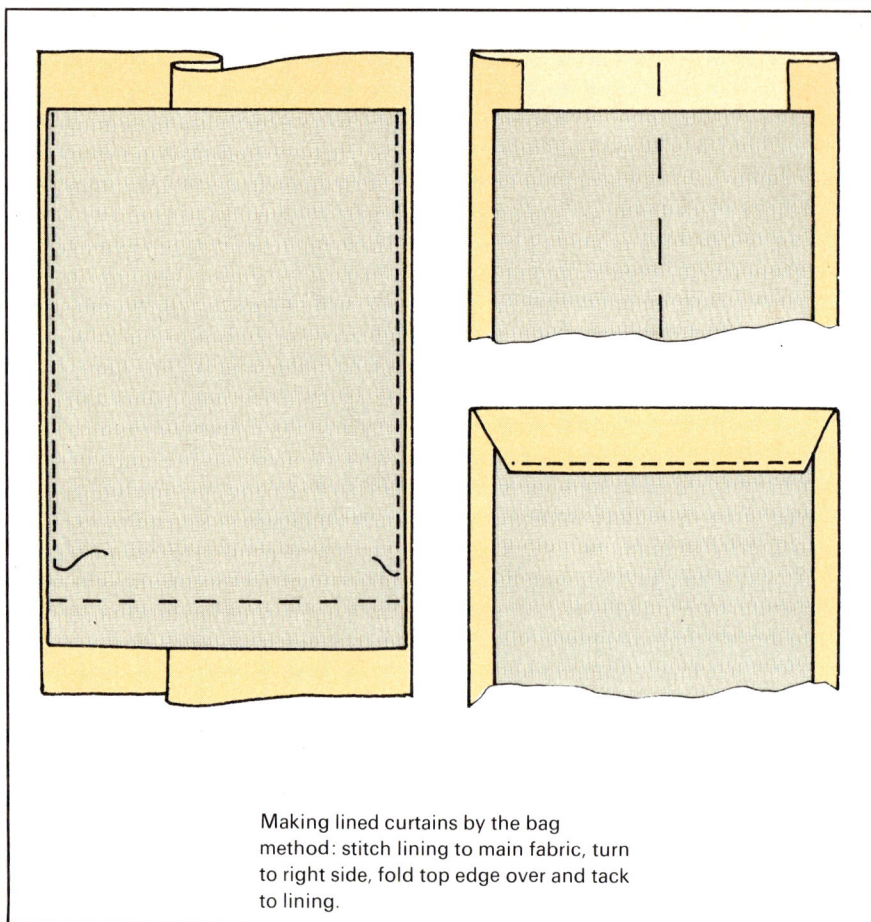

Making lined curtains by the bag method: stitch lining to main fabric, turn to right side, fold top edge over and tack to lining.

Pull up the cords to gather the curtains but do not cut the cords short. Knot the ends so that the gathers can be released easily for cleaning or laundering.

Pleating tape Tack the pleating tape to the right side of the curtain fabric, wrong side up. Machine stitch. Turn the tape over to the inside of the curtain so that there is 9 mm ($\frac{3}{8}$ in) of the curtain along the top edge. Press. Turn the sides of the curtain over onto the tape and slip-stitch. Hem the bottom edge of the tape to the curtain lining.

Finishing the hem

Allow the curtain to hang for several days before finishing the hem. Turn a doubled hem to the correct length, mitring the corners (see page 169). Slip-stitch the hem. Slip-stitch the side hems to the lining. Thus the lining is free of the curtain on the bottom edge and overlaps the curtain hem by about 5 cm (2 in). For a professional finish, make 'ties' at about 30-cm

(12-in) intervals along the hem catching the curtain to the lining.

Locking method (for multi-width curtains)

Turn 5 cm (2 in) hems down each side of the curtain and sew down with herringbone stitch, see page 192. Turn a 12 mm ($\frac{1}{2}$ in) then a 2.5 cm (1 in) hem along the bottom edge of the lining with basting stitches.

Spread the curtain out, right side down, on a flat surface. Lay the lining on top, right side up, so that the centre tacking marks and seams match and the top edge of the lining lies 4 cm ($1\frac{1}{2}$ in) below the top edge of the curtain. Pin curtain and lining together along the centre mark. Turn back the lining for about 46 cm (18 in) or to the first seam. Catch the lining and curtain together with locking stitch, starting about 23 cm (9 in) from the bottom of the curtain. Continue locking across the width of the curtain at 46 cm (18 in) intervals and on the seams.

Attaching interlinings

If the curtain is being interlined as well as lined, lay the interlining on the wrong side of the curtain, turn 5 cm (2 in) hems down the sides, tack and then herringbone stitch the curtain and interlining down together, attaching the lining with locking stitches as before. If interlining widths have to be joined, use a lapped seam to be sure that the interlining lies absolutely flat.

Unlined curtains

Unlined curtains are usually made of lightweight fabrics or nets. As nets come in widths up to 274 cm (108 in) wide, panels do not need to be joined. If it is necessary to join widths or half widths use French seams (page 38) so that no raw edges show.

To prevent the side hems curling

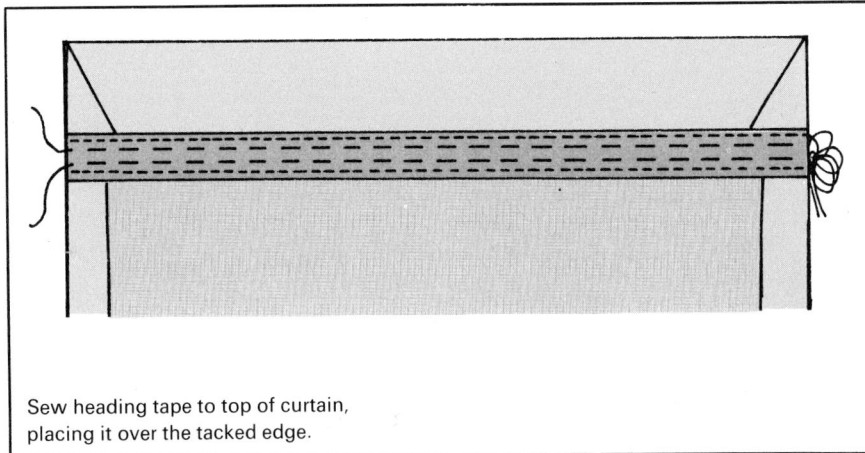

Sew heading tape to top of curtain, placing it over the tacked edge.

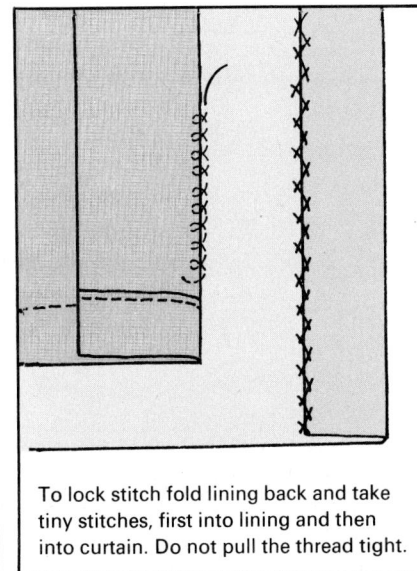

To lock stitch fold lining back and take tiny stitches, first into lining and then into curtain. Do not pull the thread tight.

back, make double 2.5 cm (1 in) hems down the sides, hand sewing or machine stitching as you prefer, but hand sewing looks more professional. Leave 10 cm (4 in) of the side seams unstitched at the top edge. Fold the top edge over and apply the gathering or pleating tape. Fold the side seams onto the tape, mitring the corners neatly. Complete hand sewing the side hems and the mitred corners. Hang the curtains for a day or two to allow them to drop. Make a doubled 10 cm (4 in) hem and hand sew using slip-stitches.

Plain casing heading

Net curtains and short unlined curtains can be hung on a wooden rod or on an expanding wire. Stitch the side hems first and then turn a 5 cm (2 in) hem on the top edge. Machine stitch. Push the rod or wire through the hem and mark the casing with pins to fit the rod or wire. Remove the rod, tack along the pinned line and then machine stitch the casing.

Sewing sheers
Net curtains

Net curtains are not difficult to machine stitch if the tension is set loose and a fairly large stitch is used. However, it is better to hand sew the side hems to prevent puckering. The finished effect is more satisfactory. If you prefer to machine stitch, make sure that you stitch the same way on both hems, from top to bottom. Use a polyester thread such as Drima. On net curtains all turnings and hems must be doubled so that cut edges do not show through the fabric.

If a deep heading is required, pleating and gathering tapes made of Tervoil polyester are available for net curtains. These are very lightweight, shrink-proof and dry quickly after laundering.

Semi-sheer fabrics

This is the term given to those fabrics which have a large open weave. They are made in a wide variety of textures and colours, usually in cotton and blends of cotton and man-made fibres. They can be a little difficult to machine sew because the threads of the weave are not really close enough to hold the sewing threads. Fold double hems very carefully, tacking so that the threads of the weave make a reasonably solid area of fabric.

Three main types of heading tape

Rufflette standard tape This is 2.5 cm (1 in) wide and makes a simple gathered heading. Two cords in the tape pull up the gathers and are knotted to hold them until the curtains are to be laundered or dry-cleaned. Ordinary curtain hooks or open rings are used with this tape. For synthetic fibres and nets there is a tape made of Tervoil polyester. Allow twice the width of the curtain track for standard headings.

Rufflette Regis tape This makes pencil pleats and is 8 cm (3 in) deep. It is made of reinforced nylon so that the heading stays crisp. Ordinary curtain hooks are used with this tape. Allow 2½ times the width of the track for this heading.

Rufflette Deep Pleat This tape makes pinch pleated headings. It is 9 cm (3½ in) deep and requires special hooks. Triple, double or single pleats can be made. When estimating fabric allow at least twice the width of the curtain track.

Café curtains

Café curtains are very short curtains, hung from a rod so that they cover only the lower half of a window. They are a useful style for windows which are overlooked from outside but where maximum daylight is required.

Café curtains are hung in various ways. Sometimes they are simply gathered and hung onto a brass rod. They can be pleated with the different heading tapes available and can be suspended from rings or hooks. The most popular styles are café curtains with scalloped or tabbed headings.

Measuring for café curtains

First, decide on the depth of the curtain. To a certain extent this will be determined by the amount of privacy required but café curtains should cover at least half the window. Sometimes two or three café curtains are used to screen a window, one for the lower window which is left in place through the day and one or two above which can be pulled back to allow more light in. These are called 'tiered café curtains'. Café curtains usually fall just to the windowsill.

Measure the track or supporting rod and allow $1\frac{1}{2}$–$2\frac{1}{2}$ times this width for lighter fabrics. For deep scallops on rings, estimate about $1\frac{1}{2}$ times the width of the track.

Allow 15 cm (6 in) for turnings, (the top and bottom hems) for ordinary, gathered headings. Scalloped headings require more allowance at the top. For instance, if the scallop is to be 8 cm (3 in), the allowance for the heading would be at least 18 cm (7 in) plus extra for a doubled hem. Allow extra fabric for matching up the pattern if you are joining widths. Linings are not usually necessary with café curtains but if the fabric is strongly patterned and would show to best effect ungathered, then a cotton lining will improve the look and hang of the curtain.

Far right These curtains have a scalloped heading and are hung from rings.

Poles, rails and rods

Wooden or plastic rods, curved fitted brass rails or decorative brass poles are fitted to each side of the window for hanging café curtains.

Scalloped café curtains

Cut off the selvedge of the fabric. Turn doubled 12 mm ($\frac{1}{2}$ in) hems on the sides and stitch. Turn a doubled bottom hem and tack, mitring the corners where the hem meets the side hems. Hand sew using slip-stitches.

Working out the scallops

There is no way in which a pattern can be given for drawing scallops because the width of the scallop and the width of the straps have to fit into your own curtain width. It is a matter of experimenting with a pair of compasses, drawing and re-drawing until the scallops fit across the width.

Café curtains have an informal appeal and look well in kitchens. They are also useful for bed- and bathrooms if they are divided, letting in light while maintaining privacy.

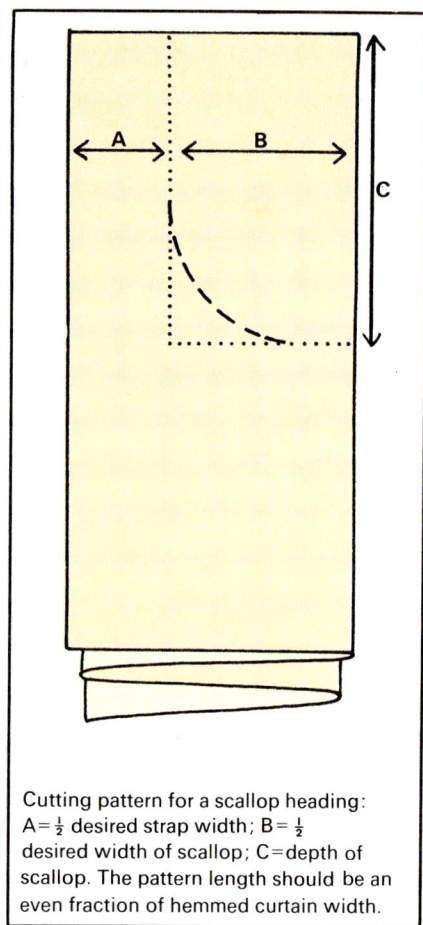

Cutting pattern for a scallop heading: A = $\frac{1}{2}$ desired strap width; B = $\frac{1}{2}$ desired width of scallop; C = depth of scallop. The pattern length should be an even fraction of hemmed curtain width.

To make a paper pattern for the scallops, first decide the width of the scallops (a) and the width of the straps (b).

Cut a piece of paper in proportion to the width of the curtain, minus the side hems which are already turned and stitched.

Fold the paper concertina-style; the depth of each fold should be exactly equal to half scallop width plus half the strap width $-\frac{1}{2}$ (a) $+\frac{1}{2}$ (b).

Now mark the scallops and straps on the folded paper as shown in the diagram. Then mark the depth of the scallops on the edge of the fold. Draw two lines at right angles to each other at these marks as shown. Use a cup or plate edge to obtain a rounded corner where the lines intersect.

Cut out the scallop pattern. Pin to the fabric placing the first strap the extra distance away from the hemmed edge to make it a complete strap width.

Making the curtain heading

Spread the curtain right side up. Fold down the top edge (right sides together) to the depth of the scallop plus 8 cm (3 in). Tack. Pin the pattern so that the top of the strap is against the folded edge. Mark the scallops with tailor's chalk. Remove the pattern and tack roughly to hold the two layers together firmly. Machine stitch on the chalked line, outlining the scallops. Cut out the scallops, 6 mm ($\frac{1}{4}$ in) away from the stitching line, leaving the folded edge intact. Clip into the curves. Trim off the corners diagonally.

Remove the tacking threads and turn the heading to the right side, poking the ends of the straps through with a blunt pencil. Press carefully. Turn up the hem, press and slip-stitch to the curtain and sides of the curtain, making sure that the stitches do not show on the right side.

Sew brass rings or hooks to the scallop straps, using a strong buttonhole twist thread in a matching colour.

Using straps for hangers

To use the straps as hangers make them much deeper – as much as 10 cm (4 in) perhaps. Fold the finished straps to the wrong side and stitch down to form loops. Alternatively, they can be folded to the front of the curtain and fastened with press fasteners, finishing with a fabric-covered button. Slip the pole or rod through the strap loops.

Pelmets and Valances

A pelmet is a stiff border hung across the top of the curtains. It may be decorative or simply covered with fabric which matches or tones with the curtains. Pelmets are often cut or trimmed to many shapes and designs.

The proportion of a pelmet to the curtains needs careful planning as the wrong proportion can spoil the appearance of a window and the room.

A valance is a form of pelmet which is rather like a very short

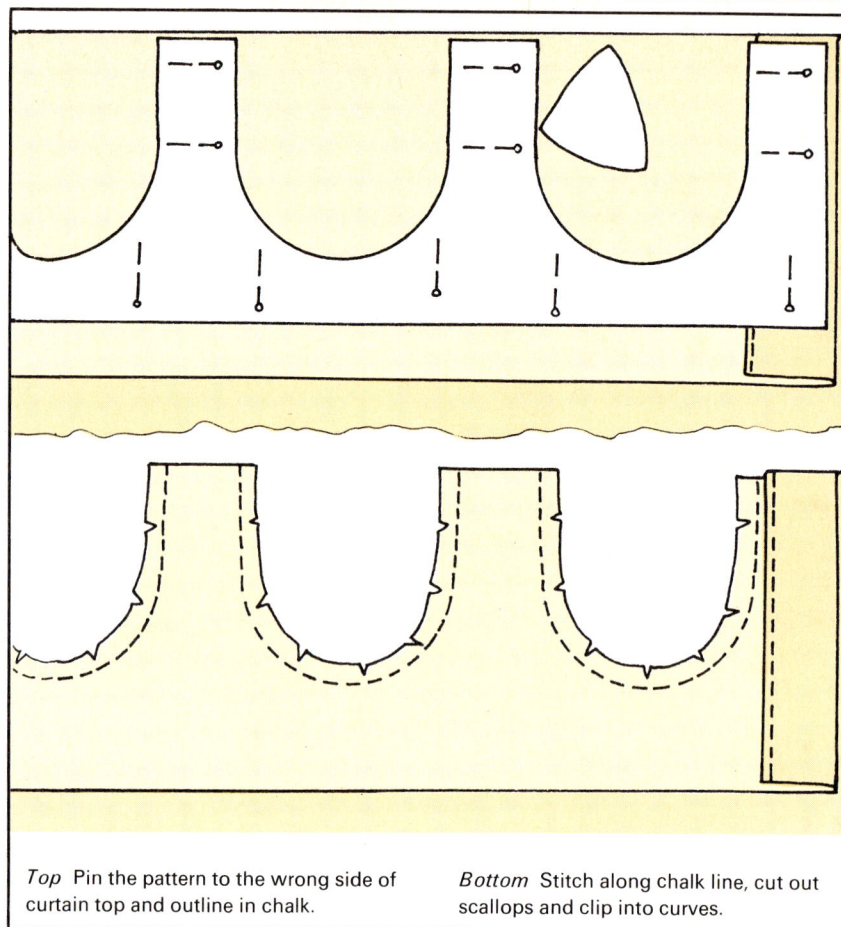

Top Pin the pattern to the wrong side of curtain top and outline in chalk.

Bottom Stitch along chalk line, cut out scallops and clip into curves.

curtain and is usually hung from a separate track above the window. The method for making a valance is very similar to that of making lined curtains by the 'bag' method (see page 156). Valances can be plain, gathered or pinch-pleated.

Making a pelmet

Make a paper pattern first. Measure the length of the pelmet board plus the returns at both ends. Cut a piece of stiff paper to this measurement by the intended depth of the pelmet. Draw out one half of the design you have chosen and trace this off for the second half so that the design is symmetrical. Cut out the paper pattern.

You will need special pelmet buckram or the heaviest possible grade of Vilene or Pellon for stiffening. To obtain sufficient width, machine stitch pieces together with a flat seam. Lay the paper pattern on the stiffening and draw round with a soft pencil. Cut out the stiffening.

Pin the paper pattern to the fabric which is being used for the face of the pelmet and cut out, allowing 25 mm (1 in) all round. Make sure that the grain of the fabric is kept true. If it is necessary to join pieces of fabric to obtain the width, keep the main piece for the centre and join half widths at each end.

Cover the buckram or stiffening with 'Bump' interlining. This is easy to do because buckram has glue in the surface. Lay the interlining on top of the buckram and press with a fairly hot iron. When the interlining has cooled, it will have adhered to the buckram.

Spread the face fabric right side down and lay the buckram on top, 'Bump' side down. Have a bowl of water handy with a piece of cotton wool. Place some kitchen weights along the buckram to hold it in place on the fabric. Proceed to fold the edges of the fabric over onto the buckram, dampening the buckram slightly and pressing the fabric

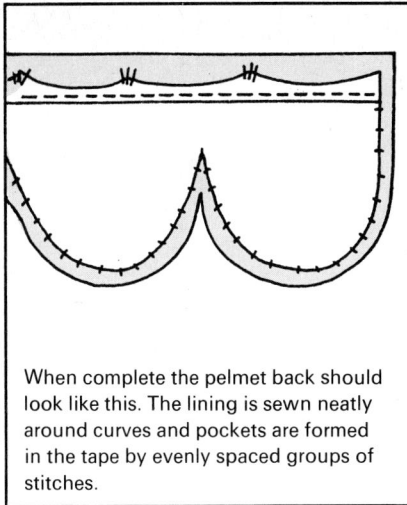

When complete the pelmet back should look like this. The lining is sewn neatly around curves and pockets are formed in the tape by evenly spaced groups of stitches.

down onto it. Alternatively, catch-stitch the fabric to the stiffening. It will be necessary to make small clips into the allowance to achieve smooth curves.

Attaching trims
Fringe edges or braid are attached at this point. Stitch fringes to the wrong side of the pelmet using stab stitches, making sure that the stitches do not show on the right side. The braid heading of the fringe should just show on the edge. Stitch braid with stab stitches or glue in place.

Preparing the lining
Pin the paper pattern to the lining fabric and cut out with 12 mm (½ in) allowance all round. Unpin the pattern and turn 18 mm (¾ in) to the wrong side. Baste and press.

A length of tape is stitched to the top edge of the lining so that the pelmet can be pinned to the pelmet board. Here is how it is done: cut a length of 2.5 cm (1 in) wide tape to the width of the pelmet plus 2.5 cm (1 in). Turn under the raw ends. Pin the tape to the prepared lining across the top, 12 mm (½ in) below the edge. Machine stitch the ends and lower edge of the tape only to the lining. The top edge is left free. Place the lining on the back of the pelmet, smooth it out and slip-stitch to the fabric turnings. It is better not to pin and tack because there is always the danger that pinholes will show

through on the right side.

Now make 'pockets' along the tape. Hand sew at 10 cm (4 in) intervals, catching the tape to the pelmet, stitching through the buckram and the interlining but *not* through to the face fabric.

The pelmet is fastened to the board with thumbtacks in the 'pockets' of the tape and should hang smoothly without sagging.

Valances on pelmet boards
For a softer pelmet effect, a gathered fabric valance can be made and attached to the pelmet board in exactly the same way, stitching the tape to the wrong side of the gathered heading.

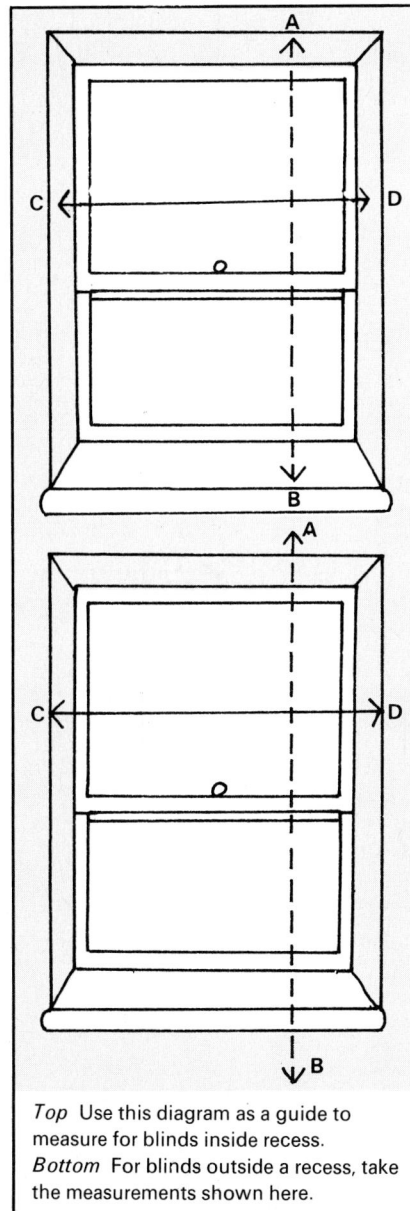

Top Use this diagram as a guide to measure for blinds inside recess. *Bottom* For blinds outside a recess, take the measurements shown here.

Roller blinds

Sometimes, a roller blind does a better job than curtains – to screen off a dreary outlook perhaps or to cover a window which is too small to curtain. Used with curtains, roller blinds are almost the perfect window dressing. They can be made of the same fabric as the side curtains or in a toning fabric. Roller blinds allow maximum natural light by day, are very efficient as sun-blinds and provide absolute privacy at night. With an inexpensive kit, you can make and install a pretty and practical roller blind in an afternoon.

Measuring the window
Decide first whether the blind is to fit inside or outside the window recess. The blind should cover the window panes completely but if this is not possible because the frame is too narrow, hang the blind outside the recess.

If the roller is hanging inside the recess, measure the width very accurately and subtract 2.5 cm (1 in) at each end. This is for the 'pin width' – the metal pins and caps at each end of the wooden roller, and the brackets which hold the blind within the window frame.

For a roller blind to hang outside the recess, add 2.5 cm (1 in) at each end for the pin width and then add a further 15 cm (6 in) to the measurement. This ensures that the window is adequately covered by the blind.

Measure the drop of the blind from the brackets to either the window-sill or to the apron, and to this measurement an allowance of 23 cm (9 in) for fixing the fabric to the roller, and to make a pocket for the lath at the bottom.

Choosing the right fabric
Holland is the ideal fabric for roller blinds because it is smooth and firm. It can be obtained in patterns and plain colours and in a variety of widths. PVC-coated fabrics are

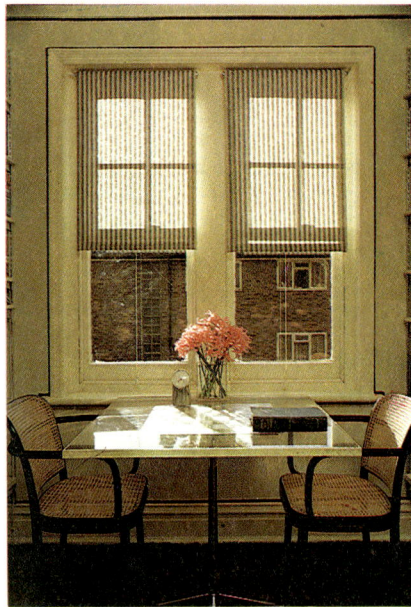

Left For a simple room scheme, roller blinds are an obvious choice. Make them up in a firmly woven fabric, perhaps in a colour or pattern that provides an accent to the existing furnishings.

Right Have fun with a giant roller blind suspended from the ceiling. Use it as a simple room divider or as here, where it turns a bunk bed into a very private sleeping space for young children.

ideal for kitchens and bathrooms. Closely woven hessian and firm cotton are also suitable fabrics.

If the blind is simply for decoration then fabrics such as cotton lace and other textured fabrics can be used, but the roller will not work successfully.

It is possible to have cotton furnishing fabrics plasticised for making roller blinds and many furnishing stores provide this service.

Cutting the fabric

It is preferable not to have seams running down the length of the blind. Seams double the bulk of the fabric and can fault the smooth running of the roller. If the window is particularly wide and fabric of sufficient width is not available, use the fabric sideways so that the seam is across the blind rather than down it.

Cutting out is the most important stage in blind making. If the material is not cut absolutely square it will roll unevenly and catch in the brackets. Check the grain lines and cut exactly along a weft thread or, if the fabric is suitable, withdraw threads and use these as cutting lines.

Making up the blind

The side hems should be as flat as possible. Ideally, the hem should be one turn only, but if the fabric is likely to fray excessively it will be necessary to make a double hem, but be sure to press the hems flat before machining.

Plasticised fabrics, of course, cannot be pressed or pinned. Secure hems in these fabrics with rubber-based adhesive.

Work two rows of straight machine stitching to secure hems or one row of zigzag stitching. The raw edge should be in the centre of the zigzag.

Measure the width of the blind at the top and bottom again to make sure that the width is still constant all down the length. Check that top and bottom edges are square. If you have made a mistake in turning hems, you must unpick and do it again. *The blind will not work if it is not square.*

Lath casing

On the bottom edge turn 12 mm ($\frac{1}{2}$ in) to the wrong side, then turn 4 cm ($1\frac{1}{2}$ in) and press carefully. Stitch close to the hem edge across the width of the blind and across one end. Cut the lath 12 mm ($\frac{1}{2}$ in) shorter than the width of the blind, push it into the casing and oversew the open end. Attach the cord holder and acorn to the lath casing.

Attaching fabric to roller

Iron the blind fabric until there are absolutely no creases in it. Lay the fabric out right side up. Put the wooden roller across the top of the fabric with the spring mechanism on the left-hand side.

Apply a strip of strong contact adhesive to the roller along the line which is marked on the wood. Apply adhesive to the edge of the fabric on the *right side*. When the adhesive is 'touch dry', lay the fabric along the roller and press down firmly. The edge of the fabric should be along the marked line.

Now tack the fabric to the roller, working from the middle out towards the ends. Tacks should be about 15 cm (6 in) apart. Now roll up the blind. (The right side of the fabric is *inside*.)

When fixing roller, place it on the *right* side of the blind fabric.

Fitting the roller

In the roller blind kit there should be the wooden roller, a metal cap and a lipped nail for the other end of the roller, two wall brackets, one slotted and the other with a round hole, a cord holder, acorn and cord, and a wooden lath for the bottom of the blind.

Screw the brackets to the window frame, or the wall or the ceiling – wherever you have decided to hang the blind. Remember that if the brackets are being positioned near the ceiling you must allow clearance for the roller and fabric. The bracket with the slot goes on the left-hand side and the one with the round hole goes on the right. Check to see that the brackets are exactly horizontal.

Place the rolled-up blind on the brackets and pull it down by the cord. Take the blind off the brackets and roll it up again by hand. Replace the blind on the brackets. Pull it down again and this should have tensioned the spring. It should now be locked in the down position.

Be sure not to over-tension the spring because if the blind is released so that it snaps up, the spring may become damaged.

Trimming roller blinds

The bottom edge of the blind can be trimmed in a variety of ways – with cotton lace, fringing, bobble braids etc. – or the surface decorated with appliqué designs, stitched on or glued with fabric adhesive.

Roman blinds

Roman blinds are made by sewing tapes to the back of a fabric blind. Rings are stitched to the tapes and cords run through the rings. When the cords are pulled, the fabric is drawn up into horizontal folds or pleats.

Roman blinds are more graceful than roller blinds and are best used wherever curtains would hide an attractive window frame. Roman blinds can be made of almost any kind of light or medium weight fabric. They are particularly useful in rooms which have a number of small or narrow windows and can be hung from the ceiling to give the illusion of greater height or made wider than the windows to make dramatic colour areas.

Calculating fabrics

Measure the height and width of the window. If the blind is to be fitted inside a recess, make it 2.5 cm (1 in) narrower than the recess. If it is to hang outside, the blind should be at least 8 cm (3 in) wider to cover the window adequately. Add 8 cm (3 in) for side hems and 12.5 cm (5 in) for top and bottom hems – a casing is made in the bottom hem for a wooden lath. Roman blinds should be lined unless the effect of the light through the fabric is part of the design appeal.

Fitting the blind

Roman blinds are tacked onto a wooden batten which is fixed to the wall above a window or inside the frame. A wooden curtain pole can be used but it must be wider than the blind by about 10 cm (4 in) and very firmly fixed on brackets.

Materials and equipment required

2.5 cm (in) wide cotton or Terylene tape, cut to the depth of the blind, 1 length for every 30 cm (12 in) across the width.
12 mm ($\frac{1}{2}$ in) brass rings to be spaced on the tapes at 20 cm (8 in) intervals.
Nylon cord, twice the estimate for the tape plus the width of the window.
Wood lath for the bottom of the blind.
Tacks, screw eyes (same number as lengths of tape) and holding cleat.

Prepare the batten from wood 5 cm × 2.5 cm × width of blind (2 in × 1 in). Paint or stain. Do not fix to the wall at this stage.

Make up the blind fabric and lining in exactly the same way as for the lined curtain (page 156).

Turn a 9 cm ($3\frac{1}{2}$ in) bottom hem, tack and press.

Cut the tapes to length. Pin the tapes down the blind so that the spaces between them are equal – approximately 30 cm (12 in) apart. Begin 2.5 cm (1 in) below the top edge and pin down to the folded edge of the bottom hem. Tuck the cut end of the tape under the bottom hem. Machine stitch from top to bottom of tapes on both edges.

Machine stitch the hem just on the edge and then again 4 cm ($1\frac{1}{2}$ in) away to make a casing. Insert the lathe into the casing as for the roller blind. Stitch the rings

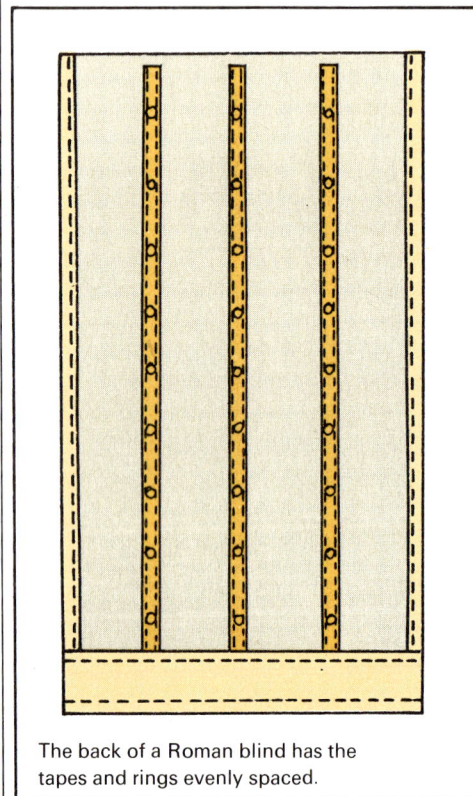

The back of a Roman blind has the tapes and rings evenly spaced.

to the tapes at 20 cm (8 in) intervals, making sure that the rings are absolutely level with each other across the blind. Stitches should not show on the right side.

Tack the blind to the batten. Screw in the screw eyes to the batten so that they exactly line up with the rings on the tapes. Thread the cords through the bottom rings of the blind and knot securely. (Later, wind thread round the cords to hide the knots – it looks smarter.) Thread the cords through all the rings and then through the screw eyes on the batten.

Take all the cords to either the left or right, through the screw eyes, depending on which side of the window the holding cleat will be fixed. Now fix the batten to the wall or window frame. Draw up the cords and leave the blind pulled overnight to set the pleats.

Other kinds of curtains

Curtains have other decorative uses in the home besides that of covering windows – for hundreds of years, they protected the occupants of four-poster beds from draughts!

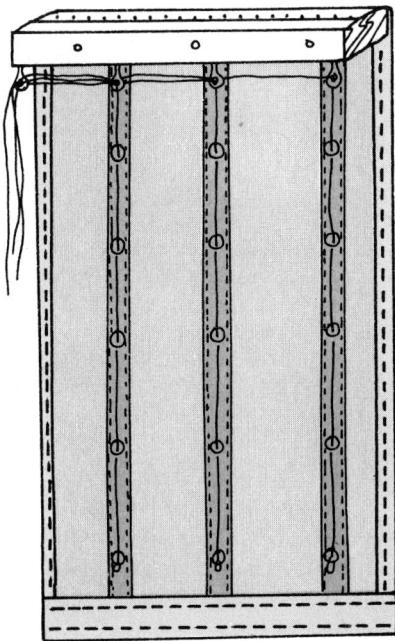

Nowadays, bed curtains are simply for decoration, made to hang from a pelmet board fixed over the bedhead.

Bed canopies, which effectively bring the height of the ceiling down visually, should be made of lightweight fabrics, hemmed on all four sides and hung across thin rods suspended from the ceiling on nylon line. A mock four-poster can be made by hanging a scalloped-topped curtain (see page 160) on each side of the bed. Suspend two white-painted poles from the ceiling with white, cotton cords. Fit decorative finials to the ends of the poles. Make the curtains with rings sewn to the scallop straps. Run gathering threads across the curtains to draw them back into attractive folds or make ties of matching fabric. This is a pretty effect for a little girl's bedroom.

Cupboard curtains

Removing cupboard doors and replacing them with curtains may seem a little drastic but in a small bedroom or a passageway, a curtain pays dividends in terms of extra space. Make the curtains with a neat, pleated heading and fit a curtain track to the underside of the cupboard surround. In a bedroom particularly, a curtained cupboard looks far softer and prettier than a blank wooden door.

Wall curtains

Curtains are often used for room dividers, the track being fitted to suspend from the ceiling. Wall curtains, often simply tacked to wood battens, are more easily removed for cleaning if they are hung from ceiling-high curtain tracks.

Curtaining off shelving

When it is necessary to curtain off shelving, do not be tempted to use expanded wire to support the curtains. Wire is really only suitable for net curtains and very light fabrics and sags if used in over 1.50 m (5 ft) lengths. Fit a hanging curtain track under the shelf edge or to the front edge and make sure that the curtain heading is positioned to hide the track.

Frilled curtains

Curtains with frilled edges are one of the favourite treatments for bedrooms and kitchens. They are usually made of lightweight or sheer fabrics and tie back at the sides to the window frame. Frills should be as full as possible – at least three times the length of the fabric although twice the length is permissible for a narrow frill. Cut frilling on the lengthwise grain of the fabric and join pieces with a narrow French seam (see page 38). The raw edges are hemmed on the sewing machine, using the foot attachment provided for the purpose. If your machine does not have a hemming foot, you must roll and hem the edges by hand.

Frill with a heading

Neaten both long edges of the frill strip by machine stitching or hand hemming. Run two close rows of gathering stitches along one edge 6 mm ($\frac{1}{4}$ in) from the edge. This can also be done on the sewing machine, setting the stitch as long as possible. Make a single narrow hem to the right side on the curtain. Baste the frilling along the curtain edge, the heading covering the raw edge of the hem. Machine stitch the frill to the curtain.

Dressing tables

Dressing table skirts look far better if they are fitted onto a curtain track. The most suitable tracks for the purpose are made of flexible nylon which can be easily curved to follow the shape of the dressing table top. Fit a clip-on valance rail in front of the track to hold a frilled valance which will hide the gathered heading of the skirt.

Again, do not attempt to do the job with expanding wire. It never works well and the wire quickly sags. For a very small dressing table, you might try using Velcro – a touch-and-hold fastener – glueing strips of it to the wrong side of a gathered heading and the wood of the dressing table.

Curtain trims
Braids and fringes

Curtains can be made to look even more individual with trimmings. This is your chance to use your imagination because there is a very wide range of trimmings to choose from. Fringes in cotton and silk, braids to match fringes, wide, patterned braids to combine with plain coloured braids, gimps, bobbles and cut-pile edges.

Generally, a plain-coloured curtain fabric sets off trimmings best but for very formal or dramatic settings, patterned fabrics can be enhanced with a rich trim. The brocade curtains in the dining room setting on page ??? are set off superbly with a scarlet silk fringe, edged with a matching gold and red braid. The scarlet placemats are also edged with the gold braid for an extra, imaginative touch.

Contrast edgings

If a patterned fabric is being used for other furnishings in the room but would be rather overpowering used for a large area of curtaining, make the curtains in a plain colour and 'bind' the inside edge with a wide band of the patterned fabric. This is sometimes a good way of using a very expensive patterned fabric in small touches in a room, matching it up to a less expensive, plain colour fabric.

Linings can be used for trimmings too. Choose a good quality fabric for the lining in a strong, contrasting colour or pattern and cut it 15 cm (6 in) deeper and wider than the curtain itself. Make the curtain and lining up together, bringing the lining over to the front of the curtain on the inside edge and hem. The corner must be mitred neatly. You might add a braid trim to outline the lining edge.

Tie-backs and cords

Straight tie-backs are suitable for lightweight, simple curtains of any length. Shaped tie-backs look superb on long curtains in richer fabrics.

Here are ideas for making straight tie-backs of all kinds.

Braid, ribbon and self-fabric ties

Loop a tape measure around the curtain and pull it back to the wall. It should not crush the curtain or be so loose that the folds do not hang well. Estimate the length of the tie and add 2.5 cm (1 in). Tie-backs can be any width at all but, generally, they should not be narrower than 5 cm (2 in).

For two tie-backs, you will need the following:

23 cm ($\frac{1}{4}$ yd) of curtain fabric.
6 cm ($2\frac{1}{2}$ in) wide braid or ribbon for two ties.
23 cm ($\frac{1}{4}$ yd) 69 cm (27 in) wide buckram.
23 cm ($\frac{1}{4}$ yd) non-woven interlining.
23 cm ($\frac{1}{4}$ yd) lining fabric.
Sewing and basting threads.
4 brass rings, 5 cm (2 in) diameter.
Wall hooks.

Pelmets and tie-backs add the finishing touch to a well thought-out interior, helping to turn what could be a very ordinary room into an elegant one. The pelmet around the shower curtain is an interesting way of using this feature.

Home sewing

Self-fabric tie-backs

Cut a strip of fabric 6 cm (2½ in) wide and 2.5 cm (1 in) longer than the required length of the tie-back. Cut the interlining and the buckram 5 cm (2 in) wide and to the same length. Cut the ends of all the strips to a point. On the fabric strips, measure 2.5 cm (1 in) in from the ends, and on the buckram and interlining measure 18 mm (¾ in) in from the ends.

Lay the interlining on the wrong side of the fabric. Lay the buckram on top and baste through all thicknesses. Fold the edges of the fabric onto the buckram and secure the edges by taking long

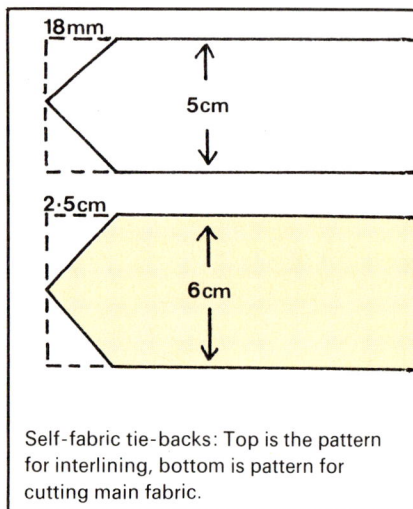

Self-fabric tie-backs: Top is the pattern for interlining, bottom is pattern for cutting main fabric.

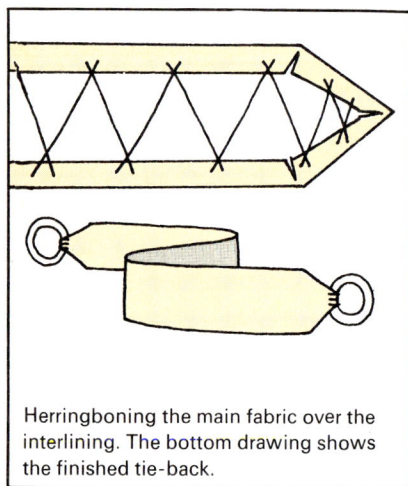

Herringboning the main fabric over the interlining. The bottom drawing shows the finished tie-back.

herringbone stitches right across the tie. Press carefully using a just-damp cloth. On the lining piece, fold in 9 mm (⅜ in) turnings all round. Press and then slip-stitch the lining to the back of the tie.

Using buttonhole stitch and strong button twist thread, sew a curtain ring to each end of the tie. Make a second tie in the same way.

The same technique is used for making ties from ribbon or braid.

Pleated, ruffled tie

This is a simple tie to make for ruffled curtains, using pieces of the ruffled curtain fabric. Cut the curtain fabric into a rectangle to the length of the required tie and about 17.5 cm (7 in) deep plus the ruffle. The ruffle is on the lower edge. Neaten the two short ends with narrow heams. Pin and baste pleats across the width until the

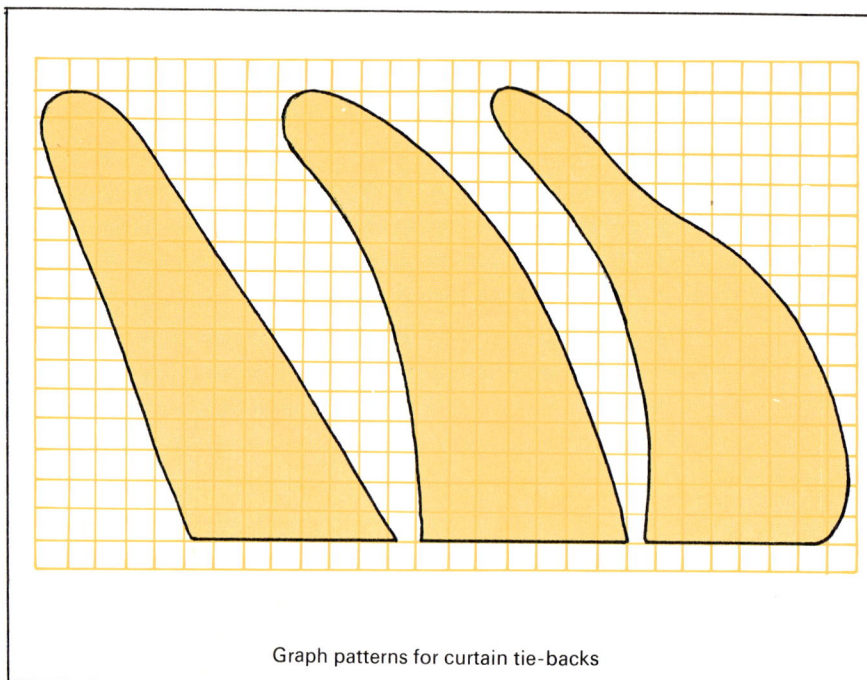

Graph patterns for curtain tie-backs

rectangle is approximately 8 cm (3 in) deep. Machine stitch each pleat flat. Sew white plastic-covered rings to each end of the tie, just above the ruffle.

Ties such as this can also be made of wide broderie Anglaise edging for tying back white cotton curtains.

Shaped tie-backs

Make a pattern first The diagram gives some shapes for tie-backs. If you decide to use one of these, enlarge to a scale of 1 sq = 2.5 cm (1 in). Measure the length of the tie-back required and alter the pattern if necessary on the dotted line. Draw up the shape and trace off a paper pattern.

Fold the curtain fabric on the grain, right sides facing. Lay the pattern on the fabric with the straight edge to the fold of the fabric. Pin and cut out with 8 cm (3 in) turnings all round. Cut out two, one for each tie.

Unpin the pattern and cut the shape out again in lining fabric but with 2.5 cm (1 in) allowance all round. Once again, remember to place the straight edge to the fold of the fabric. Unpin the pattern and cut out the same shape twice in buckram and interlining, without

seam allowances. Lay the interlining on the wrong side of the curtain fabric and then the buckram on top. Baste through all three thicknesses. Turn the edges of the fabric over onto the buckram and glue down with fabric adhesive. Snip into curved edges to get the fabric to lie flat. Leave to dry under a weight. Turn under the edges of the lining and press. Lay the lining on the wrong side of the tie and slip-stitch together all round the edges. Sew a curtain ring to each end. Rings can be covered with matching thread to make them less obtrusive.

Tablecloths

The greatest advantage of making your own tablecloths is that you can make them to exactly the size and shape you want. Bought cloths are mostly square and look wrong on rectangular tables. Round cloths for round tables are often expensive to buy and it is more economical to make your own.

Fabrics and materials

For day-to-day use, choose a fabric such as seersucker, gingham or an easy-care blend such as polyester-cotton. Cotton-backed PVC or cotton fabrics with a PVC surface treatment are easy to wipe down after children's meals.

For more formal entertaining, nothing looks more beautiful than freshly laundered linen. Real linen is expensive but there are good-looking fabrics in blended fibres with an authentic looking linen finish, ideal for table linen. Cotton sheeting makes superb tablecloth fabric and as it comes in very wide widths it is particularly suitable for circular cloths.

For round occasional tables, floor-length velvet or brocade cloths look charming. Delicate fabrics, such as voile, or a fine cotton lawn make pretty afternoon tea cloths.

Square cloths

Square or rectangular cloths should never be ground length. The actual depth of the drop (the amount of material hanging over the edge of the table) depends on your taste, but it should not be less than 30 cm (12 in).

If the table is wider than the width of the material, divide a width and seam it to the sides of a length. If possible, the seams should be on the edges of the table but if this is not possible, position seams so that they become a decorative feature.

If the fabric is geometrically patterned, for instance, you might turn the central panel the other way around. A small floral printed material could have ribbon stitched over the seams or a delicate material could be seamed with insertion lace, applied between panels. Embroidery stitches of all kinds can be worked along seams lines or strips of fabric can be joined with an insertion stitch. When joining panels, match the fabric pattern carefully and use a flat felled seam so that it looks good on both sides of the cloth.

Side seams and corners

Cut a tablecloth 5 cm (2 in) larger all round than the finished size.

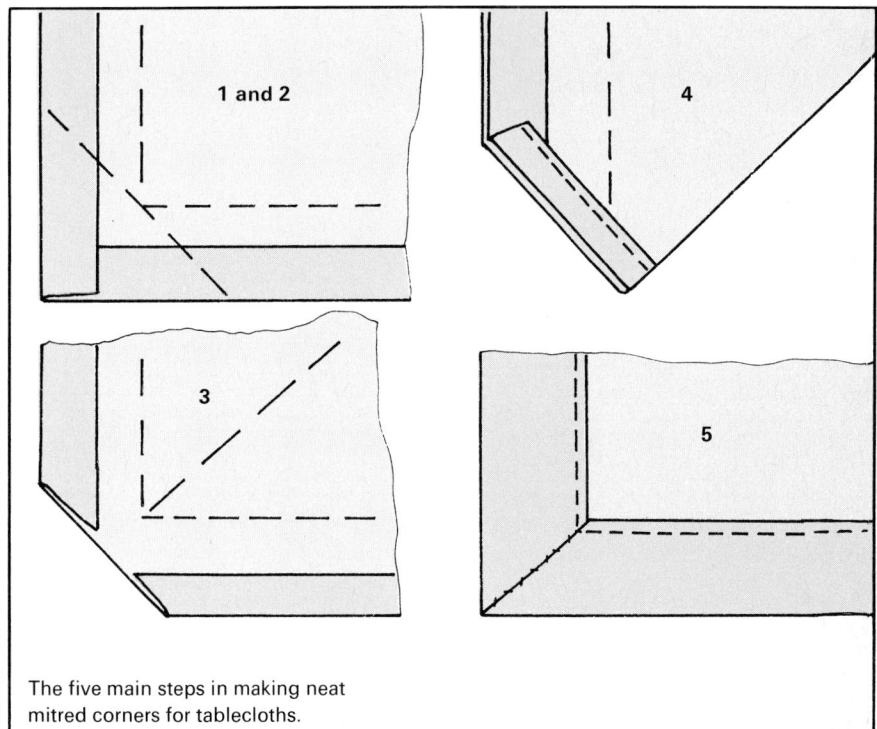

The five main steps in making neat mitred corners for tablecloths.

Draw threads to make sure that the cloth is quite square. Turn a 12 mm ($\frac{1}{2}$ in) hem all round and press. Turn a second hem, 4 cm ($1\frac{1}{2}$ in) wide, mitring the corners. Pin, placing pins across the hem and then baste. Press and then machine stitch close to the edge, using a closely matching thread and a medium-sized machine stitch.

Very fine fabrics, such as voile or lawn, can either be hand-rolled and shell-edged or machine hemmed. Machined hems should be at least 5 cm (2 in) deep and doubled so that the cut edges do not show through. Cut the cloth 10 cm (4 in) larger all round. Fold a 5 cm (2 in) hem twice, tack and stitch. If you are shell-edging (see page 69), cut the cloth 6 mm ($\frac{1}{4}$ in) larger all round.

Mitred corners

1 Fold in the raw edges of the cloth 12 mm ($\frac{1}{2}$ in) and press. Make another fold 4 cm ($1\frac{1}{2}$ in) from the fold edge and press again.
2 Open the fabric flat. With wrong side up, turn in the corner on the second pressed line. Crease this corner by pressing.
3 Trim off the corner 6 mm ($\frac{1}{4}$ in) from the pressed line.
4 Fold the corner, right sides together so that the edges are at right angles. Machine stitch along the crease line to the edge.
5 Turn the corner right side out and push the point through gently with a knitting needle.

Finish the cloth hem with machine stitching. Take care when pressing that you do not press over doubled fabric or a mark will result on the right side. Slip a piece of brown paper under the edge.

Round tablecloths

Measuring for fabric

Decide the depth the drop is to be. Measure the diameter of the table and add twice the depth of the overhang. Add 2.5 cm (1 in) for a hem. This measurement is the length and width of material you need for a round tablecloth.

Fabric width and length

A round tablecloth is made from a square of material but apart from sheeting, which can be as wide as 254 cm (100 in), you will probably have to join lengths to get the

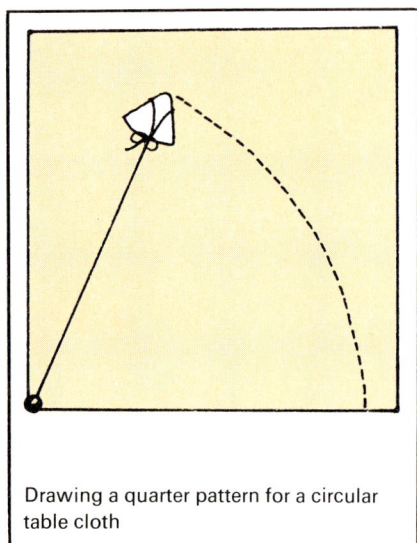

Drawing a quarter pattern for a circular table cloth

width you need. Join lengths with flat fell seams (see page 38).

Making a quarter pattern

You need a square of brown wrapping paper with the sides of the square a little longer than the radius of the tablecloth. (Estimate the radius by measuring from the centre of the table to the floor or wherever the drop ends.)

Lay the brown paper on a flat wooden surface. Anchor a length of tape to the bottom left-hand corner with a drawing pin. Tie a piece of chalk to the other end of the tape. Hold the drawing pin down with one hand and, holding the chalk with the other, draw an arc from the top left corner round to the bottom right corner. Cut out the paper pattern on the chalk line.

Cutting out the material

Join panels if necessary to get the required width. Press the cloth and then fold lightly in half and then in quarters. Pin the paper pattern to the folded fabric. Cut along the curve of the pattern edge.

Making hems on round cloths

If the cloth is to have a braid, bobble or fringed edge, a single hem is turned and tacked to the right side, and the trimming machine-stitched over the raw edge. For a plain hem, you will need bias-cut strips of the same fabric cut from the wastage (see

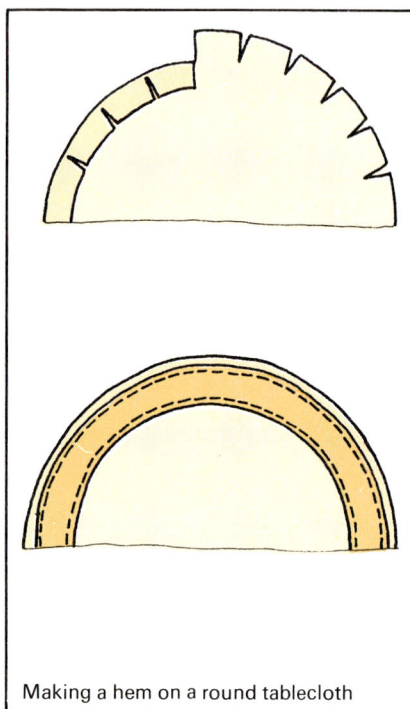

Making a hem on a round tablecloth

pages 144-145) or bought bias binding in a matching colour. Prepare the hem first; snip 9 mm ($\frac{3}{8}$ in) deep 'v's into the edge at 2.5 cm (1 in) intervals. Turn a 12 mm ($\frac{1}{2}$ in) hem to the wrong side and press.

Open the hem up again and tack and then machine stitch the bias strip all round, matching raw edges and right sides of fabrics facing. Turn the hem to the wrong side 3 mm ($\frac{1}{8}$ in). Tack and machine stitch the other edge of the bias strip. Neaten the ends of the strip by turning them under 6 mm ($\frac{1}{4}$ in) and slip-stitching to join.

The bedroom

No other room in the house can be given a new look with sewing as completely as a bedroom. You can make a new bedcover, curtains, a loose cover for a chair, cover a lampshade or a small stool, or make cushions, all from the same fabric.

Cotton sheeting is available in wide widths and comes in a range of patterns, pretty and feminine for a country house look or crisply smart. Cotton sheeting is easily laundered so it is worth considering for bedroom furnishings.

The bed is usually the largest area for a piece of sewing in the room so make a start with the bedcover.

Simple counterpane

A counterpane is a throw-over bedcover and is just a piece of fabric made to cover the bed from head to foot and extend down to the floor on all sides. It can be simply hemmed or have a decorative edging attached. You can line it to make it hang better or quilt it for a luxurious look.

Almost any kind of fabric can be used to make a throw-over, from tweeds and chunky wool fabrics to silk, cottons and glazed chintzes. Patchwork makes attractive counterpane throw-overs because the complexity of the patchwork does not need added frills or pleats to make it effective.

Measuring up

Ideally, the bedcover should be in one piece on the top with no seams but this may not be possible with large single and double beds. If you have to join pieces to get the width, either arrange the seams so that they fall on the edges of the bed or join pieces so that the seam does not lie down the middle of the cover.

Make a feature of an occasional table with a round tablecloth.

One solution is to use a full width of fabric for the centre panel and divide a width, joining the half widths to each side. You can make a decorative feature of seams by covering them with braid, ribbon or lace, depending on the fabric pattern. Or you might join panels with an embroidery stitch chosen from the Embroidery section.

Measure the bed, complete with blankets and pillows, from behind the pillow (allowing enough fabric to fall between the pillow and the headboard) along the top to the foot and then down to the floor. Measure the width so that, when the bedcover is on the bed, the sides are the same level as the end – just touching the floor. Add 2.5 cm (1 in) on all four sides for hems. If you want to tuck the bedcover under the pillow, add an extra 30 cm (12 in) to the length.

When you are working out your fabric requirements, remember that you will be taking up 2.5 cm (1 in) on each seamed panel. Also, if the pattern you choose has a large motif, you will probably need to allow one whole pattern (called a repeat) for each length of fabric for matching.

Linings and interlinings

A plain washable cotton lining will suit most heavy and medium weight fabrics. A very lightweight fabric such as silk should have a lining of similar weight. If you are quilting the coverlet, use washable synthetic wadding between top cover and lining.

Cutting out

A large table is best for cutting out but if this is not available, take up the rugs and use the floor. Check that the ends of the fabric are straight before starting to cut the lengths (see pages 28 to 29). Measure carefully and mark cutting lines with chalk and a ruler.

Making up the bedcover

Pin and tack the panels together, right sides of fabric facing. If you are matching a pattern, use the slip

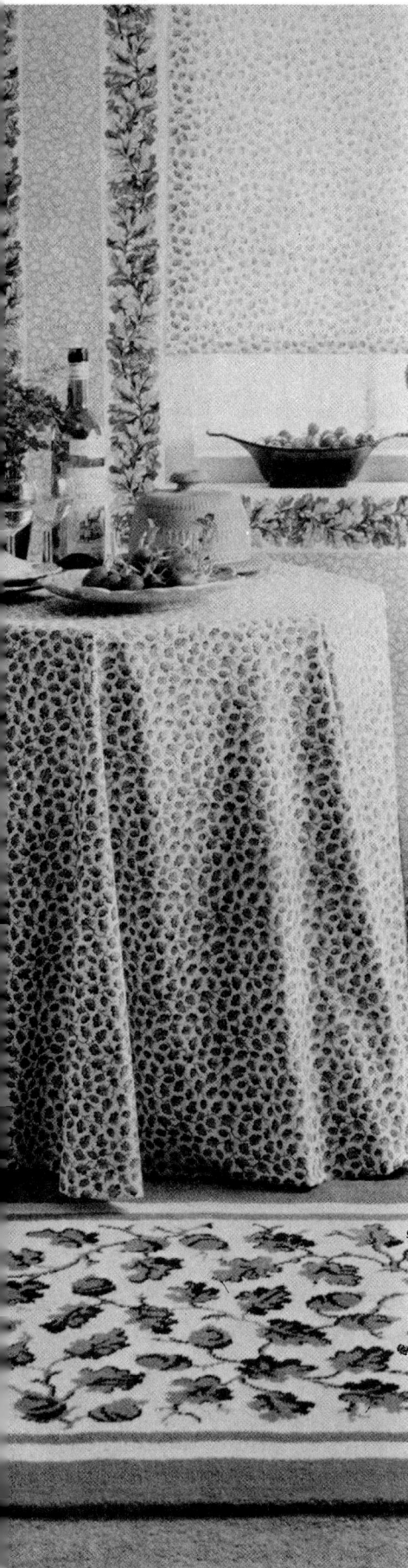

basting technique described on page 34. Now machine stitch the seams using a medium length stitch. Remove the tacking stitches and clip into selvedges at intervals, this helps the seams to lie flat. Always machine stitch in the same direction on each seam, from top to bottom of the bedcover or from bottom to top. Press the seam open. Neaten the raw edges of the seams with hand overcasting or by machine stitching if the bedcover is not to be lined.

Finish the side hems by turning a narrow 6 mm ($\frac{1}{4}$ in) hem to the wrong side on both long sides. Make a second fold 18 mm ($\frac{3}{4}$ in) deep so that the raw edge is enclosed. Tack carefully and then machine stitch along the first fold so that the line of stitching is 18 mm ($\frac{3}{4}$ in) from the edge. Remove tacking stitches and press the hems. Turn the same double hem on the top and bottom edges, making sure that the corners are square. Machine stitch, taking the line of stitching right over the line of stitches worked on the side hems.

Lining a counterpane

Make up the lining in the same way as the bedcover but make it 2.5 cm (1 in) smaller all round so that when it is attached it does not show on the right side. Catch the lining to the cover along the seams, using the technique for lining curtains on page 156.

Make sure that you pick up only a thread or two of the top fabric because the catching stitches should not show through on the

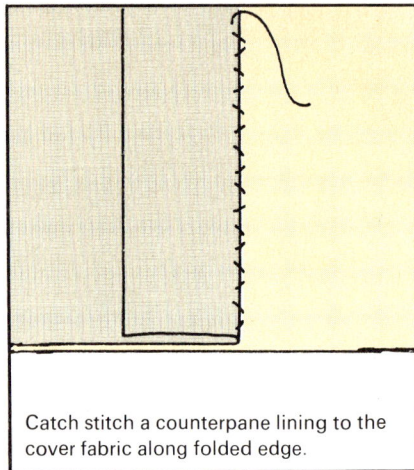

Catch stitch a counterpane lining to the cover fabric along folded edge.

right side. Finally, catch-stitch the lining to the cover round the sides.

Rounded corners at the foot end

Rounded corners look more elegant on a divan bed and can be worked in two ways.

Method 1 After seaming panels together, put the cover on the bed and mark the rounded corners with a line of pins. The curve should just skim the floor when it has been hemmed up. Cut off the excess fabric, leaving 2.5 cm (1 in) for a hem. Run a gathering thread round the curve and pull up the gathers before attempting to turn the hem. This technique makes it easier to turn a smooth hem.

Method 2 Put the seamed cover on the bed and mark the place where the corner of the mattress falls at the foot of the bed. Remove the cover and fold it in half lengthwise

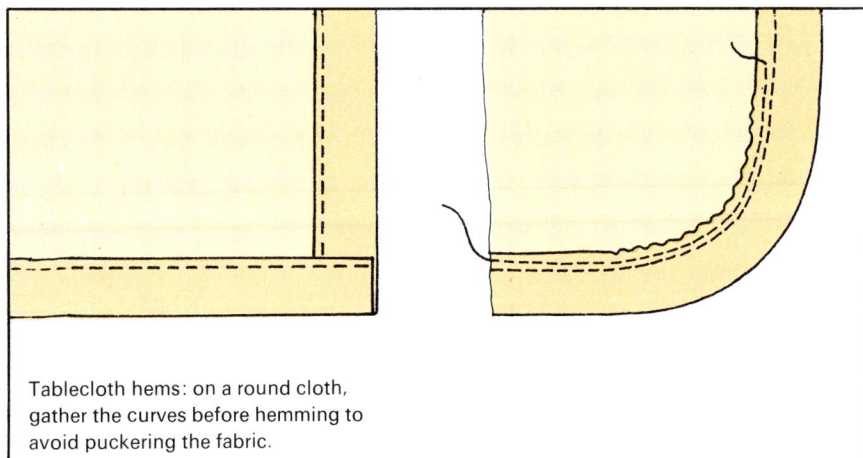

Tablecloth hems: on a round cloth, gather the curves before hemming to avoid puckering the fabric.

right side facing. Spread on the table or the floor and pin the layers together round the edges. Pin a piece of tape to the pin mark and hold the other end of the tape in your hand. Swing the end of the tape in an arc to find the natural curve for the rounded corner. When you have found it, hold a piece of tailor's chalk in your fingers with the end of the tape, and draw the arc. Cut out on the line through both thicknesses of fabric and then finish the hem.

Flounced bedcovers

Gathered flounced covers are almost as simple to make as throw-overs. The trickiest part is in handling the weight of the gathered fabric, pinning, tacking and finally stitching it to the top panel evenly. Use only soft, lightweight fabrics for flounced covers. Firm or heavy fabrics are difficult to handle.

Estimating for a flounce

The gathered flounce falls from the edge of the top panel to the floor and is seamed on the wrong side.

Measure for the top panel first, from the head end of the bed to the foot, adding 4 cm ($1\frac{1}{2}$ in) for seam allowance and then the width, adding 4 cm ($1\frac{1}{2}$ in) for seam allowance. For a bed with a foot board, add 51 cm (20 in) to the bottom of the panel to tuck under the foot end of the mattress.

Flounced covers look best if they lie flat on the mattress and the pillows are covered with a pillow scarf. (This is a piece of fabric seamed to the head end of the cover, which folds over and round the pillow on top of the bed.)

If the bed has a headboard, the flounce will be on three sides only. A bed with a footboard has the flounce on two sides with a tuck in piece on the end of the cover.

A day divan should be flounced on all four sides.

Measure the sides of the bed and double the measurement for the total amount of fabric to be gathered for a flounce this will give a reasonable fullness in the gathers.

Measure from the edge of the bed to the floor for the fall of the flounce, adding 37 mm ($1\frac{1}{2}$ in) seam allowance and 5 cm (2 in) for a hem. Cut pieces of fabric to this depth from the full width of the fabric. By dividing the total amount of fabric to be gathered by the width of the fabric you will know how many lengths you must join. To the total of the top panel plus the lengths you need for joining, add a further 100 cm (40 in) for a pillow scarf.

cover make two lengths and hem the short ends of each piece. For a divan cover with a flounce all round, join the lengths and then join up the short ends. Press all seams open, and neaten raw edges. Turn a 6 mm ($\frac{1}{4}$ in) hem on the hem edge and then fold again to make a 4 cm ($1\frac{1}{2}$ in) hem. Machine stitch and press.

The next stage is important if the flounce is to be evenly gathered; using tape measure and pins, mark the raw edge of the flounce into

that the gathering is quite evenly distributed round the cover. Pin the flounce to the panel, inserting pins at right angles to the gathering. Tack and remove the pins. Machine stitch on the gathering line, taking 18-mm ($\frac{3}{4}$ in) seams. (Work on the gathered side so that you can control the gathers while machining, ensuring that they are not flattened in stitching.) Remove the tacking and trim the seam allowance to 12 mm ($\frac{1}{2}$ in) and then neaten either by over-casting

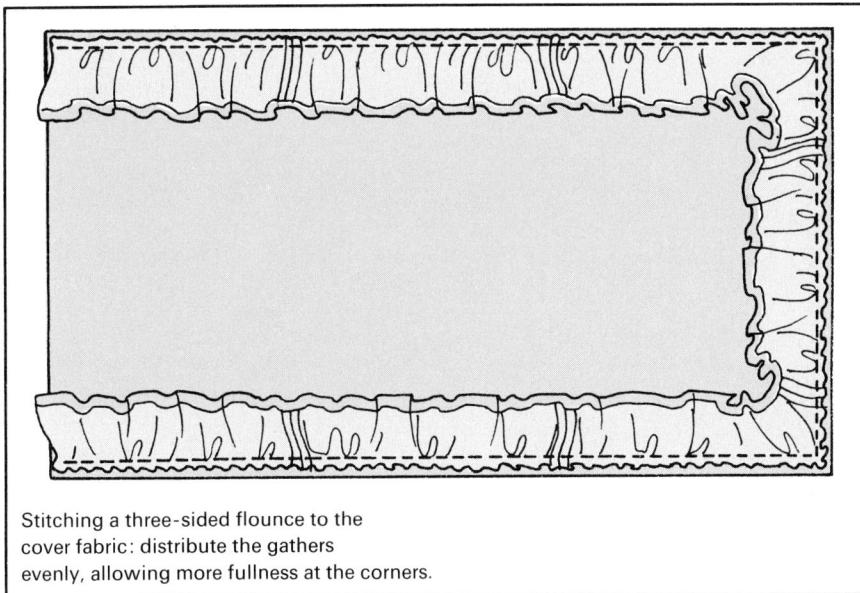

Stitching a three-sided flounce to the cover fabric: distribute the gathers evenly, allowing more fullness at the corners.

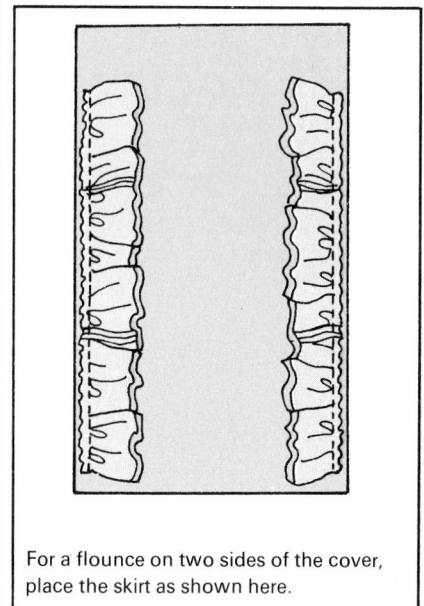

For a flounce on two sides of the cover, place the skirt as shown here.

Cutting out and making up the cover

Make the top panel without joins if possible, allowing a minimum of 12 mm ($\frac{1}{2}$ in) on all four sides for seam allowance. If panels have to be joined to each side of the centre panel, match the pattern and join the panels with 12-mm ($\frac{1}{2}$-in) seams. Clip selvedges and neaten the raw edges. Press seams open.

Flounce

Cut and then join together all the pieces for the flounce, taking 12 mm ($\frac{1}{2}$ in) seams. Take as much care as possible in measuring and cutting. It is so easy to cut one piece to the wrong depth.

For a flounce on three sides of a cover, join the pieces into one length and make a neat machine-stitched hem on the two short ends. For a flounce on two sides of a

sections, first in half, then quarters, then sub-divide into eighths and sixteenths. Lay the top panel out on the floor and mark the sides of the panels which are to be flounced in the same way.

Make the first mark 18 mm ($\frac{3}{4}$ in) in from the top edge for three-sided and two-sided flounces and 50 cm (20 in) in from the bottom edge for a two-sided flounce.

Gather the flounce 18 mm ($\frac{3}{4}$ in) from the edge either on a machine using a long stitch or by hand. Gather sections separately because if gathering threads are too long, they are liable to break. Wind the thread ends around two pins inserted vertically.

Lay the top panel flat, right side up and lay the flounce along the edges matching raw edges, drawing the gathers up to fit the markers, so

the edges or by bias binding. Press the seam towards the top panel.

Pillow scarf or 'sham'

Cut the pillow scarf fabric 50 cm (20 in) deep and to the full width of the bed plus 60 cm (24 in) on each side so that the ends hang down on the sides of the bed. Join panels to each side of the full width of fabric.

Make a narrow hem on two short sides and one long side of the pillow scarf. Now seam the pillow scarf to the top end of the cover, wrong side of the scarf to the right side of the cover, matching raw edges. Neaten the seam with bias binding.

When the cover is on the bed, the pillows are placed in position at the head of the bed and the scarf then folded forward over the pillows and tucked under them.

Bed base cover

Modern beds often have a sprung base, the mattress being on top. A base cover with a valance ensures that the bed looks just as well-dressed at night when the cover is off, hiding the legs and the bed base.

A bed base cover consists of the 'platform', which covers the top of the base (under the mattress), and a valance, which is seamed, gathered or pleated onto the platform piece. If the valance is a plain one, it is usual to have an inverted pleat at the corners. This is used on divans and beds with headboards. The hem of a valance can be machine-stitched or trimmed with braid or fringe.

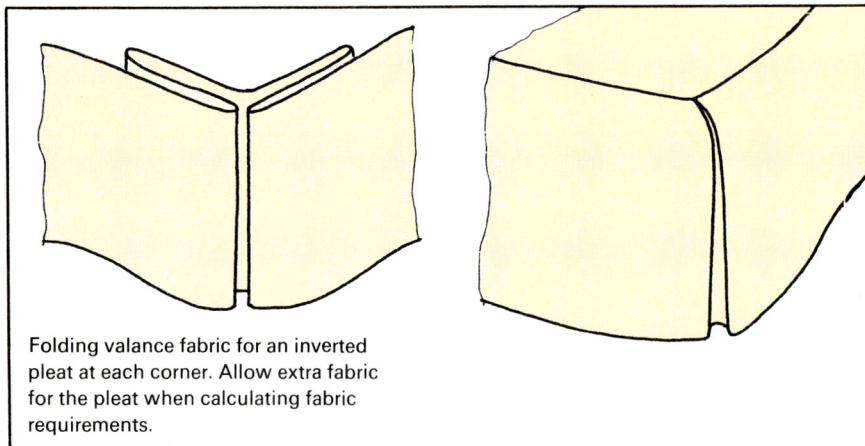

Folding valance fabric for an inverted pleat at each corner. Allow extra fabric for the pleat when calculating fabric requirements.

Estimating for fabric

Valances can be made for divans, beds with a headboard and for beds with both a head- and footboard. Measure the length and width of the bed for the platform piece. Subtract 8 cm (3 in) from the overall measurement on the sides which are to have the valance attached. This is because the seam of the valance is 8 cm (3 in) in from the bed edge and hidden when the mattress is in place. On a divan this would be on all four sides, on a headboard bed, on three sides, and on two sides of a head- and foot-boarded bed.

Measure the fall from the edge of the bed and add 8 cm (3 in) for joining to the platform and 4.5 cm (1¾ in) for the hem. For a gathered valance, estimate twice the length

of fabric, for a box-pleated valance three times the length and for an inverted pleat at each corner of a plain valance, allow an extra 60 cm (24 in) for each corner.

To make up the valance

Cut and join the lengths of fabric for the valance, taking 12 mm (½ in) seams. For a divan, join the last two short ends to make a continuous strip.

Fold a 6 mm (¼ in) hem to the wrong side of the bottom edge, and fold again to make a 4 cm (1½ in) hem. Machine stitch and press. Pleat the top edge to make box pleats. (Try to ensure that any joins are inside a pleat.) Pin the pleats; measure and pleat for inverted pleated corners.

Gather up the long edge. For a bed with a headboard, turn and stitch a narrow hem on the top edge of the platform piece. For a bed with head- and footboard, turn a narrow hem on both ends. Place the platform right side up on a flat surface.

Tack the valance to the platform, right sides together, matching edges. On a three-sided valance, you will need to pleat the corners to fit. Machine stitch the valance to the platform, working on the valance side. Over-sew or bind seam allowances.

Valances are topped with a simple throwover cover.

Fitted cover

A fitted cover gives a divan a neat box-like look for daytime use.

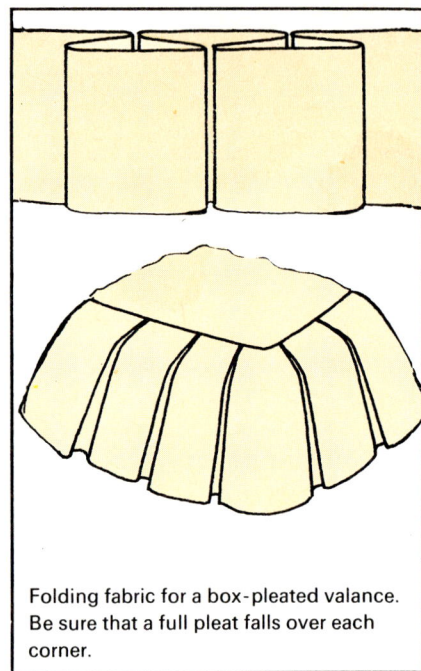

Folding fabric for a box-pleated valance. Be sure that a full pleat falls over each corner.

Choose a heavy, crease-resistant fabric, such as repp, denim, cotton or linen union. A plain fabric or a pattern without a one-way motif, such as a stripe or all-over spot, is best. Make sure that the fabric is pre-shrunk.

The fitted cover is made in five carefully fitted pieces, sewn into a box shape. One side of the cover, the side that goes against a wall, is made with a flap-over opening, so that the cover can be put on and taken off more easily.

Estimating fabric

Measure the top of the divan (with bedclothes on and tucked in, if the divan is used for sleeping in at night). Add 12 mm (½ in) all round for seam allowances.

The pieces for the sides of the divan should be cut in one piece if possible, seams occurring only at the corners. Measure the length of the side and add 2.5 cm (1 in) for seam allowances. Measure the fall from the top edge of the mattress to the floor. Add 12 mm (½ in) seam allowance and 4.5 cm (1¾ in) for the hem. The side which goes to the wall has an overlap of 15 cm (6 in) in the middle, so add 33 cm (13 in) to the length of this side piece.

Making up the cover

Cut three side pieces to

measurements. Cut the fourth side 33 cm (13 in) longer. Cut this piece into two equal pieces and make a neat, machine-stitched 6 mm ($\frac{1}{4}$ in) double hem on the cut edges. Overlap the hemmed edges 15 cm (6 in) and pin the overlap. This side piece should now be exactly the same length as the piece on the opposite side. Join the four side pieces. Press seams open and oversew seam allowances to neaten. Turn and machine stitch the hem.

Lay the top piece on the floor, right side up. Pin and tack the side piece to the top, right sides facing and matching the seams at the corners. Snip into the corners of the top piece for a neat fit. Machine stitch sides to top. Cut corners off

fillings for continental quilts are duck down and down and feather mixtures. Quilts filled with these are not washable and so must be dry cleaned. The cover material has to be 'down-proof' and a specially woven cambric is the only material that should be used. Down and feather fillings are purchased from specialist suppliers. You can use an old eiderdown to make a continental quilt, transferring the feathers from one to the other, but this is not really an economy. Feathers lose their warmth efficiency at a rate of about 1 per cent a year and you will probably have to buy additional filling to make up the loss.

For the home sewer, Terylene

It is less wasteful if you cut both single quilts and double quilts from 230 cm (90 in) wide sheeting. Use Terylene filling of the same width.

Making up the quilt
Cut two pieces of sheeting exactly the same size, adding a 12 mm ($\frac{1}{2}$ in) seam allowance all round. Spread one of the pieces on the floor, wrong side up. Lay the wadding on top so that the edges are flush with the edges of material. Pin and then tack them together all round the edges. Machine stitch 12 mm ($\frac{1}{2}$ in) from the edge, using a medium-sized stitch of about 12 to 2.5 cm (1 in).

Spread the cover on the floor again, sheeting side up. Spread and pin the second piece of the cover on top, right sides together. Tack, and then machine stitch round the edge on three sides and most of the fourth, leaving enough of the seam open to turn the cover to the right side. Turn the quilt cover right side out, and fold in the edges of the open seam. Close with machine stitching, working on the right side. Lay the quilt flat on the floor and with tailor's chalk and a ruler, mark lines down the quilt from top to bottom between 23 cm to 30 cm (9 in to 12 in) apart.

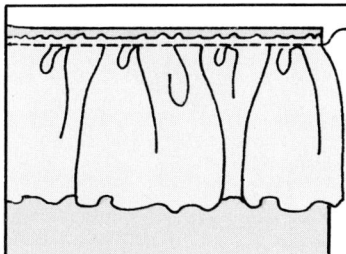

A gathered valance is perhaps the simplest type to make. The seam edges are finished with binding or they may be overcast.

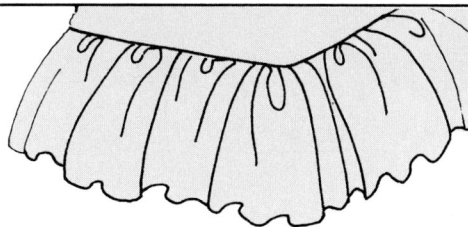

diagonally. Press seam allowances downwards and oversew raw edges together.

If you decide to pipe this seam, pin the piping to the top piece before pinning the side piece in position. Tack all three units together and then machine stitch, using piping foot on the sewing machine.

Continental quilts
More and more people are giving up top sheets, blankets and eiderdowns and replacing them all with a continental quilt – or duvet as it is sometimes called. A duvet is a bag of fabric filled with a soft insulating material, such as down, and it is said to be warmer than an eiderdown in winter and cooler than traditional bed covers in summer.
Fillings
The best, and most expensive,

fibre filling of a type called P5 is the best, because it is simple to work with, is cheaper than down and feathers, is comparatively easy to obtain and is washable. Cotton sheeting can be used for the cover.

Estimating fabric for the primary cover
For adult beds, the quilt should be at least 46 cm (18 in) wider than the bed itself. Bunk beds need a quilt 38 cm (15 in) wider. The length of the quilt is very important. It should be at least 195 cm (6 ft 6 in) long but for a tall adult, over 2 m (6 ft) the quilt should be 210 cm (7 ft) long.
For a double bed
You may find that two single quilts are easier to handle than one large quilt. A single quilt is usually about 140 cm wide by 195 cm long (55 in by 78 in) and a double quilt about 200 cm (80 in) square.

A prettily patterned fitted cover will turn a divan bed into a settee: piped edging will add to the upholstered effect.

Set the sewing machine to its biggest stitch and stitch along these lines, working through all thicknesses of the quilt. You may need to raise the presser foot of the machine a little to allow the fabric to move through smoothly. Alternatively, hand sew along the lines using back stitch.

Quilt cover

Basically, the duvet cover is the same size as the primary cover but there is an extra piece on one end for a closure flap. The flap should be about 25 cm (10 in) deep. Cut one piece of the cover 25 cm (10 in) longer. Make a narrow hem to the wrong side on the top end of both pieces. Machine stitch. Lay the two pieces together, right sides facing, matching the raw edges.

Fold the flap over and pin the sides and bottom of the cover together. Tack, then machine stitch on the three sides. Neaten the raw edges with either zigzag machine stitching or oversewing.

Turn the cover to the right side and press. The flap closes the opening adequately when in use but, if you prefer, stitch snap fasteners 20 cm (8 in) apart along the hemmed opening, or sew on tie tapes.

Sheets and pillow cases

If you are sewing furnishings for a co-ordinated look, and using sheeting material for curtains, chair covers etc., it is a good idea to make your own bed linen to match.

The top sheet is simplicity itself to make. Choose the width of sheeting you need for the bed – 177 cm, 203 cm, 229 cm and 274 cm (70, 80, 90 and 108 in) widths are available. Cut off a length 278 cm (110 in) long and turn a double 2.5 cm (1 in) hem on three sides with a deeper hem at the top – 5 cm to 6 cm (2 in to 2½ in) is sufficient. Mitre the corners (see page 169). The top edge can be trimmed with cotton lace, tatted or crocheted edging, or you could apply a length of pretty washable ribbon. Trim the pillow cases to match.

Fitted bottom sheet

To estimate the size of the sheet, measure the top of the mattress, both length and width. Measure the depth of the mattress and double the measurement adding 2.5 cm (1 in). Cut a piece of fabric to the size of the mattress top plus this total all round. Lay the sheeting out on the floor, wrong side up. With tailor's chalk, draw the outline of the mattress on the sheet. Make a mark 12 mm (½ in) away from each corner of the mattress and then draw a vertical and horizontal line from the point to the edges of the sheet. Cut this square of fabric away on each

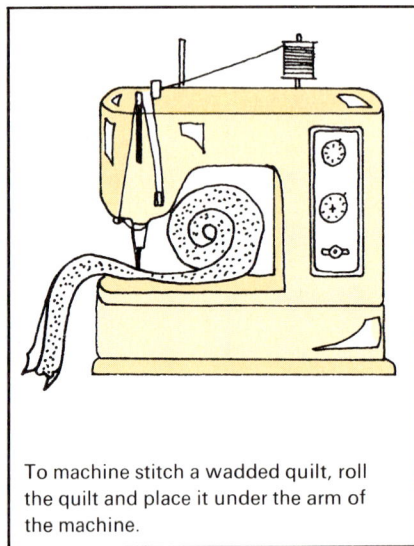

To machine stitch a wadded quilt, roll the quilt and place it under the arm of the machine.

corner. Hold the cut edges together, right sides facing and tack, taking a 12 mm (½ in) seam. Machine stitch. Press the seam open.

Now turn a 6 mm (¼ in) hem and then a 12 mm (½ in) hem on all four sides, to the wrong side of the sheet. Tack and then machine stitch to make a 10 mm (⅜ in) casing, but leave a 12 mm (½ in) gap in the stitching 15 cm (6 in) from each corner. These are for inserting elastic into the casing at the corners. Fasten a safety pin on the end of a 23 cm (9 in) length of 6 mm (¼ in) elastic and thread the other end of the elastic onto a bodkin. Run the elastic through the gaps in the casing at the corners, using the safety pin to prevent the elastic being pulled

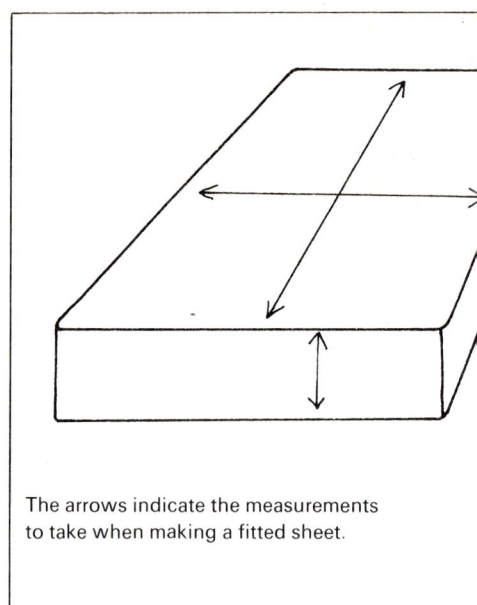

The arrows indicate the measurements to take when making a fitted sheet.

through. Hand sew the elastic to the inside of the casing at both ends and close the casing with back stitches.

The sheet fits onto the mattress with the elasticated corners underneath. An ordinary sheet can be turned into a fitted bottom sheet by the same method.

Pillowcases

Perhaps of all bed linen, pillowcases are the most worth making because they are quick to sew and you can pretty them up in so many ways.

The 'housewife' style

This is the plain type of pillowcase with a tuck-in flap to protect the end of the pillow. As pillows vary in dimensions, make pillowcases to fit each pillow. Cut sheeting twice the length of the pillow plus 25 cm (10 in), by the width plus 2.5 cm (1 in). Fold in a 6 mm (¼ in) hem and then a 12 mm (½ in) hem at one end and a 5 cm (2 in) hem at the other. Machine stitch using a medium-length stitch. Press.

Fold the fabric across the width right sides together so that the end with the narrow hem extends 17.5 cm (7 in). Fold this narrow hemmed end over so that the wider hemmed end is enclosed. Pin, baste and then machine stitch, taking special care to see that thread ends are fastened off securely. Trim off

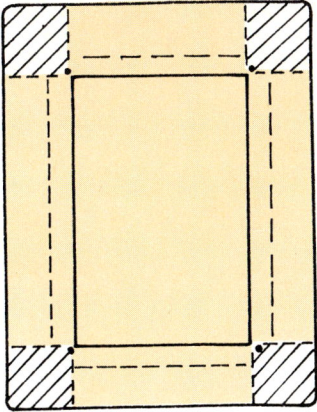

Sheeting fabric marked up for making a fitted sheet. Cut away the shaded areas and seam the raw edges to make the fitted corners.

the seam allowance ends diagonally for neat corners to the pillowcases.

For an extra finish, zigzag stitch the raw edges of the seams – it helps to give the pillowcase a longer life through laundering. Turn the pillowcase to the right side and press. (If you are planning to decorate the pillowcase, complete this before making up.)

Frilled pillowcases

There are two ways of making a frill; it can be made from single fabric, turning a narrow hem on one edge with the sewing machine attachment provided for the purpose, or shell-hemmed by hand. French seams must be used for joining up the strips, so that the frill looks neat on both sides. Alternatively, the frill can be made from doubled fabric.

Doubled frill Cut two pieces of sheeting to the dimensions of the pillow plus 12 mm ($\frac{1}{2}$ in) all round for seams. Cut a strip to the width of the pillow plus 2.5 cm (1 in) for seams by 22 cm ($8\frac{1}{2}$ in). This is for the flap. Measure round the pillow and estimate for a length of fabric twice this measurement, by 17.5 cm (7 in) deep. This is for the frill.

Join strips cut across the width of the sheeting to obtain a strip long enough for the frill. Join the strip into a circle and then fold it along the length. Run a gathering thread

along the raw edges through both thicknesses. Pull up the gathers so that the circle of frill fits one of the pillow pieces. Lay the pillow piece right side up on a flat surface and pin the frill round, adjusting the gathers so that they are even, but with a little extra fullness at the corners. Baste the gathers and then machine stitch, working on the gathered side. Stitch on the seam line 12 mm ($\frac{1}{2}$ in) from the edge.

Prepare the flap by stitching a double 12 mm ($\frac{1}{2}$ in) hem along one long edge, to the wrong side. Lay the flap on the frilled pillow piece, the raw long edge matched to the edge of the frill. Stitch these

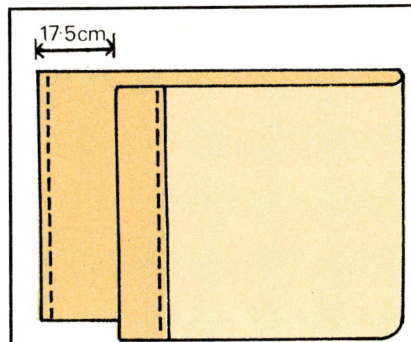

On a 'housewife' style pillowcase, fold the extension over the deep hem end and then machine down the sides.

together, machining along the same stitching line as before. On pillow piece 2, turn a narrow double hem on one short end. Slip this under the flap, right sides facing; now smooth the flap over this second pillow piece and tack through all fabric thicknesses along both long sides of the pillowcase and across the bottom. Machine stitch these three sides, finishing off ends securely. Turn to the right side and press. The method is the same for a single frill; simply machine stitch the gathered frill to the pillow piece as before.

Bolster pillows

Traditional bolsters are long pillows, made to the width of the bed. Covers are made like a 'housewife' pillowcase, with a tuck-in flap at one end. The continental bolster is like a cushion. It is plump and round and can be left on the top of the bed during the day and makes a comfortable back rest for a divan.

Ideally, the bolster should be filled with feathers but foam crumbs can be used if the fabric is heavy enough. If you are using foam crumbs, choose ticking for the bolster case. Use down-proof cambric for a feather filling.

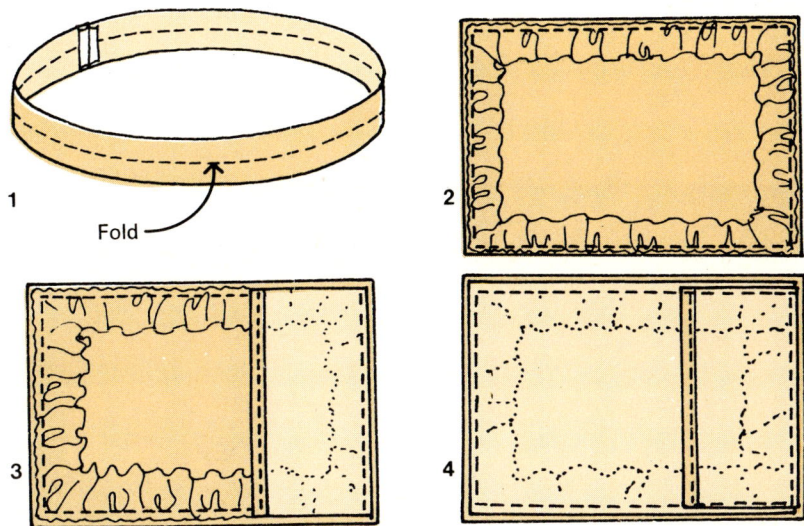

Frilled pillowcases: 1. Make the frill.
2. Sew frill to one pillow piece then,
3. sew on the flap, and 4. put last piece under flap and sew up sides.

Loose covers

If you own a sewing machine, know how to sew a straight seam and have a small degree of patience, you can make your own chair and sofa covers. The golden rule for making loose covers is 'measure twice and cut once'. Always make sure that the measurements you have taken are correct by double checking.

Most furnishing fabrics are 120 cm (48 in) wide, but check the width of the fabric you are going to buy before measuring up the piece to be covered. If the fabric has a prominent motif in the pattern, this must be placed centrally on the inside back, on the seat cushion, on the outside back, on the front facing and on the arm pieces. This is probably going to mean some wastage and you must allow extra fabric. However, it is sometimes possible to cut out the valance and the piping strips from the fabric left over after matching up the pattern.

Do take the extra trouble to pipe loose covers; it is not nearly as difficult to do as it looks, and it will make all the difference to the finished look, besides strengthening the cover at weak points. About 9.15 m (10 yd) of piping cord is required for an armchair and about 19 m (21 yd) for a settee. Piping must be pre-shrunk before using it (see page oo). When calculating fabric quantity, allow about 20 cm (8 in) for a generous tuck-in round the seat and arms, otherwise the cover will never stay in place.

Covering sofas and settees

Covering a sofa is no different from covering a chair except that the extra width of fabric required means there will have to be a seam. The seam must never occur in the centre of the back; place the full width panel down the centre and join a half width to each side. The seams should meet at the same

point on the outside back, the seat and the valance.

When it is necessary to match the pattern in two pieces of fabric, do it this way; fold the selvedge plus 6 mm ($\frac{1}{4}$ in) of pattern to the wrong side of one piece and press. Place it right side up on the table and slip the selvedge side of the second piece of fabric under the folded edge and match the pattern. Pin. Sew by hand, slipping the needle first through the fold of the top fabric and then through the under piece, until the seam is joined. Press the fold open and machine stitch exactly over the hand stitches. Press seam open. You now have a perfect pattern match and the seam is hardly noticeable.

Equipment required

Assemble the following equipment before starting. You will need a quantity of long, sharp pins, sharp dressmaker's shears, a tape measure and a piece of tailor's chalk. A yardstick or long ruler is useful too. You will also need a set of hooks and eyes for the cover closure and a zip fastener for the seat cushion. You can use snap fasteners on tape if you prefer—or touch-and-close tape. All the machine stitching is done using a zipper or piping foot on the machine. Prepare all the piping you will need before starting.

Fabrics for loose covers

Whatever the fabric, the main

Add years of use to worn furnishings, or give a new look to a room with a set of perfectly made loose covers.

motif must be centred on each section. This can be rather wasteful of fabric, so, if you are economising, choose a plain fabric or one with a small motif or an all-over pattern.

Loose covers should keep their shape and be sturdy enough to stand up to fairly heavy wear. Ideally, the fabric should not snag too easily or pull. Heavy furnishing cottons, chintzes, needlecord or corduroy, linens and furnishing velvets are all suitable. (Incidentally, check to see that your sewing machine will take six layers of the fabric—in certain areas of the cover it will have to!)

Stretch fabrics which are sold for making loose covers present no problems in making up, except that the machine stitch used should be larger and the machine tension looser.

Measuring

Remove the cushions and take off the loose cover. Brush away dirt and vacuum clean into the creases. Mend any tears or splits. Measure as follows:

1 *Outside back, A-B:* Measure from highest point of back to point where the valance will be attached, plus 5 cm (2 in) for seams. If you are covering a sofa, measure the width to see how many widths of

fabric will be required.

2 *Inside back, C-D:* Measure from point C to point D and add 23 cm (9 in) for the tuck-in at the seat back. Add 23 cm (9 in) to the width for a tuck-in into the arms at the sides. (For a sofa, measure the width to check number of widths required.)

3 *Inside arm, F-E:* From the point F, where the arm turns over to point E, plus 23 cm (9 in) for tuck-in into the seat. Measure the width of the arm from point L to V and add 23 cm (9 in) for the tuck-in at the back of the arm. Two arm pieces are required.

4 *Outside arm, F-G:* Measure from point F to point G, adding 5 cm (2 in) for seams. Two pieces will be required.

5 *Seat, D-H:* Measure from point D to point H, adding 23 cm (9 in) on both sides and at the back for the tuck-in. (Measure the width for number of widths required if it is a sofa.)

6 *Front arm facings, L-M:* From point L to M. These two pieces can usually be cut out of the surplus from the inside arm pieces.

7 *Skirt or valance:* Measure from the bottom of the chair to the floor (N to O), plus 8 cm (3 in) for seams and hems, plus 5 cm (2 in). For a valance with an inverted box pleat at each corner, estimate that you will be cutting the full depth of the valance from the full width of the fabric, four times. Widths will have to be joined for a sofa. For a pleated skirt, allow three times the measurement round the back, front and sides. For a gathered skirt, twice the measurement is sufficient.

8 *Piping:* Allow approximately 120 cm (48 in) of fabric.

9 *Cushions:* Estimate twice the top width and depth plus 25 mm (1 in)

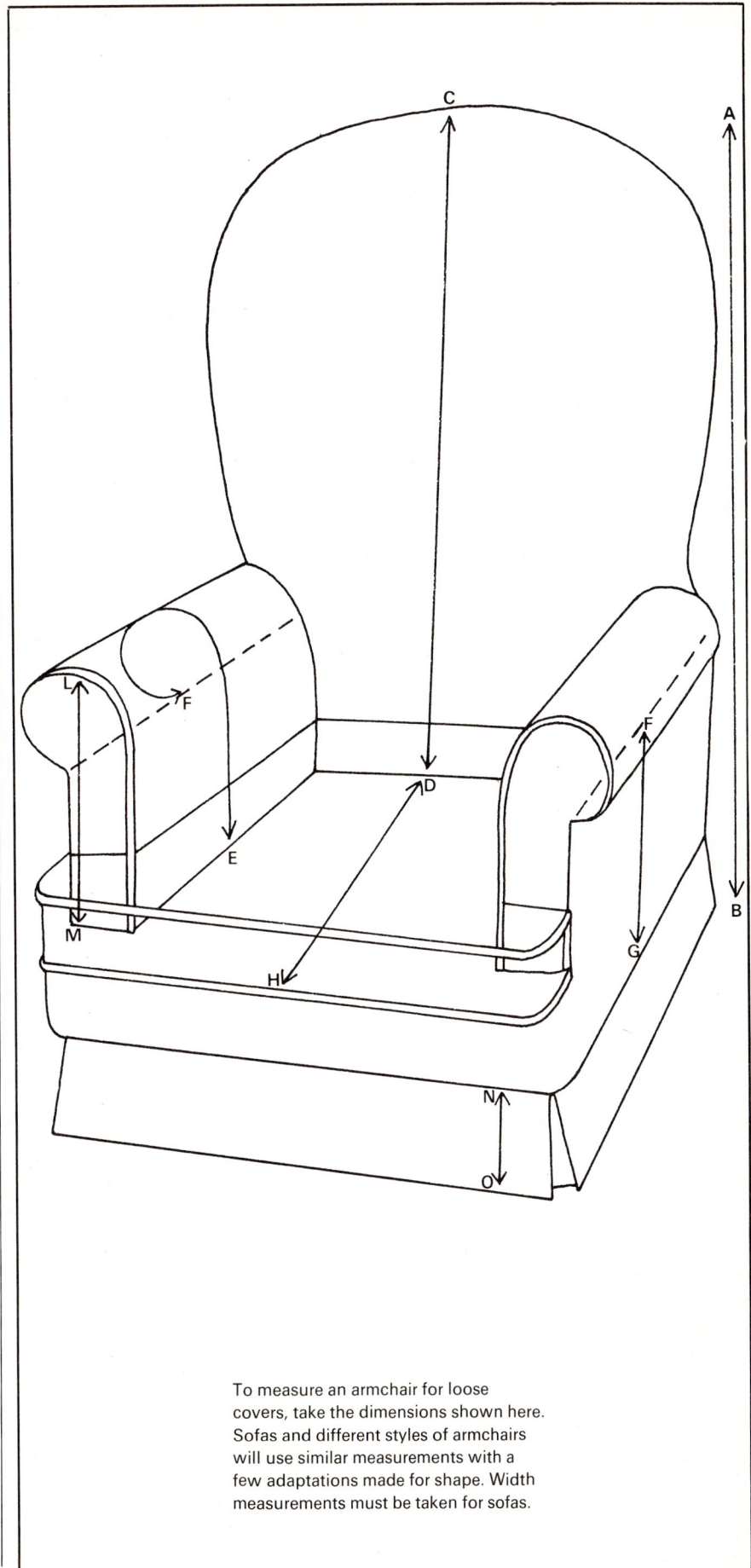

To measure an armchair for loose covers, take the dimensions shown here. Sofas and different styles of armchairs will use similar measurements with a few adaptations made for shape. Width measurements must be taken for sofas.

all round for seams, plus two pieces the depth of the cushion plus 25 mm (1 in) top and bottom for seams.

As a rough guide, the average armchair cover requires 6.90 m ($7\frac{1}{2}$ yd) fabric and a sofa 9.60 m ($10\frac{1}{2}$ yd).

To make up the cover

With tailor's chalk, mark a line down the centre of the outside back, the inside back and down the seat. Place the fabric right side up with the central motif at the centre on the inside back of the chair. Pin to hold in place and cut out roughly with 2.5 cm (1 in) turnings, except at the point where the back meets the seat and the inside arms. Snip into turnings where necessary. Here a 23 cm (9 in) tuck-in must be allowed. Pin the fabric in place with several pins.

Place the fabric on inside arms (F-E), centering the pattern if necessary, and allowing 23 cm (9 in) where it tucks into the seat and the inside back; cut out. Cut outside arms (F-G) allowing 2.5 cm (1 in) all round for seams.

Making up the arm pieces

Pin and tack piping to the top of the outside arm. Tack outside arm piece to the edge of the inside arm piece. Remove the fabric and machine stitch these seams. Oversew the raw edges to neaten. Replace the arm piece on chair and pin in place.

Fitting the back piece

It is now necessary to slash the fabric of the inside back to fit the curve of the arm – three cuts from point V to X will be enough; this should be done on the cross of the fabric to avoid the fabric tearing. Turn under the back seam edge of the inside arm piece and tack to the inside back between these two points (V to X).

The seat

Place the fabric on the seat, centering the pattern, and cut out, allowing 2.5 cm (1 in) where it meets the valance but adding 23 cm (9 in) on both sides for tuck-in and where it meets the back piece.

Front facings

Pin outside and inside arm pieces to the chair where it will meet the front facings. It will probably be necessary to make several tucks in the fabric to shape it round the curve of the arm. Make these at the same place on each arm and fold away from the chair. Pin and tack piping cord round these two pieces. Cut the front arm facings and pin and tack to inside and outside arm pieces.

Remove arm pieces, inside back and seat, and machine stitch all tacked seams. (Use the zipper foot on the sewing machine when sewing seams which have piping inserted.)

Stitching the seat

Stitch the bottom of the inside back to the rear of the seat piece with right sides facing. Stitch each of the inside arms from point X to Y and continue along bottom of inside arm. Neaten seams, oversewing by hand or with a machine oversewing stitch. Replace the cover on the chair and pin in place.

Outside back

Cut out the outside back allowing 2.5 cm (1 in) turnings all round. Pin and baste piping at the correct point round the outside arm, inside back and down round other outside arm.

You will find it necessary to have one or two tucks on the 'shoulders' of the inside back to get the material to fit nicely. Try to place them at the same spot on each corner, and turn the tuck away from the centre.

With back of chair facing, and starting at bottom right hand corner, tack outside back to outside arm, and outside back to inside back until you have worked right across the top of the chair and have reached a point about 10 cm (4 in) below the top of the back. Fasten thread off securely. The remaining part of the seam will have hooks and eyes to enable the cover to be put on and taken off.

Valance with inverted pleat corners

Pin and tack piping to the outside

arm, round the front, across other outside arm and finally across the back. The average skirt is approximately 15 cm (6 in) deep so you will have to place the seam of the piping 16 cm ($6\frac{1}{2}$ in) above the floor.

Where the skirt piping crosses the front face piping (and at any other place where one row goes across another), it will be necessary to cut the actual cord inside its piping case.

Place a pin on the edge of the piping at the point where you wish to sew across. Unpick the casing seam to a point 6 mm ($\frac{1}{4}$ in) above this pin, thus revealing the cord. Cut it off, then baste the empty casing back in place. It will now be possible for you to machine stitch right across the empty casing.

Measure front, back and two sides from corner to corner, and cut out four pieces to this measurement plus 2.5 cm (1 in) where the skirt joins onto the cover. Add 5 cm (2 in) on each side for seams and 5 cm (2 in) on the bottom for a hem. This will give a 12 mm ($\frac{1}{2}$ in) clearance from the floor. With the wrong side of fabric uppermost, turn a hem on the bottom edge and sides of all four pieces. Stitch and press. Still with wrong side facing upwards, turn down the top edge to 12 mm ($\frac{1}{2}$ in) and press. With right side out, pin and tack the skirt pieces to the bottom edge of the cover, just below the piping.

Underpleats

Cut four small pieces of fabric, 25 cm (10 in) wide and to the same depth as the valance pieces were before hemming. Hem these in the same way and press. Pin and tack the underpleat pieces to the corners under the main skirt of the valance. By making the valance in this way some of the bulkiness is avoided which often results from using one continuous piece of fabric.

On the chair back seam, mark the spacing of the hooks and eyes. Press fabric under at the point where the outside back will touch the piping cord of the outside arm. Remove the cover from the chair.

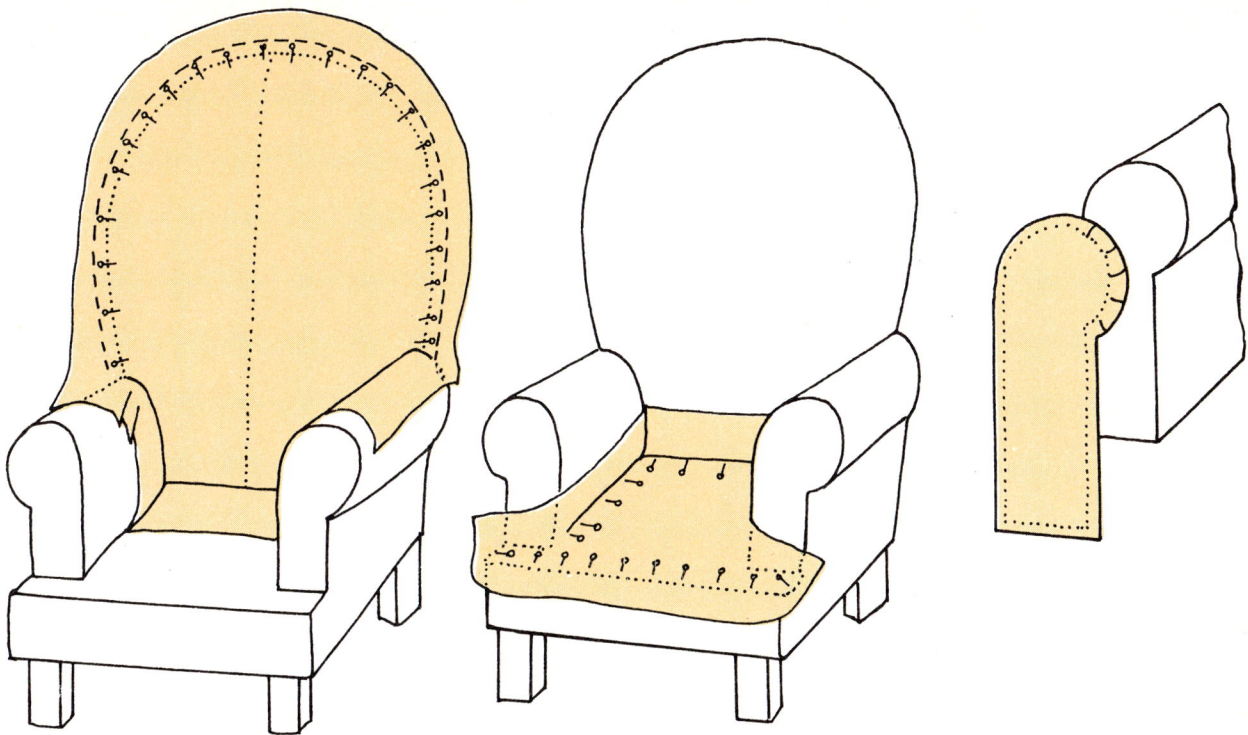

Three steps in making loose covers: from left to right — fitting the back piece, fitting the seat piece, fitting the front piece to the arm.

From the scraps of fabric remaining, cut a piece 10 cm (4 in) wide and to the length of the back opening. Fold the fabric in two lengthways, right side out, and pin the raw edges to the raw edge of the outside back. Machine stitch on the seam allowance. Press the doubled strip of fabric to inside on the seam line. Stitch across the three thicknesses at the top, and down to the bottom of the back about 18 mm ($\frac{3}{4}$ in) in from the edge. This will give a strong edge onto which to sew hooks, necessary since they will be subjected to a considerable amount of strain. Repeat on the other open edge, this time sewing the strip of fabric next to the piping. Sew on the hooks and eyes.

Machine stitch the valance to the main cover. The corner flap which goes across the corner where the opening is will also have to have hooks on it, so that it can be fastened under the side skirt once the cover is in place. Place cover back on chair and position remaining eye.

Cover without a valance
If a valance is not required, the front facing, outside arms and outside back must all be cut 10 cm (4 in) longer than the actual depth of the chair. The corner edges must be cut to make room for the castors or legs. Turn back these corner edges, and neaten on the wrong side with strong tape. Four pieces will be left hanging down. Turn under the raw edges, and make a 12 mm ($\frac{1}{2}$ in) casing. Thread strong tape through the casing. When the cover is on the chair the tapes are drawn tight to hold the cover in place. Tie the tapes in a bow and tuck the ends back into the cover out of sight.

Covering the cushion
Cut out a top and a bottom piece. Join pieces to make a gusset to go round all four sides. It will probably be necessary to join two or more widths for the side pieces. Allow 12 mm ($\frac{1}{2}$ in) all round for seams and remember that the pattern must be in the centre of both top and bottom pieces so that the cushion can be turned over should one side get soiled. With tailor's chalk, mark the piping line. (If the cushion is made of foam, take the exact measurements of the foam; if it is a feather cushion, make the cushion cover 18 mm ($\frac{3}{4}$ in) smaller all round than the inner cover.)

Make the cushion cover, following the instructions on pages 148-149 for a box cushion.

When the time comes to wash the cover, if there is any doubt that the material might shrink, place the cover back on the chair while it is still damp. This will prevent distortion and will, incidentally, make the ironing much easier, as there will be no undue creasing.

Equipment and designs

Since earliest times, women have embroidered their clothes and their home furnishings to make them more beautiful and more personal. Embroidery is a satisfying creative outlet and one which any needlewoman can master and enjoy.

There are dozens of stitches to work with to achieve all kinds of effects and modern technology has provided modern craftswomen with a wider range of exciting fabrics and threads then ever before.

Although embroidery patterns are easily obtained from haberdashery counters and needlework shops, it should be remembered that embroidery is a craft through which you can express your own personality. You should aim to get to the stage of creating your own designs rather than using traced-off patterns.

Embroidery for your homes is a wonderful opportunity for you to enjoy this absorbing and rewarding craft and in this section you will find all the techniques and stitches you will need.

Cushions are a favourite item for decorating with all kinds of stitches and patterns. Besides surface embroidery, cushions can be decorated with smocking, drawn thread work, goldwork, crewel embroidery, black work, drawn fabric work and so on.

Table linen is another area where the creative needlewoman can enjoy doing embroidery, and handmade bed linen can be personalised with sprays of beautifully worked flowers or initials and monograms.

Appliqué and machine embroidery are used on bath towels as well as a variety of other home furnishings. Curtains, quilts, headboards and wallpanels will all give you scope for creating beautiful effects. You will also be able to use embroidery techniques for upholstered furnishings, using canvaswork and needlepoint. Small accessories, boxes, pincushions, picture frames, runners and mats, etc., can all carry the loving touch of a talented needlewoman and help to create a beautiful home.

Equipment for embroidery

Most of the equipment needed for embroidery is found in the average sewing basket but there are one or two extra items which make working easier and more enjoyable.

Embroidery frames

You will find you will get a better effect if you get used to working with an embroidery frame. If the fabric is held taut it is easier to place stitches accurately, and the fabric stays fresh and crisp because it is handled less.

There are two basic types of frame. The tambour or Swiss embroidery frame is either round or oval in shape and consists of two hoops, one slightly larger than the other. The fabric is placed over the smaller of the two hoops and then the larger hoop is fitted over the top, thus stretching and holding the fabric taut. Some frames have a screw on them which tightens so that fabrics of different thicknesses can be held securely. Some of these

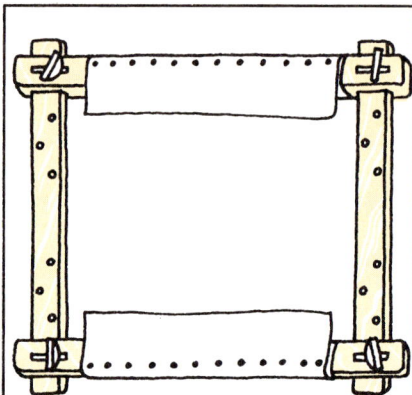

The floor-standing slate frame is most used for tapestry, needlepoint and other large works of embroidery.

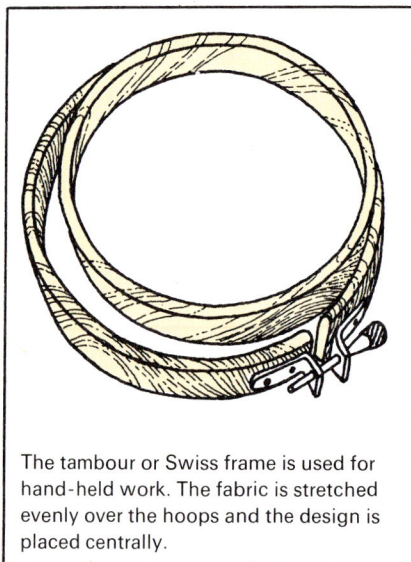

The tambour or Swiss frame is used for hand-held work. The fabric is stretched evenly over the hoops and the design is placed centrally.

frames have a clamp so that they can be fixed to a table, leaving the worker's hands free. Other types have a wooden base so that the frame can be stood on the table or held on the knee.

Large pieces of embroidery should be worked on a slate frame. This consists of two horizontal bars and two side pieces which fit into the horizontal bars. The bars have tape nailed along them, and the embroidery fabric is oversewn to the tape for working. Then the sides of the embroidery fabric are laced to the side pieces to stretch it and keep it taut.

Needles

You will need different needles for different kinds of embroidery. Needles should be smooth and sharp and kept in a needlecase. Run them through an emery cushion occasionally to clean them.

The chart on page 184 provides a guide to needles and threads used in embroidery.

Crewel needles These are long and sharp with an egg-shaped eye.

Chenille needles These are shorter in length and have a long, wide eye. You will use them with wool yarns and thicker threads.

Sharps These are sewing needles but you will find them useful for working with fine threads.

Tapestry needles These are thicker needles with a rounded point. Use them for embroidering on canvas or net and for counted thread embroidery.

Pins
Choose fine, glass-headed dressmaker's pins so that fine fabrics are not marked with holes.

Scissors
You will need two pairs, one medium-sized pair for cutting fabric and the other small-sized with sharp points for snipping threads.

Thimble
A thimble is not essential except when working with heavy fabrics.

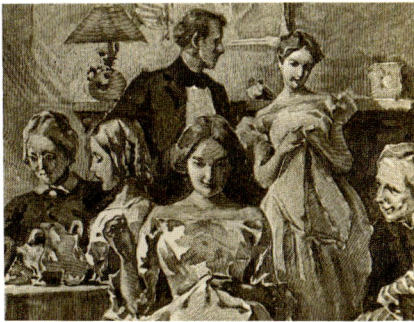

In the past, needlework has served as the central activity of social gatherings.

Other equipment
You will need basic drawing and pattern transferring equipment:

Tracing paper This is sometimes recommended for tracing designs.

Squared or graph paper Use this for enlarging designs.

Dressmaker's carbon paper This is useful for transferring simple designs to fabric.

Pouncing powder This is powdered charcoal or French chalk.

Fabrics in embroidery
Almost any kind of fabric can be embroidered in some way. The only rule of thumb is that you should choose fabric to suit the purpose for which the item is intended. Even-weave linen is excellent for practising stitches.

Threads
Stranded threads are washable, colourfast and have a sheen. They consist of six fine strands twisted together, and different effects are achieved by working with one or two strands on fine fabrics, or all six strands on coarse fabrics.

Pearl cotton is a smooth, corded thread available in different weights. No. 8 is used on fine fabrics and No. 5 on thicker fabrics. It is used in counted thread embroidery.

Embroidery cotton is thick and soft and has a matt finish. It is available in different weights.

Coton à broder is a twisted, lustrous thread and is used for drawn-thread work, drawn fabric and cutwork techniques.

Tapisserie yarns are wool threads used for canvaswork and crewel embroidery.

Crewel yarns are high-spun two-ply yarns with a beautiful finish, used for crewel or Jacobean embroidery.

Rug yarn is used for making needlework rugs but can also be couched down in bold surface embroidery.

Machine embroidery thread is used for sewing machine embroidery.

Lurex and gold threads – untarnishable threads in gold and silver colour are available in a variety of thicknesses for embroidery. Real gold thread, which is gold leaf on tissue over a silk core, is difficult for beginners to use.

Dressing a frame
Tambour frames
Small pieces of embroidery can be worked in the hand but if you prefer to use a frame, cut the fabric large enough to fit the frame. If for any reason the piece of fabric is too small for the frame, mount it on a piece of fabric of similar weight, matching the weave. Place the fabric over the smaller hoop and then press the larger hoop on top. Pull the fabric all round until it is taut and smooth, the threads straight. Adjust the screw on the outer hoop. Cut away the mounting fabric behind the embroidery fabric. If delicate fabrics are being used, protect them by winding strips of tissue paper around both hoops.

Slate frame
Dressing instructions are usually supplied with modern slate frames, but here is the traditional method in case you obtain an old or second-hand frame.

Mark the centre of the webbing or tape on both horizontal rollers or bars. Stitch a hem on upper and lower edges of the embroidery fabric. Mark the centre points. Pin the edges to the webbing or tape, keeping the grain straight. Sew with overcasting or herringbone, stitching from the centre outwards. The sides of the fabric are laced to the side strips with fine string in different ways depending on the weight of the fabric.

Strong, sturdy fabrics
Stitch a strip of fabric of similar weight to both sides of the embroidery fabric. Turn and stitch a hem. Take the lacings through the hems.

Medium-weight fabrics
Fold the edges over fine string and stitch a hem. Take the lacings through the hem so that the lacing string pulls on the edging string and not the fabric.

Fine fabrics
Mount these on a medium weight fabric. Turn a hem over string and lace as for medium weight fabrics. Cut the backing fabric from behind the embroidery fabric.

Transferring designs

The care you take when transferring the design to the fabric is almost as important as the embroidery itself. There are several methods of putting the design on the fabric, and the type of fabric you are embroidering determines the method you should use.

Transfers

A variety of designs is available in commercial transfers. To get the best result, pin the fabric on a padded board or wooden surface. Pin the transfer in position face down and then iron over it with a fairly hot iron. If the iron is too cool a smudgy line will result. Avoid ironing over the pins. If the fabric is rough-textured and the design will not transfer, tack the paper to the fabric, and then work tiny running stitches along the lines of the design. Tear the paper away carefully afterwards. If you need several reproductions of the motif trace them first on tissue paper.

Transfer pencil

The mark made by an embroidery transfer pencil is ironed onto fabric in the same way. Hold the pattern up to a window and draw over the design on the wrong side of the paper. Lay the prepared pattern on the fabric and pin it in position. Iron with a fairly hot iron to transfer the design. You may need to go over the outlines with a paintbrush and watercolour.

Dressmaker's carbon paper

This will work well on smooth-textured fabrics. Pin the fabric, right side up, to a drawing board or a wooden table. Lay sheets of carbon paper on top, chalked side down. Pin the pattern on top, making sure that the pins do not go through the carbon, and trace the lines with a hard (H or HB) finely pointed pencil. You should get a good image of the design but if it seems faint, go over the lines with a watercolour paint, using blue on light materials and yellow on dark materials.

Fabric	Thread	Needle
Traced or transferred designs		
Fine linen, lawn, organdie, sheer silk or fine synthetics	Stranded cotton – 1, 2 or 3 strands	Crewel No. 8 for 1 or 2 strands; No. 7 for 3
	Pearl cotton No. 8 Coton à broder No. 18	Crewel No. 6 Crewel No. 7
Medium weight linen, rayon, sail cloth, satin, etc.	Stranded cotton – 2, 3 or 4 strands	Crewel No. 8 for 2 strands; No. 7 for 3; No. 6 for 4
	Pearl cotton No. 8 Coton à broder No. 18	Crewel No. 6 Crewel No. 7
Heavy linen, or furnishing fabrics	Stranded cotton – 6 strands	Crewel No. 5
	Pearl cotton No. 5 Soft embroidery Tapestry wool	Crewel No. 5 Chenille No. 19 Chenille No. 19
Counted-thread work		
Fine even-weave linen	Stranded cotton – 1 – 6 strands	Tapestry No. 24 for 3 strands; No. 23 for 4; No. 21 for 6
	Pearl cotton No. 8 or No. 5	Tapestry No. 23 for No. 8; No. 21 for No. 5
	Coton à broder No. 18	Tapestry No. 24
Coarse even-weave linen and fabrics	Stranded cotton – 4 or 6 strands	Tapestry No. 23 for 4 strands; No. 21 for 6
	Pearl cotton No. 5 Soft embroidery Tapestry wool	Tapestry No. 21 Tapestry No. 19 Tapestry No. 19

Before beginning an embroidery project, consult this list for correct materials.

Trace-line method

This is the only method which works on rough-textured fabrics or piled fabrics. Pin the paper pattern to the fabric. Using sewing thread and a fine needle, work small stitches along the lines of the design. Take up only a few threads of fabric on the needle each time. Tear the paper away carefully afterwards.

Pouncing

This is one of the oldest methods of transferring designs to fabric. You will need a dabber made from a rolled-up tube of felt, pouncing powder, (charcoal for light fabrics or French chalk for dark fabrics), a pricker, which can be a large darning needle stuck in a cork, tracing paper, watercolour paint, a brush and a pad of felt or a folded blanket.

Method Trace the design onto tracing paper. Lay the tracing paper, the drawing side down, on the blanket pad. Prick along the design lines making the holes quite close together. Pin the embroidery fabric to a drawing board. Lay the tracing, smooth side down, on the fabric and secure it. Dip the dabber in the pouncing powder and rub it all over the tracing. Use a lot of powder. Remove the tracing carefully. The design should be clearly defined. Blow off the surplus powder. Paint along the lines of dots with watercolour paint.

Direct tracing

This method is used on transparent

fabrics. Pin the design to a board. Pin the fabric over the top. Draw or paint the design lines in watercolour.

Transferring designs in canvaswork

Either paint the design directly onto the canvas or lay the canvas on the design. Paint the outline of the design, which you can see through the canvas, in watercolour or oil paint.

Enlarging designs

Very often, designs are actual size and only have to be traced off before transferring. If they are provided as graph patterns or reduced in size, one of the following techniques must be used to enlarge it to the correct size.

Reduced-size patterns

The only way complex, reduced-size patterns can be used is to have them enlarged to size photographically, then trace them off and use the trace-line, carbon paper or pouncing methods of transferring.

Simple reduced-size patterns

To enlarge simple motifs, you use a squared-up method. Measure the width and depth of the motif. Draw a box around it and then divide the box into equal-size squares, across and down. Draw a similar box to the dimensions to which you wish to enlarge the motif. Divide it into the same number of squares, across and down. Now copy the motif into the prepared grid. Design motifs can be reduced in the same way by reversing the procedure.

You may find it easier to copy a design by sub-dividing squares into quarters with diagonal lines.

Graph patterns

Graph patterns are simply patterns reduced in size on a squared grid. You will usually be given a scale such as '1 square = 2.5 cm (1 in)'. To enlarge a graph pattern, you need squared dressmaker's paper to

Make a sampler in the form of a picture from the stitches you have learned.

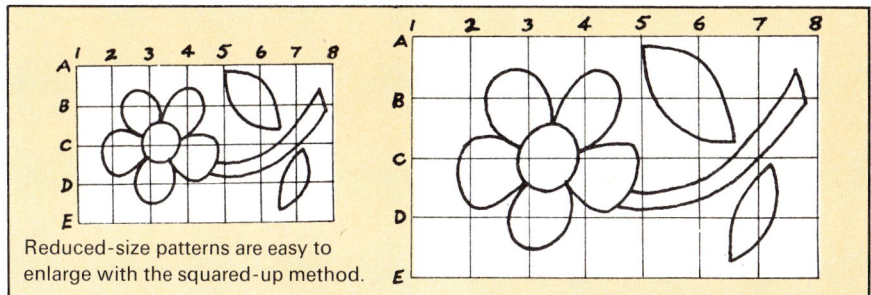

Reduced-size patterns are easy to enlarge with the squared-up method.

the scale suggested. Alternatively, you can draw a grid on brown paper or tracing paper. When you have a grid of the correct scale, simply copy the lines of the graph pattern, square by square.

Enlarging designs in canvaswork

This is a fascinating technique and provides a needlewoman with endless possibilities for patterns and designs.

If you have a motif which has been designed for canvas – perhaps 10 threads to 2.5 cm (1 in) – you can enlarge or reduce the motif by working over more or fewer

threads. Supposing you have a flower motif with 40 lines of stitches in it, then on a canvas of 10 threads to 2.5 cm (1 in), the flower will come out 10 cm (4 in) deep.

If you work the same design over 2 threads of the same canvas, the apple will come out 20 cm (8 in) deep. Worked on a coarser canvas, perhaps 6 threads to 2.5 cm (1 in), the apple will be almost 18 cm (7 in) deep.

If you wanted to reduce the size of the motif, a canvas with 16 threads to 2.5 cm (1 in) would produce a motif about 6 cm (2½ in) deep. The permutations are almost endless.

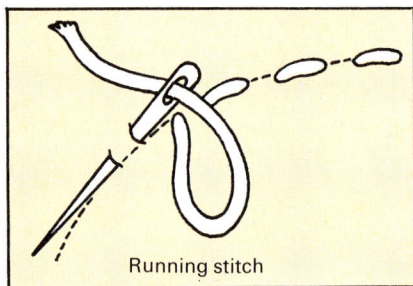
Running stitch

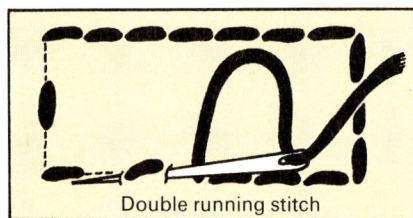
Double running stitch

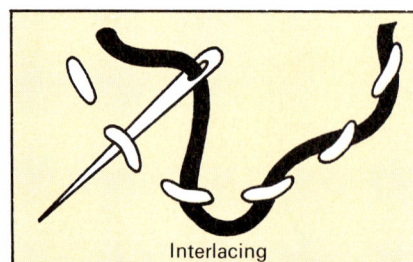
Interlacing

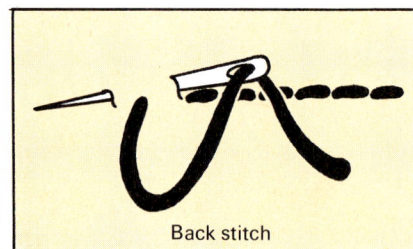
Back stitch

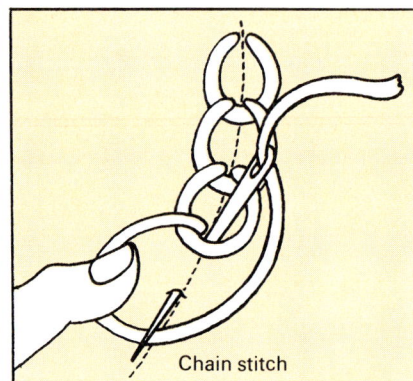
Chain stitch

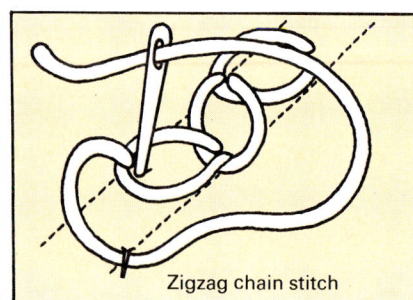
Zigzag chain stitch

Stitch library

In this chapter, you will find all the familiar basic stitches and some variations on them that might be less familiar. Some of them you will meet again in the chapters which deal with specific types of needlework. You will find that you enjoy embroidery more and more if you spend time practising stitches and discovering the effects you can achieve with them. Your repertoire will increase and you will feel more confident about creating your own embroidery designs.

All the basic embroidery stitches are easy to do and fall into one of six groups. The groups are: line, flat, looped, chained, knotted and couched stitches. When you see what looks like a complicated piece of embroidery you will find that it is usually the result of a number of stitches combined to produce an effect.

Line stitches

The stitches in this group are used to make fine lines to outline motifs, to link motifs as decorative lines of stitchery, or else they are worked close together in rows to fill motif shapes. Some of them can be used as padding stitches.

Running stitch

This very easy stitch has a great many uses in sewing and decorative needlework. A number of threads of the ground fabric are picked up on the needle and then pushed back onto the thread. In even running, the stitches are of the same length on both the top and wrong side of the fabric. In embroidery, the stitches underneath are half the length of those on top.

Double running stitch

The stitch is worked in two journeys so that both sides of the work look similar. The main pattern line is worked first.

Begin from the right and work over a given number of threads, the spaces between stitches being of the same length. When the end of the pattern line is reached, work back again, filling in the spaces between stitches. It is important that no stitches cross an area on the back. This method is also known as Holbein stitch and is used in Assisi embroidery (see page 211).

Quick Holbein

The advantage of the double running stitch method is that it looks neat on both sides of the work. If it is being used on something where the wrong side is hidden, such as a cushion cover, you can get the same effect with back stitch and thus, only one journey is needed.

Interlacing

Interlacing is used on a variety of stitches – you will meet it again in this section. Here it is used in conjunction with running stitch and double running stitches. Interlacing looks effective as an edging on home furnishings and clothes but it also looks well used as an overall patterned area, such as on a cushion. Experiment with different types of yarn for the interlacing – use knobbly wool or Raffene or try the effect of thin string or lurex threads. You should use a blunt-ended needle for interlacing so that threads are not pierced.

Method Work rows of running stitches first. Thread a blunt-ended needle with a contrasting thread. Weave, oversew or lace the needle through the stitches as shown in the diagram.

Another example of an interlaced stitch may be seen on page 192.

Back stitch

This is another basic sewing stitch but in embroidery it makes a firm outline and can be used for quilting.

Work from top to bottom or from right to left. Begin with a

small running stitch and pick up a few threads of fabric. Insert the needle into the end of the last stitch and bring it out the same distance from where the thread emerges. Back stitch can also be interlaced with other threads.

Overcast back stitch

A line of ordinary back stitch is worked first and overcasting is worked over it. If the stitches are made close together, and very little of the fabric is picked up under the back stitch, it will make a high, raised outline.

Holbein stitch

This has the appearance of back stitch but it is really two lines of running stitch, worked in two journeys. Work a row of even stitches to the end of a line and then return, filling the stitches missed on the first journey. This stitch is used in Assisi work. See also double running stitch.

Overcast stitch

This is useful for making fine raised lines and is frequently used in white embroidery. It is worked from left to right over a couched or running thread, and the covering stitches pick up as little material as possible. They must be parallel and close together.

Stem stitch

This stitch can be used for outlines or solid fillings and a raised effect can be obtained by working it over a laid thread. It is one of the most useful stitches for working stems in floral motifs. Stem stitch is also used as padding in white embroidery.

Work from the bottom of the line. Pick up a short vertical stitch diagonally across the line. Keep the thread on the same side of the needle throughout.

Overcast stem stitch

Work a line of stem stitch and then overcast it with a contrasting colour.

Chain stitches

There are a number of stitches in this group which may be used as single units for filling large shapes, or as line stitches which can be used successfully for working a whole embroidery. There are also variations of chain stitch which may be used for working broad bands.

Chain stitch

Start at the top of the outline and work downwards. Hold the thread with the left thumb to form a loop. Insert the needle where the thread emerges and bring it out a little farther down the line over the loop formed by the thread. The needle is then inserted just inside this loop and the movement is repeated. The reverse side should show a row of back stitches.

Zigzag chain

This is worked in a similar way to chain stitch, but the stitches are made between two parallel lines. Insert the needle first on the right side and then on the left to form a border.

Twisted chain

Similar to chain, but instead of the needle being inserted in the loop where the thread emerges, it is inserted to the left and to the outside of the last loop and brought out a little further down over the loop formed by the thread.

Double chain

A useful stitch for bands and borders. It is worked with a chain stitch movement from side to side between two lines about 6 mm ($\frac{1}{4}$ in) apart; the width of the band is determined by the thickness of the thread. Insert the needle in the last loop, first on one line and then on the other, alternately forming triangular loops.

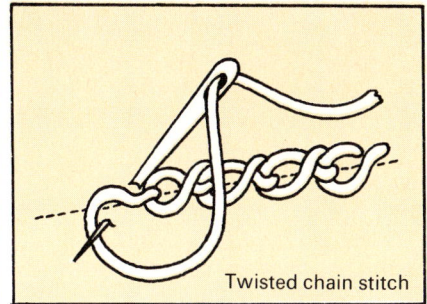
Twisted chain stitch

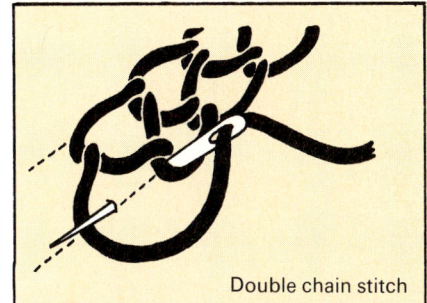
Double chain stitch

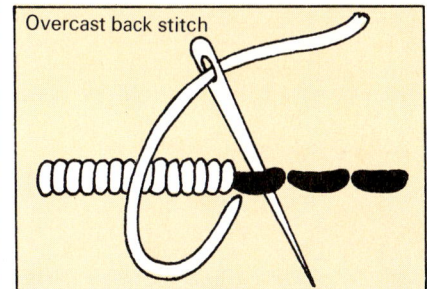
Overcast back stitch

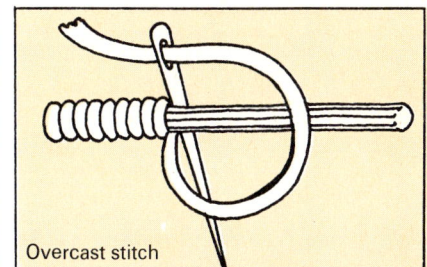
Overcast stitch

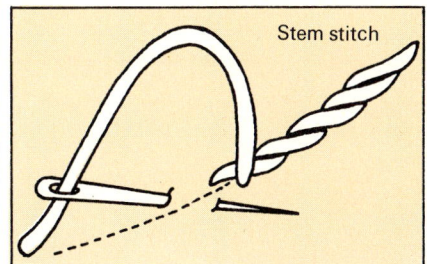
Stem stitch

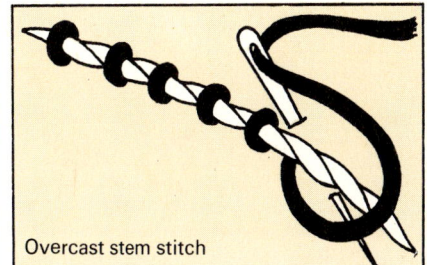
Overcast stem stitch

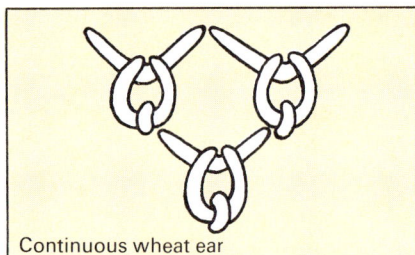

Continuous wheat ear

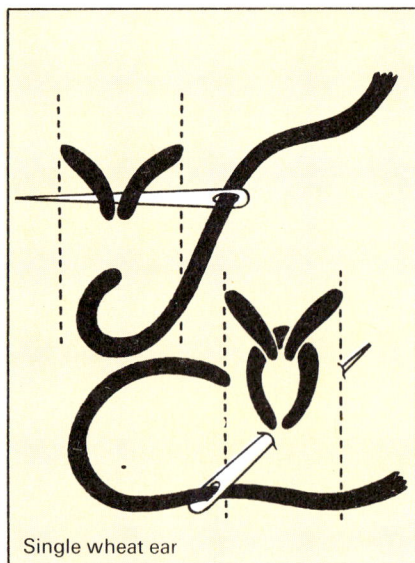

Single wheat ear

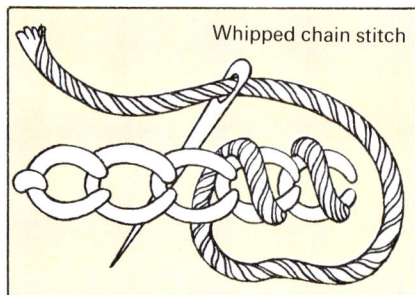

Whipped chain stitch

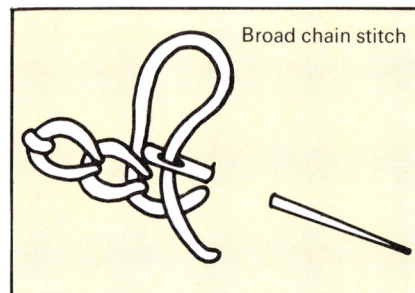

Broad chain stitch

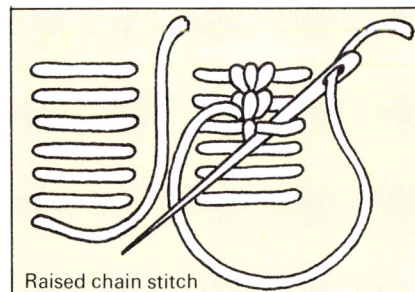

Raised chain stitch

Open chain

Another stitch suitable for bands or broad stems, it is worked between two lines. The needle is inserted in the loop, first on one side and then on the other with a chain stitch movement. The needle emerges immediately below where it is inserted and the making of the next stitch pulls the loop into a square shape.

Chequered chain

This is worked with two threads of different colours, both threaded into the same needle; as the name implies, one loop is of one colour and the next of the other. Make an ordinary chain stitch looping one colour around the needle, then for the next chain stitch, loop the second colour around the needle. The colours are used alternately to give a chequered effect. Pull the loose thread tightly each time.

Cable chain

In appearance this is like ordinary chain stitch with a single stroke between each loop. The first stitch is made as ordinary chain. To make the second and subsequent loops work as follows: take the needle under the thread and twist the thread over the point. Insert the needle in the line of sewing just below the last loop made and bring it out vertically downwards.

Lazy daisy or link stitch

A single chain stitch tied down with a stroke stitch. It may be used singly to form a spot pattern over a large area, or may be clustered together to make small flowers.

Wheat ear

This is a combination of lazy daisy and fly stitch worked together to form a wheat ear formation. They may be worked singly as a spot motif, or to form a continuous line. This is suitable for working grasses and leaves.

Continuous wheat ear

This stitch is worked between two parallel lines. The ears of the stitch are made first with two single stroke stitches: bring the thread through in the centre of the lines and pick up a horizontal stitch from left to right, inserting the needle in the left-hand line and bringing it out immediately opposite on the right-hand line; these three points should form a triangle.

Pull the thread through and insert the needle again in the centre where the thread emerged, bringing it out immediately below this point. The size of this last stitch should be the same as the two stroke stitches.

Taking a simple object and interpreting its colour, texture and shape in a variety of threads and stitches is a good way to develop a design sense and repertoire of stitches.

Whipped chain

A decorative rope-like stitch which consists of a line or ordinary chain stitch whipped with another colour. The thread used for whipping does not enter the background material.

Broad chain

This should be worked with a firm thread or the finished result will be spidery. Start at the top and make a small running stitch along the sewing line, bringing the needle out the length of the broad chain below the running stitch. Slip the needle under the running stitch or previous chain, from left to right (but not through the fabric) and insert it again in the place where it last emerged and bring it out again below ready to make the next chain. In this stitch, there should be a line of back stitch on the wrong side.

Raised chain band

A good border stitch which is worked on a basis of straight threads made at right angles to the direction of the border. Insert these threads first, making them about 1.5 mm ($\frac{1}{16}$ in) or more apart, according to the thickness of the thread.

Start at the top and work downwards, making a chain stitch on each thread: the needle is slipped up under the thread on the left to emerge above it and down under the thread on the right, with the loop thus formed passing under the needle point. Then slip the needle up to the left under the next transverse thread. This forms the tying-down stitch and the commencement of the next loop.

If the foundation threads are worked farther apart the finished effect will be more open. A contrasting shade can be used for the chain to give added interest.

Back stitched chain

This is an interesting variety of chain stitch, especially if worked in thick thread. First, work a line of chain, then with contrasting colour make a line of backstitch down the centre.

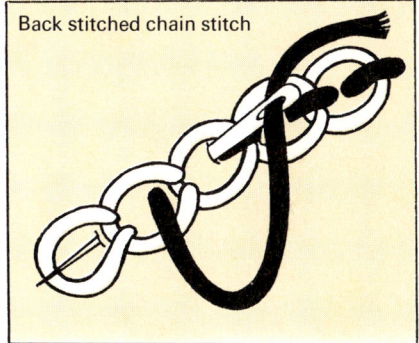

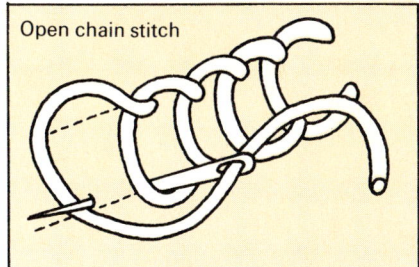

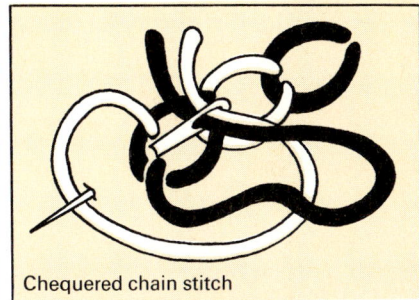

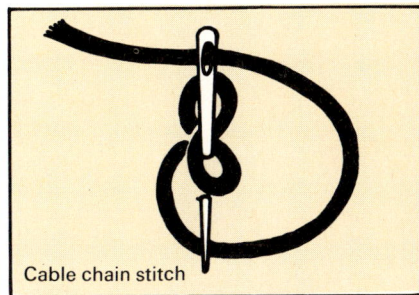

Back stitched chain stitch

Open chain stitch

Chequered chain stitch

Cable chain stitch

Lazy daisy or link stitch

Next, slip the needle under the stroke stitches from right to left.

Complete the movement by picking up a diagonal stitch parallel with the first stroke stitch. The first stroke stitch of the next and subsequent wheat ears is made by inserting the needle at the base of the last loop.

Single wheat ear

A fly stitch is made first; this is like a lazy daisy opened out. A lazy daisy stitch is then worked with the tips of the loops hooked into the base of the fly stitch.

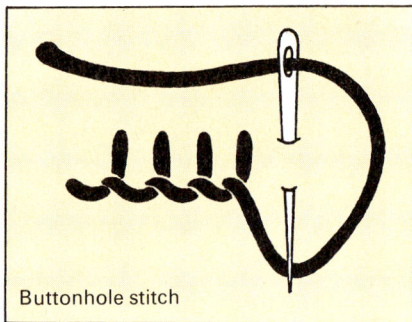

Buttonhole stitch

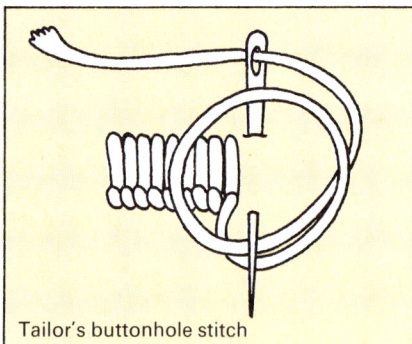

Tailor's buttonhole stitch

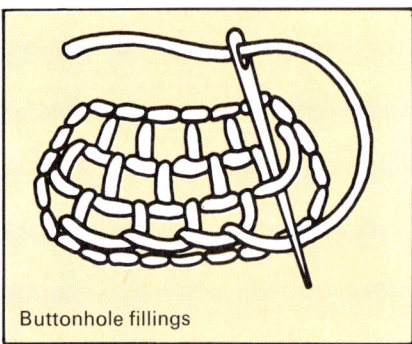

Buttonhole fillings

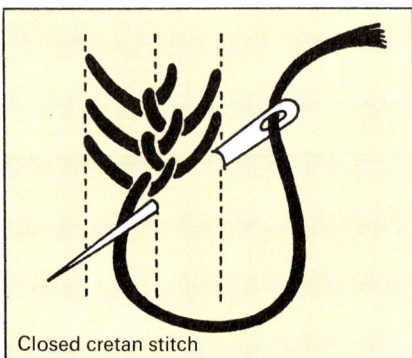

Closed cretan stitch

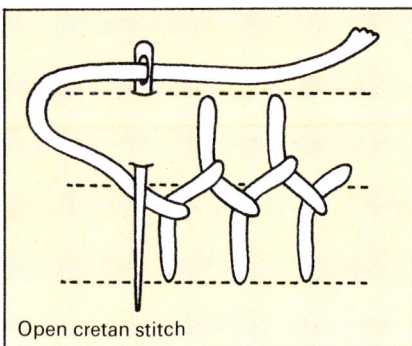

Open cretan stitch

Loop Stitches

There are a number of popular loop stitches – buttonhole stitch is one of them. They can be used for line work, for fillings, for edgings and they are used for making bars and picots. There are many variations and you may be able to invent one or two yourself.

Buttonhole stitch

Work the stitch from left to right or from right to left. Bring the needle through on the line of stitching and insert it vertically a little to the right, picking up a small quantity of fabric, the width you want the stitching to be. The loop of thread passes under the needle point and then the needle is pulled through.

There are many variations of this stitch which can be made by changing the length of the stitches, working one short and one long or two long and three short.

Buttonhole stitch can be worked over a laid thread of a contrasting colour or a second row can be made with the knots at the top and the stitches between those of the first row. Then, to be more elaborate, the direction of the stitches can be changed such as three radiating from one point or two to the left and two to the right working from the top.

Tailor's buttonhole

This is a knotted stitch and is much firmer and thicker in appearance than simple buttonhole. The stitches are always worked close together but they must lie flat on the surface of the fabric, side by side. Insert the needle vertically as for buttonhole with the material end of the thread under the point from left to right. Pass the eye end of the thread under the point from right to left and pull the thread through, pushing the knot close to the material.

Buttonhole fillings

In these stitches do not enter the material and the shapes to be filled are first outlined with back stitch, into which the buttonhole stitches may be looped at the edges. The buttonhole stitch may be worked evenly spaced or in groups to make interesting patterns. This method of work gives interesting lacy effects which can be combined in white work.

In early embroideries, petals and leaves were sometimes worked in fine buttonhole stitch, giving the effect of lace. The stitches were left detached, except for the first row of work so that the embroidery looked as though leaves and flowers were lying on the background fabric.

Cretan stitch

This is a variety of buttonhole stitch which, as the name implies, is taken from Eastern embroideries. It may be worked with the stitches close together to form a solid border or leaf filling, or openly as a thin braid-like border. In each case the stitch is worked between two parallel lines.

Closed Cretan

Bring the thread through a little to the right of a central line between the two parallel lines and, with the thread under the point, pick up a horizontal stitch, from left to right, bringing the needle out the same distance from the central line, on the left, as the thread is on the right. With the thread under the point, repeat this procedure to the right.

The stitch may be varied by spacing the stitches a little and by bringing the needle out on the centre line each time. In this case the needle is inserted diagonally.

Open Cretan

This may be worked vertically as in closed Cretan, or horizontally. The movement is the same and the needle emerges a little to each side of the central line. The length of the stitches may be varied to be more decorative.

Feather stitch

Similar to Cretan and the working movement is the same. It is a useful, decorative stitch in plain needlework as well as in embroidery. There are several variations on this stitch.

Single feather
Bring the thread out in the centre of two parallel lines. Insert the needle in the right-hand line lower down, and bring it out diagonally a little to the right of the centre, thread under point. Repeat this movement to the left.

Double feather stitch
This is worked in the same way as single feather, but two stitches are made each side of the central line, each a little lower than the other.

Triple feather stitch
Three stitches are made to each side.

Closed feather stitch
The working movement is the same as single feather but the needle is inserted vertically into the side lines and close up to the previous stitch, forming a solid band of filling.

Roman stitch
A stitch found in Eastern embroideries which makes a quickly worked solid band, or it may be used for leaf fillings. It can be worked with horizontal or slanted stitches. Three lines are needed as guides for working.

Start at the top left-hand side bringing the thread through, insert the needle again just below the thread, tying it down with a small stitch; bring the needle through to the left side again for the next stitch. If the stitches are made slanting, the needle is inserted diagonally.

Fly stitch
This is similar in working to Roman stitch and can be worked as a decorative edging or as a spot pattern. It combines well with other stitches to make a wide border. The stitch can be worked from left to right or right to left and consists of tied-down loops.

The needle is inserted level to where the thread emerges and it is brought out between the two points and an equal distance away. To tie down the loop insert the needle just below it and bring the point out where the last thread emerged.

Rows of this stitch joined together make a good filling stitch.

Flat stitches
These are the stitches which are most used as fillers, although some make good borders. In crewel embroidery some flat stitches may be used to work wide outlines to motifs.

In some varieties, stitches are interlaced, in others they lie side by side, flat on the fabric.

Many of the flat stitches can be used with other stitches for special effects.

Flat stitch
This is one of a group called fishbone stitches. Start at the top and bring the needle through on the left edge. Insert the needle at right of the centre line, a little way down, and bring it out on the right-hand line, opposite the top of the first stitch.

Now insert the needle to the left of the centre line, the thread crossing the first stitch at the bottom and bring it out on the left edge just below the first stitch. The stitches must always cross in the centre.

Fishbone stitch
This is another stitch which can be worked with the stitches close together or apart and, like flat stitch, between parallel lines. It is sometimes used for working leaves. It also makes a good solid border.

Closed fishbone stitch
Start at the top of the motif, bringing the thread out on the left-hand line. Move diagonally to the centre and insert the needle to the right of the central line, picking up a diagonal stitch upwards to the right-hand line. Repeat this to the left.

Open fishbone stitch
Work from the top as for close fishbone and pick up a small diagonal stitch under the central line, from right to left, then take a horizontal stitch from the right to the left, just below where the thread enters the fabric for the last two stitches.

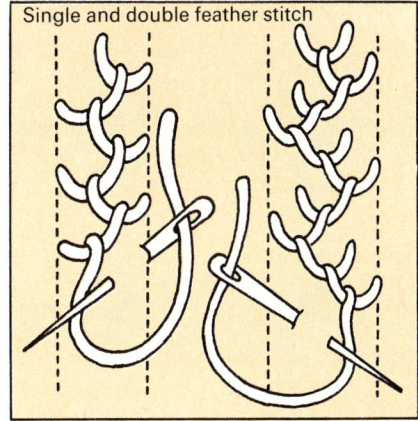
Single and double feather stitch

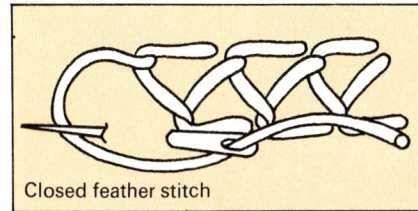
Closed feather stitch

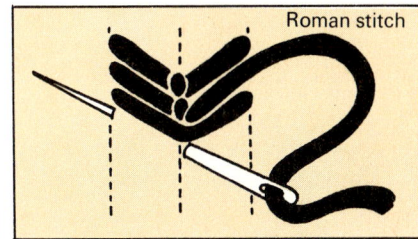
Roman stitch

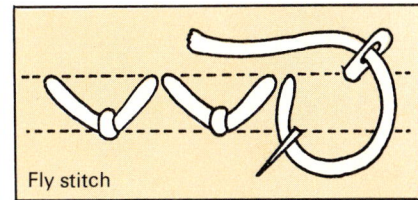
Fly stitch

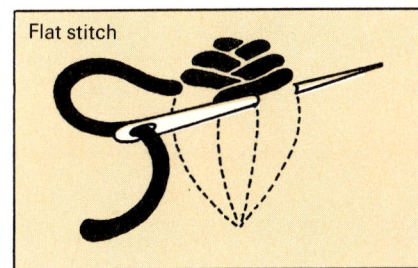
Flat stitch

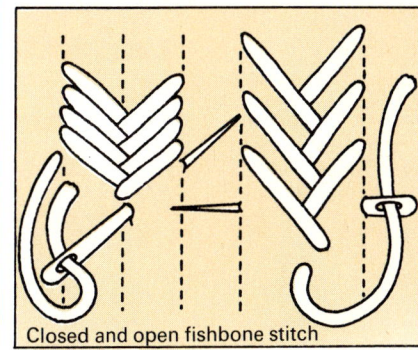
Closed and open fishbone stitch

Decorative needlework

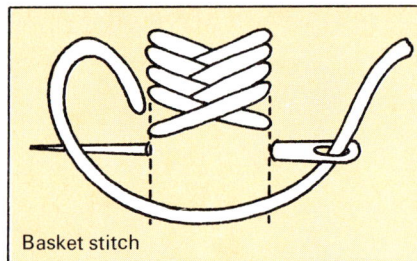

Basket stitch

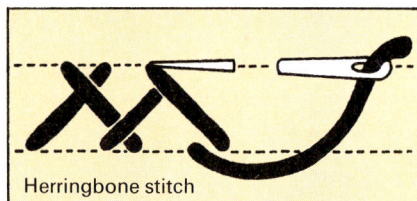

A solid border stitch, which is worked between two lines, giving a raised effect with a stout thread. Bring the thread through on left-hand line at the top and make a slanting stitch by inserting the needle on the right line about 3 mm ($\frac{1}{8}$ in) below the point on the left. Bring the needle point through, horizontally, to the left line.

The next stitch is worked over the one already made, by slanting 3 mm ($\frac{1}{8}$ in) up from the left to the right-hand line and crossing over the first stitch. Insert the needle just above the first stitch. The whole process is repeated.

Herringbone stitch

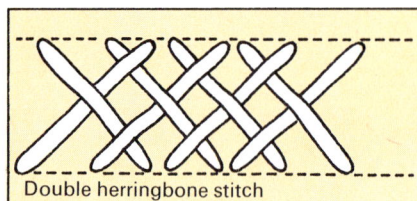

Herringbone is both useful and decorative, and it is the basis of many interlaced stitches. It is used in plain needlework and dressmaking as well as in embroidery. The stitches are made between two parallel lines and worked from the left to the right.

Start at the bottom left-hand corner and insert the needle from right to left on the top line, a little farther to the right, taking up a small piece of material. Return to the lower line and pick up a similar piece of material. Continue in this manner to get an even trellis effect.

Double herringbone

Two rows of herringbone, one interlaced into the other. It is worked slightly differently from ordinary herringbone, and the two rows form the basis for interlacing stitch. Instead of the threads crossing under and over alternately, all the same threads are on the top. After each stitch on the top line is worked, the needle is slipped under the last thread instead of over it. The stitches should be spaced far apart, to leave room for the next row.

When the second row is worked between the first stitches, the thread is taken under the diagonal stitch when working from the bottom to the top line to produce the interlacing.

Double herringbone may be worked in one colour or, to be more decorative, in two different colours.

Woven herringbone

The first movement of double herringbone is worked and a contrasting thread is woven up and down around the crosses.

Interlacing stitch

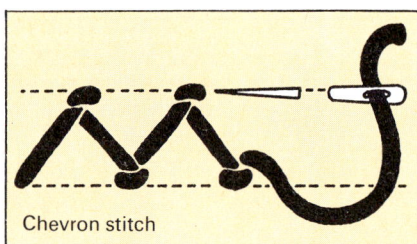

Worked on a base of double herringbone, the interlacing thread is woven under and over the cross of the foundation; working from left to right along the top row and centre and back along the bottom row and centre. This makes a very decorative border and it can also be used as a strong insertion stitch.

Chevron stitch

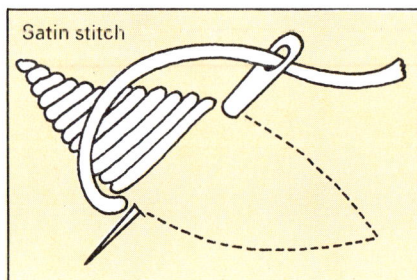

This is worked between two parallel lines. Start at the bottom left-hand side, and take the thread diagonally to the top line a little farther along. Make a small stitch from right to left, draw the thread through and hold it up with the thumb. Make a small stitch immediately to the right of the previous one and below the thread. Repeat this alternately along the top and bottom lines.

Satin stitch

A stitch which must be worked very evenly to give a good effect; silk thread is the most suitable to use. The stitches must be parallel and touching each other, they are alike on both sides and the edges should be very smooth. It may be worked between two parallel lines, or over counted threads, with all the stitches the same size, or to fill a leaf or flower shape.

The thread is brought out on the left and the needle is inserted in the opposite line and brought out just below the thread on the left. The

Basket stitch

Herringbone stitch

Double herringbone stitch

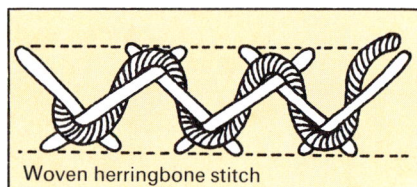

Woven herringbone stitch

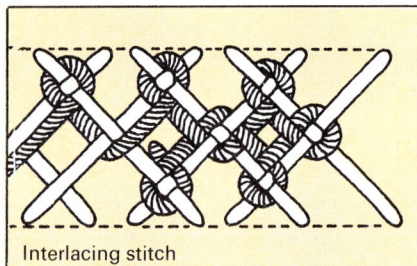

Interlacing stitch

Chevron stitch

Satin stitch

Samplers such as these from Spain were the traditional way of displaying the needlewoman's skill.

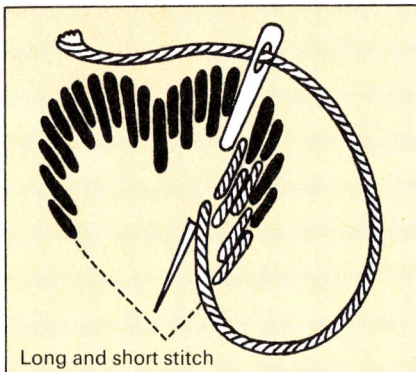

Long and short stitch

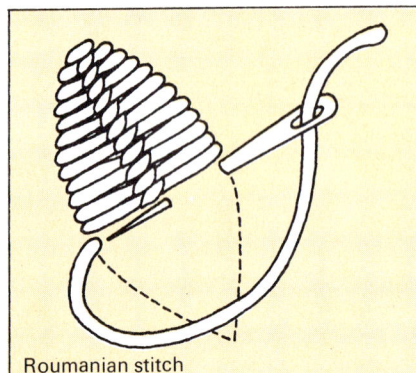

Roumanian stitch

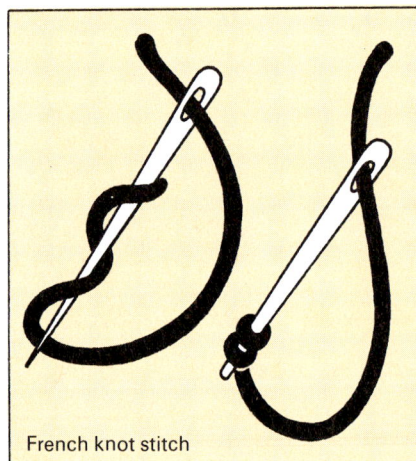

French knot stitch

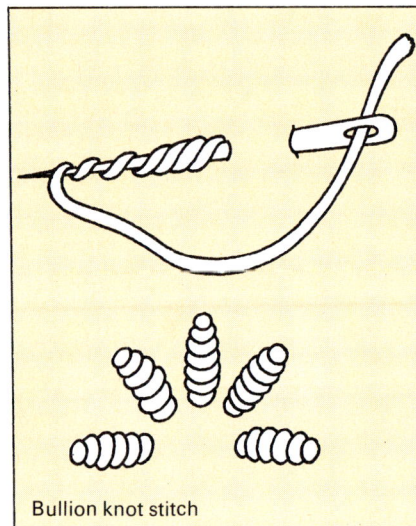

Bullion knot stitch

stitches may be worked over padding to give a rounded raised effect, but they should never be made too long, or they will pull away from the ground material.

Long and short stitch

A variation of satin stitch, it is used to obtain shaded effects either by the direction of working the stitch, or by the use of graduated colours of thread. The stitch is found in Chinese and Japanese embroideries and in 17th-century Jacobean work. Long and short stitch is useful for filling large areas where satin stitch would be unsuitable.

The first row of stitches consists of one long stitch and one short stitch, worked in the same way as satin stitch, giving a smoother outer edge but a broken inner edge. The stitches in the succeeding rows are all the same length and fit into the broken line, continuing the short and long effect. The last line of stitches is the same as the first, only in reverse.

When you are working a shaped motif, the stitches should radiate.

Roumanian satin stitch

This is worked in a similar way to satin stitch but each stitch is anchored in the centre with a small slanting stitch. It is useful for filling large shapes as the size of the satin stitch can be increased. More than one of the slanting anchoring stitches can be worked on each long cross thread. Variations on this stitch are known as janina, figure stitch and Roumanian couching.

Knotted stitches

These vary in formation from the single French knot to the line of stitches known as the coral knot. They have a wide variety of uses in surface embroidery and crewel work and are usually used in conjunction with flat stitches.

French knot

French knots can be worked very close together as a filling giving a knubbed texture, or they can be

used in clusters to break up an even surface.

To work, bring the thread to the front of the material where required and hold it down with the left finger and thumb. Twist the point of the needle twice through the thread, still holding it down with the left hand.

Insert the point close to where the thread emerges, drawing the thread tightly through the twisted piece and forming a neat knot on the surface.

Bullion knot

This long knot must be tightly coiled, but it may vary in length according to the thickness of the thread used. Bring the thread to the surface and insert the needle 3 mm to 6 mm ($\frac{1}{8}$ in to $\frac{1}{4}$ in) from that point, according to the length of stitch required, taking it through to the first point, keeping the needle in the material.

Twist the material end of the thread around the needle the number of times required, keeping the left thumb tightly on the coil, draw the needle and thread through the twist and the material, keeping the threads even.

Tighten the coil by pulling the working thread and insert the needle at the end of the knot, bring it out again in position for the next bullion knot.

Knotted chain stitch

A decorative stitch with a rope-like effect. Work between two parallel lines from right to left. Bring the thread through in the centre of the lines on the right. Insert the needle a little to the left on the top line and bring it out immediately below on the bottom line. Pull the thread through to make a short stitch.

Slip the needle from left to right under this stitch and, leaving the loop loose, pass it from top to bottom through the loop. Repeat the procedure all along the line.

Coral knot

This is a simple line stitch rather like a beaded thread. It is worked from right to left or downwards. Bring the thread through at the end of the line and hold it with the left thumb along the line. A little to the left of where the thread emerges insert the needle at the top of the thread and pick up a very little of the fabric under the thread. Pull the point through and over the loop. Repeat the procedure.

Double knot stitch or tied coral knot

If worked in a thick thread this is a very decorative stitch and it lies mostly on the surface. It can be worked either from top to bottom, or from left to right.

Make a small stitch along the line and bring the needle out a little to the left. Pass the needle under this stitch from right to left. Pull the thread through and insert the needle again at the other side. Take another small stitch along the line and continue as before.

Couching

This is an ancient embroidery technique frequently seen on old Chinese and Indian embroideries, on Spanish leather appliqué, in 17th-century Jacobean embroidery and in ecclesiastical embroidery.

In couching, a thread is laid on the surface of the fabric and then another thread is used to make a stitch or stitches over it, holding it in place. Cords, braids, metal threads, feathers, and so on, can also be applied to fabric in this way.

When couching is worked solidly as a filling it is called laid work. Any thread can be used for the couched thread and you will find it easier if you put the work in an embroidery frame. A bodkin is needed to push the ends of the couched thread through to the back of the work. The ends are overcast on the wrong side.

Simple couching

Lay the piece of thread across the fabric. Leave enough at both ends of the thread to allow the ends to

be pulled through to the wrong side and secured when the couching is completed. Tie a knot in the end of the contrasting thread which is to be used for the tying down and bring it through to the right side. Make a small stitch at right angles over the couched thread bringing the needle out below the thread a small distance away ready for the next stitch.

Finish thread end securely and then push the couched thread ends through. The couched thread (or threads) can also be tied down with other more decorative stitches, such as open chain, feather stitch, buttonhole stitch, herringbone or fly stitch.

The same simple tying technique can be used to hold down the crosses of long herringbone stitch for a decorative effect.

Snail trail

This is a quick method of couching which can be used on firm materials. It is worked with one thread and knots are made at intervals, attaching the thread to the ground fabric. See coral knot, on this page.

Bokhara couching

One thread only is used for this stitch, the tying down being done with the self-thread in slanting stitches. It is used for filling shapes.

To work, the thread is laid along the fabric and on the return journey slanting stitches are made over the thread. The needle is brought up just below the thread and inserted a little farther along just above it. The stitches of each alternate row are made between those of the last row.

Laid work

Similar to couching and used for a solid filling in large shapes. Silk or wool may be used for this; the sheen on silk makes laid work look particularly attractive. By the graduation of colour or direction of stitch, an effect of light and shade may be obtained. To get a really good result, laid work must be done

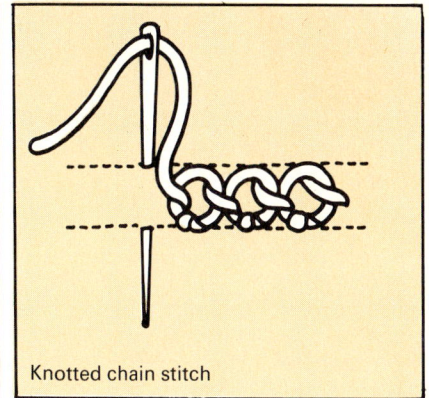
Knotted chain stitch

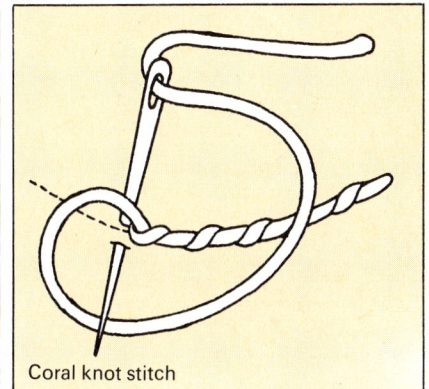
Coral knot stitch

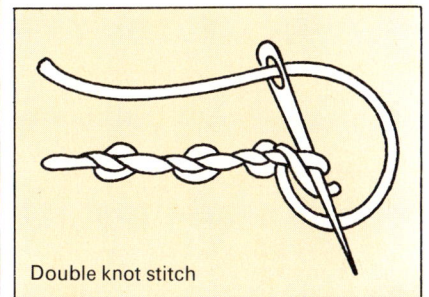
Double knot stitch

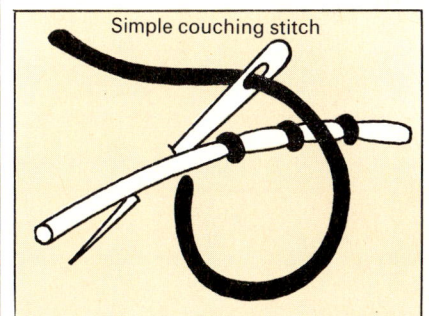
Simple couching stitch

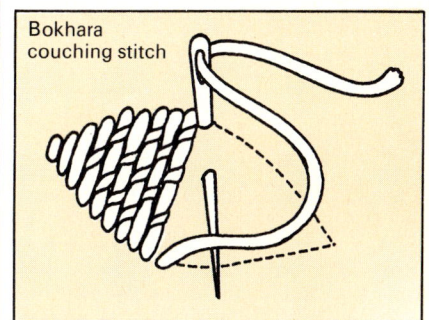
Bokhara couching stitch

Decorative needlework

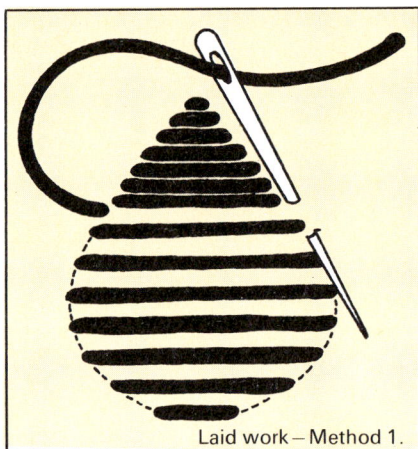

Laid work – Method 1.

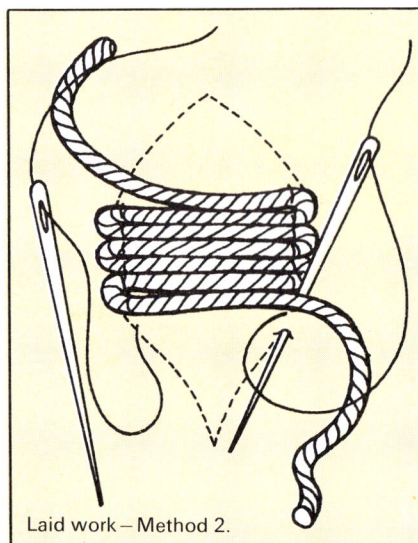

Laid work – Method 2.

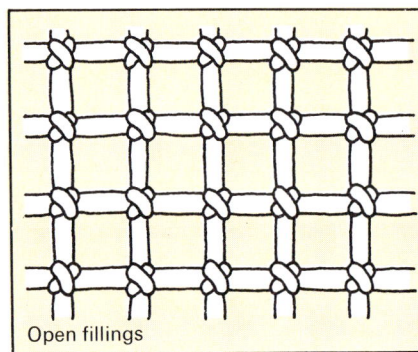

Open fillings

in a hoop or slate frame.

The threads are laid close together across the shape. They are then tied down with a couching thread which is stitched at definite intervals to make patterns. A second set of laid threads may be taken across the first ones in an opposite direction, or diagonally, and these are tied down as in simple couching. There are two good methods of laying the threads.

Method 1 As only a very tiny stitch can be made into the material, the work will be stronger if each alternate row is laid in the first working and the gaps are filled in on the return journey. The thread is brought through at one side of the shape to be filled and inserted immediately opposite on the other side. A small piece of the fabric is picked up down along the outline, and another thread is laid parallel with the first. Continue in this way until all the area is covered. Then work the in-between threads in the same way.

Method 2 Three threads are used in all, the laid thread and two finer sewing cottons, one at each side of the shape, with two needles. The end of the laid thread is passed through to the wrong side on one edge of the motif, it is then taken across to the opposite side, in a straight line, and is held down with a tiny back stitch, worked with the sewing cotton at that side. Twist the thick thread back on itself and stitch again on the outline, pass it back to the first outline close to the first laid thread, and stitch it with the second sewing thread.

Open fillings

Threads can be laid on the fabric, or over closely laid threads, to form a pattern. Crossed threads, about 18 mm ($\frac{3}{4}$ in) apart, tied down at the corners with a cross stitch, make a charming filling.

Left A basket of flowers embroidered in padded satin stitch has been used to brighten up a ready-made blouse, and is an idea to try on other articles of ready-made clothing.
Right A stunning example of how canvaswork can be used as an interpretive art: the fine colourings and subtle curves of a waterlily are portrayed in a wide variety of stitches.
Below Embroidery and canvaswork have always been used to enrich furnishings, so why not create a beautiful collection like these cushions by making covers from the pieces worked as you learn the skills of each new technique you try?

Shadow work

Shadow work is worked on semi-transparent fabric from the wrong side. Only outline stitches appear on the right side with areas of opaque fabric where stitches have been worked across the back.

Shadow work was popular in 18th-century England and was extensively used to decorate the thin clothing of fashionable ladies, usually in white on white or on pastel-coloured fabrics with a matching thread. Indian shadow work is quicker to work, but it is not quite so effective.

Nowadays, although shadow work still looks beautiful on lightweight clothes – blouses, shirts, nightwear, lingerie, scarves and so on, it is often used for delicate home furnishings such as teatime tablecloths and lampshades. In modern embroidery, brightly coloured threads are sometimes used.

Fabrics and threads
Fabrics must be fine and semi-transparent. Georgette, muslin, organdie, chiffon, fine cotton and lawn are all suitable.

Choose a thread to match the weight of the fabric. One or two strands of stranded embroidery floss or pure silk thread will probably be most suitable. Use a fine needle.

Designs
Shadow work is usually applied to floral designs but abstract designs can look effective if the design is simple with no small details.

There are two methods of working, one uses a herringbone stitch and the other, sometimes called Indian shadow work, uses a zigzag stitch.

Method of working
Pin the design to a drawing board.

Pin the fabric on top, right side down. Trace the lines of the design lightly but firmly in pencil. If the fabric is very soft, you may have to work in watercolour using a fine paint brush. Use a pale colour but one that you can clearly see. Set the work in a frame, wrong side of the fabric uppermost. (See page 183 for method.)

Tie a knot in the thread end. Make two or three stitches to secure the knot and start working from the left. Stitch library page 192 shows the basic principle of working herringbone stitch. The stitches should be placed fairly close together and angled to follow the shape of the area you are filling. On the right side of your work, the design area will be outlined with backstitch. The criss-crossed thread shows as an opaque area against the surrounding transparent fabric.

When all the petals, leaves (solid areas) have been worked, lines and other outlined areas are worked from the right side in stem stitch or double running stitch. Small areas of satin stitch can also be added to the design.

Indian shadow work
This has a lighter, less opaque effect on the right side. Begin working from the right on the design line. Take the needle up across the area, picking up a small piece of fabric. Work in a close zigzag, back and forth across the area, picking up the fabric on the outline of the design.

In home embroidery, use shadow work on organdie tablecloths, on muslin curtains, for beautiful silk bed covers, on a fabric lampshade, or on a sheer cushion cover, mounted over a coloured fabric.

The decoration on the yoke and shoulders of this cotton nightdress from the 1920s is of cutwork roses and leaves, showing that large motifs such as these are well suited to this embroidery technique.

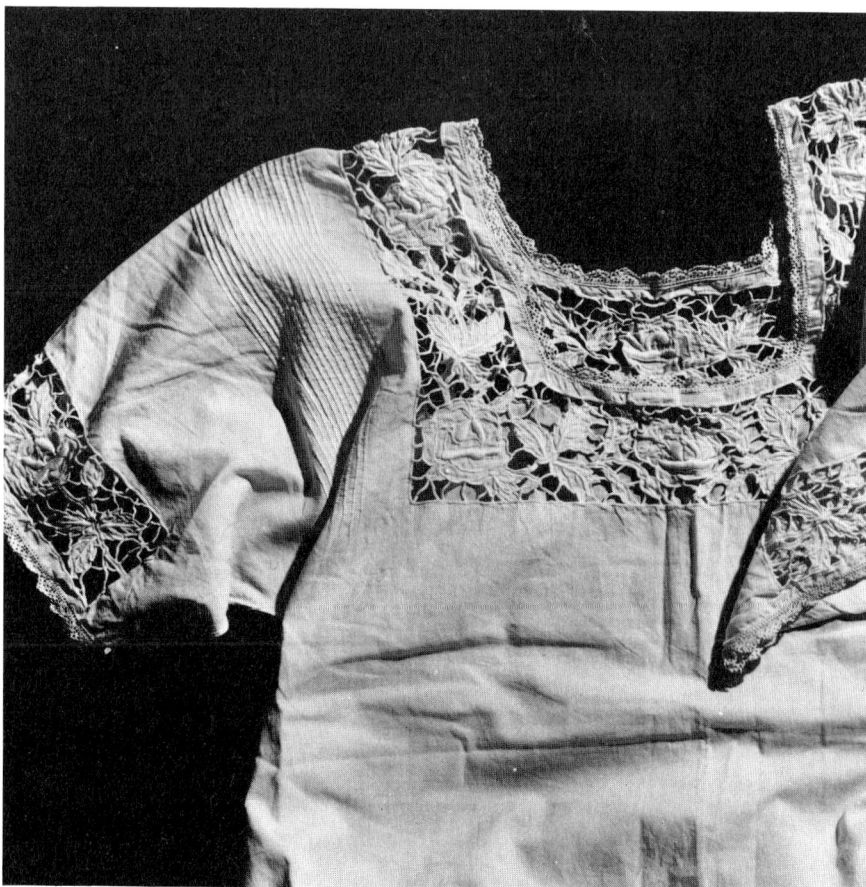

Cutwork

Cut work is a form of embroidery where shapes are outlined with closely worked buttonhole stitch and the fabric within the shape is cut away. It is mainly used on table linen but it also looks elegant on bed sheets and pillowcases. Cut work looks pretty on clothes too, on a collar or down the front of a blouse.

Fabrics and threads

It is essential that the fabric is fine, stiff and firmly woven. Linen is best, but good quality cotton can be used. The embroidery is worked with coton à broder although three strands of stranded embroidery floss can be used.

Preparing the work

Designs are transferred to the right side of the fabric either with a commercial iron-on transfer or by using dressmaker's carbon paper. The fabric should be stretched on a board so that the weft and warp are straight.

Mount the fabric onto a sheet of stiff strong paper, tacking it around the edges and stretching it until it is smooth.

Thread the needle with coton à broder or three strands of embroidery floss. Work small running stitches around the lines of the design through the fabric only. When you come to a bar, fasten the running thread with a tiny back stitch on the right side of the fabric. Do not cut the thread. Pass over the marked bar and pick up two or three threads of fabric, pass back to the other side and continue with the running stitches. Bars are usually placed at about 12 mm ($\frac{1}{2}$ in) intervals on a pattern. When a large space is going to be cut away, branched bars are worked to strengthen the place.

Branching bars The illustration shows how a branching bar is worked. Threads are worked between A and B. A to C is buttonhole stitched, then threads are made to D. Work buttonhole stitching from D to C and then finish buttonholing to B. Cover the remaining threads with buttonhole stitching.

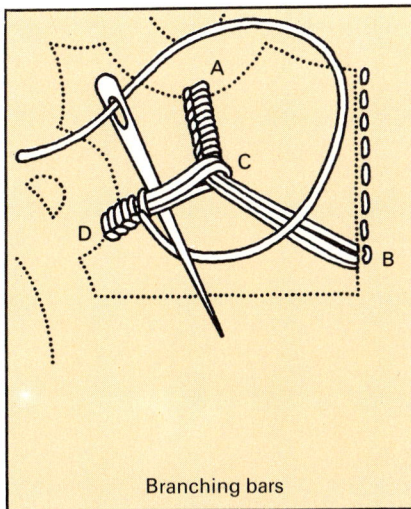
Branching bars

Working cut work

When all the running stitches have been completed and the threads for the bars worked in position, you begin to work buttonhole stitch over the marked lines of the design, up to and including the running stitches.

To strengthen the edge, lay another thread of coton à broder along the running design line and embroider over this. Lay another thread along the bar threads also. Make sure that you do not pick up the fabric underneath when you are buttonholing the bars. The buttonhole bars can be decorated with picots if you like. Fasten off thread ends by running the thread under the lines of the design where they will be covered with buttonholing. Do not end a thread at a bar because it will spoil the look of the work.

Keep tension even throughout.

Cutting the fabric

When all the embroidery is complete, snip away the tacking stitches holding the paper in place. Press the embroidery carefully on the wrong side of the work over a soft pad and using a damp cloth. With a very sharp pair of fine-pointed embroidery scissors, trim away the fabric inside the design up to the buttonhole-stitched edges. Cut as close as possible to the stitching so that no raw edges of fabric show. You must be careful not to snip the stitches. Press the cut embroidery again under a damp cloth.

Broderie anglaise or eyelet embroidery

This technique is related to cut work. Holes are outlined with a running stitch and then punched with a stiletto. The cut edges are then overcast and surface embroidery in padded satin stitch is added to the design. Fabric for broderie anglaise should be fine and closely woven – lawn, muslin or cambric are ideal.

Stitches used in cut work

Buttonhole

This can be padded with several rows of stem stitch, or worked over a running thread. It is used for scalloped edges, and the outlining of cut work. See page 190 for method of working.

Buttonhole bars

These are used to connect one part of the design to another across the background. Three or four threads are laid across the position of the bar and secured to the edge at each side with tiny back stitches. The buttonhole is then worked over these threads to hold them together.

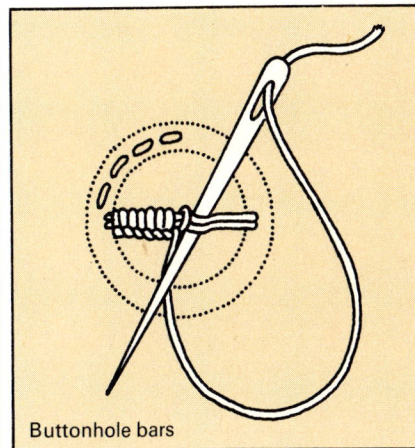
Buttonhole bars

Decorative needlework

Woven bars

This is another method of working the connecting bars in Renaissance embroidery. Four threads are laid across the background and simple weaving is worked under and over two threads at a time.

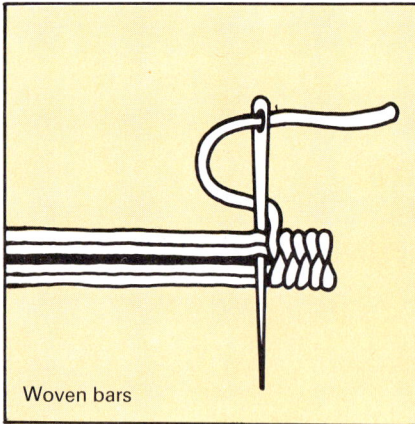

Woven bars

Picots

Used to decorate buttonhole and woven bars and edgings. There is a great variety and, once the method of working has been mastered, others may easily be invented. Three of the simplest ones are described here.

Loop picots A single loop of thread secured close to the edge with a knot. Insert a pin into the edging, in the position of the picot, preferably through the fabric. The thread is passed under the pin and a stitch is made into the fabric edge, leaving a loop the correct size for the picot. To make the knot the needle is then passed under the left-hand thread of the loop, over the pin, and under the next two threads with the working end under the point. Then continue to work buttonhole stitch.

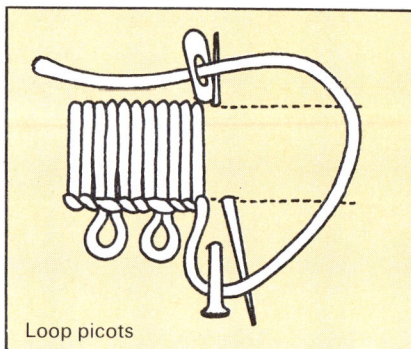

Loop picots

Below Children's clothing looks especially nice with the addition of an embroidered motif. Simple shapes and stitches are best, like this moon and star design worked in stem stitch.

Right Traditional Florentine patterns such as Carnation (top), Zigzag (middle), and Flame (bottom) provide the needlewoman with an opportunity to explore the use of vivid colour.

Decorative needlework

With a bar the pin is passed under the loose strands and through the material, which is not yet cut away.

Buttonhole picots The edging is completed until the end of the picot is reached. A loop of thread is then made by taking a stitch into the eighth knot from the last one made. Buttonhole stitch is worked over this loop and the working of the edging is continued as before.

Bullion picots These are made in a similar manner to bullion knots. The buttonhole stitch is worked to the position of the picot, the thread is then twisted five or six times around the needle point, according to the size of picot required; the needle is inserted into the fourth stitch away from the last one made and pulled through. Care should be taken to arrange the twist neatly and evenly on the thread. Pass the needle along the buttonhole knots and continue working until the next picot.

Antwerp edge or knot stitch

A simple edging which is decorative and firm. Work from left to right, inserting the needle through the fabric, from front to back, to make a single loop; then pass the needle under this loop, with the working thread under the point. Pull the thread through to make a tight knot.

Scallops

These may be made various shapes, semi-circular, pointed or serrated. Buttonhole is the most usual stitch for working scallops, but satin stitch or overcasting may be used. The scallops can be padded with several rows of running, back stitch or stem stitch, according to the effect required. Stem stitch will, of course, give a more raised effect than running stitch.

If no padding is used, a line of running stitches should be made along the outer edge to give strength to the fabric. The background material is cut away

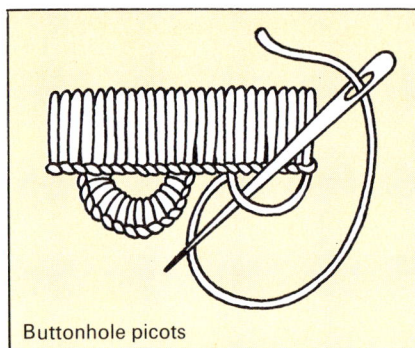
Buttonhole picots

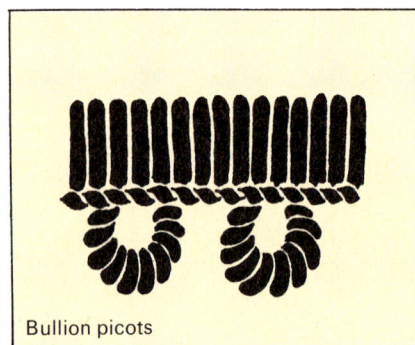
Bullion picots

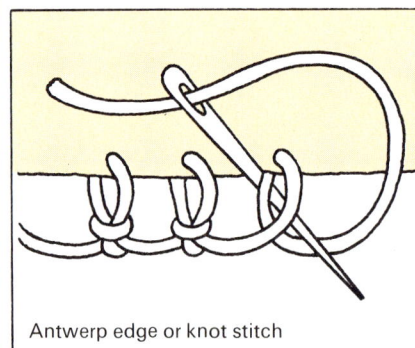
Antwerp edge or knot stitch

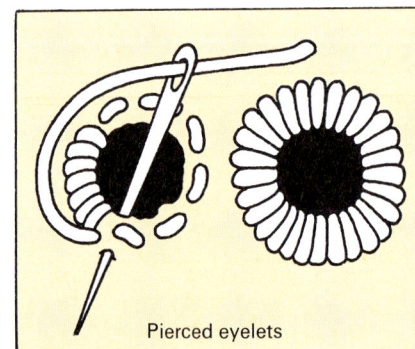
Pierced eyelets

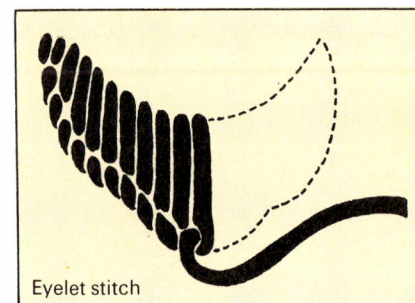
Eyelet stitch

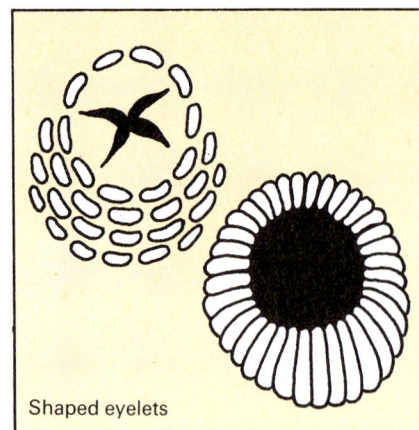
Shaped eyelets

close to the knots after all the stitching has been worked.

Eyelet holes

If the holes are to be tiny they are pierced with a stiletto; when larger, or of an uneven shape, the fabric is cut.

Pierced eyelets Make tiny running stitches around the hole, then pierce through the centre with the stiletto. Neat overcasting is then worked over the edge thus formed and the running stitches. Insert the stiletto again to make a good round hole.

Buttonhole stitch may be used instead of overcasting for round eyelets if preferred.

Shaped eyelets Outline the shape with running stitch, then snip the fabric four times to form a cross. The loose corners are folded to the wrong side and the overcasting is worked over the fold. Cut away the surplus fabric afterwards.

Eyelet stitch If used for larger circles worked close together, it makes a good background. Back stitch is worked from an outer circle to the centre. Two back stitches are made on the outer circle, then bringing the needle out at the beginning, two back stitches are taken to the centre of the circle, and then two on the edge again, continuing the circle. The threads should be drawn tightly together to form small holes where the needle pierces the fabric.

Drawn thread work

Drawn thread work is a form of counted thread embroidery. Threads are cut and pulled from even-weave fabric and the threads left are stitched together.

Fabrics and thread

Beginners will find embroidery linen the easiest to handle. Threads can be stranded cotton or coton à broder, but the thread should be close in weight to the background fabric. On linen, you would use three strands of embroidery floss.

Method of working

Here is the technique for working a traycloth. Apply this basic technique to whatever you are working. Find the centre of a piece of fabric by working a line of tacking stitches vertically and horizontally. Now measure 25 cm (10 in) to the right and to the left of the centre point to find the width of the traycloth. Measure 17.5 cm (7 in) up and down from the centre point. Mark the area with pins and then work tacking stitches all around, making sure that you follow the grain of the fabric. From the line of tacking measure 2.5 cm (1 in). Pick up a thread with a pin and snip it with sharp scissors.

Still using the pin or needle, unpick the thread you have cut, working from the centre. Cut a similar thread on the other three sides and unpick these too. Don't unpick any further than the corners where the threads meet. Leave the ends because you are going to darn these back into the fabric. Draw another two strands and no more, because that would weaken the fabric. You now have a sizeable hole at each corner. Thread the ends onto a needle and darn them into the fabric for 12 mm ($\frac{1}{2}$ in). Trim.

Now measure and tack the hem depth outside the line of tacking, 2.5 cm (1 in) away. Trim off the surplus fabric 12 mm ($\frac{1}{2}$ in) away from this second line of tacking. Fold and press on the first line of tacking and then on the second so that you have made a 2.5 cm (1 in) hem. Tack the hem, mitring the corners. You are now ready to do the hemstitching.

Hemstitching

There are a number of variations of hemstitching.

Plain hemstitch Make the hem and tack it down with the fold to the top edge of the drawn threads. Work from left to right, on the wrong side of the material. Bring the thread through just inside the edge of the fabric, at the end of the drawn threads. Pass the needle under four of the threads, from right to left, and make a stitch through the edge at the right of the group. Pull the thread through, tying the threads into a small group. Repeat this procedure for the length of the hem.

A second row may be worked in the same way along the opposite side with the stitches securing the same bundles or splitting them to make a chevron drawn thread border.

Double hemstitch For this, two sets of threads have to be withdrawn, and they should be about 6 mm to 12 mm ($\frac{1}{4}$ in to $\frac{1}{2}$ in) apart. If the drawn borders are not very wide, the method of work is to hemstitch the outer edge as described above and then work the second row.

Bring the thread through at the left-hand end of the inner edge of the unworked border, make a back stitch around the next four threads, then pass the needle down between the first and second border, making a diagonal stitch on the working side. Complete the whole row in this way. If several borders are worked in this way a charming lattice effect will be achieved.

If the drawn thread borders are wide, both outer edges must be hemstitched and the bundles are back stitched at both sides of the centre fabric; the second back stitch being made after the diagonal stitch, and before returning to the first borders.

Wide borders

Undrawn threads, hemstitched at each side, may be twisted into interesting lacy patterns. This is done with the embroidery thread, the eye end of the needle is passed under one group of threads and back under the previous one, and so on. Three or even four groups can be twisted together, and with practice, many ideas can be devised.

Corner motifs

When two borders meet at a corner a hole will be made. If the borders are wide this should be filled with a corner motif.

These motifs are built up on foundation threads of embroidery cotton, and they are usually worked with thread which tones with the fabric.

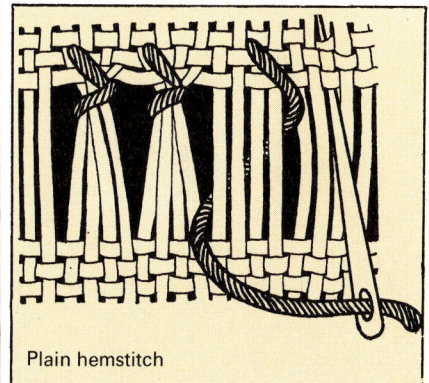
Plain hemstitch

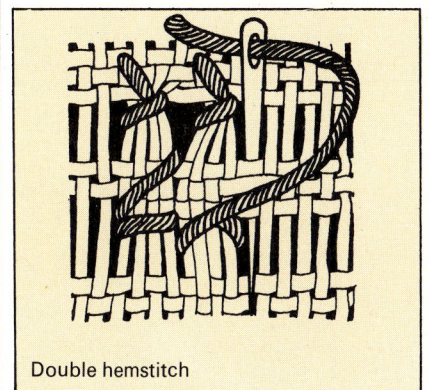
Double hemstitch

Decorative needlework

Spider's web This is one of the most usual corners and it is very simple to work. The foundation threads are laid from side to side and also diagonally between the corners. A form of back stitch is worked over these threads in a spiral, starting from the centre. A tiny stitch is made around each foundation thread. Many other corners can be designed on this foundation. A very simple one is the woven wheel, where threads are woven under and over in flat weaving.

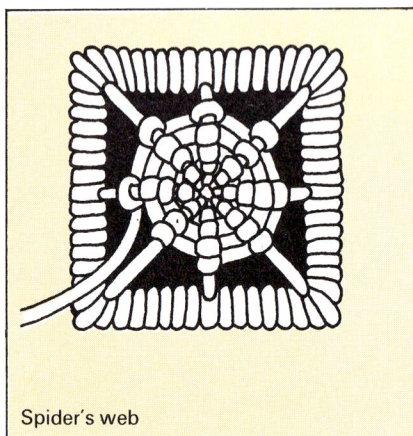

Spider's web

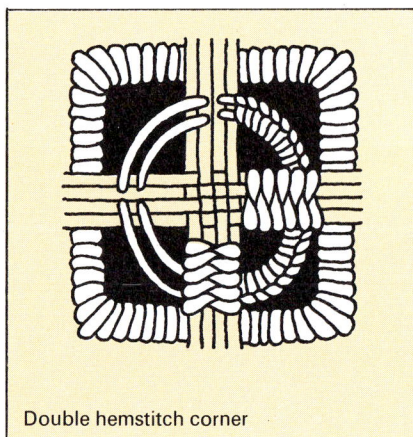

Double hemstitch corner

Double hemstitch corner With a double hemstitch border a cross of undrawn threads passes across the corner square. These are strengthened with simple weaving, under and over two threads at a time, and the four holes are enriched with a worked motif. A most attractive way to work this corner is to pass threads between the bars and work simple buttonhole stitch over them, making a complete circle.

Alternatively, four tiny spider's webs could be worked – one in each hole. There are many ways of finishing corners, and a little practice will show you ways of devising pretty designs.

Left Drawn thread work has been used to decorate the border of this tablecloth.
Above A beautiful curtain made with square net embroidery.

Both of these techniques produce a lace-like appearance. The first is done by withdrawing threads from the ground fabric and decoratively stitching the remainder together. The second makes use of a variety of stitches to fill in the meshes of an open-weave ground fabric.

Drawn fabric work

Drawn fabric work is similar to drawn thread work but the threads are not cut, instead they are pulled together in groups to make decorative effects. Drawn fabric work is stronger than drawn thread and the effect is still delicate and lacy.

This is a counted thread technique and therefore can only be worked on an even-weave fabric – linen, muslin, lawn and organdie. Beginners should choose a fabric where the threads are easy to count.

Threads and needles

The charm of drawn fabric work lies in the threads being almost invisible, so a thread closely matching the weight and colour of the background fabric should be used. Coarser threads can be used for outlining motifs or adding surface embroidery. A blunt-ended needle should be used for working the drawn fabric stitches because it is important that the needle pass between the threads and does not split them.

It is not essential to use a frame for this work; it can be worked quite well held in the hand.

Designs for drawn fabric work

Choose an embroidery pattern where there are large areas which could be worked decoratively. Plan to work a bold outline around the design. Transfer the design to the fabric, making sure that it is placed straight on the grain of the fabric.

Stitches in drawn fabric work

There are a number of stitches to use in this type of work, some worked diagonally, some horizontally. They all depend on accurate counting of the background threads.

It is recommended that beginners practise the stitches on a piece of suitable fabric in order to choose the various effects they want for a project. If done on a piece of cream-coloured linen using a matching thread, a charming sampler might be made.

Four-sided stitch

Worked horizontally and frequently used for borders. If several rows are worked together it makes a good filling. Work over four threads of fabric from the right.

There should be a cross stitch on the wrong side of the fabric. Bring the needle through at A and insert it at B, four threads up. Bring it through again at C, four threads to the left of A. Insert it at D (same hole as A) and bring it out again diagonally at E. The third side of the square is made by taking the needle diagonally from B to C. The first stitch of the next square completes the fourth side, and this is worked between C and E.

To make an overall pattern the rows are worked close together, the bottom stitches of the second row being made into the same holes as the top ones of the first row.

Drawn buttonhole

Diagonal rows of buttonhole stitch are worked back to back, the top of the stitches of the second row being worked into the holes of the first row. Each stitch is worked over six threads vertically and three horizontally.

Single faggot stitch

A diagonal stitch worked over four threads of the fabric. Start at the right, bringing the needle through to the front at A. Insert the needle horizontally, four threads to the right at B, and bring it out diagonally exactly under the starting point and four threads down at C. Then make an upright stitch from C to D with the needle inserted diagonally from D to E and four threads to left of C. Complete this first row in this way. The second row is worked similarly in the reverse direction by turning the work upside down.

Diagonal raised band

A series of crosses worked diagonally, pulling the fabric up

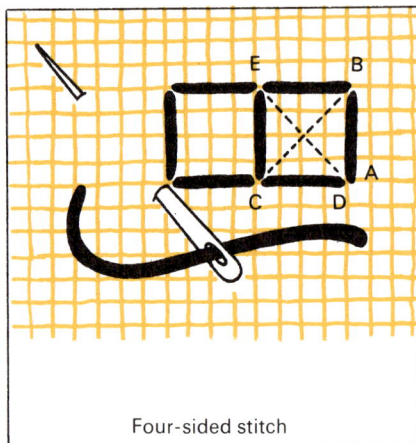
Four-sided stitch

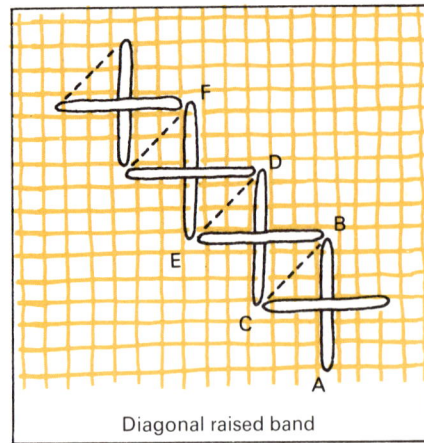
Diagonal raised band

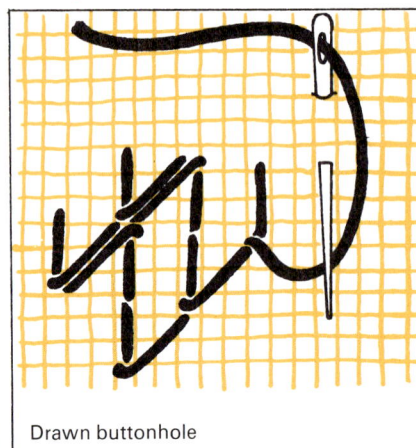
Drawn buttonhole

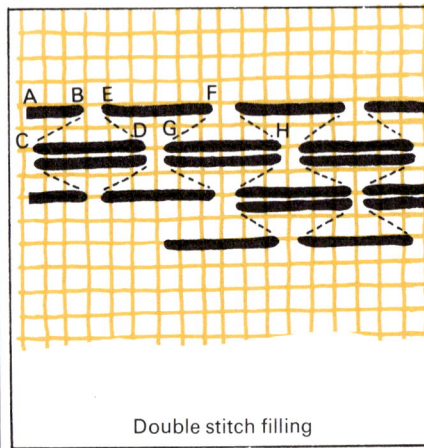
Double stitch filling

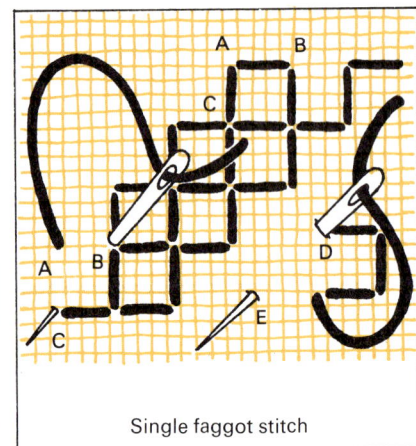
Single faggot stitch

into a tight ridge and giving a striped effect.

The stitches are made over six threads of the fabric, the first row is worked upwards, starting at A. Insert the needle at B, six threads above A, and bring it diagonally to C, three threads down and to the left. Repeat this into D, E and F, and for the full length of band.

The crosses are completed on the return journey and these stitches

should cut those of the first row in half. Work the stitches of the next row touching those of the first row to cover the ground completely.

Double stitch filling

A simple stitch worked horizontally from left to right. Two rows are worked at the same time. Bring the thread through at left of top row at A, and insert the needle two threads to the right, bringing it out two threads down and two to the left, B and C. Insert it again five threads to the right at D, and bring it back two threads up and to the left at E. Make another stitch the same as the first over five threads to F, then two threads down and to the left at G and onto H. Continue in this way for the full row.

The next and subsequent rows are worked in the same way, the top stitches being made into the same holes as the previous bottom row. The working thread should be pulled very tightly and should be fastened off at the end of each row.

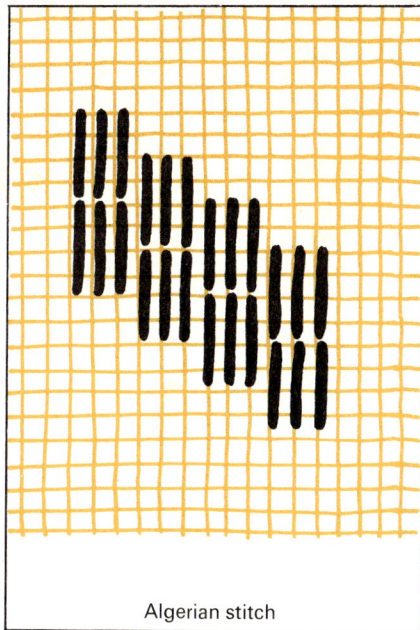

Algerian stitch

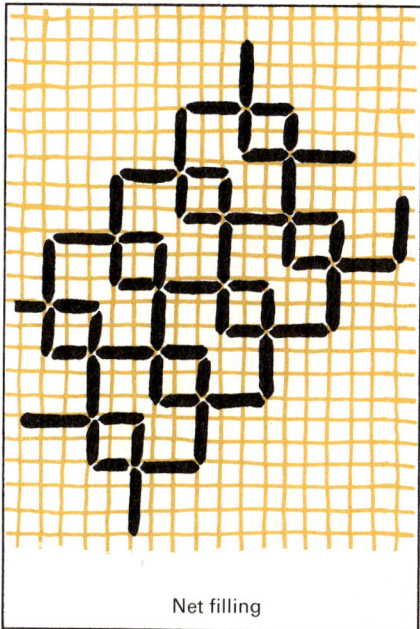

Mosaic filling

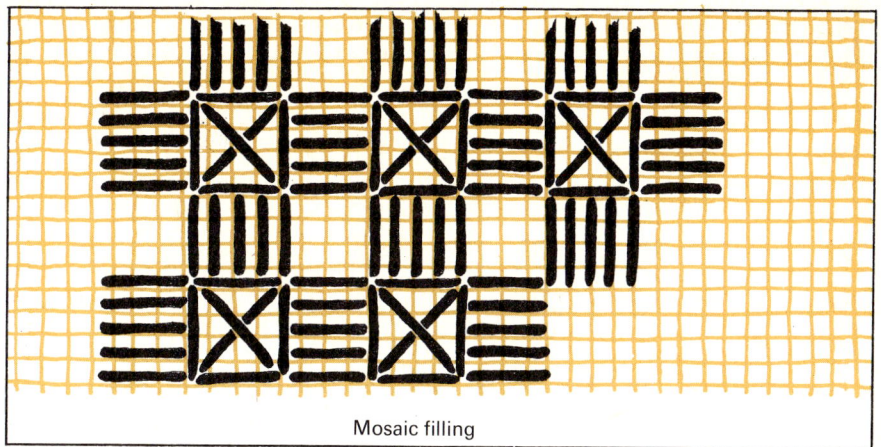

Net filling

Algerian stitch

A solid filling, which consists of groups of three satin stitches worked over four threads of the fabric. It is worked diagonally and the groups are stepped up two threads each time.

Net filling

Based on single faggot stitch. First, work a row of single faggot over three threads. Then work two rows of single faggot in the reverse direction, one over two threads and the other over three threads. Repeat these four rows as required.

Mosaic filling

A series of satin stitch groups, with four-sided stitch and a cross in the centre of each group to make a solid overall pattern. The satin stitches are worked over four threads, and if the pattern is to be repeated at intervals a complete cross is worked, including the centre. If the pattern is to cover the ground completely, the lines of satin stitch are worked diagonally first of all, and the crosses are put in afterwards.

Work the satin stitch from right to left, making five stitches in each group, each stitch over four threads. Start at the top right and work five upright stitches, with the last stitch take the needle diagonally four threads down and to the left. Then work five horizontal stitches. Continue in this way, turning the work for the next row, which will complete the cross. When all the area has been covered with this first movement, take the needle to the centre of the cross to work the four-sided stitch, completing it with a cross stitch in the very centre.

Ridge filling

This is a similar stitch to diagonal raised band. In this case the crosses are made over four threads of the fabric. The upright stitches are made first, starting from the bottom. Pass over four threads and pick up two to the left. Complete the crosses on the return journey, pulling the thread tight. All the rows must be made close together

to get a ridged effect.

Greek Cross filling

Worked diagonally this stitch is based on simple buttonhole stitch. Bring the thread through on the left and pick up a stitch four threads deep and four threads to the right catching thread under the needle at A. Make a back stitch to the right over four threads B, and a straight stitch down over four threads C. Move eight threads to the left before commencing the next cross. The stitches of the second row are worked into the same hole as those of the first row.

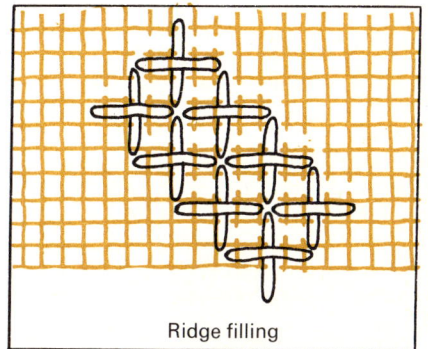

Ridge filling

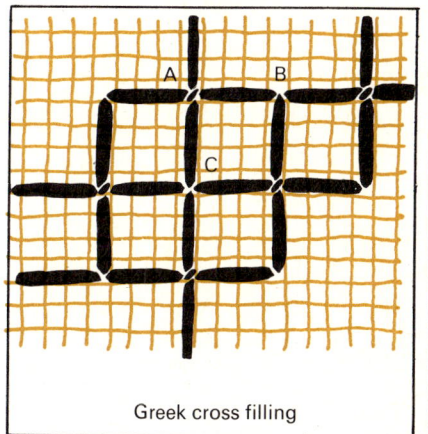

Greek cross filling

207

Insertions

Insertion is a method of joining two pieces of fabric with decorative stitches. It is most popularly used on table linen and items such as guest towels, but it is a pretty finish on clothing too. The technique is particularly effective as a way of adding a false hem when lengthening a garment.

Fabrics and threads

There is no limit to the type of fabric that can be worked with insertion, but for making table linen use an embroidery linen or a closely woven cotton or cotton mixture. The thread used should be strong, and pearl cotton number 5 is recommended. You can pull threads from linen or woven wool fabric and use this for insertion stitching.

Preparing the fabric

Make neat, narrow stitched hems on the edges to be joined. Tack the prepared fabric to stiff paper with the edges 6 mm to 12 mm ($\frac{1}{4}$ in to $\frac{1}{2}$ in) apart. You may find it helps to draw pencil lines on the paper as a guide. Join the two edges with any of the following insertion stitches.

Faggoting

This is the most simple insertion stitch and it is similar in movement to herringbone stitch. Work from right to left, joining the thread to the bottom edge; make a small stitch into the top edge a little to the left. Pull the thread through and pass the needle under the stitch just made, ready to make another stitch to the left on the bottom edge. Then thread the needle under the last stitch made and continue in this way, first in the bottom edge and then in the top.

Left A dress from Jerusalem worked in cross stitch on coarse linen, and a silk dress from Bulgaria decorated with tent stitch show the use of traditional embroidery patterns.

Buttonhole insertion

As the name implies, this is buttonhole stitch worked first on one edge and then on the other. The number of stitches made in a group may be varied.

Bar faggoting

Working from right to left, pass a straight thread across the gap from bottom to top, twist the needle round this once and make a stitch into the bottom edge, then pass the thread along the back to the position of the next bar.

Knotted insertion

This is a stronger insertion stitch and it is worked downwards. Join the thread to the right-hand edge and pass diagonally to the left, picking up a small stitch from the right side. Work a chain into this thread close to the fabric edge. Pass diagonally to the right side and repeat the procedure.

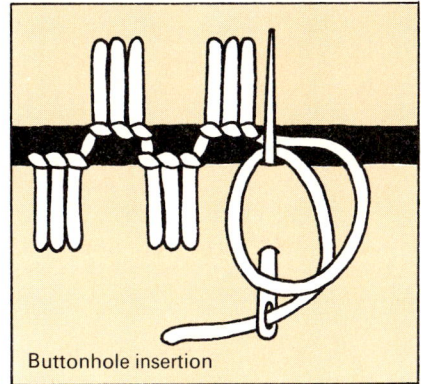
Buttonhole insertion

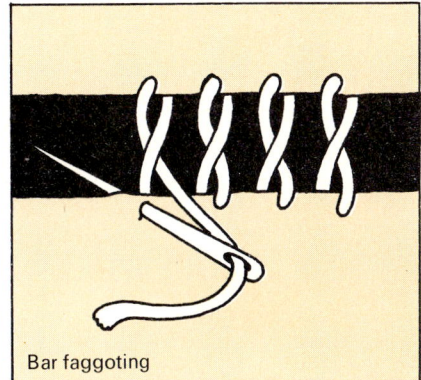
Bar faggoting

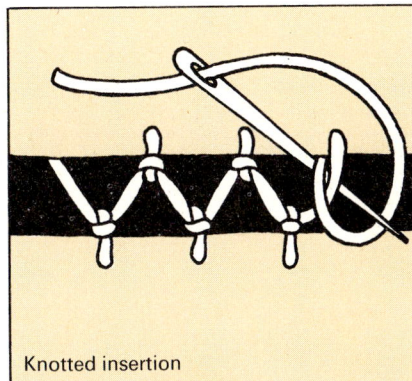
Knotted insertion

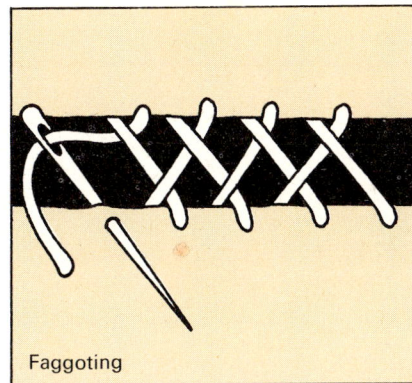
Faggoting

Right Drawn thread work stitches, including Spider's web and hemstitch, were used to make this border, which is part of a highly decorated cover for a small square pillow.

Cross stitch

Cross stitch is one of the most versatile of stitches and can look pretty and simple or dramatic and colourful, depending on the design and the way in which it is worked. Cross stitch is often seen on traditional ethnic embroideries, decorating costumes and soft furnishings, usually worked in red or black threads. The designs are often purely geometric or stylised shapes derived from nature. Cross stitch is frequently used for heraldic work and for church vestments, worked in massed areas of brilliant colour with gold and silver threads added.

Lettering worked in cross stitches looks very effective and small motifs are quite easy to work. Both of these attributes can be seen on 18th and 19th century samplers. These embroidered pictures were often the work of quite young children and they usually included an alphabet, their name and age, and little houses, gardens, birds, fruit and animals, all worked in cross stitches.

Modern uses for cross stitch work

Cross stitch designs can be used on almost anything as long as the ground fabric is suitable. Clothes can be decorated with motifs or initials around cuffs and pockets. Skirt hems, blouse collars, scarves, caps, bags and belts can all be decorated with gay patterns. In the home, the uses of cross stitch are almost endless for decorating soft furnishings – curtains, bedcovers and cushions – or for designs on lampshades, household linens etc. Cross stitch letters can be used to mark linens with initials or names.

Fabrics and threads

An evenly woven material is most suitable for cross stitch, as long as the threads can be seen clearly. Special embroidery linen can be bought in needlework shops but fabrics such as huckaback, hopsack, woven wool, coarse cotton, medium-weight cotton, voile and muslin can all be used. Very fine materials such as chiffon, ninon or lawn can be worked but the technique is different: the fabric is mounted on fine canvas first and then the stitches are worked from the canvas side. When the embroidery is completed, the threads of the canvas are carefully drawn out. This technique is used to work the miniature cross stitch motifs sometimes seen on fine handkerchiefs, the stitches being worked over organdie.

Fabrics with a checked pattern or gingham can be used for cross stitch embroidery, the fabric pattern being followed for the size and placing of the crosses. Striped fabrics can be used but it is a little more difficult to keep lines of crosses straight when working across the stripes.

Threads

Any kind of thread is suitable for the embroidery as long as it is relative in thickness and weight to the background fabric. If you are using wool yarn, be careful not to pull the stitches too tightly, as wool is springy and liable to pucker the fabric.

Needles

If you are working on a fabric where you are counting threads, use a blunt-pointed tapestry needle. For other fabrics, use crewel needles.

Designs in cross stitch

Cross stitch designs can be bought as iron-on transfers but they are not very satisfactory to use. The motif is almost impossible to place on the straight weave of the fabric. It is far better to work your own designs, either freehand directly onto the fabric or from a chart. Almost any shape or design can be translated into a cross stitch pattern. You simply draw the rough shape on squared graph paper and then work around the outlines, relating the shape to the lines. Choose motifs from books and magazines, copy them from other embroideries, or use abstract designs from wallpapers or furnishing fabrics. Work out your colour schemes by filling in squares with coloured pencils or felt-tipped pens. Keep to two or three colours for the best effect, although cross stitch designs look just as effective in a single colour.

Calculating motif size and materials

When you have worked out your design on graph paper, the next stage is to decide how big the design will be on your fabric. To do this, work an area about 2.5 cm × 5 cm (1 in × 2 in) of cross stitches, working over two or three threads. Compare the piece with your design. You can count up how many crosses fill the area and by comparing these with the number of squares on your charted design, you can work out how big your design or motif will be. By working over fewer threads or more, you can make the design smaller or larger.

To estimate the amount of thread you will need for a big piece of embroidery, cut two or three pieces of yarn to the same length, about 38 cm (15 in) long. Work a piece of embroidery and count how many crosses you made with each length and then work out the average number of stitches per length. Then count up the number of stitches in the design and divide the total by the average number of stitches. This will give you an estimate of the number of lengths. Multiply this by 15 for the total overall length; you can estimate how many lengths you will use. Skeins and balls usually have their overall length marked on them and you will then know how many skeins or balls you will need to complete your design.

Working the stitch

Cross stitches can be worked in two ways. Each stitch can be worked completely before going onto the next or half a stitch can be worked and then completed on the way back. Whichever method is used it is essential that each stitch is exactly the same size and that the top stitch in each cross lies slanting in the same direction.

You might want to use both methods in one piece of embroidery if this would make working easier.

(Note: if you are working on canvas, such as when making a needlework rug, it is better to complete each stitch before doing the next or the work may pull out of shape.)

Method of working

If you are placing a motif in the middle of an area, measure to find the centre of the charted design first. Then mark the centre of the fabric with lines of tacking vertically and horizontally. Start working the design from the middle and work outwards. If you are working a border, work from the middle towards the ends.

Assisi embroidery

Assisi embroidery evolved in central Italy during the 13th and 14th centuries and is traditionally worked on white or cream linen. Typical designs are grotesque birds and animals with leaves and flowers added. These are outlined in rust-brown thread in Holbein stitch with the background filled in with pale blue cross stitches. Assisi embroidery techniques can be adapted to make smart, modern embroideries for cushion covers, bedheads, book covers and wall panels.

Voiding technique

This is a similar technique to Assisi but the design and the background are both worked in solid cross stitches, leaving an outline of the background fabric around the design.

Table runner worked with Assisi embroidery; the wrong side is shown at the bottom.

Square-net embroidery

This type of embroidery, also known as *lacis* is older than either bobbin lace or needlepoint lace. The pattern is achieved with different types of darning and filling stitches. The net mesh should not be larger than 6 mm ($\frac{1}{4}$ in) for this type of embroidery, but a wider mesh can be decorated with running stitches and filet filling for net curtains. Use soft embroidery cotton, pearl cotton, crochet cotton, stranded embroidery floss or linen thread for working. The embroidery thread should be finer than that of the net. The net should be stitched to a covered, rigid wire frame for working but if you find this difficult to obtain, thumbtack the net to a paper covered board, stretching it smooth and taut. Smaller pieces of net can be mounted in a slate frame. Stitch wide tape around the edges first.

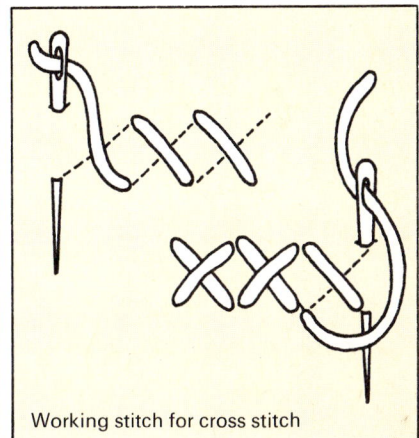

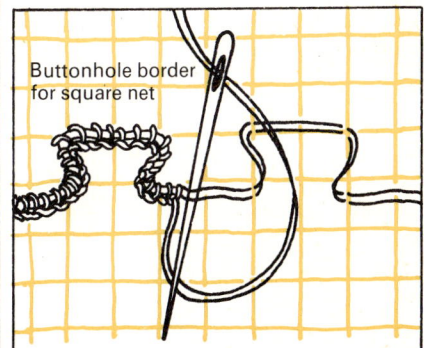

Working stitch for cross stitch

Buttonhole border for square net

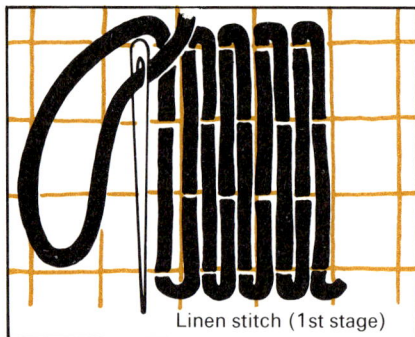
Linen stitch (1st stage)

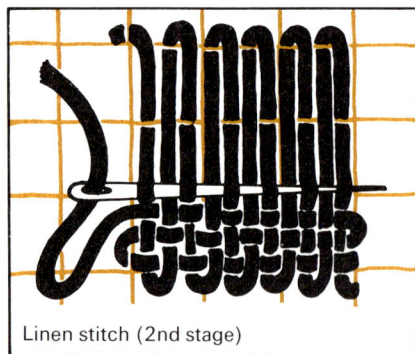
Linen stitch (2nd stage)

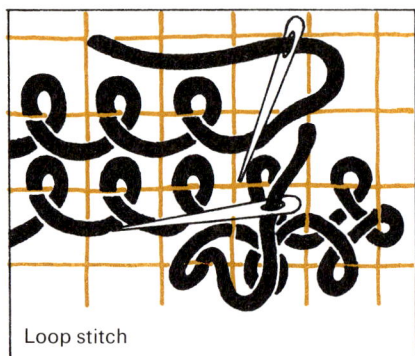
Loop stitch

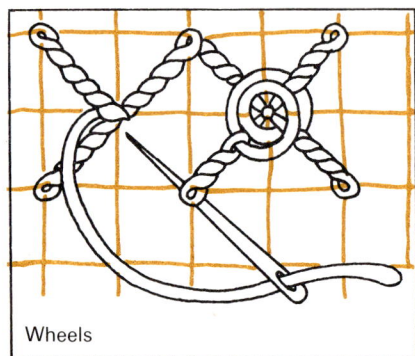
Wheels

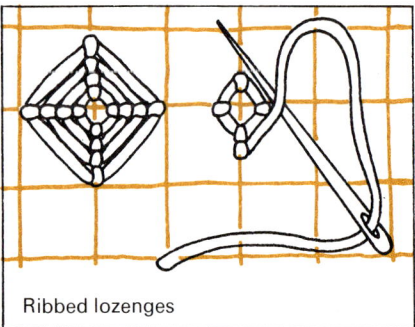
Ribbed lozenges

Designs

As net embroidery is always worked on or across squares, designs can easily be planned on graph paper. Each square will represent one mesh of the net.

Making a start

To start, tie the thread end to the bottom left corner of a square using a reef knot. Here are some of the stitches used in this fascinating embroidery.

Buttonhole border

This makes a scalloped edge. With a single thread, outline a scallop two mesh deep and two mesh wide. Work back along the same scallops so that there is a double thread out. Now work buttonhole stitch over the two outlining threads and the thread of the netting. Finally, cut away the surplus net, close to the knots.

Linen stitch

Join the thread to one corner of the mesh and darn over and under the threads of the mesh to fill the desired area with linen stitch.

Take care not to pull up the threads of the net. (If a thick needle is slipped under the loops at the end, it will keep the threads loose; then the extra will be taken up as the cross weaving proceeds.) 6 mm ($\frac{1}{4}$ in) square mesh should have about four threads across each mesh square.

Complete the stitch by darning over and under the net in the opposite direction.

If thread ends are finished off neatly, this is an ideal stitch for decorating net for curtains.

Squares and rectangles of linen stitch can be used to build up all kinds of geometric block designs and motifs.

Loop stitch

Join the thread end to a corner of the mesh square. Make a loop stitch as for buttonhole stitch into the top thread of each mesh in a row. At the end of a row, a loop stitch is taken into the side thread of the end mesh.

On the second row, work in the reverse direction with loop stitches worked into the bottom thread of the same row of mesh.

Between each stitch, weave the thread over the stitches of the first row and under the thread of the mesh.

Wheels

Four squares of mesh are used to make a wheel. Join the thread end to the knot in the middle. Pass the needle under the knot of one corner of square moving diagonally, and overcast the thread back to the centre. Repeat this with all three corners. Then darn over and under these threads and the threads of the net, making a small circle or wheel.

Ribbed lozenges

This comes out as a diamond shaped filling worked in the middle of four squares. Tie the thread end to the middle knot. Take the needle to the right of the knot and make a back stitch over the horizontal strand of the mesh. Take the needle to the vertical strand above and make another back stitch. Next, work the left hand horizontal strand and then the vertical strand below. Keep working around and around until the diamond fits the area of the four squares.

Satin stitch

This can be worked over one or two squares to fill areas. Tie the thread end to the bottom left corner of a square. Take the needle across the square and make a back stitch over the right hand vertical strand. Pass the needle under the square and make a back stitch over the left hand vertical strand. Continue, working up the square until it is filled.

Embroidery on tulle

Tulle or net with a hexagonal mesh is used for this embroidery. When the net is richly embroidered, it looks like genuine lace. Worked with simple motifs or as an edging, it makes a pretty bride's veil or could be used as an overskirt for a Christening robe. The net should be of good quality so that the mesh fibres do not break during embroidery.

Equipment

Net embroidery should be worked in a frame, small pieces in a tambour frame rings or by slate frame. Protect the delicate fabric by winding tissue on the tambour frame rings or by mounting the fabric before putting it into a slate frame (see pages 182-183). Use only a blunt-ended needle, so that the tip does not pierce the fibres of the net.

Designs can be either geometric or free style. Simple geometric patterns can be worked from a graph pattern, simply counting off the meshes as you work. More complex designs are drawn out in Indian ink on blue tracing linen first. Tack the net to the tracing linen all around and then mount the net in a frame. If you prefer, outline your design in running stitches first and then remove the net from the pattern before starting embroidery.

Threads

Generally, embroidery on net is worked in self-coloured threads. You can use colours if that is the effect you want, but colours must be in delicate shades or the effect is lost.

Coarse net can be embroidered with soft embroidery cotton or even dishcloth cotton. Good quality cotton, rayon or silk net or tulle is embroidered with lace thread, stranded embroidery floss or pure silk thread. Outlining is worked with doubled thread and fillings are worked with a single strand of thread.

Making a start

Thread both ends of the thread through the needle leaving a small loop near the needle eye. Pass the needle through the net, under a strand of the mesh and back through the loop so that the thread is secured. Darn over and under the net, one mesh at a time, all around the design, keeping the tension even. If a new thread has to be joined in, begin by running it through the back of the last few stitches of the old thread. Run old thread ends back under stitches in the same way. Wherever possible, complete a motif with a single length of thread so that there are not too many joins.

Geometric borders and simple, free style motifs can be worked entirely in running stitch.

Decorative and filling stitches

Darning

This can be worked back and forth in rows as a filling stitch.

Double darning

Work running stitch darning diagonally across the net. Then work diagonally in the opposite direction.

Diamond filling

This is a good filling for large areas. It is worked in two rows. Bring the needle through the net and make two stitches over two mesh diagonally to the right. Make the next two stitches diagonally to the left, coming back to the centre, then the next two to the right. Continue right across the area. Complete the diamonds with the second row, working two double stitches from the same centres. (See diagram.)

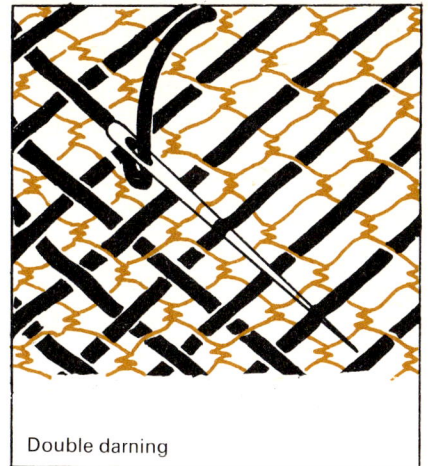
Double darning

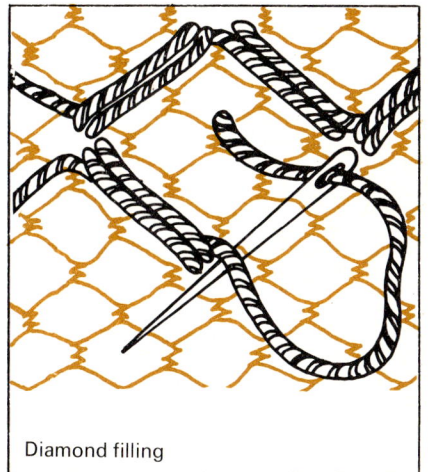
Diamond filling

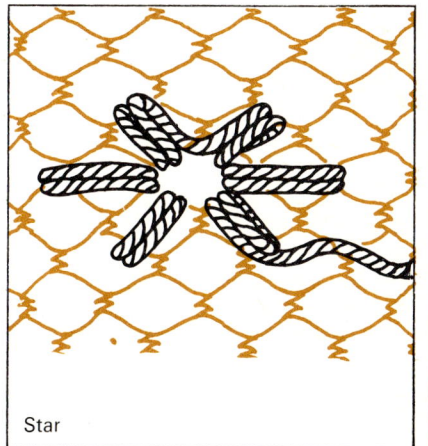
Star

Overcasting

Work along a row of mesh from left to right. Work overcasting stitches over two or more mesh solidly. Use two strands of thread.

Star

Two stitches are worked for each arm of the star. Work from the centre over two or more meshes to make a six-armed star.

Decorative needlework

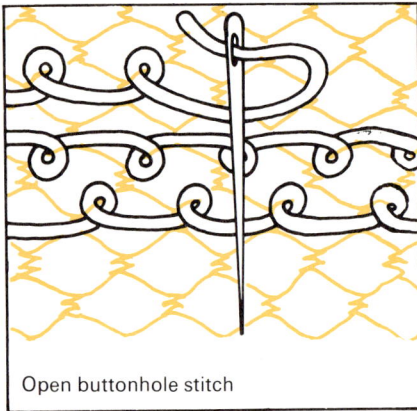
Open buttonhole stitch

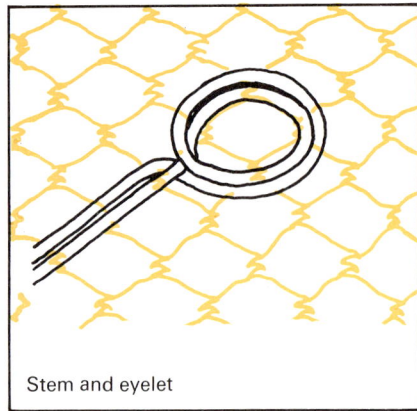
Stem and eyelet

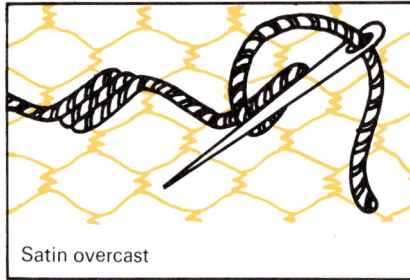
Satin overcast

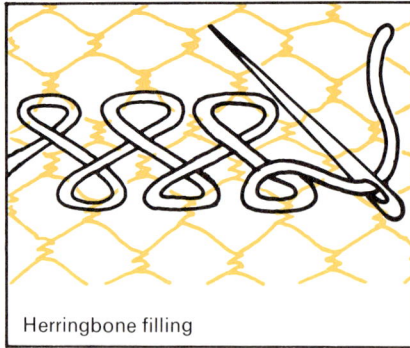
Herringbone filling

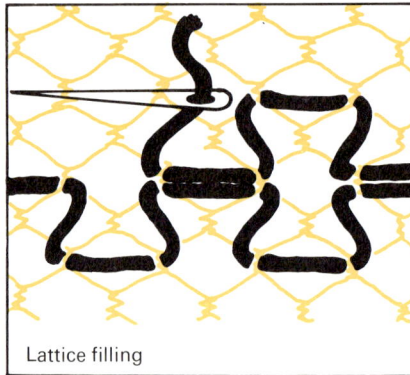
Lattice filling

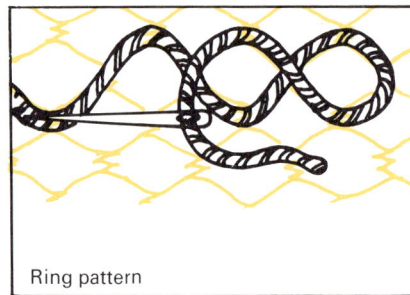
Ring pattern

Open buttonhole stitch

This is worked in exactly the same way as ordinary buttonhole stitch on fabric. Make one buttonhole stitch into each mesh of the net. You can work this stitch in rows horizontally, vertically or diagonally.

Closed buttonhole stitch

This is usually worked with a single strand of thread. Work a number of long buttonhole stitches into a single mesh hole, so that the hole is filled. Work this stitch in rows.

Couched buttonhole

Work a line of running stitches first. Then work open buttonholing over the stitches.

Eyelets

This is worked in two rows. Work running stitches for the first row. Work the second row as shown.

Stem and eyelet

Darn a line for the stem. Now work around a single mesh hole twice and back down the stem.

Satin overcast

Make three small satin stitches over each alternate mesh.

Herringbone filling

This is ordinary herringbone with the stitches picking up one intersection at top and bottom and passing over one whole mesh.

Lattice filling

Pick up one mesh and two intersections with the needle working horizontally. Then pass the needle down to the mesh row below crossing the mesh diagonally and re-insert the needle on the third row, passing it under two intersections and across one mesh. Work up and down like this, making diagonal threads and horizontal stitches to the end of the row.

The second row is worked in a similar way, with the top stitches picking up the same mesh as the stitches of the previous row.

Ring pattern

This is done with simple darning worked diagonally over two mesh to make a wavy pattern. On the second row, the ring effect is achieved by picking up the unworked intersections.

Practise these stitches on a piece of scrap net and then work out a design to make use of them.

Today there are many sewing machines equipped with special embroidery stitches. Below is a chart provided by the manufacturers of Elna, showing the wide selection available on one electronically controlled machine.

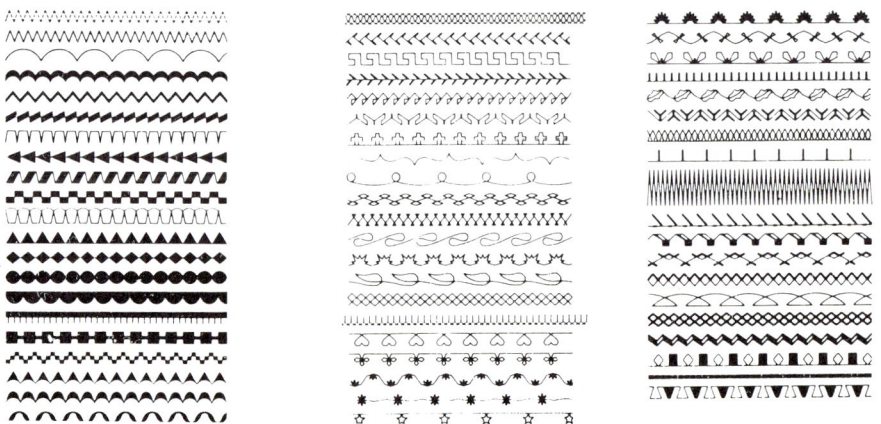

Introduction to machine embroidery

Modern fully automatic sewing machines have a variety of embroidery stitches built into them. The picture on this page shows some of the wonderful effects that can be achieved with this type of machine; try the technique on clothes and furnishings. Free-style embroidery can be worked on any semi-automatic machine which has a zigzag stitch setting. You will find it fascinating to experiment with your machine, trying various threads, tensions and stitch lengths, to find out what you can do.

Machine embroidery cotton up to size 30 can be used on the top of the machine with a needle of suitable size. (See needle and thread chart on page 98.) Heavier threads can be wound onto the bobbin by hand. In this case, you may need to loosen the tension screw on the spool for a really thick thread. Check with the manufacturer's handbook for method of doing this.

Free-style embroidery is worked with the foot of the machine removed and the feed teeth lowered or covered. (Again, check with your manufacturer's handbook for the correct method of doing this.) A hoop embroidery frame is essential for this work.

Method of working freestyle
If the embroidery thread is on the top of the machine, transfer the embroidery design to the right side of the fabric. If you are working with the thread in the bobbin, trace the design onto the wrong side of the fabric, and also stitch the design from this side, so that the decorative thread is on the right side of the fabric.

Place the fabric over the larger hoop. Press the smaller hoop down into the larger ring. Tighten the screw to hold the fabric taut. The fabric is now level with the machine bed.

Thread up the machine and remove the foot, then lower or cover the feed teeth.

Place the embroidery hoop under the needle and lower the needle into the fabric. Hold the embroidery hoop so that your fingers are only just inside the hoop and not near the needle. This is very important. Look at the diagram and make sure that your fingers are no nearer the needle than illustrated. Start the machine, slowly at first and, holding the hoop firmly, move it under the needle. You must keep the work moving because the feed teeth will not do it for you. Follow the design lines.

Combine free-style embroidery with the other embroidery stitches your machine can do. Work a kind of sampler, couching down thick wool yarns and metallic threads with different stitches. Work satin stitch motifs and combine them with free-style embroidery.

Delicate embroidery is possible with a machine, allowing you to use very fine threads and fabrics.

Monograms and initials

Embroidering initials to personalise household linens and personal accessories is a pleasing way of using this needlecraft. Multi-use transfers can be bought providing a whole alphabet of letters. From these you can use just one letter or combine two or more in a cipher or monogram. A cipher is two letters arranged one over the other. A monogram is a combination of two letters together sharing a common upright stroke.

Alternatively, you can find letters to trace in newspapers, books and magazines.

The ground fabric will determine the style of lettering and the embroidery technique you will use. Even-weave linen is a suitable background for cross stitch letters, for Roumanian stitch, outlining, blackwork and for eyelet and drawn thread work. Cording can be used on simple letters and wears well, so is ideal for items that will be laundered. Chain stitch worked as a filling looks effective on boldly designed letters.

Bold initials can be worked in appliqué techniques too, and this is particularly suitable for thick, pile fabrics, such as towelling. Edge appliqué with cording or machine-worked satin stitch. Padded satin stitch is the most popular stitch for initials, monograms and ciphers. It is best used on cursive lettering where there are curves and swashes.

These alphabets can be used for monograms; the top one is best suited to cross stitch, while satin stitch could be used for that below.

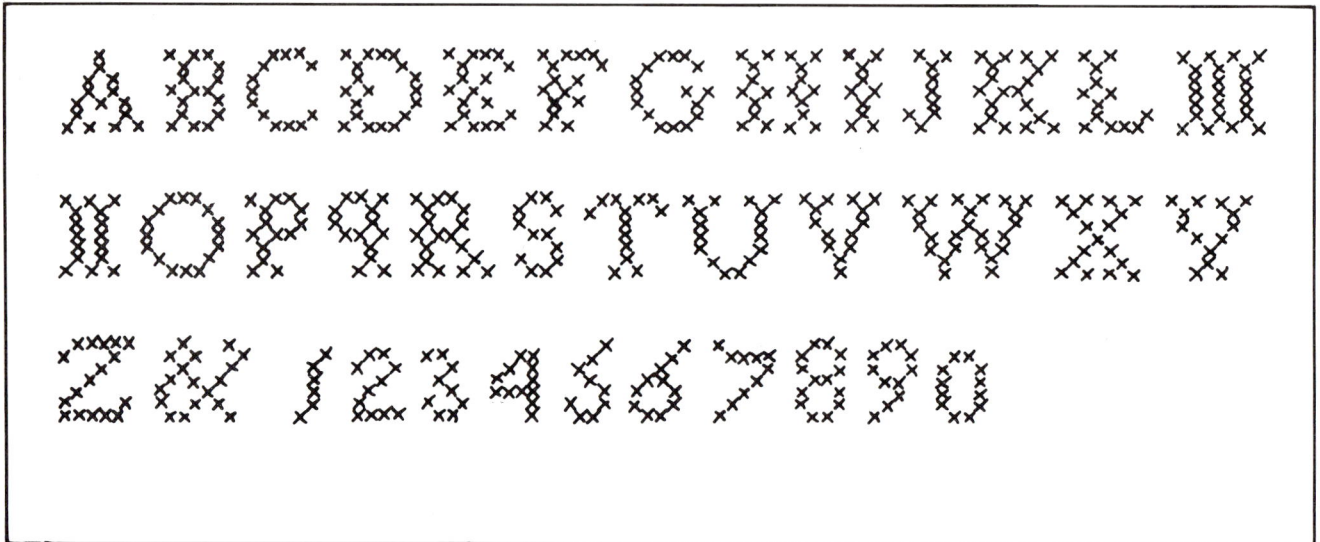

Transferring letters to fabric

Apart from letters being worked in counted thread techniques (cross stitch, blackwork etc), transfer letters to smooth fabric using dressmaker's carbon paper so that a clean, sharp outline is obtained. On rough-textured or thick fabrics, use the thread tracing technique.

Transferring cross stitch

You can work cross stitch initials on fabrics other than even weave by the following method. Cut a piece of fine canvas or firm linen to the size of the motif and tack it firmly to the background fabric. Work the embroidery over the threads of the canvas or linen and through to the fabric beneath. When the stitchery is complete, snip the tacking stitches holding the canvas or linen to the ground fabric. Gently withdraw the weft and warp threads of the canvas or linen so that the embroidery is left on the surface of the ground fabric.

This technique can also be used for working small cross stitch motifs on fine fabrics such as cambric, lawn or muslin, where counting threads would be difficult.

Padded satin stitch

Outline the letter or letters with small running stitches. Then fill the outline with small chain stitches. Work rows of chain stitches until the thick areas of the letter are filled. If you want the initials to be really embossed, work another layer of chain stitches over the top of the first. Using crochet cotton, pearl cotton or stranded embroidery floss, work satin stitches over the padding, all the stitches sloping the same way.

Included here are two complete alphabets for you to use in embroidery on household linens and personal accessories. Embroidered letters can be used large on cushions or bedcovers as a decorative motif. You can also use them individually for pictures or wall panels, experimenting with various stitches and threads for exciting effects. On personal accessories embroidered and appliqué letters can be worked on scarves, pockets or collars, on bibs and playclothes, on bags and purses. Try the effect of embroidering letters around a belt to spell the wearer's name.

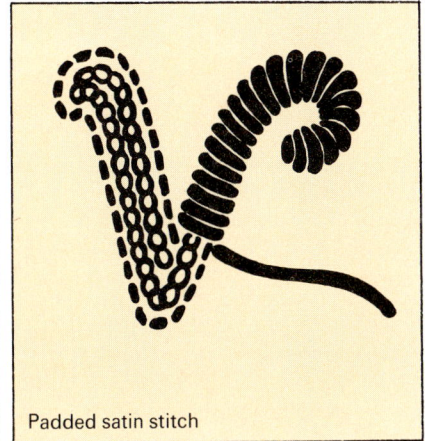

Padded satin stitch

Raid the sewing box to make an array of colourful cushions, each one embroidered differently, using up beads, sequins and ribbons with patchwork and appliquéd fabric scraps for a truly varied result.

Candlewicking

Candlewicking is an easy technique to learn and produces beautiful results quite quickly. It originated in North America more than 200 years ago and was used to decorate cotton and linen quilts with the cotton wick usually used for making candles.

Originally, candlewicked quilts were worked white on white, but now that cotton yarn is available in a wide range of colours, candlewicking can be done in colours to match room schemes, coloured fabrics or in a mixture of different yarn shades.

Use candlewicking for throwover bedcovers, cushions and for making bathmats.

Fabrics and yarns

There are two methods of doing candlewicking: one has a tufted finish and the other, called smooth candlewicking, leaves beads of thread on the surface. For both techniques bleached calico or linen is used. Thin fabrics such as cotton are not suitable for candlewicking. The process involves the fabric shrinking when it is washed to hold the stitches in position, so fabrics must not be pre-shrunk.

Yarn Soft cotton thread, sold in skeins is used for candlewicking. Twilley's Lyscot is available in a range of colours.

Needles A special candlewicking needle is used for the work. It is large, has a flattened, curved point and a large eye.

You will also need sharp embroidery scissors, and the materials for transferring designs onto the ground fabric by the carbon paper method.

Designs for candlewick
Designs for candlewick are usually large and flowing because they are best appreciated from a distance. You can work out designs on a block basis, repeating a block pattern over the work. Look at commercial patterns for cut work as these sometimes have the simplicity of design required and it is possible to adapt patterns.

Stitches for candlewick

The stitch used for both techniques is running stitch. You will find it easier if the fabric is set in a frame but, alternatively, spread the work on a table top and work sitting in front of it.

Tufted candlewicking
Thread the needle with a long length of yarn and pull the two ends even. Start on the right side of the fabric at the end of a design line. Leave the ends of the yarn on the right side of the fabric.

Work even running stitches in and out of the fabric – the stitches should be about 12 mm ($\frac{1}{2}$ in) apart. Pull the thread through so that small loops are left standing on each stitch. Form the loops over a pencil as you pull the thread through to make sure that they are all the same size.

When all the work has been completed, cut the loops evenly and cleanly with sharp scissors. In massed areas of stitches, the rows of running stitch should be worked as closely as possible without straining the fabric weave.

Smooth or beaded candlewick
This technique looks best when used for simple geometric designs and large massed areas of stitches.

Transfer the design to the fabric. Thread the needle with doubled thread. Start at the end of a design line but leave the thread ends on the wrong side of the fabric.

Work small running stitches, 6 mm ($\frac{1}{4}$ in) apart and leaving a bead of thread on the right side, slightly raised from the surface, but not a distinct loop. Always finish threads on the wrong side of the fabric. Overcast the ends when the work is completed.

Finishing candlewick
To set the stitches, wash the finished work in warm to hot soapy water and let it soak for about four hours. If you are using a washing machine, set the machine for at least a 20 minute wash. Rinse carefully several times. Do not squeeze or spin dry. Hang the wet quilt to dry naturally so that it dries with as few creases as possible. Brush the cut tufts with a soft brush, such as a bristle nail brush, to make them fluffy. You should never iron a candlewick fabric – it flattens and spoils the tufts.

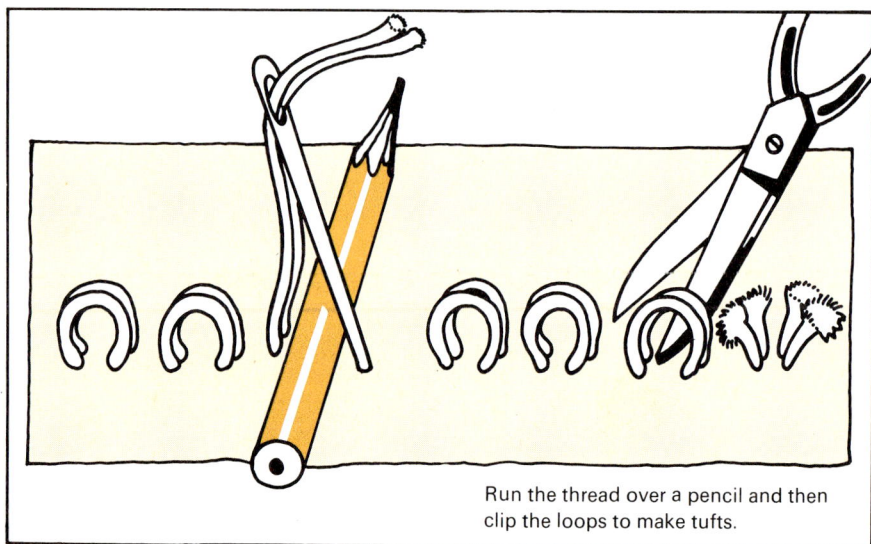

Run the thread over a pencil and then clip the loops to make tufts.

Smocking

Smocking, which is embroidery on gathered fabric, was originally used to decorate the work clothes of farmers and labourers during the 18th and 19th centuries. The garments were made of coarse cotton or linen and cut in a simple T shape. The smocking controlled the fullness on the shoulders, back and chest areas, and the thickness of the gathered fabric also made the garment more weatherproof.

Wives, who made the smocks for their husbands displayed their needle skills by combining emblems and motifs with the smocked areas, depicting the wearer's trade or occupation. A gardener might have tools and flower motifs, while a dairyman's smock would be decorated with yokes and buckets, churns and grasses.

The embroidery was worked in stem stitch, chain stitch, feather stitch and other surface stitches. These smocks were usually made in a natural-coloured fabric and the embroidery was worked in a matching colour.

Later, smocking was used mostly on children's and babies' clothes in areas where elasticity was needed.

Today, smocking is used on adult clothes as well and can be adapted to decorate a wide variety of home furnishings.

Fabrics and threads in smocking

Fabrics should be soft so that they gather easily. Gathering must be evenly and carefully done and to achieve this a transfer of dots is ironed onto the fabric. The iron must be fairly hot, so make sure that fabrics made of synthetic fibres will take the heat of the iron.

Patterned fabrics look very effective when smocked. All-over spot patterns, stripes or checks are simple for a beginner to use. No spot transfers are needed with these

In rural England, men traditionally wore tunics with smocked shoulders and yoke; the stitch pattern varied by region and profession.

fabrics; you simply use a line of spots, stripes or checks as a guide for the gathering stitches. The distance between lines of gathering should be from 6 mm to 12 mm ($\frac{1}{4}$ in to $\frac{1}{2}$ in).

Preparing the fabric

When calculating fabric requirements, allow about 3 times the desired finished width – less for fine fabrics and a little more for medium weight fabric. Join panels, if necessary, with a plain seam. Iron transfer dots onto the wrong side of the fabric. Thread a sewing needle with enough strong thread to work right across the width of the fabric. Tie a large knot on the end of the thread. Work running stitches across, picking up a few threads on each dot. Work right across and leave the thread end hanging loose. Work rows of gathering as dictated by the transfer dots or, on patterned fabric, about 12 mm ($\frac{1}{2}$ in) apart. When all the gathering is finished push the fabric back along the threads evenly. Use a pin to stroke the pleats until they are regular and even. Pull two or three thread ends together and wind them around a vertically inserted pin in a figure-of-eight. The pleats should be tightly drawn up, and from this point they are called *reeds*. It is important that all the gathering threads are left in position until all the smocking is completed. Smocking should always be done before a garment is made up. On home furnishings, turn a single 12 mm ($\frac{1}{2}$ in) hem on the top edge of the fabric and work the first row of

gathering through the double thickness.

Threads

You will find three strands of stranded embroidery floss is right for cottons, with perhaps two strands for finer fabrics. Coton à broder and pearl cotton can also be used for medium weight fabrics. Choose a matching thread or pick a colour from the fabric design for a contrasting effect.

Stitches in smocking

There are several stitches which can be used in smocking, but you

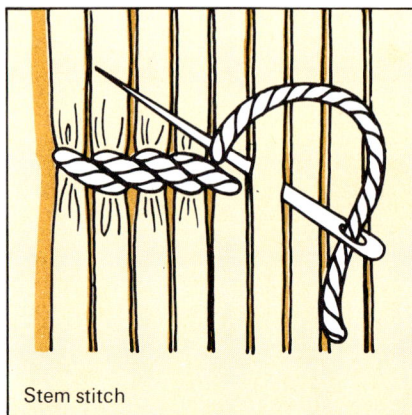
Stem stitch

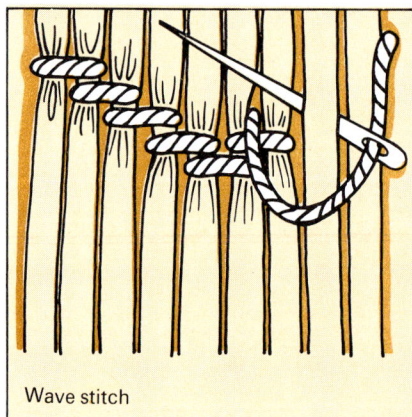
Wave stitch

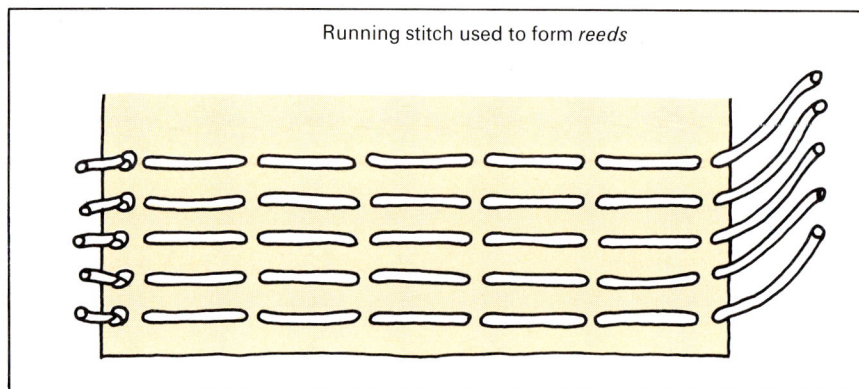
Running stitch used to form *reeds*

do not have to use more than three – stem stitch, cable stitch and chevron stitch. Some stitches have more elasticity than others, and those with the tightest hold should be used at the top of a piece of smocking, with looser-hold stitches near the bottom edge so that the released fabric flares prettily.

Stem stitch

This is a tight hold stitch and should be used at the top edge. Working from left to right, secure the thread end on the gathering thread line.

Bring the thread through beside a reed. Pass the needle to the right over 2 reeds and insert the needle, from the right, under the second reed to come out between reeds 1 and 2. Keep the thread below the needle.

Stem stitch is worked in a straight line across the reeds and is also called outline stitch.

Wave stitch

Wave stitch is a pattern using stem stitch. It is worked in a zigzag from left to right.

Pick up the second reed, but keep the thread above the needle. The next stitch is worked a little lower, picking up the third reed.

Continue until you reach the second line of gathering. Now continue working up the reeds, with the thread below the needle until you are back on the first gathering line. Carry on, zigzagging up and down between the lines of gathering.

Cable stitch

This is a medium hold stitch, and similar to a double stem stitch.

Working from left to right, join the thread to the left of the first reed. Pass the needle over two reeds and insert it from the right under the second reed, bringing it out between the two, keeping the thread below the needle. For the next stitch, the thread lies above the needle. Repeat these two movements to the end of the row.

Chevron stitch

Chevron stitch is a surface embroidery stitch. When used in smocking, it is sometimes called diamond stitch. It is a loose hold stitch and is used towards the bottom of a piece of gathering threads.

Secure the thread at the left on the lower line of gathering, and with thread below the needle, pick up the second reed. Pull the thread through.

Take the needle up to the third reed on the upper line of gathering, pick it up and then pick up the fourth reed to complete the stitch, bringing the needle out between the third and fourth reeds, with the thread above the needle.

Take the needle down to the lower line of gathering and pick up the fifth and then the sixth reeds. Take the needle up to the upper row for stitches seven and eight. Continue right across the row.

To complete the diamond effect, the second row of chevrons is worked between the third and fourth rows of gathering. The top stitches of the second row take the same reeds as the bottom stitches of the first row.

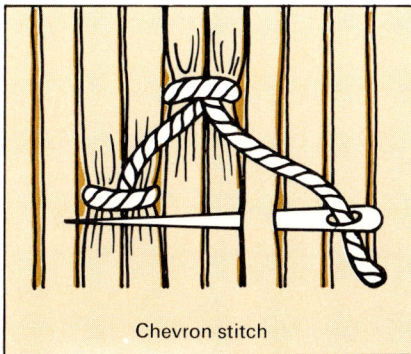

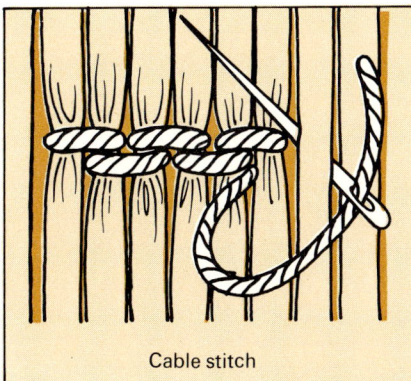

Chevron stitch

Cable stitch

Smocking has always been popular for little girl's dresses, but when used on adult clothes it can add softness and interest to otherwise ordinary lines.

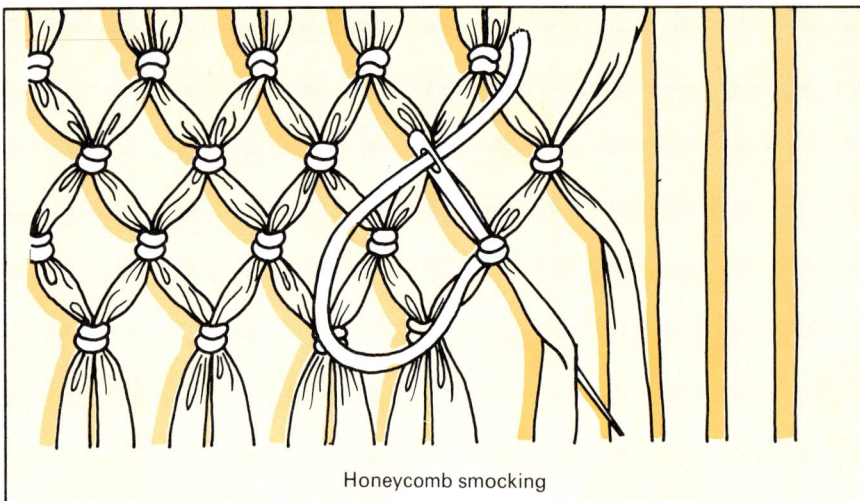
Honeycomb smocking

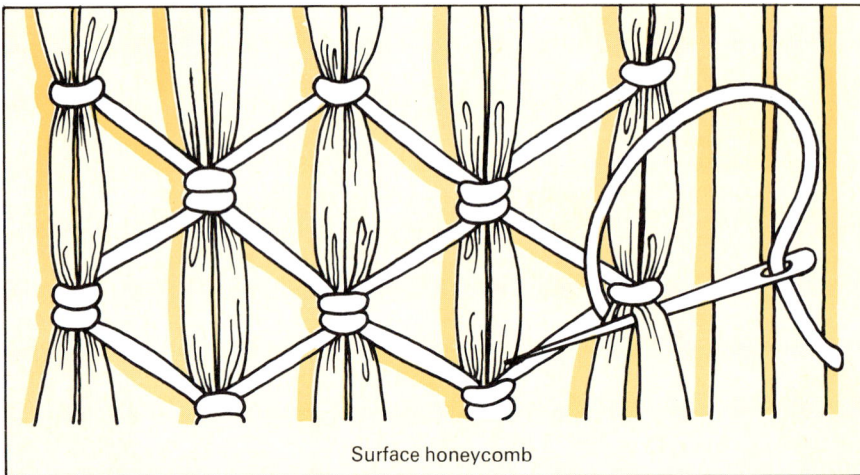
Surface honeycomb

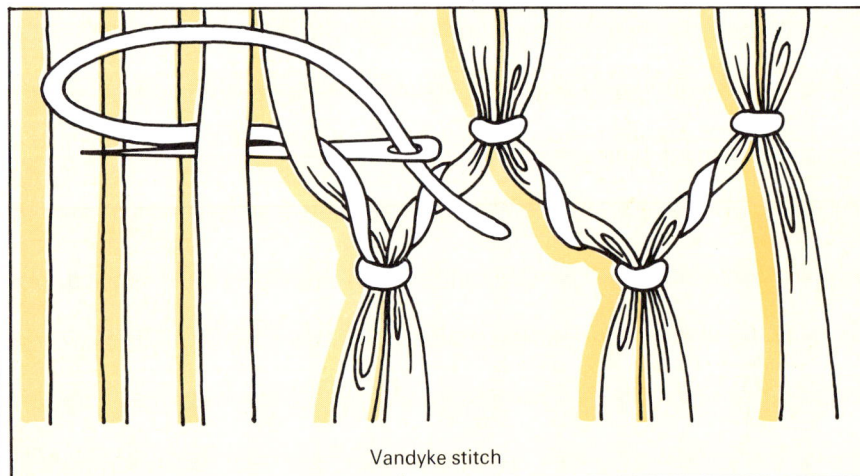
Vandyke stitch

To complete the diamond pattern, work honeycombs on gathering rows three and four. The back stitches of the upper row are made over the same reeds as the lower stitches of the first row.

Surface honeycomb
This is worked in the same way as honeycomb, but instead of taking the needle down inside a reed, the thread is left on the surface.

Vandyke stitch
This is a loose hold smocking stitch, and is the only one which is worked from the right. It can be worked between two rows of gathering, or over three or more rows so that the stitch makes large 'V's.

Join the thread to the lowest row of gathering on the right. Make a back stitch over the first two reeds.

Pass the needle over the second reed up to the uppermost row of gathering. Pick up the second and third reeds and make a back stitch over them.

Take the needle to the bottom row of gathering again and pick up the third and fourth reeds and continue to the end of the row.

If you are working over three rows of gathering, begin on the bottom row, work up to the second, then up to the first, down to the second, and then down to the third.

Finishing smocking
Unwind the gathering thread ends and pull the threads out by the knotted ends. Smocking will not need pressing but you may want to touch up the fabric below the smocking. Hems on smocked pieces look pretty if finished with a row of cable stitch or feather stitching worked along the stitch line.

Use smocking in home furnishings in the following ways:
Smock the top of curtains instead of gathering them with tape. Smock stool covers instead of gathering the skirt. Smock box covers, tea and coffee cosies, or straight-sided lamp shades.

Honeycomb smocking
Honeycomb, a medium hold stitch, is not really a smocking stitch, but it is popular and quick to work and looks particularly pretty on children's clothes.

Join the thread at the left on the top row of gathering. Make a back stitch over the first two reeds and slip the needle down inside the second reed to the lower line of gathering.

Bring the needle through and make a back stitch over the second and third reeds and take the needle up inside the third reed to the top gathered row. Continue to the end of the row.

The variety of stitches and fillings used on this carefully preserved 16th-century border piece shows the many textures that can be achieved, and stitch patterns which are common to this type of work.

Beading

Working with beads and sequins is a fascinating form of embroidery, and the techniques can be used to decorate clothes, bags, hats and scarves, as well as small home accessories such as book covers and fabric boxes. Soft jewellery, neck collars, satin or velvet waistbands and hair bands are exquisite when decorated with pearl and crystal beads.

Bead decoration can be worked onto readymade clothing. But it really is best to work the areas before a garment is made up. Beads should be stitched up to the seam line and not beyond it. Stitch the seam and then add individual beads if there seem to be gaps in the design.

Needlework counters stock a wide variety of beads in all colours and sizes. The small round beads of opaque and transparent glass or in metallic finish are called *rocaille* or seed beads. Long shaped beads, usually in glass, are called bugle beads. You will often find larger beads, some prettily carved and shaped and in a variety of materials – glass, crystal, wood, ceramic pottery etc. – in arts and crafts shops.

Sequins come in all sizes, shapes and colours and have a hole in the middle for stitching. Sequin material is sold in sheets and can be cut into shapes. Sequin waste is the material left over after sequins have been cut out and has a variety of decorative uses in bead work. *Paillettes* are large oval or round sequins with a hole on the edge.

Equipment

Beading needles are used for sewing beads and sequins. These come in sizes 10 to 13 and are long and thin with a narrow eye. Always make sure that the needle you choose will pass easily through the smallest bead you are using.

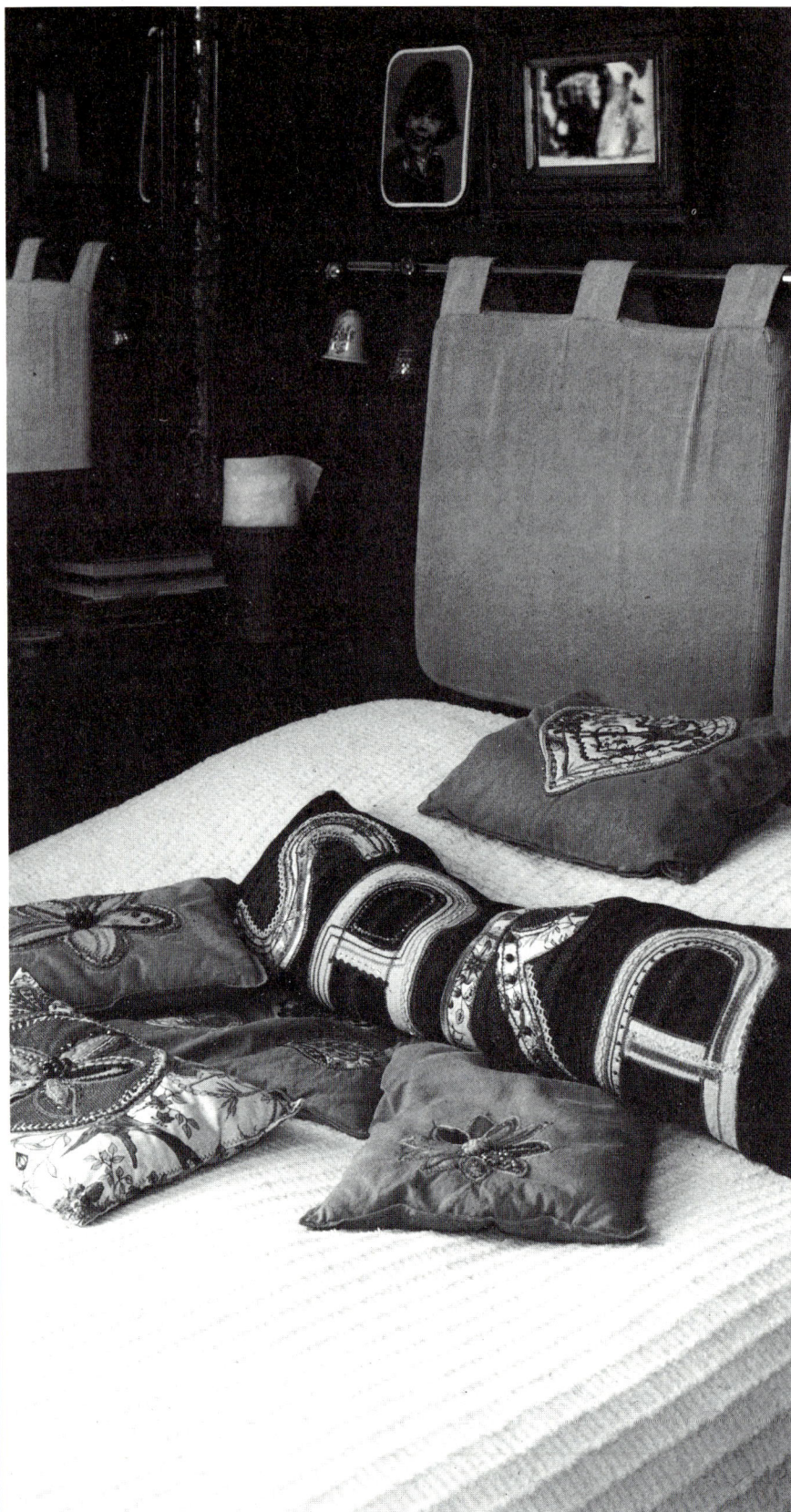

Don't feel that beads can only be used to decorate evening bags. Combined with a variety of stitches and embroidery techniques like appliqué, many creative uses can be found.

These cleverly monogrammed cushions have the initials appliquéd to the covers in bits of velvet and ribbon. Wooden and glass beads travel up and down the letters with the odd sequin added for sparkle.

Sewing threads Pure silk or all-purpose threads are used for attaching beads and sequins. The thread should be almost invisible, so choose it to blend in with the fabric and the beadwork. Draw the thread over a block of beeswax to smooth and strengthen it.

Frame It is best to use a frame for working beadwork. You will find that even small pieces of work are easier to do and have a better finish.

Preparing the work

Mark the design on the fabric using either the trace-thread method or

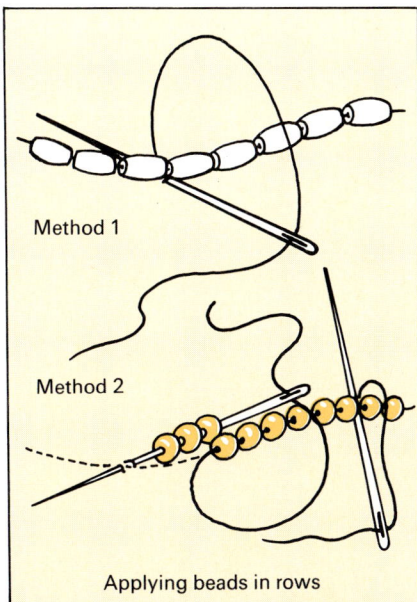

Method 1

Method 2

Applying beads in rows

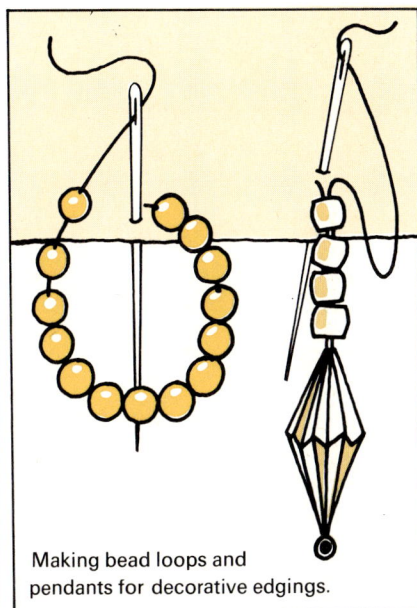

Making bead loops and pendants for decorative edgings.

dressmaker's carbon paper. It is inadvisable to use iron-on transfers because the marked lines are difficult to remove and will show under the beads.

Applying beads

Always start the thread with a secure double back stitch on the wrong side. Bring the needle through to the right side of the fabric to begin.

Applying single beads

Pick up the bead and slip it onto the thread and then make a back stitch in the fabric, bringing the needle out for the next bead. This method can be used to work beads in rows, or for a scattered effect.

Applying beads in rows

Method 1 Thread beads onto a length of thread. Lay the beads along the design line, holding them down with a finger. Bring the stitching thread through from the wrong side of the fabric. Couch over the bead thread between every three or four beads if they are very small, and between every bead if they are large as shown in the diagram.

Method 2 This method holds the beads down more securely than Method 1 so that they are less inclined to catch or snag. For this method, two needles and thread are prepared. Needle 1 picks up two or three beads and then a small stitch is made in the background fabric to hold them down. Needle 2 follows, making a small stitch over the thread between each bead.

Bead pendants and loops

Secure the thread in the folded edge of fabric. Pick up the beads. Take the needle back through the last bead but one and then through all the beads back to the fabric. Fasten off thread securely.

To make bead loops, fasten the thread in the fabric, pick up the beads to the desired length for a loop. Then take another stitch through the fabric edge a short distance away from the first so that the loop hangs nicely.

Sequins

Single sequins are applied by bringing the thread through from the wrong side of the fabric, up through the sequin hole, over its edge and into the fabric making a small back stitch. Thus a thread lies over the surface of the sequin. A row of sequins can be stitched on in this way.

Invisible stitching

Bring the thread up through the fabric, slip the sequin onto the thread and then pick up a small bead. Pass the thread back through the sequin and fasten off the thread on the wrong side.

Fish scale sequins

Bring the needle up through the fabric and then through the hole in the sequin. Place the sequin in position on the fabric and take a tiny stitch to the left of it in the fabric. Pull the needle through and pick up the next sequin and stitch down in the same way.

Bead and sequin tray

Beads are generally sold in small plastic boxes and are easy to pick up on the needle point.

Sometimes they are sold in skeins, threaded onto soft cotton thread. The thread is not very strong and you should transfer the beads to a box as quickly as possible.

When you are working a design with a number of beads of different colours and sizes, you will find working easier with a bead tray. Line a shallow box – a shoe box lid will do – with velvet or felt. Arrange your beads and sequins in piles according to colour, shape and size. You will find that they are less inclined to jump about as the needle touches them and fewer will be lost.

Crewel work

Crewel work, or Jacobean embroidery was popular in 17th-century Britain.

The designs are worked on cream-coloured linen and cotton mix fabric and are based on Indian and Chinese patterns. The main motifs of these embroideries, which were originally used for bed curtains and wall hangings, are the Tree of Life, composed of strange leaves and flowers sprouting from a curving trunk; curved hillocks, similar to the waves in Chinese designs, are used under the Tree. Interspersed with the Tree are various Tudor and Elizabethan images, animals, birds and plant forms.

Jacobean embroidery lasted from the reign of King James I (1603-25) to that of Queen Anne (1702-14), so there are many differences to be seen between the work of the earlier and later periods. Much of the earlier works were limited in the use of colour, the two main schemes being either greys, blues and silvery greens or reds shading to pinks.

Strong outlines with a great deal of decorative filling was a feature of the early Elizabethan works. Later, after the Restoration in 1660, crewel work designs became more exuberant with large fantastic trees worked boldly and in bright and varied colour schemes. Decorative fillings more or less disappeared and the work on the whole seems to lack in good taste. Modern crewel embroidery still uses the Tree of Life motif, with flowers, leaves, animals, birds and insects. Some designers are trying to work in more abstract forms but the old designs are still the most popular for home furnishings.

Material

The background fabric should be a cream coloured twill or firmly woven linen. Crewel wools, which are fine and twisted, are best. Tapisserie wools can also be used, but knitting wool is generally too soft for this type of work.

Schemes are best if kept to a limited range of colours. Reds and blues with a little grey or black, or perhaps a scheme of blues, greens and yellows.

Traditionally, only a few stitches are used in crewel work. These can all be found elsewhere in this chapter.

These are:

Buttonhole stitch Used for outlines and solid fillings.

Chain stitch For outlines and solid fillings.

Coral knot For outlines and veining.

Couching For open and solid fillings.

Double back stitch For veins and stems.

Filling stitches Darning, star stitch, satin stitch, cross stitch, French knots, Cretan stitch, fly stitch.

Long and short stitch For shading, for thick branches and leaves.

Stem stitch For outlines, veins and leaves.

Look at the crewel examples illustrated and see how the various stitches have been used for decorative effect.

On the next page is a traditional Jacobean pattern for you to work.

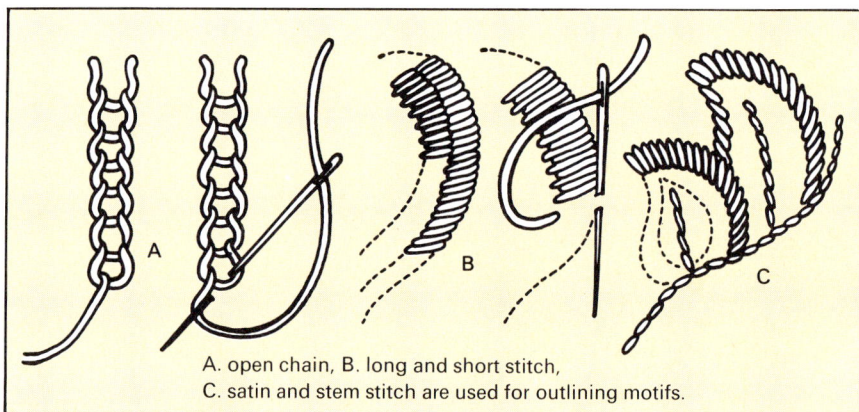

A. open chain, B. long and short stitch, C. satin and stem stitch are used for outlining motifs.

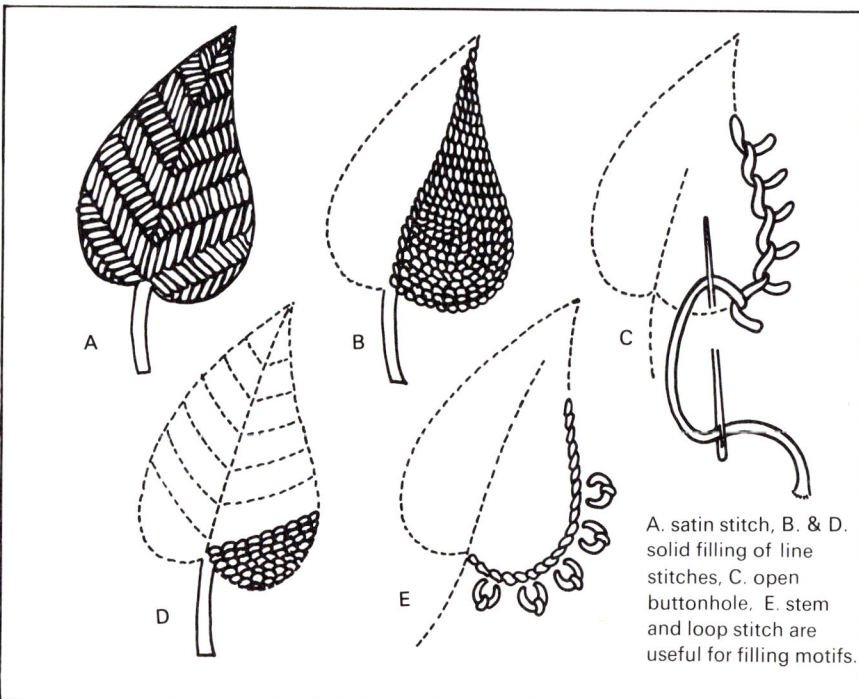

A. satin stitch, B. & D. solid filling of line stitches, C. open buttonhole, E. stem and loop stitch are useful for filling motifs.

Right These are examples of the smaller motifs typical of Jacobean work. Such designs usually 'grow' from larger ones: the branch and bird breaking up the background and the leopard resting on hill shapes at the base of a design.

Below Flowering trees and rampant wild life add vitality to the strong Jacobean pattern. Frequently the colours of wool used ranged from golden yellows at the top of the design to deep shadowy blues and greens at the base, thus adding a touch of reality to a fanciful scene. In this border pattern each area can be allocated a different stitch treatment. Knot and chain stitches, buttonhole fillings, satin stitch and cross stitch can be used in combination to create fabulous textures and shadings.

Canvaswork

Canvaswork, or needlepoint as it is sometimes called, is embroidery in wool on a canvas ground. Tapestry is a quite different technique. Tapestry is a woven fabric and sometimes this term is used, incorrectly, for canvaswork.

A wide variety of stitches can be used in this absorbing needlecraft but sadly, many needlewomen use only tent stitch, and thus never experience the richness of the other stitches.

Although canvaswork patterns can be purchased from any good needlework shop (the design marked out on the canvas and, sometimes, the colours to be used indicated for the needlewoman), there is a greater satisfaction in developing a repetoire of stitches and then designing your own canvaswork. Cross, tent, Holbein and back stitches are the most popular for this technique.

Materials, tools and equipment

Canvas
Basically, there are two kinds of canvas: single thread canvas, sometimes called Mono, and double thread canvas known as Penelope canvas. These canvasses are available in a wide range of meshes. Mesh is the term which describes the number of threads to 2.5 cm (1 in). Canvas varies from fine mesh with 32 threads to 2.5 cm (1 in), to the coarse canvas used for rug making which has only four threads to 2.5 cm (1 in). Examples of the various canvas meshes in both single canvas and double canvas are illustrated on page 000.

Canvas is supplied in various widths, from 30 cm (12 in) wide to 150 cm (60 in) wide. When you buy canvas for a project, you should always state both the length you require and the width so that you do not waste on the width.

Choosing canvas
If you are following a prepared pattern, the correct mesh will be stated. If you are designing the pattern yourself, the project or the type of design you are planning will determine the canvas mesh.

If your design is fairly bold without too much detail, you can safely choose a mesh of 12 or 14 threads to 2.5 cm (1 in). A more finely detailed design would need a mesh of 16 or 18 threads to the 2.5 cm (1 in). As a general guide, 14 or 16 mesh is suitable for making chair seats or cushions where there is going to be some wear. For large wall pictures, 12 mesh would be better.

If you are making a pincushion or a box top, or a small accessory such as a bag, you should choose a canvas with 20 threads to 2.5 cm (1 in), or even finer if the detail is intricate.

Florentine embroidery is easier to work on double thread canvas; but as a general rule you will find single thread canvas better to work on for most stitches.

Yarns and threads
The most popular yarn for canvaswork is wool. It is easy to use, covers the canvas threads well and is durable if the canvaswork is to be used for furnishings. For items which are not going to receive hard wear, such as pictures, wall hangings and some home accessories, other types of wool yarn can be used. Knitting wool, crêpe or bouclé wool, metallic threads, raffia, silk, embroidery threads and string can all be used in canvaswork, providing a large range of interesting colours and textures.

Needles
Canvaswork needles are short, large-eyed and blunt. They are called tapestry needles and come in a range of sizes from 13 to 26, 13 being the largest size. Have a range of needles available so that you can use all kinds of threads and yarns.

Thus, you are sure of always having a needle through which your thread will pass easily.

Frames
Canvaswork is generally done in a slate frame but small pieces can be worked in the hand. If canvaswork is worked without a frame, there is always the danger that the canvas will be pulled out of shape during working, and it may not be easy to stretch the piece back into shape afterwards.

'Moses in the Rushes' is the title of this 17th-century needlepoint picture. Religious and allegorical stories were frequently the subjects for such pictures worked, as this one is, in a rich multitude of coloured wools using a very fine tent stitch.

Canvaswork is still popular today for its picture-making potential and needlewomen can make use of the many stitches and materials available to explore the colour and texture of simple subjects such as a tree branch or single delicate leaf.

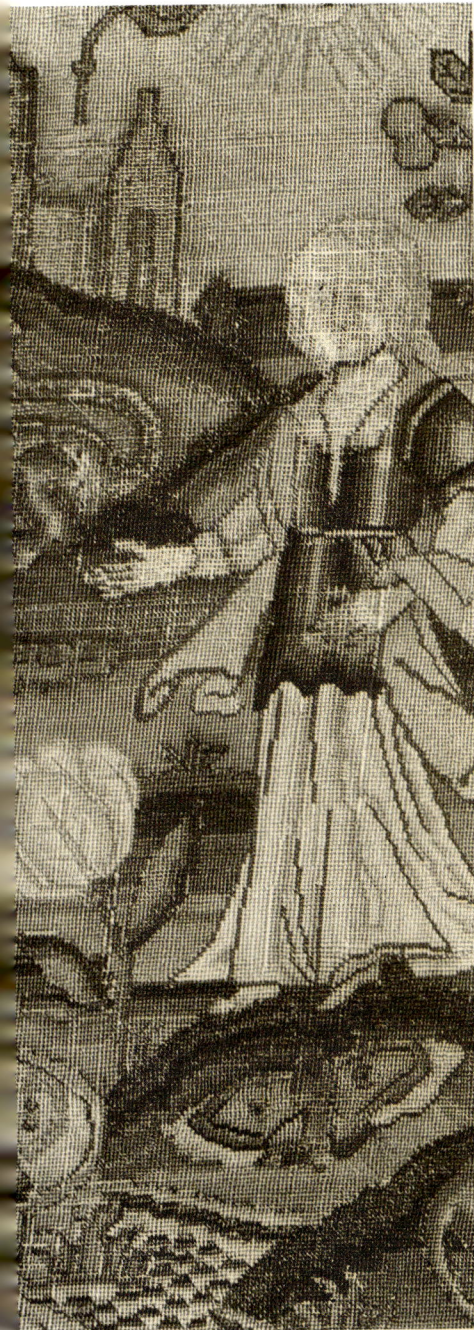

Transferring designs to canvas

Work out your design on paper. Then fold the paper in half across the length and then across the width, to find the exact centre. Go over the lines in black felt-tipped pen so that they can be clearly seen through the mesh of the canvas. Pin the design to a drawing board. Measure and mark the centre of the canvas with cotton thread and pin the canvas over the design so that the vertical and horizontal lines match the folds of the paper. Trace the design onto the canvas using black watercolour paint and a fine brush. Keep the lines light and fine – you do not need to apply very much paint to your canvas. You can use felt-tipped pen if you prefer, but use it very lightly because there is always the danger that the colour will rub off onto light-coloured wools.

Method of working

Cut a piece of yarn about 60 cm (24 in) long. If you use anything longer than this, the yarn will wear thin as it passes back and forth through the canvas. Get into the habit of pulling a piece of yarn between finger and thumb before starting to work. It removes any fluff which can clog the holes of the canvas and also wear the yarn out quicker.

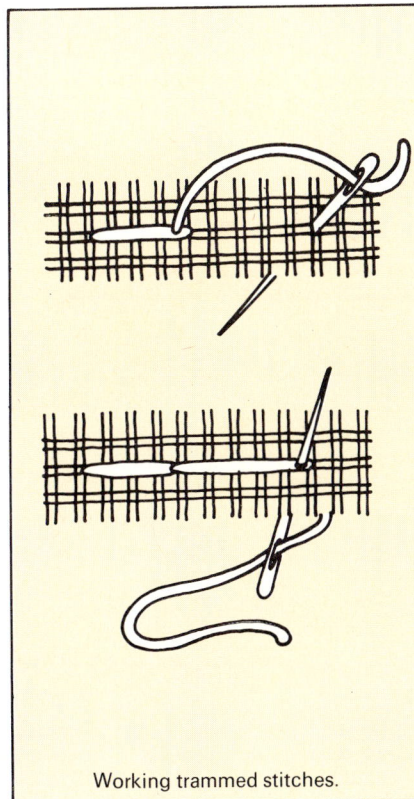

Make a knot on the end of the yarn. Take the needle down through the canvas a short distance into the pattern from where you are going to start, leaving the knot on the surface. Start embroidery and then, when that length of yarn is finished, bring the end up onto the top of the canvas, a few holes away from the last stitch, and leave it there. The advantage of this method of working is that the short ends are worked over with subsequent stitches, and the wrong side of the canvas stays neat. When the work is complete, you simply snip off the knots and ends on the top.

Work the design areas first and then the background. If you begin on the background, you may go over the edge of the design and lose the true outline.

Trammed stitches

Tramming is used when a rich effect is required on a piece of canvaswork intended for upholstery. Long stitches are worked over the canvas and stitches are then worked over the thread. The technique is particularly suitable for tent stitch on double thread canvas.

Method

Bring the thread through from the back at a point where a pair of vertical threads cross the horizontal threads. Carry the thread across the work for up to 12.5 cm (5 in) and take the thread through to the back of the work. Bring the thread through a vertical thread to the left on the same line, thus making a split stitch. Continue tent stitch across the trammed thread line. When you are making tramming threads, do not always start and end them under previous lines. Vary the lengths so that the lines are staggered.

Working trammed stitches.

Florentine or Bargello embroidery

Florentine is the name given to a style of canvaswork done in straight stitch over four or six threads of canvas. The designs are worked in striking colour schemes, two of the most distinctive being flame and the zigzag pattern. Florentine, or Hungarian embroidery as it is sometimes called, was originally used to upholster cushions and chair seats. Today, the embroidery is used for all kinds of furnishings and personal accessories.

Florentine is quick to do once the base line, or first line of stitches, has been worked across the canvas. The beauty of the work lies in the wool colours chosen; these can be tones of a single colour, from a pale tint up to a striking full colour or a mass of vibrant colours used in one design.

Florentine patterns are usually worked from a graph pattern which gives the base line or pattern sequence only. Once you have learned how to do the basic patterns you will be able to work out your own colour schemes. Shown here are a few of the most popular Florentine patterns – zigzag, ogee, flame – with base line pattern charts for each. The following list provides a guide to canvas and needle sizes.

	Canvas	Needle
Anchor Tapisserie Wool Appleton's Tapestry Wool	Single thread 14 and 16 threads to 2.5 cm (1 in)	18
Appleton's crewel wool and Anchor stranded embroidery floss	Single weave canvas 24 threads to 2.5 cm (1 in)	22

Practising the various patterns and experimenting with colour combinations in Florentine embroidery can produce the most attractive samplers.

As well as pattern and colour, it is advisable to try out different threads.

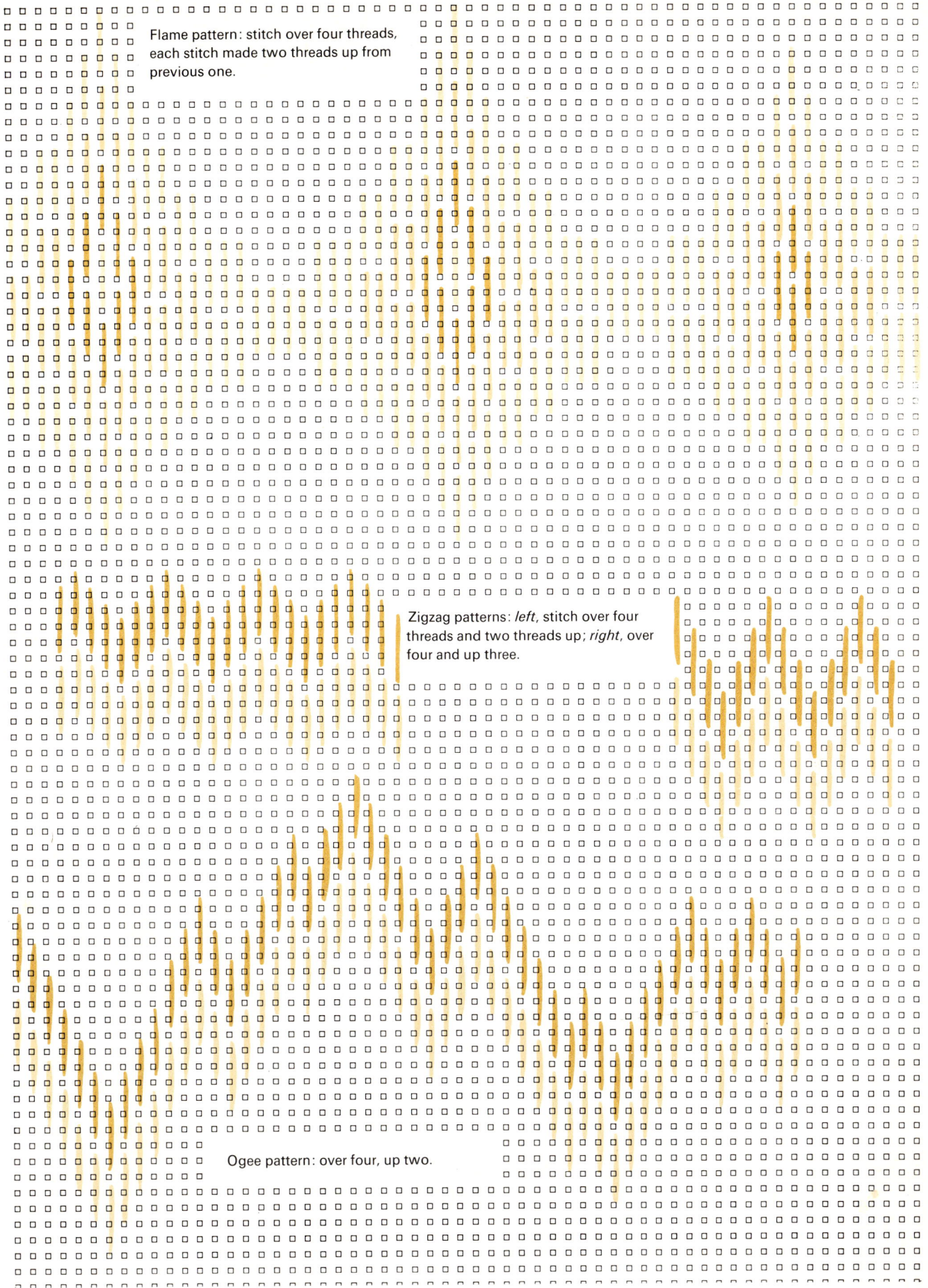

Flame pattern: stitch over four threads, each stitch made two threads up from previous one.

Zigzag patterns: *left*, stitch over four threads and two threads up; *right*, over four and up three.

Ogee pattern: over four, up two.

Quilting

Throughout the ages, quilting has been used to make warm, protective clothing: the soldiers of ancient Rome wore quilted garments under their armour. By the 16th century household items, such as cushion and bed covers were being quilted.

The craft travelled to the new world with the Pilgrims, and a new needlework art form developed in America, combining quilting techniques with piecing and patchwork.

In Britain, quilting almost died out as a needlecraft and survived in only one or two places, namely Wales and the North of England, where women still quilted warm petticoats and jackets and made bed covers in the old designs.

In recent years, with the revived interest in patchwork, quilting has become popular again, but the difficulty of obtaining full-sized quilting frames has brought about machine quilting.

Hand quilting is still the best technique and produces the finest results, and for small pieces of work, it will continue to be the method used.

Designs

The purpose of quilting stitches is to hold the layers of fabric together. The design can be as simple as straight, parallel lines or lines intersecting diagonally across the piece. However, needlewomen have evolved a number of shapes and patterns which have become essentially quilting designs, based on natural forms. These include feathers, shells, ferns, waves, flowers and leaves. There is a selection on page 235 for you to enlarge and use.

Fabrics and threads

Most fabrics can be quilted as long as they are soft and not transparent. Quilts are usually made of cotton and cotton mixtures so that they wear well and can be laundered. Silks and satin fabrics quilt beautifully and these are sometimes used for making quilted garments.

Quilting consists of three layers of fabric stitched together. The top fabric is the outer, then comes the wadding in the middle, and then the backing fabric. For a bed quilt, the backing fabric should be rough textured to stop the quilt slipping off the bed.

Originally, carded sheep's wool was used for the middle layer and then, later, cotton wool became popular. Cotton wool is really not very suitable because it absorbs moisture and thus is never quite dry. Muslin-backed synthetic wadding, available by the metre, is ideal for quilting. Domette, a wool and cotton mixture fabric, is suitable for quilted garments.

Stitches

Three stitches can be used in quilting: running stitch, back stitch and chain stitch. Running stitch is the one traditionally used. When a piece of quilting is being worked in a frame, one hand is above the work and the other below so that the stitch is worked as a kind of prick stitch – the top hand passing the needle through the fabric to the hand underneath and back again.

Preparing the fabric

Whether you are preparing the fabric for quilting in the hand or for putting onto a frame, the procedure is the same.

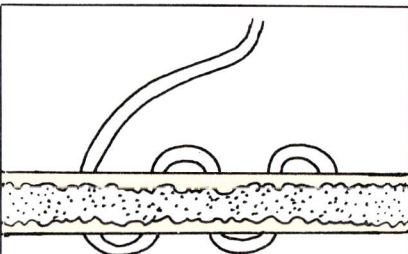

Use an even running stitch when quilting fabric by hand.

Spread the backing fabric smooth, wrong side up. Lay the wadding on top. If you are using several widths of wadding, butt the edges. Lay the top fabric over the wadding, right side up, and smooth it out from the centre. Thread a needle with a long length of tacking thread and tack the three layers together, working from the centre towards the edges and then diagonally across the quilt.

Transferring designs

The design is marked on the top fabric. Designs can be drawn free hand or traced onto the top fabric

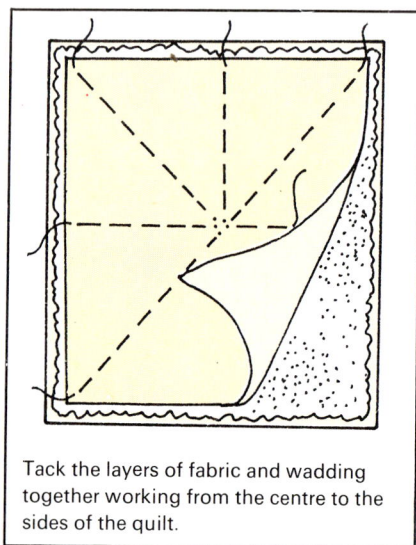

Tack the layers of fabric and wadding together working from the centre to the sides of the quilt.

with dressmaker's carbon paper; there is a risk that the chalk lines may not brush off after the stitching is finished. The best way to mark out designs is the traditional method of marking with a needle.

Draw and then cut out templates from thin cardboard. (For circles you could use wine glasses, cups, plates or lids for templates.) Push a thick darning needle into a cork. Hold the tip at an angle and holding the template firmly with one hand, mark around it with the needle. A resulting outline of dots will be clearly seen, and it will remain in the fabric.

Quilting can be used in many ways, and these simple items can be easily made from squares of fabric. If you choose a gingham, use the printed design to guide the lines of quilting stitches.

Hand quilting

Set the quilting in a frame. Thread several needles, one for each line of the design. You will find that you will keep the tension even if you work a few inches along a line, then move to another. Start off with a knot on the end of the thread and gently pull the knot through the fabric until it is inside the wadding.

Work running stitches with one hand above the quilt and the other below.

Far left One corner of hand-stitched cotton quilt shows a typical quilted border pattern. Notice also the simple background filling of crossed diagonal lines forming a diamond pattern.

Below are some traditional patterns for hand-stitched quilts. They can be used in combination to form borders, or singly as corner motifs or centrepieces.

Leaf

Rose

Shell

Rose

Cowslip leaf

Feather crown

Straight feather

Straight feather border

Machine quilting

The work is prepared in the same way as for hand quilting, the three layers being tacked both vertically and horizontally. Fit the sewing machine with a quilting foot – this has a short front and moves over the thick layers easily – and gauge. The gauge is a stitching guide and helps you to keep a uniform distance between rows of stitching.

Choose the thread to match the top fabric and the needle size for the thread and fabric. (Check with the chart on page 98).

Set the stitch size for medium to large. Roll the quilting up and fit it under the machine arm. Stitch along the first design line and leave the thread ends loose. Turn the quilt the other way round to stitch the second design line. Stitch alternate design lines in this way because it helps to prevent drag on the seams.

If you are working individual motifs, you do not have to change the direction of stitching. If the thread runs out in the middle of a seam, finish the thread ends by hand using small back stitches. Do not run the machine backwards and forwards because this would spoil the look of the seam.

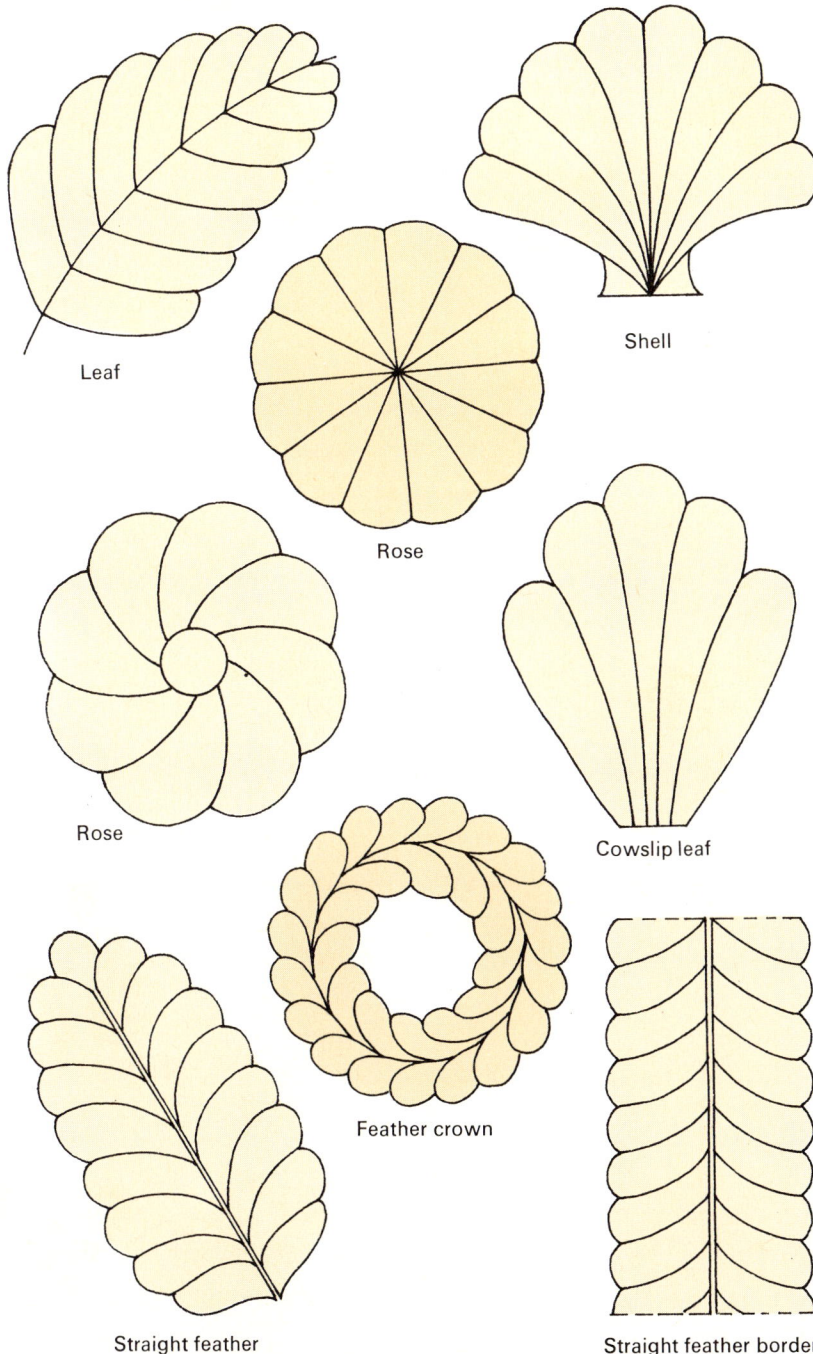

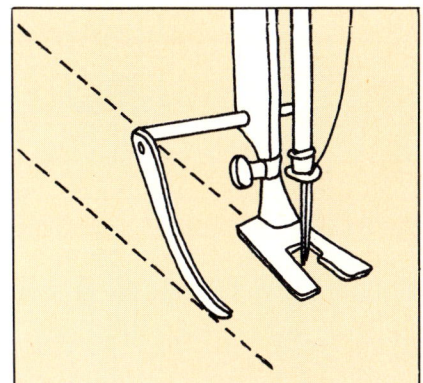

Many machines have a quilting guide which can be fitted to the presser foot so that lines of stitching can be kept even as you sew the layers together.

Finishing quilt edges

There are three different ways of finishing the edges of a quilt.

Traditional method

Work quilting to within 2.5 cm (1 in) of the quilt edges. Pull out the wadding up to the end of the stitching. Finish threads off with back stitching. Fold in the edges of the top and backing fabric. Trim some of the fabric off at the corners diagonally to reduce bulk. Pin, then tack all around. Work 2 rows of machine stitching close to the quilt edge. (If you prefer hand stitching, use small running stitches.)

Bound edge finish

Finish thread ends of quilting by hand using small back stitches. Cut strips of fabric to twice the width of binding required plus 2.5 cm (1 in) for turnings. The fabric can be the backing fabric if it is good quality or it can contrast with the top fabric. Stitch the binding to the top of the quilt and make either neat mitred corners or overlap the ends. (Mitring corners on hem edges, page 169.) Turn the binding to the wrong side of the quilt and hand sew to finish.

Self binding method

This method looks particularly attractive if the backing fabric is of a good quality and has been chosen to complement the top fabric. Cut the backing fabric 5 cm to 7.5 cm (2 in to 3 in) wider than the top fabric all around. When quilting is completed, finish off thread ends then fold the backing fabric over to the top side. Turn in edges, mitre the corners neatly then machine stitch or hand sew.

Pieced quilts

If a bedcover has been made up of appliquéd squares or patchworked squares, you might prefer to quilt each square by hand, joining up the quilted squares afterwards.

To do this, separate the top fabric from the wadding for about

Top Protect yourself from chilly breezes by making a quilted jacket.
Above A similar quilt could be made by over-stuffing a hand-stitched quilt.
Right Make a pretty quilted floor rug by sewing strips of fabric together to make the top piece. For the bottom piece use a heavy, close weave like canvas. Sandwich a layer of wadding between it and the top piece and tack the layers together. Stitch the lines of quilting along the strip seams and finish by binding the edges with a contrasting fabric.

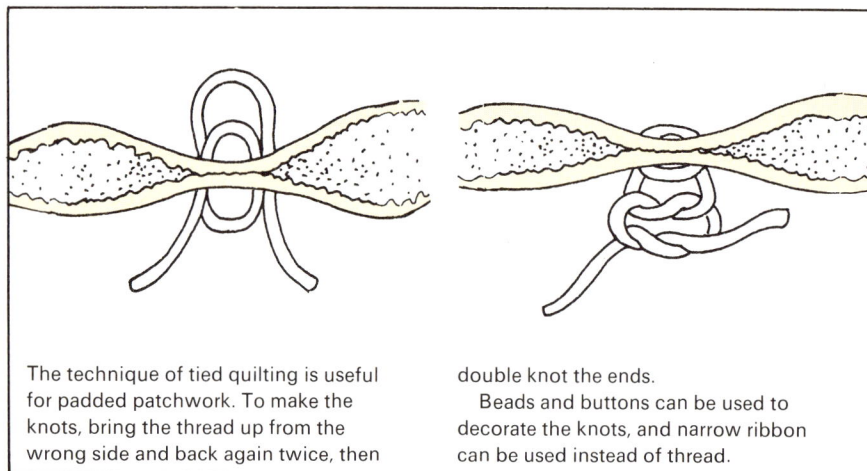

The technique of tied quilting is useful for padded patchwork. To make the knots, bring the thread up from the wrong side and back again twice, then double knot the ends.

Beads and buttons can be used to decorate the knots, and narrow ribbon can be used instead of thread.

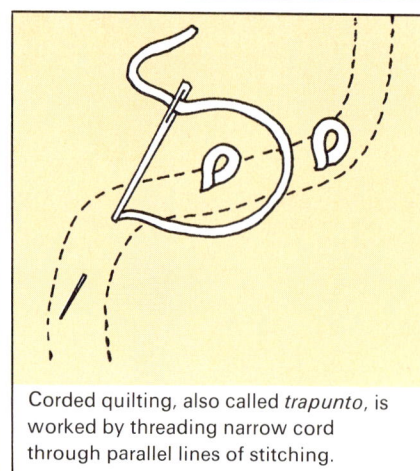

Corded quilting, also called *trapunto*, is worked by threading narrow cord through parallel lines of stitching.

1.2 cm ($\frac{1}{2}$ in). Lay the two squares together, right sides of fabric facing, and machine stitch (or hand sew with back stitches).

Lay the squares right side down. Trim the wadding from one square. Turn a narrow hem on one side of the backing and overlap the other side. Stitch with small slip stitches. Join all the quilted squares in the same way. You will find it easier if you join squares to make long strips, then join the strips.

Alternative method After quilting the individual squares, join them together with strips of contrasting fabric, working first on the top side of the quilt, then on the backing.

Other quilting techniques

Tied quilting

This technique is sometimes used on patchwork quilts where a domette interlining has been used. The ties can be made of thread and be simply functional or a small bead or button can be slipped on the end just before the second knot.

For a pretty feminine effect use a very narrow satin-finished ribbon in a large-eyed needle tying tiny bows on the top side of the quilt.

Method for tying

Prepare the quilting in a frame. Mark where the ties are to be made with crossed pins or chalk marks.

Thread a needle with pearl cotton. Bring the needle up through the quilting to the top side, holding about 8 cm (3 in) of thread below. Push the needle back through the quilt, then up to the top side and down again to the wrong side. Cut the thread. Pull the two threads gently to make a hollow on the top side of the quilting and tie a knot. Tighten and then tie a second knot. Trim off ends.

To decorate the tie with a bead or button, slip the bead on the needle just before it is passed down through the quilting on the second stitch.

For a decorative bow in thread or ribbon, start the tie from the top side of the quilt so that both ends are on top at the end of the stitch.

Stuffed quilting

Stuffed quilting, where only certain areas of a design are quilted is sometimes used in conjunction with flat quilting. Flat quilting consists of only two layers of fabric stitched together decoratively.

To work stuffed quilting, mount the top fabric on muslin or a similar loosely woven fabric. Mark out and stitch the design.

Lay the work right side down and slit open the muslin backing where stuffing is to be inserted. (For small areas you may be able to push threads apart without cutting.) Tease wadding out and push small pieces into the hole. Close the cut slit with oversewing.

Stuffed quilting is backed with fabric after all the quilting has been completed.

Corded quilting

Prepare the top fabric and muslin backing in a frame. Work parallel rows of stitching on the design lines. Turn work over. Thread a rug needle with cotton cord or thick knitting wool. Push the needle through the muslin backing and along the stitched channels. Bring the needle out at intervals and pull the cord through. Re-insert the needle at the same place. On curves, leave a small loop of cord hanging so that the curve is worked smoothly. Cut the cord off to make sharp corners or intersections in the design and then start again.

Quilting on patterned fabrics

This is a pretty and simple way to get a quilted effect and can be used to make all kinds of small accessories as well as cushions and bedcovers.

Choose a fabric with a fairly simple pattern. Prepare for quilting with wadding and backing. (If the fabric is thin, an interlining of a thicker fabric such as a non-shrink wool mixture may be sufficient padding.) Machine stitch or hand stitch on the lines of the fabric pattern, using a matching thread or a contrast thread if you prefer. Running stitch, back stitch or chain stitch can be used for hand working.

Appliqué

Appliqué is the technique of sewing a motif cut from one piece of fabric to another fabric. This needlecraft has a wide range of uses from decorating clothing and accessories to making pictures. There are several methods to choose from, some worked by hand and others by machine, depending on the effect you want to achieve.

Fabrics and threads

The use of the item being decorated, and the method of appliqué chosen determines the fabric. Clothing or household items which will receive frequent laundering should be decorated with appliqué designs cut from washable fabrics and applied using a hard-wearing technique. Things which will be dry cleaned or not need frequent cleaning can be decorated with a wider choice of fabrics – velvets, brocades, silks and so on – and be decorated with rich surface embroidery as well.

Pictures, panels and banners which will receive very little wear can be worked with fabrics which are beautiful but inclined to fray and need certain finishing techniques.

Read through the various appliqué methods and then decide which method best suits the purpose.

General hints about appliqué

Wherever possible, use fabrics of similar weight for ground fabric and appliqué, otherwise one may pull away from the other. If necessary, mount lightweight fabrics on iron-on interfacing before using them.

Cut appliqué shapes on the true grain of the fabric and match the grain to that of the background fabric. The only instance where you do not have to follow this rule is when making appliqué pictures.

Appliqué pictures can also have a mixture of different fabric weights in them, as well as two or three different techniques.

Old fabrics can be used with new but if the item is going to receive hard wear, check that the old fabric has not perished, that it is colourfast and that it will not shrink in laundering – or your delicate work may be spoiled.

Blind or hemmed appliqué

This method is worked by hand and wears well. It is therefore suitable for clothing and household linens. Lightweight, closely woven fabrics are ideal.

Having chosen your design, transfer it to the right side of the ground fabric on the straight grain.

Make a template by transferring the design onto stiff paper or the wrong or smooth side of fine sandpaper – some needlewomen find the 'cling' of sandpaper helps them to cut motifs more accurately. Cut out each area of the design. Keep the original design tracing as a working guide.

Pin each template to the fabric making sure that there is at least 12 mm ($\frac{1}{2}$ in) space between shapes. Templates should be set on the straight grain of the fabric. Cut out the shapes with 6 mm ($\frac{1}{4}$ in) for turnings all around. Snip into the turnings on curves so that the turnings can be folded under smoothly.

Applying shapes

If shapes are going to overlap, apply the lower ones first. Lay the shape, right side up, on the right side of the background fabric and secure with tailor's tacking stitches (see page 32) first down the middle of the shape, then around the edges. Make sure the fabric is lying quite smooth. Thread a fine sewing needle with matching thread. With the needle point and fingers, fold under the turning. Hem neatly making the smallest stitches possible all around the shape. Do not press the completed appliqué.

If you like, work a single row of tiny running stitches around the finished appliqué to raise the motif from the background fabric.

Alternative stitch

Appliqué lends itself to extra decoration with a variety of embroidery stitches. If you are planning to embroider the edges of the shapes, slip stitch can be used instead of hemming.

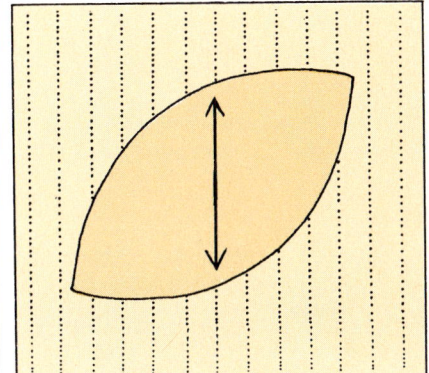

Cut appliqué shapes on the straight grain of the fabric.

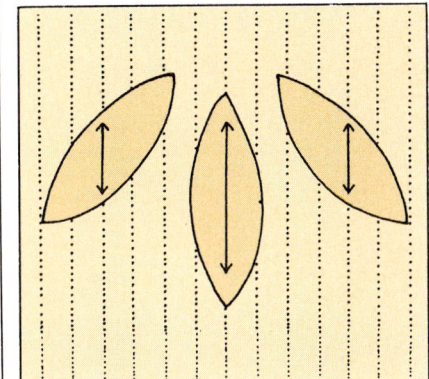

Position shapes on the background fabric matching the straight grain.

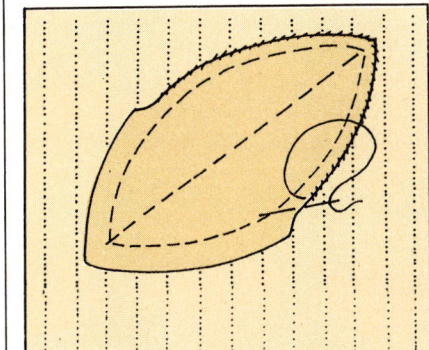

Tack the shapes in place and then hem stitch them to the background, turning under the edges as you sew.

Decorative needlework

Overleaf The techniques of patchwork and appliqué were combined to make the Flower garden pieced quilt.

The attractive appliqué headboard repeats the design of the wall mural behind it.

The pretty tablecloth has an appliquéd border and central motif. Fruit shapes have been cut out in plain coloured cottons and details are embroidered onto them in stranded cotton.

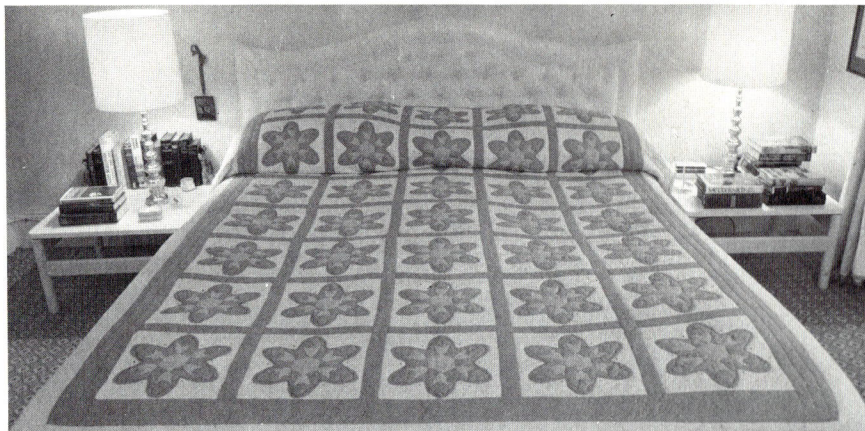

Machined appliqué

This is a strong, hardwearing method and if it is being used for children's clothes or household items, make sure that fabrics are similar in weight and washable.

Draw or transfer the design onto the background fabric. Draw or transfer the design areas separately onto the appliqué fabrics, making sure that there is at least 12 mm ($\frac{1}{2}$ in) between shapes. Machine stitch just outside the marked line. Cut out the shapes, 3 mm ($\frac{1}{8}$ in) away from the stitched line. Fix the shapes to the background fabric using tailor's tacking (page oo). Set the sewing machine for a narrow satin stitch, with a contrasting thread. Stitch around all the shapes, working over the raw edges. Afterwards, add hand or machine embroidery to your design.

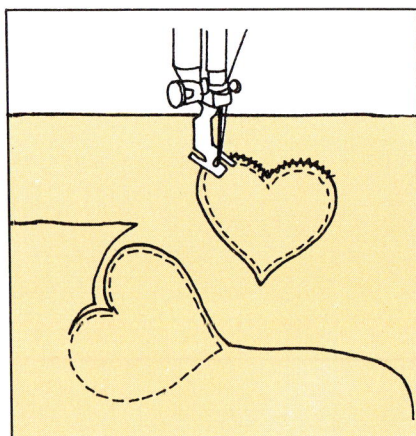

To machine appliqué, stitch around the outline of the shape and cut it out. Tack the shape to the background fabric and then zigzag stitch around the edges.

Persé appliqué

This is a technique that works well in making co-ordinated home furnishings. You can select a motif from a furnishing fabric and appliqué it to a plain fabric to make, for instance, a cushion cover.

Persé appliqué is suitable for a wide range of items from clothing to furnishings, and can also be used to make appliqué flower pictures, choosing flowers and leaves from floral fabrics.

Always wash and iron the appliqué fabric before cutting out a motif to avoid shrinking, and fabrics which are not colourfast.

Cut the motif from the fabric and tack it right side up on the ground fabric. Firm tacking is important, particularly around the edges. Work machine satin stitch over the cut edges using a thread that closely matches the background. Add surface embroidery to enhance or add to the design.

Decoupé appliqué

This technique is particularly suitable for making banners or simple pictures. Transfer the design to the right side of the top fabric. Tack a piece of the contrasting fabric to the wrong side of the ground fabric, right behind the marked area.

Work a line of machine stitching on the marked design line. Then, with sharp scissors, cut the top fabric away, just outside the stitched line.

Appliqué techniques are here combined with patchwork to make a beautiful quilt.

Cover the cut edge with machine-worked satin stitch. Trim away the excess fabric on the wrong side of the work.

Appliqué pictures

Embroidery pictures usually combine appliqué techniques with collage. After planning the

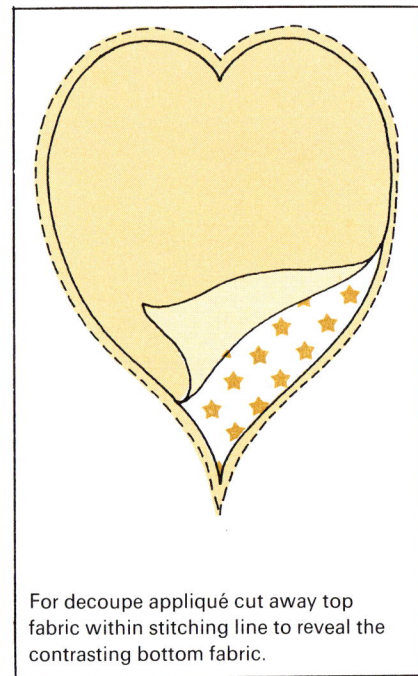

For decoupe appliqué cut away top fabric within stitching line to reveal the contrasting bottom fabric.

background fabric, which is usually mounted onto a board, individual design areas are made up in appliqué and embroidery and then attached to the background by sewing or by gluing. Additional decorative items are either stitched or glued to the picture.

Patchwork

Anyone who can sew even the simplest of stitches has the ability for patchwork, one of the most absorbing and satisfying of needlecrafts. It is entirely portable so that you can carry it with you, and has the added advantage that it can be a re-cyling craft using up cast-off clothes or fabric scraps. There are two basic techniques in patchwork: English patchwork which is worked over a paper template and American patchwork or piecing which is hand or machine stitched without a backing paper and is most used for quilt making. Both techniques are based on geometric shapes, although piecing can sometimes include appliqué techniques.

Origins of patchwork

Patchwork, or the sewing together of fabric shapes, goes back thousands of years to the ancient Egyptians. In the past 400 years, patchwork has become a needlecraft of economy: when the Puritans left Britain for the new world, the women took the craft with them. Life was hard for the pioneer women and sewing materials were difficult to come by. As clothing and furnishings wore out, these thrifty women carefully cut away the good fabric and re-used it to make warm clothes and bedcovers. Their lives were hard and with little beauty or culture, and so their creativity found expression in the patchwork patterns they developed. Some of these patterns have been passed down over the years and are the familiar patchwork designs – Grandmother's Garden, made up of hexagons, Baby Blocks, Star of Bethlehem, and Star and Hexagons are just a few of the romantic and evocative names of traditional patterns.

Star and Hexagon pattern

Baby Blocks

Star of Bethlehem

Patchwork shapes

The shapes used in patchwork are the square, triangle, diamond, pentagon, hexagon, octagon, church window, bar, and lastly the clamshell which is not a geometric shape. From these eight shapes a wide variety of patterns can be built up. On page ooo there are just a few of the wonderful patterns you can try. You will see that, apart from the clamshell, most shapes need other shapes to make up a flat design. Only the square, triangle, rectangle, parallelogram, diamond and hexagon can all be used alone. The pentagon, octagon, church window, coffin, rhomboid and bar need other shapes.

'Baby Blocks' is made of diamond shapes. Depending upon how the coloured patches are arranged, three-dimensional or striped effects can be achieved.

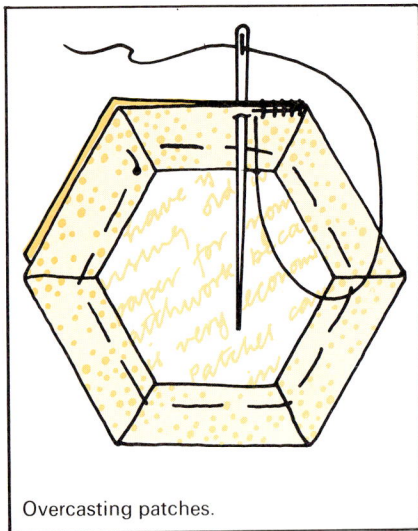

Overcasting patches.

Patchwork templates

Needlewomen used to have patchwork templates cut for them in wood and metal. Nowadays, most needlework counters sell patchwork templates in a range of sizes, made of plastic or metal. A patchwork template set contains two pieces. One is solid and is used for cutting backing papers. The other is a 'window' and is used for cutting out fabric. The window effect makes it possible for you to choose a particular motif of a patterned fabric.

Fabrics and threads

Although patchwork is essentially a way of re-using fabrics, you should always make sure that the fabric has not perished in any way and that it is colourfast and shrinkproof. Wash and iron all fabrics before using them and pull them firmly between the fingers to check for wear and weak spots.

If the finished item is going to be washed, fabrics must be washable and fairly new. Do not mix fabrics of different weights unless the patchwork is for decorative use. If you are using cottons with fine lawns, mount the lighter fabric on iron-on interfacing before using it.

Man-made fibre fabrics are ideal for washable patchwork but they do not fold easily and beginners should avoid using them.

Silks and satins look superb in

Top Make something special of a simple cushion by adding a colourful patchwork motif to the cover.
Above These shorts were made from coloured squares machined together in a random pattern.
Left Hexagons are the easiest patches for beginners to work with, and with careful colour planning it is easy to make a stunning quilt like this.

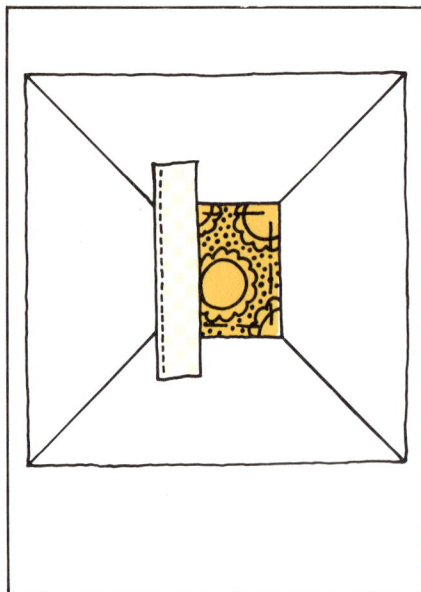

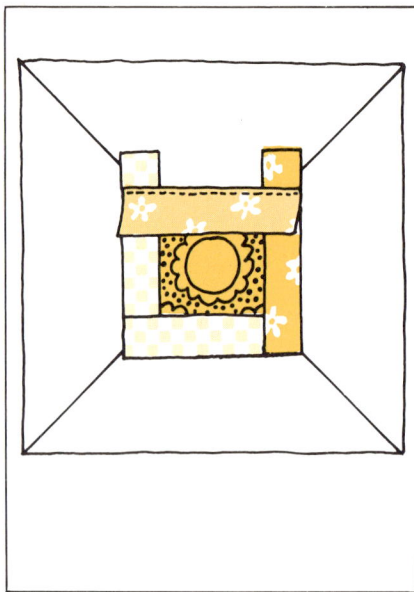

Top left The first step of a Log Cabin block is sewn to the left of the central square.

Left The second strip is sewn over the bottom of the first.

Below left The third strip is sewn over the end of the second, and to the right of the central square.

Above Stitching on the fourth strip.

Below The first row of 'logs' sewn around the 'fire'. Subsequent rows are sewn in the same sequence, each set of strips longer than the preceding one.

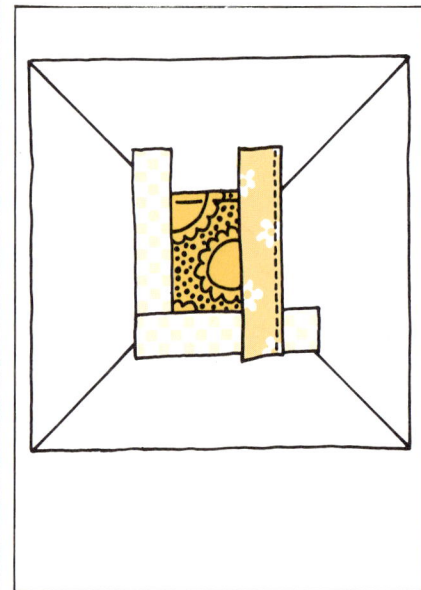

patchwork but they need careful handling and it is advisable to leave these until you have gained some experience.

Fabrics which are firmly woven and do not fray easily are best for patchwork, and fine cotton is ideal. Some types of patchwork, Log Cabin and Crazy Patchwork for example, can use mixed fabrics as long as the finished item is not going to be hard-worn or frequently laundered.

Use all-purpose thread or pure silk thread and a short fine needle for both English and American patchwork.

English patchwork

Basic technique
The smaller template is used to cut out a paper shape. The larger template is used to cut out the fabric. The fabric is mounted on the paper shape and then shapes are stitched together with oversewing.

Backing papers
Postcards, greetings cards or stiff notepaper are all suitable for backing papers. Hold the smaller template down on the paper and draw around it with a sharp pencil. Cut out very carefully with scissors. Careful cutting is important because it is the paper shape which decides the accuracy of your patchwork.

Cut several papers. You will re-use them, but it is advisable to have a good supply.

Cutting fabrics
Hold the larger template down on the straight grain of the fabric and draw around it with chalk or a soft lead pencil. Mark out several patches. Cut them out carefully. Use the 'window' template to select special areas of pattern.

Mounting patches
Patches are mounted on the papers with tacking stitches. Experienced patchworkers fold the turnings and the paper, pleating the corners and work the tacking stitches through the fabric only so that no holes are

246

made in the paper. Beginners should pin the fabric to the paper patch then fold and pin the turnings. Tack the turnings and remove the pins. Press the mounted patches under a dry cloth.

Stitching patches together

Thread the needle. Hold two mounted patches together, right sides facing and corners exactly matching. Lay the thread end along the edge of the patches. Beginning from the right, work straight oversewing stitches over the thread, joining the two patches. Work stitches through the fabric only and not through the paper backing. Keep stitches even and small. You need not fasten off the thread when you reach the end of the patch side, simply join other patches in, continuing the line of stitches onto the next patch. Finish thread off with a double back stitch.

Positioning a template on patterned fabric patches.

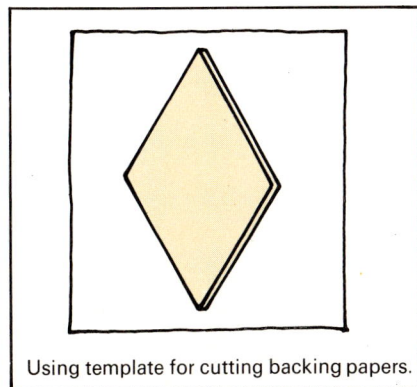

Using template for cutting backing papers.

The paper patches are left in place until all the patchwork is finished.

Dry-press the work on the wrong side. Snip the tacking threads and shake the papers out.

Mounting patchwork

Patchwork should always be mounted, with muslin if it is being used for something like a cushion cover, and with lining fabric if it is being used for a quilt or for a garment. To attach muslin to

An American pieced quilt made from blocks of Drunkard's Path.

patchwork, make tiny holding stitches at intervals to hold the two layers together.

If a patchwork bedcover is not being quilted, stitch ties at intervals between the top fabric and the mounting to prevent the quilt 'ballooning' when it is picked up.

Other patchwork styles

Log Cabin is an American block pattern and is worked without a template and consists of fabric strips sewn around a central square or block onto a fabric base. It can be worked with handsewing but looks neater if it is machine stitched. A variety of plain and patterned fabrics can be used, but they should be distinctly light toned and dark toned. The effect of Log Cabin depends on one side of the square appearing to be in the shadow and the other in firelight.

The squares of finished patchwork can be any size you like depending on the use of the finished item. For a quilt, the squares are usually made about 30 cm (12 in) across. For a cushion or a bag, you might want to make the block square 15 cm (6 in) across. The base fabric should be a firm, new cotton. Do not use old fabric because this could quickly wear out and weaken the finished work.

Start by drawing diagonal lines on the base fabric from corner to corner. Cut a square of light fabric for the centre square and tack it in position. Once this square is tacked, you can draw in the bars or bands for the rest of the patchwork.

Cut strips of fabric to size for band 1, about 2.5 cm (1 in) wide.

Place the first strip, which should be light toned, on the left hand side of the centre square, right sides facing, and raw edges together. Machine stitch (or hand back stitch) about 6 mm ($\frac{1}{4}$ in) from the edge. Open out and press the strip flat.

Apply the second light strip to the bottom edge of the centre square, overlapping the first and stitch in the same way. Continue cutting and applying strips to fit around the square. It is traditional to keep the strips the same width but, if you prefer, you can cut them progressively wider on each band for a different effect. Join blocks of Log Cabin with machine stitching or running stitches, working from the wrong side (see diagrams, p. 246).

Quilting Log Cabin If you are quilting a Log Cabin bedcover, work the quilting along the lines of the bars.

Crazy Patchwork

Crazy patchwork can be used to make quilts, cot covers, cushions and curtains, or cover small home accessories. It can also be used to make dramatic looking clothes. The same rules about fabrics apply to this type of patchwork as apply to English patchwork. If the item is going to be laundered, the patches must be colourfast and the fabrics washable and similar in weight.

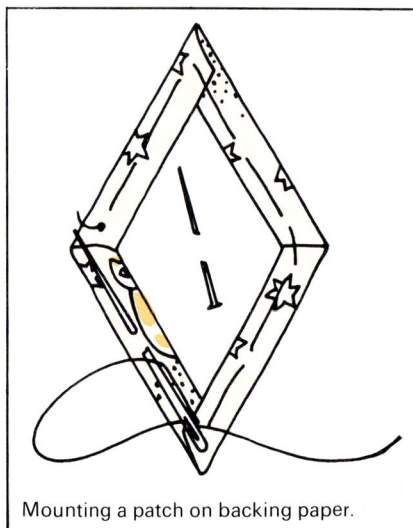

Mounting a patch on backing paper.

For purely decorative pieces, a wide variety of fabrics can be used, mixing cottons, silks, satins and velvets with metallic fabrics and then decorating the seams with embroidery or beading.

The ground fabric should be firm and new.

Method

Mark out the area of the finished item. Iron or press the patchwork fabrics smooth. Cut the first piece to fit the top left corner and with one crazy or random edge. Work running stitches along the top and left straight edges. Cut a second crazy patch to any shape desired, and slip it under the first patch. Pin in place and then work running stitches along the overlapping edges. Prepare the third patch and slip it underneath the second, working running stitches as before. When the patchwork is completed, cover the cut edges of the patches with a variety of embroidery stitches. Chain stitch, herringbone stitch, buttonhole stitch, feather stitch and Cretan stitch are just a few that might be used. Use contrasting colours and textures of threads for a truly crazy effect. If bands of embroidery are worked across some of the plain-colour patches, this heightens the rich effect.

Above This detail from a crazy patchwork
clearly shows how the style lends itself to the
use of rich fabrics and colours which are
framed in embroidery stitches and patterns.
Top left Cathedral window is a more time-
consuming patchwork technique than others,
but the results are striking due to the depth
created by the fabric folds which frame the
coloured squares.
Right By arranging the light sides of Log
Cabin blocks so that they touch, a striped
effect can be created.

Machine crazy patchwork

For large items, you might try machine stitching crazy patchwork. Plan and tack the patches onto the ground fabric. Work zigzag stitching over all the raw edges. This technique is particularly suitable for cotton fabrics and items which will receive a lot of wear. Handwork embroidery stitches to decorate some patches if you like.

Clamshell patchwork

Clamshell is a different kind of patchwork in that it does not make use of a geometric shape and takes more time to master. But it is worth the effort as the finished effect is very beautiful, the patches overlapping each other like fish scales. There is a variety of ways in which clamshell patchwork can be used. Worked in a mixture of plain and patterned fabrics, clamshell makes pretty bed covers, cushion covers etc, or used as an appliqué motif, it can be used as a border for hems or to decorate a variety of home accessories. Clamshell templates are used in the same way as other patchwork templates.

Cut the backing papers from stiff paper. Cut the fabric patches and pin them to the paper templates.

The top edge of the patch is turned onto the template and tacked smoothly to form a perfect curve. Thread a needle and tie a knot in the thread end. Make tiny pleats in the fabric and tack it neatly with tiny stitches to follow the curve of the backing paper. There must not be any points at all – the curve must be perfect.

Press and then unpin the backing paper. Prepare all the patches in the same way.

Assembling the patchwork

The best surface to work on is a piece of cork but a large piece of thick cardboard will do.

Lay the first line of patches in a straight row, right side up. Arrange the side edges so that they just touch. Pin to the work surface.

Lay the second row of patches over the first so that the curved tops just cover the raw edges of the clamshell 'stems'. The centre of the second row of patches should lie exactly on the spaces between the patches of the first row. Tack the second row to the first, around the curved edges. Remove the pins. Sew the clamshells together with tiny hemming stitches worked around the curved edges of the second row and into the first row. Add subsequent rows of clamshells in the same way.

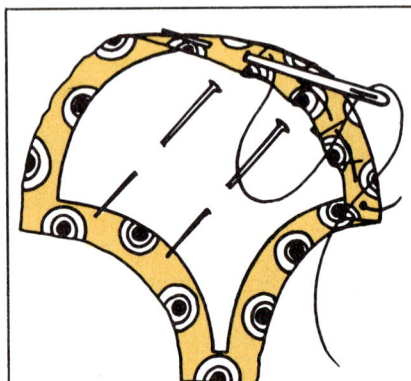

Mounting a clamshell patch.

Turning folded edges over centre patch for Cathedral window.

Cathedral window patchwork

Cathedral window is another modern patchwork style but it has a limited use, as it is best suited to quilts and bed covers. It looks complicated to do, but it is surprisingly easy once you master the basic technique. The fabrics for this patchwork should be soft yet firm. Cotton is ideal for the framing fabric. A bright, contrasting fabric of a different weight can be used for the 'window'.

Method of working

Cut a square of the plain fabric, 15 cm (6 in) across. Press a narrow 3 mm ($\frac{1}{8}$ in) turning to the wrong side on all four sides. Lay the square wrong side up.

Fold the four corners to the centre and pin. Crease the folds with your fingers.

Fold the four corners of the new square to the centre and pin, removing the first pins. Make two squares in the same way.

Sew these squares together along one edge folded sides facing, with tiny oversewing stitches. Lay the joined squares flat.

Cut a piece of contrasting fabric 4.5 cm ($1\frac{3}{4}$ in) square on the straight grain. Pin it over the seam of the two squares. Turn the top right folded edge of the upper square over onto the edge of the coloured patch. Stitch it down with small stitches worked through from the back of the large patches and through the coloured patch. Make two tiny stitches at the corners to give a neat finish.

Work all four sides of the coloured patch in the same way. This is one unit. To make up a piece, you need not put windows in all the squares. Some patches can be left plain and the folded points stitched together at the centre.

Do not press the finished patchwork because it spoils the effect of the folds.

Machine patchwork

A patchwork of squares and rectangles is easy to sew by machine but great care must be taken when cutting the shapes because any inaccuracies will spoil the finished effect. Therefore, it is best to mark the shapes in on the wrong side of the fabric with chalk and a ruler, working on the straight grain. Cut each piece individually and carefully.

Pin and tack the patches together into strips, always taking the same seam allowance. Match strips up, pinning and tacking. If one patch is out of alignment, unpick and rework it because one badly worked patch will throw the rest out of line.

Mounting patches

Mounting the fabric patches on the backing papers is the hardest part for a beginner. It is very important that you learn to do it properly because the sharpness of the patch edges will determine the quality of your finished work. If patches are clumsily made, the patchwork will have tiny holes at joins and patches will not fit together neatly. Practise mounting patches using a hexagon template. It has wide angles and is the easiest to work with.

Hold the paper on the wrong side of the fabric patch and put one pin in the centre. Have a needle threaded with soft tacking thread knotted at one end. Fold the first turning onto the paper. Bring the needle through from the right side near to the first corner of the patch. Make two or three small tacking stitches through both fabric and paper. Fold down the turning on the next edge so that you make a sharp corner and a small pleat. Work two tacking stitches to hold the corner in place. Continue tacking along the second side and then fold over the third turning making the second sharp corner.

Mounting diamond patches

Diamond patches are the most difficult to mount because the angles are so narrow. Begin as for the hexagon, bringing the thread through from the right side. Tack the top right edge of the diamond first. Fold the tip of the folded turning down and then make the second turning. If you follow this procedure, you should be able to make fine, sharp points.

Piecing

Piecing is the American method of patchwork, differing from the European method in that the patchwork pieces are assembled into squares and then in blocks, usually 35 cm (14 in) square, which are then stitched together and framed with a wide fabric border.

Traditionally, the block area cover the top of the bed only, and the border falls over the edges.

The designs and the names for these blocks (each pattern is identified by a specific name) were developed by pioneer families drawing upon the experiences of their daily lives. Crown and Cross, Garden of Eden and Jacob's Ladder reflect their religious beliefs; Churn Dash, Hen and Chickens and Monkey Wrench, their daily chores on the farm, and impressions of their new surroundings are revealed in block patterns such as Cactus Flower, Rocky Road to Kansas and Flight of Geese.

Pieced quilts have always been assembled by hand, using running stitch to join the patches and blocks. Today, of course, the sewing machine is widely used as it is quicker and makes stronger seams.

Fabrics and fabric quantities
Fabrics for a pieced quilt were gathered from friends and family, cast-off clothes being the main supply. Although this is still a favourite source, contemporary quilt-makers often use fabric purchased especially for the purpose.

To determine how much fabric you need, you must first work out how many blocks will be required to cover the top of the bed. First measure the length and width of the bed over bedclothes and pillows. Then decide the dimension of the block size of the blocks (usually 35 cm [14 in]). Now divide the bed measurements by the block

Churn Dash block

Palm Leaf block

Lone Star block

Rocky Road to Kansas block

size. This will give the number of blocks across and down. Multiply these for the total number of blocks.

Next, decide the colour scheme of the blocks, drawing the design on squared graph paper and colouring in the areas with pencils or pens.

Once you have your quilt design

worked out it is possible to estimate how much of each colour of fabric you need. To do this, draw up a paper pattern of each colour shape in the block. Sort the various shapes into groups of colours. Cut a piece of paper 90 cm (36 in) wide and begin to trace out each pattern shape, side by side, with 6 mm ($\frac{1}{4}$ in) turnings between the shapes, and always on the straight grain. Measure how much fabric is taken up by the shapes for one block and mutliply this by the number of blocks in your quilt. You now know how much fabric you should by each colour for the top of the quilt. Work out the border quantities in the same way.

Working out blocks

If you look at the designs on these pages you will see that some blocks are made of nine squares (three across and three down). Lone Star and Jacob's Ladder are examples of square blocks. Sometimes the nine squares are divided into triangles. Some have a centre square and parallel lines. Others are divided diagonally.

To copy a design, cut a square of paper 35 cm (14 in) and then fold the square until you have achieved the lines of the design you are copying. Draw over the folded lines and use a pattern for assembling the patches.

Drafting templates

Having worked out the components of your design, the next stage is cutting the templates. Another way piecing differs from patchwork is that you use only one template for each shape. This must be carefully and accurately cut.

Cutting

Cutting the pieces is the most important stage in piecing. You have to be accurate or the quilt will never look well.

Method Cut a shape in stiff, smooth cardboard 6 mm ($\frac{1}{4}$ in) larger all round than the finished piece will be when stitched. Smooth the edges with sandpaper. Mark the number of pieces you are going to cut from this template.

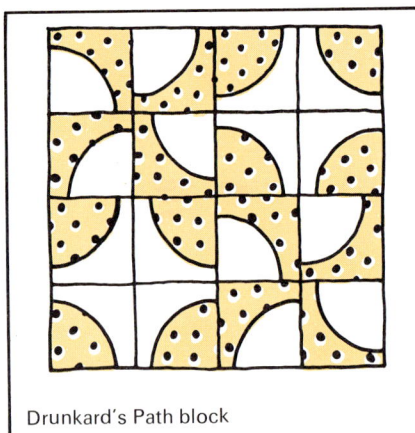

Drunkard's Path block

Press the fabrics. Lay the template on the fabric and draw around it with a sharp soft pencil. Make sure that the template has one long edge lying to the warp threads. Allow at least 3 mm ($\frac{1}{8}$ in) between each shape.

Cut the pieces out carefully on the pencilled lines. Gather the pieces together according to shape and colour of fabric and thread them onto a length of thread with a knot tied in the end.

Appliqué shapes are cut in the same way except that you may sometimes be cutting free-form shapes on the bias. If you are cutting flower stems for flowers, cut these as bias strips. (Check with the techniques for appliqué on pages 239-42 for applying appliqué shapes to a background.)

Sewing patches together

The traditional stitch for piecing is running stitch. Whether you are hand sewing or machine stitching, it is important that corners are accurately and sharply stitched. Hold two pieces together, right sides. Each seam should be securely finished off at both ends with a few back stitches. The seams should be 6 mm ($\frac{1}{4}$ in) and as straight as possible.

Stitch pieces together to make up squares and then press the work on the wrong side. Press all seams flat, not open.

Stitch the squares together to make up complete blocks

Setting the quilt

Lay all the completed blocks on the bed and see whether you need to link the blocks with strips.

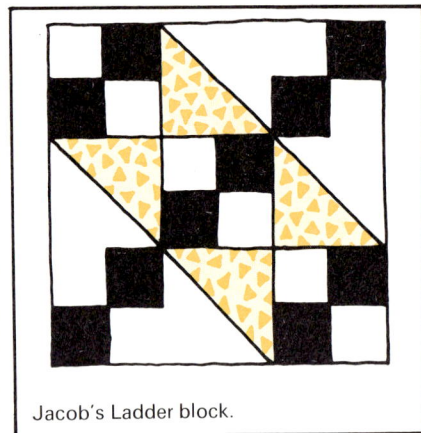

Jacob's Ladder block.

To join blocks, tack a row together and then stitch them with a 6 mm ($\frac{1}{4}$ in) seam. Make up all the rows and then sew the rows of blocks together. You can do this stage by machine, but you will find that it is easier to control the shape of corners if you are hand sewing.

When you come to sewing on the borders, stitch on the top and bottom borders first and then add the side pieces.

Above Grandmother's Fan is a traditional American block pattern for quilts.
Right Depending upon how Log Cabin blocks are arranged, different pattern effects can be achieved.

Finishing embroidery

Between work sessions, embroidery should be kept in a fabric or plastic bag to keep it clean. While working handle the fabric as little as possible and be sure to keep hands scrupulously clean. It is advisable to wear light clothing and, if possible, an apron while working. Dark clothing will inevitably leave dark-coloured lint on the work, making it look grubby.

If the finished work looks dirty it will have to be laundered in which case, treat it very gently. Wash the piece in warm, rich suds and swish it through the water. Do not squeeze or rub. Rinse several times in warm water but do not squeeze, wring or spin dry.

Roll and press the work in a soft, dry towel to remove moisture, and then lay it flat on a towel to dry. Press on the wrong side.

Canvaswork can be freshened by gently cleaning the surface with a proprietary dry cleaning fluid.

Pressing embroidery

Hemmed articles, such as tablecloths and napkins, have to be pressed. Use a well padded surface, a pressing cloth and a regular or steam iron. If the fabric is very wrinkled (as could be the case if it had been embroidered in the hand rather than a frame), sprinkle the fabric with water and roll it in a towel. Place the embroidery face down on a padded, smooth surface and press very lightly.

If there are sequins or beads in the design, make sure they will not melt under the heat of the iron. If an embroidered picture is being finished, it should be mounted immediately after pressing (see Mounting embroidery).

Removing transfer marks

Transfer marks will almost always wash out of fabrics, but if the fabric is not washable, soak it in cleaning fluid for about ten minutes. Lay it on clean blotting paper to dry. If the marks persist, rub with a soft cloth dipped in cleaning fluid.

Silk and rayon fabrics may need the cleaning fluid procedure followed by a gentle washing in soapy water. After rinsing carefully, lay the embroidery face down on a padded surface and press under a cloth.

Blocking embroidery

Embroidery can sometimes become puckered during working. This is more likely to happen if the work has been done in the hand without a frame. If the puckering is very slight, it can sometimes be shrunk out by pressing under a damp cloth.

To prepare a piece of embroidery for framing, it should be blocked first. First work a line of tacking stitches around the picture to align with the inner edges of the frame. Before beginning the embroidery, measure and mark the exact centre of the four sides of tacking.

When the work is finished, wash the embroidery if it needs it or dampen it down. Tape a sheet of brown paper over a drawing board or other flat wooden surface. On the paper, draw a shape to correspond exactly to the inner dimensions of the frame.

Place the embroidery right side up on the brown paper and pin to the board, matching the four corners. Next, pin the centres of the four sides, gently pulling the embroidery to match the guide lines. Continue pinning all around, dividing and subdividing the sides, placing pins equidistantly. Leave to dry.

Blocking canvaswork

If the piece is fairly small, simply sponge the work on the wrong side, then lay it on a damp towel on a board. Pull the embroidery into shape and pin it out. Lay a damp cloth on top and press with a medium hot iron.

Larger pieces may need blocking. Mark out the correct shape and size on a board covered with brown paper. Pin out the canvaswork, stretching it to shape and pin, first the corners and then the sides. Place pins about 12 mm ($\frac{1}{2}$ in) apart. Dampen the back of the embroidery with water and leave it to dry naturally.

Mounting embroidery

Cut a piece of thick card 3 mm ($\frac{1}{8}$ in) smaller all around than the inner dimensions of the frame. Lay the embroidery on the card to position it. At the corners, push dressmaker pins into the thickness of the card edge to hold the embroidery. Then begin to insert pins from the centres of the sides, working towards the corners. Pins should be about 6 mm ($\frac{1}{4}$ in) apart. You will need to use a small hammer to secure the pins. Turn the picture over and glue the surplus fabric to the card, mitring the corners. Alternatively, you can lace the edges with long zigzag stitches. Remove the pins with pliers.

Mounting canvaswork

Follow the same procedure as above, but for large pieces you may have to mount on hardboard or plywood.

Several toys that can be made from the patterns in the Toymaking chapter are shown on page 256:

The towelling dog is ideal for a baby. It is very soft and washable and there are no bits to pull off and swallow.

Everyone loves a Teddy and this one is particularly appealing. He has moveable arms and legs and is made up in durable corduroy.

The rag doll, a favourite toy with little girls, is so called because you are meant to use up fabric remnants for the clothes. Finally, a cuddly rabbit with pink velvet ears. A few carefully placed darts give this toy its realistic shape.

Toymaking

There is no end to the variety of soft toys that can be made at home. For baby it is best to make simple cloth or wool dolls, without wires, buttons and so on, that might work loose. It is most common to choose animal shapes for these toys. The older child will like jointed toys with movable heads and limbs. The most usual jointed toy is a Teddy Bear with movable arms and legs.

Toddlers will love toys that are mounted on wooden platforms with wheels, which can be pulled along.

Lastly, for the little girl who loves dolls there is a rag doll, fully dressed. In this chapter there is a representative selection of the various types of toys and the construction and patterns are described in detail.

General instructions for simple soft toys

The main details of construction are the same for all kinds of toys; the pattern is made, the fabric cut out and sewn up and the toy is stuffed – all these methods are described generally in this section. The more intricate details for making jointed animals, doll faces and so on are described later in this chapter.

Accessories, tools and fabrics are not very elaborate or expensive, and are available from craft suppliers.

Accessories

These are the little extras that are needed for the more complicated toys. Metal washers; wooden and metal discs; and cotter pins for jointed toys. Glass eyes, made in various sizes. Hair for dolls, ribbon for bows.

Fabrics

Fabrics suitable for toy-making include cloth coatings which are closely woven, such as velour or flannel, but not tweeds or materials which fray, felt is best for small shapes because seams do not have to be turned.

Synthetic fur fabric These are available in realistic patterns and textures and thus are ideal for toy animals.

Fur Best suited for very simple patterns, but is difficult to handle. It should not be used for toys for small babies.

Leather Makes very good small toys with decorative outside stitching, good for noses, paws and so on.

Kapok or other synthetic stuffing.

Calico, muslin and other firm, closely woven cotton fabrics are used for doll's bodies.

Wire and wood for leg supports.

For the dressing of toys, most fabrics can be used. The main thing is to choose a fabric suitable for the toy being made. Toddlers' toys should be made of colourful and hard-wearing material, and for a small baby's toy a washable soft material is best.

Tools

Scissors for cutting pattern and fabric.

Sewing needles and a darning needle for attaching eyes.

Sewing thread and button thread.

For jointed toys you will also need wire cutters and small-nosed pliers for bending wire and cotter-pin ends.

Pompon Bunny

This is a very simple toy made from two little woollen balls or pompons which are clipped to shape. It is soft and bright and will amuse and delight baby if hung in the cot or pram.

About 50 g (2 oz) of white or yellow wool is required; but various colours may be mixed together from oddments, or from discarded and unravelled sweaters.

To make the bunny

Cut two circles of cardboard 9 cm (3½ in) in diameter, and two 5 cm (2 in) in diameter. Larger circles are used for larger toys.

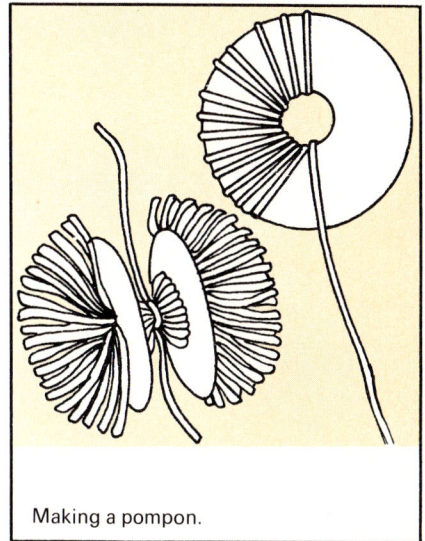
Making a pompon.

Cut out a 12 mm (½ in) diameter circle from the centre of each of the larger circles, and a smaller hole from the smaller ones. Place each pair together and wind the wool around the cardboard through the centre until the hole is completely filled in and the cardboard covered. Insert sharp scissors between the two boards at the edge and cut through the wool all around, cutting every loop. Pass a length of strong wool or fine string around the wool between the circles and tie firmly. Clip the cardboard circles and pull off from the wool, then shake the ball well. Repeat with remaining circle.

Clip the larger ball to an egg shape for the rabbit's body, then shake the smaller ball in a similar manner for the head, clipping it flat on the neck edge.

Sew the head firmly to the narrow end of the body, then sew on a tiny red nose made from a scrap of cloth or velvet; do this by passing the needle and thread through the tied centres of the pompons. Two circles of black patent leather, or felt, cut from an old belt will serve as eyes, and should be sewn firmly with white or green thread. Ears are made from scraps of felt, cut 2.5 mm (1 in) wide at the base, and pointed at the top.

Make a tiny tuck or fold at the base of each ear and sew them to the top of the head in a perky manner.

Cut a little semi-circular cape, 5 cm (2 in) deep, from a piece of bright flannel or felt and a tiny waistcoat of a different shade. The waistcoat is sewn to the front of the bunny and the cape around his neck. Sew the cape to the waistcoat or, if preferred, the waistcoat may be omitted and the cape left to fall open at the front. A bow tie, cut from black felt and a tiny collar of white felt can be sewn to the neck of the cape. Turn up the cape at the back. Sew a loop of ribbon, felt, or twisted wool to the back of the neck, so that he will hang in pram or cot.

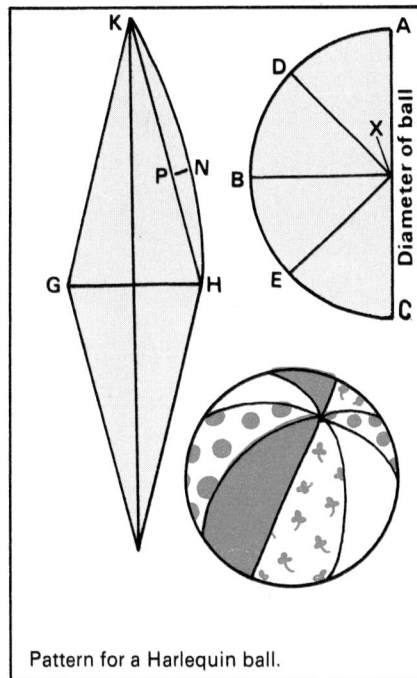

Harlequin ball

An attractive ball, made of odd scraps of fabric, all different colours and patterns, or with various coloured felts, may be easily made from the pattern given here.

Any sized ball, with any number of strips in it, can be made, although eight or twelve strips is the usual number, unless the ball is very large.

The pattern

Decide upon the height of the ball, that is, the diameter. The diagram gives a pattern for a ball 16 cm (6 in) high. Line AC is the diameter of the ball and therefore one third of the circumference, therefore ABC = one and a half times AC = 24 cm (9 in). This gives the length of the strips for the ball.

Any number of strips can be put into a ball, this one has eight, so half the ball has four strips. The 24 cm (9 in) curve divided by four makes the strips 6 cm (2¼ in) across. AD, DB, BE, EC each = 6 cm (2¼ in).

Draw a diamond 6 cm × 24 cm (2¼ in × 9 in), GH = 6 cm (2¼ in), KL = 24 cm (9 in).

Draw a curved line from K to H. The distance from the straight line depends on the size of the ball. For this size, make the widest part PN

Pattern for a Harlequin ball.

just under 6 mm (¼ in) across.

Fold pattern down the centre and across to get each curve alike.

Making the ball

If felt is used, no seam turnings are necessary. The edges are oversewn on the right side, and an opening is left at one side for stuffing. The stuffing may be flock, kapok or very small pieces of rag cut up. Stuff very firmly, pressing it down into a good round shape, then sew up the opening.

If woven fabric is used, allow narrow turnings and oversew the pieces on the wrong side, then machine them about 6 mm (¼ in) from the edge. Leave an opening and stuff as for the felt ball, slip stitch or neatly oversew the gap.

A kitten

From this pattern a kitten, baby tiger, or leopard may be constructed, the variations being governed by the material and decoration used. For the kitten fur fabric is best with applied felt for the nose and eyes, but an amusing tiger or leopard could be made with appropriately patterned fur fabric. If this is not available you could use a plain yellow or orange cloth, with stripes or spots embroidered, or applied in black felt. An alternative pattern of a tail is included in the design; this is suitable for the leopard or tiger. To make these animals realistic, bristles of thin wire, wool or thin plastic wire should be threaded through the face on either side of the mouth for whiskers, as indicated by the dotted line.

Draw out the pattern following the diagram; the squares represent 2.5 cm (1 in), and cut out in the fabric leaving slightly more turnings when fur fabric is used. With pile fabric the pile should brush towards the back of the animal.

Place the under paws to the upper paws with right sides facing and stitch, starting from the centre back at D to the centre front at P. Seam from O about 2.5 cm (1 in) along the centre seam of the under body. Now stitch up the back seam from the back legs, over the centre back, to the nape of the neck C. Fit in the centre side of the fronts of the face. Join PO to the under legs and stitch.

When stuffing the kitten begin with the head, then the forepaws, back paws and finally the body. Over-sew the under body seam neatly.

Seam up the tail, stuff, and oversew to the body at AB for tiger and YX for kitten. Line the ears and make a small pleat in the lower edge, then attach by slip stitching the turned-in edges to the head.

Whiskers may be attached if desired.

In the case of the tiger or leopard, spots or stripes are now sewn to the body and the eyes and nose pieces are slip stitched into position. These can be embroidered in wool instead of being made in felt. A bow with small bell attached will complete the kitten.

A terrier

This soft toy requires 25 cm (10 in) of 90 cm (36 in) wide fabric if the under legs can be cut from the opposite way of the material. If the material has a nap or patterned surface you will need 30 cm (12 in) of 90 cm (36 in) wide fabric. Gingham, velveteen, fur fabric, felt or firmly woven woollens are all suitable, with contrasting scraps in a bright colour for the linings of the ears. Two glass eyes may be bought, or buttons used, or the whole face may be embroidered with nose and eyes in coloured wools or silks.

Method

The pattern is drawn to scale, as each square representing 2.5 cm

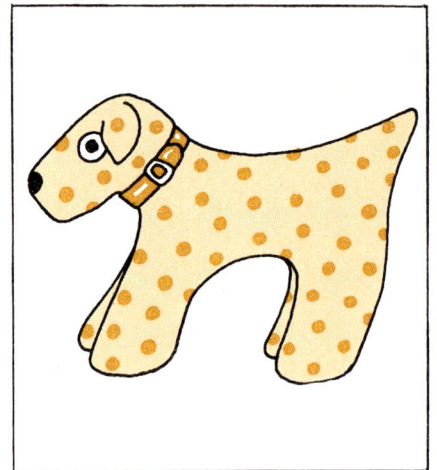

(1 in). The pattern may be made by folding the paper or by using squared paper. No turnings are allowed on the pattern, so from 1 cm ($\frac{3}{8}$ in) extra should be added, according to the type of fabric used.

Draw the pattern full size, and place it on the fabric with the arrows following the straight grain of the fabric correctly. Cut out two bodies A, two underlegs E, two ears F, and two ear linings. Mark with thread the dotted line on the underlegs and the position of the eyes, nose and ears. If using napped fabric, place pattern pieces so they all run in the same direction.

To make the dog

Place the right sides of the fabric together and fit the underlegs to the outer legs, up to the points of the centre back and front; stitch these seams. Now fit from the centre front neck, around the face and head and along the centre back of the dog, to the point below the tail where the underlegs meet in a point. Stitch this seam, also stitch from the centre front and the centre back 2.5 cm (1 in) along the under line of the body, starting from the points where the underlegs finish. Press all seams, clip or notch any seams or points which are bulky or to make curves sit properly, turn the dog the right side out and he is ready for stuffing.

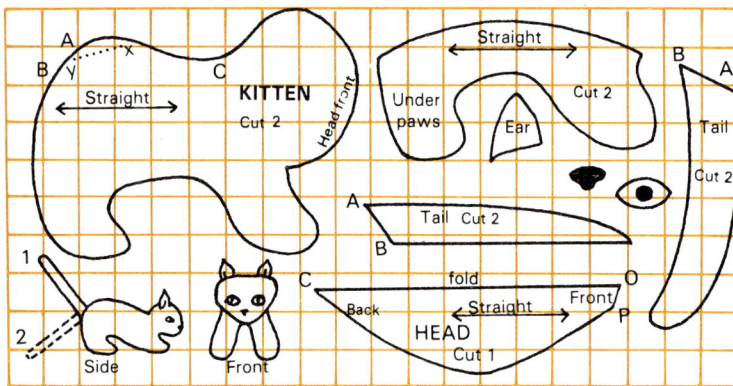

Kitten pattern

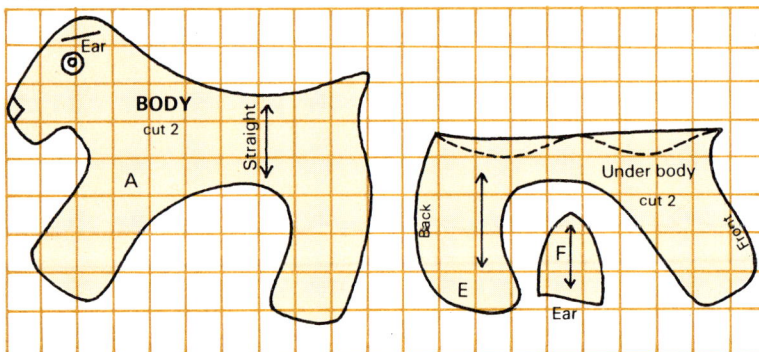

Terrier pattern

To stuff

Start with the head, then the front paws, then the back paws, then the body. A long pencil will help to push the stuffing into the corners. Make sure that all the stuffing is very even, and as tightly packed as possible so that there are no loose gaps which will make the dog sag.

Oversew the remainder of the underbody seam very neatly. It will be found that the dog's legs spread out too much, this is remedied by pulling the fabric on the dotted lines, with thread into a tuck, which is oversewn with fine stitches; this should give the dog a good standing position.

Seam up the ears around the two curved sides, right side of linings to right sides of outer ears, clip corners, turn right side out and press. Turn in the lower ear edges and slip stitch, pleat and place in position on the head, slip stitching them on firmly.

The eyes are now attached, either sewn on or embroidered in satin stitch, according to the kind chosen, a nose is embroidered, and a ribbon bow or wrist-watch strap placed around the neck for a collar.

If a plain fabric has been used for the dog's body it may be made more colourful by sewing on patches of contrasting felt or embroidering spots in different colours. If a squeaker is inserted before the final sewing up, a small child may find the dog more fun.

If felt is used to make this toy all the work is done on the right side.

A glove puppet

Glove puppets are easy to make, even young children can attempt them, and a number of different characters can be made from one basic pattern. The decoration of the head and change of costume is all that is needed to give variety to each puppet.

Method

The materials required are few. The head is made from a cotton knit fabric stuffed with rag or

kapok. The body lining may be of sateen or calico and the dress can then be changed if wished. Felt is used for the hands. Three cardboard tubes can be bought or made for the fingers of the hand which manipulates the doll. The pattern shows a body suitable for a child, but it can be made larger to fit an adult's hand.

The tubes should be 2.5 cm (1 in) long, and are fitted into each hand of the puppet. The thumb and second finger are inserted into these tubes when working the puppet. The tube for the head should be long enough to go right inside the ball with about 2.5 cm (1 in) outside for the neck and the centre must fit the first finger. If these tubes cannot be bought they are easily made by wrapping stiff paper around a stick and gluing it until a sufficient thickness is obtained.

Make the head from a piece of knit fabric; for the clown which is illustrated, white is preferable; the size is 24 cm (9 in) wide by 14 cm (5½ in) deep. Seam the 14 cm (5½ in) edges together and put the seam to the back of the head. Gather the bottom edge about 2.5 cm (1 in) up and place the cardboard tube in the opening. Draw up the gathering thread and wind strong

thread a number of times around the outside to keep the tube and gathers in position. A little glue may be smeared on the outside of the tube and the material pressed over it to make it stronger. Now stuff the head firmly, draw up the top opening as tightly as possible and overcast the edges together.

Decorate the head by painting or applying felt features and patches to suit a clown. Sew on a nose, D, which is slightly stuffed and applied to a shape as C, also white felt ears, I. Two tufts of hair made of loops of wool are sewn one over each ear and the head is completed with a conical hat of paper or felt. Cut this from the pattern given and sew it to the head at a rakish angle.

The body is a rectangle of fabric gathered around the neck, and glued over the cardboard tube. The pattern is made to fit a child's hand, for an adult allow at least 5 cm (2 in) extra at the centre front.

The arms are two small fabric rectangles fitted into seams or slits in the front of the body, as shown. The large rectangle shown with the dotted line represents the full sleeve of the dress, it is gathered at the armhole and wrist. The pattern is drawn up to scale, each square representing 2.5 cm (1 in).

Make the hands of felt, stuff them lightly and indicate fingers by stitching. Glue the two tubes into the hands so that half a tube is in the hand and half in the arm. Oversew the bottoms of the arms to the hands, E, fix the arms into the slits of the body and sew strongly. K shows the complete construction before the face is finished. Hem the bottom of the body and then dress the puppet.

The clown has a gathered skirt of bright yellow cotton, cut from the same pattern as the body only a little fuller, and with extra length. The sleeves are cut as shown and gathered. The decoration is in green and black felt, it may be painted instead of being sewn to the dress. A stiff frill of muslin at neck and wrists completes the clown's costume.

Steps in making the glove puppet.

Ear
I

Hands
Cut 2
fold
F

Cut
Nose
D

C

G

E

Fabric for head
J

B

H

K

L

Neck
gather

FOLD

FOLD
SLEEVE
Cut 2

Wrist

FOLD

Seam

gather

Extra length

Centre
FRONT

1 sq = 2.5 cm (1 in)

Frock and hat pattern for puppet

A little girl

This charming rag doll could easily be turned into a little boy by changing the hairstyle and by slight alteration of the features.

Materials

A closely woven smooth cotton is most suitable for the body in natural or pale pink, although dyed calico could be used; you need 45 cm (18 in) of 90 cm (36 in) wide fabric. Rug or knitting wool makes good hair, or even raffia could be used. Kapok or other suitable material is needed for stuffing. The features are embroidered, as a change from using felt. Cotton is used for the dress and calico for the underclothes. The shoes are cut from small pieces of felt.

Making the doll

The patterns are drawn to scale, each square representing 2.5 cm (1 in) and turnings of 1 cm ($\frac{3}{8}$ in) should be allowed when cutting out. Place the pieces correctly on the fabric with the arrows on the straight grain, mark any darts and centre lines and cut out.

Stitch up the arms leaving the curve at the shoulder open, turn right side out and stuff the hands thinly, then indicate the fingers by stitching. Finish stuffing the arms; it is important to see that these are stuffed firmly. Turn in the shoulder line and tack flat, seam to seam, ready for oversewing to the shoulders.

Stitch the side seams of the legs, then insert the soles by oversewing. Stuff the legs to the top, tack the ends flat with the seams in the centre back and centre front of the legs, ready for attaching to the body.

Stitch the side and shoulder seams of the body, turn in the lower edge and tack, sewing the base of body half circle to the back. Turn right side out, fit the legs between the front and back edges of the hip line and slip stitch very strongly all around. Now stuff the body up to the neckline.

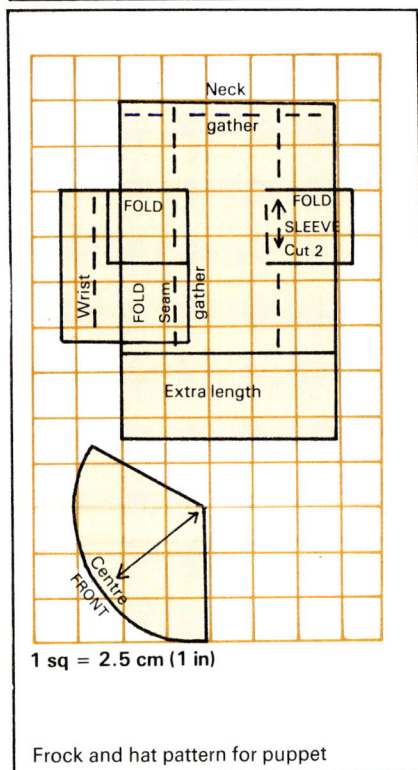

The head is made next. Sew up all darts, then the centre back seam and over the crown; insert the front of the face to the side pieces and stitch. *Note*: if the doll's face is to be embroidered, it is much easier to do it before stitching on the body.

The mouth is worked in satin stitch, the nose, eyebrows and around the eyes in stem stitch with brown or black thread, using one or two rows according to which looks best. The eyes may have the whole shape applied in white cotton or silk, with the pupil and iris embroidered in satin stitch in black and a colour. The cheeks are worked in running stitches.

Attach the head to the neck after stuffing by turning in a narrow hem on the neck, fitting the head into the neck and overcasting with very small stitches.

Only the arms remain to be fixed. Curve the top arm over the shoulder and slip stitch or overcast firmly into place.

Attach the hair and the doll is finished. If wool is used it should be sewn with back stitching at intervals, starting with a parting and working from the front to sufficiently far over the back of the head to keep it firmly in place. Style the hair into two plaits with a centre parting.

Clothes

The patterns given for a dress, petticoat, panties and shoes are all drawn to scale. A vest and socks could be knitted. 16 cm (6 in) of 90 cm (36 in) wide fabric is sufficient for the dress, while a piece of fabric 23 cm × 46 cm (9 in × 18 in) wide fabric is enough for petticoat and panties. The shoes are made of felt or leather.

The dress

Cut out, allowing sufficient turnings at the neck edge and lower sleeve edges to make a deep hem. The frills around the pockets may be of lace or a straight gathered strip 12 mm (½ in) wide of matching fabric. There are no fastenings except drawstrings, which should

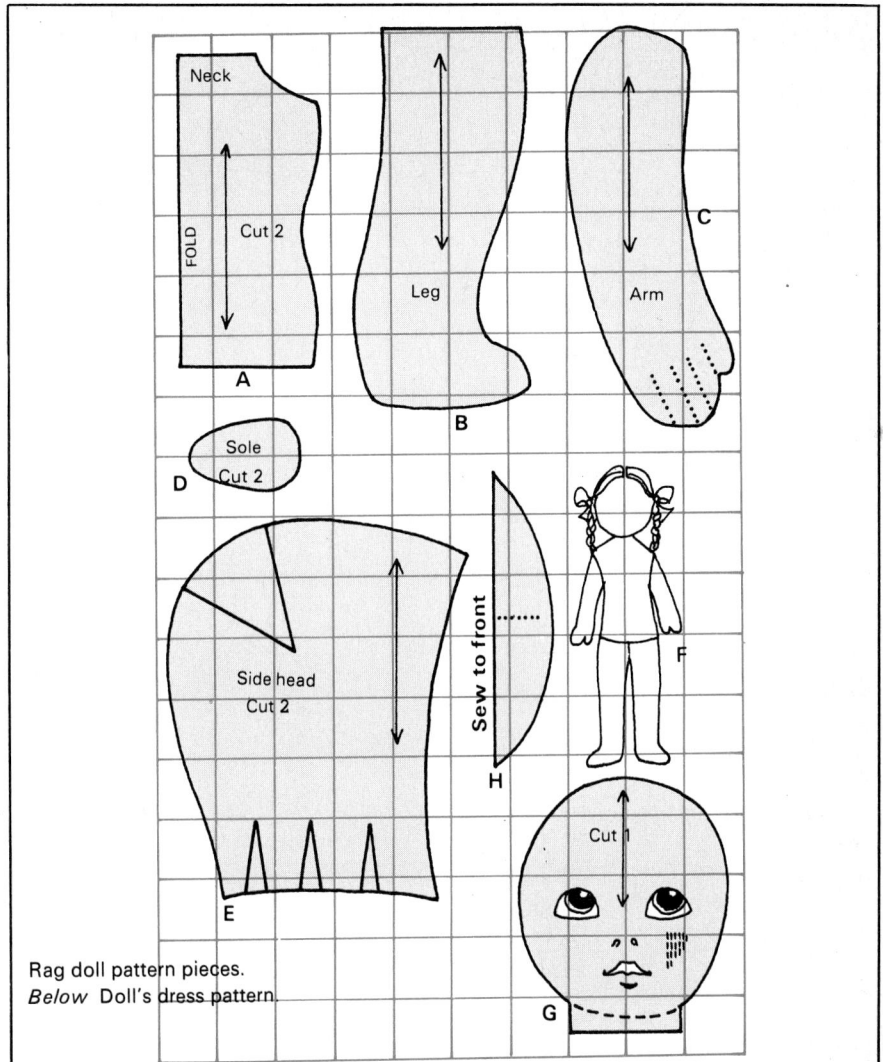

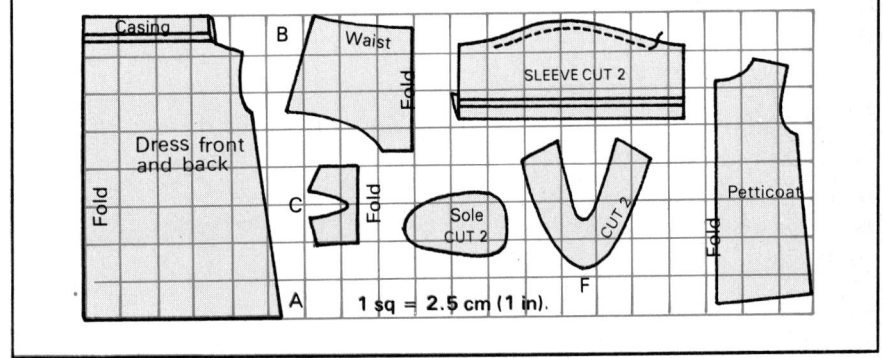

be of narrow ribbon. The dress irons out completely flat and is easily taken off and put on.

Sew up the side seams and shoulder seams of the body. Turn in the neck edge and make a double hem on the neckline through which the ribbon is threaded, work an eyelet at the centre front of the neck for the ribbon ends. Tack the frills around

the pockets and stitch the pockets in position on the front of the dress, then turn up the bottom hem.

Seam up the sleeves turning double hems at the bottom of each sleeve and thread with ribbon pulled through an eyelet, as indicated. Gather the sleeve heads and fit into the armholes and stitch. Give a final press and the dress is complete.

Rag doll pattern pieces.
Below Doll's dress pattern.

1 sq = 2.5 cm (1 in).

The petticoat and panties

Cut out with turnings, allowing 2.5 cm (1 in) for a hem on the lower edge of the petticoat. If there is sufficient material, the panties may be cut out without any seams between the legs.

Stitch up all seams of petticoat, bind the armholes and neck with a bias cut strip. Make a short opening at the back to allow the head to pass through, with a button and loop for fastening. Make a hem on the lower edge and sew with neat hemming.

Turn in a hem around the top edge of the panties, deep enough for threading with elastic, after the seams have been sewn. Turn up the lower edge of legs and hem neatly.

The edges may be trimmed with narrow lace.

The shoes

If made in felt or leather the shoes are cut without turnings and overcast to the sole on the wrong side. The centre front strap is slit and tied with a lace or ribbon.

If you wish to make socks cut them as for the pattern of the doll's legs and seam centre back and front.

Realistic soft toys

Designing patterns and making a rabbit

For those who would like to design for themselves, here is a simple method which gives good results. First draw the outline of the animal to be reproduced, either from memory or by copying a good illustration. The diagrams here show how to make the pattern for a rabbit but the principles remain the same for all animal shapes.

Omitting the eyes, ears and tail, items which are usually put on last, draw a single outline of the basic shape.

If two pieces are cut for this pattern, sewn together and stuffed, the toy will have a head which is flat, rather like a fish, and a body without breadth. To give width across the head a dart is made; to allow for this the head outline has to be enlarged, as the dotted lines on diagram.

When this dart is sewn up there will be fullness towards the lower point of it, but, because of the enlargement in outline, the head will remain the correct size. This method also gives width to the body.

The base or underbody on which the rabbit is to sit must now be made. Cut out the pattern just drawn and lay the lower part of it on a piece of folded paper, the fold touching the dotted line, which extends from 6 mm ($\frac{1}{4}$ in) above the neck to 6 mm ($\frac{1}{4}$ in) above the base of back. Cut around the part of the pattern resting on the paper. When opened out the underbody pattern should have an outline as shown in the diagram.

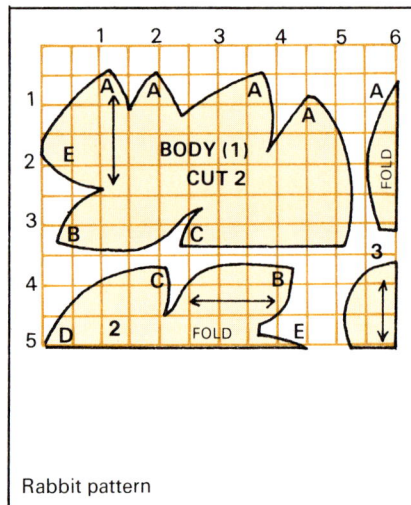

Rabbit pattern

Cut a quarter of the back portion away, rounding out the remainder as shown. This will give a perfect-fitting base, the point between the front paws adding width to chest and throat.

The ears should be about the same length as the head and measure about one-third of their length at the base. The powder-puff tail can be a circle of white fluffy fur or white fabric gathered at the edge and pulled tight over a ball of stuffing.

When designing soft toys thought should be given to the placing of the features; for instance, all young things, animal or human, have nicely rounded foreheads. If the eyes are kept low and widely spaced they look appealing. In general, the eyes of animals which are normally hunted by others, rabbits for instance, are placed to the side of the head. The 'hunter' animals, such as lions and tigers, have them more to the front.

Patterns

It is best to draw the pattern diagram on to squared paper, each square representing a given dimension. This way it is possible to enlarge the pattern pieces by transferring them to paper ruled into actual-size squares. All the diagrams are drawn on squared paper, and to scale. The numbers along the top and down the sides of the diagrams represent inches; see the pattern of the rabbit.

To enlarge a diagram work as follows. Number the squares to correspond with the diagram, along the top and down the sides, making each small square on the diagram correspond with the larger drawing. It is now an easy matter to reproduce in each larger square, the small section of drawing shown in the corresponding small square. This gives the larger pattern required, true to scale. It is the correct and most accurate method of enlarging or reducing only illustration or pattern, but the original must be squared up in proportion to the size required.

Cut out the pattern and place the pieces on the fabric with the body of the animal sitting or standing squarely on the straight grain. If two pieces exactly the same are required the pattern is reversed for the second one. When cutting out fur fabric, place the pattern on the wrong side of the fabric. Note the direction of the pile and lay the pattern according to the instructions. In general, the pile should lie from head to legs, or head to tail.

Ears

Ears are usually lined with a contrasting colour; the two pieces are sewn together on the wrong side and attached to the head with ladder stitch.

Eyes

Glass eyes are obtainable in several sizes and colours; choose a pair that is most suitable for the toy being made.

Specially designed safety eyes are available and should be used when possible, particularly on toys for toddlers.

To attach eyes

The two methods generally used for attaching eyes are described in this chapter.

The eyes are obtained in pairs attached to each end of a wire; for both methods of inserting prepare the eyes first.

Cut the wire about 12 mm ($\frac{1}{2}$ in) away from each eye and, with the pliers, bend the end back to form a loop, like the loop on a metal-shank button.

Method 1 Poke a hole through the fabric for each eye with the point of a scissors. Thread a very long needle with doubled button thread, knotting the ends together. Pass the needle through the shank of an eye and then through the loop of double thread, so that the eye will be firmly attached to the knotted end. Push the needle into the head through the scissor hole and bring it out behind, and slightly under, the ear on the opposite side of head. Pull the thread tightly to embed

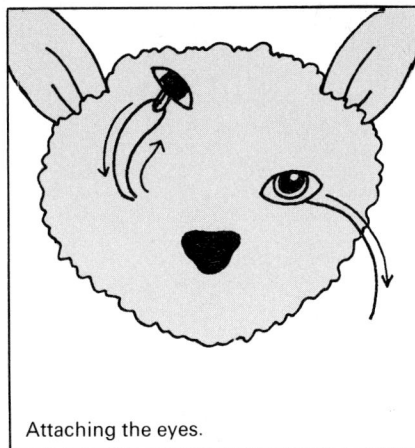

Attaching the eyes.

the shank in the stuffing and to sink the eye and form a socket. Hold the eye in this position, pressing on it with the left thumb, while fastening off behind the ear with a firm stitch or two. Attach the other eye in the same manner.

Method 2 This method is used for the rabbit. Pierce holes for the eyes, thread one on a doubled button thread, and insert needle in one hole, bringing it out at centre of hole made for the other eye. Pull tight, but do not fasten off. Thread the second eye on the same needle, returning it to the first hole. Pull tight again, so that both eyes are embedded, cut off the needle. Separate the two ends of thread, give a turn round the shank and tie tightly under the eye. Snip off the ends quite close.

Nose

The working of animal noses is usually done with embroidery thread; a square of satin stitch, or a few stroke stitches to suit the animal being made.

Paws

Four stroke stitches with double embroidery thread, or lines of back stitch, are used for these.

Pile

If fur fabric has been used a wire brush will fluff the pile, particularly along the seams.

With non-fraying fabrics place the two pieces together, edges level and right sides outside, then stitch.

The right sides of fraying fabrics are placed together, the tacking and stitching is made along the sewing line and the animal is turned right side out. Most animals are improved in appearance if they have a gay-coloured ribbon tied around the neck; a colour that tones with the ear lining is a good choice. For inside sewing a small back stitch or machine stitching is best. For outside work on leather, blanket stitch in coloured silk is decorative; on felt, oversewing or machining in matching thread; and for sewing up all cloth toys after stuffing, or for putting on ears and other features, a ladder stitch will be found best.

Ladder stitch

Take up a small piece of fabric on the needle 6 mm ($\frac{1}{4}$ in) from the edge, first one side of the opening and then the other, each stitch forming one ladder rung. When several stitches have been made, pull gently but tightly together, whereupon cut edges will disappear inside and no stitches will be visible.

Extremities should be stuffed first, firmly and without lumps. Much can be done in the way of modelling at this stage. Strands of stuffing can be lightly twisted over the end of a narrow stick and inserted as far as possible into the toy, side by side, until it is quite firm; it should not be rammed in hard balls.

Supports sewn inside limbs are used to give firmness to limbs and will help the toy to stand up.

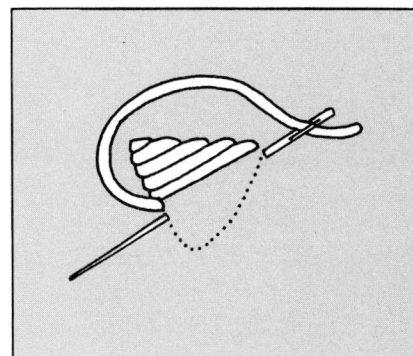

Embroidering a nose shape for the bunny.

Bracing stitches

Invisible bracing stitches are put in after the toy is otherwise completed. Firstly, to help in modelling limbs, head or other features; secondly, to brace limbs against spreading when they are not wired.

Leg supports

Firm galvanized wire is used to give support to the legs of toys which are required to stand. It is bent in the form of an arch with looped ends at the feet, upright for straight-legged animals, or slightly bent for hind legs. These wires should be bound with strips of cloth before inserting them into the legs. They should be secured by a strong stitch under the foot, in the centre of legs so that the stuffing can be placed round the wire.

Wooden stand

If this is made with wheels it will appeal to the toddler, as he can pull the toy along. The stand also acts as a brace to the legs of the animal, making them quite rigid. Metal washers and wooden discs are slipped into the feet from inside before stuffing, cotter pins are passed through the centre; the split ends are pushed through holes made in the wooden stand and opened underneath.

Wooden supports

For the large soft toys, such as an elephant or horse, upon which a toddler can sit, it is advisable to insert lengths of wooden rod, about broom-handle thickness, into legs. This method is used for the elephant.

Whiskers

Some animals have whiskers and these can be bought ready for use. To insert, thread one whisker into a needle, pass it through the head at the side of the mouth, leaving a length protruding for the first whisker. Make a small stitch and bring the needle back, making two whiskers on one side. Repeat this as required.

Jointed toys

A toy that can move its head and limbs has a fascination for a child, as it seems more lifelike. Many animals and dolls can be jointed, and in every case the method of making the joints is the same.

For making the joints metal washers, wooden discs and cotter pins are used; the size of these is governed by the size and type of toy being made.

The wooden discs can be made from thin plywood; the edges are sawn with a fretsaw and a hole is made in the centre with a small drill. If there is difficulty in obtaining wood, strong cardboard may be used. Is is sometimes possible to purchase jointing sets, complete with cotter pins.

Method

Sew up the body pieces, leaving an opening for stuffing. Make up and stuff the head, leaving the neck unstitched.

Thread a small metal washer or disc and a large wooden disc on to a cotter pin. Place the threaded cotter pin inside the neck opening of the stuffed head, with the ends pointing outwards. Fold the edges of the material 12 mm ($\frac{1}{2}$ in) over the edge of the disc and sew with criss-crossed threads. Push the cotter-pin ends through the unstuffed body and thread a large wooden disc and a large metal disc on the ends.

Make sure that the material between the two wooden discs is stretched flat and that the cotter pin is pulled through as tightly as possible, or the joint will be loose. Open out the ends of pin and curl them, with a pair of pliers, tightly on to the metal disc.

Sew up the arms as instructed. Thread a small wooden disc on to a cotter pin, as for neck, and when the arm is nearly stuffed place the disc inside, piercing the fabric with the cotter pin at the correct position. Complete the stuffing and sew up the opening. Fasten the arm to the body by pushing the protruding ends of the cotter pin into the side seam, and complete joint, inside the body as for neck.

Sew up the legs, leaving an opening for jointing and stuffing, as instructed. Make the joints as for the arms.

A selection of cotter pins and eyes for stuffed toys. Tiny children should not be given a toy containing these.

Teddy bear pattern.

Teddy bear

Try using heavy corduroy to make up Teddy, with velveteen paw pads and ear linings.

Materials required for a 30 cm (12 in) teddy

23 cm (9 in of fabric 114 cm (54 in) wide
Eight 3.5 cm ($1\frac{1}{4}$ in) wooden discs.
Two 4.5 cm ($1\frac{3}{4}$ in) wooden discs.
Five metal washers.
Five 3.5 cm ($1\frac{1}{4}$ in) metal discs.
Five 5 cm (2 in) cotter pins.
Black silk thread.
Stuffing.

Method

Cut out the teddy from the pattern. Sew the four body sections together from E to F in the manner of a football, leaving the last seam open from X to X for stuffing at centre back. Sew the two head pieces together from A to B. Then fit the crown piece between the two sides of head, placing centre front of crown A across the seam A on head, matching C to C, D to D, and sew together. The neck, BD is left open for stuffing, which may now be done. Before sewing up the opening insert a metal washer and a wooden disc threaded onto a cotter pin.

Arms

Take the two underarm pieces and the arm-pads and sew together from G to H. Then lay an outer arm piece on each, right sides facing, and sew from I to J and on to K, leaving open from I to K at top of arm for stuffing. Thread up a cotter pin onto a smaller wooden disc, and when the arm is stuffed almost to the top, place the threaded cotter pin inside, piercing the material at the spot marked L so that the points protrude. Complete the stuffing and sew up the opening, when the arm will be ready to fasten to the body.

Push the arm cotter pins through the side seams of body at L and complete the joint inside body with a wooden and a metal disc, then bend back the ends of pin.

Legs

Make up legs by sewing from N to O and P to Q. Sew foot-pads in the openings between NQ and leave open between OP for stuffing and joints. Fix to body at M on side seams, in the same way as the arms. Fasten the head to the body in the same way as the arms. The body is now ready to stuff.

After stuffing sew opening neatly with invisible ladder stitch.

Sew on the eyes as described taking the needle down to the back of the neck and fastening it off there.

With thick black silk thread work a square of solid black for the nose at A with an inverted V underneath. Make four stitches on each foot for claws.

Line the ears, turn inside out and neaten the raw edges. Sew to the head along the upright dotted line, with the top quarter of the ear length folded forward at right angles and sewn along the line of crown, with velvet lining facing front. A ribbon tied around the neck with a bow on one shoulder completes the toy.

Acknowledgements

Artwork

Jill Shipley pp 13-181 and 232, 235, 238, 239, 242, and 256

Janet Allen pp 185, 190-229, 243-252

Margaret Saunders p 231

Photographs

Michael Plomer pp 10, 41, 98, 119, 234, 241, 256 and 264

Singer Co. (U.K.) Ltd. p 12

Elna Sewing Machines Ltd. p 12

Mansell Collection p 15

Mary Evans pp 21, 35, 183 and 219

Simplicity Patterns Ltd. pp 27, 39, 49, 58, 63, 64, 67, 72, 73, 76, 81, 84, 94, 99, 122 and 136

Style Patterns Ltd. pp 47, 50, 58, 77, 81, 84, 87, 92 and 93

Mike Wilkins p 131

Liz Whiting pp 142, 147, 163, 166, 178, 204-5, 217, 224, 236, 240, and 242

Arthur Sanderson and Son Ltd. pp 149, 150-51, 154-55, 167 and 170-71

Barbara Snook pp 185 and 230

John Webb pp 193, 198, 201, 208, 211, 215, 223 and 229

Camera Press pp 196-197, 200, 221, 233, 236, 237, 244-45, 248-49 and 252-53

The American Museum in Britain, Bath pp 240, 243, 347 and 349

Samples of embroidery for the photographs on pages 193, 198, 201, 208, 211, 215, 223 and 229 are from the collection of the Embroiderer's Guild, Hampton Court Palace.

Back cover photograph by Paul Williams.

Index